OLIVER CROMWELL: COMMANDER IN CHIEF

OLIVER CROMWELL: COMMANDER IN CHIEF

RONALD HUTTON

YALE UNIVERSITY PRESS
NEW HAVEN AND LONDON

For information about this and other Yale University Press publications, please contact:
U.S. Office: sales.press@yale.edu yalebooks.com
Europe Office: sales@yaleup.co.uk yalebooks.co.uk

Set in Adobe Garamond Pro by IDSUK (DataConnection) Ltd
Printed in Great Britain by Clays Ltd, Elcograf S.p.A

Library of Congress Control Number: 2024940500

ISBN 978-0-300-27894-1

A catalogue record for this book is available from the British Library.

10 9 8 7 6 5 4 3 2 1

To Clive Holmes, in memoriam

CONTENTS

PLATES AND MAPS

PLATES

MAPS

ACKNOWLEDGEMENTS

I am very grateful to the staff of all the libraries and archives in which I have worked during the research for the book. Interestingly enough, both of the institutions in which I have found them to be superlatively so are in Oxford: the Bodleian Library, and especially its manuscripts division, where I have read items happily since 1976; and Worcester College Library, which I entered for the first time in the course of the present project. I am very grateful to Ian Gentles, for reading the whole manuscript in draft, and to the publisher's readers for their comments. My final debt is to Heather McCallum, who is the reason for my fidelity as an author to Yale University Press over the past one and a half decades.

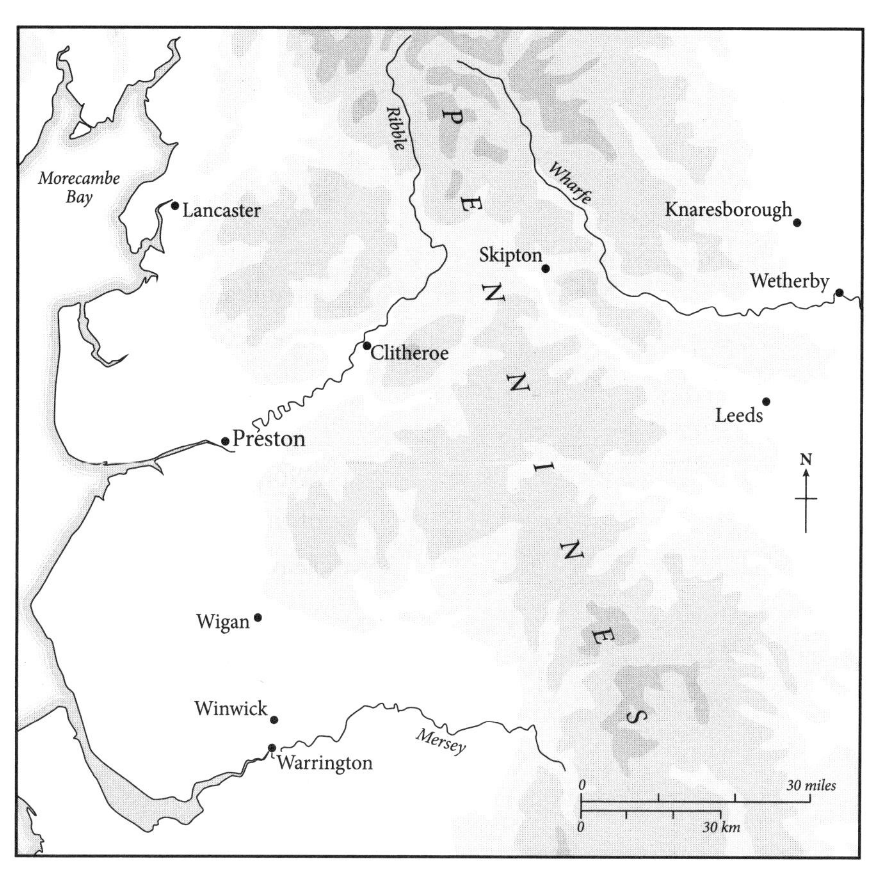

1. The Preston Campaign Area, August 1648.

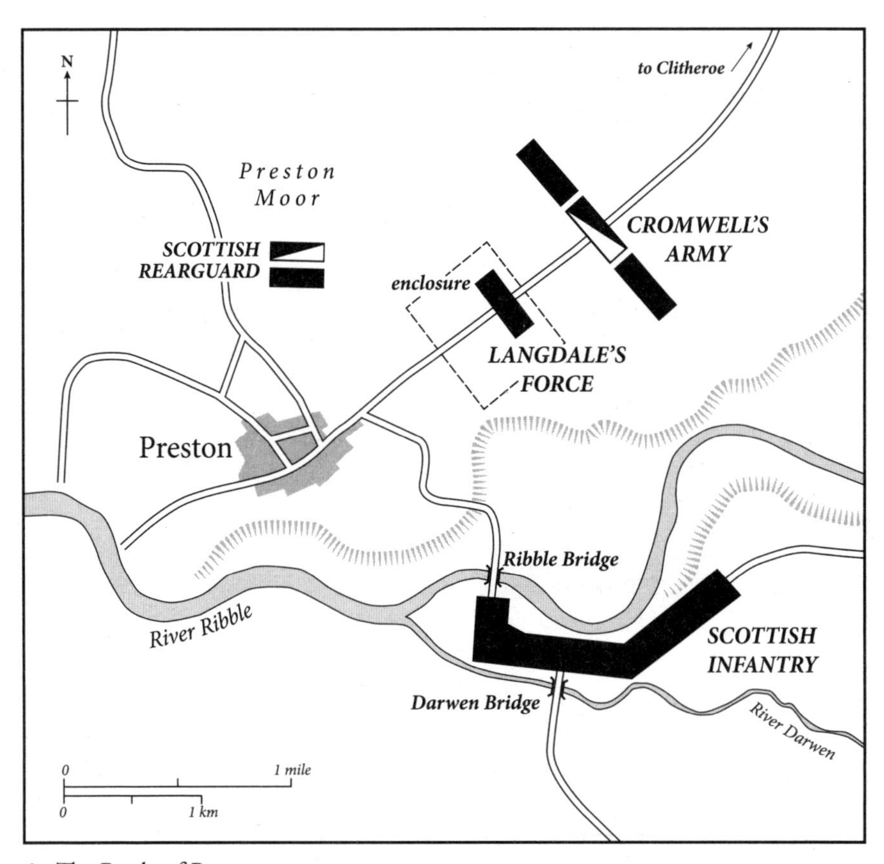

2. The Battle of Preston.

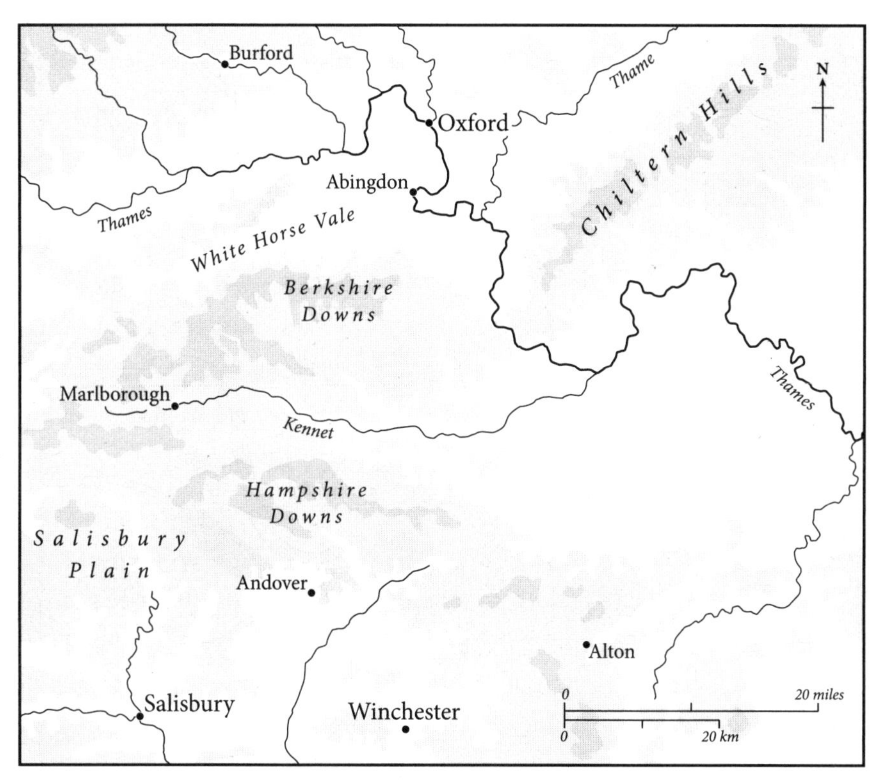

3. The Area of the Army Mutiny, May 1649.

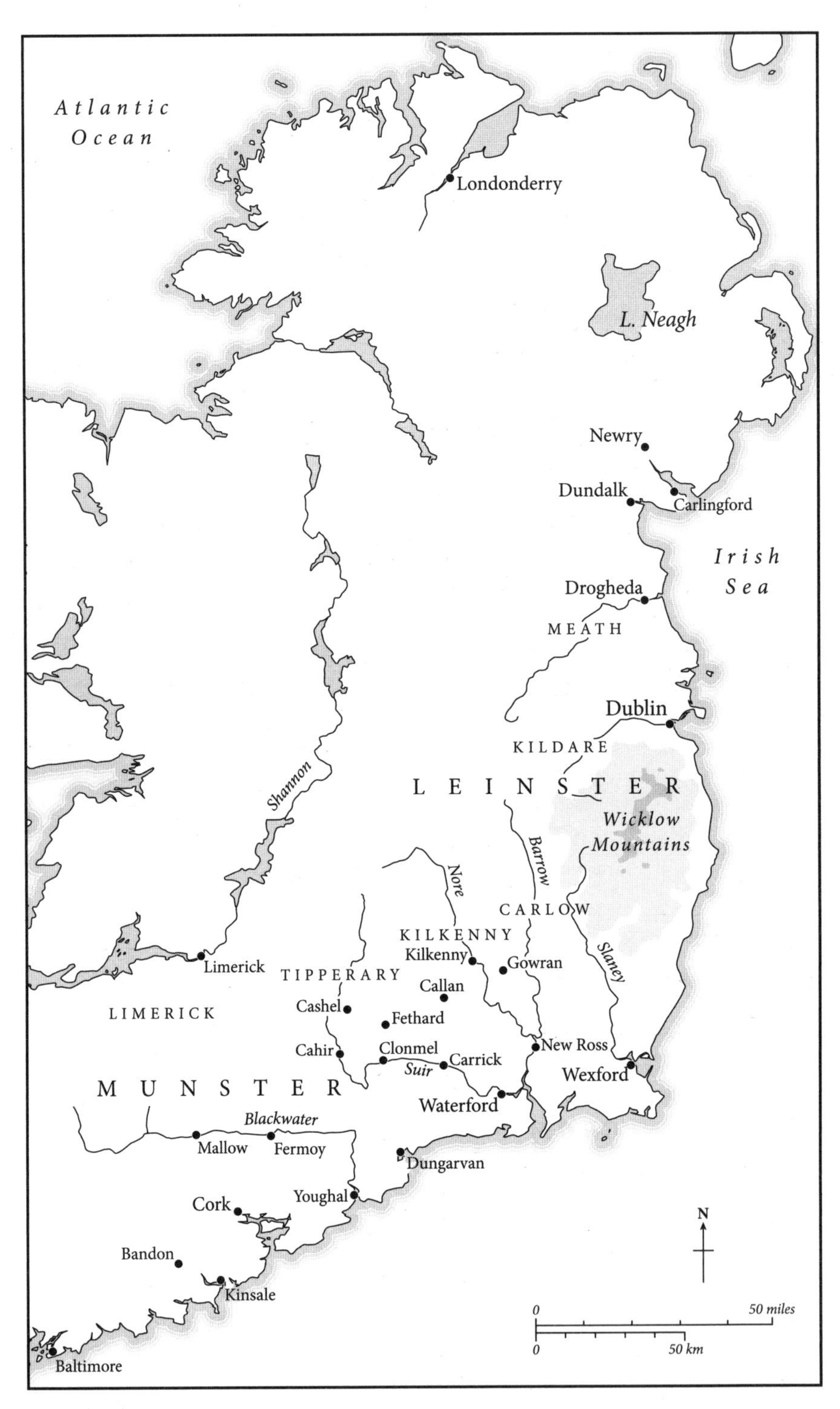

Atlantic Ocean
Londonderry
L. Neagh
Newry
Dundalk
Carlingford
Irish Sea
Drogheda
MEATH
Dublin
KILDARE
LEINSTER
Wicklow Mountains
Shannon
Barrow
Nore
CARLOW
KILKENNY
Slaney
Kilkenny
Gowran
Limerick
TIPPERARY
Callan
LIMERICK
Cashel
Fethard
Cahir
Clonmel
Carrick
New Ross
Suir
Wexford
MUNSTER
Waterford
Blackwater
Mallow
Fermoy
Dungarvan
Youghal
Cork
N
Bandon
Kinsale
0
50 miles
0
50 km
Baltimore

4. Ireland.

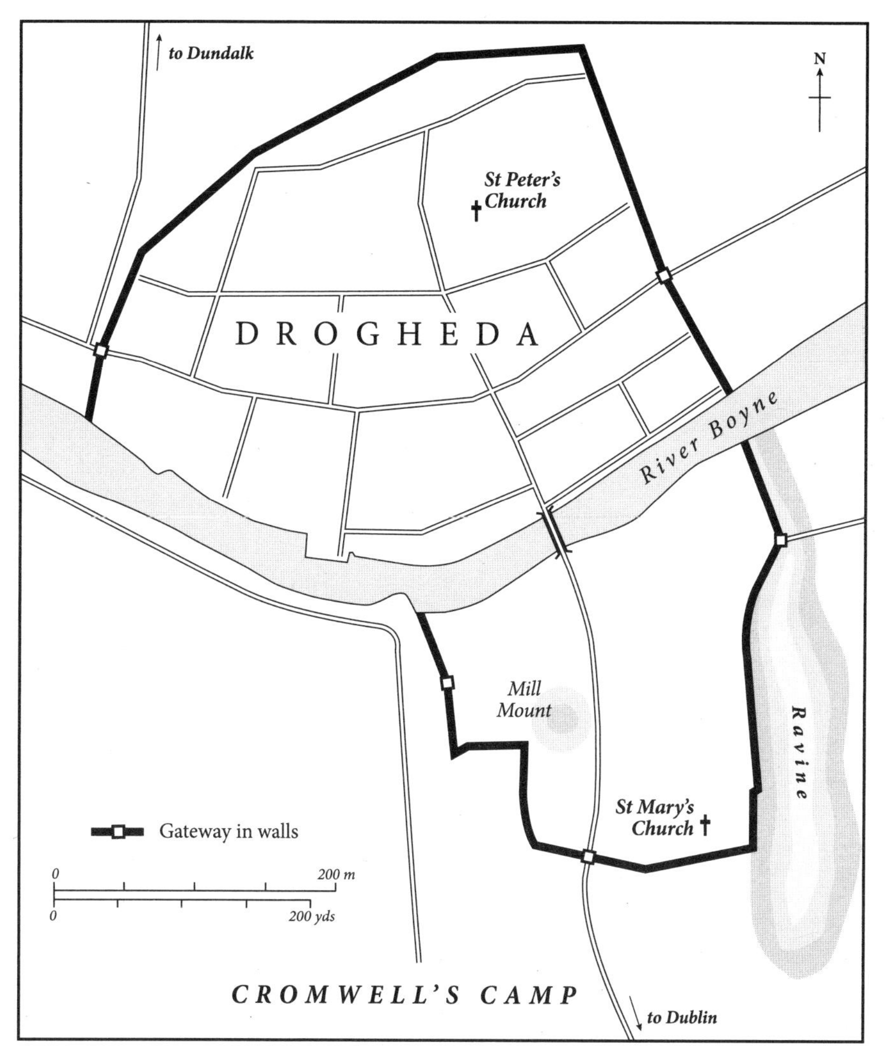

5. Drogheda, 1649.

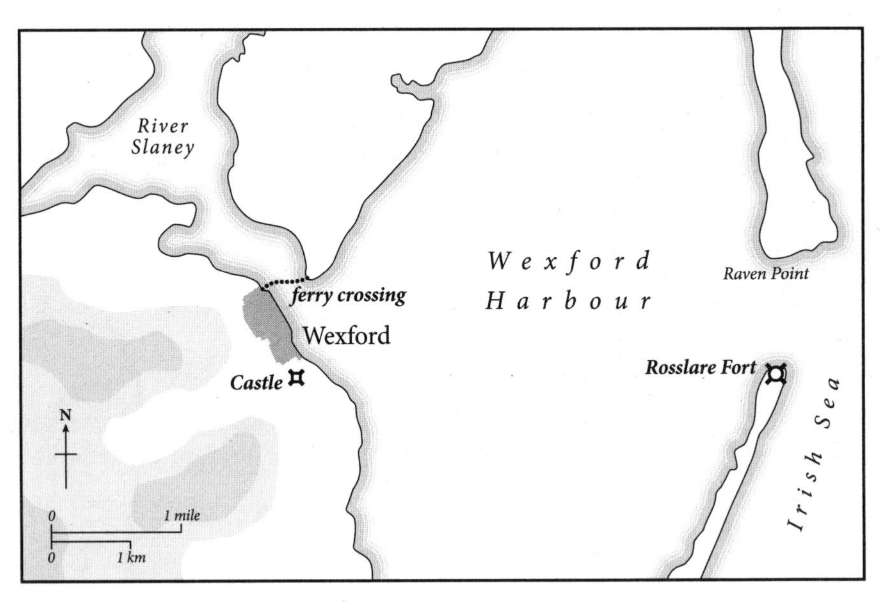

6. The Setting of Wexford, 1649.

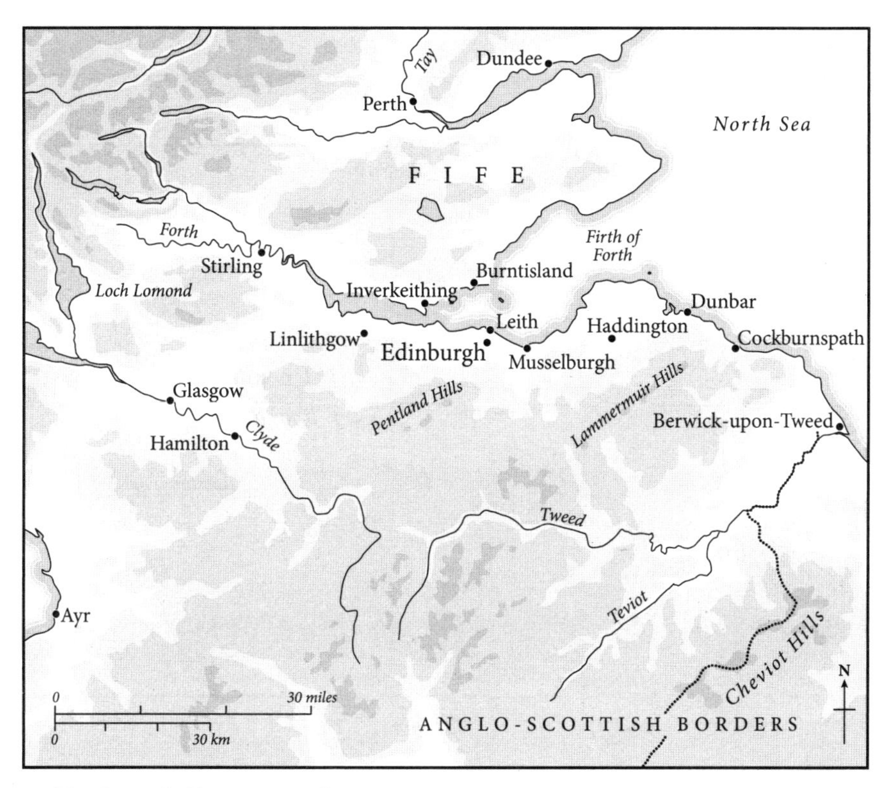

7. The Scottish Campaign, 1650–1.

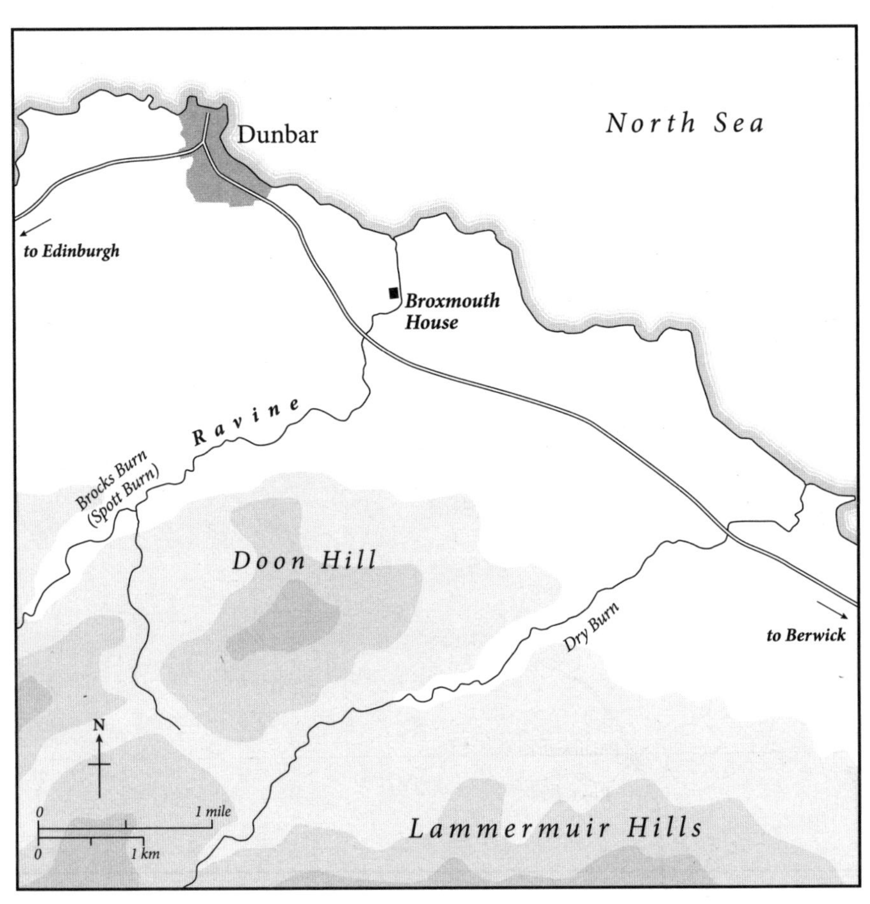

8. The Battlefield of Dunbar, 3 September 1650.

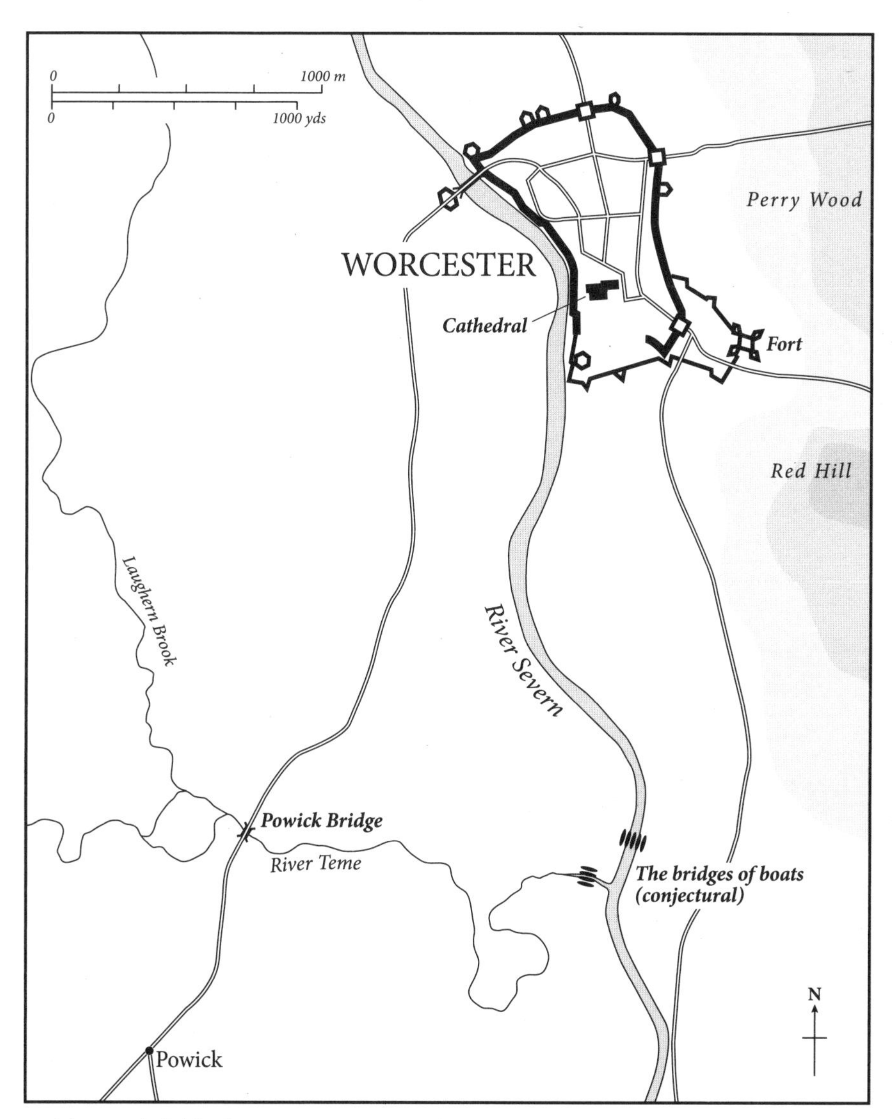

9. The Battlefield of Worcester, 3 September 1651.

INTRODUCTION

In the later 2010s, I wrote a book entitled *The Making of Oliver Cromwell.* It engaged with his career up until the end of the year 1646, enabling me, as the title suggests, to describe its formative stages, during his youth, his time as an active member of Parliament and (above all) his service in the Great Civil War. I had been intending to write a study on him for thirty years before, and prepared for it over that time, and decided to undertake it for this period because it was the one that I knew best. I did not at that time have any definite ambition to follow it with any further books upon Cromwell, wishing to monitor its critical reception before deciding whether to follow his life further. This was because I had adopted two distinctive strategies in that first book, both of which I thought risky and likely to provoke negative responses.

The first was to avoid the usual policy of previous biographers of Cromwell, which was to use the man's own letters and speeches as the basic framework on which to hang a narrative. This was a natural enough approach, given the length and intensity of his public career, the voluminous nature of his recorded words, and the vivid insight that they appeared to provide into his thinking. I wanted, however, to check those off against other evidence at each point, both the recorded sequence of events and the testimonies of other people involved. Such a process was lengthy and difficult enough to preclude a full one-volume study of his life, which is why I chose a section of it instead. It also involved questioning much of what Cromwell himself wanted people to believe of him, and in doing so questioning the generally accepting and admiring tone of most previous scholarly writing on him. My work confirmed the prevailing impression of his military and political brilliance, but also showed him to be more devious, ruthless, manipulative and self-seeking than he had previously been taken to be in modern times.

My other strategy, which might have provoked a different kind of disquiet in readers, was to paint the physical surroundings of Cromwell's life as vividly as possible. This was the kind of technique more commonly employed by historical novelists than by professional historians, let alone previous biographers of Cromwell, and might jar with many readers. There is no evidence that he himself regarded the landscapes around him in this way, though equally there is none that he did not. My objective in providing such lush descriptions was instead to enable readers to imagine themselves there with him and, looking around them, to set the scenes for action. In the event, both gambles paid off, for the book produced reactions, both formal and informal, that were overwhelmingly of a generosity much beyond what I regard as its deserts. Many included encouragement to proceed to a second instalment, and that is what I have done here.

In embarking on that course I was aware of at least three considerable prospective problems in the section of Cromwell's life that I now selected for treatment, from the opening of the year 1647 to April 1653.The first was the year 1647 itself. Somebody had once told me a story about one of the historians of the period whom I had most enjoyed reading in my early adolescence, Dame Veronica Wedgwood. I was informed that she had intended to follow her two hugely popular narrative histories, which covered between them the history of Britain and Ireland in the period between 1637 and 1646, with a third volume to carry her story up to the death of King Charles I. What had prevented her was her encounter with the records for the events of 1647, which proved to be so numerous, complex, difficult and (often) dull, that she, the mistress of narrative, abandoned hope of making them intelligible and enticing to a wide readership – and, with that hope, the book (instead she wrote a short one on the eventual fate of King Charles). I had somehow to try to succeed in the endeavour which she had allegedly disowned (and the fact that the story was told of her at all indicated the reputation of the events of the year among experts).

My second daunting prospect was how to deal with the massacres at Drogheda and Wexford in Ireland in 1649, which presented the opposite difficulty to the previous one. They were all too exciting, and notorious. For over a hundred years, they had represented a pair of the most appalling episodes in Irish historical memory, especially the killings at Drogheda, and the greatest blot on Cromwell's reputation. As such, they had always been a subject of contention between Irish and English historians, and also within both groups, and recently the controversies had hotted up again. As a result, whatever I wrote of them, I was going to make some people disappointed, unhappy and resentful.

My third problem was with the evidence for political events in England during the period. It was not one of a shortage of material, but of the quality of that material. There was a critical lack of internal evidence, in which the main actors explained their motivations and manoeuvres or were observed by those close to them. Instead there was an abundance of gossip, rumour, propaganda and assertion, usually of unknown provenance and almost always of dubious veracity. No previous historian had accepted this in its entirety, but there had never been any consensus over how much should be rejected or set aside.

In a broad historiographical context, the project of contextualizing Cromwell's words and actions was a piece of revisionism of a kind classic for the period since the 1970s. The work being revised was that of the great Victorian and Edwardian historians, who had established the basic story of the British past that was taught as orthodoxy in my youth. This version of events had not been challenged since, but constantly amplified and augmented in details, and given a social and economic underpinning by the influence of Marxist theory. Cromwell and his allies had a special place in this story, as proponents of religious and political liberties that came to define constitutional modernity in the Western world. They were seen as harbingers and ancestors of that modernity, and particular phrases in Cromwell's letters and speeches could be picked out to exemplify such a role. The actions of the regime he led – of making the parliamentary system more equitable by reforming constituencies and the franchise, and safeguarding the right of Protestant dissenters from the national Church to participate fully in the nation – were those of the nineteenth-century reformers. His fervent Christian religiosity matched that of the Victorian and Edwardian era, and his protection of Protestant nonconformists chimed with the powerful alliance between political liberalism and religious dissent in that period. That alliance transferred subsequently to the socialist movement, as Methodism and other nonconformist denominations proved to be nurseries of trade union and Labour Party leaders. Cromwell and his followers, with their republicanism, their revolutionary army and their association with gathered community churches, made even more obvious forebears and heroes for modern America, and were hailed as such.

The project of revising this construct stemmed from the profound changes that occurred in British and American societies from the 1960s onwards, when many of the assumptions of the nineteenth and early twentieth centuries began to be questioned. That process was especially intense in the United Kingdom, which lost the colonial empire and great power status that had underpinned its identity, and which began to lose the heavy industry that had been another of its modern foundations. Christian cultural hegemony atrophied swiftly, and so did the restrictive traditional morality which had accompanied it. As these anchors of the British world picture fell away, so all manner of established assumptions and mental structures came to be questioned, and with them the history (and prehistory) that had been written to justify them.

It was inevitable that Cromwell's period should come under that scrutiny, as it had played such an important role in the historical self-image of modern Britain and America. Indeed, though from the 1970s revisionism came to affect many areas of the British past, it first became widely employed as a term among British historians with respect to a questioning of the accepted picture of events in England in the first half of the seventeenth century. The result was a prolonged and at times heated controversy in which divisions ran within rather than between generations, and the consequences of it have not quite worked themselves out. At its best, however, the revisionist enterprise was a worthwhile one, consisting collectively and in the long term not of an iconoclastic attack on the traditional version of history but of an examination of its Victorian and Edwardian underpinnings, to ascertain which are still sound and which seem in need of replacement. Such an attempt has not yet been made in the case of the career of Cromwell, and the present series of books represents a tentative attempt to begin one.

No historical writing can escape its contemporary context, however, and if that attempt produces in some respects a different Cromwell from the traditional one, then that is partly because the contexts of the two are now very different. It cannot be stressed enough that my project does not represent a right-wing attempt to debunk a liberal and socialist hero. My own politics embody a passionate attachment to liberalism, socialism, cultural and ideological pluralism and democracy. The problem is that the Cromwell revealed by my researches no longer matches up well to those values as they are understood in the early twenty-first century. Fervent religious belief remains an admirable component of individual identity and of private life, but it no longer seems as reliable a force for communal cohesion as it did 150 years ago, when, even in an island with as many different forms of Christianity as Britain, a broad-based allegiance to that faith, and especially to a Protestant denomination, served as a unifying factor. Now religious devotion has come once more to function commonly as an intractably divisive force in public life, as much within states as between them. Cromwell's militarism, evangelism, piety and republicanism can make him look more akin to the current American radical Christian right than to a

Victorian British liberal. Likewise, as a leader of military coups that installed puppet regimes against the will of the majority of his compatriots, claiming a superior ideology, he bears a resemblance to figures who have held that role in developing nations in recent decades. Nonetheless, the present is never the past, and there remain important differences between him and these modern counterparts, as significant as those between him and his nineteenth- and twentieth-century English admirers.

I continue in this book stylistic conventions and modes of proceeding followed in the last. I follow prevailing convention in using dates for events according to the calendar employed by the British of Cromwell's age, and not that in use in his time across much of Europe (and subsequently adopted by the British), which reckoned the same dates ten days earlier. On the other hand, I follow the same scholarly convention in starting each year on 1 January, instead of 25 March, on which date Cromwell and his contemporaries held that the year changed. I have modernized spelling in quotations from documents, to make their sense clearer to a wide readership. As a matter of personal taste, I have avoided reference to political groups by the insulting names accorded to them by contemporaries, which have often stuck down the centuries. Thus, I speak of the London radicals rather than the Levellers, and of the purged Parliament rather than the Rump.

As before, also, whenever my conclusions reproduce and confirm those drawn by specific colleagues, I draw attention to the fact. However, except when explaining and contributing to an established historiographical debate, I have not drawn attention to points at which I disagree with particular fellow scholars. As I have written previously, those who are already expert in the period will recognize these points easily enough, and those who are not are unlikely to be interested. All of the current fellow experts in Cromwell and his times are either friends or respected companion workers of mine, and I see no reason to turn difference into conflict. In my earliest published work, in the 1980s, I declared my allegiance to the concept of a republic of letters, and I have never experienced anything to disillusion me with it.

1

MAY EVE 1647

A MORNING JOURNEY

On the morning of 30 April 1647, Oliver Cromwell stepped out of his newly acquired house in Drury Lane in order to attend the House of Commons. A passer-by would have seen a powerfully built man in middle life, of average height, with a broad face and reddish-brown hair, just starting slightly to recede and go grey, and falling just below his collar. This was a modest length for a male hairstyle of the time, and likewise he wore the fashionable moustache and beard, but clipped close, the beard a mere tuft below his lower lip. This impression of restraint and austerity would have been reflected in his clothes: normal apparel for a gentleman of his period, but lacking ostentation. Posterity was to make much of a further distinguishing feature of his appearance, the three warts on his face, the most prominent below his lower lip. Satirists among his contemporaries, however, were to devote much more attention to two other features: the long bulbous nose, which was a family trait, and the reddish flush in it and his cheeks. Nevertheless, it was not a strikingly ugly face, any more than it was a strikingly handsome one: the long nose balanced the broad cheeks, and the heavily lidded eyes and stubbornly firm and resolute mouth were both attractive.[1]

At this time Cromwell was one of the more prominent members of the House of Parliament for which he was bound, but he was also well known as one of the foremost soldiers to emerge from the civil war which had just ended. In that war, his party, representing around three-fifths of the House of Commons and a third of the House of Lords and claiming the full authority of a Parliament, had defeated the supporters of the king, Charles I. Cromwell had played a leading part in that victory, as commander of the cavalry in the main field force which had won the war, commonly known as the New Model Army. In this role he had operated occasionally on his own, with a detachment, but mostly as the able lieutenant to the equally able commander of the New Model, Sir Thomas Fairfax. It may be tempting, therefore, to downplay his importance by this time – after all, few now remember the name of the duke of Wellington's second-in-command at Waterloo – but it would be misleading. For one thing, Cromwell was a front-rank politician as well as a general, and for another he had emerged as one of the great cavalry leaders of English history, equivalent to Joachim Murat in the Napoleonic Wars and Jeb Stuart in the American Civil War.

Having said this, his own status was unusually insecure at this time. Parliament had voted during the closing period of the war that he should be rewarded for his services in the settlement with the defeated king that was then expected. The reward was lavish: to make him a baron and support his title with an aristocrat's landed estate, worth £2,500 a year. No settlement with the king had been made, however, and the lands had not been fully secured to him. If his opponents within his own party became leaders of that party, as they seemed to be doing, then there was a real chance that neither estate nor title would ever materialize, and he would be left with his pre-war standing as a minor gentleman: socially, he was still just 'Oliver Cromwell Esquire'. He could also be known by his military title of Lieutenant-General, but even there his exact standing was in doubt.[2] Two years before, Cromwell had been disqualified from holding any military office, together with all other members of both Houses of Parliament, as part of a complete renewal of the command structure to clear away serious quarrels and rivalries. His position in charge of the New Model's horse regiments was made possible as an emergency measure by granting him a series of time-limited exemptions from this regulation. The last of these had expired when his military service ended in the previous summer, and he had duly left the army and returned to the Commons; so it might be supposed that he no longer held any command. However, Cromwell had never surrendered his commission, and Fairfax had continued to sign pay warrants to him as if he was still in service: apart from anything else, the money would have been a useful supplement to Oliver's meagre private income. His standing as an army officer, therefore, like his standing in society, was ambiguous and imprecise.

His new home in Drury Lane, to which he had moved his family from their native East Anglia in the previous winter, was itself testimony to his ambitions. It was ideally positioned for a public figure, being halfway between the City of London, the commercial and financial hub of the realm, and Parliament. It was also a very prestigious address, in a recently built street of handsome residences occupied by aristocrats.[3] His journey to the House could have taken one of two routes. The first was a northerly one, down Long Acre, which was another new-build street of homes for the wealthy, well known to Oliver because he had lodged there during his attendance of Parliament during the early part of the decade. The second was southerly, along the Strand, the main highway connecting London and Westminster. Whichever he chose, he would have been aware of the enormous city behind him to the east. In the previous century and a half the population of London had increased ten times over, to near 400,000, making it one of the three biggest urban centres in Europe, with Paris and Constantinople, dwarfing its nearest competitor in the British Isles (Norwich) by a factor of twenty to one. Possession of the city had been one of the key factors which had enabled Parliament to win the war, because of its tremendous resources of manpower, money and manufactures. Even at this relatively warm time of year, there would still have been a constant haze over it, of coal smoke and other fumes rising from domestic chimneys and industrial processes. Even more apparent would have been the noise – of footfalls, voices, wheels and hooves, like a great wind or sea in the distance. For Cromwell this constant background hubbub may have had a menacing quality, for at this time it is likely that the majority of politically active Londoners were his enemies.

If he had chosen the route along the Strand, he would have passed a series of reminders of the destructive impact which the parliamentarian cause had made upon religion, politics and society, clearing away what people like Cromwell saw as corruption and ungodliness. His own street of Drury Lane had contained a theatre, but that had been closed as part of a general ban on such entertainments. On reaching the Strand itself, he would have seen the medieval church of St Mary, in which, as in all parish churches in Parliament's power, the focus of devotion would have been shifted from a communion table draped and railed in at the east end, as the main setting for ceremony, to a pulpit in the body of the nave, from which the word of God should be preached. The rails had been taken out, and the table banished to a less conspicuous position in the nave, overlooked by the pulpit. Before the church in the street had stood a tall maypole, around which Londoners had danced and made merry in summers past; but three years earlier, Parliament had ordered the removal of all such poles in England as incitements to idolatry and disorder.

The Strand itself was lined with the mansions of great nobles, among them the official London residence of the queen, but some now had been confiscated by Parliament because of the royalism of their owners (the queen herself having fled to France) and were used to house foreign guests and administrative committees. Where Long Acre and the Strand converged had stood Charing Cross, a tall stone medieval pyramid surmounted by a cross and carved with saints and other figures, which had been demolished during the war as a monument to superstition and false religion. Beyond its site, Cromwell would have passed through a tall turreted Tudor gateway, decorated with a chequered pattern of flint and stone, onto a street running straight to a second gateway. On either side of it, and especially on the left, were the jumbled buildings of the main royal palace, Whitehall, the most impressive being the massive stone banqueting house with its classical pillared facade, halfway down. The palace had been shut up for half a decade, since the king had fled his capital and so triggered the war.

For Cromwell, as for all of his fellow countrymen, the overarching question of the moment was what could be put in place of all this removal in order to build a better England and so justify the expense and bloodshed of the war. For those embarked upon this task as the war ended, it must have seemed an appallingly daunting one. The defeated royalists included most of the traditional leaders of social and political life, who were now excluded from any role in central or local government for the foreseeable future. Parliament had only won the war with the help of the Scots, who had a large army on English soil and expected a double reward for their aid: a huge cash payment to cover their expenses, and a reform of the Church of England to make it more compatible with their own. Most obviously, this involved removing the bishops who were the Church's accustomed leaders, and reforming its liturgy to abolish most ceremonies and seasonal festivals. Meanwhile, as long as Parliament continued to maintain its own armies after the war, the heavy wartime taxes had to be continued to pay them, and those taxes were very unpopular. Despite their scale, the army was still employing twice as many soldiers as the taxes could support, and by early 1647 the state debt had reached a total of £2.8 million, with no evident means by which it could be repaid.

The Church had lost a third of its clergy, expelled for royalism or unpopularity. The worst harvest failure of the century had commenced in the previous summer, and would be repeated for three years, further undermining the tax base and the patience of tax-payers, and forcing an increase in soldiers' pay as the price of food rose. To complete the mess, at the end of the war the king had surrendered to the Scottish army in England, hoping to turn it against Parliament. Meanwhile, Ireland had for over five years been engulfed in a brutal civil war of its own, sparked by the rebellion of the majority of the inhabitants, who adhered to the Roman Catholic religion which had been overthrown in England and Scotland during the previous century. Irish Catholics had risen to protect their Church, to secure their own property and to regain access to political power; those in the island who had remained loyal to the government in England had become divided between the adherents of king and Parliament when the English Civil War broke out. When that ended, the royal lord lieutenant in Ireland, the marquis of Ormond, still held Dublin and its region in the name of King Charles, so ensuring that one of the three capitals of his realms remained loyal to him.

In the course of the autumn, winter and spring, the parliamentary leadership had responded to this nightmarish set of problems with imagination, daring and considerable success. It had already replaced the traditional liturgy of the English Church with one much more acceptable to the Scots, and had now abolished the bishops, using their lands as security for loans which paid the Scots enough up front (with promise of more) to persuade them to go home. The Scots failed to reach a deal with the king, and on leaving England in early 1647 they handed him over to Parliament. In Ireland, the marquis of Ormond opened negotiations to surrender his territory, including Dublin, to Parliament, and these proved successful.

In late 1646 some of the provincial parliamentarian forces in England were disbanded and in early 1647 the number of garrisons began to be reduced. The end product of this process would be to disband the New Model Army itself, retaining much of its cavalry for a home guard for England and Wales and sending some of the remaining horse soldiers and much of the foot to reconquer Ireland. The rest of the infantry would be disbanded, and England guarded by the regular local militia, put in hands loyal to Parliament, and paid from local rates. This would allow a considerable reduction in taxation. Once all this had been accomplished, the king would be left isolated and forced to accept what Parliament had done. His acquiescence in the new state and Church, with reduced royal powers, would oblige the royalists to embrace it too, and all but the extremists among them would eventually be allowed back into the political fold. It was a programme which, by April 1647, had secured the support of a majority in both Houses of Parliament and the City of London and among parliamentarians in the provinces. There was, however, a minority of people in all those places who were deeply worried by aspects of the plan, and Cromwell was one of them.[4]

He would have been aware of all this as he prepared to end his journey on that last April morning, passing through the second gateway and along the straight street that continued beyond, seeing in front and to the right the church of St Margaret, and looming behind it the enormous bulk of Westminster Abbey. To the left was the huddle of buildings, of different ages, sizes and materials, that made up another royal palace, the medieval one of Westminster which the monarchs had vacated for Whitehall over a century before. He crossed the broad yard of smooth earth in front of it and entered, finally reaching the lobby of the tall medieval chapel, with its lancet windows, in which the Commons met. Inside, he took his seat in one of the wooden stalls which ran along the side walls, four deep, and prepared to play his part in the business of the day. That promised to be important, and perhaps pivotal. The first three months of the year 1647 had been a depressing experience for him; but now things were looking up.

PRELUDE (1): JANUARY TO MARCH

An aspect of Cromwell's character that has been justly highlighted by all his biographers is his intense religiosity, unusual even in a generally religious age. This was partly a reflection of his own nature and of the profundity of the conversion experience that he had undergone in his thirties. It was also, however, an aspect of his anomalous social and political position. His astonishing rise from genteel obscurity in the provinces to national political, social and military prominence, made possible by the war, could only be explained to himself and his allies by a special divine favour, which he had to continue to earn if he were to maintain his position. This meant that misfortune had an even more profound implication for him than most people, in suggesting that this favour might have been withdrawn.

For the past seven years he had enjoyed an astonishing sequence of good luck, which, allied with his own talent and skill in exploiting advantages, had enabled his ascent. Even the rare moments of unhappiness that he had suffered during that period had been immediately followed by dramatic achievements of glory: for example, the death of his eldest surviving son, at a point when his own military career seemed to be stagnating, was succeeded within a few months by his leading role in the spectacular victory of Marston Moor.

In early 1647, however, it might have seemed that the foundations of his success were giving way. For one thing, having come through the entire war in robust health, despite its considerable risks and strains, he fell seriously ill in late January or early February, with what seems to have been some kind of abscess in his head.[5] For a time he thought he might die, and he did not recover until March.[6] Next his career prospects took a slide, when on 8 March the House voted without a division to bar its members from holding any command in the home guard that would replace the New Model Army.[7] Later in the month Cromwell was observed to be holding 'long talks' with a Protestant German prince, the Elector Palatine, and it was thought – perhaps correctly – that he was thinking of taking up a high position in a new force to be raised by the latter, and so seeking his fortune abroad. The foe he would fight in Germany would be Roman Catholics, the most feared and hated division of Christianity to a Protestant of Cromwell's extreme kind, which would give his service the character of a crusade, and so suit his view of the world as divided into the followers and enemies of God.[8]

In February his allies in the Commons put him forward as one of the generals to command the army sent to Ireland, but this was quashed in early April, when the House agreed to give the overall leadership to Philip Skippon, who had been general of the foot soldiers of the New Model Army as Cromwell had been of the horse. The cavalry of the expeditionary force were entrusted not to Oliver but to Edward Massey, who had been a very successful garrison governor in the earlier part of the Civil War but had turned in a lacklustre performance as general of a local army in its last year. He was, however, in favour with the party that now dominated Parliament.[9] Cromwell was being sidelined, and he knew it.

Coupled with these personal woes was a broader problem: that the political and religious ideals for which he had fought the war seemed in danger of being rejected. The parliamentarian cause had become more or less synonymous in religious affairs with that of the Puritans, that wing of the pre-war Church of England which wanted fundamental reform in it, to shift it away from ceremony and hierarchy towards a greater emphasis on preaching and the Bible. This had been one of the principal causes of the war itself, as the royalist cause had been supported largely by people who wished to retain the traditional nature of the reformed Church, as one led (under the monarch) by bishops, associated with cathedrals and their clergy, and having a large surviving component of ceremony embodied in the official Prayer Book. In 1645 and 1646 major steps had been taken by the increasingly victorious Parliament to commence the programme of further reformation: the bishops had been abolished, and the Prayer Book replaced by the Directory, a set of services much sparer in ritual and more absolutely dominated by the parish minister.

What remained unclear was the future structure of the Church, because of a major rift among Puritans and parliamentarians, which had appeared by 1643. Those on one side acquired the label of 'presbyterians'. They were inspired by the Church of Scotland and those Churches in parts of Europe which favoured a Christianity based on the teachings of the Swiss reformer John Calvin. These Churches were composed of a hierarchy of parish, provincial and national bodies, mixing clergy and laity, and a uniformity of faith and practice of the kind attempted by the traditional Church of England. The other side of the rift awarded a much greater degree of authority to the parishes, allowing ministers and congregations a broader amount of latitude in doctrine and practice. The clearest model for this was provided by the colonies of New England, and proponents of it were generally known as 'independents'.

In practice, matters were neither as simple nor as polarized as this summary may suggest. Rather than representing two clearly defined parties, among clergy or laity, the attitudes concerned made up a continuous spectrum, with a stark and sustained polarity only between people grouped towards its extremes. Some patrons appointed churchmen of both views to livings, and there were people who preferred modified versions of each system, such as a presbyterian structure at parish level but not at that of region or nation.[10] Moreover, even those who gravitated towards the extremes were themselves divided by a different clash of instinctual belief, between individuals who believed that clergy should be entrusted with ultimate power over religious affairs, and those who thought that they should not. To complicate matters further, there was a third split in the Puritan movement, which was caused by the collapse of national Church discipline at the opening of the 1640s and much accentuated by the disruption of the war. The suspension of mechanisms to police religious beliefs and behaviour had allowed a proliferation of Protestant sects, such as baptists, gathered around particular leaders, sometimes ordained clergy and sometimes not. Most of these wanted to worship outside the established Church, no matter which form that Church took, and many thought that the Church itself should be abolished.

The crucial question for the great majority of English Protestants was whether these gathered churches should be allowed to continue to exist, alongside the national ecclesiastical system, for at least a time after the new form of the latter was settled. By every detectable sign (petitions, publications and recorded comments), majority opinion in the nation was hostile to this approach, regarding sectaries as heretics, alike offensive to God and destructive to communal cohesion from national to local level. It was also plain, however, that many of those who belonged to the sects had made contributions to Parliament's victory, and it was believed by many members of both Houses that some measure of what was often called 'liberty of conscience' should be their reward. One of the most prominent of these had long been Cromwell. He had shown himself flexible when it came to the actual form of the post-war Church, being willing to accept a presbyterian system if it did not enforce conformity on those who did not wish to join it, though his natural allies were among the independents. He was, however, viscerally opposed to any kind of religious institutions that gave churchmen coercive power over the laity. In general, the independents did not want anybody to separate themselves from the national Church, but increasingly came to ally with the sectaries against the powerful threat represented to both by intolerant presbyterians. Cromwell's tenderness towards the sects, in contrast, seems to have been genuine, and to have stemmed from his recognition of the service many of their members had given to his cause, and the genuine and fervent piety that they displayed.

These tensions and disputes had made an impact on the national political scene, so that halfway through the war Parliament itself, and its supporters, divided into two loose alliances, generally known as Presbyterians and Independents after the religious groupings. Broadly speaking, the Presbyterians were more inclined to favour a strong and intolerant national Church, based on the presbyterian structure, and a negotiated peace with the king. As such, they made natural allies with the Scots. The Independents tended to want a looser Church structure, with some degree of liberty of conscience, and therefore usually supported a war effort designed to defeat the king outright, as he and his supporters were much less likely to accept a peace treaty which honoured their principles than those of the Presbyterians. As part of this stance, they were also more inclined to want stricter controls over royal power after the war, to keep the gathered churches safe from royal hostility, than their opponents. And they had a mutual antipathy with the Scots.

The religious divisions did not map precisely onto the political: notably, many individuals who themselves were perfectly happy to belong to a presbyterian Church supported the Independents because they were also prepared to allow freedom of worship to fellow parliamentarians who did not want to belong to one. Furthermore, few if any people in Parliament were themselves members of the sects for whom some were seeking at least a limited tolerance.

Just as important, the two political groups were not organized and cohesive parties. Some MPs and lords belonged very clearly and consistently to one or the other and provided their leadership, but most MPs, and perhaps lords, cannot be attributed confidently to either, but swung their support between the two according to the moment and the issue.

Nevertheless, by the end of the war, the core groups of partisans were consistent and entrenched in their opinions and their opposition to each other. Most commentators deplored the existence of parties: but this was in itself a testimony to their presence.[11] In the course of 1646, the House of Commons came to divide over issues more and more frequently, and generally the tellers on each side of a division – those prominent proponents of the rival arguments who were chosen to count the votes – were taken from the leadership of the rival parties. In particular, Denzil Holles and Sir Philip Stapleton tended to act as tellers for the Presbyterians, and Sir Arthur Hesilrige and the Wiltshire gentleman Sir John Evelyn for the Independents. Cromwell, again, had a firmly established place in this pattern, as one of the best-known leaders of the Independents.

What would have exercised and troubled Cromwell's mind strenuously in early 1647 was that his party seemed to be losing power. It had mostly been the Presbyterians who had pushed forward the programme which had, as described, done much to tackle the post-war problems of the nation in the previous half year and had promised to settle the rest. In the first quarter of the new year they achieved a steady majority in the Lords and were coming to dominate the Commons as well, and in April they took control of Parliament's main executive body, the committee of representatives from both Houses that met in the confiscated mansion of the royalist earl of Derby to administer the nation.[12] The process by which Cromwell was pushed out of future military employment was a consequence of this shift of power. Equally alarming to him, or even more so, were the implications of that shift for his religious ideals. By this point it was clear that Parliament was establishing a presbyterian Church, but the question of liberty of conscience remained completely unsettled. There seemed now to be an increasing risk that it would never be granted, as the proponents of it seemed ever more clearly to be a minority in both nation and capital, and even among the former wartime parliamentarians, while the ever more dominant Presbyterians had no commitment to it. Nonetheless, those who favoured it remained a significant number among those who had supported Parliament's cause, well scattered through the provinces and with a particular concentration in London and in the New Model Army.

In both of the last two, in particular, the war had generated people who combined a commitment to liberty of conscience, and often also to independency or sectarianism in their own religion, with a growing desire for fundamental change in the political constitution. These may henceforth be termed 'radicals', as a trans-historical expression for those who want to reform the foundations of a system rather than only to repair or modify it: this usage neatly reflects the Latin origins of the term as signifying a willingness to root something up.[13] By 1646 a group of London intellectuals had formulated a programme based on the principle that power should reside in the majority of the people of the nation, embodied in the elected House of Commons. They called for a removal of the traditional right of the king and House of Lords to veto the Commons' proposals, so shifting the constitution from a balance between these three component parts of a Parliament, with the monarch having the ultimate decision, to a dominance of the people's representatives, with king and Lords acting more as advisers and mediators to the latter. Increasingly, this programme also incorporated a call for liberty of conscience not just for all kinds of Puritan but for Christians in general, and perhaps even people in general. Again, those who articulated such a religious view looked abroad for a model, this time to the Dutch Republic. Their approach to politics drew in part on their experience of popular participation in the local government of London and in the formation of gathered churches, and on the practical problem that, with both king and Lords seemingly hostile to liberty of conscience, the Commons was the only remaining hope for that liberty among the traditional trinity that comprised a Parliament.

This programme was articulated most prominently by three men, John Lilburne, Richard Overton and William Walwyn.[14] Cromwell had especially strong links with the first of them, a dome-headed bundle of nervous energy with a bob of hair and a natty moustache. He had launched his own rise to prominence in the current Parliament with a speech in favour of Lilburne's release from prison, into which the royal government had clapped the man for attacking the bishops. During the war, Oliver had acted as a patron and protector to Lilburne, but in 1646 both Lilburne and Overton had been locked up on parliamentary authority, and held indefinitely without trial because they denied the right of Parliament to act as a court of law in this manner. Had Cromwell wished to help either – though by now their political views were outpacing his as he had shown no interest in popular sovereignty – he was powerless to do so.

Through the winter and spring, the pressure built up against liberty of conscience. In 1646 some intolerant presbyterian ministers had begun to preach and write systematically against the proliferation of sects and to call for their suppression.[15] These ministers sometimes targeted the New Model Army as a breeding ground for such heresy, and indeed both sectaries and independents were prominent in some of its units. The nature of the army was to mix together Puritans of different kinds in the single enterprise of winning the war, and so provide a model for how such religious liberty might operate in practice. From its creation, the New Model had in addition often been identified politically with the Independents, as their prime, and very effective, instrument for their aim of winning the war outright and without conceding anything to the king. Moreover, by the end of 1646 a few members of the army were starting to echo the political views of the London radicals.[16] Accordingly, the Presbyterian programme to disband the army won especially enthusiastic support among the more politically and religiously conservative parliamentarians.

In December 1646 the corporation of London petitioned Parliament to disband the army because it was a breeding ground for sectaries, to abolish the property tax on which the soldiers most depended for their pay, and to suppress preaching by anybody not an officially ordained clergyman.[17] The Lords responded warmly to this, as they did to petitions from Suffolk and Essex that followed in February and March, to suppress unorthodox religious opinions, reduce taxes and remove the army.[18] Between December and March, members of both Houses listened to a barrage of sermons from ministers calling for the crushing of heresy, and increasingly for the disbanding of the New Model as well.[19] In March Parliament decreed a day of prayer and humiliation before God for the nation, in repentance for the 'abominable heresies and blasphemies' that were spreading in the army.[20]

In Cromwell's few letters to survive from this period, his fear for the loss of liberty of conscience is a major theme. Writing in March to the New Model's commander, his old friend and ally Fairfax, he declared that he hoped to earn a place in heaven by being ready 'to love the Lord, his poor despised people, to do for them and to be ready to suffer with them'. A short while later he wrote to Fairfax again, that a bitter spirit was abroad, spread by the Devil, and that slanders cast on religious radicals, such as a rumour of a planned uprising by them in London, were 'fine tricks to mock God with'.[21] His despondency was reflected in his poor attendance of the Commons, even when he had recovered his health. In April a royalist newsletter writer concluded that the 'Presbyterians now carry all before them with a high hand', and noted how seldom Cromwell and other leading Independents were to be seen in the House.[22] Likewise, they ceased to attend Parliament's executive agent, the Derby House Committee.[23] What seemed to them to be ominous portents, however, were to many mainstream parliamentarians signs that the nation was being settled, and returned to normality after the terrors and disruptions of war. At the end of March, one of the most reliably supportive of parliamentarian newspapers, the *Kingdom's Weekly Intelligencer*, proclaimed that 'all things do seem to promise fairly'. Four months later, its editorial stated instead that 'there were never times in such a general distraction and so woe-begone as these'.[24]

The transformation that was for the editor a source of dismay and despair was for Oliver Cromwell a source of relief and opportunity.

INTERLUDE: CHARLES AND SAMUEL

Before explaining how that reversal of fortunes came about, it is necessary to remove for a short while from London and Cromwell, to the hilly Midland county of Northamptonshire, and a huge country mansion called Holdenby House, then a royal property. It was there, far from the centres of national power and activity, and guarded by a regiment of foot soldiers, that Parliament had placed King Charles in political cold storage, after the Scots had handed him over and while it carried out the vital preliminaries to settling the nation. As he is to become a key player in the story about to be told, it is worth taking a closer look both at his intrinsic nature and at his attitudes and beliefs at this time. Charles was the smallest English king for whom we have a reasonably reliable sense of size, standing at or just under 5 feet tall, and was also afflicted by a stammer that was the result of psychological rather than physical strains, because it was episodic. Neither of these afflictions should have counted for very much, because he had an older brother and sister who were of normal height (and diction), and also charismatic, self-confident and very popular; but the former died in his teens and the latter married and moved abroad, leaving Charles, the runt of the litter, to inherit the throne. Unsurprisingly, he remained shy and fond of privacy, and coped with his unexpected royal role with a frigid dignity and a repetitive daily routine, which included a great deal of prayer: it was after all apparently his God who had put him in this difficult position, and to whom he answered for his performance in it. Charles wanted his three kingdoms brought into a much greater uniformity and order, and efficiency, regularity and predictability of government: in effect, laid out like one of the art galleries that he loved, or made to function like one of the clocks that ordered his day. In both Church and state he prized beauty, hierarchy, ceremony and obedience.

With this bundle of characteristics, and his resolute devotion to duty, he was not a guaranteed failure as a ruler. He would probably have made a good enough Italian duke or German prince, or even a king of Spain or Portugal. Instead, he was put in charge of three different kingdoms, each of which had emerged from the Reformation with a different religious complexion and a different set of divisions, problems and tensions. Aware of these, his response was to attempt to tidy them all up and resettle them according to his own tastes; the result was that he stirred up severe trouble in all three and that government eventually broke down in each.

He was not a bad man. He was a very good husband and father, did his best to reward faithful servants with an equal loyalty, and completely lacked ruthlessness, let alone cruelty: his time in actual power was notable for its lack of executions of front-rank politicians, and he was the first English monarch for one and a half centuries under whom nobody was burned at the stake for their religious opinions. He was infinitely well meaning and stubbornly brave, caring nothing for his own safety if to preserve it would compromise his causes and ideals.

As a statesman, however, he had three great weaknesses. One was that he was incapable of understanding other people, either individually or in the mass. He accordingly entirely lacked the ability to entice or manipulate them, and, as he truly believed that everything he did for his subjects was for their good, he could not comprehend opposition to it. His second fault was largely evolved in an attempt to compensate for the first: that he was a conviction politician of utter rigour, believing that to do what was expedient rather than what seemed right risked the damnation of his soul. The third was that, adrift in increasingly complex, traumatic and baffling public affairs, he often tried to cut his way through them with sudden bold strokes and dramatic solutions. These could take an aggressive form, by striking at foreign or domestic opponents: examples were the two wars he had declared soon after becoming king, and his bungled attempt to arrest the leaders of Parliament in 1642, which had lost him control of his capital. They could also be defensive, in that he was inclined to panic and make flights from situations, without any clear idea of where he was going and what he was going to do: it had been his dash into the provinces in 1642 which had precipitated the Civil War, and he had similarly fled from his base at the end of the Civil War with no clear idea where he was going. The most dangerous aspect of this bundle of qualities is that, while he was a disaster as ruler of any of his three nation-states, he could be effective as the leader of a faction or party. An utterly inept, unprincipled or nasty monarch would not have attracted the support to enable a civil war to occur in any of his kingdoms, let alone, as transpired, in all of them.

It was in character that, at end of the war in England, when it was clear he had been defeated, Charles chose neither to flee to safety – and ignominy – abroad nor to surrender himself to Parliament and submit to its constraints. Instead he tried to drive a wedge between Parliament and the Scots who had helped defeat him, by handing himself over to the Scottish army in England. In doing so he was counting on the undoubted resentment that this army felt at the way in which Parliament had starved it of resources to supply the New Model, and the horror felt by most Scots at the prospect of liberty of conscience in England. He was, however, unable to offer it concessions which represented a better deal than the one it still expected from Parliament.

As a result, the Scottish army held him prisoner at Newcastle while the English and Scottish leadership compiled a joint set of terms to which both required him to agree as a post-war settlement for England. Charles and all his subjects were to swear allegiance to the Solemn League and Covenant which had allied Parliament to the Scottish government and committed them to reform of the English state and Church. He was to consent to the abolition of bishops and cathedral clergy, and of the traditional Prayer Book; nothing was said of liberty of conscience. New laws were to be made to intensify the persecution of English Roman Catholics, and the truce that the king had made with the Irish rebels was to be voided. Charles was to annul all the declarations he had issued during the war, so admitting that his waging of it had been illegitimate. Parliament was to control the armed forces for twenty years, with no guarantee that they would revert to the Crown after that, and to nominate all ministers of state. Those who had actively supported the king during the Civil War were to be severely punished, with thirty-seven of them sentenced to death if they were apprehended, and their estates confiscated, and all barred from Parliament and central or local government. In effect, the traditional constitution was to be preserved, with the Lords and Commons taking over most of the powers of the monarch, and the Church was to be transformed from one governed by bishops, under the sovereign, to one governed by presbyterian committees, under Parliament.[25]

These 'Newcastle Propositions' were presented to the king in that town in July 1646, and to general surprise he refused acceptance of them, asking instead that he be allowed to discuss them further with a view to amendment.[26] The surprise was due to the fact that, seven years before, he had surrendered royal power over the Scottish state and Church to much the same degree, and had also accepted some limitations on it in England. The difference now was due to two factors. The first was simply that he regarded England as his core and home kingdom, and the basis for his authority, and was not prepared to sacrifice as much of the latter there. The second was that he had concluded that his earlier concessions had brought him no settlement, and only encouraged his opponents to demand more from him. Indeed, he had come to believe that his defeat in the war had been a divine punishment for making those concessions.

His resistance to the further surrenders now demanded derived from two immovable emotional impulses. One was his wish to hand onto his heir the traditional powers of the English Crown that he had inherited from his own father, and regarded as entrusted to him by God. Without bishops, rulers had no control of the Church, and without command of the armed forces and the right to choose ministers of state at will, they had none over the kingdom. He was willing to part with all such powers temporarily, to give his enemies security and dominance for a limited period after the war, and perhaps for the rest of his own lifetime, but not to cripple the Crown permanently. His other impulse was a deep loyalty to those who had supported him during that war, and who had suffered and sacrificed so much for him. He was not prepared to let them be punished in his stead. While he was ready to have them banned from politics and government for a limited term, he wanted to leave open the opportunity for them to be reintegrated thereafter.[27] In this he had a point: a large part of the nation had supported him during the war, and only a minority had been enthusiastic parliamentarians; if the aim now was to restore stability and unity, then a settlement based on vengeance and obdurate partisan principle was hardly likely to achieve that. Those who now controlled Parliament, however, had an equally reasonable position: that they had fought a long, bloody and expensive war in order to achieve their vision of a better England, and were not prepared to forgo any part of it. Moreover, they had to satisfy the expectations of their Scottish allies.

As a result, both Parliament and the Scots concentrated through the autumn and winter on trying to persuade Charles to accept their whole package of requirements. When he still refused, the Scots handed him over and Parliament put him into Holdenby House, proceeding to get on with things without him. From their refuge in France, the queen and the coterie of exiled royalists who had gathered round her pressed him to agree at least to the loss of the bishops, in the hope of securing greater political and military powers and with the reassurance that he could always return the Church to its former government if he regained control of the nation. He firmly refused this, on the grounds that, once carried out, major reforms would be very hard to undo.

By September 1646, however, Charles had come round to the view that the deadlock in negotiation needed to be broken by concessions. He obtained the consent of his bishops to offer presbyterian Church government for three years, after which the final form would be decided by Parliament, advised by an assembly of churchmen of whom a third would be named by the Presbyterians, a third by the Independents and a third by himself. He was willing to hand over the armed forces for ten years, or for his own lifetime if they were then guaranteed to be restored to his heir. He was also prepared to confirm all Parliament's wartime ordinances and declarations, which would recognize its actions as legitimate without condemning his own. If all this was accepted, he would annul the truce with the Irish rebels.[28]

When the Scots handed him over to Parliament, the French ambassador took these proposals to the Presbyterian leaders in London, but was unable to persuade most to respond. By April they were telling the ambassador that their position was now so strong that they did not need to concede anything to the king.[29] For his part, Charles could only wait and hope that God would dispose matters to make them more flexible. He may have been possessed of a belief that the state could not be settled without him, and so if he hung onto his principles long enough then events would inevitably move in his favour; but he did not actually say this. Instead his justification for his stance, expressed to his wife, his supporters and the Frenchman, was simply that in conscience he could not offer more than he did without risking damnation, whatever the practical consequences. He was as devout a person as Oliver Cromwell, and as determined to discover and fulfil the wishes of his God.

Before proceeding to recount the king's part in the events which were now to unfold, it may be necessary to emphasize that the way in which this has been commonly represented has been strongly influenced by a writer who lived over 200 years later. This was Samuel Rawson Gardiner, perhaps the greatest historian of the Civil War period. Between 1863 and 1901 he produced a narrative account of the British Isles from 1603 to 1656, in eighteen volumes. It was based on a huge trove of pioneering research in foreign and domestic archives, which enabled him to establish, once and for all, the sequence of events through that long period, and its cast of characters. For anybody seeking a basic narrative of the events, his text remains the fundamental one, and will probably never be surpassed. His interpretations of them are a different matter. He wrote with very strong beliefs and prejudices, being a classic Victorian Liberal, ardently supporting William Gladstone in the twin causes of religious toleration and the extension of democracy. Both were contested issues at the time. Gardiner himself had suffered in the former, because his parents, although wealthy and able to give him an excellent education, were members of a small Protestant sect. Membership of that sect initially barred their son from an academic career under the prevailing regulations, leaving him to support his own family by odd jobs as a teacher, mainly in schools. These rules were relaxed during his lifetime, and in any case he converted to mainstream Anglicanism. He subsequently held a professorial chair and was loaded with academic honours, but his sympathy with religious dissenters remained. Meanwhile, over the course of his life the parliamentary franchise was extended to include first middle-class men and then most of those from the working class; but the process was slow, incremental and the subject of intense debate.[30]

Gardiner's history was therefore in part a contribution to contemporary political and religious discussion, representing early seventeenth-century England as the arena in which the crucial ideas in favour of religious pluralism, constitutional monarchy and representative democracy were developed, in opposition to the Stuart kings. The heroes of his story were naturally the leaders of that opposition, and the greatest of all, dominating the last volumes of it, was Oliver Cromwell. Gardiner had some qualms about the militaristic aspects of Cromwell's career, but he still regarded him as a person of exemplary virtue as well as talent, at once a reflection and leader of popular will, of the kind he felt to be needed in his own lifetime both to guide and to control an increasingly empowered populace. Conversely, Charles I was, if not exactly the villain of the tale – as Gardiner recognized him as a tragic and flawed figure rather than an evil one – certainly the antihero. As Gardiner represented him, not only was Charles always opposed to what Gardiner vaguely but potently called the spirit of the nation, but he was possessed of political vices, rather than merely political failings, of which the greatest were untrustworthiness and duplicity, coupled with an unwavering desire to regain supreme, and ultimately absolute and divinely ordained, power.

In portraying the king's role in the politics of 1647, Gardiner therefore constantly glossed it as that of a man in whom no faith could be reposed and whose aim in adversity was always to play off his opponents against each other to regain authority for himself. This representation of the king has retained acceptance in recent decades among the great majority of historians to write upon the period.[31] It was far from being one that originated with Gardiner: rather, it was repeatedly made by Charles's enemies in the 1640s, to justify first their attempts to disempower him, then their war against him and finally their failure to reach a settlement with him. In later centuries it became a trope of the 'Whig' history that was written by admirers of the Civil War parliamentarians.[32] It may therefore give some pause for thought that, in reiterating it now, scholars are endorsing a vehemently partisan claim: but this does not itself mean that the claim is wrong. What it should mean is that such a representation cannot necessarily be taken to be correct, and that, in telling a tale of what followed in 1647, each part of the evidence needs to be checked anew with some care.

PRELUDE (2): MARCH TO APRIL

The chain of events which was decisively to change national politics, and Cromwell's fortunes, began with the decision of Parliament in February to disband most of the New Model Army's infantry, and some of its cavalry, or send them to Ireland. In late March the common soldiers (perhaps with the collusion of officers) drew up a petition to their commander in chief, Fairfax, for security that the arrears owed to them would be paid, and for indemnity to be given to them for their actions in the war. These were very important issues. It was clear that the huge scale of the arrears would preclude the payment of more than a portion of them at the time of disbanding, and there was no evidence of how the remainder could be funded and handed over subsequently. The amount likely to be offered on disbanding was six weeks' pay, when the foot soldiers were owed eighteen weeks' worth and the horse and dragoons forty-three. Indemnity was a problem because the soldiers were uncertain of how far they would be vulnerable once out of arms to prosecution for wartime actions such as the commandeering of the materials of war, especially horses. The open hostility shown to the army by preachers, writers and petitioners over the past few months suggested that, once vulnerable, its former members would be subject to persecution. The soldiers also wanted reassurance that they would not be conscripted for further military service once demobbed, and that pensions would be given to men crippled in action and to the widows and orphans of those who had been killed.

These were reasonable requests, but they were linked to a refusal to volunteer for Ireland until they were addressed, and they were reported to the House of Commons with the information that threats were being used to force reluctant soldiers to endorse them. On 30 March the Presbyterian leaders persuaded both Houses to declare the petition mutinous, and threaten any who continued to promote it with being proclaimed enemies of the state. They further ordered that the volunteers for Ireland be drawn into a single body, but the rest of the army be scattered across a wide area and far from its headquarters.[33]

This was a fatal error. The right of subjects to petition Parliament or the government for redress of grievances and for justice was a traditional one in England. Now the soldiers were being forbidden even to ask their own commander for help, while petitions for their removal were being received without disapproval by both Houses. The order for quartering suggested a plan to divide the army and use those who accepted the Irish service as a strike force to keep their comrades in check. In April the Derby House Committee sent a commission of leading Presbyterians to Fairfax's headquarters at Saffron Walden in Essex to encourage volunteers for the Irish expedition. Thereafter it became apparent that only a minority of the soldiers were responding. When the names of the generals who would command the expedition were announced – Skippon and Massey – officers called instead for Fairfax and Cromwell, the partnership that had given them victory in the Civil War.

The commissioners, and therefore the two Houses, concluded that firmer action was needed to cow resistance to enlistment, although the Commons also started work on measures to satisfy the requests made in the suppressed petition.[34] They were conscious that pamphlets were circulating among the regiments (and had been since March) calling upon them to resist both engagement in the Irish venture and disbandment.[35] It was not known then, and cannot be known now, where all of these originated, whether in the army itself or in London among independents, sectaries and political radicals (three overlapping groups whom the Presbyterians were forcing into an alliance). One of the most notorious was said to have been sent up from the capital for dispersal among the soldiers' billets.[36] The pamphlets warned that the Presbyterians in Parliament and London were plotting to gain power and to destroy the liberties of the nation which the war had been fought to save. The project to remove the New Model Army and the increasing attacks on independents and sectaries were linked together in the tracts as aspects of this plot, and the army was urged to resist it.[37]

Developments of this kind lent especial significance to another during April, which was triggered by Parliament's decision to borrow £200,000 from Londoners to finance the disbanding of the soldiers. The Lords had suggested that the City corporation be induced to support the loan by being granted one of its key desires: to have returned to it control over the militia units that provided a home guard for the capital. During the war this had been vested in a committee of citizens chosen by Parliament, which had come to be dominated by Independents. The Presbyterians who now dominated both Houses thus had a double reason for gratifying the corporation, and the transfer of power was duly made. By the end of April, the City leadership had both purged the committee of many Independents and replaced them with their political rivals, who then purged the militia officers in turn. This really mattered, because the trained bands of London made up the largest and most effective local armed force in the nation, on which Parliament had drawn repeatedly to reinforce its field armies in the earlier part of the war, and which had performed outstandingly well. The Presbyterians now had a potentially formidable military power at their disposal, totalling 18,000 concentrated men, who almost matched the 19,340 – currently widely scattered – in the New Model Army.[38]

So where was Cromwell in all this? The answer is that wc do not know. As said, he kept a low profile in Parliament during this period. On 24 March Lilburne had written from his cell in the Tower of London to inform Cromwell of a story he had heard, that Oliver was advising the soldiers to drop the petition they were then framing and assuring the Commons that they would disband obediently if required. With characteristic tactlessness and intemperance, the imprisoned radical told his old ally and protector that, if it were true, he would believe Oliver to have been corrupted by his prospective ennoblement and enrichment, as the army was the last hope of the people of God (those who believed in liberty of conscience).[39] He did not, however, know if it were true, and neither do we. A royalist enemy of Cromwell subsequently asserted that, when the New Model had first tried to present its grievances to Parliament, Oliver had spoken in the Commons against the presumption of the soldiery and advocated the arrest of some officers.[40] But this is a hostile account, written long after and relying on information of uncertain quality. All that is certain is that from mid-April Cromwell was active in the Commons again, being named once more to sit on various committees, including one to consider the apparent sedition in the army.[41]

Events now began to move rapidly. On 27 April the House of Commons voted that the soldiers of the New Model would indeed be paid six weeks' worth of the arrears owed to them on disbanding, with no evident security for the rest.[42] This was the allowance made to Parliament's provincial armies that had already been put out of service, and none of them had yet received the residue owed to them.[43] On the same day, the House received a reply to Parliament's 'Declaration of Dislike', condemning the soldiers' petitioning movement, signed by scores of officers in the New Model.[44] It claimed the right to petition to be a fundamental one, and the requests embodied in the soldiers' petition to be reasonable, and asked for Parliament's declaration to be withdrawn.[45]

The MPs agreed to debate it on 30 April, and it was on that morning that Cromwell made the journey to the House which was described at the opening of the chapter. He had just received a still more provocative document from the army. This was a letter delivered to him by three common soldiers: one from his own horse regiment, one from Fairfax's and one from Henry Ireton's, Cromwell's son-in-law and loyal deputy in commanding the cavalry. It was signed by elected representatives of those and five more cavalry units, representing four-fifths of the units in the New Model, and it appealed to him for help, holding that the Irish expedition was just a stratagem to destroy the army and so introduce tyranny. The troopers therefore refused to join the expedition until their desires were satisfied.[46] After Cromwell had entered the House, Philip Skippon rose and revealed to the members that he had been given the same letter, and disclosed its contents. It was reported that Fairfax, currently in London seeking medical treatment, had been sent one too. Whatever Cromwell's intentions had been, once this happened it became too dangerous for him not to declare the receipt of his own copy.[47] It turned out that the three troopers who had acted as postmen were in the lobby – which must have been agreed and arranged beforehand – and they were called in to be interrogated. With superb composure, they parried every question with the response that the letter was a joint production of the ordinary soldiers of all their regiments, and that therefore the latter needed to answer collectively.

After a long debate, the MPs decided on a compromise. They did not annul the Declaration of Dislike, permit any petitioning or reply to either the officers' or the troopers' document. On the other hand, they did nothing to punish the troopers, accelerated work on an indemnity ordinance of the sort that the suppressed petition had requested, and sent a new set of commissioners to visit the army and try to allay its fears and suspicions. This time the commissioners were not Presbyterians but MPs who were also trusted and popular officers of the New Model Army. One was Skippon and another was Ireton. The third was one of the leading regimental colonels in that cavalry and another old ally and protégé of Cromwell's, a young Midland gentleman with long curling blonde hair and a long austere face called Charles Fleetwood. The fourth was Cromwell himself. His inclusion gave him a renewed importance and agency, as a mediator between Parliament and the army who might produce an outcome acceptable to both. In recognition, the MPs gave him two marks of favour. The first was to style him 'Lieutenant-General', so formally recognizing his position (and his right to pay) as a continuing leader of the army. The second was to confirm the award of £2,500 per year to him, and to set about assigning the remaining land to support it, from the estate of a royalist nobleman.[48] God was smiling once again.

2

MUTINY

SAFFRON WALDEN

As May opened, the four officer MPs made their journey to the army headquarters at the Essex market town of Saffron Walden. Their route took them up successive river valleys, and over a watershed to the vale of the Cam, where the town sat, a cluster of rose-coloured brick and magpie timber like the other settlements on the way. The landscape through which they passed was one of the lushest in England, at one of the loveliest times of year, when the young grass and corn sprouted thickly in the farmlands, and the trees were whorls of unfurling foliage, in shades of emerald, lime, bottle green and the intense yellow of the young oak leaves. The floors of woodlands would have still had the azure haze of bluebells, and returning swallows would have skimmed across the fields. Like most river towns of the time, Saffron Walden consisted of a high street running up from a bridge to a market square and a medieval church (in this case with a tall and graceful spire), and a huddle of smaller streets around those two foci. From there on 3 May the four men summoned all the regimental commanders plus one commissioned officer from each troop or company, to report on the feelings of their men. They also wrote to the whole New Model Army, encouraging its members to volunteer for Ireland.[1]

Even as they were on their journey, the mood in that army was heating up further. On the day on which the four issued the summons, the horse soldiers who had sent the letter to Cromwell, Skippon and Fairfax published its text, followed by a still more incendiary declaration. This not only repeated the requests made in the suppressed petition, but demanded punishment of those who had framed the Declaration of Dislike and a formal vindication of the honour of the army, and threatened action if all these desires were not met.[2] On arrival in the town, Cromwell and his fellows found the soldiers quartered around it, on guard against what they expected to be a surprise attack on them by forces loyal to the Presbyterians.[3] At the same time, a plan was circulating among the soldiers to set up a council of their representatives, arrest Presbyterians across the kingdom, get redress for all 'arbitrary and exorbitant' proceedings by the country's present leadership, and demand an improvement of the national provision of justice.[4] News was reaching them that the clamour of many Londoners against them had been worsened by a speech made by a Presbyterian peer, the earl of Pembroke, to the City corporation in which he asked for the loan Parliament required to disband the army. He had emphasized the danger that the soldiers represented to order, and asserted that they had been seriously infiltrated by royalists.[5]

By 7 May, 180 officers had crowded into Saffron Walden's church to meet Cromwell and his fellows. The latter urged them to calm their men and discover what was worrying them, and also to find out who had framed the letter from the horse regiments at the end of April.[6] They were instructed to report back in seven days; during that interim, Parliament increased the amount of arrears of pay to be offered to each man on disbanding to eight weeks, and completed an ordinance indemnifying members of the army for all actions during the war.[7] The reaction of the ordinary soldiers to the return of the officers from Saffron Walden was to choose a committee from each troop and company to formulate grievances. Representatives from these committees then met at Bury St Edmunds, in west Suffolk, and handed over lists of the desires of their units to the officers to take back to Saffron Walden.[8] The officers were back in that town on 15 May, and immediately factional rancour was apparent between those who supported the Presbyterians and those who did not.[9]

On the following day, Skippon reminded the officers that they had been asked not just to report the grievances of their men but to allay them, and wanted to know what had been done in that cause. One after another they replied that almost none of the men would volunteer for Ireland until their concerns had been addressed. Cromwell now intervened at Skippon's prompting, urging the officers to return to their units and press the men to accept Parliament's latest terms for disbanding, leaving him and his companions to read the grievances. He ended by saying that, if Parliament's terms were rejected, then 'nothing can follow but confusion'. He was answered by a young Yorkshire cavalry colonel with collar-length wavy brown hair and a chunky, clean-shaven face called John Lambert, who replied that, on the contrary, Parliament needed to change its policy. The representatives who had been appointed by the regiments to carry their views to the officers, and who were now acquiring the name of 'agitators', concluded that the Presbyterians had concluded a secret deal with the king to destroy the army, and sent a warning to every regiment to be ready to resist.[10]

The reports submitted by three-fifths of the units survive.[11] They overwhelmingly concentrated on the material concerns that had been expressed ever since the March petition, and on the aspersions cast on the army since then, especially the Declaration of Dislike. Only occasionally was there a mention of liberty of conscience or the gaoling without trial of people like Lilburne. However, some of the officers at Saffron Walden admitted that they had toned down the original submissions from their units, which were probably rather more radical.[12] On 17 May, Cromwell and his fellows signed a despondent letter to the House of Commons admitting that even after great efforts they had failed to pacify the army. It reached the MPs on the next day, and they replied immediately, ordering Skippon to remain at Saffron Walden but one of his colleagues to return with a full verbal report.

On receiving this response, the commissioners decided that both Cromwell and Fleetwood should go.[13]

Two other very significant developments occurred on the day on which the Commons ordered this report. One was that it voted by 139 to 100 to proceed with the disbanding of the army, ordering the Derby House Committee to draw up a plan for this. The other was that it received a letter from the king. Charles had decided that the increasing tension between different groups of his old enemies could mean that they would be more amenable to the compromise package of terms that he had assembled in response to the Newcastle Propositions, which he now duly sent to both Houses. They won a positive response from the Lords, which voted that he should be brought to a royal palace near London to open negotiations, but were ignored by the Commons. Three days later, both Houses read an intercepted letter to the king from one of his supporters in the queen's circle in France, urging him not to make concessions, because he was likely now to receive military aid from both the Dutch and the Irish. There was nothing to indicate that Charles himself approved of this advice, but it acted as a reminder that the royalist threat was not dead. Simultaneously, the Houses agreed to allow a Scottish politician, the earl of Dunfermline, to visit the king for the first time since the Scots had handed him over, though not to reside with him.

A few days later, the Commons dealt with the last of three petitions that had been presented to it by the London radicals since March, a petition that hailed it as the supreme authority in the nation and called for the release of their imprisoned comrades and the fundamental reform of Church and state, which was the programme of this group. They also demanded an end to the vetoes of Lords and king over the Commons' measures; reform of the legal system to make it simpler, cheaper and more transparent; liberty of conscience; and the abolition of tithes, the compulsory payment levied on parishioners to support their minister. The MPs had reacted to each petition with increasing severity, referring the first to a hostile committee, condemning the second and now reacting to the third by ordering both it and the first one to be burned by the public hangman. The vote was a close one, ninety-four to eighty-six, and it also represented a clear contest between the parties, as the tellers on each side were respectively leading Presbyterians and Independents. The same had been true of the vote in the Lords to respond to the king's overture, with the Presbyterians again winning.[14] During this time, too, the Presbyterian-dominated committee completed its takeover of the London militia. The Derby House Committee simultaneously sent Presbyterian officers to commands across the provinces, to limit discontent among the soldiery.[15]

None of these developments were related, but they would all have served to reinforce suspicions among the New Model Army of a conspiracy between Presbyterians, royalists and Scots, to destroy it and impose a more conservative and repressive settlement upon the nation. Had the Presbyterian leadership acted at any point in May to defer both the Irish expedition and the disbanding of the army until the soldiers' material and moral grievances were satisfied, while granting all the provisions for both the expedition and the demobilization that they had requested, repealing the Declaration of Dislike and issuing statements praising the army for its services and essential worth, then these suspicions would probably have been contained among a minority.[16] They did not, however, and, in lieu of such action, belief in the conspiracy could flourish unchecked.

Cromwell and Fleetwood retraced their route to London, through what would already have been a changing countryside, the grass and corn thicker and lusher, the meadows brimming golden with buttercups and the roadside blooming white with cow parsley and hawthorn. On 20 May, Oliver made his report to the Commons, delivering the composite set of grievances and a set of individual returns from regiments. He emphasized that the army was seriously unhappy, and expressed the hope that the MPs would use the information to their advantage.[17] What they did was to thank him, publish the new indemnity ordinance, and order the proper calculation of the army's arrears of pay and the production of two measures: one to aid widows, orphans and maimed soldiers; the other to enable demobbed soldiers to get into work immediately without being obliged to complete apprenticeships for it.[18] That was all. The indemnity which the army was offered did not cover actions committed since the war and could be rejected by the king if he were restored to power. The hostility displayed to its members in sermons and petitions augured badly for their future once disarmed and scattered, and many soldiers apparently did credit the rumours of a plot to destroy them, hatched between Presbyterians, royalists and Scots. A motion for a parliamentary declaration praising the army as friends and supporters of the regime – which Cromwell must have supported – was debated but never put to a vote.[19]

On 25 May the Commons took the final, fatal, step, when it voted by 136 to 115 to disband the New Model Army immediately, giving those who would not volunteer for Ireland a more generous amount of the pay owed. The process would start in a week, and be completed in two more. It was the Presbyterian leader Denzil Holles who delivered the plan from the Derby House Committee, which he and his fellows dominated, and the vote was a contest between Presbyterians and Independents (with Cromwell certainly among the latter), which the former won yet again. One MP whose support was solicited by Holles and his fellows noted that they were motivated by a personal loathing of the army, coupled with an expectation of the popularity they would win in the nation by this measure. Three days later, the Lords approved the measure, on the timescale proposed, with just three Independent peers protesting against it.[20]

As soon as the Commons passed their resolution, a London ally of the army sped a letter to the agitators chosen to represent the common soldiers, urging them to arrest Skippon and the Presbyterian officers, and to refuse to disband. Fairfax had by now returned to his headquarters from his sick leave in London, on the express orders of Parliament. He had issued an order forbidding members of the army to hold any more meetings, and had moved his base from Saffron Walden to Bury St Edmunds, thereby occupying what had been the agitators' meeting point. There, on 29 May, he gathered the officers to discuss Parliament's decision. They voted overwhelmingly not to allow the disbanding to be attempted when the soldiers were in their present dangerous mood, but to call the whole army together to restore discipline. They blamed Parliament for constantly provoking unrest. By that date, ordinary soldiers had started to seize and expel their Presbyterian commanders, while a party of them had secured the artillery train, stored at Oxford. When the commissioners sent by Parliament to pay off the first regiment due for disbanding arrived at its quarters on 31 May, they found that it had marched off to join other units. Instead they were met by Skippon, who told them that their mission was hopeless.[21]

Did Cromwell play any clandestine part either in encouraging the army to resistance or in fomenting a breakdown in its relations with Parliament? Several of his political enemies subsequently accused him of doing both, and especially of privately urging on the soldiers to recalcitrance while reassuring the House of Commons that its current treatment of the army was the correct one.[22] We may certainly believe that he was shocked by some of the behaviour of Parliament towards the New Model, not least because we have the subsequent memory of an MP who opposed the Presbyterians and sympathized with the soldiers, that Oliver turned to him during a debate and whispered that 'these men will never leave till the army pull them out by the ears'.[23] There is also good evidence that he kept in close contact with the political and religious radicals of London during this period, and advised them on the formulation of their doomed petitions to Parliament. One of their most prominent members, William Walwyn, later recalled that he regularly visited Oliver at his house in Drury Lane, with friends and allies, and was warmly received, while Oliver's friends frequented Walwyn's own home in the City.[24] After all, Cromwell had been firmly associated with the cause of liberty of conscience for several years, and would not have stopped encouraging it now. A royalist who had contacts in the army recorded around this time that Cromwell was the person who worked hardest to reconcile its members with Parliament; indeed, this was the job that he had been sent to Saffron Walden to accomplish, and the success of which would have made him a hero to both sides.[25]

All this is consistent with honourable behaviour, and would tend to indicate that the retrospective accusations of hypocrisy and duplicity were the work of embittered enemies. Cromwell's recorded declarations to the officers at Saffron Walden and his report to Parliament would seem to bear that out. However, there are pieces of evidence which would support a different view. One is the testimony of Robert Huntington, who in May 1647 was the major of Cromwell's own horse regiment, one of the units which had been foremost in challenging Parliament's policy towards the army. In the following year, having resigned his commission in disillusion with Oliver and his cause, this individual made a statement to Parliament that at Saffron Walden Cromwell and Ireton had tacitly encouraged the officers to resist both the Irish service and disbanding. This is significant, as Huntington was in precisely the position to know what was going on. What is equally significant is the fact that his testimony was subsequently challenged by enemies of his; but, instead of attempting to disprove his assertions about the two generals, these enemies tried instead to discredit him by alleging that he was heavily implicated himself in the actions that he now denounced.[26]

It is also noteworthy that, while the text of Cromwell's report to the Commons on his return from Saffron Walden is, like that of his speech in Parliament, a model of apparent honesty, probity and duty, he seems to have said more to the MPs than is contained in that report. A citizen of London wrote in his private journal that Cromwell and other Independents had assured the House that, if the soldiers did not submit to Parliament's wishes, they would abandon the army's cause.[27] A correspondent of Fairfax's father wrote that the MPs had been deeply reassured by Cromwell's speech, which seemed to promise a fair accord with the New Model; this is not reflected in the text we have.[28] Nor is the report of a royalist correspondent in London, who recorded that Oliver had told the House that the army would not volunteer for Ireland, but that it would disband.[29] Finally, there is a strange contrast in the subsequent fortunes of Cromwell and Skippon. On the face of things, they seem to have behaved in exactly the same way at Saffron Walden, in encouraging the officers to persuade their men to obey Parliament's wishes. Yet afterwards it was Skippon who was treated by the soldiers as a foe, while Cromwell was welcomed back by them. It is tempting to conclude that, off the record, he was saying things to the officers that, at the least, served to reassure them of his fundamental sympathy and loyalty.

This is probably as much as can be said at this distance in time. The charges of systematic treachery to Parliament, and a design deliberately to create a crisis in its relations with the army, are unproven. Nevertheless, some hints remain that Cromwell was trying to keep in with both sides, by telling each what it wanted to hear.

GENERAL RENDEZVOUS

On 4 June 1647 the New Model Army mustered upon Kentford Heath, 4 miles north-east of Newmarket, in the centre of the line of chalk hills that runs across south-east England from Berkshire to Norfolk. It was an open landscape of grazed turf studded with gorse and hawthorn bushes, which would have rung by day with the song of skylarks, and a few weeks before the muster would have been melodious at dusk with that of nightingales. The hawthorn blossom would still have been rich, but in decay, with a heavy stagnant scent and some sprays flushing a deep pink. In other places elder would be opening its creamy saucer-shaped blooms. The heathland was wandered in places by flocks of England's largest flightless bird, the bustard, now long extinct but then abundant, with long grey necks and heads, and ruddy backs striped in black.[30] The birds would have soon fled on that particular summer day, when over 10,000 men, in 6 horse regiments and 7 of foot, paraded up onto the turf and halted, the foot soldiers in the standard New Model uniform of red coats and grey breeches, the horsemen in body armour of helmet, breastplate and backplate. Fairfax rode up and was cheered loudly, and the agitators handed him a statement which repeated the soldiers' claim to the right to petition and attacked the Declaration of Dislike. It pronounced Parliament's terms for disbanding to be inadequate, but added that the soldiers would not be safe to disband at all as long as their enemies remained in power. This was a clear and public statement that the army was now aiming at regime change and not merely satisfaction of grievances.

The following day the regiments reassembled on the heath and subscribed a 'solemn engagement' which formally charged the Presbyterian leaders with trying to start a new war. They undertook not to disband until those leaders had been removed from public life. The army requested a formal council to be elected to negotiate with Parliament, composed of trusted generals plus two commissioned officers and two privates from each regiment. To reassure moderate public opinion, the document also denied that the army aimed to put the Independents into power or impose an unlimited liberty of conscience.[31] It trumpeted instead that the soldiers intended to promote a 'common and equal right and freedom'.[32] In their attack on the Presbyterians, the authors reflected two very widespread themes of English politics in the early to mid-seventeenth century, both of which were rooted in a belief in a naturally well-ordered and harmonious cosmos ruled by an all-good and all-wise deity. One was a love of conspiracy theories, a tendency to credit any malfunctions in the political world to the machinations of evil men. The other was a corresponding desire for scape-goats, based on an assumption that to identify and remove those bad men would automatically restore the natural health and harmony of political life. Such instincts had helped to produce the Civil War, and they acted to propel the army now.

It seems to have been on that day that Oliver Cromwell joined the muster, having fled the capital. Years later, a royalist enemy provided a dramatic account of this event, according to which the Presbyterian leaders, coming at last to suspect his collusion with the recalcitrant soldiers, had decided to send him to the Tower of London. He got warning of this and left his home at dawn the next day with a single servant, to meet some horse regiments at a prearranged point and then write to the Commons that the troopers of his own regiment had invited him to join them, with the assurance that if he did then their discontents would be composed.[33] The account of events by this particular writer is badly garbled, and there is no record of any such letter to the MPs. Another garbled and retrospective account left by another of Cromwell's enemies – though this time somebody who was an ally of his in 1647 and sat in the Commons – contains the information that Oliver fled to the army on the afternoon of the day on which the Presbyterians were going to arrest him.[34] The story of his impending arrest was also recorded much nearer to the time, later in the same year, by yet another opponent, who said that repeated appeals from the soldiers to Cromwell to join them had failed until that moment. It was this writer who stated that Oliver appeared in the army on the second day of the Kentford rendezvous. As the writer was one of the London radicals and had good contacts among the soldiery, he can be believed in this particular.[35] When the Presbyterian leaders came to write their own accounts of events, however, none of them mentioned a design to arrest Oliver, although by then they hated him and would have had no reason to conceal it.[36] Almost ten years later, somebody wrote to Cromwell to repeat a tale he had heard from a close associate of Oliver, that the latter had received three appeals from the army to join it, and had yielded to the third because it carried the threat that the soldiers would abandon him if he did not respond.[37] This is another which confuses the details of events, but there may well be some truth in it.

What is abundantly clear is that Cromwell had ample reason now to throw in his lot with the army, because his role as a mediator between it and Parliament had completely failed, through obstinacy and conspiracy theories on both sides. He was left having to pick one of those sides. The New Model contained the men whom he had commanded in the recent war, many of whom shared his own religious views, whereas the Presbyterians who currently led Parliament were his traditional political and religious opponents. Moreover, in a contest of physical strength, the soldiers held all the advantages. At any rate, there were apparently no cheers for Cromwell when he showed up on the heath as there had been for Fairfax – perhaps because his formal speeches in support of Parliament's policy, during May, still rankled among some of those drawn up there. Indeed, there was not even a notice of his arrival. Instead he slipped back immediately into his old role as lieutenant-general and one of Fairfax's Council of War, and re-emerges into the historical record as established there a couple of days later. Back in London, the Presbyterian leaders naturally regarded what they saw as Cromwell's defection as an unpardonable betrayal.[38]

In part, Cromwell's return to the army may have been unremarked because it was overshadowed by the arrival of a very different personage, none other than King Charles I. In the early hours of 3 June, an assemblage of troopers from different cavalry units had ridden up to the king's prison at Holdenby House, with a cornet – the lowest grade of commissioned officer – called George Joyce as spokesman. He claimed he was there to prevent a plot to remove Charles and put him at the head of a new-raised army intended to start a new war: the evidence for this plot was confidently promised to follow, but was never produced. The Presbyterian colonel in charge of the house then slipped away, and Joyce and his fellows began to fear that he had gone for reinforcements. In the course of the day, they decided that it was necessary to remove the king to the quarters of the army itself. Early the following morning, Joyce therefore invited Charles to accompany him, with an acknowledgement that if the king refused he would be compelled. Charles responded to this coercion with courage and charm, and was duly tucked into a coach and drawn eastwards in the midst of the cavalcade of troopers, the commissioners whom Parliament had previously sent to attend him trailing along with them. On hearing that his monarch was approaching, Fairfax immediately sent a horse regiment under Cromwell's cousin Edward Whalley to return him to Holdenby and guard him there. On 5 June, Whalley and his men ran into Joyce's contingent in Cambridgeshire, where they found the king refusing to go back to a place of which he was thoroughly weary. Fairfax therefore ordered him to be put into the nearest big house, at Childerley Hall, 4 miles from Cambridge, while his future was worked out.[39]

It is absolutely certain that the decision to abduct the king from Holdenby was taken by Cornet Joyce and his comrades as a panic-driven response to the possibility of being attacked. There was in fact no plan to mount any such attack, just as there was none to remove Charles to launch a war against the New Model Army. There was indeed a report by the Dutch envoy to England, a fortnight before, that the Presbyterian leaders were discussing the removal of the king to a safer place; but this was credited not to a wish to use him to start a war but to fear that the New Model would seize him.[40] What is *not* completely clear, and has been debated by historians for over a century, is who sent Joyce to Holdenby in the first place. He himself was always careful to conceal this, claiming vaguely to the king and parliamentary commissioners that he had been authorized to secure the royal person by the whole of the New Model Army. This could be taken to mean that the agitators elected from each regiment had collectively instructed him to do so, but he wrote to an unknown confidant at the end of the day on which he carried off the king, instructing him to inform the agitators that he and his men had acted in the name of the army in general, but would not have dared to do so had they not known that 'you and my best old friend' had consented.[41] This does not sound as if the agitators were in charge of the operation, and clearly indicates a couple of powerful individuals as having given the necessary encouragement, while carefully concealing their identities.

Subsequently, the most commonly identified of those individuals has been Cromwell. Later in 1647, a London radical who had turned against Oliver published an account of a meeting at his house in Drury Lane on 31 May where it was decided that Joyce would secure the artillery train at Oxford and then lead a party to Holdenby to remove the king.[42] During the next year, Cromwell's estranged major, Robert Huntington, provided a slightly fuller account: that Cromwell and Ireton had advised the agitators to secure or remove the king after seizing the artillery train, and that the agitators had sent Joyce. He added that, when Fairfax heard that the cornet had abducted Charles, and demanded to know who had authorized this,

Ireton had replied that he had only encouraged the securing of the king not his removal. Cromwell then arrived from London and said that, if Joyce had not acted, Charles would have been removed either by order of Parliament or by its commissioners. When, later that day, Joyce was told that Fairfax was displeased with his action, he answered that Cromwell had ordered him at London to do what he did at Oxford and Holdenby.[43] Huntington was in the right place at the right time to know all this, and it accords with the movements of Fairfax, Ireton and Cromwell at the time concerned. If it is true, then Joyce's action in removing the king, though his own decision, was one option that had been given to him by those advising him before he set out. It is just possible that Huntington hated Cromwell so much by the next year, when he gave this testimony, that he was prepared to pick up stories told against his former general by others, and repeat them as his own. He was, however, testifying in person to Parliament; if he was indeed playing that game, then it was a very dangerous one.

There are other pieces of evidence for the matter. One is a letter written by Joyce at Holdenby, confirming that the king had been secured and desperately asking for instructions as to what to do there, as the colonel in charge of the garrison had escaped and could be fetching more soldiers.[44] Still protecting his patrons, the cornet carefully avoided naming the intended recipient(s), but it is almost certainly the same letter as one from him which was intercepted en route to London and read out in the House of Commons.[45] That was directed to Cromwell, or in his absence to two allies of his, the Independent political leader Sir Arthur Hesilrige and the cavalry colonel Fleetwood. Once more it points to Oliver as the main figure behind the coup, but the House could not question him about it, as he had already fled. Another relevant source is a pamphlet written a dozen years later, after Cromwell's death, and hostile to him, which claimed that Joyce had been shocked when Oliver disclaimed any knowledge of his mission, but was talked into accepting Cromwell's attitude. This could be slander, but the account added that, when the pamphlet which published the story of the 31 May meeting came out, Cromwell demanded that Joyce publish a refutation of it (which Joyce failed to do), a detail so precise as possibly to be true.[46]

Many years later, when he was struggling to defend his actions at this time, Fairfax stated that he wanted to court-martial Joyce for his action, but his officers refused to support him.[47] This reflects a glaring fact. What Joyce did was a mighty affront both to military discipline, by overruling a superior officer (the colonel at Holdenby), and to legal and political tradition, by defying the wishes of Parliament. Yet not only was he never punished for it, he went on to receive promotion, eventually rising to the rank of lieutenant-colonel. Clearly he had powerful protectors, who kept their promise to shield him in exchange for his fidelity in hiding their role. The evidence for the identity of the main one remains inconclusive, but it has always pointed very strongly to Cromwell.[48]

On 7 June Oliver came face to face with King Charles, almost certainly for the first time. It was at Childerley Hall, whither Fairfax had led a set of senior officers, also including Ireton, Lambert and Whalley, to work out what to do with their royal captive. It was a tense meeting, as Charles discovered that, despite Joyce's claim that the entire army had approved it, neither Fairfax nor any other officer accepted responsibility for his abduction. It was also noted that, while all of them kissed his hand in the classic gesture of recognition of royalty, neither Fairfax nor Cromwell knelt to do so. Nonetheless, all treated him with respect and it was observed that he talked most with Fairfax, Cromwell and Ireton. It was eventually agreed that he should be granted his desire to take up new quarters at his hunting lodge at Newmarket, which he liked and which was a safe distance from Parliament and the capital. Whalley remained in charge of him with two horse regiments; one commentator noted that he was in political cold storage again: 'more guarded than regarded'.[49]

Meanwhile, Parliament was reacting to the unexpected news that the New Model Army was out of control. There had in fact been no need for the Presbyterian leaders to concoct an elaborate conspiracy to raise a fresh army to attack the New Model, because they thought that they were about to pay it off. Clear testimony that they had no such scheme is provided by the French ambassador, who attended a meeting of them and realized that they had no plan to use military force against the army. He now watched them debate different models for one without agreeing on any.[50]

Parliament's initial reaction to the soldiers' refusal to disband was to persuade them to do so by conceding everything they had wanted between March and May: full payment of arrears, the erasure of the Declaration of Dislike, and an ordinance to guarantee full indemnity for acts committed by soldiers. Commissioners were appointed to carry these offers to the New Model Army.[51] Then came the news that the army had seized the king and was demanding a purge of the parliamentarian leadership, and the Houses found themselves suddenly preparing for war. On 6 June the Scottish representatives in London informed Parliament that the abduction of the king had breached the treaty between the two nations, which now had to join forces to retrieve him from the New Model. Two days later, the Commons decided by one vote not to deal with that army any further.

By then the earl of Dunfermline, the Scot who had been allowed to visit the king and who had fled Holdenby when Joyce arrived, had hastened to the queen in France, with a plea to her from the Scottish commissioners in London, and from some Presbyterians, to send the prince of Wales to Scotland, to lead an army from there to free the king.[52] It was a hare-brained idea, because there was almost no chance that she would put the royal heir into the hands of the Scots, and no guarantee that the Scottish government would attack England if it had him. In any case, any such expedition would come far too late to remedy the current crisis.

There was in theory much more potential for military resistance to the New Model closer at hand, in those 18,000 London militiamen, who could be reinforced by thousands of soldiers demobbed from the provincial armies who had come to the capital in pursuit of their promised arrears.[53] There was also Parliament's regional army in the north of England, commanded by a Presbyterian, and around a thousand soldiers who had left the New Model to join the Irish expedition and were gathering around Worcester, with some in London. The City and Westminster were still surrounded by 11 miles of powerful fortifications constructed to protect them during the war. If the New Model tried to attack those fortifications, it would now find them held by a larger body of armed men, presenting a formidably daunting prospect. The big question, however, was how many of those men would actually be willing to fight the New Model.

On 10 June Fairfax drew up the New Model Army to hear Parliament's latest terms for disbanding, on another verdant chalkland pasture, this time Thriplow Heath, 8 miles south of Cambridge.[54] It now mustered 14,000 strong. Cromwell and the other senior commanders looked on as Parliament's commissioners rode up first to Fairfax's own foot regiment and delivered their list of offers, after which Skippon made a soothing speech urging the men to accept them. The reaction was uproar, the men shouting 'Justice! Justice!' to indicate that they still wanted revenge on the Presbyterian leaders. Other regiments took up the cry, and the commissioners withdrew defeated.[55] The whole army now began to move towards Westminster and London, marching first south-west along the great chalk ridge to the market town of Royston. There that evening Cromwell joined the other senior officers, including Fairfax, Lambert and Ireton, in signing a letter to the corporation of London, stating that they now wanted not only the satisfaction of their army's desires but the punishment of those who had slandered it and tried to start a new war which would remove the privileges of Parliament. They claimed to be defending the cause for which parliamentarians had fought the Civil War, against a 'few self-seeking men', and that they had no intention of altering the form of government, preventing the presbyterian Church settlement or imposing a 'licentious liberty' of religious belief and practice. To secure its aims, the army was now advancing on the capital, but intended no harm to it or to Parliament as long as neither assisted 'that wicked Party'. If its requirements were met, it would halt and disband, but if the Londoners resisted, then they could expect their city to be ruined.[56]

Around the four leaders, their army was changing. Not only was it growing in size as more units came up, but virtually all of the Presbyterian officers in it had departed or been ejected since April, representing just over a quarter of those above the rank of captain. On the other hand, only around 4 per cent of the rank and file had left, showing how completely the ordinary soldiery identified with the grievances and resentments that had caused the army's revolt. The places of the Presbyterians were filled with Independents and others of a more radical hue, so converting the New Model more fully into a force determined to prevent the settlement of the nation that the Presbyterians had intended.[57] As the majority in both Houses had supported that settlement, this now meant that they had to view the New Model as an active and aggressive enemy, and on receiving news of what had happened at Thriplow Heath and Royston, they directed the corporation of London to take urgent measures to defend both the City and Westminster. They also ordered Fairfax to halt his advance and encouraged his soldiers to desert.[58]

At this the New Model surged forward again, down from the chalk hills onto the rolling farmlands of Hertfordshire, and so to St Albans, with its huge abbey church, and pieces of Roman masonry protruding from hedges where pale wild roses and purple foxgloves were now in flower. There, on 14 June, it moved a stage further, from demanding regime change to setting forth a rival programme for the settlement of the nation. The impending reality of a military showdown with the legally constituted government of the nation had forced it to claim that it, and not the current Parliament, had become the true voice of the English people, and their instrument to rescue that Parliament from a corrupt clique no longer worthy to hold power – though the proof it offered of that corruption was simply that the Houses had defamed the army. The army went on to demand that, after the current Parliament was purged, it should set a date for its own dissolution, and that future Parliaments be elected for short and fixed terms, and from a more equal distribution of seats. The right to petition any Parliament was to be firmly established, and the ability of either

House to imprison people without allowing them a legal trial as firmly denied (a blow here for Lilburne and Overton). A presbyterian Church was still to be established, but with liberty granted to worthy people to worship outside it.[59]

This was essentially a blend of the Independent religious programme with some of the political ideas trailed earlier by the London radicals. A leading MP who now had close connections with the Independents, and so should have known, recorded that this, and the other army declarations of early to mid-June, were drawn up by Henry Ireton, using his previous training as a lawyer. He added that Ireton was much assisted in this work by Cromwell and Lambert.[60] At the same time, the army sent to the Commons a formal charge against eleven men representing the Presbyterian leadership in the House, headed by Holles and Stapleton. They were accused of attempting to overthrow the liberties of the English by slandering the New Model Army and trying to raise forces to start a new civil war.[61] Ironically, that last action was exactly what they were now attempting, but only in the face of what seemed to be an attack by the New Model.

What rendered Parliament's position futile was that the Londoners did not rally to them: when the corporation tried to raise the militia and put the city on a war footing, it got very little response. Certainly the army had a large minority of sympathizers among the citizens, consisting of the Independent–radical alliance to whom the New Model now represented the only barrier to a Presbyterian settlement. It counted for more, however, that, while many in London were prepared to risk their lives to save their city, they were not prepared to do so to save the Presbyterian leadership. As a result, Parliament was left with no option other than to come to terms with the army, starting with the humiliating gesture of sending Fairfax the month's pay he had demanded for his men. A further humiliation followed when the Houses tried to get the king out of the army's hands and were refused.[62] Up in Scotland the government debated sending a force into England to oppose the New Model, but reached no decision after two weeks, by which time the opportunity to intervene had passed.[63]

The New Model had settled down around St Albans while it monitored the reactions to its menaces and demands, Cromwell invisible among the mass of officers and agitators who discussed responses. The army continued to grow as more of its scattered units came up and the few gaps in its ranks were filled by recruitment: because it was clearly now so strong and Parliament so weak, service in it was an attractive prospect. By 20 June it had 13,000 foot in twelve full-strength regiments, and 7,000 horse in eight more.[64] On the 22nd and 23rd, Fairfax and his Council of War (made up of senior officers) informed Parliament and the corporation of London that their men would have to take offensive action unless the accused MPs were removed from the Commons, all new forces raised around the city were disbanded and the army was properly paid. Between the 23rd and the 25th they tightened the screws on Parliament further by advancing south-west, to quarter the army in the prosperous farming villages of western Middlesex, within an easy day's march of Westminster.[65]

At the same time, the army leaders were starting to take advantage of their possession of the king, bringing him south from Newmarket, and placing him in a series of mansions just to the rear of their own positions. As they had shifted their political position, from merely removing the Presbyterian leaders to formulating their own settlement for the nation, it seemed possible that they might be able to enlist royal support for that settlement. They accordingly began to pamper the king as Parliament had not done, allowing him the company of former royalist courtiers and councillors, and the use of chaplains for religious services who employed his preferred form of worship, with the traditional Prayer Book. His continuing popularity with many of his subjects was demonstrated by the way in which the cheering people of the villages through which he passed strewed green boughs and roses before him to welcome him.[66]

Meanwhile, Parliament found itself in an impossible situation with respect to the charge presented by the army against eleven of the members of the Commons. There had been no plot to bring in foreign forces or raise new soldiers to crush the New Model, and everything that the accused men had done had been legitimately enacted with free will by a majority of MPs and peers. The House accordingly did not know how to proceed. The problem was only resolved when, on 26 June, the eleven men volunteered to withdraw themselves from the Commons. Two days later, Fairfax declared on behalf of his army that its immediate requirements were satisfied and it would now withdraw westwards into the Chiltern Hills and up the Thames, from where to discuss the settlement of the nation, providing that the army was regularly paid, that Parliament made no more attempts to raise other soldiers, that the eleven MPs kept out of public life and that the New Model retained possession of the king. The crisis was over, leaving the army effectively in the position of being an independent power in the realm, with which the Lords and Commons now had to negotiate in order to frame a future for the nation.[67]

The army's declaration of 14 June had laid out a framework for a future English constitution which, in its provisions for regularly elected Parliaments with fixed terms and a reformed system of constituencies, and for liberty of conscience alongside an established national Church, prefigured reforms that were actually to be carried out over the following two centuries and would lead to Britain's current liberal representative democracy. It is perfectly in order for historians of ideas to place the declaration in such a sequence of developments and also for those who value this democracy to hail the New Model Army as ideological ancestors. It is a much more questionable exercise to write the history of 1647 in these terms, and to treat Cromwell and his fellow soldiers as the heroes of this narrative as a result. The Presbyterian leaders, and the bulk of MPs and peers whom they had swayed, had certainly treated the army shabbily and foolishly, especially in view of the invaluable service it had performed in winning the war for them. On the other hand, they had ended up conceding to all of the demands that its members had made in the course of April and May, once they had realized the true strength of the soldiers' feelings. At each stage, they had been persuaded by reasoned arguments and apparent information into supporting particular lines of policy, and so exercising their rights as elected or hereditary representatives of the nation, even if a large part of the politically active members of that nation, the royalists, was now excluded from the process. In doing so, they had planned a settlement which was likely to have the support of a majority of the parliamentarian party and the acquiescence of many who had been neutral or even royalist during the war: in sum, the greater part of the English and Welsh people.

By contrast the behaviour of the army had been much worse. However reasonable the fears and needs of the soldiers had been with respect to their prospective demobilization, they had in the last analysis served their own selfish interests. The pretext which they had articulated to justify their armed opposition to Parliament – of saving the liberties of the nation from evil people who had intended to start a new war and impose a tyranny – was a fantasy and a delusion. They may have developed it as the result of an understandable misreading of various signs, but they had been mistaken nonetheless. Their assertion that they were not acting on behalf of any party when demanding the removal of the leading Presbyterians was pure hypocrisy, for the crippling of that leadership was itself bound to bring about a shift of power in the nation. Furthermore, as soon as Parliament had shown signs of resistance to having that shift imposed upon it, they had not only swept this aside with a blatant display of military force but had articulated a rival programme for settlement with the specious claim that they represented the generality of the people better than its elected representatives. Like many throughout history who have seized power in self-defence, they had rapidly come to enjoy wielding it and to persist in doing so. What they had done is understandable, and the basic duty of the historian is to attempt to understand the past: but it cannot be lauded as justifiable by the claims either of law or of necessity.

THE FALL OF LONDON

At the end of June, the army's headquarters were pulled back from Westminster as promised, to Wycombe, which nestled in a valley in the centre of the pastures and woods which muffled the slopes of the Chilterns, one of the broadest portions of the great finger of chalk that southern England thrusts out towards the North Sea. On 2 July nine new commissioners arrived there from Parliament to discuss the New Model's plans for the nation. In response, the army commissioned nine senior officers, headed by Cromwell and including Ireton, Fleetwood and Lambert, to meet them at their inn and inform them that talks could not commence until Parliament had annulled the last of its votes to raise forces against the New Model and settled regular pay and supplies for it.[68] Instead, three days later, Fairfax's Council of War (comprising the leading officers) sent Cromwell, Lambert, fifteen other commanders and two agitators to meet lawyers in order to draw up a full list of charges against the eleven Presbyterian MPs. The following day this was delivered to the Commons. It repeated the vague accusation of trying to start a new war and subvert English liberties, accompanied by a host of assertions dredged up against individual men from gossip and factional fighting stretching back years.[69]

By then the headquarters had been moved again, to settle at Reading, Berkshire's largest town, situated where the River Thames carves a broad gap through the chalk and joins a smaller river, the Kennet, flowing in from the west. These were now slow green summer waterways, reflecting the leaves above them, with insects dancing over them in the evenings. King Charles was installed in a stately mansion across a bridge from the town, ready to be involved in the impending settlement. Ireton spent the whole evening of 3 July in private with him, sounding him out on his views and wishes, and the following day Fairfax arrived to see him, with Cromwell and other military leaders. These discussions were resumed on succeeding days and seemed very promising. On the first Sunday after the king's arrival, his chosen churchmen preached to him in an upper room, while one of the New Model's favourite independent chaplains, Hugh Peters, performed for Cromwell and his fellow officers and the parliamentary commissioners who still accompanied Charles, in the room below: a fine example of liberty of conscience at work. As part of this pampering, the army allowed the king to be visited by his younger children, who had been held apart from him since the end of the war. He was also permitted to carry out the traditional royal rite of touching people afflicted with the disease of scrofula in an attempt to heal them. Fairfax defended all this to Parliament as intended to incline the king to agree to a settlement, and Cromwell talked round the agitators to it with the same argument.[70]

As part of this charm offensive, the generals invited in royalists to act as intermediaries to persuade Charles into compliance. The first to arrive was Sir John Berkeley, of whom the leaders of the New Model had formed a good impression when they had negotiated with him during the Civil War, and who had been sent by the important royalist circle around the queen to see if a deal could be struck with the soldiers now. He was warmly welcomed at Reading, but also given warnings against unreasonable expectations. Two royalists already established in the town told him that Ireton had cautioned Charles that the army intended to arbitrate between king and Parliament, and would not allow the king to arbitrate between Parliament and army. Cromwell informed Berkeley that both the sovereign and his subjects needed to be secured in their rights, and that the army would do its best to find a deal which would reconcile royalists, Presbyterians and Independents. During the next couple of weeks, Berkeley decided that Fairfax had little influence, and that his Council of War was effectively led by Cromwell and Ireton. However, the representative body of the army which had been formed in June, the General Council, on which leading officers sat with the agitators elected from junior officers and other ranks, was now coming into session. Berkeley thought that Cromwell and Ireton had a strong party there but that it was dominated by the agitators, many of whom were jealous of Oliver's power and apparent ambition. These men also retained an intense suspicion of him, following his attempt to persuade the army to accord with Parliament in May, and thought that he was not only a dissembler but somebody who would actually change his views to suit the occasion. They suspected that his apparent new warm feelings towards the king were an act, and that his only constant aim was to 'prosecute his ambitious ends through all means whatsoever'. Cromwell had effectively manoeuvred himself again into the position of a mediator, this time between king and army, which carried the same discomforts and problems as his previous one between Parliament and army, and an even greater scale of possible reward.

Despite these suspicions, the signs of rapprochement remained promising. Berkeley himself thought that Cromwell's wish for one was sincere, and was impressed by an encounter with him just after Oliver had witnessed Charles's reunion with his children. Cromwell burst into tears and admitted that the untrammelled affection that the king had shown his family had finally convinced him that Charles was a decent man. He added that the king's refusal of the Newcastle Propositions had demonstrated that Charles was a man of principle, whose word could be trusted, and not a dissembling opportunist. Berkeley warned two of the other generals that the king probably could not be persuaded to give up bishops, ruin any royalists and their families or relinquish the armed forces for more than his own lifetime. The generals, however, thought that these points could be accommodated. Sir John's main problem was with Charles himself, who remained deeply resentful and suspicious of the army after its crushing of his own soldiers during the war and its abduction of him a month before. He believed that Cromwell and its other leaders were trying to use him for their own designs. On the other side, Berkeley found that the agitators and chaplains of the army were less willing to treat, and make concessions, than their commanders, and suspected that they had more influence with the ordinary soldiers.[71]

Meanwhile Parliament was still struggling to accommodate itself to developments. It was ever plainer that the New Model was in control of the country, as in early July the members of the northern army, acting through their own elected agitators, arrested and disowned their Presbyterian general. All the parliamentarian soldiers in the country now gave obedience to Fairfax. Pressed by his subordinates, he therefore requested Parliament to place all of them formally under his command; on the 17th the Commons faced reality and voted overwhelmingly (though in a thinly attended House) to do so. Two days later the Lords agreed, and from that moment onward the New Model Army technically ceased to exist as a separate force: all the men under arms in the nation in the theoretical name of Parliament were under the control of Sir Thomas and can henceforth be called simply 'the army'. On the same day, the eleven MPs charged by the soldiers delivered a full defence to everything alleged against them, but the risk of provoking the army again was obvious, and the following day the House gave them permission to leave the country for six months, which would completely remove them from the political scene. In the same period, Parliament acted to banish any former soldiers from London who might be suspected as representing a potential alternative force.[72]

A large part of the reason for Parliament's compliant behaviour was that the attitude of the soldiery remained menacing. On 16 July, in the General Council at Reading, the agitators advocated a march on the capital to enforce the enactment of the requests sent to Parliament. Over a hundred officers and other ranks were present to debate this, and Cromwell, Ireton and other senior commanders opposed it successfully in favour of allowing the Houses more time to acquiesce with what was asked of them: Cromwell was especially to the fore in doing so. On the other hand, the actions requested of Parliament multiplied. They now included the release of Lilburne, Overton and other radicals who had been detained without trial; and the return of the London militia committee, which controlled the still potentially formidable military resources of the capital, to the Independents and radicals who had dominated it until April. To allay the soldiers' ongoing fear of invasion plots, it was decided to ask for a declaration that it was treason to attempt to bring any foreign forces into the kingdom. Cromwell assured the agitators that a response would be demanded within days, and the army could move on Westminster and London, and purge Parliament, if none were forthcoming. He emphasized, however, that the army had faithful friends in both Houses who could probably be relied upon to do its work for it, and Ireton added that the withdrawal of many Presbyterians ought to have shifted the balance of power in Parliament to the army. At midnight the debate was concluded in their favour.[73]

On 20 July the fresh requests reached Parliament, and once more it buckled. Two days later the Commons resolved to declare it treason to attempt to bring in foreign soldiers and voted to restore the City militia committee to its former hands, removing the Presbyterian majority. The Lords rapidly concurred. Only the matter of the prisoners held without trial was ignored.[74] Cromwell's policy of trusting to Parliament seemed vindicated, and between the 21st and 23rd Fairfax and his Council of War withdrew the army further from the capital, quartering its regiments across a swathe of country between Wiltshire and Norfolk. The headquarters, including Cromwell, moved up the Thames and then into the neighbouring broad clay vale of Aylesbury, before settling at Bedford on the great Midlands river called the Ouse, beside which he had been born and grown up. The king was also moved again with the headquarters, being installed in the earl of Bedford's home at Woburn Abbey, up in the chalk hills of Bedfordshire where the cornfields were now turning yellow.[75] There, for the first time, he had a view of the settlement that the army was intending to offer him and Parliament.

This had been in preparation since early July, a summary of the key points being put together by Ireton, the fiery Nottinghamshire gentleman with legal training who was Cromwell's son-in-law and close ally. He was now just in his mid-thirties, still with thickly hanging light brown hair and the fashionable moustache and triangular beard framing an intent gaze. He was as committed a religious independent as Oliver, but had a keener interest in political reform, and the scheme that he drew up – doubtless after extensive discussions among different interest groups which are hidden from view – reflected both.[76] The records give us a few glimpses of this process. Berkeley discussed the initial proposals with Ireton for almost the whole of a night; on 17 July they were presented to the General Council of the army, when it was agreed that both the agitators and Fairfax's

Council of War could offer additions to them. Interestingly, Cromwell was unsure then of the meaning of one of the clauses and Lambert clarified it for him, suggesting that Oliver had not been as closely involved in the production of the draft concerned as some of the other senior officers. A committee of twelve of these officers (including Ireton, Fleetwood and Lambert) and twelve agitators was appointed to 'perfect' it, with the proviso that Cromwell would attend when he could. They worked fast: on the 20th the result, which had become known as the 'Heads of the Proposals', was delivered to Parliament.[77]

The first draft of the terms seems to have represented a modification of the Newcastle Propositions, to please Independents, London radicals and royalists. Thus, bishops were still to be abolished and a presbyterian Church established, but with some liberty of conscience to those who did not wish to belong to it. An alternative way of supporting the established clergy would be found to replace the traditional system of tithes levied on all parishioners, which was resented by those who did not wish to belong to the Church. The number of royalists to suffer execution (if they did not stay in exile) and loss of estates was reduced to seven, and the fines on the rest were lightened, though all were banned from the next three Parliaments and from holding office for five years, unless given a special dispensation. Legal actions were to be made simpler and cheaper. In the most dramatic change, the current Parliament was to dissolve and be replaced by successors elected every two years to sit for eight months, the elections to be based on a more regular system of voting rights and on constituencies redistributed across the nation to reflect taxable wealth. Any bill passed by the Commons in two successive Parliaments would have to become law even if the king vetoed it, and the monarch would further be restrained by a Council of State which wielded many of the traditional royal powers, including that of declaring war or peace. Members would be chosen in the first instance by joint agreement between king and Parliament to serve for seven years. The council would also control the armed forces for ten years; after that time, Charles would be able to appoint military commanders with the approval of Parliament, while his successor could apparently do so with the approval of the council. Government ministers would be appointed by Parliament for ten years and then chosen by the king from a list of three named by Parliament; his successor would still have to take account of Parliament's wishes when making such appointments.[78]

The king had begun to respond to his relatively good treatment by the army with a willingness to treat with it and with the Independents, but when Berkeley showed him a first draft of the proposals he was shocked. He had probably been expecting a softer version of the Newcastle Propositions, close to the compromise he had offered in May. Instead he was asked to agree to a radical change in the traditional political constitution, which still crossed all the lines that he had established as not negotiable in the summer: he was expected to agree both to the abolition of the bishops, and so of royal control of the Church, and to the permanent loss of key political powers of the Crown. In this bitter mood he paid attention to the most active of the Scottish representatives in London, the earl of Lauderdale, who visited him with hopes that the Scots would now send an army into England to defeat the New Model. Charles apparently allowed the earl to sound out his countrymen concerning this possibility, while also hoping that the army would make more concessions.[79] Its leaders responded with a major one, of allowing king and Lords to keep their vetoes over the Commons' legislation; but this in turn violated a key aspiration of the London radicals, who sent a letter of protest on 24 July.[80]

At this moment, a second royalist negotiator, sent by the queen to broker a deal between the king and the army, arrived on the scene. This was John Ashburnham, who was supposed to reinforce Berkeley's efforts. Unhappily, it soon became obvious that the two men did not get on, and their lack of co-operation confused the talks and the king still further. According to Berkeley, when the 'Heads of the Proposals' were formally presented to Charles at Woburn by Ireton and a deputation of other senior officers, at some point in late July, he appalled them and Sir John by receiving them angrily and insisting on the retention of bishops. He also (if we can trust

Berkeley's memory) informed his military visitors that they depended on him for any political credibility, giving permanent offence to some.[81]

One reason for Charles's irritability with the army – if Sir John's account of the meeting is correct – may have been that he was being pressed by both the Scots and the Presbyterians not to deal with it.[82] When the king was first courted by the officers, and wrote to one of his most important supporters in Scotland that he was prepared to deal with them, he received the withering reply that, if he accepted the kind of settlement the army was likely to offer, he would lose all his Scottish followers.[83] As for the Presbyterians, they were starting to push back against the soldiers. The eleven accused MPs had not yet left the country, and the bullying of Parliament by the army into giving Fairfax control of all the soldiers in the nation, along with the Independents' regained control of London's militia, had provoked serious anger among many Londoners. On 14 July large numbers of the city's apprentices had already petitioned both Houses to restore the king to his 'just' rights, suppress religious sects and pay off the army.[84] A week later, a crowd of citizens gathered at the hall of the Skinners' Company and drew up an engagement to have the king brought to the capital to treat on the basis of the terms he had offered in May, while the army kept its distance. Immediately, news of this engagement was carried to Bedford by an ally in the city; the army's leaders informed both Houses that if they did not act to suppress it then the soldiers would. On the 24th, the day after Parliament had ordered the London militia to be returned to the army's allies, it tamely declared the new engagement to be treason.[85] Charles would certainly have known of these events, and his feelings would have been embittered by the fact that the same officers who were treating with him were ruthlessly quashing an attempt by his subjects to allow him exactly the basis for negotiation that he had been proposing since the winter.

Far from imposing calm, these latest actions of Parliament in response to the army's demands and threats only served to apply a match to the political powder keg which London had become. Infuriated by what they now perceived as a military tyranny which denied them their freedoms and desires as citizens and subjects, many of the inhabitants now reacted, led by their corporation. On 26 July a deputation from the corporation presented a petition to Parliament to return its militia committee to those, mostly Presbyterians, who had populated it earlier in the summer. This was followed, however, by a mob, consisting largely of young men, which invaded first the House of Lords and then the Commons, and coerced the members of both into passing the desired measure. The Commons were also forced to invite the king to the capital to settle the nation, with their Speaker being held down in his chair: the Londoners, having suffered from the results of the army's willingness to submit Parliament to menaces in order to get its way, had now copied the tactic. In the evening, members of the corporation arrived and persuaded the crowd to leave.

The Houses adjourned for four days. When they regathered on 30 July, it was found that many members of both were missing, mainly Independents but also some Presbyterians, and including both Speakers. Nevertheless, both were still quorate, and so technically their actions were both legitimate and free, the crowd not having returned and the corporation guaranteeing that it would not. Both Houses therefore took advantage of a restored Presbyterian majority to shake off the army's control and pass a set of measures on the last two days of the month that were designed to produce a different sort of national settlement from that being proposed by the soldiers. The militia committee was restored to its former membership; Fairfax's command was limited to regular field units and removed from garrisons and militias. By majority votes in the Commons, it was first agreed that the king was to be removed from the army's control to that of Parliament, and then (on 2 August) that he should be brought to London to treat. The City of London was empowered to take measures for its defence against a counter-strike by the army, and it promptly did so, with the Presbyterian general Massey in charge of them.[86]

By then it was clear that the counter-strike was coming, because Fairfax and his senior officers, including Cromwell, had immediately reacted to the news of the coercion of Parliament by the mob by proclaiming that neither House was now free to act and that their army was coming to rescue both. In reality, as the City corporation was guaranteeing the safety of both Houses by the time that their members reassembled on the 30th, the soldiers were acting to crush the counter-revolution that threatened their grip on the nation. Back across the great chalk ridge streamed their regiments, through the fields where the ripe wheat, barley and oats now made golden ripples in the breeze. When the Houses were reoccupied, the army's vanguard was already back in the villages of western Middlesex, and a part of the reason for the decision of many members not to return may have been a desire to get out of the way of the impending attack, and then align with the victorious power in the contest.[87]

The legitimacy of the army's attack on a Parliament which was plausibly claiming to be free to act again and quorate, in partnership with a City government which could equally claim to be following the will of most of its citizens, would be greatly enhanced if it could be seen to act in collaboration with the king. Its negotiations with Charles therefore took on an even greater intensity. For his part, he was now in the even more agonizing position of being asked to support military action against people who were now explicitly offering him what he had been asking earlier in the year: it is indeed possible that the 'Heads of the Proposals' were first offered to him by the officers after 26 July, and that his angry reaction (at least according to Berkeley) derived from his resentment of the situation. Nonetheless, he continued to respond to them and, feeling out of his depth among the radical implications of the army's intended reforms, sent for a set of royalist judges, clergy and former courtiers to advise him. Probably after this consultation, he presented his own suggestions for amendments to the 'Heads' which would enable him to accept them: the return of the armed forces to him after ten years; his ability to name a third of the Council of State; a general indemnity for all wartime royalists; the acceptance of grants (including peerages) that he had made in the war; royal control of diplomacy; the return to him, after a period, of control of the great offices of state; and the retention of bishops (with their lands) and the Prayer Book in the Church, but without any coercive powers for the former or an imposition of the latter on those who refused to use it. In return, he would accept the main points of the 'Heads': biennial Parliaments on a reformed electoral system, liberty of conscience for those who wanted to worship outside the Church, a breadth of practice and belief inside it, and temporary extensive limitations on royal power.[88]

It must be borne in mind that, strong as the army was, it did not know at this point that it could defeat the Londoners. There was a real chance at the opening of August that, if Parliament and the citizenry remained resolutely defiant, it would have a tough fight on its hands, against large numbers of well-armed men, many with considerable military experience, defending powerful fortifications. The army's leaders therefore made significant further concessions to get an immediate deal with the king: the retention of bishops and the Prayer Book with the status he proposed; the exclusion of just five royalists from pardon; and reduced fines for the rest, with a ban from office for five years. Nonetheless, a significant gap remained between Charles and the army – over royal political powers, the treatment of royalists and the status of the king's wartime grants – while the future structure of the Church and the fate of the bishops' lands were left undecided. The fact that the king did not feel able to accept immediately what was now on offer to him was both a demonstration of this gulf and an indication that he did indeed intend to keep – or recognized that he would be obliged to keep – a deal to which he agreed.

At any rate, the army leaders, including Cromwell, felt it necessary to publish the terms they were now offering, from their headquarters at Colnbrook on the Thames on 1 August.[89] If they could not yet get an agreed settlement from the king, they could get a different and more urgent document out of him: a declaration disowning the proceedings of the present Parliament at Westminster and of the City, and supporting the army in its action against them. Charles, who was now once more lodged in a succession of mansions in the army's rear, hesitated a day over this, knowing full well that among those preparing for resistance in the capital were not only Presbyterians now inviting him to treat with them but also wartime royalists. On the 3rd, however, he provided it, declaring the 'Heads of the Proposals' to be the best basis for a lasting peace, supporting the army in marching against London as a prelude to this, and warning his followers not to offer resistance.[90]

On that day, Fairfax and his Council of War, including Cromwell, declared that the army was moving to attack Westminster and London, on what they still proclaimed to be a mission of liberation, from a Presbyterian conspiracy fomented by the eleven accused MPs, to restore the king to powers limited only by the meagre concessions he had offered in May. In its accustomed menacing manner, it now promised not only to arrest the eleven men but to punish all who had promoted the invasion of Parliament on 26 July.[91] Parties of the army had already surrounded the city, seizing the forts on the Thames downriver from it to cut it off from the sea. One led by Cromwell's brother-in-law Desborough had found a troop of armed horsemen at Deptford, and dispersed it, killing some.[92] As soon as the Council of War issued its declaration of offensive action on the 3rd, it hastened to review its army, mustered on the yellowing grassland of Hounslow Heath, the largest open space to the west of the capital. Nine thousand foot and six thousand horse were drawn up in a line one and a half miles long, and Fairfax rode along it accompanied by the lords and MPs who had joined him, to the cheers of the men. All then surged towards Westminster, halting for the night between Brentford and Hammersmith and sending a force to occupy Southwark, where sympathizers let it into the defences in the small hours.[93] That evening too, the MPs and peers with the army drafted a declaration supporting all that it did, which was published the following day.[94]

On 4 August, the corporation of London surrendered. It had called out the militia to the defences, but – in a repeat of their performance in June, most of the trained bands did not appear. It seems that, once more, even the many citizens who supported the developments in Parliament since 26 July did not want to risk being killed and having their homes sacked for the sake of a better national settlement, once the army had shown itself to be determinedly aggressive.[95] The speed and suddenness of the City's collapse took the king by surprise, leaving him high and dry without any bargaining position; and from that moment Cromwell and the rest of the army ignored him while they followed up their victory. The French ambassador shrewdly summed up the two aspects of Charles's predicament: that he was now at the mercy of the army and the Independents, having lost his chance to make a deal with them when they were vulnerable; but that the terms he had been offered even then were 'hard and destructive and subversive of all the foundations of royal authority'.[96]

The following day, the 5th, Fairfax entered Westminster accompanied by three horse regiments, the riders crowned with bay and laurel leaves as a sign of victory and peace. With them came the returning peers and MPs in their coaches, including both the former Speakers. Cromwell went ahead with an advance guard to line the way to the doors of the Houses of Parliament with soldiers, which both honoured the members and showed them who was in control.[97] On the 6th both Houses received Sir Thomas to give him and his army their thanks, with the Speakers restored, treating him with an honour usually reserved for visiting royalty or ambassadors, handing over the Tower of London to him and granting the soldiers a month's pay.[98]

It only remained for the army to stage a victory parade through London, which it did on 7 August, with all of its horse and foot, and its train of artillery. It was noted that Cornet Joyce, the abductor of the king, was among the six or seven troopers chosen as the elite personal guard of Fairfax's coach. Cromwell was again conspicuous, on horseback in command of the rearguard, which consisted of the cavalry regiments of Fleetwood, Whalley and an ardent young religious radical, Thomas Harrison, who had been promoted to colonel during the removal of Presbyterian officers in June. The whole event lasted twelve hours, not ending until dusk, when the last of Cromwell's horsemen clattered through the gates of Southwark into the Surrey countryside.[99] In the records for much of the previous two months, Cromwell had only intermittently been clearly in view, most often being subsumed in the mass of senior officers. Nonetheless, he had obviously been at the centre of events, and the surrender of London and Parliament to the army of which he was second-in-command now made him one of the most powerful men in the nation, in both political and military affairs. This was a position the full potential of which somebody with Oliver's talents was certain to realize.

HAMPTON COURT AND PUTNEY

In the rest of August, the army headquarters settled on the River Thames above Westminster, first at the market town of Kingston and then, from the 27th, at the village of Putney, which was within easier reach of Parliament. Cromwell found lodgings there in a private house.[100] The General Council met in the parish church, a grey medieval building with a square tower, directly next to the river. It continued to do so as the Thames swelled with the autumn rains and began to carry down the first yellow and red leaves of the year, while the sunlight coming through the church windows became gentler and more dappled. Initially the soldiers, embodied both in the General Council and in Fairfax's elite Council of War, were most preoccupied with three issues, fruits of victory. The first was revenge, as the agitators called for action against the perpetrators of the attempted counter-coup in the capital, and Fairfax required the demolition of the defences of London. The second was to consolidate the army's grip on England, most clearly signalled by sending John Lambert to command what had been the northern army of Parliament. The third was to obtain further conquests. A sense of divine favour must have been strengthened when the easy conquest of London was followed by news of a great victory in Ireland, by the force that Parliament had sent to occupy Dublin when the marquis of Ormond handed it over. That force had proceeded to destroy the army maintained by the Catholic rebels in the eastern province of Leinster, which included Dublin, in a battle at Dungan's Hill in County Meath. The success provoked an immediate resolution to send a full-scale field force over to undertake the reconquest of the island that the Presbyterians had planned in the spring, to be gathered as soon as Parliament put up the money for one.[101]

It soon became obvious that the money wasn't coming, because it wasn't there. Moreover, it wasn't there for the army of England itself, because the shortfall of taxes to pay the soldiers, especially from London, had suddenly become serious. This mattered acutely, as not only did the failure of regular pay make the soldiers in general restless and resentful, but the number of men in pay had swollen greatly at the end of July, when many additional recruits had been taken on in a hurry for what seemed likely to be the siege and storming of London. These men, now not needed, had to be paid off, and not only could this not be done but, while they remained, uselessly, in service, they were running up further arrears of wages. The people of the capital, having given way to the threat of military force, retained one single, silent, means of resistance to the soldiers who had humiliated and bullied them. It was to withhold the money on which their oppressors depended; and they were deploying it. By September the shortfall was serious and the army was already threatening to re-enter the City and collect what was due to it by force. On the 16th the General Council agreed to meet in Putney church every Thursday to debate the affairs of the kingdom.[102]

The soldiers also had to deal with Parliament. The events of early August had resulted in a change in relations between its two Houses. Hitherto the Lords had been more conservative, and prepared to treat with the king and secure a settlement that preserved as much of the old order as possible. Now, so many of the peers who had supported that policy had fled that the upper House had a secure Independent majority and was prepared to take more reformist action. By contrast, although the eleven members charged by the army had gone abroad, the Commons retained a much larger number of Presbyterians and of moderate men who had supported their programme. The contrast showed almost immediately after the army reimposed its control, when the Lords agreed to annul all the measures passed by Parliament between 26 July and 6 August, and the Commons refused to do so by two votes. In part this may have been due to a legal issue, in that to declare those measures void would expose anybody who had acted in obedience to them to prosecution. It may also, however, have been due to a genuine feeling on behalf of many MPs that the Parliament which sat on 30 July had been a free and legitimate one. A tussle ensued between the Houses until 19 August, when the Commons received a furious remonstrance from the General Council of the army, requiring them to adopt the 'Heads of the Proposals' as a basis for settlement, punish those responsible for the pressure on Parliament in late July, annul the measures passed as a result, and bar all who had passed them from sitting in either House unless they gave guarantees of future good behaviour.[103]

Great pressure was exerted on the Commons to comply. Both Cromwell and Ireton made speeches in the House warning against the dire consequences of defying the soldiers, as did several leading Independents. A body of cavalry was stationed in Hyde Park and foot soldiers guarded the corridors of the palace of Westminster: ostensibly to protect the Houses, but sending out a clear threat. That threat was very real, because the regimental agitators were demanding a fresh march on Westminster to remove all those who had sat in the Commons from 30 July; this would have represented a major purge. The MPs caved in over the annulment, although they protected from prosecution any who had obeyed the measures concerned. They also agreed to prosecute three of their own members and seven Presbyterian lords for their actions in late July and early August. Cromwell supported these steps, partly to gratify the army of which he was a part but also reflecting a pattern which he had shown from the opening of his political career, of dealing ruthlessly and vindictively with adversaries. When a Presbyterian MP, leaving London for the provinces, was arrested by soldiers, Fairfax released him but Cromwell had him secured again as an enemy. Oliver allegedly informed the major of his own regiment that the Presbyterians should be 'pulled out by the ears' from Parliament, that across the nation their leaders should be gaoled and that those responsible for the tumult on 26 July should be executed. The

Commons, however, made no general attempt to call to account those who had remained at Westminster during the critical period. Nor did they pay any attention to the army's terms for settlement. The Houses certainly did act swiftly to send proposals to the king, submitting them on 7 September in concert with the Scottish commissioners in England. These were, however, not those drafted by Ireton in July but those tendered to Charles at Newcastle in the previous year, amended in only a few small details which did nothing to meet the objections he had raised to them.[104]

As the army had established its headquarters at Putney, it had installed the king at Hampton Court, Henry VIII's great red-brick Tudor palace beside the Thames, as easily accessible to the west of Putney as Westminster was to the east. This was a situation agreeable to Charles, as it seemed to grant him what he had desired for much of the previous year: to reside in a royal house near London and negotiate a peace settlement. The generals resumed the good treatment of him that they had accorded in July, allowing him to keep the state of a sovereign, to receive throngs of visitors and to attempt to cure people with the royal touch.[105] Following the army's complete takeover of the nation in early August, he had decided to make a firm alliance with it in an attempt to obtain a peace he could accept. The royalist courtier John Ashburnham daily carried messages from him to Cromwell and Ireton in the last warm days of the year, passing through the rich Surrey countryside of shaved gold cornfields and orchards heavy with fruit. Cromwell was plainly nervous about the constructions that enemies might place upon these private negotiations, and reported a rumour that he was to be made earl of Essex and captain of the royal guard as a reward for a settlement favourable to the king. He was especially angered by talk in the army's General Council that he had become more a partisan of Charles than of his own soldiers. He asked Ashburnham to limit his visits, and to send messengers instead.[106]

The king seems to have expected that the terms he would be sent by Parliament would be those offered to him by the army in late July. If so, it must have been a shock when he got the Newcastle Propositions back instead. Nonetheless, he continued to work closely with Cromwell and Ireton, and allowed them to advise on the reply that he made to these terms on 14 September.[107] It was calculated to be exactly what the army desired, stating that he preferred to treat on the basis of the 'Heads of the Proposals', as much better suited to the interests of the soldiers and the nation. In particular, he noted that those proposals offered freedom of conscience as well as securing the liberties of his subjects and the privileges of Parliament.[108] In his room in Putney, Cromwell instructed his major, whom he used as his own messenger to the king, to reassure Charles that he could trust to the 'Heads' and (Oliver at this point putting his hand on his heart) that the king could be sure of getting what he wanted through them.[109]

Leading army officers and Independent politicians were certainly delighted with the royal answer, but Parliament was not.[110] After a week both Houses voted it to be unsatisfactory, and the following day the Commons divided over whether to consider it at all. Cromwell acted as a teller for those believing that they should, with another leading Independent politician. His side won by a comfortable fifty votes. On the 23rd the House voted again, to send further propositions to Charles, again by a large majority.[111] All this opened the way to a settlement closer to the one proposed to the king by the army officers in July, but there was no good prospect that any could be agreed which would satisfy the soldiers, Parliament and the king. On the 21st, the day on which Parliament censured the king for his reply to its terms, the General Council of the army had submitted a set of specific desires. They were concerned with the material needs of the soldiers, during and after service, but one term was a request that the accumulated arrears of pay due to the army be provided by selling off not only the remaining bishops' lands but also those of the deans and chapters of cathedrals and the royal forests.[112] This immediately supported one of the reforms to which the king had always refused to agree, the alienation of Church property.

A large part of the problem for Cromwell, in steering the way to a settlement which he himself wanted and which the king would accept, was that he was now opposing not just Presbyterians and other conservative parliamentarians, but radicals who had hitherto been allies in the broad Independent coalition. The process had started rapidly in the case of the most celebrated of these, the civilian Londoners John Lilburne and Richard Overton, who had been imprisoned by Parliament. The actions of the army in June, of turning on that Parliament and driving out its Presbyterian leaders, had raised natural hopes in those men that their release would be imminent. When it did not occur, both as naturally felt betrayed, and blamed the generals. In June and July Lilburne sent Cromwell a series of letters accusing him of selling out the cause of liberty in hope of material reward, and being seduced by the 'silken Independents' in Parliament, such as Sir Henry Vane and Oliver St John (who were indeed Oliver's usual allies there). He added the accusation of robbing the agitators elected by the soldiers of all influence over the actions of the army, and in late July published these diatribes to show Cromwell's 'villainy to the world'.[113] In the same month, Overton published the charge that the agitators were the true representatives of the army, and that its generals, like Cromwell, could not be trusted.[114] As shown, the soldiers did ask Parliament to release Lilburne and Overton, but were ignored on this point, while the key radical demand for the abolition of the vetoes of the king and Lords over legislation was dropped from the 'Heads of the Proposals'.

In early September, Cromwell visited Lilburne in the Tower of London to strike a deal with him, after Lilburne had written to Fairfax proposing that negotiations be opened to discuss the differences between him and Oliver. Cromwell had, moreover, presented a paper from Fairfax to the Commons, drawn up in Sir Thomas's new capacity as constable of the Tower, asking it to consider again some relief for the men Parliament was holding prisoner. On arrival in Lilburne's cell, Oliver allegedly offered to obtain his release and give him employment in the army if he would stop his attacks, but Lilburne refused to co-operate unless the soldiers' leadership changed their ways. Cromwell said that he would try to help notwithstanding; he visited other prisoners of Parliament held in the great medieval fortress, mostly royalists, and undertook to get them freedom or better conditions too.[115] A few weeks later, after no further action seemed to have been taken on his behalf, Lilburne published another set of letters blaming Cromwell and his 'lordly interest' for his continuing incarceration, and terming Oliver one of the 'enemies of liberty' who kept the General Council of the army subordinate to the higher officers and one of a clique of Independent politicians who kept the English people in bondage under a corrupt Parliament.[116] The great radical had in common with King Charles both considerable courage and an utter devotion to high principle, and an almost complete absence of a sense of political reality: Cromwell was cut from very different cloth.

Part of the problem created by Lilburne was that his accusations might resonate with radicals inside the army, especially in view of the distrust which some of the agitators had already expressed of the generals, and especially of Cromwell. In August one of the royalists shut up in the Tower, who had developed contacts with agitators through Lilburne, reported that these 'desperate and dangerous firebrands' in the army were discussing arresting some of the chief officers as traitors.[117] The regular meetings of the General Council gave an opportunity to contain such feeling. Cromwell still took the tone of a mediator and conciliator in it: he was reported as having declared there on 9 September that he was prepared to support a (tolerant) presbyterian Church because he desired 'nothing more, than to see this poor tattered nation established in truth and peace, and this languishing commonwealth restored to their just rights and liberties'.[118] One hot-headed agitator, who declared in the council around this time that there was no rightful power in England except that of the army, was expelled.[119] A more dangerous development for Cromwell was that he had quarrelled with one of the senior officers, a quick-tempered Londoner from a seafaring family called Colonel Thomas Rainsborough. The two men had been allies but (according to Sir John Berkeley) Rainsborough had been especially offended by the king's initial hostile reaction to the 'Heads of the Proposals', and had become averse to further dealings with him.

This had put Rainsborough on a divergent course from Oliver, but the occasion of their falling out was a personal one. It arose from the army's effective takeover of the nation, which meant that it needed to put all of the armed forces, including the navy, in loyal hands. That entailed installing one of its own officers or political supporters as vice-admiral, the person directly in command of the fleet, and Rainsborough, with his nautical family background, wanted the job. It was said that Cromwell and his friends had decided that the colonel was too self-willed, and that he and his main political allies, the leading Independents in Parliament – above all Viscount Saye, Sir Henry Vane and Oliver St John – wanted a more malleable man. In the end another soldier was chosen, one who had allegedly been a servant to Rainsborough's family. Rainsborough's response was volcanic, and a story was told of how, in mid-September, he had barged into a room where Cromwell was discussing matters with Ireton, Vane and St John and demanded the appointment.[120] After high words, table-pounding and threats from the angry colonel, it was agreed that the appointment was his, but the atmosphere between him and Cromwell remained tense.

This mattered the more in that Rainsborough had also been elected to the Commons. There he formed a partnership with a radical wing of the Independents, which was starting to separate off from the main party leadership over the issue of national settlement, objecting to any arrangement which left significant power to the king and the Lords. As such they were natural associates of the London radicals, especially the most lively and consistent of these MPs, a short, merry Berkshire gentleman with dark hair lapping over his ears, dark short beard, dark eyes, deeply lined face, sardonic mouth and large nose and chin, called Henry Marten. In the votes against further dealings with the king, on 22 and 23 September, Rainsborough and Marten acted as tellers against Cromwell and his allies.[121] As we have seen, they were defeated by a safe margin, but this required a major concerted effort by the mainstream Independents. According to the radicals, Cromwell met the Independent leaders to decide on tactics for it, and the decisive one was to persuade the MPs that the army wanted negotiations with the king to continue, with Ireton supplying inside testimony to that effect: once more, the implied threat of armed force proved effective. Cromwell was especially active in the debate on the king's behalf, while some of his opponents now drew on stereotypes of accursed characters from the Bible to call their sovereign an Achan or a Jonah. The radicals, thwarted, turned instead to further collaboration with their fellow believers in London, and – above all – in the army.[122]

From the Tower, Lilburne noted bitterly that, despite Cromwell's promise to help him, it had been Marten who had spoken for him in the Commons, while Cromwell sat silent. Marten got the case referred to a committee, in which Lilburne was informed that Cromwell had given testimony against him, while an ally of Oliver's did the same in the Commons. Lilburne's position was improved as a result of the investigation, for he was allowed out of the Tower while it was in progress (his friend Overton had been released), and in further publications he lambasted Cromwell without restraint, calling him 'my now grand adversary'.[123] Observers noted the 'snapping' between members of the former Independent alliance in the Commons, and the manner in which what one termed the 'root and branch men' (those demanding fundamental political change) had turned on Cromwell and Ireton. That writer reported how an ally of Marten's called Thomas Scot had accused Ireton (correctly) of secret dealings with the king through Ashburnham and Berkeley, and demanded an inquiry into them. Cromwell had sprung to the aid of his son-in-law (and himself) by declaring their complete innocence in the matter and their willingness to obey whatever Parliament decided, and that if Scot's inquiry proceeded he wanted another into attempts by the 'violent party' which Scot represented to suborn members of the army. That quashed the matter.[124]

All through October Parliament worked hard to agree its new terms for settlement, with Cromwell attending the Commons almost daily, and able to visit the army headquarters only sporadically.[125] The results were a compromise between the Presbyterians and the Independents and army leaders, and between the Newcastle Propositions and the 'Heads of the Proposals'.[126] This was itself an achievement, but one which could not easily be the basis for a general agreement because it failed to satisfy the minimum requirements of either the king or the radicals. Although Cromwell continued to speak favourably of Charles in the House and to urge a treaty with him as soon as possible, the actual terms agreed represented a major retreat from the offers that the army had made to the monarch in late July.[127] Bishops, deans and chapters were to be completely abolished in the Church and their lands sold, and the traditional Prayer Book, so beloved of the king and many of his subjects, was similarly to be abolished.[128] Some form of liberty of conscience was to be allowed, but only to the independents and sects, and not to Roman Catholics or Anglicans of the king's sort. Moreover, those who worshipped outside the established Church would still have to pay tithes to it. Presbyterianism was to be established, and though this was only to be until the end of the next Parliament after the present one, nobody knew when this would come: Cromwell acted as a teller on a motion to get an exact period set, but was defeated. When the time to review Church government did arrive, there was a chance that bishops might be restored, but with the lands on which their traditional state and their cathedrals had depended long gone, meaning that it would not be in any form that the king wanted.

The number of royalists to be sentenced to death was fixed at seven, and the fines on the others were to be moderated, as the army had wanted, but this was far short of the general pardon for the king's old followers, with a time-limited exclusion from power, on which Charles insisted. Moreover, many more royalists would lose their lands, all were to be excluded from pensions as well as any offices, and Parliament was to name ministers of state and viceroys of Ireland, apparently indefinitely. The king was required to annul all grants, including of titles, that he had made during the Civil War, and all his publications against the declarations and actions of Parliament, effectively forcing him to admit that his cause in the war had been wrong. The royal veto over laws passed by both Houses would be abolished, and the armed forces were to be put in Parliament's hands for twenty years, not the ten requested by Charles and stipulated in the 'Heads of the Proposals', with no certainty of whether they would then revert to the king or his successor. The reform of the parliamentary system desired by the army would go ahead, but probably with general elections every three years and not two, and without a date yet set for the change. The list of things to be demanded of the hapless sovereign became less rather than more accommodating as the month went on. As before, the proposals were to be handed to him by commissioners, to be accepted or rejected without allowing him any freedom to bargain over them. According to Cromwell's major, Robert Huntington, Oliver confided at this time that the best interest of the kingdom was simply the interest of the 'honest men' in it (by which he meant those of his own persuasion), and that any tactics, including a purge of Parliament, and any forms of government, could be adopted to pursue it. As for political manoeuvres, he allegedly told Huntington that 'it is lawful to play the knave with a knave'.[129]

The harshness of the terms prepared for the king was taken by some observers as a sign that Cromwell and Ireton were losing influence in Parliament.[130] What would really destroy their power base, however, would be if the army turned against them, and developments in October pointed disturbingly towards such a possibility. Trouble began among the junior officers and ordinary troopers of the horse regiments, precisely the group which had been most aggressively insurrectionary in April. After Parliament had decided to offer revised terms to the king, and when the shortfall of pay was starting to bite hard on the army, five of these regiments – or some sections of them – appointed new agents to represent them. As was to be noted ironically by observers, the units concerned were Cromwell's own and those of his closest supporters in his efforts to achieve a settlement with the king, including Ireton, Whalley and Fleetwood.[131] In the first half of October, six more regiments did the same, two of them infantry. On the 18th these new agents handed Fairfax a manifesto entitled *The Case of the*

Armie Truly Stated, which they claimed to have been inspired by God, and which they had already published. It complained of the generous treatment given to the king and to Parliament, and asked that the latter be purged immediately of all members who had sat in it from 30 July and the rest be forced to dissolve themselves within a year. They were to be replaced by biennial Parliaments, in which supreme power lay with Houses of Commons elected on a much broader franchise (though one which excluded royalists). The declaration taxed the army leadership with how little had been done since June to secure the people's liberties.[132]

Fairfax always kept scrupulously clear of politics as far as he was able, leaving such affairs to Cromwell, Ireton and the other generals who sat in Parliament, and concentrating on the material and military needs of his army. True to form, on this occasion he said that he had to refer the inflammatory document to the General Council; but he did make plain his dislike of it, and when the council discussed it on the 21st there was uproar. A committee was appointed to find the authors. With Cromwell away in Parliament, this was headed by Ireton.[133] In Parliament, Oliver reassured the Commons that the senior officers disowned the tract.[134] He was, however, back at Putney church to chair a discussion of the results in a meeting of the General Council a week later, which was attended not just by a few of the new agents but by some of the most prominent and active of the London radicals. By then it seemed as if the trouble in the army might be more serious than supposed, because news was arriving that an infantry regiment, commanded by John Lilburne's brother Robert, had mutinied on its march to garrison duty in the north. On having *The Case of the Armie Truly Stated* read to them, the soldiers had decided to go no further, and disowned their officers. A letter by a now unknown hand reached them, informing them that Fairfax and Cromwell would not oppose them if they made a stand for English liberties and soldiers' rights, and this strengthened their resolution to do so.[135] As a result, the meeting in the church on 28 October became an occasion not to punish the composers of the declaration, but to discuss it with its supporters and to try to reach an understanding. The result was the opening of the now famous Putney Debates, a week of discussions within the General Council, of which the first three days were meticulously recorded, and which were to become regarded in the twentieth century as one of the seminal occasions in the development of British democracy. Cromwell's is one of the voices eloquently represented in the minutes.

He found himself facing a formidable radical challenge from existing agitators as well as from a few of the new agents and from civilian allies of both. He and Ireton were immediately accused, by an established trooper-agitator called Edward Sexby, of having lost reputation with the soldiery because of their support for a worthless king and corrupt Parliament. Both denied that they had betrayed the army's interests, and Cromwell claimed that he had only acted as the General Council had wished. They were then wrong-footed again because, instead of letting them discuss *The Case of the Armie Truly Stated*, the radicals presented them with a completely new document, a draft plan for a new constitution entitled *The Agreement of the People*. It was founded on the radical conviction that all political power should derive ultimately from the English people in general, embodied in the House of Commons, which should control all the functions of the state. It also, however, recognized certain fundamental rights which not even the Commons could remove: liberty of religious conscience, freedom from military conscription, and equality before the law. Parliament was to be based on new constituencies formed according to the number of their inhabitants. There was no mention of the king and the Lords, or of how government would operate between Parliaments. The provisions of the document looked forward to the modern democratic revolutions, including the French and American, but in 1647 there was no apparent chance that it would be acceptable to the great majority of the English and Welsh, of all social ranks, let alone the political nation embodied in the current Parliament.[136]

Cromwell immediately saw the enormity of what was being proposed, calling it potentially the biggest change in English constitutional history. He stated that it was, in theory, entirely viable, but questioned how the

English people could be brought to go along with it, and what was to stop others among them proposing their own alternative constitutions ad infinitum. He suggested that all there wait for God to show a way forward and that in the meantime they unite in a review of the existing engagements and declarations of the army, which he held up as solemnly binding in divine eyes, to see how far the new constitution was compatible with those. This was the man at his political best: he had not opposed or disparaged a single clause of the document as a matter of principle, but instead cast doubts on its practical viability, and also raised an issue of conscience which was likely to force its amendment or abandonment. Immediately he found himself facing Rainsborough, who declared that any previous engagements could be voided if duty compelled, and that all English laws had once been new and so could be replaced.

Cromwell kept calm, and played on his theme of unity by declaring that all there were people of integrity, and that most (including the fiery colonel) were soldiers who did God's work. He agreed that unrighteous engagements should be abandoned, and the *Agreement of the People* should be considered, and he proposed that a committee do the work. He announced dramatically that he would rather resign from the army than be a hindrance to it in the work of settlement. Another of the senior officers present, Lieutenant-Colonel Goffe, proposed that the next day be spent in prayer for divine guidance, and both Cromwell and Ireton supported this, so that it was agreed that those who wished to do so collectively should meet in the spacious lodgings of the army's quartermaster-general, and go on to further business if desired. A fresh wrangle broke out over the issue of existing engagements, with Cromwell urging that a willingness to compromise was essential. He also denied that people like him were 'wedded and glued to forms of government', indicating that the whole constitution was up for debate. He welcomed the radicals' civilian allies to attend on the morrow, if they wished, and a committee of eighteen was set up as Oliver had advised, headed by himself and Ireton, and mixing senior and junior ranks of the army, and allies of Cromwell with radicals like Rainsborough and Sexby.[137]

On that same day, 28 October, the pressure on the senior officers was racked up by a preacher who had been greatly favoured in the New Model Army, the religious independent John Saltmarsh. He wrote to the Council of War, siding with the army radicals and accusing its members of having failed both God and the people. He added an admonition not to esteem 'the kisses of an enemy', by which he fairly clearly meant the king.[138] The following morning the prayer meeting occurred, and when Cromwell tried to postpone any further discussion of the *Agreement* until after the committee reported, Rainsborough urged an immediate resumption of it. He was supported by other soldiers of different ranks, and got his way. Moreover, Goffe, the senior officer who had suggested the meeting, had declared that he now interpreted the Biblical Book of Revelation as a warning that the king had become the representative of Antichrist, and that dealings with him therefore represented compliance with the enemies of God, and a forsaking of some of the saints (meaning religious radicals) with whom the soldiers had formerly joined to oppose those enemies. This probably shook Cromwell badly, as it showed that feeling against Charles was penetrating further through the higher ranks of the army.[139]

The debate over the *Agreement* that Oliver had tried to avoid opened with a discussion of the franchise that became one of the great political exchanges of seventeenth-century history. In it, Ireton, calling for the right to vote in parliamentary elections to be restricted to people with property, was opposed by a range of proponents of a wider electorate, both soldiers and civilians. One of the soldiers was Rainsborough, whose declarations in favour of true democracy, such as 'I do think that the poorest man in England is not at all bound in a strict sense to that government that he hath not had a voice to put himself under', have echoed down the centuries. Cromwell mostly stayed out of the discussions, but did intervene to support Ireton in arguing that universal manhood suffrage was not just. His main argument was, however, still one for unity: that all were agreed on extending the franchise, and that he would probably be persuaded to a wide extension. He called for another committee to be set up, to agree proposals. After further disputation he admitted that he was out of ideas, and that there would probably never be agreement over whether the proposed new constitution was superior to the old one. Ireton then found himself up against a young civilian Londoner called John Wildman, who accused him of confirming the vetoes of both the king and the Lords over the will of the people in the 'Heads of the Proposals'. Ireton gave ground, claiming that the matter of the royal veto was still open and that the king would only be restored to power if he agreed to the package of limitations on his power to be offered by Parliament.[140]

Once more, as the day's debates unfolded, the radical cause was being promoted by another publication, this time a pamphlet directed at members of the army which warned it against the crafty speeches of politicians in the General Council. By this it clearly meant Cromwell and Ireton, whom it accused of misleading the soldiers about the merits of *The Case of the Armie Truly Stated*, and of betraying the cause of liberty by embracing the king's. It actually labelled them 'venomous serpents', though it held out hope that Cromwell might return to greatness if Ireton were removed. It called for a purge of both Parliament and the chief army officers.[141]

On the following day, the 30th, the committee set up to consider the *Agreement* agreed upon its proposals. Parliament was to be dissolved by 1 September the following year, and succeeded by Parliaments elected every two years, which would appoint an executive Council of State. The constituencies would be redrawn to reflect population. Before dissolving, the current Parliament was to agree on the bounds of religious toleration and on a broader franchise which would include all the army's soldiers, a request that had first been raised by Sexby on the previous day. Royalists were to be excluded from voting.[142] This was indeed a compromise between the 'Heads of the Proposals' and the *Agreement*. Nothing was said of vetoes. Two days later, on 1 November, the General Council reconvened in the old grey church. It was its first meeting since it had agreed that all should pray for divine counsel, and Cromwell began by asking those who had done so individually to feed back what they had felt God had said to them.

One captain immediately replied that the vetoes of king and Lords should go; another said that he could not pray for the king; Goffe, supported by Sexby and another captain, spoke again against dealing with him. Oliver made a last attempt to defend doing so, saying that, though the king was at fault, he was part of contractual government, and that the authority of Parliament had to be maintained if military discipline was to be. He also, however, acknowledged that *The Case of the Armie Truly Stated* had much good in it, that Parliament had to be required to reform the kingdom and that the royal veto might be abolished. He repeated that forms of government were of little account, as God's ancient people, the Israelites, had many, but he also now adopted the language of the radicals, that the English government should depend on the will of the people. Again he faced objections from Goffe that dealing with the king was sinful, and from another senior officer that Charles needed to be declared guilty of the Civil War. He countered by saying that clearer evidence had to be demonstrated of the divine will before any such decisions were taken. He now shifted his ground again to agree that God probably wanted to destroy both the king and the Lords, but insisted that this needed to be made more apparent. A committee was set up to consider the question of the vetoes.[143] A royalist writing rumours on that date about the debates at Putney used a new and abusive term for the supporters of the *Agreement*, which was to become current for the radicals both in London and in the army: Levellers.[144]

The following day, 2 November, more of the *Agreement* was adopted, as it was agreed that the judiciary and ministers of state should account to the House of Commons rather than the king and the Lords; that the House would have power over all matters that affected commoners; and that the concept of fundamental liberties, reserved from legislative change, be accepted.[145] Two days later the General Council agreed that the Commons alone should control the armed forces for twenty years, and that all adult English males except servants and beggars should be able to vote in parliamentary elections.[146] On the 5th it sent a letter to Parliament stating that it did not support any offer of terms to the king at this time, and the radicals won another considerable victory by obtaining an agreement that the army would be called to a general rendezvous to decide what sort of national settlement it preferred.[147]

That, however, was the high point of radical success in the council. In the following days, Cromwell and Ireton somehow rallied their supporters to push back against it. The detailed record of debates stops on the 1st, and so the manner in which they managed this cannot be reconstructed; but its consequences were plain. On 8 November Cromwell reproached the radicals for their conduct as being divisive, and condemned the *Agreement of the People* as tending to anarchy. The prospective parliamentary franchise was restricted to the traditional one for county elections, of freehold owners of land, and the letter to Parliament was recalled. The generals refused any further discussion of the king's powers, and dissolved the Council until after the general rendezvous, ordering its members to their regiments. To put the army in the best possible humour, Parliament was to be asked for six weeks' pay immediately, and to raise the property tax which supported the army by 40 per cent to keep payments regular thereafter.[148]

Following Cromwell's denunciation of the *Agreement* in the council, on the following day, the 9th, the House of Commons condemned the whole document as destructive to fundamental government and asked Fairfax to seek out its authors.[149] The general was present that day at Putney in a select body instructed by the General Council to conclude its business. A final gesture of possible compromise was held out to the radicals, as the committee that Cromwell had previously suggested was set up to see if any of the army's existing declarations could be found to be compatible with either *The Case of the Armie Truly Stated* or the *Agreement*. The list of members was headed by Oliver and Ireton, and it was large, eventually numbering thirty-one. There were radical spokesmen like Wildman and Rainsborough on it, but it was not to meet until after the army had gathered and made its views clear. At the same time, Parliament was explicitly declared to be free to act as it wished in sending terms to the king, and it was decided that the army would muster not as a single body but at three different places, ostensibly to make the concentration of soldiers simpler but patently to make containment of discontent easier.[150]

The army radicals were naturally infuriated by all this, and published a letter to their comrades urging them to resist both the senior officers and Parliament.[151] At the same time, those senior officers themselves remained divided over how to deal with the king. On 11 November they met in Fairfax's Council of War, and Thomas Harrison, the godly young colonel who had been given command of a horse regiment in June, called Charles a 'man of blood', a phrase echoing a text in the Biblical Book of Numbers, and demanded he be prosecuted. Still Cromwell and Ireton urged moderation, pointing out that there were cases in the Bible of blood guilt being pardoned, and that it might be sinful to proceed against their monarch. Cromwell was, however, no longer advocating negotiations with Charles, and he now conceded that it might be necessary to act against the king: his counter-argument was to suggest that the army should wait until it became absolutely clear that it was necessary to do so.[152]

This was quite a considerable shift of ground, which seems to have occurred in the course of the Putney Debates. As ever, we cannot see inside Cromwell's head, and so cannot tell what it was that brought this change about. It is possible that his eyes had been genuinely opened to the extent of Charles's unworthiness by the speeches of comrades such as Goffe and Harrison, and that he had undergone a profound personal conversion experience during the discussions in the church. It is also possible, however, that the political realist in him had realized that a deal with the king was no longer a practical option. In the course of October, Parliament had put together terms for a deal which Oliver must have known would be unacceptable to Charles. The only chance of having those terms moderated in such a way as to attract the royal consent would be if the army put pressure on Parliament to do so. By the time that the officers dispersed from Putney to their regiments, it must have been plain to Cromwell that this was not going to happen. Too many of them still regarded the sovereign as an enemy, whose followers had tried to defeat and kill them only a year or two before, and who had not accepted the terms they had offered him, with important concessions, during the summer. Feeling against Charles was hardening at every level of the army, and this doomed the whole negotiation that had commenced in July. From this moment, Cromwell showed no more interest in renewing it. It is clear that he had realized, with whatever degree of reluctance or sorrow, that the captive monarch had become inconvenient, and so dispensable.

CARISBROOKE AND CORKBUSH

All this time the king himself had remained at Hampton Court, keeping the same state as before and holding to the agreement he thought he had reached with the army leadership: that it would get Parliament to offer him terms based on the 'Heads of the Proposals' (with the hope that these would be still more favourable to him). When the five newly commissioned representatives of the Scottish government presented themselves to him on 22 October, offering to assist his speedy restoration to power, he informed them that he was in the hands of the army, which had treated him much better than the Scots had done, and would only deal with it and Parliament.[153] In the last week of October, he warmly received at his court the wives of Cromwell, Ireton and Whalley (the colonel being still in command of his guards).[154] By this time, however, his prospects were darkening. It was becoming ever more clear that the terms Parliament would offer him were not such as he could accept, and the Putney Debates were a huge additional shock. The hostile expressions used against him by many of the participants leaked out widely, and with them the manner in which the speakers escaped serious reproof, which destroyed the prospect that the army's leaders could be counted upon to support Charles in gaining a better deal. Instead, it now seemed that some of the army might be an actual danger to the monarch; by the opening of November, observers sympathetic to him generally believed his position to have become desperate.[155]

Charles himself had come to share that view. After the first two days of the debates, the king's negotiating agent, John Ashburnham, visited Cromwell and Ireton for reassurance that they were still well disposed towards the king, and found that they now refused to see him: as the king had entertained their wives only the week before, this must have been a shock. At Hampton Court, Whalley allegedly admitted that he might not be able to protect Charles against hostile elements in the army, and the king decided to consider the option of escaping from the palace. At Newmarket in June, he had formally given his parole to the army that he would not attempt to leave its custody, and he now formally and honourably sent word to the generals through Ashburnham that he could no longer guarantee that. Their reaction was immediate and dramatic: on 1 November all his royalist companions and agents, including Ashburnham and Berkeley, were banned from Hampton Court, and the following day the king was confined to it without visitors and with doubled guards. He found the new soldiers rude and intrusive.[156] Over the next few days, tension rose still higher. Since their rebuff, the Scots had continued to lobby Charles to deal with them instead, and on the 5th they asked Parliament to remove him from the army's control and agree joint terms with them again.[157] At the same time, some of the army radicals published a tract for their fellow soldiers, ahead of the approaching musters, that accused Charles of being a cruel tyrant and the chief officers of aiming to restore his ability to crush English freedoms.[158] Cromwell wrote to Whalley instructing him to post a strong guard against a possible attempt to murder or kidnap the king. The colonel showed this letter to the unhappy sovereign, who also received an anonymous note warning that he was in danger of assassination by radical soldiers.[159]

At this point, Charles's nerve broke, and he told Ashburnham to prepare an escape route. This was duly done, with Berkeley brought into the plan. On the night of 11 November, the king slipped out of Hampton Court, leaving a letter to Parliament that he was propelled into his action by the growing hostility of the army and fears for his own safety. He said that he was seeking a more secure and secluded place from which to continue negotiating a peace which would content all parties and (especially) ensure the liberty of conscience that the army required. This was sincere as, when their monarch arrived at the rendezvous point, Ashburnham and Berkeley found that he refused to adopt the one course that would win him real safety and freedom, which was to leave the kingdom. Instead, he wanted to carry on negotiating a settlement from a safer place, preferably with the army but, if that would no longer talk to him, with the Scots. The trouble was that he had no idea where that might be. As previously in moments of political crisis, Charles had bolted from a situation with a very clear sense of what he was fleeing, but no firmly settled plan as to where he was going. After much argument, they all agreed on what seemed to be the least impractical suggestion, from Ashburnham, which was to head for the Isle of Wight. The island had a new governor, a former New Model Army colonel related to Cromwell, called Robert Hammond, who had expressed sympathy for the king, and who was based in the medieval castle of Carisbrooke in the centre of the island. The king and his companions arrived on the south coast a day later, and Hammond reluctantly gave them shelter. All promised him not to try to escape and were given the freedom of the isle, though under close watch and with other royalists banned from joining them.[160]

Almost immediately, a story appeared that Cromwell, with or without the collusion of Ireton and other senior officers, had cleverly frightened the king out of Hampton Court and into the Isle of Wight, where he could cause less trouble.[161] In subsequent years, this idea enjoyed wide circulation among both his admirers and his detractors, but it has justly failed to gain much credit among historians.[162] After all, when Charles fled the palace he had no idea where he was going, and the plan to reach the Isle of Wight was only chosen after other options had been discussed. It was entirely possible, as far as people like Cromwell knew, that the king would be talked into going abroad and out of the army's and Parliament's reach. The immediate results of the royal flight were potentially uncomfortable for Oliver himself. The king's keeper, Whalley, was his own cousin and protégé, and could be held guilty of negligence, while Cromwell's own warning letter to him might be blamed for scaring Charles into absconding. In the event, Parliament exonerated both, but only after a long debate by the Commons in which Rainsborough accused both Cromwell and Ireton of responsibility for the royal flight. The House's response to the event itself was savage, as it decreed by eleven votes that anybody found to have sheltered the fugitive monarch was to die a traitor's death, while all the ports were closed to stop Charles from getting overseas. On hearing that he was safely in Hammond's custody, the House ordered the arrest of Ashburnham and Berkeley, and was only persuaded to desist when the governor bravely protested that both of them, and Charles, had voluntarily put themselves into his hands. There the king was still held securely by the army, and in safer conditions.[163]

Once the initial fallout had been negotiated, it probably did suit Cromwell to have Charles out of the way while he concentrated on the approaching vital confrontation with his soldiers. Observers expected that this would be a crucial moment in his career, perhaps its ruin or salvation, and that it was likely that the regiments who appeared at the first rendezvous, on 15 November, would be deeply divided over the conduct of their generals and the best policy for settlement of the nation.[164] He and other senior officers therefore prepared carefully for it, when Fairfax's Council of War gathered on the 13th at the Hertfordshire market town of Ware, north of London, in the broad, fertile valley of the River Lea. On the following day, they agreed on a document to be read to the assembling regiments, designed to isolate and outflank the radicals. It assured the soldiers that the army's leaders and its General Council had remained steadfastly devoted to their welfare, according to the engagement of June, and condemned the new agents as slanderers and mutineers. It promised the final attainment of the objectives agreed in early June, plus a dissolution of the present Parliament, to be followed by successor Parliaments elected freely and equally according to more proportionate representation.[165]

The place chosen for the rendezvous was Corkbush Field, a large open space between Ware and Hertford. At each of the gathering points of the army since the opening of June, the soldiers present had proved to be even more radical than many commentators had expected, and it was a fair supposition that this would occur now. Once more the units tramped and trotted their way to a designated place, now an expanse of frost-bitten dead grasses, and bushes to which the last withering leaves were adhering, instead of the summery vistas of Kentford, Thriplow and Hounslow. The radicals had been busy with their own preparations: Rainsborough, Scot and some of the new agents were there at the start, handing out copies of the *Agreement of the People* and accompanying propaganda to the assembling men; John Lilburne was at hand in nearby Ware. The units invited to this first and pivotal rendezvous – for it would almost certainly influence the tone and outcome of the other two – had been carefully chosen to mix some which had chosen new agents, and so might be considered more critical of the leadership, and some which had not. However, the radicals had tried to tip the balance by inviting two regiments which seemed especially well disposed to their cause and which had not been summoned by the generals to any rendezvous: Harrison's horse and Robert Lilburne's mutinous foot soldiers.

The senior officers reacted to these challenges promptly and decisively. The document composed at Ware was read at the head of each regiment; Fairfax promised the men to stand by it and them, and he was cheered. All then consented to a declaration to submit to the general and his Council of War. That emboldened Fairfax and the other senior officers to arrest Scot and most of those who had been handing out tracts. Harrison's and Robert Lilburne's men then arrived on the field with some of those pamphlets in their hats, a gesture especially provocative because it mimicked the custom of putting tokens in hats before going into battle to distinguish comrades from the enemy. Again, the official response was fast and effective. Harrison's men were persuaded to remove and discard them; when Lilburne's proved more recalcitrant, senior officers rode into their ranks and tore them out, seizing the most obdurate men. Some accounts, though not by eye-witnesses, stated that Cromwell commanded the officers who carried out this action and engaged in it himself, charging through the foot soldiers on his horse with drawn sword. This is quite likely, given his character and the circumstances. When the regiment was subdued, a court martial was held on the field to try the ringleaders of the mutiny, sentencing three to death and executing one – chosen by lot – by firing squad immediately.[166]

Cromwell and the senior officers had not, after all, allowed the men to debate the respective merits of alternative national settlements, but had turned the occasion into a straightforward issue of obedience and discipline, confronting the radicals directly; and their policy had worked. After that, the other two musters, comprising most of the rest of the army, passed off without incident. The next was on Ruislip Heath on 17 November and the last at Kingston the following day. Among those present at the latter, and completely tractable, were the horse regiments of Cromwell, Ireton and Whalley. On the 19th, Cromwell triumphantly reported to the House of Commons that the army was now entirely obedient, and received its gratitude and an invitation to Fairfax to send addresses from the soldiers whenever they desired. Harmony between army and Parliament was thus confirmed, and Fairfax was subsequently thanked for the execution of the mutineer at Corkbush Field and encouraged to prosecute others. When more of the London radicals presented the *Agreement of the People* to the House again on the 23rd, they were arrested, so confirming their apparent defeat. Cromwell, in the House at the time, urged this action. He told the MPs that the radicals had been allowed to address the General Council of the army in the hope that 'their follies would vanish', but that now he thought it 'high time to suppress such attempts'. He added that he had allowed the Council to debate the franchise in order that they should see that the attempt to extend it was unreasonable, but that the proposed extension had reached the point where he had to oppose it. All this is compatible with the record of what happened at Putney. The military headquarters was now moved to Windsor for the winter.[167]

Meanwhile, the king was living in a fool's paradise on Wight. His decision to move there seemed to him and his companions to have been an inspired one. He had the run of one of Britain's largest and most beautiful offshore islands, with a courteous and sympathetic keeper in Hammond, the services of his royalist chaplains, and the company of his loyal followers and advisers who had accompanied him from the mainland. When news of what had happened at Corkbush Field arrived, it appeared that the crushing of the radicals opened the way for the army leaders to resume their collaboration with him to make a mutually acceptable settlement. He accordingly framed a new approach to Parliament, stating that he could never agree to the abolition of bishops, deans and cathedral chapters, or the sale of their lands, but that he was prepared to reduce the power of bishops considerably and allow the lands to be leased out on easy terms. He would accept a presbyterian Church for three years, as long as those who did not wish to submit to it, including himself, could have liberty of conscience. After that he still proposed that an assembly of clergy, to which he would name twenty, would devise a permanent settlement, and king and Parliament would decide upon it, but with continued freedom given to all who could not accept it, save Catholics. He offered Parliament control of the armed forces and of government appointments for the rest of his reign, as long as his heir could regain that control. He promised to do his utmost to pay the army's arrears from a range of different sources of revenue, and to use Church land as security for loans to do so. A comprehensive act of indemnity was promised to the soldiers for all actions during the war. He offered to annul all oaths and declarations he had prescribed or issued in the course of it, and to discuss the titles he had granted in it case by case. Finally, he agreed to full consideration of the electoral reforms that the army had requested.[168]

This was a package which genuinely seemed to give the king, Parliament and the army the most important outcomes which each desired, and it was delivered to the Houses on 17 November. It took no account, however, of two of the realities of the situation. One was that the financial measures proposed to guarantee payment of the soldiers' arrears were simply not robust enough, especially compared with the sale of Church and royal lands which the army was requesting and with which Parliament was agreeing. The second was the smouldering resentment and distrust which many in the army felt towards Charles, as their adversary in the war and (to them) the cause of it, which was now hardening into a sense that he should be called to account for it. At Putney, and in the radicals' publications, it had been asserted that any act of indemnity granted by him to the soldiers for their actions was worthless as he could always have it repealed. The contemporary sense of a need to identify and punish scapegoats was now starting to fasten on the king, as the greatest malefactor of all, responsible both for the war and for the failure to reach a settlement after it.

Near the end of the month, perturbed by the lack of response to his offer to Parliament, Charles sent Berkeley to the generals at Windsor, to ask for their support for it. Hammond added a letter from himself to Cromwell and Ireton urging them to comply. Sir John hastened north through the Hampshire forests, now shedding the last of their yellow leaves, and nearing Windsor ran into George Joyce, the junior officer who had abducted the king from Holdenby. Joyce told him that he now agreed with many other soldiers that Charles should be tried for causing the war. That was unsettling, and worse came when Berkeley delivered the royal letter to Fairfax and received the reply that the army was now leaving all such matters to Parliament. Cromwell and Ireton treated Sir John coldly and disdained Hammond's letter. Another (unnamed) general who had also previously been friendly met Berkeley in a park at midnight and said that Cromwell and Ireton had turned against the king because of the growing feeling against him in the army and the unrest it was causing. They had jettisoned co-operation with him to reunite the soldiers, lest the divisions among the latter ruin their own careers. That very day, the general said, Ireton had proposed in council that Berkeley be arrested and the king put on trial. He added that Cromwell's volte-face was succeeding in winning back the disaffected officers to him, and that Oliver had compounded this success with a request to the 'saints' in the army to pray to God for forgiveness for his mistake in dealing with Charles, and a promise that those still under arrest from Corkbush Field would be pardoned. Berkeley made an attempt to see Cromwell in private, but received the reply that Oliver dared not comply and that giving any further help to the king would be his own ruin.[169] All this is entirely in accord with the other evidence from the time and the preceding month.

Publicly, of course, the generals presented an entirely different justification for their volte-face, which was to blame it on Charles. Ireton informed Hammond that they did not believe that the king had intended to remain in the hands of the army, or to go to Wight, when he left Hampton Court. He offered no evidence for this, but went on to suggest that Charles's royalist companions and chaplains be expelled from the island and more soldiers sent there from the army to guard the king closely.[170] He was correct, of course, that Charles had not formed any settled plan when he began his flight, but the royal fugitive had nevertheless been determined to carry on negotiating – as he had done – and had decided voluntarily to trust Hammond. In the following decades, a feeling persisted among some writers that Cromwell and Ireton must have had some better reason for turning against Charles than was provided at the time. Rumours circulated that the two men had uncovered solid evidence of the king's insincerity in negotiating and his determination to destroy them.[171] It was never, however, produced. Had it ever existed then, the army and Parliament would surely have made it public in order to justify their subsequent treatment of him. When they had captured his private correspondence near the end of the war, the portions of it which seemed to convict him of plans to bring in foreign armies, and of a disinclination to make peace, were immediately printed to harden opinion against him.[172]

By late November, Charles had become aware that his initiative in offering fresh terms and concessions had been a disaster. Not only had the army abandoned him, but the Scots wrote to tell him that what he had conceded, especially with regard to liberty of conscience (which they took as a permanent toleration of heresy and schism), meant that they could no longer offer him any service.[173] When his offer reached Parliament, it made a great initial impression there on moderates, but they soon turned out to be outnumbered by the hard-liners, once again.[174] After considerable discussion, on 27 November the Commons agreed by nine votes to accept a suggestion by the Lords, that the king be allowed to come to Westminster to negotiate a treaty providing that he accepted four measures beforehand, which would immediately pass into law.[175] He was asked to give control of the armed forces to the Lords and Commons for twenty years, no matter who was reigning, after which they would decide whether they wanted to keep it. This was a tougher requirement than even the Newcastle Propositions had made, and opened up the prospects both of removing one of the fundamental powers of the English Crown and of keeping Fairfax's army in existence indefinitely. The second demand was for the king to justify all acts by Parliament during the late war and declare all his own void. He had consistently offered to do the former but refused the latter, which might expose his old supporters to prosecution for their actions. The third demand was that all titles granted by Charles during the war were to be annulled and Parliament was to consent to any he awarded in future, so removing another of the traditional prerogatives of the Crown and forcing the king to betray his former followers again. Finally, the Houses were to be given the power to adjourn themselves to any place that they chose, instead of only meeting at Westminster. This could be taken to mean that they would meet where the army decided that they should, but it also implied a fear of their unpopularity with Londoners, given the policies they were now pursuing.

These requirements could not be discussed by the king, or bargained over, and he was given the option only of acceptance or rejection. To accept them would require his abandonment of the whole position of principle to which he had adhered since the end of the war. They trailed behind them terms which were up for discussion if the king accepted the four non-negotiable demands. He was asked to consent to the abolition of bishops, deans and chapters and to the sale of their lands; to the annulment of his truce with the Irish rebels; to the right of Parliament to choose ministers of state (without a time limit); to the establishment of a presbyterian Church with some liberty of conscience outside it; and to the punishment of royalists in three tiers of severity, with seven sentenced to execution and loss of lands.[176] Overall, and with the four immediate demands, this was a harsher package even than the one that Parliament had prepared for the king in October, though still more favourable to the army. The French ambassador, who was sympathetic to Charles, was appalled by this treatment of him, as were some Presbyterian MPs and also the Scottish commissioners, who sent a protest to Parliament.[177] Many in both Houses, however, seem genuinely to have expected that he would cave in and accept the initial four requirements.

At this period, Cromwell seems to have spent more time in the Commons than at army headquarters, partly because the latter were now much further away, at Windsor.[178] He did, however, have some opportunity to attend the Council of War and General Council, and to share in its discussions and resolutions, which, now that the soldiers had withdrawn from national politics, were devoted mainly to two different causes. One was a continued attempt to secure regular pay for the men, in the face of persisting resistance by the general population, especially in London, to pay the tax on which the army depended. Through Fairfax, the officers bombarded both Parliament and the City corporation with a succession of remonstrances and menaces, including a renewed threat to send in soldiers to collect the money directly, and demands to increase the tax level still further and make its national collection more efficient. They were successful in obtaining measures to improve the gathering of the money, to disband the extra forces raised since summer to reduce the cost of the army, and to secure payment of arrears.[179]

The other main activity of the officers and agitators, in their meetings in Windsor town hall and in the great hall of the royal castle sprawling across the hill above, was to reintegrate the radicals who had been defeated at Putney and on Corkbush Field, and so complete the reunification of the army. Cromwell was certainly involved in this at times. The most high-ranking of the defeated faction was Rainsborough, who made a complete submission and apology, whereupon the officers agreed to request Parliament, through Fairfax, to forgive him and appoint him to command its fleet as had been agreed previously.[180] The Council of War sentenced a corporal from Robert Lilburne's regiment to death, but reprieved him, and then discussed whether to release those arrested on Corkbush Field.[181] On 6 December, the former army chaplain who had criticized the army leadership in October, John Saltmarsh, appeared at the castle on the edge of death, just as the General Council was about to meet there. Like an Old Testament prophet, he informed several officers that God had forsaken them because they had forsaken God. He met Fairfax and Cromwell in the great hall, refused to remove his hat to them and told them that the army would be divided and ruined if they did not release the 'saints' whom they had imprisoned at the muster. He repeated the message to Cromwell on the next morning, and thought that Oliver seemed responsive, so that the ailing minister remarked that 'there is some tenderness of heart in you'. Saltmarsh then returned to his home, where he died.[182] This visit may have helped to inspire a fast held by the soldiers at Windsor in mid-December, at which Cromwell and Ireton both delivered public prayers for unity.[183]

In the last week of the month, two deputations arrived in the Isle of Wight to see the king: that from Parliament, bearing the Four Bills for his consent; and the Scottish commissioners who had just denounced them. The presence of the latter may have reinforced Charles's decision to reject the proffered measures, but it is practically certain that he could not have accepted them in any case. The realization that England had passed into the power of people who were now determined on a political and religious settlement which was anathema to the Scots pushed those commissioners into a pivotal decision: to make significant concessions to the king as the English Parliament had consistently failed to do, and as the army had failed to do sufficiently. They accepted the religious settlement he had offered Parliament in May, and on 26 December signed a secret agreement with him which became known as the Engagement. It provided for the establishment of a presbyterian Church in England on the Scottish model (without liberty to worship outside it) for three years, after which an assembly of divines would review it, with twenty of that assembly's members added by the king. The new Directory of Worship would remain imposed on the nation during that time, but the king could use the old Prayer Book. If the English Parliament failed to allow him to negotiate after his rejection of the Four Bills, Scotland would send an army into England to restore him immediately to his control of the armed forces, and the granting of honours, government offices and the veto over legislation, and to dissolve the Parliament.[184]

Charles had at last found a party among his former enemies which was prepared to accept a genuine compromise settlement with him, but even he must have realized that in agreeing to it he was taking a very long shot. There was no guarantee that the Scottish government would accept the deal, or that if it did it would be able to raise an army capable of defeating Fairfax's. If the Scots in power at home did recognize the treaty and act on it, the disclosure of its existence would seriously provoke the very people in whose hands the king was gripped, leaving him utterly vulnerable to whatever they chose to mete out to him. All that Charles was doing, as before, was acting according to his principles and hoping that God would somehow reward him for doing the right thing. Those who value consistency in a ruler may well wonder how this one could offer liberty of conscience in England in November and agree to crush it a month later. The king had, however, a different kind of consistency. Unlike the Scots and many of his English subjects, he seems to have had no instinctual horror at the prospect of some of his subjects being allowed to worship outside the national Church: after all, he was married to a Roman Catholic. Instead, he regarded liberty of conscience as something which he was prepared either to concede or to discard in order to rescue the traditional ecclesiastical structure.

It is correct that the 'Heads of the Proposals' offered at the end of July were the most generous terms presented to the king by any English group after the end of the war. To fault him for declining them, however, is to miss two important points. One is that Charles's objective was not to accept the best deal that he could get, but to refuse any which seemed to remove permanently the traditional powers of the English Crown over Church and state, which he believed that he had undertaken to protect at his coronation. The 'Heads' did not quite go far enough to pass this test. The other point is that they were not the work of a settled government but of an army which appeared at that moment to be locked in a struggle with forces apparently more favourable to Charles, which might prevail. Once he realized that the army had taken control, he expressed a consistent willingness to negotiate on the basis of the 'Heads', only to find that they proved to be unacceptable both to Parliament and to a significant party within the army. His behaviour during 1647 does not suggest somebody trying to play off different groups against each other. Instead he first offered a compromise settlement to Parliament, and then, finding himself captured by the army, slowly came to work with that body towards a peace deal, only to find himself betrayed and abandoned by it. It was only at that point, in desperation, that he signed terms with the Scots, because they became the first people who, becoming desperate themselves, offered him something that he could accept. We cannot say how far he would have adhered to any settlement had he made one with Parliament or the army, let alone whether his ultimate aim was to regain all the power that he had lost in the previous seven years. Both are matters for endless speculation, and all that can be said is that his care to refuse concessions which he felt would compromise the basis of the monarchy proves that he was not prepared to agree to things in the expectation that he would be able to renege on them later. In the last analysis, he was flawed not just by a lack of political aptitude and insight but by an innate optimism: a faith that, if he just stayed put and kept trying to do the right thing, then his God would not let him down in the end. He was prepared to be punished himself for his political misjudgements, but not to let those permanently alter the monarchy.

For the time being, he was about to face still crueller disillusion than that which had beset him in October and November. Two days after he had secretly agreed with the Scottish commissioners, he refused the Four Bills, on the grounds that one gave the Lords and Commons an indefinite power over the armed forces and that the whole package would alienate the Scots. He asked for a personal negotiation of terms instead. His reply reached the Commons on 31 December, together with news of an inept and easily crushed attempt by royalists in Wight to rescue the king from Hammond's custody. Their response was savage: to order that he be made a close prisoner in Carisbrooke Castle henceforth. His royalist attendants, including Berkeley and Ashburnham, and his chaplains, were expelled from the island. The Lords confirmed the Commons' decision the next day.[185]

On 3 January the Commons debated whether to proceed with any further negotiation with the king. The leading Independent Sir Arthur Hesilrige opened by proposing that Parliament should receive no more messages from its sovereign, and that anybody who ventured to open talks with him should be guilty of treason. A member called Sir Thomas Wroth proposed that Charles be prosecuted for his crimes and the nation settled without him. Ireton then said that, as the king had denied security to his subjects, they owed him no further loyalty. A discussion followed that lasted ten hours, candles being brought in as the winter daylight faded beyond the lancet windows. The Independent leaders lined up against Charles. Cromwell himself sat silent for most of the time, but rose furiously near the end and declared that the nation needed to be taught to expect nothing more from 'an obstinate man whose heart God had hardened'. He quoted the Biblical text (from the Book of Job) that 'thou shalt not suffer a hypocrite to reign'. He added that monarchy itself should continue but then said that there might come a time when necessity forced its abolition. He continued that Parliament needed its army to defend it, and that to deal further with the king would make the soldiers feel betrayed and drive them to dangerous courses. As a hint of what these might be, he laid his hand on his sword. His words, and his clear threat, allegedly had a powerful influence on the House, and Hesilrige's motion passed by a comfortable fifty votes. The Lords initially divided equally over whether to agree, whereupon the army officers issued a declaration in support of the Commons – so fully supporting Cromwell's declaration that the soldiers insisted on the measure – and the peers gave in.[186]

Looking back on the year 1647, Oliver must have felt some satisfaction. He had spent the first third of it fearing the loss of his health, his place in public life and much of the cause for which he had fought in the Civil War. Events, which he would have seen as the work of his God, had restored all three. He had twice boldly seized the opportunity of acting as a mediator – first between army and Parliament, and then between army and king – and so of making himself pivotal to an ensuing settlement of the nation. In both cases his efforts had ended in complete failure, but he had nimbly extricated himself in time by assessing accurately the feeling of his soldiers and adjusting his politics to align with it. How much this process rested on expediency, and how much on a genuine conversion experience, we can never know. In both cases the process concerned appears to have been a rapid and sudden one: for example, he seems to have arrived at the Putney Debates still convinced of the need to make a deal with the king, but left them convinced that one was no longer practicable. In a sense, his relationship with Charles fell into a previous pattern, whereby he had co-operated with aristocratic generals to fight the war but, on realizing that they had become liabilities, turned savagely against them and worked for their ruin: John Hotham, Lord Willoughby and (above all) the earl of Manchester were examples of such individuals. It could be said that King Charles, the greatest aristocrat of all, was the last and most eminent in the sequence.

Now Cromwell had reaffirmed his position as second-in-command of the army that had seized control of the nation and dictated its politics, and also as the most important of its soldiers to sit in Parliament. He had survived an apparently serious challenge to his leadership in that army and, by changing his own political strategy, he had confirmed its loyalty. In the process he had earned an increased amount of hostility from royalists and Presbyterians, and had made new enemies among London radicals. All three groups had begun in the course of the autumn and winter to publish attacks on him as a hypocrite, traitor and dissembler, who only sought power for himself.[187] For the time being, however, his position in both army and Parliament was secure, as one of the dominant figures in each and the most important of those who linked the two. The problem for both bodies of men, which neither at this point seems to have seen coming, was that they had alienated not only most of the Scots and the Londoners, but also a very large number – almost certainly the majority – of the people of England in whose name they claimed to speak and to wield authority.

3

REBELLION

GATHERING STORM

In the first three months of 1648, the army and the Independent-dominated Parliament continued to pursue successfully and confidently in partnership the policies which they had adopted at the beginning of the year. In January Parliament established a new executive body, sitting like its predecessor at Derby House and termed the 'Committee of Both Houses'. It had a nominal thirty-nine members, mixing Presbyterians and Independents, with a majority of the latter, but the actual attendance was usually around six, with the same political weighting. Cromwell was one of the most dedicated of that handful of attendees, turning up to most meetings until mid-April.[1] As a further sign of military and political co-operation, and also as both a tacit admission of its own new unpopularity and a snub to the king, Parliament asked in January for 2,000 soldiers to be quartered in the deserted royal palace of Whitehall as a guard for it.[2] On 9 March the Commons agreed to require all MPs to concur with the engagement made by those members of both Houses who had fled to join the army in late July, to support the soldiers and link their fortunes to them. They did so by eleven votes, after a full day of argument and after many Presbyterians had left; once more, the Independent leaders warned those present not to provoke the army, and Cromwell spoke for the measure as promoting unity between the latter and

Parliament.[3] Unanimity between the current regime at Westminster and the new leadership of the City was signalled on 8 February, when Cromwell was among a large party of prominent army officers, MPs and lords entertained to dinner by the lord mayor. A huge serving of food and drink was consumed to the music of fifes, drums and trumpets.[4]

In this period, too, Parliament continued to harry those who had become a nuisance to it at both political extremes. This included the wretched king, in his new prison of Carisbrooke Castle, where in February, on Parliament's orders, he found his attendants both reduced in number and replaced by men chosen by Fairfax.[5] This was a security measure, but the removal of familiar servants made life still more unpleasant for him, and this was compounded in the same month, when Parliament issued a declaration to justify its Vote of No Addresses to him.[6] The declaration not only blamed the failure of negotiations entirely on him, alleging that he had consistently refused to co-operate, but dredged up a list of old partisan accusations against him. The most scandalous and wounding was an allegation, never before made officially, that he had covered up the possible murder of his father, King James I, by his own friend and favourite, the duke of Buckingham. This was originally asserted by embittered Roman Catholic enemies, to undermine Charles's new government when it had failed to do anything to make things easier for British Catholics. The allegation had been investigated by a parliamentary committee at the time, and a story now circulated that in the debate over the new declaration a distinguished lawyer who had sat on that committee, John Selden, had told the Commons that the charge had been found to be baseless. It was said that, accordingly, he had urged the House not to include it, only for Cromwell to move that Selden be expelled.[7] The story went that this caused another MP well versed in the case to complain about lack of freedom of speech. If the motion was made to expel Selden, it was not followed up, but the allegation was retained in the declaration, and Cromwell was noted as having spoken vehemently against Charles's rule as part of the general debate concerning the measure.[8]

Simultaneously Parliament acted against the London radicals. On 18 January a London minister denounced John Lilburne and John Wildman to both Houses for having spoken about forcing Parliament to adopt their reform programme at a meeting in the London riverside suburb of Wapping. The following day both men were summoned to Westminster to answer the charge, after which they were committed to prison to await trial.[9] One of the allegations was that Lilburne had told the meeting of a secret agreement between the king, Cromwell and Ireton, to restore the king to his full traditional powers, with Cromwell made earl of Essex and a knight of the Garter, and Ireton sent to rule Ireland. He had added that both men had changed sides in fear when they had discovered that some of the radicals were ready to murder Cromwell if he tried to put this plan into action. Wildman admitted that this (unconfirmed and implausible) story had been told at the meeting: it is a good example of the kind of rumours circulating about Oliver in such circles.[10] After this, it was said around London that, if Cromwell did not ruin Lilburne completely, then the latter would ruin him.[11]

A good insight into Cromwell's handling of the remaining radicals associated with the army, and into his mode of operation in general, is provided by his dealings with a troublesome character called William Thompson. Thompson had been thrown out of his regiment in the previous autumn, after a nasty tavern brawl, and had then hung around with the soldiers propagating the ideas associated with *The Case of the Armie Truly Stated* and the *Agreement of the People*. In the crackdown which followed Corkbush Field, he was court-martialled for these activities (once in a session at which Cromwell presided) and made the defence that, as he was no longer in the army, he could not be tried by a military court. He had a private meeting about the matter with Oliver, who told him that he had a case but that Cromwell himself could do nothing to help it. Nevertheless, he was allowed to go free, and he travelled to London, seeing Cromwell again privately at Derby House and being promised his arrears of pay and other help into civilian life. Clearly these assurances were contingent on his good behaviour but, instead of giving it, Thompson published an attack on the army's proceedings against him and tried to suborn the soldiers at Westminster. In February Cromwell recognized him there when coming out the House of Commons with Ireton, and ordered his arrest for sedition, calling him 'a bold impudent fellow'. Thompson was imprisoned in the new military headquarters of Whitehall; again he came in front of a court martial and again he refused to recognize its authority. This time Cromwell, who was present, called him 'a mutinous fellow' and ordered him to be put in chains. He was subsequently sentenced to death, but kept imprisoned at Whitehall instead.[12] The episode is an early example of an abiding pattern in Cromwell's treatment of radical critics: to try to win them over privately but, if they failed to respond, to have them proceeded against formally and severely.

In the same months, Parliament and the army collaborated closely and effectively in other respects. In early January Fairfax dispersed the concentration of regiments around London to wider quarters and dissolved the gathering of officers at Windsor, giving them a dinner in the castle before they left.[13] On the 17th he and his Council of War – among whom, of course, was Cromwell – formally reassured the House of Lords of their loyalty and support (including, implicitly, in the matter of its veto over legislation).[14] In February Fairfax appointed a committee of field officers, led by Cromwell and Ireton, to sit twice weekly at Whitehall to deal with all matters that concerned the soldiers.[15] Parliament and the generals also collaborated in the first four months of 1648 in a major initiative to reduce the size of the army, which resulted in it getting better paid. Twenty thousand soldiers were demobilized, representing almost half of the total in service at the end of the previous year. The units chosen for disbandment or reduction reflected a clear political programme, for they were overwhelmingly from provincial forces that might have represented a counterweight to Fairfax's main field army. They also tended to be regiments associated with the unrest in November.[16] The result was that the grip of the generals over the national military machine was tightened still further.

The overall size of the main field army nevertheless remained slightly larger than it had been a year before, and there was no reduction in the property tax levied on the nation to support it. Instead, that tax was increased by a third to provide resources for another attempt to reconquer Ireland from its Catholic rebels.[17]

Throughout these months, correspondents sympathetic to the king, including English royalists and Presbyterians, agents of his Scottish supporters, and foreign ambassadors, reported rumours of secret attempts by leaders of Parliament and the army to reopen negotiations with him. The same writers also recorded stories of an equally clandestine mission to the queen to persuade her to allow the prince of Wales to become ruler if his father abdicated, and of quarrels between leading Independent politicians and the army leaders. The element of wish-fulfilment in all these is obvious, and there is no supporting evidence for any of them, meaning that there is only a slight chance that any were true.[18] One piece of evidence used to substantiate some of the tales of covert approaches to the king was that Cromwell undoubtedly went to Hampshire in February and March, but the proven reason for this was to pursue a very different kind of negotiation: of a marriage for his eldest surviving son, Richard. The projected match was with the heiress of a gentleman in that county, which would bring Richard a manor house and Oliver a handsome endowment for his two youngest daughters.[19]

The exchanges involved putting a figure on Cromwell's income at this time, which was just under £3,000 per year, making him a wealthy man for the age. It could have been significantly larger, because on 9 March, as a sign of his high standing in the alliance between Parliament and army, the former granted him a large landed estate in Monmouthshire, Glamorgan, Gloucestershire and Hampshire, confiscated from a royalist nobleman. This comprised the residue of the reward promised to him near the end of the Civil War, and added £1,680 to his annual income. However, Oliver immediately donated £1,000 of that each year to the reconquest of Ireland, and in addition discharged all claims to the remaining arrears of pay due to him for his service in the Civil War.[20] This was both an ostentatious gesture of generosity and devotion to the public good, and simultaneously a reply to those who had accused him of being propelled by personal greed and ambition. It probably also derived from his own sense of duty and wish to avoid falling into sins of pride and avarice; as so often, actions that promised to please his supporters likewise provided a prospect of pleasing God. To get his son set up with an independent income and social position in Hampshire, a county in which Cromwell himself now held much land, was also prudent. If Oliver's position in power was ensured, then Richard would eventually inherit his estates there to add to his wife's dowry. If, however, Oliver fell from power and forfeited most of his income and his new landed endowment, then his son would have salvaged something from the wreckage. As yet, however, this plan was not to be, because the prospective father-in-law broke off the discussions.

This may have been because Cromwell's own prospects were suddenly in jeopardy, along with those of his political and military allies. The fundamental weakness in their position was their unpopularity, and their reliance upon the army's grip on the nation. The Presbyterians had secured the loyalty or co-operation of a large faction in Ireland and the dominant parties in Scotland and Wales, as well as of most of the English who had supported Parliament in the war. Their programme would probably have received the acquiescence of those who had remained uncommitted in that war and the submission of most royalists. The Independents, with their commitment to some form of liberty of religious conscience, and their now harsh treatment of the king, were pursuing a policy which lacked support from the majority even of the English, let alone the inhabitants of the other lands. Moreover, they had been put into power by an army which had seized control against the will of most of Parliament and which imposed a now seemingly indefinite severe tax burden on a nation that was entering into a third successive year of harvest failure.[21] As the campaigning season of that year drew on, a series of challenges began to be mounted to the regime.

The first to be fully registered was also the most easily crushed: a rising in London on 9 April which started when the lord mayor, who had so flamboyantly demonstrated his loyalty to the current national leadership, decided to enforce recent legislation for stricter observance of Sunday as a day dedicated to religion. He sent a party of militia to disperse youths playing sports in a traditional manner in fields to the north of the city; the militia got into an altercation with the young men, fired on them and killed one. This aroused onlookers to fury, in which they overpowered and disarmed the militiamen. Having thus gained their weapons and flag, the crowd decided to attack the hated regular soldiers quartered at Whitehall, and surged towards it, reinforced by many more citizens. On hearing that this was happening, Fairfax, Cromwell and Ireton ordered their men to form up and meet the attack. This they did, hitting the mob when it appeared with a cavalry charge led by Cromwell that drove the crowd back broken through the streets and along the muddy foreshore of the Thames. The fleeing Londoners retreated behind the medieval walls of their city, closed the gates and took over the whole area inside: the militia ignored the appeals of the mayor to resist them.

For a night the rebels were in control, but during that night Fairfax held a council of war and decided to take the city with the available regular troops. Those soldiers were let in at dawn, through a gate unlocked for them by sympathizers, and crushed the uprising, meting out more death and injury to any who resisted. By noon everything was over, but it had been a bad shock for the army and parliamentary leadership. It was probably symptomatic of their ongoing tense relationship with the capital that at some point since the autumn Cromwell had moved his family home again, from Drury Lane to King Street, Westminster, next to the palace (and garrison) of Whitehall. This was certainly more convenient for attendance at the Commons, Derby House and the army committee, but it also put a safer distance between him and the City. The move had been made by the time of the uprising, and proved its wisdom then.[22]

Much more menacing developments were occurring in Scotland, where a new Parliament had met in early March to discuss relations with England after the breakdown of co-operation with the Parliament there during the winter. Its leaders were furnished with the secret agreement that the king had made with their commissioners in December, and in the course of the next two months, the MPs gathered in Edinburgh swung towards support for him. By April it was clear that they had decided to intervene in England to reverse the political revolution that had resulted from the army's take-over of power there. On 26 March the Scottish Parliament sent its ultimatum to Westminster, accusing its English counterpart of ignoring Scottish wishes, tolerating religious separatists and threatening the monarchy. It therefore demanded that an intolerant presbyterianism be imposed on England, that Fairfax's and Cromwell's 'army of sectaries' be disbanded, and that the king be freed and brought to London to make a settlement which gave him his old rights. A week later the Edinburgh Parliament ordered the raising of over 30,000 men to provide an expeditionary force.[23]

It was, however, the Welsh who proved to be the most immediate and serious threat to Cromwell and his allies. During the Civil War, almost their whole nation had thrown its support behind the king, save for the heavily Anglicized enclave in the south-western corner, which formed a steadfast parliamentarian redoubt. At times this was reduced to the single town of Pembroke, governed by its mayor John Poyer, which became the base for a regional army led capably by another local man, Rowland Laugharne. Supplied from the sea by Parliament's navy, this army eventually succeeded in conquering most of South Wales, and subsequently continued to hold down the region. In March 1648, however, the seizure of the national military machine by Fairfax, Cromwell and their commanders led to a decision to disband Laugharne's army and replace Poyer in control of Pembroke with one of Fairfax's officers. The parliamentarians in Pembrokeshire were already badly worried by the Independent takeover in England, because they had allied with the Presbyterians while their local enemies (who ironically included former royalists) had accordingly associated with the Independents and the New Model.[24] The sudden destruction of their local position pushed Poyer, Laugharne and their faction over the edge. In March they refused to obey Fairfax's orders; when Parliament reinforced those, they rebelled against it. They and their army were then reinforced by large numbers of former royalists, and issued a joint declaration in favour of the king and the traditional Church that he supported. By mid-April the whole of Wales west of Cardiff and south of Aberystwyth had passed into their control.[25]

In the course of this spring, as threats to him, his army and its political allies steadily mounted, Cromwell worked hard to broaden support for their cause. First he tried the Presbyterians, giving dinner to their leaders in Westminster, together with leading Independents. This initiative failed to reach agreement over the form of the Church, so next he tried the radicals, holding meetings between them and prominent politicians and soldiers at his new King Street address. One of those invited, who was also an MP, was a young man with a broad, burly face, high-arched eyebrows and a sardonic set to his mouth, called Edmund Ludlow, who had supported the agitation for fundamental constitutional reform in the previous November. He and his friends were now frustrated by the refusal of Cromwell and his companions to commit themselves to a form of future government, and their insistence (which Cromwell had expressed at Putney) that God had not yet made his views clear. According to Ludlow's later account, his own group declared themselves firmly against monarchy, on the grounds that the king had forfeited all claim to obedience and needed to be called to account for his misdeeds. Cromwell professed himself to be still undecided on the matter, and ended the discussion with rough horseplay, by throwing a cushion at Ludlow's head and then running downstairs (the younger man overtook him and hit him with another).

The next day, Cromwell passed Ludlow in the Commons and told him that he thought his ideas desirable but not feasible; Ludlow suspected him of saying such things to try to keep the radicals friendly, while expressing himself differently to people of other opinions. These uneasy exchanges continued at times, Cromwell sometimes railing against the radicals for their pride and their overestimation of their own importance. Eventually, as the number of threats to Parliament and the army multiplied, he came across Ludlow in the yard in front of the palace of Westminster. According to Ludlow, Cromwell complained of having now seemingly turned most of the nation against him by supporting actions (by which he seemed to mean the army's mutiny against Parliament and the Vote of No Addresses) which had seemed to be just. He added that his own allies in those actions seemed suspicious of him, and so he appeared to have ended up with the worst of both worlds. Ludlow advised him henceforth to throw his lot in with the radicals, consistently, to regain their trust; and Cromwell seemed grateful. If the reported exchange is true, it provides a valuable insight into Oliver's feelings at this time.[26]

At any rate, by the end of April, decisive action was clearly needed. On the 28th the House of Commons scrambled to placate the Scottish Parliament and moderate opinion in the nation, resolving that government would continue to be by king, Lords and Commons, and that the Vote of No Addresses would be reviewed, with the option of renewing negotiations with the king on the basis of the terms presented to him at Hampton Court in September (which had the endorsement of the Scots). The Lords rapidly concurred. Parliament also agreed to return control of the Tower of London and the City militia to the corporation. On 2 May it rushed out an order for the punishment of radical religious opinions. This decreed not only death for denial of the existence of God, the divinity of Christ or the authority of the Bible, but also indefinite prison for those who asserted that all humans could get to heaven, that only adults should undergo baptism, that an established Church was unnecessary, or that Church and state had to be separated. This latter provision outlawed the sects for whom Cromwell and the army had sought liberty of conscience, thus representing a sudden dramatic rejection of that policy. Meanwhile, the military news got worse, as first Berwick and then Carlisle were taken by English royalists, giving the Scots easy entry to the north of England.[27]

The volte-face in Parliament was caused not merely by the majority of members switching their support back from Independents to Presbyterians, but by the support of some of the Independent leaders who were Cromwell's traditional allies. Cromwell was said to have been furious when he learned of it.[28] He himself was almost certainly not present in the Commons for any of these measures, probably being at Windsor Castle instead for a crisis meeting of the army leadership, which commenced on 27 April.[29] It continued for a week, and discussions, punctuated by prayer, centred on three issues. The first was to deal with renewed radical agitation among the soldiers, most obviously expressed by a meeting of representatives of one horse regiment at St Albans on the 25th to discuss a new petition to Parliament for a reformed parliamentary system, liberty of conscience, equality before the law and changes in land tenure. Those there were arrested by their officers and sent to Windsor, where it was decided to release most with an admonition to postpone such discussions until the various new threats to the army were defeated. The second issue consisted of a consideration of the causes of the sudden threats to the army's existence, which seemed to indicate a withdrawal of divine favour. Cromwell urged a concerted effort to discover them, and after two days they decided – according to a single account, published long after but seemingly reliable – to blame everything on King Charles, and call him to account if they won the coming war. This decision was not made public, but confirmed that army and Parliament were now set on radically opposed courses if the latter did not rescind the decisions that it was simultaneously taking to woo moderate opinion.

The third issue was, of course, the response to be made to the burgeoning military emergency. On May Day it was resolved to despatch Cromwell to Wales with a large force to crush the rebellion there, and to endorse the measures taken by Parliament to placate the Londoners, making easier the withdrawal of regiments from around the city. Three days later, it was decided that Fairfax would take most of the rest of the army north to regain Berwick and Carlisle and face the Scots if they invaded. Cromwell expected to be able to defeat the Welsh rebels very swiftly, and so to join Fairfax on his march before he made any contact with northern enemies. For the first time in almost two years, both men were setting out to war again.

MARCH INTO THE WEST

Fairfax lingered in the London area into mid-May, making careful preparations for his northern expedition, while Cromwell, true to his word, headed for Wales with all possible speed. He gathered a force immediately from the units near the city, initially finding some discontent among the soldiers over both the arrest of their fellows at St Albans and their unpopularity in the nation, but managing to allay it.[30] He led them across the Chilterns, and by the time that he reached Abingdon in the broad middle basin of the Thames, he had around 5,000 men, made up of 3 foot and 2 horse regiments. Parliament already had a few thousand field soldiers stationed near Cardiff under a capable leader called Thomas Horton; this, combined with Cromwell's force, promised an army easily capable of defeating the rebels.[31] Once more, as in the previous year, Oliver was journeying through the luscious landscapes of an English early May, but this time going to war and into unfamiliar country. He reached unknown territory west of Oxford, as his soldiers began to climb the long dip slope of the Cotswold Hills, a limestone land in which the walls and houses were made from the local rock. When newly hewn it was like freshly minted gold, weathering first to honey and then to dove grey. All around were sheep runs, the flocks wandering like clusters of small clouds across the vividly green and fast-sprouting new grass of the year, and stands of planted beech trees, wreathed in a lighter and more delicate green. Banks would have been starred with pale yellow, gold and silver: cowslips, buttercups and daisies. At last the scarp of the hills was reached, and the glittering serpent of the Severn, Britain's greatest river, became visible in the distance below, and by it the walled city of Gloucester, with the tall grey tower of its cathedral rising from one side.

On 8 May Cromwell assembled his army in a field 2 miles from that city. As each regiment came up, he rode to its head and reminded its men of the previous campaigns on which they had risked their lives together and triumphed, and was roundly cheered. New recruits had swelled the ranks, so that he led 6,500 soldiers into the Forest of Dean, passing through its small, restless hills, dense stands of oak, ash and hazel, all aureoled in brilliant young leaves, and rosy sandstone villages hazed with the smoke of ironworks.[32] Before they reached Monmouth, a small walled town dominated by a castle, Oliver learned, with what must have been mixed feelings, that Thomas Horton had just accomplished his main task for him. Horton had not meant to jump the gun, but was awaiting Cromwell's arrival at a village 3 miles west of Cardiff called St Fagans. There Laugharne decided to attack him while he was still isolated and vulnerable. Horton was outnumbered, perhaps by two to one, but had a much more cohesive force, better trained and equipped, and with many more cavalry and dragoons. When he realized that his enemy was approaching, he drew up on terrain which broke up the oncoming army while keeping his own men together. He then launched a series of attacks on different units of Laugharne's force, perfectly co-ordinating horse, foot and dragoons, until he shattered and routed it, killing and capturing over 3,000 men. Laugharne fled back to Pembrokeshire, abandoning the rest of South Wales.[33]

Cromwell now had the worst of both worlds. On the one hand, his subordinate had just earned the glory of the decisive military victory. On the other, he could not simply march his army back to rejoin Fairfax's, because Horton by himself did not have the men and equipment to reduce the strongholds which the defeated rebels still held. Oliver was thus condemned to an interlude of siege warfare, which he could only hope would be short. On 11 May he advanced down the winding, wooded Wye valley to Chepstow, another little walled town with a castle, this time a huge one sprawling down to the riverside. It actually now belonged to Cromwell himself, being the local centre of a corner of Monmouthshire in which Parliament's recent land grants had made him the dominant magnate. This must have made it the more galling that it was held against him, having been surprised and captured by local royalists. His foot soldiers broke through a gate and took the town, but the defenders retreated into the castle and fired on the drummer Oliver sent to demand their surrender. He had to leave a foot regiment behind to besiege it.[34]

Cromwell led his remaining force westwards along the south Welsh coast towards Pembrokeshire. This involved crossing a long series of rivers by bridge or ferry, often at more small walled towns dominated by castles. Occasionally the huge stone carcass of a ruined abbey church rose into the landscape: in Wales the structures of the Middle Ages still dominated the scene in a way no longer the case across much of southern and midland England. The gentry and urban delegations who greeted him along the way would have spoken English, as would many in the streets of the towns, but he would also have heard there the lilting syllables of the native language. This had once been the land of his paternal family, and he would have passed close to the village in Glamorgan which had been its seat one and a half centuries before. Indeed, his very name was still legally 'Cromwell alias Williams', but we have no sign of any connection that he may have felt with the people now around him. He would certainly have been conscious of the line of mountains that bounded his horizon to the right hand after he had marched only a day from Chepstow. Sometimes it was blue in the distance, and sometimes it was close enough for him to see the green bracken, gorse and trees upon its slopes. Golden eagles, which nested among the peaks, would have soared overhead at times.[35]

From the 18th to the 22nd he was at Swansea, where once again he was now the local lord, having been granted the whole of the wildly beautiful and intensely varied lands of the Gower Peninsula to the west.[36] Beyond Carmarthen the mountains slowly diminished and receded from sight, and the roads led on through a low green pastoral land until the broad shining expanse of Milford Haven, the inlet of the sea which divides the western end of Wales, opened ahead. The peninsula to its left contained the towns of Pembroke and Tenby, upon opposite sides of its coastline, and into these the remnants of Laugharne's army had retired. Cromwell settled down to besiege Pembroke on the 24th, leaving Tenby to Horton. In the last week of May, news arrived that the regiment left at Chepstow had blown a large gap in the castle wall with heavy siege guns from Gloucester, and had taken the fortress by storm. A few days later, Tenby surrendered, and so in the whole of Wales only Pembroke now held out.[37] That was, however, a different matter. For one thing both Poyer and Laugharne were inside, with up to 2,000 of the best of their veterans from the former civil war. Enough time had been left while Cromwell was marching across South Wales for them amply to supply the place. The two commanders and their followers had, as said, experienced before the situation of being cooped up there by besiegers, and had survived. Pembroke had, moreover, been the centre of first Norman and then English power in south-west Wales all through the high and late Middle Ages, and had never fallen to an enemy. It was the strongest fortress town in the region.

If those inside were in a strong position, then the besiegers were in a weak one. They completely lacked siege guns, because those from Gloucester, which had enabled the reduction of Chepstow and were then to be sailed round to Pembroke, had been lost in the River Severn when they were being loaded back onto shipboard. Weeks would be needed to salvage them. Another problem was that the terms of surrender offered to the defenders were unusually harsh. A decision had clearly been taken to make a severe example of the rebels: the former royalists as repeat offenders and the former parliamentarians as turncoats. As a result, at Pembroke, as at Tenby and Chepstow, the only conditions offered were 'mercy', which was not as it sounds to a modern ear. It did not mean that mercy would be granted to those who surrendered, but that they would be at the mercy of the victors, to be dealt with as they or Parliament decided. Poyer, Laugharne and their followers therefore preferred to hold out, in the hope that luck (or God) would turn their way as had repeatedly happened in the previous war, and that their enemies would become distracted by developments elsewhere and march away.

As May turned to June, it seemed increasingly possible that this would be so. The Scottish invasion had been badly delayed by dissensions at home, as the governing body of the Scottish Church, allied to a large party of politicians, had refused to support it on the grounds that the king had still not firmly agreed to a lasting remodelling of the Church of England along Scottish lines. The proponents of the alliance with Charles, now called Engagers, nonetheless retained the approval of most of the political nation, and of the Scottish Parliament. They managed to subdue their opponents and to gather an invasion force, which was almost ready by the end of June. Meanwhile, Fairfax and the rest of Parliament's field army had become badly distracted by developments nearer home. In the course of May, the counties around London, which had been the mainstay of Parliament during the Civil War, had petitioned the Lords and Commons for a settlement with the king and the disbanding of the army. Parliament could not agree to the latter, and dragged its feet over initiating fresh negotiations with Charles, although it did pardon all the Presbyterian leaders who had been chased out of power in the course of 1647. As a result, a serious popular uprising took place in Kent and Essex at the end of May, with support from Hertfordshire. Fairfax defeated the Kent rebels in a hard-fought battle at Maidstone on 1 June, but the remnant of them joined those from Essex and Hertfordshire, to form a sizeable army which shut itself up in the town of Colchester.

Fairfax and his commanders, who included Ireton, then found themselves pinned down outside Colchester as surely as Cromwell was at the far end of Wales. If they left the siege to face the Scots, then the royalists in Colchester could immediately take London and Westminster. Thus, most of the field army was neutralized. Inspired by the rebellion in the south-east, a rash of further royalist risings occurred in many parts of the Midlands, North Wales, the north of England and the Thames valley in the following six weeks. Most were put down by local forces, but one captured and held the huge medieval castle of Pontefract in Yorkshire, from which the rebels raided as far as Lincoln. To make matters still worse, when Rainsborough arrived at last to take command of Parliament's fleet, with the office of admiral that he had sought so hard in the autumn, a whole section of it promptly mutinied. Rather than be led by a man of his political and religious views, the crews put him ashore and sailed off to offer their services to the prince of Wales.

Faced with this increasingly appalling situation, Cromwell did his best outside Pembroke. He encircled the town completely and attempted to starve it out. By early June the horses for Laugharne's troopers were being fed on thatch pulled from roofs, and by the end of the month the human population was relying on biscuit and water. The crucial difference from the First Civil War was that the town had then been supplied from the sea, which Parliament's warships had controlled. They still did, but were now hostile, leaving no relief from that direction for the besieged. Instead Cromwell borrowed heavy guns from one warship in the haven and tried to break open the wall of Pembroke. The guns were, however, medium-weight siege weapons, culverins and demi-culverins, which could crack open medieval masonry but not demolish it. When a breach was made in late June, it was too high for horses to enter, and too narrow for infantry to do so in force. A party of musketeers was sent in, but it was not followed fast enough by pikemen, whose spears could hold off horsemen. Charged and smashed by Laugharne's cavalry, it lost up to forty men, and the survivors fled back through the crack, after which no further attempt was made. Instead Cromwell and his officers relied on hunger and acts of terrorism, such as using the ship's guns to fire into the town from a nearby hill and set houses alight. By late June a proper siege train was ready at Bristol, but contrary winds prevented the shipping of it to West Wales. The poverty and remoteness of Pembrokeshire was such that the besiegers were reduced to straits almost as severe as the besieged, living mostly on bread and water and receiving no pay.[38]

From early June onwards, Oliver found himself bombarded by orders from the Committee of Both Houses to make some kind of deal with Poyer and his associates that would free him to take his army to face the Scots.[39] By early July it was clear that he would have to moderate his terms, and he duly did, insisting now that only Poyer, Laugharne and two other former parliamentarians should be left at mercy, their fate to be decided by Parliament (which in the end had only Poyer shot). The royalist leaders were allowed to go into exile, all the other soldiers could go home and the townspeople were protected from plunder. Given their increasing hunger and the impossibility of relief, this was enough to induce the defenders to surrender on 11 July. Sections of the town and castle walls were blown up to render them indefensible, and then at last Cromwell could lead his men away.[40] The expedition had been a success: after all, Oliver had become the first person to conquer Pembroke. It had however, been protracted, messy and not very lucky, which counted when both the general and his men looked anxiously for signs of divine favour or disfavour. Moreover, success had not come a moment too soon, for on 8 July the long-expected Scottish army had at last crossed the border.

MARCH INTO THE NORTH

The most direct route from Pembroke to the English Midlands, and so to the north, was across the centre of Wales, but the mass of mountains that occupied it meant poor and winding roads and little food or shelter. Cromwell therefore decided to retrace the course of his outward march, back to Gloucester, which he reached on 25 July. At Carmarthen he put most of his foot soldiers on ships which transported them to the Severn, while he pressed on overland with the cavalry. His men were still unpaid, and the infantry were already wearing through their shoes and stockings from hard marching, and had much more of that ahead of them. Fortunately, he was dealing with a very efficient body of committed allies on the Committee of Both Houses, which promptly despatched a large supply of both to depots in the Midlands on his expected route. It also ordered all commanders in the north to obey Cromwell without question.[41] On the 26th he marched from Gloucester with 4,000 men.[42] They had been in Wales so long that summer was already starting to wind up, the cornfields in their golden harvest colours, the long grass yellowed, and the woods in heavy and uniform bottle-green foliage. Not that they would have regarded this scene as idyllic as they tramped or sat or led their horses through it, as the summer of 1648 had been as bad as those of the past two years. Wind and rain had been almost constant, and continued to be so; much of the cereal crop had rotted or been flattened; and a third widespread harvest failure, leading to continued high food prices, was on the way.

The route led through Warwick and Leicester, on forced marches which got Cromwell to Nottingham on 4 August. En route, more military bad news arrived, of the loss of another of the strongest castles in the north, Scarborough on the Yorkshire coast, to a local rising.[43] The political news was also disheartening. Cromwell was already angered by Parliament's willingness to persecute religious sects, published in May. He had written to Fairfax that the latter's victory at Maidstone had to be a sign that the 'poor godly people' of the nation should not 'be made the object of wrath'.[44] Parliament had not only maintained its harder religious policy but had repealed the Vote of No Addresses in May. On 28 July, by a majority of four, the Commons agreed to treat with the king again, on the basis of the terms sent to him at Hampton Court in the previous September, and without prior conditions. As he had rejected those terms then, and now stood a good chance of being restored by the Scots and their English royalist allies, there was little chance of him accepting them now. The offer, however, conceded one of the demands of the Scots and would conciliate many Presbyterians further.[45] It also widened the gap between Parliament and army: but the series of measures that Parliament had passed since the opening of May not only represented attempts to win back moderate opinion but also followed the natural inclination of many members, now that the military emergency had rendered the soldiers unable to threaten them any further.

On 29 July Parliament formally ordered Cromwell to fight the Scots, who had now entered England.[46] Their declared purpose was to destroy the English army, so freeing Parliament from coercion by it and enabling both the establishment of a full presbyterian Church in England and negotiations with the king at a palace near London. On receiving this declaration, Charles gave the Scots his implied support, saying that he required nothing except the opportunity to negotiate with Parliament personally and without duress.[47] On 2 August the House of Lords refused by two votes to declare any English who aided the Scottish invaders traitors, so holding open a possibility that the invaders themselves were not actually enemies. This was a clear insurance policy against the chance that Cromwell was going to be defeated by them, and on the very same day another step was taken to undermine his position. His former major, Robert Huntington, delivered a testimonial to the House of Lords concerning Cromwell's dealings with the king in the previous year. It revealed the full extent of those secret negotiations, including Cromwell's advice to Charles to reject the terms offered by Parliament and prefer those of the army, and the manner in which he had turned against the king when treating with Charles no longer seemed opportune. An inquiry was ordered into the allegations.[48] If Cromwell did suffer defeat in battle, then his removal from political power was already being prepared. Meanwhile Fairfax, Ireton and their thousands of men were still pegged down helplessly outside Colchester, with more being held outside the castles still occupied by royalist rebels in Kent.

One beneficial effect for Oliver of the preparations being made by many in Parliament to accommodate a Scottish victory was that they pushed the radicals back towards support of the army leadership, as such a victory would doom them as surely as the soldiers. Ludlow claimed later that he had been invited to add his own hostile evidence for Cromwell's dealings to that provided by Huntington, but refused to do so, writing instead with some of his allies to Oliver to offer his support.[49] One of those allies was the arch-Leveller John Lilburne, who had now been released from the Tower of London again by Parliament, in a further attempt to hedge bets by making friends on all sides. He, too, was asked to support Huntington and he, too, refused, sending Cromwell a letter on 3 August, via the former army agitator Edward Sexby. It informed Oliver that Lilburne was now his friend once more, as he seemed to have returned to his old principles.[50]

Cromwell moved on through the rain into Yorkshire. This was country he knew well from the Marston Moor campaign four years before, a rolling land of small hills, pastures, copses, coal diggings and ironworks. He reached Doncaster and waited there two days to receive a train of field artillery. On 9 August he attacked the royalist defenders of Pontefract Castle, driving them into the fortress itself and penning them there. He left the castle, and Scarborough, blockaded by local levies from the East Midlands, taking with him the veteran soldiers from Yorkshire. Then he pressed on, to meet Parliament's northern army in the hilly country between Knaresborough, Wetherby and Leeds on the 12th and 13th. More news arrived from elsewhere: some bad, that North Wales had now rebelled in the name of the king; and some good, that a brother of John Lilburne had declared for King Charles at Tynemouth Castle, near Newcastle, but had been killed when the fortress was immediately retaken by storm.[51]

The general of Parliament's northern army, with which Cromwell now united his own and who thereby became his lieutenant, was well known to him and seemingly liked and trusted by him. It was John Lambert, the able young Yorkshireman alongside whom he had fought on the Marston Moor campaign, who had been prominent in the politics of the army in 1647, and who had been sent to command in the north later that year. In the month since the Scots had invaded, he had fought a skilful rearguard action with inferior numbers to pen them into Cumberland and Westmorland, until reinforcements could reach him.[52] Though there is no doubt that Lambert handled his men well, there is also little that the Scots made no sustained attempt to press forward, because their army was not ready to do so. Even now, contingents of it were arriving from Scotland, and those already assembled were mostly inexperienced and badly trained and disciplined, as well as short of pay, food, artillery, ammunition and equipment, all of which were expected, or at least hoped, to follow. In the meantime, the animals that the army needed to draw its baggage and munition waggons had to be conscripted from impoverished local farmers. The dreadful weather sent the turbulent upland rivers and streams of the region into flood, and laid roads deep in mud. In addition, the Scottish generals were torpid and timid (of which more will be said), but it is not clear how well they would have fared at this stage, given their logistical weakness, had they attempted a more aggressive strategy towards Lambert.[53]

Without Lambert's men, Cromwell would not have been strong enough to engage the Scots as he had been ordered to do, which was why he had come up into Yorkshire instead of heading straight for the Cumbrian region through Lancashire. As soon as the two generals were united, they moved west to attack the Scots, who were now at last going south, although slowly. The combined parliamentarian forces pushed up Wharfedale into the land of Craven, which lies at the heart of the Pennine Hills, the backbone of northern England. This was Lambert's home country, but an area which Cromwell had never entered before, although he had reached its edge on the Marston Moor campaign. The slopes around rose ever higher and more barren, some with concave slopes and some with convex, and some with pavements of bare limestone on their crests. On 14 August they reached the little town of Skipton, around the drum towers of its medieval castle, and then struck across the open moors on the next day to Gisburn in the Ribble valley. Down that vale lay Preston, which was now known to be the Scottish headquarters.

By now, advance parties of the army were skirmishing with bodies of its enemies, and so on the 16th they advanced more cautiously downriver, past another old town and castle at Clitheroe, and out of the great hills. The Ribble was growing broader, and so they needed to decide whether to move down its left or right bank: to face the Scots from the south across the line of their own advance or to attack them in the flank. A council of war called at Hodder Bridge chose the latter course, along the right, northern, bank, because this would enable them to engage the foe much faster, before the remaining reinforcements intended for the Scots, a force of veteran soldiers shipped back from the Irish war, could join them from the north. That evening Cromwell made his headquarters at a mansion on a slope above the river, Stoneyhurst Hall, 9 miles from Preston and 3 miles from the nearest enemy outposts, while his regiments mostly slept in the wet park around it. Battle would be joined the next day. It was clear that, by moving up to the assault so quickly and directly, he and his commanders were taking a huge risk. They knew, vaguely, that their enemies had superior numbers; they also knew that if the Scots were well led and well briefed on the movements of Parliament's army, then they could receive the attack in such a way as to deal a lethal blow to Cromwell's force.[54]

By an extraordinary stroke of luck – or, as Cromwell and his men would view it, an act of divine providence – neither of those two contingent conditions prevailed among their foes. The latter were led by three men in particular, of very different character. The commander in chief was James, duke of Hamilton, the premier peer of the Scottish nation, related to the royal family and the king's natural lieutenant in his northern kingdom. This inheritance explained his prominence in national life. Otherwise he was a genial, hesitant, diffident and well-intentioned man, of average intelligence, with no experience in or aptitude for military affairs. His portraits show him as an exquisitely dressed figure with delicate features, an immaculately trimmed beard and moustache in the king's style, and dark hair carefully cut to fall over his collar. His political record had been one of sequential failure, partly because of his own failings and partly because he was a natural moderate, who had repeatedly been caught between the king and his more extreme opponents in Scotland. The seizure of power by the army and Independents in England had swung Scottish opinion back towards the political centre ground. Hamilton's position there, and social eminence, had then made him the natural leader of the Engagers, who supported the deal with the king, and he had chosen to command the resulting invasion of England himself.

This being the case, it was obviously necessary for him to appoint a lieutenant-general who had military experience and could advise him, and this role was given to another Engager nobleman, James, earl of Callander. His features in his portrait sum up his character well, and also its contrast with Hamilton's: a coarse jowly face with a mop of dark curly hair and simple tufts of beard and moustache. His nature was forceful, touchy, imperious and self-confident, which might have been an asset had his undoubted record of previous service in armies been combined with any actual talent as a soldier. In reality he had none, and his standard reaction in the face of any military problem was to reach for the rule book.

These were the men in charge of the Scottish army. They were accompanied by, and had some authority over, a local force of northern English royalists led by a Yorkshireman, Sir Marmaduke Langdale. His long, dour, clean-shaven face, with its determined gaze and trailing straight – almost lank – hair, again well expresses his character, which was one of devoted loyalty, courage, intelligence and ability. During the Civil War he had commanded the king's Northern Horse, one of the finest cavalry units in the royal armies, and had done so with considerable flair and distinction. His unit should not, strictly speaking, have been marching with the Scots at all, because the Engagers, in an effort to win more support at home, had promised their critics that they would not ally with royalists, who had been the enemy of the Scottish government in the preceding war. Langdale himself had fought against the army that Scotland had sent to aid Parliament against the king. The quality and number of his men, and their local knowledge, nonetheless made them invaluable to Hamilton and Callander.

Although the combined Scottish and royalist armies clearly made up a force larger than that which Cromwell was leading against them, it is difficult to say by how much. Cromwell himself provided a breakdown of the numbers in his own army, which has long been persuasive because of its detail: 4,000 foot and 2,500 horse and dragoons made up of the conjunction of his and Lambert's forces, plus a body of levies from Lancashire comprising 1,600 foot and 500 horse.[55] That gave him 8,600 men in all, a figure confirmed by other parliamentarian sources: a newspaper which put the total at 9,000, and one of Lambert's officers, who reckoned between 8,000 and 9,000.[56] We are also quite close to certainty with Langdale's English royalist contingent. Cromwell, who had good opportunity to observe that force, estimated it at 2,500 foot and 1,500 horse.[57] Langdale himself said he had around 3,000 foot and 700 horse a few days before, and Cromwell's figure for the cavalry contingent may include some Scottish units that Hamilton had in the rear of the English royalists, as will be recounted.[58] The real uncertainty is with the Scottish army, which Cromwell estimated at a gigantic 12,000 foot and 5,000 horse. One of the junior Scottish generals put it as less than 14,000, which would match Cromwell's figure if it excluded Langdale's brigade but not otherwise.[59] Nor is it certain whether Cromwell included in his total the Scottish force from Ireland that was far in Hamilton's rear and unable to reinforce him in time. Modern historians have accordingly differed in their calculations.[60] It seems safest simply to conclude that the Scottish army was larger than Cromwell's, even without the addition of Langdale's contingent, but we cannot now tell by how much.

The crucial factor, which those who have written upon the ensuing battle have always identified, was that the foes upon whom Oliver was now launching his attack were both unsuspecting and dispersed. This turned out to negate their superiority in numbers. Because of the problems of supply experienced by the Scottish army, and the poverty of the surrounding countryside, its units had been quartered widely apart in order to find food and accommodation, and forage for the horses. As day broke on 17 August, its cavalry were almost all 12 miles to the south, at Wigan. Most of the infantry were at Preston, preparing to cross its bridge over the Ribble and then move on to follow the horse regiments. For two days, the advance parties of Cromwell's army had been clashing with the outposts of Hamilton's and Langdale's men, and forcing them back towards their main body. Not all of the retreating units reported these encounters to their commanders, however, and those that did furnished the latter with a problem of interpretation: for one and a half months there had been skirmishing in the Pennines between their detachments and Lambert's, and there was no sign thus far that the latest encounters were anything other than more of the same. No news had reached the allied generals of Cromwell's approach. As a result, when reports were brought to them of these actions, they decided to continue to discount them as minor raids, and to march the Scottish infantry over Preston Bridge, covered by a rear-guard of horse and foot units stationed on Preston Moor to the north of the town, and Langdale's brigade in a compact mass to the north-east. Langdale's men were therefore directly in the path of Cromwell's attack.[61]

This attack was spearheaded by a party of Lambert's northerners, whom Cromwell ordered in front of his main body to probe the enemy's position. When they nervously asked for greater numbers, he peremptorily repeated his command.[62] This advance guard drove in Langdale's outposts to a group of enclosures that surrounded the road into Preston, where Sir Marmaduke massed his infantry. It was a strong position, blocking the road and giving the royalist pikemen and musketeers shelter behind a series of banks and ditches, above which their flags and the spearheads of their pikes rose. Cromwell and Lambert now led up their main body to the enclosures, launching an assault in late afternoon. The small size of their advance party had served to reinforce the belief of the allied commanders that they were facing only a raid by detachments of local parliamentarians. Langdale and his men would gradually become aware that this was wrong, as the full size and weight of the attack became apparent, in the teeth of another wet and windy day. Cromwell sent two horse regiments to push up the road to Preston, which ran through the centre of Langdale's position, three foot regiments to attack the enclosures to its right, and two more against those to the left.[63] He kept the Lancashire men in reserve.

None of these attacks made any initial headway. The roadway was too deep in mud, and too much raked with fire from the enclosures, for the horsemen to get up it, and the foot assaults on the enclosures were held at their banks, hedges and ditches. Above all, Langdale's royalists fought heroically, though outnumbered around three to one in infantry alone and unsupported by cavalry. They held their ground for hours, enabling Sir Marmaduke to get a desperate appeal to the Scottish generals for help, and leaving time for them to bring up reinforcements. There seems little doubt that had the thousands of Scottish foot soldiers in Preston and to its south come to the aid of their English allies, then, given the terrain and the numbers involved, Cromwell's army would have been outflanked, worn down and forced to retire. Instead, all the while that the English royalists fought on, the Scottish regiments continued to march in the opposite direction, over Preston Bridge and out of the town. Afterwards, their leaders agreed that it had been Callander who had persuaded Hamilton that it was against the practice of war to send infantry into battle unsupported by cavalry. He therefore argued, successfully, that the Scottish foot should be moved to the south of the river to await the return of the horse from Wigan, holding the line of the river in the meantime. He reasoned that, if Langdale were indeed facing the full force of a major army, then he should continue to hold it off as long as he could, and then retire to rejoin the Scots across the river. Hamilton sent Sir Marmaduke some units from the Scottish rearguard stationed north of Preston, but they were too few and too late to be of help.[64]

The flaw in Callander's plan was that it was simply not credible that Langdale's men would be allowed to disengage from Cromwell's when they had had enough, and to make their way to and across the bridge in an orderly fashion with the Scottish rearguard. What happened instead is that they fought on desperately until they were exhausted and running out of ammunition. At that point, Cromwell's reserve of Lancashire men came into action, and its foot soldiers found a sunken lane running to the left of the royalist position which allowed them to get round the flank. The combination of all these factors caused Langdale's northerners to break and flee at last towards the town; once they were in the open ground beyond the enclosures, Cromwell's cavalry could overtake them and cut them down. The slaughter went on for an hour, without mercy, the falling fugitives being trampled into the mud by the horses. The pursuit carried on into Preston, where the streets became littered with discarded weapons and equipment. The Scottish rearguard on the moorland to the north was overwhelmed by the advancing victorious army and its foot soldiers killed or captured, while the horse fled towards Cumbria with the remnants of Langdale's. Hamilton had lingered ineffectually in the town, wondering what to do to help Langdale, and he and his bodyguard now had to cut their way through the advancing enemy to the river, which they swam to safety on their horses, joined by Sir Marmaduke.

Callander's strategy had depended on regrouping the bulk of the Scottish army across the river and holding its line: but it embodied a lack of understanding of the terrain. The only point at which infantry could cross was Preston Bridge, over which the Scots had been passing all day, and which they now defended strongly, as Cromwell's foot regiment and the Lancashire men came down to attack it. On the bridge itself, the Scots were completely exposed to musket shot, and they were equally vulnerable in the open ground at their end of it. Cromwell's men, by contrast, could shelter in a medley of banks and hedges on a slope above the northern end, from which they poured a withering fire onto their helpless opponents. When those were depleted enough, the Lancashire pikemen charged across the bridge, points levelled, pushing away the remaining Scots. The momentum of the attack carried them on to seize a second bridge, over a smaller river, the Darwen, which flowed into the Ribble just below Preston. This operation exposed both the front and the flanks of the main Scottish position, and Cromwell's cavalry poured across the rivers to harass its enemies. Some captured part of the Scottish baggage train, including Hamilton's possessions, so that his gold and silver dinner service was spilled across the hillside, a prey to looting troopers. Darkness, however, was now falling. Cromwell and his officers decided to hold the ground that they occupied at that point, and attack again on the morrow. Most of their men could sleep snugly in the houses of Preston, as the rain and gale that had raged through the day continued into the night.[65]

Hamilton now called a council of war to decide what to do next, and Callander persuaded most of the officers present, and Hamilton, to support a withdrawal to the south overnight.[66] It is easy to see the appeal of such a plan. The action of the day had left the surviving Scottish infantry exposed to attack, and its vulnerability was much increased by its continuing lack of cavalry: its horse regiments had been recalled, but had not appeared. To move south to meet them on a night march held out the prospect of regrouping, as a complete and coherent army, to meet the enemy on a field of the generals' choosing the next day. They probably had no idea of the size of the army now facing them, and poised to strike; they may have thought it larger than it was, and superior to their own. In this situation, to retire, consolidate and offer battle on favourable ground must have seemed attractive to many. In fact, it was the fatal error that lost them the war because, like the strategy on the previous day, it did not correspond to practical reality. That evening, the surviving Scottish infantry still probably outnumbered Cromwell's and it was drawn up in a strong position among enclosures on a hilltop, equivalent to that which Langdale's brigade had held but in much greater strength. It was well supplied with food and ammunition, and its men had used the afternoon to make huts in which to shelter from the dreadful weather. The cavalry was in fact on its way, at a pace which would bring it all up by dawn. Had the Scots held that ground and prepared to receive the enemy on it, they might well have beaten them off and then routed them.

Instead, the tired Scottish soldiers were ordered out of their shelters into the dark, raging night, to march south through it, and along strange lanes deep in mud, without guides. It was discovered that the local people whose horses and oxen had been taken to draw the army's waggons had taken advantage of the confusion to steal them back. As a result, the Scots now had no means of moving their ammunition. Musketeers were accordingly issued with a full flask of powder and ration of lead balls each, which increased the weight under which they marched, and the bulk of the munitions were left in the waggons to be blown up. This had to be delayed in order to avoid warning the enemy that the Scots were pulling out; in the end, the job was left too long and all the waggons were captured, with their stores. When dawn broke after that terrible night, on 18 August, and the Scots tried to muster again, it was found that about half of the infantry was missing, having lost its way and straggled in the darkness and storm. So was all of the cavalry, because it had taken a different route back to Preston to rejoin its comrades, and had passed the foot soldiers marching towards it. The Scottish horsemen arrived at the town at daybreak to find it full of enemies and their own comrades gone. Drums and trumpets called Cromwell's soldiers to arms, and his own horse units swarmed out to attack the Scots. The latter were driven south again and continually harassed, although they fought back with determination and one of Cromwell's cavalry colonels died with a lance through his heart.

The remaining Scottish infantry stood in a body for a few hours in the morning. Seeing neither its own comrades nor the enemy, it was ordered to move on to Wigan to quarter for the night. As a result, it became vulnerable once more to attack when spread out on the march, and the woods and fields on its way became the scene of a series of running fights, as first Cromwell's cavalry and then his infantry began to catch up with Scottish units and pick them off, killing many. On a moor outside Wigan the remainder were rallied again, but the ground was decided by the commanders to be unfavourable, and the ammunition carried by the men was now running out. The decision was taken to march the survivors further south through yet another night, in an attempt to cross the River Mersey over Warrington Bridge, which could then be held against their pursuers. The Mersey was broad enough, and the bridge long enough, to present a real natural defensive line at last. Cromwell's army spent the night lying in the drenched fields north of Wigan, and mustered in the morning to find their foes gone from the town.

Once more the pursuit was resumed, and once more natural conditions had damaged the Scots as much as their attackers had done. A second trek through darkness, along unfamiliar, narrow and muddy lanes, by men who had now not slept for two nights, thinned out their ranks still further. When day returned, many had not reached the sanctuary of Warrington, and fell prey to Cromwell's better-rested and better-fed soldiers, following at greater speed thanks to local guides. Near Winwick church a large body of them turned at bay, in enclosed ground that favoured defenders, and fought hard. However, local people, who hated them both as foreigners and as plunderers (to which they were driven by lack of pay and supplies, so that Wigan had been looted bare), led Cromwell's men around their flanks and rear, and so turned their position. The survivors broke and fled, to be attacked repeatedly by cavalry as they ran, so that the lanes, cornfields, meadows, woods and ditches between there and Warrington became littered with bodies. The sorry remainder of the Scottish infantry crossed the bridge, exhausted, demoralized and with their ammunition spent or soaked through, to be informed that their generals had just abandoned them and fled with the cavalry, leaving an order to make the best terms with Cromwell as the infantry could.

Oliver and his fellow commanders arrived at Warrington to find that the campaign was suddenly over. The few thousand surviving Scottish foot laid down their arms for nothing more than a promise that their lives would be spared. Hamilton, Callander and Langdale fled east with the cavalry, seeking a way back northward and losing men steadily as they dropped out in fatigue or were picked off by local parliamentarians. Cromwell despatched Lambert to follow them with a strong mounted force, and in Staffordshire on the next day the Scottish troopers mutinied and demanded a surrender. Hamilton remained with them to conduct it; he and his men became Lambert's prisoners. Callander and Langdale preferred to keep fleeing, and both eventually escaped to safety.[67]

This protracted, messy, running fight, which historians were to put under the umbrella term of the 'battle of Preston', had been Cromwell's first large-scale field action in which he had been in overall command of an army. The result was a total victory, and one which, indeed, was barely believable. His army had faced a well-armed one that had superior numbers and no obvious weaknesses, and yet never had to fight it as a body. Instead, his soldiers had needed to deal first with Langdale's heavily outnumbered, isolated and unsupported brigade, then with a few Scottish units cut off to the north of Preston, and finally with the taking of a bridge under circumstances that strongly favoured the attackers. After that the Scottish army had simply run and kept running until it disintegrated: its commanders had been allowed to defeat themselves. Cromwell's attack plan had been both crude and risky: to engage the enemy as swiftly as possible and from a direction which ensured that the foe under attack could not be reinforced, and then see what happened. What happened was that the assault, by astonishing good luck, had maximized both of the Scots' major weaknesses: their lack of intelligence concerning the approach of a powerful enemy, and the extreme dispersal of their forces. Sequential mistakes then ensured their defeat. On their part, Cromwell and his men, including the local Lancashire levies, had made not a single error, but had fought with consummate skill, making perfect use of opportunity and terrain. For all that, had the Scottish infantry reinforced Langdale's brigade en masse, or simply held its position on the following night, it is likely that none of this exemplary military conduct would have saved Cromwell from defeat. No wonder he concluded that he had been the recipient of an extraordinary manifestation of divine favour.

On 20 August, the day after the surrender of the Scottish foot soldiers at Warrington, he wrote the official despatch announcing the victory to Parliament. It was the longest and most detailed that he had written after any military action to date. He naturally played up, and perhaps exaggerated, the huge size of the defeated army, and his own much smaller numbers – in his opinion, even at Warrington. As naturally, he used this to argue that his success could only be ascribed to the will of God. He concluded by saying that he would not presume to advise Parliament on how to make use of the Almighty's favour, and then proceeded to do so, though in veiled language. He bade the MPs and Lords not to 'hate His people, who are the apple of His eye, and for whom even kings shall be reproved', and to ensure that 'they that are implacable and will not leave troubling the land may speedily be destroyed'.[68] In the prevailing context, the reference to God's people was clearly to the sects whom Parliament had proscribed in its ordinance in May. The call to take retributive action against those who had fomented and led the rebellions and invasions against Parliament and the army that year left open the possibility that it might include the king; but the preceding declaration that even kings might be reproved on behalf of the godly was a patent hint that Charles might indeed be intended. In this manner, Oliver declared against the policy of negotiation with Charles and rejection of liberty of conscience that Parliament had adopted in the summer to conciliate moderate opinion. In conformity with the strategy he had followed since Putney (and which, as said, may have been based on conversion as well as expediency), he was very much in accord with the feelings of his soldiers in doing so.

MARCH ACROSS THE BORDER

The destruction of the Scottish army effectively ended the war further south, for on hearing of it the royalist defenders of Colchester and of the Kentish castles surrendered, and those who had risen in North Wales retreated and prepared to make terms. Parliament immediately dropped the investigation into Cromwell's conduct in the previous year, initiated by Huntington's evidence, and Huntington found himself no longer welcome at Westminster: Oliver's political and military careers had both been saved at Preston.[69] The war itself continued, however, because the reserve of the Scottish army survived in the far north of England, with many local royalists in arms, and might be reinforced from Scotland. On sending him its thanks for his victory, the Committee of Both Houses ordered Cromwell to destroy these remaining enemies.[70] He duly turned his men north again, and once more they squelched along the miry roads, through sodden fields from which the wretched harvest had been gathered, and pastures brimming with puddles.

The remaining Scots had stripped Cumberland and Westmorland of supplies, and now moved east into Northumberland. Oliver therefore retraced his route through Skipton into Yorkshire, and by 7 September had reached Durham, the infantry footsore, and the horses galled, with marching. En route he wrote to some of his traditional allies in Parliament, his cousin Oliver St John and Lord Wharton, sending his regards to their fellow Independents and taking notice again of the 'despised jeered saints' threatened by the religious policy adopted in May. On the 9th he entered Newcastle, where the cannon were shot off to welcome him and the corporation treated him and his chief officers to a banquet. The Scots he now faced were the veterans from Ireland, led by a tough, aggressive and capable commander called George Monro. But just when it seemed possible that Monro and his English allies might stand and fight, the Scot was recalled to Scotland. The loss of the army they had sent into England had left the 'Engager' party there vulnerable, and those Scots who had opposed the deal with King Charles, and the invasion, had now risen in rebellion against it. These men have been given the name of the 'Kirk Party', because they were supported by the leaders of the national Scottish Church (Kirk in Scots). The Engagers needed Monro's help to resist. Thus, as Cromwell reached Newcastle the Scottish general left England, abandoning the English royalists who had joined him to their fate.[71]

Cromwell's orders from the committee had included the recapture of the two English border strongholds still in Scottish hands, Berwick and Carlisle. He held a council of war, which decided to march on Berwick. This he did on the 13th, up through the green Northumberland hills, with the greater heights of the Cheviots showing to the left. His army was about 5,000 strong and essentially the same as that with which he had fought at Preston: his force brought up from Wales, with Lambert's northerners and some extra units from local northern forces. As before, the Committee of Both Houses gave him full logistical support, ordering up supply ships, clothes and money to keep his men in peak condition. Cromwell tried to win the support of the Northumberland villagers by promising to return them the cattle plundered from them by the Scots if he could. It was at this time that London journalists began to apply to his men the nickname bestowed upon Oliver himself by their predecessors in 1644: 'Ironsides'.[72]

On the 15th, Cromwell summoned Berwick to surrender. It would be a very hard nut to crack, because previous English governments, recognizing its strategic importance as the key to the eastern Scottish border, had given it powerful fortifications, resistant to siege guns (of which

Cromwell currently had none in any case). It had a strong garrison of Scots still loyal to the Engagers. Even before he marched on it, therefore, Cromwell tried to win it bloodlessly by writing to the Scottish government to demand its return. Events in Scotland, as events had done throughout this northern campaign, now played into his hands. The civil war there had rapidly reached a stalemate, with the Kirk Party, which had captured Edinburgh, facing off against the Engagers, who had withdrawn to a strong position at Stirling after being reinforced by Monro. The parties were equally balanced in strength, and it was clear that, if Cromwell were willing to intervene on the side of the Kirk Party, then the balance would be decisively tipped. On 15 September, therefore, the earl of Loudon, chancellor of Scotland and one of the Kirk Party leaders, wrote to him promising to surrender both Berwick and Carlisle if that party defeated the Engagers, and asking for his help in fighting them if needed.[73]

Oliver thus found himself in the simultaneously exhilarating and awkward position of effectively negotiating with a foreign power. He immediately called a council of war to discuss Loudon's letter, which agreed that his army should come to the Kirk Party's aid, without waiting for an actual invitation, and not return to England until the Engagers were beaten and Berwick and Carlisle returned. As the army could neither besiege Berwick effectively nor stay nearby, Monro having swept the area bare of food, this was the most obvious way of fulfilling its mission. On 19 September Cromwell led his force, now around 9,000 strong, into Scotland, across the River Tweed, and wrote the next day to the Committee of Both Houses to justify his action and asking to be supplied by sea. He had discovered that a new-raised County Durham foot regiment in his army had already raided across the river and returned with plunder. Anxious to win as many Scottish allies as possible, he mustered that regiment beside the Tweed and asked the local farmers to identify and claim the horses that the soldiers had taken from them. The plunderers were then sacked from service, an officer was gaoled and the colonel was suspended to face a court martial, after which the rest of the regiment was sent back to England. Next, Cromwell informed the Scots that, if the local officials along his route would give his men food, then they would not take it in any other way.[74] It was all a very neat public relations exercise.

Oliver did not initially march far into Scotland, settling his headquarters at a mansion at Mordington, 5 miles beyond Berwick. This enabled him to lodge his army in the Merse, the low-lying district of cornfields and meadows just north of the Tweed, and to keep Berwick itself blockaded. It also emphasized that he was an invited guest, awaiting further requests, and not an invader: the talents that had always served him as a politician and propagandist now aided him as a diplomat. On 22 September some of the leading members of the Kirk Party arrived to negotiate with him, including the greatest magnate of that party, Archibald Campbell, marquis of Argyll. This tall, long-faced, red-haired, squint-eyed man was a ruthless and canny politician, utterly devoted to the cause of Scottish-style presbyterianism and opposed to any concessions to the king that undermined the prospect of its extension to England. The two shrewd men, Argyll and Cromwell, must have sized each other up. The latter's main requirement was the surrender of Berwick, but Argyll could not immediately obtain that.[75]

Yet again, however, events played into Cromwell's hands. The mere presence of his army on Scottish soil to assist the Kirk Party gave the latter a potential military superiority over the Engagers of more than two to one. As a result, peace talks between the two sides rapidly gathered momentum and ran in favour of the Kirk Party. To reinforce this progress, Cromwell agreed to send Lambert deeper into Scotland with an advance party of six horse regiments and some dragoons. The young major-general duly followed these orders, halting about 5 miles short of Edinburgh, and the Engagers at Stirling rapidly finalized the treaty. It was signed on 28 September, and obliged both parties to disband their troops and submit their differences to a new Scottish Parliament to be called in the winter. In the meantime, however, the Engagers were to be excluded from the central government, though they preserved their freedom and property. Moreover, the Kirk Party was allowed to keep 1,500 soldiers to oversee the disbanding, so providing it with some residual armed strength.[76] The agreement installed the Kirk Party as the new rulers of Scotland, which enabled them to obtain the surrender of Berwick to Cromwell by its Engager governor immediately afterwards.[77] On the day that the treaty was signed, the English Parliament retrospectively approved Oliver's action in entering Scotland.[78]

Thereafter, things improved still further, as the new Scottish government invited Cromwell to lead his army closer to Edinburgh, to protect it as it enforced the provisions of the treaty. Bolstered by his endorsement from his own government, he duly did so. He and his men therefore pushed deeper into a land that was utterly strange to him and most of them. The costume of its inhabitants was slightly different, many of the men sporting broad flat bonnets. Their language was related to English and for much of the time mutually intelligible with it, but contained thousands of words unique to itself. The landscape was often harsher, and poorer, than that of much of England. To the left hand rose the bare Lammermuir Hills, now yellow and brown as their grass, heather and bracken faded towards winter. To the right was the North Sea coast, great waves breaking upon it, rising at times to cliffs where seabirds roosted in flocks. Ports and promontories were studded with castles, and further north the dark battered masses of prehistoric volcanoes began to appear against the sky. In early October Cromwell halted his men around the small harbour of Seton, and on the 4th he received an invitation to enter Edinburgh itself. He went at once, with Lambert, Hesilrige and others, in a coach provided by the Scots which rattled across the farmlands to where the volcanic mass of Arthur's Seat dominated the sky to the left, and the lesser dramatic height of Calton Hill to the right. In front was the city, crowding out its steep ridge and mounting up to the huge castle that beetled over the higher western end. Oliver and his party of chosen officers entered from the eastern one, escorted by a party of Argyll's Highlanders in their plaids, and were lodged at the new government's expense in the mansion of an earl in Canongate, close to their point of entry. That evening Argyll, Loudon and a set of Kirk Party grandees came to visit.

The following day the formal embodiment of the Scottish government, the Committee of Estates, sent representatives to ask Cromwell's desires of it, and he responded at once with a demand that measures be taken to deprive the Engagers of all public offices, permanently. Assurance that this would be done came the next day, as did several ministers from the Kirk of Scotland, the provost (or mayor) of the city and leading citizens. Cromwell's stay ended in a sumptuous reception with wines and sweets at the castle, for which coaches were sent to fetch him and some of his chief officers. Argyll was present, together with the castle's governor and the Kirk Party's leading military commander, the earl of Leven, whom Oliver would have known well from the Marston Moor campaign. As the English deputation left the castle, the artillery and musketeers fired a salute to it. Cromwell's party continued out of Edinburgh to rejoin their army and march homeward. At the request of the Committee of Estates, Lambert was left with three regiments of horse and some dragoons to protect the new government while it recruited a larger native force to embody its will.[79]

There were some uneasy undertones to all this public amity. Threats were made against Cromwell's life by Engagers and royalists, and his soldiers were attacked by local people who regarded them as interfering and invading foreigners. In Edinburgh, horses were stolen from the English delegation and they were afraid to sleep or walk the streets. It was noted by one of that delegation that Cromwell was of course treated with the greatest honour by their hosts, but that Lambert's easy charm won more hearts. At the castle, Oliver met the second most high-ranking of the Kirk Party's soldiers, Leven's kinsman and lieutenant-general David Leslie, who greeted him formally and then walked out. They knew each other very well from the Marston Moor campaign, and Leslie had commanded the Scottish cavalry on Cromwell's wing during the battle. His coldness towards his old colleague may have derived from the aftermath of that action, when supporters of each had striven to gain the credit, or it may have stemmed from religious differences, as Leslie was a strict Scottish presbyterian and Cromwell, of course, protected sectaries and independents.

It was precisely to quiz Oliver about his record on this matter and others, and to try to remove tensions, that the delegation from the Kirk had come to see him. It consisted of three leading ministers, led by Robert Blair, whom he also knew from the Marston Moor campaign, and who propelled the discussion. Blair asked him first for his attitude towards monarchy, and their current king; Oliver said he supported both, which may have been technically correct, as no moves had as yet been taken against either which he might endorse. He was then asked his opinion of toleration, and said that he was against it; again this could have been a technical truth, as at no time did Cromwell endorse toleration of every kind of opinion (for example, he consistently backed the proscription of Catholics and of Anglicans of the king's kind). Finally, he was invited to provide his view of the Scottish presbyterian system of ecclesiastical government, and this was too much even for his capacity for equivocation: he said that he needed more time to think about an answer. He wrapped these replies in lengthy and tearful protestations of his sincerity and good intentions of pursuing an alliance with the Kirk Party. His tendency to tears when speaking formally about public affairs was one of his hallmarks, and taken in his time to be a virtue in a speaker, as a proof of candour. If Blair's memory is to be trusted, Cromwell's efforts worked upon two of the ministers but not upon Blair himself, who on leaving told his companions that Oliver was 'an egregious dissembler and a great liar' and a 'greeting [weeping] devil'.[80]

Cromwell marched south on 7 October with an order from the Scottish government for the surrender of Carlisle to him. His army tramped and trotted through the barren hills of the Pentlands and the Borders, which were now settling like the Lammermuirs into the dun hues of winter. They remained lawless country, and many horses were lost to 'moss-troopers' raiding out of the strongholds of local chiefs. On the 12th the army arrived before the English border city and took custody of it from its Scottish garrison. Cromwell joined the local parliamentarian administrators in ordering the wrecking of castles in the region which had been held by royalist insurgents, and in settling local defence measures. He then moved along the line of Hadrian's Wall to Newcastle, and so via Durham into Yorkshire again, to quarter and await further orders.[81]

Cromwell's northern campaign in September and October had been as complete a success as that in August, and especially notable in that it had been achieved without needing to fight at all. Once more it seemed that divine providence had delivered everything that he sought and that he needed only to make use of the advantages that were thereby provided; and once again he did that faultlessly. This long and dramatic succession of apparent striking demonstrations of God's favour must have greatly strengthened Cromwell's feeling that the army he commanded embodied a divine plan, and that the beliefs of its soldiers must mirror that plan. If he had turned against the king almost a year before, he now began to show a similar toughening of attitude towards Parliament. In particular, his Scottish expedition had provided an example that could be used in this respect, as was explicitly noted in a letter to Robert Hammond that was probably written by Cromwell and certainly by somebody close to him. It spoke of how an honest and godly minority in an elected national assembly could remove an ungodly majority from power and call a new assembly to replace it.[82] The letter boded ill for the English MPs who had voted against liberty of conscience and in favour of treating with the king.

4

REVOLUTION

THE GOLDEN FORTRESS

As soon as the military crisis was over, with the defeat of the Scots and the surrender of Colchester, Parliament pressed on hastily to negotiate with the king. A deputation was sent to treat with him in the Isle of Wight. The talks opened there on 18 September, and represented a genuine effort on Parliament's part to make a deal with Charles at last, and so settle the nation, while the army was still distracted by mopping-up operations. Its treatment of him was remarkably, and deliberately, generous. Despite the comprehensive defeat of his supporters, the terms offered were the same as those put together in the previous November, and offered anew to him in July when it seemed that those in arms for him might win. No prior conditions were attached, and he was allowed to bargain over details, instead of, as in 1646–7, being offered a package that he had to accept in its entirety. Moreover, the terms being offered to him had already been agreed (in 1647) with the Scots, and so would be acceptable to them. In addition, the king was allowed to invite royalist grandees and clergy to attend and advise him. The hope was clearly that the complete military defeat of his supporters would finally induce him to make concessions that hitherto he had regarded as impossible.[1]

This is exactly what happened, as Charles gradually proceeded to agree to most of what Parliament had wanted. He consented to the repeal of all the declarations he had issued against his opponents during the main Civil War of 1642 to 1646, so seeming to acknowledge that Parliament's cause had been just. He approved new measures to persecute Roman Catholics in England, and agreed to ban his Catholic queen from attending services of her own religion. He awarded control over the armed forces and government offices to Parliament for twenty years, after which Parliament would decide who would exercise it. His former lieutenant in Ireland, the marquis of Ormond, had returned there to negotiate an alliance between the island's royalists, Catholic rebels and Scots, to support the king. Parliament naturally demanded that Charles disown Ormond's initiative, which he duly did. He also expressed himself willing to abolish archbishops and deans and chapters from the Church.

The remaining sticking points, after two months of talking, were those which had given the most trouble before, namely Parliament's determination to remove bishops and the old religious liturgy altogether, and to punish royalists. The king repeated his former willingness to confirm a presbyterian Church and Parliament's new liturgy for three years and then have the enduring forms of both decided by an assembly of clergy for which he would choose a minority of the representatives. He offered to allow the bishops' lands to be leased out on generous terms for a century to come. He asked first that the traditional liturgy be allowed to himself and others as a private choice, as part of a general liberty of conscience granted for three years; and when this was refused, he asked that he alone be permitted to use it in private. As for his old supporters, Parliament wanted to condemn seven to death, confiscate the estates of forty-three more, and disable all of them from entering its own Houses or government. Charles refused to let any be sentenced to death but offered to exile those whom Parliament had wanted to die. Parliament, as a gesture of conciliation, resolved to exile instead of executing Hamilton and the leaders of the English royalist risings of the summer, though Hamilton was given a huge fine and imprisoned until he paid it. Moreover, of the seven men it named as worthy of execution because of their part in the earlier

Civil War, all but one was safely overseas. All told, the gap that remained between Parliament and the king now seemed to be relatively narrow, the only substantial disagreement being the determination of the one to get rid of bishops completely, and so of royal control of the Church, and of the other to retain them. Even there, the Lords had been prepared to accept the king's formula for Church government, only for the Commons to insist on its rejection.[2]

Charles was, however, no longer negotiating in good faith. He had become convinced that he and Parliament would never be prepared to make the concessions to each other needed to reach agreement, and that the failure of the current attempt to do so would result in him being sentenced to death or life imprisonment. He therefore told supporters that he was making concessions in order to lull his captors into an expectation of impending agreement, and so cause them to relax the watch on him sufficiently for him to escape.[3] He wrote secretly to Ormond, instructing him to ignore whatever the king said until he was free, and to take orders from the queen instead.[4] In view of this, it is remarkable how much effort the amount that he accorded cost him. He tried hard to avoid promising more than the minimum apparently needed to lull his captors into carelessness, stalled the process repeatedly, and found his concessions deeply painful, at one point weeping over them.[5] Moreover, even in order to win an opening for escape, when he was convinced that to fail to do so would cost him life or liberty, he refused to give away the things that mattered most to him, such as Church government. Had Parliament only been prepared at last to make him the concessions he had always asked on those, it seems very likely that he would have agreed sincerely to a deal. He was still not somebody who could glibly negotiate with duplicity; and his sense of his most likely prospects, if he did not escape, was more prescient than that of most of those with whom he was dealing.

Indeed, the steps towards realizing Charles's worst fears were already being taken as the commissioners returned from Newport to Westminster with the results of their discussions with him. In fact, even before those discussions started, moves were under way, with a petition delivered to the House of Commons on 11 September by the London radicals, and written by, among others, John Lilburne. It hailed the Commons once more as the supreme authority in the nation and called king, bishops and House of Lords all oppressors of the realm. It then demanded an end to the treaty with Charles, as he had proved himself utterly untrustworthy. Instead, it asked the Commons to settle the nation by abolishing the vetoes of king and Lords over legislation, instituting annual Parliaments elected for short terms, freeing religion from restrictions, making all subjects of the state equal before the law, punishing those responsible for the war in the summer (who might include the king), and paying the army properly.[6] This petition was followed by more in the remainder of the month and the early part of October, from supporters in the provinces, and – more ominously – from soldiers stationed in Cromwell's command area of the north of England. These urged the Commons to heed the London petition, and especially to stop talks with the king. One from Leicestershire explicitly held him to be guilty of all the bloodshed of the civil wars.[7] A tract issued in the name of the army demanded the implementation of the London petition.[8] The response of the MPs to that and the other petitions was to make no formal reply and to press on with the treaty with Charles as if they had not been delivered.

On 16 October came a still more dangerous development, when Henry Ireton's horse regiment, ordered to disperse to winter quarters across south-eastern England, refused to do so until its requests were addressed. It formulated these, in a petition to Fairfax, as the need to put on trial those believed to be responsible for fomenting the war in the summer, especially the king. Although the petition acknowledged that the evidence against Charles was not as clear as that against Hamilton and the others, it held that to deal with the king at all was treason until the case against him was heard and determined.[9] This action could be construed as mutiny, and was a direct threat to Parliament. There were two forces operating behind it, and behind other army petitions that now appeared against the treaty and for the punishment of those responsible for the recent uprisings and invasion. One was simply that the soldiers were badly paid again, after the summer's fighting had disrupted tax collection, and Londoners in particular had taken advantage of the distraction of the troops to stop handing over their dues once more. When this was drawn to the attention of the House of Commons in October, it discussed a drastic reduction in the size of the military establishment, which probably suggested to members of the army that the MPs were more concerned to get rid of them than to care for them.[10]

The other factor in the soldiers' discontent was the combination of conspiracy theory and scapegoating that has been remarked upon as so potent in the politics of the time. To those signing the petitions, it seemed that Parliament had once more been taken over by a party of enemies, intent on destroying the army and instituting policies contrary to the aims it had professed since 1647. They regarded the king as a natural ally of such people, and many had seen him as an enemy ever since they had fought him and his supporters through the long Civil War earlier in the decade. This animosity to Charles had been smothered for a time in 1647 when it seemed as if he might be a useful helper against the Presbyterians; but when he failed to fulfil that role adequately, the underlying distrust and dislike had resurfaced. As we have seen, at Putney it was strong enough to turn Cromwell away from co-operation with him, and at Windsor in April the suspicion that Charles had fomented the new war that was erupting caused a meeting of senior officers to commit themselves to calling him to account if they won it. That account was now to be settled. As in 1647, it is very difficult to tell how much of the unrest among the rank and file was encouraged and supported, clandestinely, by those officers, especially Ireton, in whose regiment it had surfaced so rapidly.[11] What is clear is that the hostility towards the king and those who had fought for him in the summer was strongly present among the ordinary soldiers and junior officers, and that this provided a powerful momentum to what was represented as being, and may actually have been, an initiative of theirs.

More petitions from regiments to Fairfax now called for the prosecution of the king and leading royalists, and some urged the removal of royal power from England altogether, the implementation of the programme in the original London petition, and the summoning of a general council for the army.[12] Fairfax himself (who had formally been a lord since his father had died in the spring) had ignored the petition from Ireton's troopers, but, after the next one arrived, he decided to call a council of the senior officers stationed in southern and midland England to ask their advice.[13] This council met in the medieval abbey church at St Albans on 7 November.[14] As it deliberated, a group of members of independent churches at London invited John Lilburne and John Wildman to meet them at a tavern in the city. There, according to Lilburne, they informed their guests that the army now intended to kill the king and purge or dissolve Parliament. Both sides concluded that they would frame a new *Agreement of the People*, to be finalized in discussions with representatives of the army.[15] News of this was sent to the council at St Albans, and on 16 November it agreed, allegedly unanimously, on a remonstrance to Parliament, meaning not a petition, which asked somebody to do something, but a formal rebuke to a person or body for misconduct, attached to advice for better behaviour.[16]

For the first time, the officers declared not only that Parliament was the supreme authority of the nation, but that the House of Commons could embody all that authority by itself. They then accused the MPs of having been corrupted by royalists and the House of Lords into dealing with a king who had always implacably opposed the sovereignty of the Commons and godly religion. They held that the war in the summer had proved that he was determined to overthrow any settlement that limited his powers, and that he should now be accused of responsibility of all the blood spilled in the civil conflicts since 1642. Keeping to strict legal form, they allowed for the possibility that, when tried, he might be acquitted, but added that, if he were convicted, he had to be punished. They termed him a tyrant, who could not be relied upon to keep any terms that he agreed, and they invalidated the many concessions he had now made by saying that he had never possessed the right to the powers he was conceding. They therefore demanded an end to the talks with him, his trial with those of the leading royalist offenders of the summer, and the proclamation of his two eldest sons as traitors if they did not surrender themselves. The Crown lands were to be used to pay Parliament's debts (which provided a serious prospect of satisfying the arrears due to the army).

Fundamental constitutional reforms were then demanded anew by the soldiers: this time, the replacement by a set time of the current Parliament with elected Houses of Commons, annual or biennial, based on a reformed franchise, which had supreme power over the making of law and policy. These reforms were to be embodied in an *Agreement of the People*; certain basic liberties would be enshrined in that document and would be declared forever immune to amendment or restriction by future Parliaments. The remonstrance explicitly approved the London petition of September as a good model for such a future state.[17] In this manner, the army publicly aligned itself at last with the radicals in its own ranks and their civilian allies. It is probable that what had propelled it into this dramatic and decisive action was a declaration by Parliament on the day before, that, as soon as King Charles agreed to its terms, he would be restored fully to his lands, palaces and freedom.[18]

The remonstrance was delivered to the MPs on 20 November, and came as a terrible shock to most. After long discussion they decided to postpone any response to it, and they renewed that decision after a week, by an overwhelming majority. This majority was still determined to conclude a deal with the king if possible, especially as one now seemed close, and believed vehemently that the army should not be allowed to dictate a policy in which most of the House did not believe. At the same time the MPs avoided any direct rejection of the remonstrance that might provoke the officers into violent action.[19] When it became clear that the Commons were not going to act rapidly on the army's requests, the soldiers started to take matters into their own hands. On 23 November they moved their headquarters to Windsor, from which an advance on Westminster could more easily be made, and sent soldiers to the Isle of Wight to make the king a close prisoner. Hammond was replaced as his custodian, and Charles was moved to a small Tudor fort on a gravel spit of the Hampshire coast where he could be more easily guarded.[20] Meanwhile, Lilburne arrived at Windsor with a deputation of London political and religious radicals, to meet with Ireton and other officers. He found them determined to destroy the king as their top priority, but they agreed to the speedy drafting of a new *Agreement of the People* at full speed, by a committee representing Lilburne's group, London religious independents, MPs and soldiers.[21]

On the 28th the officers who were gathered at Windsor decided to march on Westminster, to put direct pressure on the MPs to heed their remonstrance. Ireton, who was probably the author of the document, was appointed to head a committee to draft a declaration to justify this move, which was published on the following day and announced that, as Parliament had failed the army, the soldiers now had to trust to natural justice, God and the people of England (which meant armed force). The declaration directed the House of Commons to expel its 'corrupt' members, or for those loyal to the army to withdraw, whereupon the army would recognize them as a legitimate House on their own.[22] MPs who approved of the remonstrance were privately invited to join the army and settle the nation's affairs with it.[23] On the 30th Fairfax wrote to the corporation of London, informing it that his men were coming, and ordering it to send £40,000 of the unpaid taxes to pay them. When the MPs heard of this, they told the corporation to comply, but wrote to Fairfax instructing him not to march.[24] He ignored them, and the strike force was assembled from crack regiments, troops and companies, totalling several thousand horse and foot.[25] On 1 December it began to surge down the Thames valley. For the third time in one and a half years, Fairfax's army moved against the capital.

By the following day, the army had arrived, occupying various mansions, palaces and villages around Westminster, with its headquarters in

Whitehall.[26] For three days after that, the Commons debated how to react, and decided to adhere to their former policy: of doing nothing directly to provoke the soldiers while continuing to try to conclude a treaty with the king. On the morning of 5 December, after an all-night sitting, they voted by a majority of 46, in a house of 212, that, although Charles's offer was not acceptable as it stood, it was close enough to make further talks with him worthwhile.[27] The outvoted minority and the army officers now conferred and decided to stop the talks, by purging the MPs down to the minority which could be relied upon do so. On the following day, therefore, soldiers occupied the entrance to the House and prevented the entry of all whom they regarded as unreliable.[28] Later in the day, Fairfax and the council of officers informed the remaining MPs that their House had been corrupted by faction and personal interest and had forgotten the public good. They demanded the continued exclusion of those who had voted in the summer against declaring the Scottish invaders enemies, the end of all negotiations with the king, a date for the Parliament's dissolution, and provision for a series of successors to it.[29] The army had decisively changed the course of national policy once again, this time with a direct and brutal physical force that it had not hitherto needed to apply.

So where was Cromwell while all this was happening? The answer is absent, on duties in the north of England which had been brought about by unforeseen and contingent events. On finishing his campaign in Scotland and along its border in mid-October, his intention had been to march south with the regiments he had originally taken from Fairfax's army in May, and report to the headquarters at St Albans by the opening of November.[30] When his force was at Durham on 21 October, however, he received an appeal from Parliament's adherents in Yorkshire to help them settle a siege of Pontefract Castle, in the centre of their county. This was a medieval royal fortress and one of the strongest in England. It had, as said, been surprised in the summer by a local royalist uprising, and contained an unusually large and active garrison, which the Yorkshire parliamentarians could not contain. Cromwell replied that he would assist, if he were given the artillery and supplies to do so. Three days later he began his progress towards Pontefract.[31]

Cromwell's part in the siege should have been brief, because another commander had already been sent from Fairfax's army to take charge of it: none other than that stormy petrel Thomas Rainsborough, for whom this employment had been found after his expulsion from his mutinying fleet in the summer. However, soon after his arrival in the area, on 29 October, the frisky royalists in the castle raided his quarters to take him as a hostage. Rainsborough resisted fiercely and was killed in the struggle.[32] That suddenly left nobody effective in charge of the job of containing and reducing the castle. Moreover, the circumstances of Rainsborough's death demanded investigation, to establish how the royalists could have identified and reached his quarters without inside help.[33]

In early November, Oliver and his men arrived in the Pontefract area, and set about their new duties.[34] They faced a huge, many-towered castle of light golden stone, with a very dark reputation. Before the Tower of London had become the main repository for state prisoners, under the Tudors, it had been Pontefract to which they had mostly been sent, and where they tended rapidly to die under mysterious circumstances: a deposed king, Richard II, had been among those to suffer this fate. It also posed a formidable obstacle to any besiegers. The castle stood on a hill of solid rock, which meant that the walls could not be undermined, and those walls had been packed with earth inside, to a depth of up to 15 feet, which made them impervious to all but the biggest siege guns.[35] There were no siege guns available of any kind. Cromwell was back in the situation in which he had found himself at Pembroke, but with a stronger, more compact, more determined and better-supplied enemy inside the fortifications he was obliged to overcome.

Immediately, he set about forming proper siege lines around the castle, with a continuous bank and ditch, and forts, to block up the garrison completely. The work was hard as the days shortened and the weather turned more bitter, but after two weeks the defenders were securely penned in. Parliament gave support by ordering winter clothes and pay for the besiegers, and siege artillery. Mostly Cromwell himself resided in a town a few miles away and visited the works to view their progress, but this could be dangerous enough: on one occasion a cannon shot from the castle passed through a room in which he was present, providing another example in his life of the remarkable good luck which preserved and promoted it.[36] By now John Lambert was on his way back from Scotland with the detachment with which he had guarded the new Scottish government until it was secure, and it was expected that he would take over, releasing Cromwell and his own soldiers to carry on south. In mid-November the siegeworks were strong enough for some of Oliver's foot regiments to be sent ahead, and Lambert and his force arrived in the last week of November. It was then thought by those with Cromwell that he would stay a little longer to oversee the disbanding of the ill-disciplined local soldiers, and after that rejoin the main army at last.[37]

While all this happened, of course, the momentous events were unfolding in the south, and the available evidence leaves Oliver's part in them obscure. Here the loss of his own archive, in its entirety, is especially important. It removes from historical view much of his private life, and costs us one of the prime sources for his political career as well; although it is also true that at pivotal political moments he and his allies would probably have taken care to keep transactions verbal to promote secrecy. At least some royalists declared that the whole agitation in the army against the treaty, and the king, had been clandestinely fomented by Cromwell and Ireton, in concert with allies such as Hesilrige and Marten.[38] It may well be that they played a part in encouraging the unrest, but the accusation that they did so may also have been another manifestation of the contemporary conviction that everything that went wrong in political life had to be due to the machinations of a few bad men. Occasionally a trace is detectable of Cromwell's concealed interventions in events, the main one being provided by John Lilburne, when he later stated that, in November, after being approached for support by Lilburne, Cromwell had sent an agent to the leaders of London independent churches. This man carried Oliver's advice to the churches to make an alliance with the political radicals like Lilburne, in order to advance the cause of fundamental reform – which, of course, was exactly what happened.[39]

In all Cromwell's behaviour at this time, there is no sign of anything except support for whatever the rest of the army leadership were doing. His own soldiers in the north were themselves among the most radical, in both religion and politics. After all, it had been some of those in garrison in his area of command who had started the military petitions against any treaty with the king. In early November, an officer wrote from Cromwell's headquarters to one in Fairfax's that God would 'break that great idol the Parliament and that old job-trot form of government of King, Lords and Commons', and that the method to achieve this would not matter.[40] More formally, on 10 November representatives of the regiments under Cromwell's command met near York and issued a declaration agreeing with the calls from other parts of the army for justice on all evildoers, including the king.[41] Cromwell's own surviving pronouncements are consistently compliant with such calls, if somewhat vague and inclined to follow rather than lead events. When Lilburne contacted him at the siege of Pontefract, he replied that he wanted a more equal and just government, and that the civil wars could only be justified as a defence of the people.[42] On 20 November, he wrote to two MPs expressing his shock, and that of his officers, that Parliament had decided to spare the lives of the royalist leaders captured in the summer. On the same day, he informed Fairfax of the desire of his soldiers to have justice executed on all who had caused the recent wars, and forwarded a set of regimental petitions to this end, with which he heartily concurred. He and his officers duly approved the army's remonstrance to Parliament.[43]

Most celebrated of all Cromwell's pronouncements at this time are two long letters which he is said to have sent from his billet near Pontefract to Robert Hammond, the king's gaoler, his old comrade from the New Model Army, and his own relation by marriage. They were personal communications, framed in warm and intimate terms, but dealing with the serious political issue of Hammond's attitude towards his royal prisoner. The first was probably by Cromwell, though there remains some doubt over this. It warned Hammond not to be hostile to radicals or too partial to the king, to whom the writer of the letter seemed to refer as 'an accursed thing', certainly calling him somebody against whom God had witnessed. He did not find any deal with the king over the Church necessary, and thought the whole negotiation with Charles evil, preferring to wait to see what God intended instead. He hoped for union between all godly people, no matter their beliefs, and that those who did not agree with Cromwell and his party would come round to their way of thinking. If Oliver was the author, then, as usual, he was more interested in religious than in constitutional matters, but did (as said before) call on Hammond to see how what had happened in Scotland showed how a minority in a Parliament could successfully expel a majority and call a new assembly, and that this might be an example for England. The second letter was certainly by Cromwell, and written in reply to one from Hammond which might have been the latter's answer to the first. This answer had expressed Hammond's alarm at the suggestion of a purge of Parliament and his reluctance to remove traditional forms of government. Cromwell held that extraordinary actions were justified by the public good and that God had always favoured 'the saints' during the decade's troubles. He recognized that he himself and others might have preferred the army to hold off from opposing the treaty with the king until it was actually made, but still called that treaty 'this ruining hypocritical agreement'. He closed by saying that God had witnessed against the king, and that active resistance to the currently constituted powers in the land was just and honest.[44] Although his language was careful and somewhat veiled, there is no mistaking the drift of his message.[45]

It is true that for a first-rank general and politician, Cromwell was rather passive during these developments, but he had always tended to be less forward, and interested, in constitutional issues than in that of liberty of conscience. Nonetheless, he did declare personal opinions, unlike, for example, Fairfax who functioned formally and passively as the figurehead and mouthpiece of his army. At the time, conspiracy theories were formulated to account for Cromwell's long stay in the north of England while the crisis burgeoned in the south. One of the radical newspapers accused the leaders of Parliament of keeping him there to stop him from opposing the treaty with Charles.[46] Conversely, a royalist journalist accused Oliver himself of lingering in the north to evade responsibility for events, while using Ireton as his tool to bring them about.[47]

A second proposition, in the more moderate form that Cromwell deliberately stayed out of the way because of caution or indecision, has had a much longer life. There is, however, no good evidence for it.[48] The military problems that he encountered at Pontefract were serious enough to warrant both his appointment to deal with them and his expectation that his reputation would be marred unless he did so effectively. He could not leave the task until Lambert arrived to relieve him, which was not until late November. Conversely, until then there was no political crisis to need his attention and presence. Before mid-November there was every chance that the talks between king and Parliament would end without a deal, leaving Charles potentially at least to face justice. Even after the army presented its remonstrance, difficulties would have been averted if Parliament had accepted it and changed policy accordingly. Only when it became obvious that the MPs were disregarding the remonstrance did the army decide to take direct action, and so precipitated a full-blown political and constitutional drama. It was at this moment, on 28 November, that Fairfax recalled Cromwell urgently from Yorkshire to play his part.[49]

Oliver had already decided to do so, seemingly as soon as Lambert arrived, and fixed as his date of departure the one on which Fairfax wrote to summon him, taking the remaining regiments that he had led out of Scotland, and leaving Lambert with his men to complete the siege of Pontefract Castle.[50] He moved at what was clearly the maximum speed, given the short and shortening daylight hours, the winter weather and the depth of mud or ice upon the roads. On the evening of 1 December he reached Nottingham, and a few days later was at Dunstable on the Chiltern chalk hills. There he left most of his soldiers to follow, and hurried on with a small guard of troopers to Whitehall, arriving on the evening of the 6th, after the Commons had been purged. He was received with great rejoicing at the army's headquarters there.[51] Edmund Ludlow later remembered that Oliver remarked that he had not known of the plan for the purge but that he approved of it and would support it. It was completely true that he had not known of it, because it was formed in a hurry on the previous day, when he was nowhere near Westminster. Ludlow, however, seems to have recorded the comment as a further example (among many that he provided) of Cromwell's political slipperiness, in going along with a policy while registering his lack of personal responsibility for it.[52]

REGICIDE

Cromwell had now plunged back into the centre of political events, and it is a mark of how central he was that he was given a bedroom in the palace of Whitehall, the new military headquarters, even though his own home and family were in the next street. On the morning after his return he made his re-entry into the much depleted House of Commons, accompanied by a current ally, the famously radical MP Henry Marten. Marten promptly proposed a formal vote of thanks to Oliver for his military services in summer and autumn, and this was heartily provided.[53] The purge was still in progress, more members being excluded by the army that morning and over the following six days. Well over a hundred of the Commons were removed forcibly in all, and well over a hundred more absented themselves in protest.[54] Some of the Lords stayed away voluntarily from their own House, leaving a bare quorum to keep its affairs going; the nation's executive body, the Committee of Both Houses, effectively ceased to meet, and Cromwell did not attend it.[55] By 13 December the reduced House of Commons had pulled itself together, formally rejected the treaty with the king and repealed the measures that had been agreed to release the royalist leaders. It ordered that Charles be kept a close prisoner by the army. He was now brought up from Hampshire to Windsor Castle. Once he was there, on the 23rd, the Commons set up a committee to prepare his trial, according to the army's wish. Five days later this committee had produced a measure to launch the proceedings, which was sent to the Lords on the first day of 1649, with a declaration that it had been treason for the king to make war on his people (which set him up for the death penalty). The Lords unanimously refused to pass either, whereupon on 4 January the Commons agreed equally unanimously to declare that under God the 'people' were the origin of all power in the nation, and that as their elected representatives the Commons could fully embody it, and act alone. Two days later, they accordingly passed the order for the king's trial, and on the 18th decided by seven votes in a House of forty-three not to seek the Lords' concurrence in their actions.[56]

Meanwhile, the General Council of army officers, mostly representing lower ranks like captains, continued to meet in the palace of Whitehall and devoted itself to two tasks. One was to prepare for the trials of the king and his supporters, ordering that the king be brought up to Windsor and establishing a committee of its own to decide how to stage the proceedings, a week before the Commons set up theirs. The other was to agree on a future constitution for the nation. Both were under way by 14 December, and the debates over a settlement lasted until 15 January. The basis was a new *Agreement of the People* drafted by the joint committee of radical civilians, soldiers and MPs set up in November. John Lilburne had expected that the officers would simply accept this, and was surprised and angered when they proceeded to discuss and revise it in detail.

The result declared that the current Parliament would dissolve at the end of April, to be replaced by biennial successors consisting of 400 members each, elected according to a reformed distribution of seats. The right to elect those members would be granted only to male householders and payers of local rates, aged over twenty-one, who accepted the whole new constitution and – for the first seven years of the new arrangements

– had not been royalists: effectively this restricted the franchise to a minority of the adult male population. Members of the first two Parliaments had to be loyal supporters of the parliamentarian cause. Each new Parliament had to appoint a new executive council to run the nation, and none would have the power to destroy property rights or force people to attend the national Church or persecute those whose views differed from that Church's, unless they were either Roman Catholics or those who, like the king, wanted the old Anglican religion of bishops and traditional liturgy.

Despite its libertarian rhetoric, the agreement was a blatantly partisan blueprint, confining power to those who either held the political and religious views of the officers or came to accept them. It was, however, not issued immediately and directly, but presented to Parliament, on 20 January, in the form of a petition, for consideration. The officers explicitly invited the Commons to accept or reject it as they pleased, or to approve parts of it. The MPs ordered it to be printed, thanked the army for its services, and promised to consider the document at some unspecified future time. That gently and effectively shelved it.[57]

In the same period, the army continued to deal with the City of London, and the loss of patience with Parliament displayed by the military was accompanied by an explosion of force towards the citizens. On 8 December Fairfax sent his men into the city to ransack houses and the halls of the trade companies, taking around £30,000 back to Whitehall. He offered to return the money if all the arrears of tax were paid within two weeks – which they were not. As part of the preparations for the trial of the king, the soldiers went back on 4 January to remove from the streets the chains that were kept there as precaution against attack, to be tied across to prevent cavalry from charging down the thoroughfares. In case of disorder, the army's horsemen were now free to cut down protestors.[58]

So where was Cromwell in all this? As part of his general lack of interest in constitutional matters, he did not attend the debates of the General Council over the new *Agreement of the People*, save for two days, on one of which it appears that he did not speak. As at Putney, it was Ireton who was fully engaged in the arguments.[59] The two clashed directly on 6 January, the other date on which Oliver was present, over the time by which the current Parliament was to be dissolved. Cromwell wanted that to be left to the MPs themselves to choose, as a courtesy, while Ireton argued that they could not be trusted to do the job; it was Ireton who carried the council with him.[60] This is the one time known when the two men disagreed in public. Oliver was more active in the preparations for the king's trial. It was he and Ireton who signed the orders for the reception and imprisonment of Charles at Windsor Castle.[61] Oliver also made a well-recorded visit to the castle himself in mid-December to talk to the duke of Hamilton, who was another captive in the fortress. He hoped to induce the duke to provide evidence that would help convict Charles and the English royalist leaders, the inference being that co-operation would save Hamilton's life. Hamilton was, however, too honourable to comply.[62] Finally, Cromwell was clearly active in Parliament, being appointed once again to committees. He was, for some unknown reason, not put onto the committee tasked with preparing the trial of the king and the royalist leaders, though he was on those named to prepare and defend the declaration of the sole sovereignty of the Commons on 4 January.[63]

Cromwell was also clearly busy with one of his favourite activities: that of political networking and attempted bridge-building. He was one of a deputation of top army officers, including Fairfax and Ireton, who visited Parliament's chief naval commander, the earl of Warwick, when he returned to London in December after seeing off the threat from the warships that had revolted against Rainsborough's leadership. The intention was to persuade Warwick to comply with the army's action against Parliament and to get him to induce his captains to do the same; he agreed to both.[64] Cromwell also tried to draw more MPs into working with him and the army to settle the nation, especially concentrating on two respected legal experts in the Commons, Sir Thomas Widdrington and Bulstrode Whitelocke. On 19 January, Whitelocke visited him in his room at

Whitehall, where Cromwell lay in one of the palace's 'rich beds'. That conversation resulted in a meeting two days later of the two of them with Widdrington and the Speaker of the Commons, which ended in the two lawyers being asked to draw up principles for a future government. Having done so, Widdrington and Bulstrode talked them over with other MPs, but all came to nothing on the 26th, when the two men decided to bolt from London rather than be implicated in the king's trial.[65] Lastly, there is a reasonable amount of testimony that, in early January, Cromwell, together with Ireton and the famous army preacher Hugh Peter, visited or summoned London presbyterian ministers to induce them to accept the current political developments, or, if they could not do so, at least not to denounce those developments publicly.[66]

This much seems relatively clear, but beyond lies a morass of rumour, assertion and speculation which any historian enters at risk. There is a dearth of direct testimony, and especially of contemporary evidence, for the opinions and discussions of those at the centre of political events, including Oliver himself. The closest to good material of this sort are the minutes taken of discussions in the General Council of army officers, but these are incomplete. In addition we have a collection of reports made by enemies of those now in power, namely royalists and Presbyterians, which are of dubious or simply unknown accuracy.[67] Moreover, they are often contradictory. The royalist press continued in general to represent Cromwell as the malign and dominant figure conceiving and directing everything.[68] On the other hand, there was a pronounced tendency among royalists and Presbyterians to credit him with doubts about the wisdom of putting the king on trial, and with either lukewarm support for it or actual opposition to it.[69] Sometimes the accounts of this are very specific, but rest on a single uncorroborated source. Thus, a royalist newspaper stated that on 25 December the General Council debated putting the king on trial, that Cromwell argued that Charles would be more useful as a prisoner, but that Ireton and Peter carried the day against him.[70] A rumour among royalists held that, a few days earlier, Ireton had similarly defeated Cromwell in the General Council by getting it to resolve to try the king before his leading supporters went to their trials.[71] Both a royalist agent and a Presbyterian MP reported that, when the Commons discussed the king's trial, Cromwell stood up and said that hitherto it would have been considered treason to do this. He added that nonetheless it did seem to be what God clearly wanted, though he would not himself direct the House one way or the other.[72] This does sound like Oliver's normally cautious way of proceeding in politics, and the emphasis on divine will is also characteristic, as is his evasion of personal responsibility for a key decision. Neither informant, however, was in the House at that time, and it is not known how good and how independent their sources were.

Whatever precisely he was doing around the capital in the short cold days and long dark evenings of midwinter, Cromwell emerges clearly into the historical spotlight again on 8 January, with the opening of that great political drama, the trial of King Charles. It was on that morning, in the Painted Chamber of the palace of Westminster, that he gathered with those of the men commissioned by the MPs to judge their monarch who had dared to turn up. The chamber concerned had been used by medieval rulers for receptions; it was a long narrow one parallel to the House of Commons, and had become employed for conferences between representatives of the two Houses. It had a ceiling of wooden planks decorated with bosses, and walls that since the Reformation had been whitewashed to conceal the medieval religious paintings which had given the room its name. It contained at least one table, and chairs, for the transaction of business. Of a total of 135 commissioners named to be the king's judges, 58 appeared, including Ireton, Whalley, Harrison, Ludlow and Marten. Another who turned up was Fairfax, who then failed to return for the rest of the trial, so distancing himself from the proceedings. He was never rebuked or questioned by anybody in or out of his army for doing so, and retained his post as general without any difficulty, so it was open to Cromwell to do the same. Instead, Oliver became one of the five most faithful attendees, throughout the whole process, and at the next two meetings in the chamber, he was recorded at the head of the list of those present on the first occasion, and first after the president on the second. Those there on the 8th agreed to order the proclamation of the trial, on the following day.[73] The commissioners met four more times in the chamber before the trial opened, to agree on procedure and to appoint the president, who proved to be John Bradshaw, an experienced lawyer from Cheshire. Cromwell was made one of a committee to select the place for the hearing, which was set to be almost next door, in Westminster Hall.

On 20 January fifty-six commissioners met in another room of the palace, the Exchequer Chamber, from where they filed into the hall, following 120 gentlemen armed with short spears known as partisans, used for crowd control. The mace of the House of Commons and a ceremonial sword were also carried in front, as symbols of parliamentary authority. Around them opened one of the most impressive buildings to survive from medieval England, with an enormous hammerbeam oak ceiling and polished flagged floor. Bradshaw seated himself in a chair upholstered with crimson velvet, an assistant on either side and two clerks sitting before him at a table covered with a richly embroidered Turkish carpet. Cromwell took his place with the other judges on seats and benches hung with scarlet cloth, on either side of the president. The public were admitted, in great crowds, to an enclosure on the right side of the hall, fenced in by both a wooden wall and railings, and they also poured into wooden galleries above. A company of red-coated musketeers from the army occupied an enclosure on the left side to control that public, and another strong guard brought in the diminutive figure of the king, garbed in black, a large hat on his head and a silver-tipped cane in his hand. He was put into a chair covered in more crimson velvet, in the centre of the hall.

Bradshaw announced the opening of proceedings, and the lawyer acting for the state declared that Charles had been entrusted with limited power over his people, framed by the law and the public good, but had sought tyrannical rule instead, for which reason he had waged war on

Parliament twice, the second time in 1648. He was furthermore charged with attempting to do so still, through Ormond's efforts to form a royalist coalition in Ireland. To the evident amazement of the court, the king responded not by denying the charge but by challenging the authority of the proceedings themselves, as they were instituted not by a proper Parliament, consisting of king, Lords and Commons, but by a minority of the Commons. That stymied any further progress for the first day. On the 23rd, Cromwell and the other judges met in the Painted Chamber again and decided that, if the king did not recognize the court, it should proceed to judge him anyway. That afternoon the public hearing was resumed, and Charles was informed of this decision. He replied that, by denouncing the legitimacy of the tribunal, he stood for traditional liberties against arbitrary power, and that he had fought the Civil War to defend those liberties. He added the point that his judges claimed to act in the name of the people without having consulted them, and that he spoke now for the freedoms of his subjects and the privileges of both Houses of Parliament. For this, he was pronounced to be in contempt of court.

The judges decided to give the king one more chance, whereupon he reaffirmed his position in the hall that same afternoon. They then went back to the Painted Chamber, where they decided to devote the next two days to summoning and hearing the witnesses they had intended to deploy against the king in open court. These duly appeared in the chamber, and gave evidence for the undoubted fact that the king had commanded his army in person during the main Civil War, and so could be deemed to have waged it against Parliament in person. On the 26th the judges present, numbering sixty-two, agreed unanimously to sentence Charles to death.

On the afternoon of the 27th, the public proceedings were resumed, and the king was informed that the sentence would now be pronounced on him. He asked that he might be allowed to address the court beforehand, whereupon the judges withdrew for half an hour into another of the palace's main rooms, the Court of Wards. There they decided to deny this request. They returned to the hall to hear the death penalty pronounced on

Charles, by Bradshaw, who had donned a scarlet gown as a symbol of the shedding of blood. The king tried to speak at this, but was led away by his guards. On the 28th the judges fasted and prayed all day in the royal chapel of Whitehall. They met again in the Painted Chamber on the next day, at which point they decided to execute Charles in the open street in front of the fine stone banqueting house of the palace of Whitehall. The warrant for this was drawn up, Cromwell signing third, after only Bradshaw and the single peer present, men who could claim precedence from office and rank. On the following day, the judges assembled for a last time in the same room, when they decided that the scaffold was to be covered in black cloth. The warrant was sent, and the king beheaded later that day.

During all these events, Cromwell is in plain view of history, sitting in the hall and chamber or moving between them or other rooms of the palace. But in another sense he is invisible, subsumed into the mass of the king's judges. Nor is it possible to read his thoughts as he watched the courtroom drama unfold. Did he do so with an implacable hatred for Charles, whom he now regarded as a perfidious and intractable individual, cursed by God? Did he instead act with a cold and calculating pragmatism, following the demands of the soldiers on whose loyalty he depended for his career, and unrestrained by the scruples that made Fairfax hold back? Did he even feel a sadness and remorse that it had not been possible, after all, to save the monarch and as much as possible of the traditional constitution within a settlement that would have secured the aims for which he had fought the Civil War?[74] All possibilities are credible, and the only seemingly sure conclusion to be proposed here is that, ever since his volte-face at Putney, Cromwell had set his face firmly against negotiation with Charles – according to all the solid evidence that we possess – and that his presence at the trial was the logical culmination of that record.

If we are uncertain of Oliver's thoughts with respect to great matters, the same is the case with regard to particular incidents. When Bradshaw pronounced the sentence upon the king, in the name of the people of England, a masked woman in the gallery called out that the great majority of the people were against it, and that Cromwell was a traitor. She escaped before she could be apprehended, and we would love to know whether Oliver thought, as many people did at the time, from her build and voice, that she was Fairfax's wife.[75] After the Restoration, a set of anecdotes were reported concerning his conduct during the trial. By that period it was generally assumed that he was the mastermind who conceived and directed the whole proceedings, which is clearly not the case, and that may well have coloured people's memories.[76] Nevertheless, some recollections are likely to have been true. Two witnesses, for example, testified that, when Charles asked to speak after hearing that he was about to be sentenced, one of the judges had proposed and obtained the adjournment to discuss the matter. They agreed that Cromwell had first told this man to be quiet when he began his proposal and then berated him in the Court of Wards as a troublemaker. One witness said that, as part of this exchange, Cromwell termed the king 'the hardest hearted man upon the earth', and accused his fellow judge of trying to stir up trouble in the army. As a result, nobody else supported Charles's request.[77]

Famously, after the Restoration one of the parliamentarians who had been commissioned as a judge of the king recalled that he had joined the gathering in the Painted Chamber on 8 January and had argued that both the proposed court and the proposed trial were illegal. Cromwell then replied of Charles that 'We will cut off his head with the crown on it.'[78] This line, which has rung down the centuries, is the more likely to be true in that it was not actually an answer to the point made, and nor is its meaning transparent. It could have signified that the king would be condemned to death directly rather than deposed, or that his fate would be decided in open and public court. Another eye-witness, an MP present in the House of Commons at the time, recollected that Cromwell came into it to solicit signatures for the king's death warrant. A former servant of Henry Marten's remembered how Oliver had come into the Painted Chamber to seek Marten on the day that the warrant was drawn up, and that he had seen both men playfully inking each other's faces with their pens. The image is so bizarre and incidental that it is unlikely to have been invented, and it fits Oliver's taste for rough horseplay (illustrated by his throwing of a cushion at Ludlow). A former colonel in the army testified to an unseemly wrangle in the room at Whitehall occupied by Harrison and Ireton, into which were crowded, on the morning of the fateful 30 January, both of those men with Cromwell and three colonels, including the deponent. Oliver ordered the latter to write and sign the actual order to carry out the execution; when he refused, angry words were exchanged. Eventually Oliver wrote out the order himself, and got one of the other colonels to sign it. Another former officer, present on the occasion, did not deny that this had occurred, although he vehemently opposed the account given of his own part in it. That man, the commander of the guard that watched the king, testified that he received his orders each morning from Cromwell and Ireton, and not Fairfax.[79]

There are a few other vivid snapshots of Oliver in the king's last days. On the evening of 28 January, a Dutch embassy which had come to England to plead for Charles's life (at the behest of his daughter Mary and her husband, the prince of Orange and first citizen of the Dutch republic) found Cromwell with other leaders of the army at Fairfax's house. The Dutch asked for a stay of execution until they had addressed Parliament, but each officer gave a different answer.[80] None of the king's judges attended his death, following the precedent whereby neither royal judges nor the monarchs whom they served were present at the execution of the traitors that they had condemned. As the axe fell, Cromwell was with Fairfax and other chief officers, in the apartment occupied by Harrison and Ireton which looked inward into the palace's private garden. They passed the time there in prayer and conversation. Fairfax later emerged into the long gallery of the palace, and ran into a royal servant and a bishop who had attended their now dead master on the scaffold. He asked how the king was, and seemed startled to learn that the sentence had been carried out. Further down the gallery they met Cromwell, who clearly knew perfectly well what had happened and told them to await instructions for Charles's burial.[81]

With Fairfax unwilling to participate in the trial, Oliver was the most senior general prepared to do so. All the available evidence homes in on the conclusion that, towards the end, he pursued the king's death with the ruthless determination with which he closed in on a military enemy, or indeed – as he had done since before the wars began – on a political opponent whom he deemed to be beyond conversion.

It is just possible, in theory, that the king's trial was itself not originally intended to end in execution, and that Charles's intransigence, in refusing to recognize the legitimacy of the court (with considerable political and constitutional right on his side), left his captors without other options. Against such an idea can be counted not only the complete absence of any solid evidence for it, but also a body of testimony that suggests that regicide was always the anticipated outcome. The very act of the House of Commons which ordered the trial began by declaring, as fact, that the king had formed a wicked design to introduce a tyrannical government, and had launched the Civil War to do so. It went on to say that he would now be called to account for this treasonable offence (and treason incurred the death penalty), as former leniency towards him had proved useless.

There was no suggestion in any of this that his guilt was in doubt.[82] When Bradshaw pronounced sentence on Charles, he declared that the witnesses called had made that guilt clear. These were the witnesses to the king's actions in personally leading his army, who were ready to be heard as soon as Charles entered a plea of not guilty: the crucial question of proving his *intention* in going to war was never addressed by the court, as the purged Commons had already stated it to be self-evident.[83] As the trial opened, the main newspaper that supported the army's cause declared that 'the death of the wicked is safety to the righteous'.[84] A letter from a supporter of the trial written shortly before it began stated that the king and the captured royalist leaders were expected to die.[85] A gentleman who talked to the leaders of the army at that time found that most of them were determined that the king had to be executed, dismissing any arguments to the contrary.[86] There is also Cromwell's own comment to the reluctant commissioner on 8 January. Just as it is hard to see how a fresh deal with Charles could have been sought after the army's remonstrance, so it is difficult to see how his death could have been prevented once his trial was ordered.

The king's violent, and unprecedented, end has traditionally been viewed in two opposing ways. One, echoing those who brought it about, has been to represent it as the outcome of his own folly and perfidy. The other, echoing the royalists, has been to see him as a martyr for the Church and monarchy that he had inherited, and which he loyally upheld to the end. The present book tends more to the latter view, with some qualifications which have been made in the text. It is also qualified by the observation that, like previous English kings who had come to be considered martyrs – the Anglo-Saxon Edmund of East Anglia and the late medieval Henry VI – Charles's own poor judgement contributed considerably to his fate. On the other hand, it must also be allowed that all three faced problems significantly greater than those encountered by most rulers of England.

In the precise context of the period between 1646 and 1648, it is worth asking what would have been likely to have occurred had Charles been less obstinate in holding out for his own minimal terms. Had he accepted those offered to him at Newcastle in 1646, then the Presbyterian majority in Parliament would have felt even more secure, and the Scots would have departed even faster. This would have made the leaders of Parliament even less inclined to deal tactfully and wisely with the New Model Army, and the mutiny of the latter in 1647 would still have happened. Had the king accepted the 'Heads of the Proposals' when first offered to him, they would have been no more acceptable to the Lords and Commons than they were when Charles actually did approve them as a basis for settlement in September 1647. That would have provoked the radicals in London and the army to propose an *Agreement of the People*, as actually happened. A more compliant king would have meant no Vote of No Addresses, and so no second civil war in 1648, but it is hard to know whether the army would have accepted a much more conservative settlement in the winter of 1647–8, of the kind that Parliament wanted, than that envisaged in the 'Heads'. Finally, if Charles had made a complete surrender to Parliament's terms in late 1648, this would still not have been acceptable to an army which had already set its face against dealing with him, and had decided to call him to account.

None of this is to suggest that the outcome of events was preordained by the political landscape. Had the leaders of Parliament dealt carefully and generously with the New Model Army in the first half of 1647, or had Hamilton and his colleagues kept their army closer together at Preston in 1648, anticipating an attack, then the history of Britain would probably have been different. Nevertheless, the story as we seem to have it makes it hard to convict the king of crass unreliability and double dealing as glibly as his executioners would have us do. There is also one factor that should invite more sympathy for him: that the people who despatched him were guilty of a double dose of hypocrisy. They accused him of seeking to introduce a royal tyranny, while themselves using armed force to coerce and purge Parliament in a way that he had never clearly intended, let alone actually done. They also spoke of acting in the name of the people, when it was as clear to contemporaries as it is in retrospect that the great majority of the inhabitants of the kingdom were opposed to their actions: indeed, the army's own remonstrance in November 1648 resentfully recognized the king's ability to win popular support. Charles's refusal to recognize the court assembled to try him was in constitutional and legal terms absolutely correct. The army's actions in the winter of 1648–9 were a blow to democracy, whether defined by the standards of its time or of ours.

COMMONWEALTH

The army's determination to remove the king had not been a mere negative act of vengeance, which wrecked the remnants of the traditional constitution in its push to get at its target. The officers had, after all, come up with a full blueprint for a new framework of government, which fused aspects of two different plans from 1647: their own 'Heads of the Proposals' and the original *Agreement of the People* proposed by the radicals. Their problem was that neither document had ever found favour with Parliament, and even the purged House of Commons had no enthusiasm for their new one. Instead, in the aftermath of the regicide, the House set about constructing what was supposed to be an interim form of government, to deal with public affairs until a permanent settlement was fully worked out. Cromwell played a full part in that. Indeed, his unique position as a leading MP, second-in-command of the army and an active member of the regicide tribunal made him in many ways the most important person in the nation.

He continued to be very active in the Commons, which now assumed the name, and full authority, of Parliament. Once more, as had been the case every time he spent extended periods in the House since he had been elected to it in November 1640, he both attended debates and was appointed to committees, most of them for the great matters that now needed consideration. These included negotiating with the Scots, excluding royalists from being returned to Parliament in by-elections, abolishing deans and chapters from the Church, surveying the value of the former Crown lands prior to selling them, and repressing criticism of the new regime in sermons or print.[87] Cromwell also continued to take his place on committees concerned with quite small issues that caught his attention, such as the regulation of elections at Norwich, and he ran errands for the House, such as carrying a merchant's petition to the Dutch ambassador.[88] All the while, the House of Commons was growing around him, as members returned who had chosen to absent themselves during the dramatic events of December and January, and so disassociated themselves from the actions taken. In at least one notable case, Cromwell was directly responsible for a return: that of his former reliable ally among the Independents, Sir Henry Vane, whom he now wooed back.[89] In the first six weeks after the king's execution, up to seventy-five MPs formally disowned the vote on 5 December to carry on negotiating with him, and resumed their seats, to be joined by thirty-one more subsequently. They therefore much exceeded the number (up to seventy-one) who had sat through December and January, but even the two groups together represented no more than a third of the House as it had existed before the purge.[90]

As an active and leading MP, Oliver played a full part in the measures enacted by the Parliament in the course of that spring to demolish the ruins of the old constitution. He was appointed to the committee charged with considering the acts to abolish the monarchy and the House of Lords.[91] The fate of the Lords was decided in early February after two days of hectic debate, in which Cromwell argued for the retention of the House in a residual capacity as an advisory body or a court of law. He always tended to use traditional forms of government if they could be made to serve his ends, and in addition probably retained a personal respect for and gratitude to Independent peers who had usually been his allies until the move against the king. He was unsuccessful, and the upper house was voted down by a majority of fifteen in an attendance of seventy-three.[92]

Even as the machinery of the old regime was dismantled, so its supporters were punished, the trial of the king being followed by those of his leading supporters captured in the war of the previous summer. They were conducted by the same mechanism, of specially appointed tribunals of reliable adherents to the new government, acting as both judges and juries. Cromwell sat on none of these, but was active in the debates that resulted when death sentences imposed on the defendants were passed to Parliament for confirmation. He had a long track record of ruthlessness towards confirmed opponents, and it seems to have operated at this time as well. A royalist commentator later alleged that he let the sentence on Hamilton be confirmed without doing anything to save him, even though the duke had surrendered to Cromwell's lieutenant Lambert on promise of his life; that he actively supported the execution of the earl of Holland, once a parliamentarian leader who had then changed sides three times before ending up a royalist; and that he also urged the death of a steadfastly royalist noble, Lord Capel, on the grounds that such an implacable enemy needed to be removed. All three were subsequently beheaded.[93] Some support is given to this portrait of severity by the fact that, when the sentence upon a fourth noble, the earl of Norwich, was debated in the House, Cromwell was one of the tellers of the votes to uphold it (unsuccessfully, as Norwich was reprieved by a single vote).[94]

The major piece of construction supplied by the newly created republic – which took the formal name of a commonwealth – in its first two months was the establishment of a new executive body. This was urgently needed to supply the day-to-day administrative direction that the new one-chamber Parliament could not, and to replace the Committee of Both Houses, defunct not only because of the disappearance of one House but because so many of its members were estranged from the new regime. The result, constituted on 14 February, was a Council of State, theoretically with forty-one members, to direct the armed forces and foreign affairs. To emphasize continuity, it was to meet in the same room in the confiscated Westminster mansion of the royalist earl of Derby as the previous two executive committees had done (though, with increasing confidence, it moved in May into the former royal palace of Whitehall).[95] Despite the key part that the army had taken in establishing the regime, Parliament was notably reluctant to appoint military men to the new council, and two of the most important and most forward in the army's political role, Ireton and Harrison, were rejected without a vote.[96] Fairfax and Cromwell, by contrast, were added without controversy, and Oliver duly became the first president of the new body and so formally the leading person in the commonwealth. He was therefore the most assiduous attendee during the first one and a half months, as well as one of the first to take his seat, and he reported regularly from the council to Parliament, and served on three of its major committees. As it met nearly every day, this was a considerable burden of work. There is no clear evidence of the personal reactions of Cromwell to all these proceedings, though it is likely that he rued the loss of Ireton to the new executive. Having established that body successfully, he stood down from the chair on 10 March, to be replaced by Bradshaw.[97]

Cromwell may well have wanted and needed to hand over the job because it was so onerous, but by that date he was also being considered as the prime candidate for a major new military command. On 17 January, as the king was preparing to stand trial, his lieutenant in Ireland, the marquis of Ormond, signed an alliance between the Roman Catholic rebels there and the royalists, who now included the Scottish soldiers in the island and defectors from Parliament's cause. This meant that suddenly most of the armed men in Ireland were available to fight for the new king, Charles II, and that having secured the remainder of the land they would be able, in theory, to stage an invasion of England. The reconquest of Ireland in Parliament's name, prepared in 1647 and then abandoned because of the renewed turbulence in England, was thereby restored as a high priority, and by early February Cromwell was already spoken of as the obvious person to lead the expedition.[98] The process by which he was chosen was launched on 2 March, when the army presented Parliament with a petition that asked, among other things, that preparations for the reconquest be commenced. It immediately ordered the Council of State to effect this. Within four days, the council had produced a plan for the 44,273 soldiers currently in pay in England and Wales. Of these, 2,500 were to be disbanded and 12,000 sent to Ireland; the existing taxes would need to be raised to £120,000 a month to support the expedition.[99] The plan was immediately accepted, but on the 13th Fairfax ramped up the pressure by replying that nothing could be done to prepare an Irish expedition until a commander was appointed for it. The following day Parliament ordered the council to nominate one; it proposed Cromwell.[100]

There was no apparent opposition to his appointment, and it is easy to believe the sour comment of a royalist: that his friends wanted him to have the honour and his enemies wanted to have him out of England.[101] He did not, however, immediately accept, moving cautiously as usual, both to head off accusations of personal ambition and to secure the best conditions for service. On 23 March he was given three days to make a definite answer. He told the General Council of army officers that he would go if Parliament wanted him to do so and if the army he was to lead was properly resourced. He then delivered a masterly set-piece speech to his fellow soldiers, telling them that 8,000 foot and 3,000 horse soldiers were needed, to attack an enemy which could number up to 30,000 and was more menacing to his and their cause than the English royalists or the Scots. He held that to deal with that enemy was to do the work of God and to protect England, and that many in the army were as fit to command as he, so that all there should be willing to go on the mission if needed. The officers agreed on the numbers Cromwell had specified and added 1,200 dragoons; they nominated a committee to decide how to choose the eight foot regiments, six horse regiments and one dragoon regiment for the service.

The committee met the following day, fasting and praying until evening, when after long debate it was decided that the units should be chosen by lot, to remove any suspicion of favouritism or victimization, as the campaign was likely to be protracted and difficult, in alien terrain.[102] On 28 March Cromwell was sufficiently satisfied to accept the post, and Parliament formally appointed him to it two days later, while proclaiming Ormond a rebel and traitor. It also accepted the army's plan to select the units to go, and sweetened their service by ordering that those chosen would get paid all their arrears for the past four years, with three months' more wages in advance. Magazines were to be established in five English ports to supply them, and a military hospital was to be set up in Dublin. The accompanying fleet of warships was to be put under Cromwell's control, as were all Parliament's soldiers already in Ireland. Hundreds of tons of food were ordered to accompany the expedition, with a full artillery train and armour for the horses.[103] On 12 April Oliver accompanied a parliamentary deputation to the corporation of London, to persuade it to lend the government £120,000 to pay for all this. He spoke last, insisting that all the money would be spent on the expedition and that the soldiers chosen would obediently go on it. The City fathers set up a committee to consider whether the loan would be sufficiently secure.[104]

Oliver's now exalted and apparently secure position had an impact on his family fortunes. In February he resumed negotiations for an advantageous marriage for his eldest surviving son, and heir, Richard, to the heiress of a Hampshire squire, Richard Major. This time they were successful, though Cromwell drove a hard bargain with Major, and the settlement was concluded in May. Richard and his bride were subsequently installed in the manor house of the village of Hursley, in rich farmland near Winchester, while Oliver's remaining son, Henry, was allowed to follow his father to Ireland.[105]

Cromwell's now accustomed mixture of generosity, wiliness and ruthlessness when dealing with people was displayed in other ways during this period. On 18 February he heard an able young minister called John Owen, who supported the independent party in the Church, preach to Parliament, urging the army to do its duty in Ireland. Two days later, Owen was visiting Fairfax at his Westminster house when Oliver arrived with many officers. On seeing Owen, he came up and introduced himself. He led the young clergyman into the garden and asked him to accompany the expedition to Ireland. When Owen refused, Cromwell harassed him unwearyingly until he agreed, even writing to the man's parish to get its inhabitants to grant him leave.[106] The lawyer MP Bulstrode Whitelocke later told an anecdote of how Cromwell and Ireton came to his house for supper in February and stayed until midnight telling stories of the marvellous providences that had proved divine favour to their army. On their return to Whitehall in the early hours, their coach was stopped by the soldiers on guard, who refused to believe in their declared identities without further proof. Ireton was annoyed, but Cromwell amused and impressed, so that he commended them and gave them money.[107]

Other accounts of this period show him in a less genial light, including another by Whitelocke, who found two surveyors operating on Oliver's behalf in the former royal forest of Windsor, with a warrant from him claiming that the traditional authority over the forest land had lapsed with the end of the monarchy. As an expert in law, Whitelocke informed them that Cromwell had no authority there, and sent them away.[108] John Hutchinson, a soldier loyal to the new regime, was invited by Cromwell to attend a parliamentary committee which was hearing complaints against the current governor of Hull. Hutchinson defended the governor, whereupon Cromwell took him aside and told him that Hutchinson himself would get the governorship if the present occupant were ousted. Hutchinson was said to have stood firm, holding the governor to be innocent, and so to have incurred Cromwell's dislike. This exchange was the more significant in that Hutchinson already believed himself to have experienced Oliver's methods of underhand dealing. When one of Cromwell's cavalry colonels took a Scottish lance through his heart south of Preston in 1648, his regiment had asked to have Hutchinson as its new commander. Cromwell, however, had served alongside the latter in the First Civil War, and Hutchinson thought that Oliver had found him too plain-speaking to want him as a subordinate. According to Hutchinson, Cromwell had first persuaded Fairfax to appoint another man as colonel, and then represented the decision to the regiment as Fairfax's, which could not be disputed.[109]

In the same period, a soldier serving in the army claimed to have carried an appeal to Parliament from his captain, who had been sacked by Fairfax for insubordination and then gaoled by the MPs when he published a complaint against this. He duly gave it to the Speaker, who went into the House and emerged with Cromwell, who ordered that the man be arrested, taken roughly to Whitehall, and then produced before the Council of State. There Oliver accused him of fomenting unrest in the army. He was eventually bailed, and visited Cromwell to protest his innocence. He was allegedly promised possible favour if he worked for peace in the army and volunteered for Ireland.[110]

LEVELLERS

Cromwell's hypersensitivity to the mood of the army was justified by dramatic events which took up the late spring and early summer. The fuse that was to lead to these was lit in late February. On the 22nd the General

Council of army officers decided to approach Parliament about the continuing shortfall in pay for their men, but also took notice of a different petition, being circulated among ordinary soldiers, for further national reform. This petition was blamed on radicals who had been expelled from the army in the previous two years. The council decided that henceforth soldiers would only be allowed to petition as individual regiments, including the officers, and only approach Parliament if Fairfax approved the text. Cromwell and Ireton were to be asked to solicit an order from the MPs against civilian agitators in the army.[111] Two important existing impressions are confirmed by this discussion. One is that the common soldiers of the army were indeed capable of taking political initiatives by themselves, without being encouraged by their officers. The other is that military and civilian radicalism were intertwined, with the meeting points mediated by individuals who had themselves been soldiers.

At any rate, the council was either too late or ignored, because four days later five cavalry troopers delivered the petition to Parliament. It asked for the legal establishment of liberty of conscience, with the abolition of tithes, which were naturally resented by those who wished to worship outside the Church. It also asked for the abolition of the excise, a tax on commodities sold in shops, which hit the poor harder than the rich, plus equality before the law and the end of imprisonment for debt, which by definition also struck at the poor. To demonstrate the collusion between military and civilian radicals, on the same date John Lilburne presented a matching petition from radicals in London, pointedly asking the MPs why they were ignoring the *Agreement of the People* presented in January. It also accused the General Council of hypocrisy by speaking of liberty while denying soldiers the right to petition Parliament, and accused the new regime of tyranny by establishing illegal courts of justice and a too-powerful Council of State. The House referred both documents to its committee for petitions, where they were ignored: a polite way of kicking both into the procedural long grass.[112] Cromwell was reported to have been among those who spoke harshly against Lilburne's.[113]

The General Council was less polite, summoning the five troopers to account for their action. On 1 March they replied with a bold letter to Fairfax, standing by a right to petition which they thought had been established by the army's revolt in 1647. They went on to endorse the complaints about the new regime made in Lilburne's document, and furthermore immediately published their letter. This sealed their fate, as they were immediately court-martialled for insubordination and four of them sentenced to death. The sentence was commuted to being thrown out of the army after being forced to sit backwards on wooden horses outside the palace of Westminster, with papers proclaiming their offence on their breasts, and having their swords broken over their heads. In the event, a blacksmith weakened the sword blades to make that ritual less injurious.[114] On 2 March the General Council presented its own petition to Parliament, ignoring all political, constitutional and religious matters, and asking only that proper wages be provided for the army from a heavier property tax, that the lands of the deans and cathedral chapters be used to pay its arrears, and that Ireland be reconquered. Parliament thanked the officers warmly, and ordered the Council of State to respond immediately to the requests. It was this process that launched Cromwell into being chosen as the commander for Ireland.[115]

The army remained quiet, but the London radicals did not. In late March, one of them – probably Lilburne's long-time collaborator Richard Overton – published a pamphlet on the treatment of the four troopers, calling for their reinstatement and for the right of ordinary soldiers to petition directly, and accusing the new regime of being tyrants as great as the king and the Presbyterians. It termed the General Council a tool of Cromwell, Ireton and Harrison.[116] A few days later, a yet more serious challenge appeared from the same group, accusing the purged Parliament of oppressing the nation and the General Council of doing the same to the army, both for their own power. It called on the soldiers to remove their corrupt leaders, and denounced the purging of Parliament, the bullying of the Londoners and the regicide.[117] This could not be ignored. On the morning of 28 March, detachments of soldiers, numbering between two and three hundred each, hauled Lilburne, Overton and two of their associates from their homes, on the orders of the Council of State. They were taken to Derby House, where they were accused by the council of having authored the denunciation of Parliament and the army. They all refused to acknowledge its authority, so were left in a neighbouring room while the councillors debated their fate. Lilburne put his ear to the door and was certain that he heard Cromwell pounding the table with his fist and calling on his colleagues to break Lilburne and his friends before they destroyed the new government: he allegedly called the London radicals 'a despicable contemptible generation of men'. As Oliver had ample reason for fury with the radicals after their renewed personal attacks on him, the story is perfectly credible. At midnight the council broke up, leaving warrants to commit the four men to the Tower of London.[118] On 11 April Parliament ordered their trial for treason.[119]

Having thus apparently crushed its radical critics in both the army and the city, the regime now attempted to win support from both bodies. In the course of April, it passed acts to raise the property tax from £60,000 to £90,000 a month, for half a year, to pay the army properly and to sell the dean and chapter lands, and it directed that £900,000 be raised from the sale of those lands and the former estates of the Crown to pay the soldiers their arrears. Many of the baptists of London, the most powerful of the religious sects which wished to worship outside the Church of England altogether, wrote to Parliament, disowning Lilburne and his friends and offering assurances of their loyalty. As these sects had formerly been one of the main sources of support for the London radical programme, this was an important development, and the petitioners were assured in turn of their freedom to worship as they chose under Parliament's protection: a notable step towards that liberty of conscience which people like Cromwell had long sought. Parliament subsequently debated the abolition of tithes, to gratify the sects still further.[120] At the same time Oliver and others made an effort to reconcile the presbyterian clergy by at last establishing a national

Church on their model, though one that could not force anybody to attend it. Cromwell moved in the House of Commons that one be settled, and that the MPs who had been purged in December be invited back into the House if they were willing to accept the new commonwealth. A set of clergymen who already accepted it were sent to woo both Presbyterian politicians and presbyterian ministers.[121] Parliament agreed in principle that a presbyterian Church settlement be indeed established, with an adequate system of payment for its clergy to take the place of tithes.[122]

On 20 April the General Council had the lots drawn to decide the army units to go to Ireland; the selection was made by a child, to rule out any lingering suspicion of manipulation.[123] The results removed only four horse and four foot regiments, and five dragoon troops, from the established army, the remainder to be provided by new-raised units, including a foot regiment for Cromwell himself. It was determined that the whole force would be placed under familiar and popular generals, and the support mechanisms for it were much superior to those prepared for previous English expeditions to Ireland. Care had thus been taken to avoid the problems which had resulted from the last attempt to launch such an expedition, in 1647. Nonetheless, even before the lots were drawn, there were already reports of discontent among horse regiments quartered in the provinces, at the imprisonment of Lilburne and his friends, and the persisting absence of adequate pay, of any sign of an end to the present Parliament, and of a general declaration of liberty of conscience.[124] Then, on the 24th, sixty troopers of Whalley's horse regiment, quartered in London, refused to march to new quarters in the countryside until they received more pay, barricading themselves into an inn. On the following day, Whalley offered them five days of wages, whereupon they demanded their arrears as well. The mutiny ended when Cromwell and Fairfax arrived with a party of foot soldiers equipped to storm the inn, threatening death and with Cromwell looking 'bloody and red'. The troopers surrendered.

Fifteen were court-martialled on the 25th; six were sentenced to die and five more to be cashiered after sitting on wooden horses in the street outside the inn, with carbine guns tied to their legs to increase the pressure of their testicles on the hard wood. Cromwell pleaded for the lives of those condemned, as well he might, as the regiment had been his own in the Civil War, and he probably knew some of them. Fairfax then pardoned all but one, a twenty-three-year-old man called Robert Lockyer who had served in the army since the beginning of the wars in 1642, but who was the leader of the mutiny and regarded as a troublemaker. He professed his guilt and repentance and begged to be spared; when that failed, he died proclaiming that he was dying for trying to rescue the people of England from slavery to the army and purged Parliament. He was shot against the wall of St Paul's Cathedral on 27 April, and two days later was accompanied to his grave on the far side of London by thousands of civilians and troopers, the latter in black, and with rosemary twigs dipped in blood draped over his coffin, as a symbol that his death should not be forgotten. Many of the huge crowd of mourners wore sea-green ribbons, which were becoming the insignia of the London radicals.[125]

On 1 May two more developments occurred. One was that Lilburne and his friends issued a new *Agreement of the People* from their prison in the Tower, which reasserted the basic points of that in 1647, while banning army officers from Parliaments (which hit at Cromwell, Ireton and others), prohibiting anybody from sitting in two successive Parliaments and calling for elected local officials and parish clergy.[126] At Salisbury the troopers of Adrian Scrope's horse regiment, which had elected new agitators from their ranks, declared that neither the freedoms of the English nor the rights of the soldiers had been secured by Parliament and the army officers. This regiment was one of those chosen to go to Ireland; it refused to do so until those freedoms and rights had been achieved. When it came to detailed complaints, however, as with the mutiny in London they turned out to be all about money: that the troopers were not being paid enough, and that those who refused to serve in Ireland were going to be discharged without receiving enough cash in hand to get them home.[127]

These two manifestoes uncorked the genie of radicalism all over southern England. In Sussex, some of Ireton's horse regiment, which had been so politically precocious in the autumn and was another selected for Ireland, mobilized and set out to join that at Salisbury. In Somerset and Bristol, most of another cavalry unit became restless as well. This was commanded by John Reynolds, a young man who had been part of Cromwell's own regiment in the Civil War and then one of the agitators who resisted Parliament's attempt to disband the army in 1647. He had raised his regiment to reinforce Fairfax in the fighting of 1648, and led it so well that it had now been added to the regular army and marked for the Irish service. Reynolds himself was detached from most of his men, with three troops of them in the south Midlands; in his absence, the remainder were inclining to mutiny. Harrison's horse regiment and Skippon's foot were reported to be restless as well.

Even more dramatically, William Thompson, the cashiered soldier who had given the officers trouble in 1647 and 1648, resurfaced and gathered a troop of mounted irregulars at the north end of Oxfordshire, near Banbury, joined by many horsemen from the local militia. On 6 May he and his men declared against Parliament and the army leadership for having broken their promises to restore the people's liberties, by instituting tyrannical government in the form of the Council of State, the courts that tried the king and his followers, and the courts martial that sentenced soldiers. They adopted the new *Agreement of the People*, promised the abolition of the property tax and tithes, and vowed to join the mutinying soldiers. The latter were themselves said by London journalists to have called for the *Agreement of the People*, in either its January version or the new one.[128]

The journalistic viewpoint is important here, because the print industry of the capital provides the best expression for what can be described as a moral panic that gripped much of the nation at this time, uniting royalists, Presbyterians and the new republicans. Back at the beginning of November 1647, the insulting and inaccurate name 'Levellers' had started to be applied to the London and army radicals, signifying people who aimed to reduce all ranks of society to a uniformity of wealth and status. The radicals concerned intended nothing of the kind, but it was a useful smear term with which to pollute their reputation among the propertied and socially respectable. It had hung around subsequently – indeed it remains today, as modern historians have found it a useful if erroneous collective term for Lilburne and his friends – but it acquired a new potency and intensity in May 1649. In April the press had been alerted to a novel kind of radical initiative, in Surrey and other parts of south-eastern England, whereby small communities of landless people, with a code of religious liberty and social justice, had occupied areas of common land and begun to cultivate them for themselves. They usually called themselves 'Diggers', but also occasionally 'true Levellers'. What happened in the journalistic milieu of the early summer of 1649 was that the Lilburne set, the Diggers, Thompson's band and the army mutineers were all mixed together under the umbrella term of 'Levellers', as an urgent and serious danger to familiar English society.[129]

These developments positioned the senior army officers, who had been destroyers of the traditional political and religious order, to function now as champions of the traditional social order, while reasserting their own control of their men, and so of their power base. Moreover, they had a strategic advantage in the concentration of soldiers around them in London and Westminster, holding down the capital and Parliament, while the rebellious units were scattered across southern and midland England. As soon as the news of the uprisings reached Whitehall, Fairfax and Cromwell decided to mobilize rapidly and crush the regiment at Salisbury, before it could link up with any that were sympathetic to it. On 9 May they mustered their own horse regiments in Hyde Park, and Cromwell exhorted them to join him in crushing the mutineers, as 'Levellers'. He praised the purged Parliament for having executed justice on the army's enemies, and promised that it would fix a date for its own dissolution. This time none of the troopers cheered, a few wore sea-green ribbons in their hats to indicate sympathy for the radicals, and one shouted that they should not obey. He was arrested, but Cromwell freed him when some of his fellows pleaded for this. After that the soldiers consented to march; they were joined by three foot regiments and moved west to Brentford on the Thames. This made around 4,000 men, easily enough to deal with the 600 at Salisbury, and one newspaper exulted that the two generals had gone to 'level the Levellers'. It remained uncertain, however, if their force would fight. Even if few held the same opinions as the mutineers – which was not clear – there was a real danger that they would be unwilling to engage and kill their own comrades, when the latter had not declared war on them.[130] It would have been some cheer to Cromwell and Fairfax that, on that same day, Reynolds and his three loyal troops skirmished with Thompson's men in Oxfordshire and turned them back from joining the mutinous soldiers.[131]

It was the seventh May in succession in which Cromwell had headed out into the English countryside to lead, fight or negotiate with soldiers, and this time he might have to do all three. He and Fairfax marched at the head of each company and troop in turn, to bolster morale and bond further with their men. They moved through the woods and heathlands of the Berkshire Barrens into the Hampshire forests. At this season the bushes of the heaths would have been full of the song of returning warblers, and the voices of nightingales would have made the evenings in particular lovely. The trees would have been wreathed in young green, of many different shades. They halted at Alton on the 11th, to take stock of the situation and to see if an understanding could be reached with the horsemen at Salisbury. That day Scrope's regiment gathered within the earthworks of the huge prehistoric fortress of Old Sarum, where they were joined by four troops of Ireton's. Together they published a response to what they had heard of Cromwell's condemnation of them in Hyde Park and his advance on them with Fairfax. It called the present political and military leaders tyrants and demanded a new General Council in which ordinary soldiers were represented in equal numbers with officers.[132] Back at Westminster, the MPs launched into a spate of responsive measures. Some were repressive, such as ordering Fairfax to suppress the mutineers as rebels and directing that Lilburne and his friends be held separately and under close guard in the Tower at their own expense. Others were conciliatory, such as discussing a date for their own dissolution and replacement by a reformed series of Parliaments.[133]

On the 12th the defiant cavalry moved north across the vast open grassland of Salisbury Plain and up into the northern chalk hills, to Marlborough, hoping to link up with Harrison's troopers. Fairfax, supported by Cromwell and the other senior officers with him, issued a condemnation of them for opening the way for a royalist rising, halting the invasion of Ireland and opposing the will of God. He offered them the customary choice handed out to rebels: a pardon if they submitted and annihilation if they did not. His force then advanced up onto the chalk as well, to Andover, where it drew up near the town. Cromwell rode to the head of each regiment to say that he would live and die with them as before, fighting the 'Levellers' as he had other enemies of the nation. Some were enthusiastic, others expressed dismay at the prospect of killing friends, but they remained obedient. Meanwhile, the mutineers replied to Fairfax's ultimatum with a fresh complaint about the demobilization payment offered to those who declined to go to Ireland, holding it to be an example of the general disempowerment of ordinary soldiers since 1647. They then moved on down from the hills northward into the woods and fields of White Horse Vale on 13 May.[134]

Fairfax and Cromwell followed them, sending a further offer to negotiate, and hurrying ahead with their cavalry. The rebellious troopers were now expecting reinforcements or representatives from six more regiments, and therefore returned Fairfax a further demand for the reinstatement of agents of common soldiers on the General Council. Some spoke with sympathy for Lockyer and the prisoners in the Tower. Joined by two troops of Harrison's horse, they were now 900 strong. On the 14th they rode towards the River Thames, west of Oxford, but found the only bridge there blocked by Reynolds and his 200 troopers. The mutineers were reluctant to start open hostilities by launching an attack, and in any case a ford was found a few miles upstream, by which they all crossed. They rode on into the evening, up onto the open limestone slope of the Cotswolds to the market town of Burford, where they halted for the night. They were worn out, thought themselves far ahead of their pursuers, and believed themselves to be engaged in talks with Fairfax, which customarily meant a suspension of military action. They were encouraged in this belief, quite sincerely, by one of Fairfax's messengers, who had elected to remain with them to negotiate further, and who seemed to be close to a deal. Accordingly, they posted no guards.

Fairfax and Cromwell, on the contrary, thought that the mutineers' last message had been a rebuff, and were determined to stop them before they grew any stronger. The two generals decided that to surprise them in their beds would offer the best chance of winning an easy victory with minimal violence, and so test the consciences and loyalties of their own men to the minimum. They pushed those men on through the early summer twilight, pounding over the Thames bridge and sweeping up Reynolds's troops from it. Turning west, they made at full speed for Burford, into which they swept from both sides at midnight. The soldiers quartered there were taken completely unawares and resistance was indeed minimal. Most of them escaped in the darkness, but scattered into the countryside without their horses or weapons. One was killed, several wounded and around four hundred herded into the church under guard. The representative sent by Fairfax who had been making a deal with them claimed to have informed the generals that the problem could have been solved without the need for the attack, whereupon Cromwell told him not to be ridiculous.[135] As news of the action at Burford spread, regimental addresses poured in to Fairfax reaffirming total obedience to the generals, especially from units which had wavered in their loyalty over the previous two weeks.[136]

The ringleaders were tried by court martial on the two days following the action, and four were condemned to death. One showed histrionic remorse and was pardoned; the others were gunned down by firing squads against the church wall while their comrades were made to watch from the roof. The survivors were then visited by Cromwell, in the sour words of one, 'making his old manner of dissembling speeches', to say that they had wanted many things of which he approved himself, but had done wrong to mutiny. He informed them that they were lucky not to have every tenth man among them executed as custom allowed. A favourite army chaplain, the independent preacher William Dell, then mounted the pulpit to berate them on their unlawful conduct. They were sent home, losing all claim to arrears of pay. The horses and personal possessions, including money, captured in the town were shared out among the victors as their reward for loyalty.

Of all the foci of resistance during the previous fortnight, only Thompson's band of irregulars now remained, and Reynolds was sent in pursuit of that with a cavalry detachment.[137] On 20 May news arrived that he had cornered his quarry in a wood near Wellingborough, in Northamptonshire, and that, abandoned by his men, Thompson had fought back resolutely and been shot dead.[138] He could be termed a genuine martyr for the radical cause, as he had openly championed popular liberties of the sort that Lilburnc and his friends had sought. On the other hand, he was so violent and unstable a character that it is hard to warm to him as a person. For their part, the Lilburne group were genuine idealists who sought a more equal, just and tolerant social, religious and political order, though they displayed a rigid attachment to principle, and blindness to political realities, which exceeded those of the king himself. The mutinying soldiers, by contrast, while expressing some informal sympathy for those ideals, had in their stated aims only been out for themselves.

By the time that Reynolds's report arrived, Cromwell, Fairfax and their men were at Oxford, where they reaped the first dividends in public acclaim for their action in suppressing the mutiny. The university had been thoroughly purged after the Civil War. It was now led by clergymen loyal to the new government and glad to lionize their guests as defenders of the nation and society against the 'Leveller' menace. Fairfax and Cromwell were accommodated in the Warden's Lodge at All Souls' College on the 17th, and the next day the university heads visited them to offer an official welcome. Cromwell replied with 'smooth words', promising that the republican regime would foster learning. On the 19th, they and their officers were feasted at Magdalen Hall, followed by a game of bowls on the college green and finally by the great event of their stay. They walked to the courtyard of fluted golden limestone buildings that contained the university schools, where Cromwell and Fairfax were given scarlet gowns and the degree of Doctor of Law, and ten of their senior commanders, including Harrison, were awarded that of Master of Arts. A sumptuous banquet in the university library followed on the next day, and they were treated to a sermon in the university church, praising the army for its achievements. On 21 May they and their men departed.[139]

Fairfax went on to Hampshire and the Isle of Wight, to deal with reported agitators in the garrisons there. Cromwell made for home and Parliament, where on the 26th he reported the events at Burford to the MPs, emphasizing the extreme danger that had been posed by the 'Leveller' threat, and the providential manner in which that had been averted. The MPs returned hearty thanks, the Speaker according Cromwell special honour by rising from his seat to do so. They then proclaimed a national day of thanksgiving, and again agreed to discuss a date for their dissolution and the form of new Parliaments.[140] The army was now docile, and Lilburne and his collaborators were left high and dry in their cells, awaiting a trial which Parliament was in no hurry to arrange. It is a measure of the passage of a long period of crisis that Oliver felt able to live in his own house next to Whitehall, and no longer in the military quarters there. The national thanksgiving was held on 7 June, and became the occasion for a public display of the security and solidarity of the commonwealth leadership. That leadership now had a tractable corporation of London, achieved by banning whole political groups from standing for election. Its current lord mayor invited the MPs currently attending Parliament, plus the chief army officers, to hear John Owen and another favoured minister preach at a City church, and then to a banquet held at the hall of the Grocers' Company.

The banquet was of course sumptuous, and Cromwell was given next pride of place at the top table after the Speaker, lord mayor, Fairfax and the commissioners of the new Great Seal of the state. The remaining MPs ate in the body of the hall, and the judges, army officers and corporation members in other rooms. Drums and trumpets provided music for each course, and several speeches were made of mutual regard and amity. At the close, the City presented Fairfax with a gold basin and ewer and Cromwell with £300 worth of silver plate, with £200 in gold coins. Their role as saviours was thus emphasized. But there were other aspects to the event that undermined its message of renewed security and unity for the realm. Strong bodies of soldiers, still stationed in London, guarded the coaches of attendees along the streets, which were also lined by the City militia. This did not prevent some of the onlookers from abusing the procession with foul language as it passed, and in Cheapside a wheel fell off Cromwell's coach, apparently because somebody had managed to pull out the pin when it halted for a moment. It was also noted that many ministers in the other parish churches did not hold the thanksgiving service, and some of those who did prayed for the new king, Charles II.[141]

It was now time to finalize the arrangements for Ireland. On 15 June Parliament accepted a recommendation from the Council of State, doubtless at Cromwell's suggestion, that Ireton be appointed his deputy in command of the expedition, as major-general of the foot soldiers. A week later it confirmed Oliver as commander in chief, with all the powers formerly granted to a royal lord lieutenant of the land.[142] It was around this time that he sat for his first full-length portrait, which was to become the most widely circulated of him and the one most commonly featured in and on modern books. It now hangs in the National Portrait Gallery. The painter was a reliable professional, Robert Walker, who shamelessly copied the portrait made by Charles I's favourite court artist, Sir Anthony van Dyck, of that king's favourite lord lieutenant of Ireland, the earl of Strafford. In the manner in which the new commonwealth adapted and refracted royal forms, therefore, the portrait deliberately situated Oliver in the tradition of viceroys of Ireland. His looks were improved as far as possible, his fine hair and eyes well represented, his colour lowered, his nose slightly slimmed down, and his figure elongated. He wore a full suit of rather antiquated black armour, carried a baton of command and was attended by a page – all features taken from the Strafford portrait. Nonetheless, the head and gaze were still clearly Cromwell's, at his commanding, intense and purposeful best.[143]

The days now romped towards his departure. On 5 July he held a feast for many of his friends, and appointed his remaining general officers.[144] Two days later, he presented several petitions to Parliament on behalf of friends and clients, and on the 9th he intervened there on behalf of a royalist cousin, Henry Cromwell, to get the latter's estate restored to him: he still, across the political divide, felt obligations towards his extended family. Around this time, too, he made spiritual preparation for his task by having three ministers pray with him, and by discussing Biblical passages that seemed relevant with his two fellow scriptural devotees in the army, Goffe and Harrison.[145] On 10 July he bade his fellow MPs farewell and returned to his house, from which he emerged at the end of the afternoon, accompanied by eighty former army officers who were to provide his bodyguard on the expedition, and many civilian attendants. The street was full of cheering well-wishers. Cromwell climbed into a coach drawn by six pale grey mares – the equipage of a great aristocrat – which drove off, followed by a chain of others carrying his entourage, to a blast of trumpets. The procession wound through Westminster in the summer evening and out into the Middlesex countryside. The new campaign had begun.[146]

5

IRELAND

AT THE WATERFRONT

After leaving Westminster, Cromwell and his entourage journeyed through the rest of the long July evening to Brentford, and then next day through the familiar farmland of the Thames valley to Reading. From there they turned up the Kennet valley, until the chalk hills closed round them again, and up white roadways into the land where smoothly folded slopes rolled around them like the hides of great green animals. Once more they were amid slow-grazing flocks of sheep, and the bright songs of skylarks and the cold mewing voices of soaring buzzards. There were also many cornfields, now ripening into yellow. The wheat and barley of that age was much taller than modern strains, so that the ears would have stood level with a person's head or shoulders. Cromwell was entertained for a night by the regional potentate, the earl of Pembroke, one of the few peers to have given active support to the new commonwealth. The reception was at the earl's local seat of Ramsbury Manor, as if Oliver were royalty on progress. From there he carried on up the Kennet, passing the enormous conical prehistoric mound of Silbury, and so westward over the chalk to dive down its scarp into the woods and pastures of the Wiltshire cheesemaking lowlands. Beyond them rose the limestone country of the southern Cotswolds, with its cottages of weathered grey masonry, and drystone walls looping around more sheep runs. On the far side, a deepening valley led down to the handsome little cream-coloured city of Bath; from there it was an easy journey down the Avon valley and out of the hills to their destination at Bristol on 14 July.[1]

Cromwell knew this city, England's second most important port, very well, because he had been among the leaders of the army that had stormed and captured it for Parliament almost four years before. He was formally welcomed by the corporation and garrison installed by the victors, and settled down to commence the final preparations for his expedition.[2] He also, of course, avidly received all the latest intelligence from the land that he was about to invade, and fitted it into the already long and complex history of relations between England and Ireland, and the different Irish factions.[3] The Tudor monarchs of England had inherited from their medieval predecessors an Ireland divided roughly equally between territory controlled by native chiefs with Gaelic names and customs (mostly in the north and west) and English settlers under their own nobility (mostly in the coastal towns and in the southern and eastern regions). By the early modern period, the latter were commonly known as the Old English and the former as the Old Irish. The Old English were traditionally loyal to the English Crown, even if most of their outlying aristocrats had to some extent adopted Gaelic ways; the Old Irish were no threat if left in peace. The whole island was technically under the overlordship of the Pope in Rome, with the English Crown ruling it as his deputy, through a government that, with its central institutions and Parliament, replicated that of England. When Henry VIII and then Elizabeth I threw off the authority of the Pope, assuming direct rule as monarchs, efforts were made to draw the whole island more closely under royal authority.

Fatefully, Elizabeth decided not to entrust that authority to either the Old Irish or the Old English, but awarded it to a succession of English deputies. These were the leaders of a large number of English adventurers, all professing the queen's Protestant faith, who crossed to Ireland during her reign to win estates and power, profiting from royal distrust of many of the existing landowners. These interlopers became known as the New

English. They gradually provoked a growing number of those existing landowners, mostly Old Irish but including major Old English nobles, to rebellion. Those risings were all eventually put down, usually at great cost to the native population, and the lands of the rebels handed over to New English successors. The task of converting the natives to Protestantism was also entrusted to those men, but they were neither interested enough in the project nor possessed sufficient resources to carry it out effectively. The Crown, likewise, was unwilling to provide sufficient funds for an evangelistic effort. The Old English and Old Irish, who were in a position to establish the new religion effectively if they adopted it, had no incentive to do so as it was associated with aggressive and self-seeking English newcomers. As a result, both groups remained overwhelmingly Roman Catholic.

This situation was maintained under the Stuarts. In 1607 the main Old Irish chiefs of Ulster, the northern province, fled to the Continent, and their former estates became the one area of the island in which ordinary Protestant English and Irish settlers arrived in large numbers and in which Irish tenants were dispossessed in equal proportion to make way for them. By 1640, an uneasy peace had been maintained in the land for almost forty years, but the situation was chronically unstable and combustible. Protestants, mostly New English, held the government offices and most parliamentary seats, while Catholics, both Old Irish and Old English, still owned most of the land and made up the overwhelming bulk of the population as a whole. Catholics enjoyed some toleration for their religion in practice, but no security for it, and little for their titles to their lands. As a result, near the end of 1641 an alliance of Old Irish and Old English Catholics staged an uprising that was intended rapidly to seize control of the island and establish a provisional government that would negotiate with Charles I to gain legal safeguards for their religion, property and political rights. This was largely a reaction to the emergence of fervently Protestant regimes in Britain – the Scottish Covenanters and the English Long Parliament (which included Cromwell) – which were especially hostile to Catholicism.

The result was that most of Ireland fell into rebel hands within a few weeks, but not Dublin itself, or a number of other ports, or some areas of the interior. Moreover, while the rebellion was intended to be a bloodless coup, it swiftly became anything but one, as the dispossessed native commoners of Ulster turned on the British settlers who had taken their lands. Between 4,000 and 8,000 Protestants (up to a quarter of the settler population) were killed, or died of exposure after eviction, within a few weeks. In other areas, Protestants retaliated by slaughtering local Catholics, adding around 5,000 to the body count.[4] The result was probably, in total, the greatest civilian massacre in the history of the British Isles. A culture of recrimination and vengeance was thereby established, right at the opening of what turned out to be a protracted civil war. Partly out of fear for their own safety, most of the Old English landowners and towns joined the rebellion, so making common cause with the Old Irish en masse for the first time in history and allowing their mutual allegiance to Catholicism to trump ethnic differences.

It did not seem initially as if the conflict would be lengthy, because the British nations responded to the uprising with a concerted effort of repression, armies being sent over by the English and Scottish governments to dispose of the rebels in the spring of 1642. What prevented such an outcome was the outbreak of the English Civil War, followed by the intervention of the Scottish government in it on Parliament's side.[5] The king's representative in Ireland was his lord lieutenant there, the marquis of Ormond, a leading Old English noble who was unusual among his people in being a Protestant. He was also utterly loyal to Charles, and a politician and diplomat of exceptional ability, respected and liked by many of the Old English rebels. On the king's orders, Ormond found himself first making a truce with the rebel Catholic confederacy, then shipping the English royal army in Ireland over to join the English royalists, and finally trying to make an alliance between the king and the Irish rebels to balance that between Parliament and the Scots. That failed because Charles and his lord lieutenant were unable to make enough concessions to Catholicism to satisfy the insurgents without alienating Protestants in all three kingdoms. The failure was partly because the terms demanded by the Catholic confederacy were driven higher by internal factional rivalries. One such division was between those who were content to gain better security for the Catholic community as it had existed on the eve of the uprising, and those who wanted to reverse some of the transfers of lands to New English owners, and of churches to Protestant use, that had taken place over the previous sixty years. This division tended to map onto the two groupings of Old English and Old Irish respectively, but not perfectly. Another tension was between Catholic clergy and laity, the former naturally tending to demand more for their faith. Yet another lay between those who regarded the Stuart monarchs as their natural leaders and those who thought of them as foreigners, heretics and usurpers, to be given at best a conditional allegiance. Militarily and politically, the rebels came to co-operate quite well, forming a provisional confederate government based at Kilkenny and operating a number of provincial armies. Negotiations with Ormond, however, highlighted their differences.

Of all of them, the commander who was most consistently supportive of an intransigent Catholic stance was the leader of the rebel army of Ulster, Owen Roe O'Neill, the dispossessed heir of the former paramount Gaelic lords of the province. He was also the confederacy's ablest general. The failure of the negotiations for an alliance with the English royalists gave him and his allies the initiative and paramountcy in Irish affairs. This development, coupled with the defeat of the king's cause in England and Wales, caused Ormond to choose loyalty to Protestantism over other factors and to hand over Dublin and its region to Parliament in 1647. Michael Jones was duly installed there to replace Ormond as the parliamentarian commander, and he proved very able. In the south-western province of Munster, with its chief city and port at Cork, Parliament had an equally effective local leader and soldier in Murrough O'Brien, Lord Inchiquin, who had deserted the king's cause some years earlier. Inchiquin was even more of an anomaly than Ormond, in being an Old Irish chief who was fiercely Protestant and who had opposed the rebellion from the start. Smaller outposts of New English Protestants gave Parliament footholds in the north of the island, and it maintained its alliance with the Scottish army still operating there. In 1647, therefore, the Presbyterian-dominated Parliament had been in a good position to launch a reconquest of Ireland, only for the revolt of the New Model Army to reconfigure English politics and destroy the whole Presbyterian programme.

These events also overturned the balance of power in Ireland, as stage by stage the army's actions undermined Parliament's position there. The army's initial revolt prevented the departure of an English expedition to retake the island. Then, in the spring of 1648, Inchiquin changed sides again, unhappy with both the policies and the personnel of the regime now in power in England. He took with him his Munster army, made up of New English settlers, and so removed the whole of that province from Parliament's control. As the soldiers in England moved against the king, most of the different parties in Ireland were appalled enough by this development, and sufficiently frightened by the prospect of an English republican government that tolerated sectaries and was hostile both to Catholics and to Protestants who wanted bishops and ceremonies, to sink their former differences. In January 1649, as mentioned, Ormond succeeded in creating a military alliance that united the Catholic confederacy, Inchiquin, the Scots in Ulster and the Protestant and Catholic Irish royalists. Only two groups stayed out: one was the Ulster Catholic army led by Owen Roe O'Neill; the other, the remaining adherents of Parliament, who were confined to a few coastal towns and their hinterlands. One of these was Londonderry, or Derry, in Ulster; the others were all in the eastern province of Leinster, comprising the three ports of Dublin, Drogheda and Dundalk, under the command of Michael Jones. These ports could provide the bridgehead for a new English army of reconquest now led by Cromwell, which would have ample resources of manpower and supplies funded by the purged and single-chambered Parliament. That body had the military muscle to force continued heavy taxation out of its subjects, and the confiscated Church lands to add further windfalls of cash, while the former Crown estates satisfied the soldiers' arrears. Action to retake Ireland was moreover urgent, as, without reinforcement, Parliament's last few holds in the land would fall to Ormond's coalition, which would then be able to launch a royalist invasion of England.

Cromwell spent almost a fortnight at Bristol, in the bustling port city hemmed in by long limestone ridges, trying to ensure that he approached his task with every possible advantage. First he demanded £100,000 from the Council of State, to cover all initial expenses. The council promptly agreed. A tenth of the sum was sent in kind from London, as wheat, biscuits and cheese shipped to feed his men, and three hundredweight of salt was despatched to Dublin to preserve meat and fish for them. By the end of July £70,000 was on his way to him in cash, with the residue promised in a few days.[6]

Most unusually, evidence has survived of Cromwell's relations with his family at this time, perhaps because the Irish expedition seemed likely to be so difficult, and protracted, that he was taking special measures to settle family affairs and maintain contact with his relations before departure. His wife followed him to Bristol; it was intended that she would accompany him to Dublin, though for some reason this never happened. On leaving London, he had sent his eldest son, Richard, to his new home and role as squire of a Hampshire village, with his equally new bride, Dorothy. With the usual hint of concern and disappointment that hung around Oliver's attitudes to this son, he asked Richard's father-in-law to counsel the youth and get him to understand business and apply himself to historical, mathematical and geographical studies, subordinating all to religious piety. He also wrote to his new daughter-in-law, urging her to seek God, so that the deity could manifest himself to her. The letter provides a further glimpse of Cromwell's own providentialism, and accompanying constant insecurity, in that he drew attention to his command of the Irish expedition as a further proof of special divine favour to Oliver himself and his supporters.[7]

In the last few days of July, he moved with his retinue to Pembrokeshire, where the great inlet of Milford Haven was to be the embarkation point for the expeditionary force. At the westernmost point of Wales, it offered the shortest crossing to Ireland for anybody coming from southern England. Cromwell retraced his route of the previous year, along the South Welsh coast through Swansea, probably making the ferry crossing of the Severn estuary above Bristol.[8] All this while, the news from Ireland was getting worse and worse. In early summer, Ormond had launched his new coalition into action, driving the single dissident Catholic group, O'Neill's army, from the centre of the island back into its power base of Ulster. There O'Neill embraced the understandable but shaky logic that his enemy's enemy had to be his friend, relieving the isolated republican outpost at Londonderry and making a truce with, and being sent supplies by, that at Dundalk. In late June, Ormond moved his army into the vicinity of Dublin but, instead of attacking that city immediately, he sent Inchiquin to mop up its outlying garrisons during July, including the two ports of Drogheda and Dundalk. Both of those soon surrendered, the defenders being outnumbered and half-hearted, and many of them joined Inchiquin, so that he returned to join Ormond for the attack on the Irish capital with a larger force than he had taken out.[9]

The effect of all this news on Cromwell's soldiers, combined with a temporary lack of pay as the money from London had not yet arrived, was demoralizing. Many chose to disband, or simply deserted, rather than go to Ireland, including almost half of Horton's horse regiment, which had so distinguished itself against the Welsh rebels in the previous year. A foot regiment being put on shipboard in Devon mutinied, and had to be forced to embark with promises of a month's pay.[10] The response of the Council of State was to hasten the money and to send units ahead to reinforce Dublin, so that by the end of July three foot regiments, a cavalry regiment and some additional horse troops had joined the garrison there. Some of these were crack soldiers: the horse regiment was Reynolds's.[11] They did the trick.

At the opening of August, Ormond forced the hand of the republican governor of Dublin, Michael Jones, by pushing forward his outposts until they prevented the citizens from using the pastures outside the walls and threatened to stop ships entering the harbour. This faced Jones with the prospect both of hunger in the city and of an end to any further relief, including from Cromwell's own expedition. Ormond, however, had blundered both by overextending his own lines and by underestimating the strength and aggression of his opponent. Jones now had an army, of 4,000 foot and 1,200 horse. It was still smaller than Ormond's, but probably not by much; moreover, it was of better overall quality and could be concentrated to strike a well-aimed blow, at an enemy spread around the west of the city. On 2 August Jones launched it, first overwhelming Ormond's advance posts and then attacking his main camp at Rathmines, taking it completely by surprise. The result was the routing of the whole royalist army, removing the threat to Dublin. Jones claimed officially that the army concerned had been 19,000 strong, and that he had killed 4,000 of it and captured 2,517 men plus its artillery train. Ormond later wrote to the king that he had lost no more than 600 killed out of fewer than 8,000 effective soldiers; he was silent on those captured, and the precision of Jones's figure lends some credence to it. Whatever the actual numbers, the marquis had lost many of his best men, and the rest were scattered and disheartened. The way was wide open for Cromwell to land, and there would now be no field army capable of facing him. The news reached him on the 12th; to him, and to all who supported his cause in England, it was a providential delivery and a divine blessing on his enterprise. The desertions and resignations of the soldiers destined for Ireland halted.[12]

While assembling his expedition, Cromwell was visited by two ambitious men who had made the crossing from Ireland. Both seem to have thus met him for the first time, and both were to play major parts in his subsequent career. One was a soldier of forty years, with a heavy build, dark complexion and large jowls, called Colonel George Monck. There was more than Monck's physique that might remind people of a bull, for he possessed a savage temper and a streak of ruthlessness. He was also equipped with a shrewd and calculating intelligence, an impressive aptitude for efficiency, and a capacity to conceal his thoughts and feelings. Born a younger son to a Devonshire squire, he had needed to make a living through the profession of arms, and after considerable experience of this on the Continent he had fought for the king in the Civil War. After the defeat of the royalist cause, he had taken service under Parliament in Ireland, and had been governor of Dundalk earlier that year. As such, he had taken two steps that between them might have ruined his career. The first was to make the truce mentioned above, with the dissident Catholic general Owen Roe O'Neill, and to send him ammunition to help him continue his fight against their common enemy, Ormond. This was understandable as a pragmatic measure in a desperate situation, but O'Neill was notorious in England, and among Irish Protestants, as the leading military supporter of the extreme wing of the Irish Catholic rebels. Moreover, his Ulstermen were regarded as the main perpetrators of the massacre of Protestant settlers in 1641. In addition to these considerations, Monck's aid to O'Neill had done nothing to save Dundalk, which he had been forced to surrender to Inchiquin soon after – as his second near-fatal action.

The unhappy ex-governor realized that he could be in serious trouble, so he hastened to Britain to plead his case, making the journey to the far end of Wales to enlist Cromwell's aid. Oliver's response, according to all commentators on the matter, was threefold. He refused to intervene directly in the matter, formally referring it entirely to the Council of State and through that to Parliament. He also, however, counselled Monck to proceed carefully when pleading his case, gave him money to assist his actions, and wrote to influential people in Westminster on his behalf. One of those letters has survived: it does not so much defend Monck as urge the recipient to hold the latter to a willingness to take full responsibility for his actions, so exonerating both Cromwell himself and the Council of State. When the colonel appeared before Parliament on 10 August he did exactly that, alleging urgent necessity. The result was a compromise formula, whereby the MPs publicly disapproved of all Monck had done at Dundalk, while expressing an understanding of his motives and refraining from any

1. Sir Thomas Farifax. This glamourized print of the New Model Army's commander captures his effectiveness as a war leader. In politics, he found himself unhappily dragged behind his soldiers.

2. Philip Skippon. The capable infantry commander of the army, who was cast aside by it as he prioritized his loyalty to Parliament above that to his men when the two fell out.

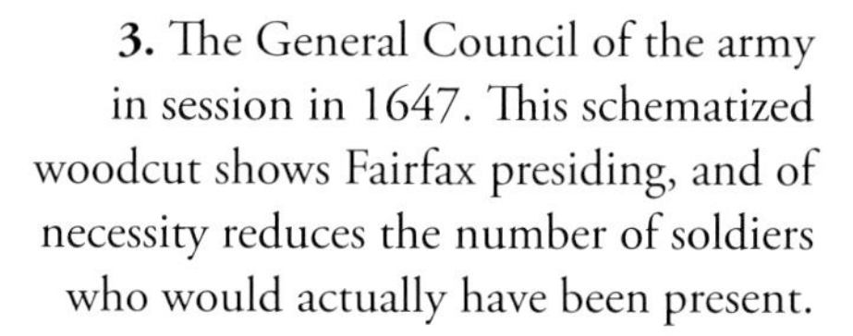

3. The General Council of the army in session in 1647. This schematized woodcut shows Fairfax presiding, and of necessity reduces the number of soldiers who would actually have been present.

4. Rowland Laugharne, the commander for Parliament in West Wales – whom shifting politics turned into a rebel against it – and Cromwell's opponent at Pembroke, in 1648.

5. John Lambert, the northern general who repeatedly proved a capable lieutenant to Cromwell in his campaigns between 1648 and 1651. This celebrated painting expresses his intelligence and dash.

6. Edward Bower's portrait of Charles I at the time of the negotiations with him in 1648 and his trial in 1649. The dignity, resilience and melancholy of the man are all there.

7. The trial of Charles I. A woodcut representation of it provides a generally accurate sense of the scene in Westminster Hall, looking towards the set of judges including Cromwell.

8. *(below)* A cartoon representing the psychological effect of the regicide, in the fall of the royal oak tree of the monarchy. As in many hostile portrayals of events at this time, it credits Cromwell – wrongly – with being the motivating personality.

9. Edmund Ludlow, the radical MP and soldier whom Cromwell repeatedly attempted to woo between 1648 and 1650. This engraving shows him later, in middle age, but his heavy and obdurate features would have been similar in his youth.

10. The most famous portrait of Cromwell, now in the National Gallery, showing him on the eve of his departure to invade Ireland. Its trappings of a conventional military hero do not camouflage the energy, determination, unpretentiousness and ruthlessness of his personality.

11. Hugh Peters, the independent clergyman who was one of Cromwell's favourite preachers and most ardent followers, on campaign and off it.

12. A prospect of Drogheda, drawn around 1680 but showing the town as it would have been in 1649. Its massive walls, formidable against medieval foes but not against cannon fire, are visible, as is the Mill Mount on which the leading defenders died.

13. Charles II, painted a couple of years after he faced Cromwell in Britain. His flamboyant charm and verve are evident, as also, perhaps, his reckless adventurousness.

14. David Lesley, the capable and patient Scottish general who held back Cromwell, and was eventually defeated by him in Scotland in 1650–1.

15. George Monck, the former royalist whom Cromwell brought into his service in 1650, with dramatically good results. This miniature captures his intelligence, coarseness and savagery.

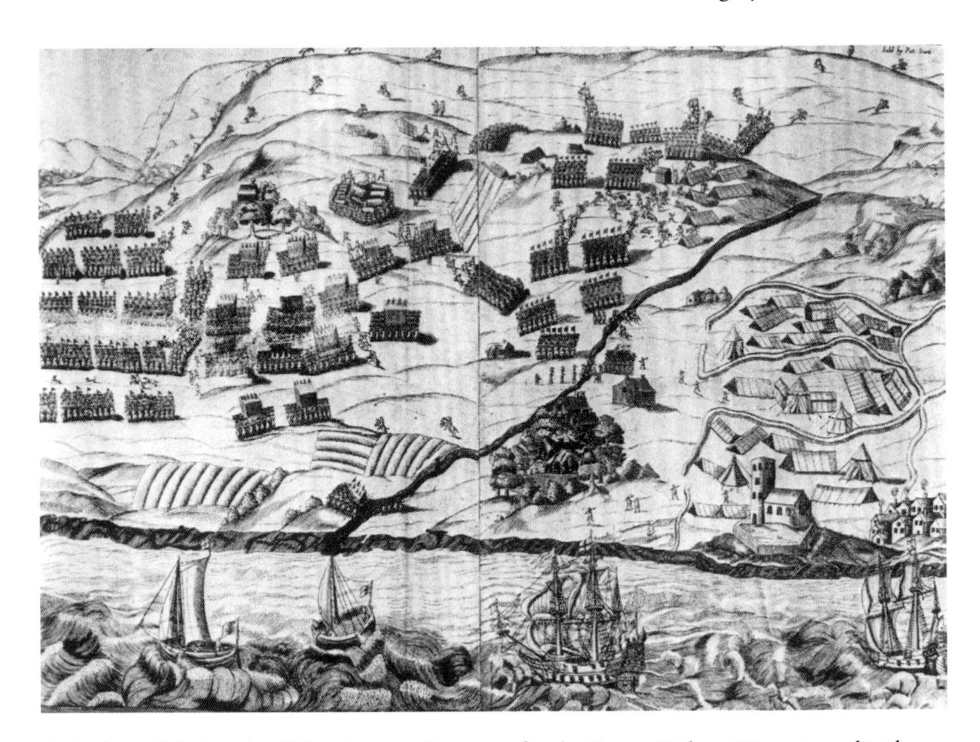

16. A plan of the battle of Dunbar, made soon after by Payne Fisher. Historians divide over how accurate a representation of the action it is, but it portrays the terrain, with the sea, town, Brocksburn ravine and the steep slope of Doon Hill, very well.

17. Cromwell at the battle of Dunbar, as imagined by a Victorian artist. The result ably sums up the stormy morning, the sodden ground and Oliver's forward role in the action.

18. Edinburgh Castle today. Not much has changed in the view since 1650, the massive fortress still occupying its volcanic plug at one end of the old city.

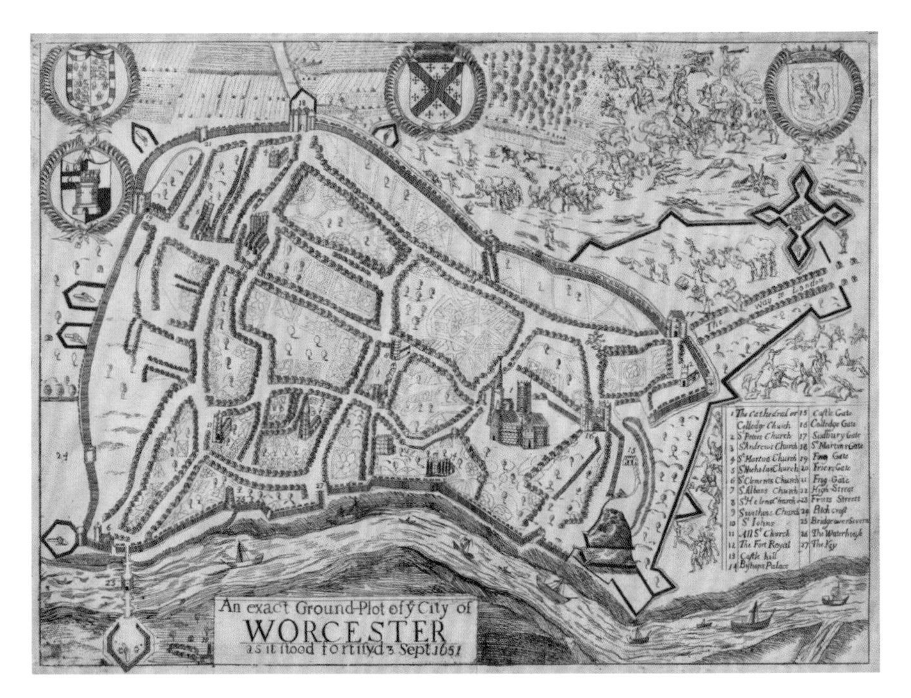

19. A plan of Worcester, showing the fortifications as they were in 1651. The vital fort outside the south-eastern gate, which King Charles's strategy rendered ineffectual, is visible to the right.

20. Cromwell's expulsion of Parliament on 20 April 1653, as imagined in a Victorian print. The soldiers would have been musketeers, not halberdiers, but the drama of the moment, with Oliver ordering the seizure of the mace, is well realized.

condemnation of him. For the time being, Monck was left unemployed; but he would not be forgotten.[13] Clearly, he had been protecting somebody by taking the blame, but whom? One obvious person is his immediate superior, Michael Jones, who was currently being so useful to the commonwealth. Monck's later chaplain and biographer, Thomas Gumble, wrote long after that Monck had told him that Jones had urged Monck to treat with O'Neill. The same writer added that Cromwell himself was rumoured to have ordered him to do so, which would explain why Oliver was so grateful to the unfortunate colonel for concealing this. Monck himself, however, seems to have said nothing to his chaplain on this matter; and so it rests.

Cromwell's second visitor was another able and ambitious younger son, but this time an aristocrat, whose father was the richest New English peer in Ireland, the earl of Cork, who had owned much of Munster. He was not yet thirty, and had a long pale face framed in streaming dark brown hair, small eyes and a wry and sardonic mouth. His name was Roger Boyle, and he had already been awarded his own Irish title as Lord Broghill. In the early 1640s he had followed his family into royalism and support for Ormond, but had defected to Parliament's side with Inchiquin in 1644, only to fall out with him and favour the English Independents. Inchiquin's subsequent repudiation of Parliament, in 1648, had left Broghill isolated; he had retired to family lands in England to review his options. His hostility both to Catholics and to Inchiquin made an alliance with the new English commonwealth a natural step. He seems to have visited Cromwell as part of that process, and on 4 August the Council of State awarded him £500 to fund a journey to Ireland to make trouble for Ormond there. Broghill did not actually commence this, however, for three months, perhaps because of distractions or perhaps – and this would have been entirely in character – because he wanted to see if Cromwell was defeated before committing himself to his cause.[14]

Through the first half of August, Oliver kept hard at the work of assembling his armada, beside the long glittering haven enclosed by the westernmost part of Wales, with its villages of English settlers and names, and small stone-walled fields of ripe corn, and cattle herded by small dogs who were the ancestors of the corgi. By the 13th he was ready to go on board ship at last. Hay, oats, wheat and his artillery train had been shipped ahead to Dublin, and now the men were embarking. He sent a last letter to Parliament, using his moral authority as the commander of a crusade to urge it once more to the work which had been his most cherished project all through the Civil Wars: the repeal of the laws that compelled godly Protestants to attend the national Church. The letter was timed to support a petition partly to the same purpose, from senior army officers. He then called a council of war on his flagship and decided to divide his force into two. He would sail at once with thirty-two ships and 4,000 men for Dublin; a second fleet, just arriving, would carry Ireton and another 4,000 to Munster to attempt a landing there. The wind being fair, he gave the order to weigh anchor and hoist canvas. The Welsh hills fell away behind them and, for the first time in his life, Cromwell faced the open sea.[15]

DUBLIN AND DROGHEDA

It was not a good crossing. Cromwell was immediately violently seasick and, to increase his misery, the wind soon dropped, becalming his fleet for a day. On the 15th, however, he saw land ahead, which resolved itself into a large bay shaped like a lobster's claw, with a long bulbous bony headland to the north and a shorter rocky one to the south, green mountains rising behind it. In the centre of the bay, the walls, castle, churches and ship masts of Dublin came into view, around the mouth of the River Liffey. Cannon fired a salute, and citizens cheered in hundreds as Oliver's soldiers marched onto the quays, and even louder when he informed them, humbly removing his hat, that God had brought him to them to restore their cause, of true religion and peace, against the barbarous and bloodthirsty Irish. He then removed to Dublin Castle, the traditional seat of royal lords lieutenant, with his huge cache of money, which was secured there.[16]

After almost a fortnight, Ireton's fleet appeared, having completely failed to find a landing place in Munster. The wind had turned contrary, and had blown the ships back and forth across the Celtic Sea before it enabled them to steer north-west to Dublin. Ten days at sea had left the horses in particular in poor shape, and so a further period was needed in which to rest them and the seasick men. Shortly after, a third fleet arrived from Milford Haven, bringing Horton's horse regiment, one of dragoons, part of an infantry unit, and 400 carthorses. There were still more soldiers due, and Cromwell pressed the Council of State to send them, but the consignments that had already arrived, joined to Michael Jones's existing force, gave him a formidable army, capable of overpowering any opposing force in Ireland.[17] A thousand men were sent off immediately to reinforce Londonderry, and debate ensued over how to use the rest. It had at first been expected that the force would be sent west to invade Munster, with its rich farmland, many ports and large Protestant settler population. Jones, whom Cromwell had tactfully and justly confirmed as his lieutenant-general, successfully argued against that, with a proposal to strike northward instead and to make regaining the important port of Drogheda the first objective. Cromwell reinforced his own godly credentials, and invited further divine approval, by issuing a proclamation against profanity and drunkenness in Dublin, among both soldiers and civilians. He also forbade his men to pillage the local civilian population, unless the people were in arms against them, or special orders were given to make exceptions, or civilians withheld the taxes intended to increase the supply of money to Cromwell's army. His huge war chest enabled him to take this approach, and to promise locals who brought in provisions to his camp and garrisons that they would be paid in cash.[18]

On the last day of August, Cromwell reviewed his full strength of men outside Dublin, and on 2 September he commenced the march on Drogheda with 8 foot regiments and 6 of horse, plus the dragoons, totalling around 10,000 soldiers.[19] In doing so, he and Ormond were adopting a complementary strategy. The marquis dared not engage his enemy's enormous army with the rags that Rathmines had left of his own. He had gathered around 6,000 men under his direct control inland from Dublin, but many of these were demoralized by his defeat and unreliable in their loyalties. On 23 August he held a council of war with his leading officers. They decided both that Drogheda would probably be Cromwell's first objective and that it should be held against him. Its surrender to Inchiquin had been partly due to the fact that its garrison at that time had been too small to defend its full circuit of walls, and so the marquis decided to pour in about half of his remaining infantry, including most of the best and most dependable soldiers. The total force comprised four foot regiments, including Ormond's own, eight horse troops and three smaller foot units. The total eventually came to around 3,000, a huge garrison for the time. It mixed together Catholics and Protestants, Old English and New English, and a number of English royalist refugees, including the governor, Sir Arthur Aston. The latter was a one-legged veteran, querulous and cantankerous, but loyal, determined and experienced in siege warfare. It was a formidable defending force, and its composition reflected the rainbow coalition of interest groups that Ormond had put together.[20]

In many ways, Drogheda now represented a model example of how the different religions and political groups in Ireland could co-operate, in harmony, reunion and forgiveness. The concentration of soldiers, however, had arrived without most of the supplies needed to sustain it, and although Ormond pumped in as many of these as he could, there remained a serious shortage both of pay for the men and of ammunition. In particular, there was no cannon shot in the town, which meant that Aston could not answer Cromwell's artillery. Ormond was, as ever, relying on his diplomatic skills to compensate for his military weakness. He had obtained the promise of reinforcements from the Catholics in the western province of Connacht, and – yet more important – was on the point of gaining O'Neill. The Ulster Catholic general had realized that the arrival of Cromwell's army changed everything, presenting him and his co-religionists with a formidable and implacable new enemy. He therefore agreed that it was time to patch up differences with Ormond, so giving the latter's coalition a complete additional army, with a formidable track record and a capable leader. He also agreed to march rapidly to the relief of Drogheda. Ormond had no need, therefore, to come to the aid of the town himself. Instead, the marquis expected that, as long as Aston could hold out for a week or two, then O'Neill would approach from the north and break the siege.[21]

Drogheda lies on the estuary of the River Boyne, which divided it into two halves connected by a bridge, the middle section of which could be drawn up. Even Cromwell's large army could not encompass both parts of the town, especially with the river cutting communications between the forces outside each, and so he would have to concentrate on the nearer, southern, half and leave most of the northern one able to receive supplies and relief. His force took two to three days to march the 23 miles through the now autumnal cornfields and pastures that spread over the small hills and valleys where County Dublin gave way to Meath. The men began to arrive before Drogheda on 3 September and established a camp near the southern wall before spreading out around it, sending 2,000 troops across the river to threaten access to the northern side of the town, and building batteries for the siege guns. Those had been loaded onto eight ships at Dublin and sent by sea to the mouth of the Boyne. They were delayed by contrary winds, but arrived after six days. Cromwell had held a council of war to decide whether to invest the town and reduce it by slow approaches or to smash a hole in it as fast as possible and take it by storm. It was decided that the latter course promised to be the more effective. So all was now up to the great guns.[22]

The walls of Drogheda (of which portions survive) were 20 feet tall, 4 feet thick at the top and 6 feet at the base, making it one of the strongest towns in medieval Ireland, then a bastion of English rule and subsequently one of Protestant resistance during the Catholic revolt of the 1640s. It had surrendered to Inchiquin in July partly because he and his men were champions of Irish Protestantism. However, there were now many Catholic soldiers, and perhaps some Catholic civilians, within the walls. The fact that modern artillery could breach those walls had not mattered before, as the town had not faced a foe with a proper siege train. Medieval walls could still be made invulnerable to cannon shot if 20 feet of soil and dung were packed behind them to absorb the impact.[23] This, however, required a huge effort of labour and expense, and the townspeople had not made it, as until now it had not seemed necessary. The walls therefore faced anything that Cromwell could throw at them without a foot of earth to stabilize them. Once more the meticulous planning which he and the Council of State had put into his expedition came into play, and he had brought to Ireland what was probably the most powerful siege train put into action anywhere in the British Isles during the 1640s.

With artillery, more than in other branches of seventeenth-century warfare, everything ultimately came down to the mathematics.[24] They were crucial in calculating the range, trajectory and elevation of shots, but were also built into the types of gun themselves. In a siege train, the three lightest pieces were the saker, firing metal balls weighing 4–7 pounds, the demi-culverin, with balls of 7–12 pounds, and the culverin, with shot weighing 12–20 pounds. The first two could knock down battlements and turrets, removing the ability of defenders to man a wall being attacked. A culverin could crack open stonework and, if that was slender enough, break it open, but not knock down a standard medieval castle or town wall. That was the job of the demi-cannon, the early modern European siege weapon par excellence, which fired balls weighing 20–40 pounds. Punching holes in medieval stonework was even easier with proper cannon, whose shot weighed 40–80 pounds. In addition there was the mortar, an anti-personnel device, consisting of a squat tub of metal that could lob explosive shells over defences onto the soldiers inside them. Ideally, these pieces were operated as a team, the sakers, demi-culverins and mortars driving off the defence while the culverins put cracks in a wall that the demi-cannon and cannon then broke open.

All the guns were, however, very hard to move. Even a saker was up to 10 feet long and could weigh 1,800 pounds, while a demi-cannon weighed up to 6,000 pounds and needed thirty to forty horses or oxen, or a hundred men, to tow it. Proper cannon were even heavier and less mobile. That was why siege trains were transported by water whenever possible. Against Drogheda, Cromwell erected two batteries, with teams of eight guns consisting of culverins and demi-cannon.[25] Constructing a battery was itself work of skilled engineering. A position had to be found that was close enough to the target to hit it hard and yet far enough away to be safe from shots or sallies from the garrison. Tall and thick wicker baskets filled with soil were then placed in front of that position to absorb enemy shot, and the ground made level and firm enough to withstand the weight and recoil of the guns. Once they began to fire, the environment became literally hellish, as those near them had to withstand the concussive impact of the blasts upon human ears, and the belches of sulphurous fumes that scorched eyes, noses and throats. It was also an appallingly dangerous environment, with the constant risk of powder kegs or gun barrels exploding. Those barrels had therefore to be painstakingly raked and mopped out before reloading; the charge, priming powder and shot all had to be applied without risk of flying sparks; and the kegs and the smouldering match on its pole had to be kept at a safe distance until the moment came for powder to be transferred to the gun and the match to be carried over and applied to the touch hole.[26]

As the batteries outside Drogheda neared completion, Ormond's plan to save the town fell apart. With one of those remarkable strokes of fortune that regularly aided Cromwell's career, Owen Roe O'Neill fell mortally ill as he started his march, and his army ground to a halt. The marquis suddenly found himself alone and unprepared. His reaction was to call on the reinforcements from Connacht to hasten, and to summon the Scottish army from Ulster. He also set about finding powder, match and musket shot for Aston, who was now running out of all of these in firing at and sallying out on the besiegers.[27] This was, however, all too late. At eight o'clock on 10 September, Cromwell summoned Drogheda to surrender. When Aston refused, the guns opened fire. Before the end of the day they had already opened two breaches in the walls, the larger beside the parish church of the southern part of the town, St Mary's. That position was probably chosen because the bulky church limited the space behind the breach in which the garrison could mass to defend it. For a time the spire provided a vantage point for snipers, but the siege guns just made it a target in turn and brought it crashing down, ruining the church. In the course of the next day, between 200 and 300 balls slammed into the walls, widening the gaps in them further. The thick base still resisted the pounding, so that it could not be levelled to the ground to let in cavalry, meaning that the foot soldiers had to go in without mounted support, using ladders in places to reach the opening. Between four and five o'clock in the afternoon the order was given to attack.[28]

The main assault took place on the big breach by St Mary's. Drums and trumpets sounded, and the red-coated infantry surged forward, representing three of the best regiments brought from England.[29] An outwork on the wall near the breach was overwhelmed and all the defenders inside killed, after which the main body of attackers climbed the wide gap in the wall. A vicious fight took place within, in which the assault force suffered heavy losses, including one of its colonels, and was repulsed. It was commented later that the ditch in front of the wall was largely filled at that point with bodies, though this, in its macabre way, made the breach easier to climb. At this moment, Cromwell himself acted, leading up two fresh regiments to reinforce and rally those who had been beaten back.[30] The new and heavier attack force went in, and Aston's men, outnumbered, tired, probably low on ammunition, and facing an apparently limitless supply of enemies, gave way. They had dug earthen defences behind the breach, but had lacked the time to make these formidable, and they could be outflanked on either side. When this occurred, the defenders broke at last, fleeing into the town behind. They were pursued so closely by the victors that, when some made the crossing into the northern half of the town, they were unable to pull up the drawbridge behind them before Cromwell's soldiers got across on their heels; and so the whole of Drogheda fell. As it did, a darkness of doubt, disputation, recrimination and rancour settled upon what happened next, together with the falling September night.[31]

MASSACRE

The actions of Cromwell and his soldiers after they entered Drogheda represent the greatest single stain on his historical reputation, and the question of how deep a stain that should be has been debated for over a hundred years. In most respects, the positions in that debate were established right at the outset, in the Victorian period. One was taken up in 1883 by an Irish Jesuit, Denis Murphy, in a work that played to the extreme nationalist and anti-British feelings of his time, and summed up his account of Cromwell's campaign as a 'history of one year's sufferings of the Irish people for their faith and country'. He declared that, at Drogheda, Cromwell had 'issued an order that the life of neither man, woman nor child was to be spared'.[32] He could not actually produce such an order, and inferred it from the subsequent atrocities in the town, for which his star witness was one of the English soldiers who took it, a young man called Thomas Wood. Wood's story of what happened was reported by his younger brother Anthony, when the latter came to write his own autobiography many years later, after he had become an Oxford academic.

Thomas allegedly related that, during the storming of the town, 'three thousand at least, besides some women and children, were put to the sword'. He then went on tell how some of the garrison took refuge in the tower of the parish church of the northern half of the town, St Peter's, and continued resistance there, raining down shots and other missiles on their attackers. He recounted how his comrades had picked up children, using them as shields as they mounted the stairs into the tower. When everybody in the body of the church had been killed, the victors broke into the vaults beneath and found women hiding there. One of the best-looking and most richly dressed of these begged Wood to save her, and so he led her out of the church intending to do so. One of his comrades, however, ran his sword into her guts. Wood, seeing her dying, looted her of her money, jewels and other valuables, and flung her over 'the works' (meaning either the churchyard boundary or the town wall) to expire. Thomas Wood rose to be a major, but died of dysentery in garrison at Drogheda the following year.

Murphy also quoted the later testimony of an Irish Jesuit, who had not himself been present. This man declared that no mercy had been shown to Catholics, whatever their age or sex, and that the Jesuit residence had been pillaged. He added that on the following day the victorious soldiers had found two Catholic priests and a Jesuit, beaten one priest to death and shot the other two men in the marketplace.[33]

These are terrible stories, but it may be noted that they do not actually support Murphy's contention, that Cromwell ordered the death of every person in Drogheda. This gap between evidence and interpretation was exploited by the main early proponent of the opposite position, one of mitigation of the actions of Oliver's army. It was articulated a few years after Murphy wrote, by Samuel Rawson Gardiner himself, who had by then established himself as the leading British authority on the period. Despite his own admiration for Cromwell, he decided that Oliver was personally responsible for the slaughter of the garrison, some of them after they had surrendered, and of the Catholic clergy. He also thought that a few civilians had died, but that most had survived. His best witness here was a Protestant clergyman resident in the town, Nicholas Bernard, who described in later years how he had sheltered the mayor and about twenty other leading inhabitants in his house, and all had been spared by the soldiers. Gardiner rejected Thomas Wood's story as a probable invention, noting that nobody else had mentioned the alleged atrocities at St Peter's church, including Bernard, who preached there. He also called as evidence a later declaration by Cromwell in which he had denied that any civilians had been killed during his Irish campaign until that time.[34]

Murphy's accusation that Cromwell had ordered a general massacre of the inhabitants became part of the national memory of an independent Ireland in the twentieth century. In 1988 I was taking coffee in a hotel in Connemara and watching an audio-visual guide to the country made by the Irish tourist board. When it reached Drogheda, it spoke of it as the setting for one of the blackest days in Irish history, when Oliver Cromwell's men stormed the town and killed every man, woman and child in it. That was also taught as the truth in the Irish mass media and in the republic's schools. As such, it came to provoke Tom Reilly, a native of Drogheda, who from the 1990s launched a campaign to disprove the claim and cleanse Cromwell's reputation. His message became fixed around the argument that there was no evidence that a single unarmed civilian was deliberately killed when the town fell, all references to civilian casualties being theoretically accountable to townsmen dying while resisting the invaders or being caught in crossfire or otherwise struck by accident.[35] This is an extreme position, and as such provoked answers from some of the best Irish and British historians of the period, who emphasized instead the extraordinary scale of the bloodshed at Drogheda and the probability that a large number of unarmed civilians were victims.[36]

These disagreements conceal the fact that there is actually a large area of consensus among current experts: that most of the garrison was slaughtered, creating a body count quite exceptional for Britain and Ireland at this period, and that most of the civilian population survived. Disputes continue over relatively minor questions, which are less easily resolved: whether any of the garrison were killed after surrendering on promise of their lives, and whether any unarmed civilians were deliberately murdered. Even these issues, however, have been sufficient to create significant disagreement among professional scholars over the past few decades, and with it a variety of opinions over how far Cromwell himself should be censured or exonerated.[37]

So what more can be made of the evidence? The first answer to that question is that there is a very firm indication that Oliver and his officers immediately realized that what had happened was out of the ordinary and might well result in reputational damage. Whatever its human cost, they had achieved a mighty victory, at minimum cost in time and resources, striking a crippling blow at Ormond's own army. After similar triumphs in the past, Cromwell had dashed off letters to his superiors and friends, crying up to the full the magnitude of the achievement and its proof of divine favour. In this case, they imposed a complete news blackout, while they clearly pondered how to package the story. Until the moment when the siege guns opened up, there had been regular newsletters sent from the siege to Dublin and England. From that moment, there was a complete cessation of information lasting several days, on which newspaper editors and correspondents commented with surprise and perplexity.[38] It was broken by a letter from Hugh Peters, the independent minister who was one of Cromwell's favourite clergy, written from Dublin to Parliament on 15 September. This announced tersely a great victory in which all of the enemy had been killed, to the number of 3,552, while only 64 of his own side had fallen.[39] The precision of the figures was designed to compel belief, but at least that for the republican lives lost is suspicious. One of Cromwell's colonels who was involved in the storming of the breach said that between 120 and 150 of the attackers had been lost.[40] He might have meant dead and wounded together, but the usual ratios of the time would have produced a much larger number of wounded for sixty-four killed. The point of the contrast in Peters's figures was to echo the Old Testament trope of a godly few triumphing over an ungodly multitude, as with the forces led by Gideon or Jonathan, with divine support. Cromwell himself had repeatedly deployed this strategy previously in his career, in keeping with the habit of the age.

On the 16th, Oliver sent in his own despatch at last, to the Council of State, giving a summary of how the town had been taken, and stating that mercy had been refused to the defenders after they had refused to treat on being summoned. He added that he did not think that thirty of the defenders had survived out of three thousand, and argued that this bloodshed would save much in the future, by terrifying other garrisons into rapid surrender.[41] He clearly did not think this report to be enough, because on the next day he wrote a second time, to Parliament. The result was one of the longest letters to survive from him, and it reflected his continuing unease about what had happened at Drogheda and his according need to explain and extenuate it. He described the storming in greater detail, and added that, once his soldiers were in the town, 'being in the heat of the action', he had forbidden them to spare any 'in arms' within it, so that during the night they killed around 2,000. About a hundred of the defenders had got into the steeple of St Peter's church (as Thomas Wood had described), and more into the fortified west gate of the town and one of the strongest towers on the walls. When summoned to surrender at the mercy of the victors, they refused, whereupon Cromwell had ordered the steeple to be set on fire, and the defenders had perished in the flames. Those in the gatehouse and tower were eventually starved into surrender. The men in one were punished – because they had fired on Cromwell's forces and wounded some – by having their officers and every tenth man killed. The rest, and those in the other strongpoint, were shipped to the West Indian island of Barbados, an English colony, to work as forced labour on its plantations.

These are some of the most famous, and most discussed, documents in seventeenth-century Irish and English history, and one of the most commonly repeated parts of them is the section in the second letter in which Cromwell justified his actions. He began by stating that he was convinced that God himself had ordained the slaughter, as a punishment on 'barbarous wretches who have spilt so much innocent blood'. The meaning of this line is not wholly clear, but the most likely one is that it referred to the massacre of Protestant settlers at the opening of the Catholic rebellion in 1641.[42] If so, it was a patent injustice as the defenders of Drogheda were Protestants or Old English Catholics, and had not been implicated in the earlier slaughter. He also repeated his claim that the killing would save much more in the future, by terrifying other enemy garrisons into immediate surrender, which he pointed out was already happening. He concluded that these two motives were 'the satisfactory grounds to such actions, which otherwise cannot but work remorse and regret', the latter phrase being an admission that something terrible had happened. He called in God again as the author of the victory, and claimed that the Catholics in the garrison and town had gained the upper hand over the Protestants and had begun to oppress them. Specifically, he added that on the day before the town fell, they had expelled the Protestants from St Peter's church, to hold a mass there, and that this act sanctified and justified the fact that his soldiers had slaughtered around a thousand people who had taken refuge there. He added proudly that all the 'friars' in the town – which seems to have been his expression for any Catholic clergy – had been killed (agreeing with the testimony of Murphy's Jesuit), and that most of the bloodshed had been committed by the regiments that had stormed the breach, enraged by having lost officers in the action.[43] If Cromwell was concerned about the possible effect on public opinion, he certainly did not need to have worried about the reaction from Parliament, which proclaimed a great victory and, when formally thanking him, approved the 'execution done at Drogheda'.[44]

So what of the issues that still divide experts: the terms on which the garrison were killed and the deaths of civilians? The conventions of European warfare in this period were not codified and formally agreed, but were a set of hazily defined assumptions. It was generally believed that a garrison which refused to surrender when summoned, and was then overwhelmed by attackers, could legitimately be slaughtered, but in practice the death rate on such occasions was rarely wholesale. There was an equally widespread belief that the killing of unarmed civilians, and especially of women and children, was barbaric. It was also accepted, moreover, that if a garrison surrendered on terms, and the victors subsequently violated those, then the action was dishonourable and deserved censure, as a gentleman's word was supposed to be trustworthy.

In the context of Drogheda, most of the doubt in this matter concerns what happened at Mill Mount, a large mound in the south-eastern part of the town. It had a windmill on top, as the name suggests, and the defenders had turned it into a citadel, with ditches, ramparts and artillery, and hedges of posts with protruding spikes driven into the sides of the mound. When the defence failed at the breaches, Aston, the governor, retreated to the top of it with many of his senior officers and soldiers, to make a stand. They were subsequently persuaded to surrender by a deputation of Cromwell's soldiers. After laying down their arms, they were all killed.

What is not clear is the terms on which Aston's men surrendered. If they had done so at the mercy of their enemies, then their deaths were technically justified, although their total annihilation was most unusual. If, however, they had given up their position and weapons on promise of their lives, then the usual code of conduct had been flagrantly breached. There is no clear evidence as to which was the case, but good reason to suspect it was the latter, for three reasons. One is that none of the victors actually stated the terms made, when a surrender at mercy would have vindicated their action. The second is that Aston and his men would have been most unlikely to surrender a position of such strength, without a fight, unless they were promised an adequate recompense for doing so. The third is that commentators on the episode kept coming up with different excuses for it. Cromwell himself said that the killing had occurred because the soldiers in charge of the prisoners remembered his order that the lives of none of the garrison be spared.[45] A report from one of his soldiers was that it happened because Castle's regiment wanted revenge for the loss of their colonel, and they were further angered because Aston had replied rudely when first summoned to surrender his position on the mound.[46] An apparent eye-witness of the negotiation with Aston said simply that, after he agreed to surrender, following an initial haughty refusal, he and his chief officers were herded into the windmill, 'where they were disarmed, and afterwards all slain'.[47] The clergyman Nicholas Bernard later stated unequivocally that they had been given assurance that their lives would be spared.[48] There must remain a strong suspicion that the conventions of war were indeed violated at the Mill Mount, but the perpetrators successfully blurred what happened in their subsequent accounts.

There is some testimony that the murder of royalist officers continued during subsequent days. Two circumstantially detailed accounts of such atrocities were contained in a letter from a family friend (himself in France) to the relatives of Sir Edmund Verney, an English royalist exile who had commanded Ormond's regiment in the town. It recounted how his life was spared, but that three days later, when he was walking beside Cromwell and so thought himself safe, a man called him aside and ran him through with a sword. The same letter reported that a Lieutenant-Colonel Boyle had also survived the fall of the town, but that when he was at dinner with a hostess, some soldiers had summoned him outside, where they had shot him.[49] There is no way of verifying or disproving this evidence. It is hard to see why Cromwell would have spared Verney only to let him die later, and equally difficult to believe that he would have been killed without Cromwell's knowledge and approval. Some of the accounts of the surrender of Mill Mount seem to imply that he was among the senior officers who died with Aston there.[50] Certainly, sixteen severed heads were sent from Drogheda to Dublin to be displayed on poles as those of traitors, which must have been on Cromwell's orders. One was Aston's and another Verney's.[51] Such savage treatment was never meted out to enemy officers by Oliver at any other point in all the wars that he fought, and it is hard to see why it would have been accorded to Verney after he had been singled out for mercy during the initial period of slaughter.

How exceptional was the massacre of the garrison at Drogheda? There is no doubt about the extraordinary scale of the killing. The body count was far in excess of that reached when any other stronghold was stormed in the course of the wars in the British Isles in the 1640s and 1650s. Even in Ireland, where the fighting was exceptionally brutal, it was four times that of the nearest figure on the fall of a fortress. On the other hand, this was not because of unusual severity but because of the exceptional size of the defending force, as Ormond had put what was virtually an infantry army into Drogheda. The worst body count notched up on the taking of a town before then was when Inchiquin had gained Cashel in Munster, when fighting for Parliament in 1647. He had killed around seven hundred men, fifty of them after surrender – seemingly the whole garrison – and about fifty women.[52] The Catholic rebels could allegedly be as savage, so that when some of O'Neill's men stormed the town of Drumrusk at the end of 1648 they were reported to have 'put all, in town and castle, to the sword', and then at Boyle to have 'burnt the town, and killed all whom they met, of whatever age or sex'. The victims were fellow Catholics, of that part of the Confederacy that was coming to terms with Ormond.[53] Again, much smaller numbers of deaths were the result simply of much smaller garrisons. In terms of scale, however, the truly comparable figures to that at Drogheda were generated not by the capture of towns but by pitched battles. When he had defeated the Catholic army of Leinster at Dungan's Hill in 1647, Michael Jones systematically butchered the fleeing Irish, allegedly killing around 3,000 out of 5,000 infantry.[54] When Inchiquin likewise destroyed the Catholic army of Munster on behalf of Parliament, later that year, at Knocknanuss, he again killed most of it, refusing quarter and allegedly inflicting 4,000 deaths.[55] Cromwell had effectively treated Drogheda like a battlefield.

In doing so, he was remaining perfectly true to his nature, because he had always been a killer. From his first actions as a commander in the English Civil War, he had exulted in the pursuit and slaughter of fleeing enemies after field actions, and the death of their commanders during their flight, in a manner unusual for that conflict. At the largest battle of the war, Marston Moor, the army of which he was one of the two main field commanders had led the massacre of up to half of the royalist infantry, numbering several thousand men. This ruthless violence was linked to two other traits in his nature. One was a tendency, more marked in his earlier life before he became more self-disciplined, to lose control of his temper and lash out. Another was a propensity to demonize opponents, and to divide the world into the followers and agents of the Almighty, such as himself, and God's enemies, who were of course his own religious, political and military opponents. He was a born holy warrior, and Drogheda was a perfect killing field for him, populated by a beaten foe who represented both a cause and a religion that he detested and regarded as ungodly, and who had resisted fiercely and killed scores of his men.[56]

Drogheda, however, was not a battlefield in the conventional military sense, because it was crowded with unarmed civilians, and here the second of the continuing controversies comes into play: whether any of those were deliberately killed as the town fell. Tom Reilly's careful work on the town records confirms the long-established impression that most of the population survived, but that significant damage was done to both life and property. The council continued to meet as before, and municipal documents contain many of the same names of inhabitants as before, but also confirm that at least two prominent inhabitants, one an alderman, had been killed, that the town hall was no longer inhabitable, and that other buildings needed to be repaired.[57] Reports from Cromwell's army suggest a bloody rampage through the streets, but are unclear with respect to damage to civilians. One said that, as the soldiers spread out through the town, they 'put men to the sword' as fast as they could.[58] Another spoke of the 'undistinguishing fury of the sword'.[59] Yet another stated that Cromwell's men killed everybody they met in the streets and who 'seemed' soldiers, but spared 'many' who stayed quietly in their homes.[60] This last report in particular does carry an implication that some innocent people died, even including some in their own houses. Ormond and Inchiquin did not speak of civilian deaths in their subsequent correspondence, but they were not interested in the people of Drogheda and concentrated on the damage to their army.[61] Furthermore, when Ormond used expressions like 'bloody execution of almost all that were within' the town, it is hard to know whether he was including inhabitants.[62]

In the following winter, Cromwell issued a major public declaration in which he challenged his Irish enemies to give evidence of a single unarmed civilian killed by his forces in Ireland, without attempts being made to bring the killers to justice. He added that he would not willingly take away the life of any unarmed person save by due process of law.[63] Unhappily, no weight can be placed on this at all, because in his previous rise to power Cromwell had regularly distorted the truth in his public statements to gain advantages for himself and his cause.[64] An uncharitable reader might also note his form of words: he did not state that his forces had not killed unarmed people, but challenged his enemies to prove that they had, and he did not claim that no such people had been killed without his will.

Other evidence is equally ambiguous. On 27 September Cromwell wrote again to Parliament and sent a list (not necessarily his own) of the senior officers and the number of ordinary soldiers his men had killed in the town. Both documents were published, and much republished in newspapers, and some versions had appended to the list the chilling addition 'and many inhabitants'. Ever since the first edition of Cromwell's letters appeared in the 1840s, doubt has been cast on the authenticity of this addition, but the argument could run the other way: that it was omitted from some published versions to conceal the fact that many civilians had died. A careful examination of the publication history of the list suggests that this is, in fact, the case, and that those three loaded final words were integral to the original document.[65] However, this still provides no testimony of how the inhabitants concerned died, and how many were not armed males. It is also possible to play a plausible numbers game with the fatality lists. Peters, as said, announced 3,552 deaths, suggesting that somebody had been carefully counting corpses as they were cleared. The reports by Cromwell and his soldiers suggest that around 2,800–3,000 of the garrison died, so the difference between the two would imply a casualty rate of several hundred civilians. But it is possible that neither number is accurate and, again, even if the conclusion drawn is correct, it tells us nothing of the circumstances in which the deaths occurred.[66]

In this context, the testimony of Gardiner's star witness for civilian survival, Nicholas Bernard, can actually operate on the other side, showing how innocent civilian deaths might have occurred. There are two caveats to be considered before an examination of it begins. The first is that his memoir was published after the restoration of the monarchy, to extenuate Bernard's behaviour in having subsequently become reconciled to Cromwell's regime and accepted a post under it.[67] He therefore had every reason to portray both his royalism and his sufferings, and danger, in 1649 as greater than they were. On the other hand, he summed up the main points of his later account in a sermon to his fellow citizens at Drogheda within two years of the Cromwellian siege, when none of those considerations applied, and the points are the same, so that most of the first concern can be discounted.[68] The second caveat is that Bernard was not an ordinary inhabitant of the town but a leading Protestant one, and a clergyman, with important personal connections with members of Cromwell's army. He might be thought to have been the very sort of person who would survive. On the other hand, he was genuinely a fervent royalist at the time, and had preached encouragement to the garrison to resist the attackers. The two aspects of his situation may therefore be thought to balance each other.

What Bernard remembered was that, as the enemy soldiers burst into the streets, the mayor and about twenty other leading citizens took refuge in his house, because it was a strong one. Soldiers arrived outside, who he learned later intended to kill him; when he refused to open the door, they shot through it. A sympathetic junior officer then appeared, and saved those within by ordering the soldiers away, leaving one of his own subordinates to watch the house. Fifteen minutes later, a horse troop came up and demanded entry, whereupon Bernard assured the troopers that all within were Protestants and he was a minister. In reply, one of them shot twice through a window, killing the officer left to watch the place and wounding one of Bernard's servants. They all then broke in through another window, but left the people inside alone as they were more interested in looting the contents of the building. At that point, one of Cromwell's colonels, who had commanded a regiment in the forefront of the storm, and who knew Bernard, saved the day by coming to the house and turning out the troopers, claiming it as his own quarters.

The next day, the colonel concerned reported ruefully that Cromwell and many of his officers had rebuked him for sparing Bernard's life (a statement which, if true, completely invalidates Cromwell's protestations that he never intended harm to unarmed civilians). The minister saw that the streets and the churchyard of St Peter's were full of dead bodies, to which more kept being added. The friendly colonel saved Bernard again by using his house as a billet for wounded soldiers, until Cromwell and his retinue of officers came to it and sent the minister as a prisoner to Dublin. His life still hung in the balance for a time, and he was committed to prison in England, before eventually being released.

If all this is true, it suggests that even an unarmed, non-resisting and Protestant inhabitant like Bernard had survived only because of remarkable luck (or, as he would have said, divine providence). It is easy to believe that other civilians, especially Catholics, would have been less fortunate. Bernard's account also brings out an aspect of the fall of the town which hardly features in modern considerations of it but would have been all-important to the victorious soldiers: loot. By the military conventions of the time, they were fully entitled to reward themselves for the perils of storming a fortified position by pillaging anything of value inside. Bernard had been careful to send his family away from the town before Cromwell's army arrived; if many others had done the same, then the number of women and children inside the walls would have been much reduced. Some of Bernard's goods would have gone with them, but not all, and in his subsequent sermon, facing his fellow townspeople, he recalled how thoroughly all of them had been plundered. The booty would have been gained by soldiers forcing their way into houses, as they did into his, and it is easy to believe that violence to the inhabitants would often have accompanied this process, as it did at his home, if they did not open their doors and stand aside immediately.

What of Murphy's star witness for atrocities on civilians, Thomas Wood? His account is a second-hand one, remembered by his brother Anthony many years later. At first sight, his memory seems at fault in a detail, because he calls Thomas a lieutenant in the regiment of Henry Ingoldsby, which had not yet been formed when Drogheda was taken. On closer reading, however, he says that Thomas held this position before he returned to visit his family and tell his tale in 1650, which is possible: he does not state the unit in which Thomas served at Drogheda. Anthony wrote about Thomas in two successive versions of his own autobiography, an initial draft and an expanded one which did not affect the account of Drogheda save in the alteration of a few words.[69] Neither was published in Anthony's lifetime, the work being edited and printed long after.[70] Both are in Anthony's own handwriting, so there is no possibility of later addition or corruption. Rejection of Thomas's story therefore depends on a plausible reason for why either he or his brother would have created a fiction.

Anthony recorded of his brother that he had been remembered by his superior officers for his 'art of merriment', which often entertained his regiment: but there is nothing merry about this anecdote. It did not show Thomas in a noble or heroic light – indeed, quite the opposite – and it was not for public consumption, but admitted in private to his family. It was not only to his own discredit but also to that of the army in whose service he remained and, soon after, died. The suspicion of invention must therefore rest on Anthony, and here again it is hard to find a credible motive. The tale put a brother of whom he had clearly been fond into a shameful light, and was, again, not a piece of published propaganda but part of an account of his own life in which no other episodes seem to have been invented. He certainly had only contempt for Cromwell and his associates, writing as he did long after the restoration of the monarchy, but said hard things about the Civil War royalists as well.

There are two further considerations which may induce belief in Thomas's dreadful tale. The first is that it was set in an exact location where it is compatible with the other actions recorded there. Cromwell himself recorded that around a thousand people who had taken refuge in that very church were massacred, without, of course, specifying if any civilians were among them. Some of the soldiers inside did indeed withdraw into the steeple and defend it, as Wood said, and the initial attack on it was repulsed so that eventually Cromwell ordered it to be set on fire. All this fits. As Gardiner noted, none of the other accounts of the fighting there mention women and children, but those by the attackers would not, and Bernard was cowering in his home while the action took place. He witnessed none of it, only hearing about what had happened later, from the colonel who had supervised the burning of the steeple.[71] The second consideration is that some of the acts described by Wood had happened before at the hands of Parliament's soldiers, during the English Civil War. After destroying King Charles's field force at the decisive battle of Naseby, the victorious infantry of the New Model Army found and looted the baggage train of the defeated royalists, while Cromwell's cavalry pursued the fleeing monarch and his horsemen. The pillaging soldiers came across many women among the train, the wives and lovers of the royalist soldiers, killed at least a hundred of them and mutilated the faces of many of the rest. Parliament, embarrassed, tried to explain the atrocity away – the worst of the Civil War – by claiming that its men had thought they were Irish women. In doing so it plugged into a long-developing stereotype of those women as murderers of vulnerable Protestants who deserved no mercy.[72]

Within this context, what Wood reported was not an aberration at all, save for the details concerning the children, but fitted a familiar pattern. Even those, even more appalling, details, would have been comprehensible in terms of other Protestant propaganda that had flourished for almost a decade, of atrocities enacted upon settlers' children by the Catholic rebels in 1641–2. Moreover, to men trying to fight their way into the steeple under a rain of bullets and missiles, to use children as shields may have seemed a potentially effective, if horrific, way of preserving their own lives. There is no reason to link any of this, if it happened, to Cromwell himself, as he does not seem to have come on the scene until later, when the initial attacks on the steeple had failed. All this makes Wood's story credible, and should warn against rejection of it out of hand, but none of it gives that story proof; and it remains a matter of individual judgement how far to accept it as evidence. I myself think that it has the ring of truth, a dark memory confessed by a young soldier racked by guilt and horror at what he had done and in what he had colluded. His brother's account of it sums up Thomas's retrospective feelings (in the two different versions) with the words 'deep remorse' and 'pity'. My conclusion is, however, a subjective one.

Moreover, even if we accept Wood's story, it does nothing to substantiate the later legend of a general massacre of the population, let alone one ordered or encouraged by Cromwell. That began as soon as the reports of the fall of the town reached England, in the royalist press that needed to tarnish the new republic's immediate and stunning victory in Ireland.[73] When in 1660 the republic fell and the monarchy returned, in both kingdoms, the story that Cromwell had ordered that mercy be denied to men, women and children became a standard royalist historical trope, which was taken into modern Irish nationalism.[74] It has spanned the centuries as a partisan lie. It is the more to be regretted in that it has served partly to cloak the fact that truly awful things happened at Drogheda in September 1649, even if one accepts only the absolute minimalist interpretation of them: the slaughter of most of the defenders and of any civilians unlucky enough to become collateral damage. The streets, Mill Mount and St Peter's church in that autumn night must have been a scene of utter nightmare, with the screams, groans and sobs of the dying and the rising stench of blood, urine and faeces as thousands of bodies were stabbed, slashed, clubbed and disembowelled.

Do Cromwell's justifications for the killing stand up? The first, that the garrison had brought its dreadful fate on itself by the previous participation of its members in atrocities against civilians, does not, for reasons stated. What of the second, that the dreadful example of it acted as an inducement to other enemy garrisons to surrender immediately and so saved many lives which would otherwise have been lost in sieges? Cromwell gave supporting examples in the very letter in which he made the argument: as soon as he had taken Drogheda, he had sent a summons to surrender to the other seaport of northern Leinster that Inchiquin had taken in July, Dundalk, threatening it with the same fate, of mass slaughter, unless its governor complied. He also detached a force of 5,000 men under one of his colonels, Robert Venables, sending it north to open operations against the port. The garrison fled before the town was attacked, and the castles of the area were likewise abandoned by the royalists.[75]

Encouraged by this, Cromwell ordered Venables to press on into Ulster, clear as much of the east of it as he could, and try to link up with the isolated republican force at Londonderry. The colonel obeyed, and within a week he had taken Carlingford and Newry, the garrisons surrendering at once. Cromwell could hold these successes up as further proof of his policy.[76] This evidence appears compelling, but there is a problem which cannot be resolved, as it runs into the question of counter-factual history. It was normal for small garrisons to surrender or evacuate if attacked by larger field forces, against which they could not hope to hold out for long. Moreover, the almost immediate fall of Drogheda, with its enormous garrison of crack field infantry, would probably have terrified and demoralized smaller garrisons in weaker towns, such as Dundalk and Carlingford, even without the mass slaughter that accompanied it. It is very likely that they would have given up as swiftly had Cromwell made Aston and the majority of his men prisoners instead of killing them. The suggestion can never, of course, be proved; but it should act as a deterrent to an easy acceptance of Oliver's defence of brutality.

It is therefore contended here that what happened at Drogheda was both dreadful and unnecessary, and that Cromwell can be held primarily responsible for it. This is the case even though it may forever remain in doubt quite how dreadful the action was, with respect to the killing of prisoners and of non-combatants. The events take their place in a context not only of previous bloodshed in the war in Ireland, but of a disposition to ruthlessness that Cromwell himself had already shown: his behaviour in the town was not an aberration but an extreme manifestation of a pattern that was long established. It is therefore to be the more regretted that partisan hostility immediately established an enduring tradition of grossly exaggerating the horror of what happened, and Cromwell's role in it, to an extent which has served to obscure the fact that what did occur was quite awful enough in itself.

WEXFORD

Cromwell's next objective was decided even as Drogheda was being cleared up. The one thing that his Irish campaign could not afford to do was to lose momentum. The pace of it had to be forced constantly, to make good use of every penny of his war treasury before it ran out, and to damage the Irish royalists beyond recovery before the fledgling English commonwealth had to face any other threats. To speed things up, his men had landed in Ireland equipped with tents, which had not been much used in the wars in England, instead of needing to be billeted overnight on local people. This meant that latrines had to be dug for them, and supplies of fresh water located and kept unsullied, and this, given the size of the army, meant that to keep them on the same site for long was an invitation to disease. In addition, the soldiers would have brought various bacilli and viruses with them from England, which thrived in crowded and static conditions. Sickness had broken out immediately, in the camp before Drogheda, and the army had to keep outpacing the germs. All these considerations outweighed the major and obvious opposite one: that the campaigning season was now over, and it was time to disperse to winter quarters where the men might wait out the late autumn and winter weather snugly under roofs and beside fires.

With Venables carrying all before him to the north, it was decided to make for Munster, the south-western province, with its many seaports at which supplies could be landed, rich farmlands on which taxes or rates could be levied, and large population of New English settlers who might be wooed from their new alliance with the Catholics. Even on the march to Drogheda, small parties of Inchiquin's Munster Protestant soldiers had begun to defect to Cromwell. This continued after the fall of the town, encouraged by his success there and perhaps by Ormond's new alliance with O'Neill's hated Ulster Catholics. Ireton had tried to land in Munster right at the opening of the campaign, and now it was time to launch the main army at it. On the march there, it was decided to attack the seaport of Wexford, in south Leinster, which was a notable stronghold of Old English Catholic rebels and a base for privateers that preyed on English shipping.[77]

The army left Drogheda on 16 September, even as Cromwell wrote his first letter to England about the taking of the town, and reached Dublin on the following evening. A week was spent there in preparation for the southern expedition. His original force had shed thousands of men, in those killed, wounded or fallen ill at Drogheda, those sent with Venables, and the garrisons that needed to hold Dublin and Drogheda strongly while the southern expedition proceeded. Some of the losses, but not all, were made up by the final wave of soldiers shipped to join him from Wales, which had landed at the Irish capital, conducted by the minister Hugh Peters, while he had been at Drogheda.[78] Cromwell therefore wrote to the Council of State pressing for further reinforcements to fill up his army later in the campaign. On 19 October it resolved to raise 5,000 new men for him, in five regiments, and ten days later it made provision for their shipping.[79]

The bulk of Cromwell's army had left Dublin on 23 September, and he followed it four days later. Their progress down the south-eastern coast of Ireland met with no resistance from Ormond's small garrisons in the castles there, which fled or surrendered as the huge column of the English army approached. To the right hand, initially, rose the Wicklow Mountains, now in their rusty red and tawny yellow autumn colours. They were one of the remaining strongholds of the Irish wolf, and it is possible that at this season the howling of packs was heard in the camp of Cromwell's men at night. They were also, however, the refuge of human predators, Old Irish clans adhering to the Catholic rebel cause, and the question of whether or not these attacked the marching Englishmen encounters a classic failure of the records to agree. Neither Cromwell's despatch to Parliament about the march nor the reports to newspapers from his soldiers mention any contact with the highland raiders. A report in a letter to Westminster, however, stated that the latter had attacked the column and been beaten back into a bog, where they were cornered and slaughtered. A later Catholic account, by contrast, testified that two notable mountain leaders, Brian McPhelim and Christopher Twoohill, had struck successfully at the army's baggage when it was strung out in narrow passes along the coast, stealing many horses and Cromwell's own furniture. What everybody agreed was that Cromwell's men were attacked by the weather, as they paid the price for keeping the field so late in the year, and wind and rain lashed and slowed them through all the 60 miles of the way.[80]

On 1 October they arrived before Wexford. At first sight, this town seemed a much tougher target than Drogheda had been. It ran north to south for a mile along the edge of a large harbour, with the sea protecting the whole eastern side of it. The estuary of the River Slaney defended the northern side, while all along the west ran a double medieval stone wall, which this time had 16 feet of soil packed behind it to render it proof against siege guns. The southern flank also had a wall, covered by a medieval castle positioned outside. When Cromwell's army camped to the west of the town, it found the ground sodden with water and mud from the rain. The force now numbered only 4,000 foot, 1,200 horse and 900 dragoons. It was running short of food and ammunition and also lacked its vital siege guns, which like the supplies had been sent by sea and could not get into the harbour because of a fort defending the entrance.[81] The men were becoming sick and hungry. With capable leadership, and a united and determined defence, Wexford would be a very hard nut to crack; but Cromwell's luck was in again, and it had neither of those.

The reason for this lay in Ormond's ramshackle alliance. On realizing where Cromwell was heading, the marquis set to work trying to secure the town, and ordered his commander in Leinster, the earl of Castlehaven, to appoint a capable governor. The townspeople of Wexford, however, distrusted Ormond as a Protestant and an old enemy; while Castlehaven was a Catholic and had fought for the Irish rebels, he was similarly distrusted, as an Englishman and friend of Ormond's. Their cause was now discredited by its defeats at Rathmines and Drogheda. The townspeople requested that they be led by a young officer called David Synnott, an Old English Catholic who had served well in the Leinster Catholic rebel army but had never yet commanded an important stronghold. Castlehaven appointed him, but Synnott found the citizens inclined to make terms with Cromwell in order to avoid the fate of Drogheda, and accordingly refusing to allow reinforcements into the town. As a result, instead of hurrying to improve the defences, governor and corporation spent the time until their enemy appeared arguing over what to do, until the latter tried to get the former suspended from his command. Synnott then attempted to quit. The really vital step would have been to strengthen the fort which protected the harbour, 6 miles from the town, but that was ignored.[82] On the day after their arrival, Cromwell sent Jones to capture the fort; the defenders deserted it without a fight, even bungling their flight so that they were captured. This let in the ships with the crucially important food, munitions and guns, and morale in the camp rose accordingly, helped by the fact that the soldiers were still fully paid from the funds Cromwell had brought to Ireland.[83]

Driven by the loss of the fort, the arrival of the heavy artillery and the pressure of the citizens, Synnott opened negotiations as soon as the town was summoned to surrender on 3 October, while the corporation cravenly sent Cromwell a present of white wine, spirits and strong beer to sweeten him. He did agree to talk, providing that his preparations to take the town continued without pause. At that point, however, it was not clear what he could actually do, faced with a wall that could not be breached, and on 6 October Castlehaven arrived on the far side of the harbour, from where he sent over 500 more foot soldiers and 100 horse to reinforce the garrison. Ormond moved the remainder of his depleted army up to New Ross, the next town to the west of Wexford, sending messages to Synnott and the mayor that he was preparing to relieve them. Both accordingly halted the treaty with Cromwell, and Ormond drew up a scheme for a combined operation by his force and the garrison to destroy the siege guns.[84] Just as at Drogheda, however, Oliver moved too fast for him. Cromwell and his officers had realized that Wexford had a fatal weakness, represented by the castle on its south side. In the Middle Ages, when it was constructed, this had represented a formidable fortress that shielded the southern town wall. Now, however, the castle's precinct was not lined with earth, rendering it very vulnerable to artillery fire. If it could be captured, it overlooked the wall, and so would threaten that instead of protecting it, allowing the town to be won.[85]

Cromwell accordingly sent Jones with most of the cavalry and dragoons to block Ormond's path and so prevent any interference from the marquis. He moved his camp to the south-eastern side of the town and constructed a battery which mounted two cannon, a demi-cannon and a culverin, a truly heavyweight kit. On 11 October these opened fire, and a hundred shots smashed down all the castle's battlements and ripped three great breaches in its walls. At this point, Synnott and the corporation, whatever else they were doing, should have been rushing their soldiers to the town's southern perimeter and preparing a co-ordinated defence there. Instead, Synnott reopened negotiations for surrender, asking for his garrison to march away with all their weapons, artillery and goods, and for the townspeople to be allowed to leave with their moveable wealth or else to remain with equal rights to new English settlers and the free practice of their Catholic religion. Cromwell was not prepared to let useful military resources escape, nor to allow freedom of worship to Catholics; he offered only to let the common soldiers go home, to make the officers prisoners and to spare the town from plunder. He was about to sign this offer, and Synnott's commissioners were waiting to return with it, when he realized that he had lost control of his own men. This was a direct result of his policy of avoiding the wastage of any time by directing that military operations continue alongside the talks, in case those broke down. The attack on the castle therefore proceeded even though negotiations were in progress, something Synnott and the corporation were clearly not expecting. When the governor of the castle saw Cromwell's soldiers preparing to storm the breaches in his walls, and realized that he and his men were facing certain death, he capitulated and surrendered the fortress, so saving their lives. The lack of communication between Synnott and his officers was so complete that the governor apparently did not even realize that this had occurred.

The defenders of the southern wall found out that it had happened only when they realized that the castle which was supposed to protect them was full of their enemies, who could fire down on them and were turning the fortress's artillery on them. Their response was to flee en masse, which was witnessed by the soldiers on the castle. Those men also saw news spreading through the town that it was falling, and citizens starting to load their possessions into boats in the harbour. Confronted with an apparently defenceless town, and seeing their plunder vanishing from it, they relayed this news to their fellows, who put scaling ladders against the wall and swarmed over in thousands. Realizing that their enemies were upon them, some of the garrison attempted resistance, resulting in a chaotic and bloody running fight through the streets, which culminated when the remaining defenders made a stand in the marketplace. This only served to turn the area into a killing ground. None of this resistance seems to have been led by Synnott, who concentrated on his own escape, getting into a boat to cross the harbour to safety; but he was shot in the head, fell into the water and drowned. By the time that Cromwell and his officers regained authority over their soldiers, the fighting seemed to have ended, leaving the town comprehensively looted and many of the garrison and citizens dead.

As at Drogheda, argument has persisted ever since over the scale and nature of the casualties. Once again, Denis Murphy started the modern debate by suggesting that an extensive civilian massacre had taken place. He cited a number of sources to substantiate this, but none were from individuals present at the time, and all were retrospective. The Catholic archbishop of Dublin subsequently wrote to Rome to state that many priests, some friars, innumerable citizens and 2,000 soldiers had been killed. In 1655 a Jesuit sent a letter claiming that the citizens had been exterminated, and a colonel noted that the town was much depopulated.

At the restoration of the monarchy in 1660, the Catholic inhabitants of Wexford petitioned the returned king for restitution, alleging that Cromwell had not only slaughtered the garrison but also 1,500 men, women and children, representing the great majority of the population. In 1673 the Catholic bishop of Ferns, a native of the town although absent when it fell, stated that the Catholic priests in it had been beaten, gaoled or killed, that the noblest citizens were massacred in the streets, hardly a family being spared, and that the whole place was plundered. He added that his chaplain and some of his servants had been cut down in his own mansion. A former resident in the town's Franciscan friary later wrote that seven of its friars had died when the town was stormed. Murphy also cited a local tradition, first recorded in the eighteenth century, that 300 women had been massacred around the market cross.[86]

Once more, Samuel Rawson Gardiner supplied an alternative account. He accepted that Catholic clergy of all kinds had been butchered, and that many civilians must also have died, though he believed that 300 had actually been accidentally drowned as the craft on which they were escaping capsized in the harbour. He rejected the story of the women perishing around the market cross as a later legend, arguing that, if there had been many female victims of Cromwell's soldiers, then it would have been mentioned in Ormond's subsequent correspondence. He accepted that by one means or another there had been many civilian deaths, as well as a massacre of those of the garrison who were not able to get away, but justified this result as the natural consequence of a prolonged struggle between attackers and defenders through the streets and houses.[87] Recent historians have naturally occupied points on the spectrum between these two great progenitors, most tending towards Gardiner's end of it.[88]

When examining the issue anew, it is important to commence by acknowledging how much we do not know about what happened. We do not know whether the unanimity in the accounts of it from Cromwell's army, from its leader downwards, reflects an objective truth about the events or an agreement on a common story that the world needed to believe. We do not have a single eye-witness testimony from a defender or resident to balance those left by the attackers. We do not know how long it took Cromwell to realize that his men had stormed the place, and whether he made any attempt to control them when he did. We do not know whether the soldiers who led the storming realized that negotiations were in progress for Wexford's surrender. We do not know the size of the garrison or the population, or how many of each perished. All this makes any attempt to determine the scale of the massacre, and responsibility for it, much more difficult.

Some things can be stated. Unlike Drogheda, which was a Protestant town, Wexford was entirely Catholic, because, led by their clergy, the rebels who seized control of it had expelled all its Protestant inhabitants.[89] Cromwell's men believed that atrocities had been inflicted on the latter when this happened. The citizens in 1649 were therefore of English descent and had English accents, but were divided from those who stormed their town by both religion and blood feud.[90] It can also be said with certainty that Wexford's capture represented another major victory for Cromwell and his cause, giving them control of 200 miles of the eastern Irish coast in all, and depriving the Irish Catholics of their major naval base. Moreover, it dealt another major blow to Ormond's reputation, authority and resources, reducing his own army to a small minority of the force that it had been in the summer, when the losses at Rathmines, Drogheda and Wexford were taken together. The circumstances of the fall, however, significantly reduced the value of the victory for Cromwell. He had been on the point of gaining a wealthy town intact, which could have provided useful resources for his army and perhaps, in due course, winter quarters. Now it had been wrecked, plundered and partly depopulated, and much of its wealth had vanished into the possession of his soldiers. Merchandise stored in warehouses was ignored by the looters, and was confiscated for the profit of the republic and its war effort, as were the ships and fishing boats in the harbour. Marketing all these would take time, however, and the place could no longer support the army that had seized it, which would have to move on. This absence of rest mattered the more in that the sodden camp sites had already taken their toll, with many men having fallen sick with fever and dysentery.[91]

So what was the scale of the massacre? The reports from Cromwell and his soldiers to England gave different estimates, being the only aspect of the taking of Wexford over which they disagreed. One said that many of the garrison had been spared, unlike at Drogheda, but that 1,500 soldiers and citizens had been killed, or drowned trying to escape.[92] Another claimed that many had been killed in the town or trying to flee it by land, or had drowned in the harbour, but that many more had got away by boat with their goods. This report added that some priests and friars had been slaughtered in the church that they served (where allegedly Protestant prisoners had been starved to death by the Catholic citizens near the beginning of the latter's revolt).[93] Hugh Peters reported 2,000 deaths among the defenders and inhabitants, for 6 among the attackers. Another letter was written by somebody who exulted at having seen pigs lapping the blood of the 'Irish' off the streets.[94] A further account stated that there had been between 1,700 and 2,000 soldiers in the town, of whom 400 escaped, many of the deaths being caused by drowning. It put the attackers' losses at only one or two.[95] Yet another confidently reported 1,000 deaths among the defenders for 7 on the other side.[96] Cromwell himself, in his official report to Parliament, said that two boatloads of refugees had capsized, drowning nearly three hundred people. He reported that the 'enemy' had lost almost 2,000 people in all, while his men lost fewer than 20. Again, the Biblical comparison in the numbers was clear. He added that scarcely one in twenty of the townspeople had any possessions left in their houses. He admitted that he had wanted to gain Wexford intact, but gave the responsibility for the resulting slaughter and wreckage to God, who had clearly been determined to punish it as a nest of privateer ships and for its cruelty to Protestants: once more a Biblical echo is apparent. This being the case, there is not the slightest sympathy for the inhabitants in his despatch.[97]

On the royalist side, as said, there is little testimony. A letter to Ormond from Kilkenny three days later complained of the burden of supporting the number of soldiers who claimed to have fled there from Wexford; if their claims were correct, a lot of the garrison did get away.[98] The beginning of a charge of wholesale massacre against Cromwell is found immediately, as in the case of Drogheda, in the English royalist press. One of its newspapers printed an alleged letter from Dublin which reported the fall of the town with the statement that the entire population, including women and children, had been killed, save for three or four aldermen.[99] This is so much at variance with the reports by the victors, especially Cromwell's reference to the number of inhabitants who had survived but were plundered bare, that it has to be discarded as a fiction. Belief in it may, however, have been nurtured by the fact that two months later Cromwell's governor of Wexford expelled the entire remaining Catholic population as a security measure; so the people were indeed removed en masse, but not at the taking of the town.[100] The story about the women killed in the marketplace appeared later. In 1660 a royalist history of the republic, which had included the claim of a wholesale massacre at Drogheda, was still saying only that soldiers and citizens had made a last stand at that place, and that all 'found in arms' were killed.[101] The addition of a slaughter of helpless women came a few years after, in a scurrilous and comprehensive attack on the reputation of Cromwell, to suit the mood of the restored monarchy, by James Heath. He claimed that 200 women had been murdered in the marketplace, a number that had been expanded by a further hundred a century later, in the version that Denis Murphy repeated. This makes it the less likely that this particular detail is true, though it has been repeated (and augmented) into recent times.[102]

We shall never really know the details of what occurred at Wexford on 11 October 1649, except that, as at Drogheda, they must be calibrated at some point on a spectrum of horror. At least 1,500 people, and probably more, died from the garrison and population, categories that blend into each other because many of the defenders would have been armed citizens.

According to all accounts, most of those who died did so at the hands of Cromwell's soldiers, in their push to seize the town and plunder it. More precise figures, and estimates of the proportions of armed and unarmed citizens, or of women and children, among the dead are futile. It is also certain not only that Cromwell never wanted the slaughter and the looting, and did not order it, but also that his motives had nothing to do with the welfare of the citizens. The loss of life and property that Wexford suffered may be squarely blamed on him in the sense that both occurred because he had not ordered a cessation of hostilities, according to accepted and expected convention, while negotiations for surrender were in progress. This was propelled by his haste to score as many victories as he could before time, money and men ran short. But it is also understandable – if not strictly pardonable – in that his terms had not yet been accepted, while Synnott had broken off talks with him before and might do so again. It is clear that Cromwell never foresaw the actual consequences of his policy of pressing home both military and diplomatic advantages simultaneously. Morally, he does not emerge well from a discussion of his taking of Wexford, though he cannot easily be cast as the villain of what happened either. Militarily, of course, he had notched up another stunning success.

NEW ROSS AND WATERFORD

For the reasons stated above, Cromwell needed to move on as soon as the military government of Wexford was organized. His next target was Ormond's recent base at New Ross, a port town lying on the River Barrow west of Wexford, which commanded the direct route further west towards Munster. Ormond had left a strong garrison there under an Old English aristocrat, Viscount Taaffe, which the marquis had reinforced to a total of 2,500 men. Oliver's army arrived outside it on 17 October. He had dragged three large siege guns with him; these opened up on the town wall the next morning and, as it was not lined with earth, soon blew a hole in it. Taaffe offered to treat at once. Although Cromwell again refused a cessation of hostilities during the talks, and his guns kept on widening the gap in the wall, the two men soon came to terms. Taaffe decided that his chances of defending the breach successfully were no better than Aston's had been at Drogheda, while Cromwell knew that the garrison could easily escape on boats across the river, which had no bridge at this point, while his own men prepared to attack. As a result, on the next day he allowed Taaffe and his men to make that passage with their weapons and baggage, and promised safety to the townspeople. He did so, moreover – as his messages to the governor were published – with heavy emphasis on the fact that this agreement proved that he did not seek bloodshed if it could be avoided, something the events at Drogheda and Wexford had cast into doubt. The reality of the matter was that Cromwell believed that the defenders would get away in any case.

He denied two things, however, that the viscount had requested: the garrison's artillery, which could not have been taken with Taaffe had he fled, and freedom for the citizens to practise their Catholic religion. The latter was a delicate and important point, forcing Oliver to make what was in effect a public pronouncement on the matter, because Taaffe had asked him to allow the people of New Ross the liberty of conscience that he had long claimed so vehemently for radical Protestants. Cromwell's answer managed deftly to express complete obedience to the regime that he served while side-stepping any personal responsibility for the blatantly partisan nature of its notion of religious freedom. The message declared that he would 'meddle not with any man's conscience', but that the Parliament he obeyed would not allow the celebration of the Catholic mass in its dominions. He therefore allowed citizens who could not accept life without it freedom to leave the town with their goods within three months. Taaffe's men were, however, not all Catholics but included 500 of Inchiquin's Protestant infantry from Munster; as the viscount withdrew, these defected to Cromwell. Oliver was therefore left with an intact town, a good harbour and a reinforcement of experienced soldiers. Nevertheless, he could still not get his army across the Barrow, as Taaffe's retreating men took the boats, and so his army had to settle down to build a bridge across it.[103]

As they did so, Cromwell received both bad and good news. The bad was that Ormond had at last finalized his alliance with O'Neill and his Ulster Catholic army, which gave the marquis the resources of an entire additional field force, experienced and renowned, and regarded as heroes by southern Irish Catholics who distrusted Ormond and Inchiquin and their followers. Cromwell feared that the united armies would now allow the royalists to challenge him in battle.[104] In fact, the benefit to Ormond was much reduced in practice by a number of factors. The first was that O'Neill himself died immediately after the alliance was made, depriving his army of its trusted and able commander and leaving it without a successor of comparable ability. It would also now not come south in its entirety; instead, large detachments of it, totalling 5,000, were offered to Ormond. Those in turn seem to have been unwilling to serve alongside the marquis's and Inchiquin's soldiers. In any case, Ormond no longer had the resources to pay, feed and equip a large combined field force, so could not unite one. What the Ulstermen could do was shore up his defences at certain key points.[105]

The good news for Cromwell represented a further major problem for, and blow to, the royalists: the gaining of the Ulster Catholic soldiers was balanced by the loss of the Munster New English. To some extent the two developments may have been linked, because, while the Protestants who had made up Inchiquin's army and its civilian supporters may have been willing (with some qualms) to ally with 'moderate' Catholic rebels such as the Old English friendly with Ormond, they may well have had greater scruples about the hard-liners epitomized by the Ulster army. There is, however, a much more evident reason for their defection at this time. From 1644 to 1648 they had been allied with the English Parliament, and had won a steady number of victories. In contrast, when Inchiquin had led them over to co-operation with royalists and Catholics, that alliance had suffered a succession of stunning defeats at the hands of the purged Parliament's agents Jones and Cromwell. There was no prospect of a reversal of fortune, given the discrepancy of resources between England and Ireland,

and the momentum of Cromwell's progress and his obvious grasp of the military initiative. These practical considerations morphed naturally into a religious one: that God seemed firmly to have set his face against Ormond's coalition and that the defeats that the New English had suffered as part of it could be regarded as a divine punishment for co-operation with a bad cause. Here the wonderful logic of the seventeenth-century mind came into play again, as repeatedly illustrated by Cromwell's own behaviour: that opportunistic and realistic motivations for a course of action could be regarded, with perfect sincerity, as submission to the divine will.

The domino effect of defection began on 16 October, when the Protestant garrison of Cork, the main city and port of Munster, revolted and joined the English townspeople in declaring for the commonwealth. They expelled the Irish soldiers; soon after, the garrison of Youghal, a smaller port eastward on the same coast, did the same. Westward from Cork, an English royalist fleet based at Kinsale, a third port, fled for the open sea; Kinsale's garrison, too, went over to Cromwell's cause. Lord Broghill had appeared at last, and immediately became very active in co-ordinating these developments, drawing on his family's considerable influence in the province and taking personal charge of Youghal. He then obtained the surrender of Bandon, a Protestant town upriver from Kinsale. Smaller seaports now came in, from Baltimore to the west of Kinsale to Dungarvan to the east of Youghal. By mid-November the whole southern seaboard of Munster, with most of the province's important harbours, was at Cromwell's service without any action needed on his part, other than to confirm the Protestant garrisons and councils in power in the rebel towns.[106] His army now had ample, and comfortable, winter quarters. God had been good again.

Cromwell would have been the more grateful for divine favour in that his protracted stay at New Ross, building his bridge, was a miserable experience. His campaign was stalled and the town not large enough to accommodate all his men, many of whom remained under canvas in the fields around. They were running short of clothing, shoes and stockings, and the decline in their morale was reflected in their behaviour: Oliver had to issue a proclamation ordering them not to steal horses and grain from the local people. The late autumn damp and chill was setting deeper, and the sickness already evident at Wexford became rampant. Cromwell estimated that only one officer in forty avoided it, and many died, including Horton, the victor in South Wales in 1648. By early November he was himself too ill to move.[107]

He had decided to attempt one more major objective before suspending operations for the winter: the Leinster port of Waterford, to the west, which was the second largest city in Ireland and a Catholic stronghold, as Wexford had been. It was also the only good harbour left to the royalists on the entire south and east coasts of Ireland. It lay on the far side of two rivers from New Ross, but there was a direct overland route to the nearer side of Waterford harbour. If Cromwell could secure the entrance to that, then he could get his fleet in, and with it the lethal siege guns. After taking New Ross, he therefore sent Ireton with a strong force to seize Duncannon, the fort that protected the harbour mouth on the east, reinforced soon after by another force led by Jones. Disappointment struck again, however, because this fortress was a modern one defended by formidable earthworks with protruding bastions, proof against storming parties and all but the most powerful artillery. In charge were not half-hearted locals but a determined garrison commanded by a renegade English parliamentarian, who knew that death awaited him if he fell into the hands of the besiegers. Castlehaven ferried reinforcements over the harbour to the fortress, enabling the governor to sally out and capture the besiegers' field guns. At that, Ireton and Jones gave up and retreated under cover of darkness, abandoning much equipment.[108] It was the first defeat inflicted on Cromwell's army since it had arrived in Ireland; but, as he himself was not present, it did little to affect his reputation, and was completely overshadowed by the free gift to him of the Munster ports.

The defection of those ports was, of course, a devastating blow to Ormond and Inchiquin. They now found themselves deserted by all but 200 of Inchiquin's infantry, and trusted their remaining soldiers so little that they did not dare risk confronting Cromwell. On paper their resources remained considerable, Ormond calculating that soldiers occupying garrisons who owed allegiance to his alliance numbered 18,000 foot and 4,000 horse. He estimated that 8,000 of the foot and 2,500 of the horse could be drawn into a field army if he only had provisions for them, but he did not. He could in reality collect no more than 5,000 foot and 1,300 horse, of dubious reliability, and had difficulty in supplying these. He therefore saw his only hope lying in bolstering the remaining garrisons loyal to his cause which stood between Cromwell and Munster, and hovering nearby with his field force in the hope of catching and defeating detachments of the enemy, so bolstering his men's morale with small victories.[109]

That, of course, left the initiative with Cromwell, who took it as soon as the bridge over the Barrow was completed, on 15 November. He was still too ill to lead an advance himself, so sent Ireton and Jones over with most of the army. To invest Waterford they now had to cross another of the broad southern Irish rivers gliding between small green fields, the Suir, normally placid but now in flood. An alternative was to stay on the east of the Suir and bring Ormond and Inchiquin to battle at last. Ireton and Jones took that latter course first, moving swiftly north up the Nore, a third of the local rivers, which flowed into the Barrow above New Ross. The rain still poured and the rivers rose higher, but progress was otherwise easy because the royalist garrisons of the small towns on their route fled before them. Once again, Ormond refused the risk of a fight, retreating from the Nore and breaking the only bridge on that stretch of the river behind him. As he was now out of reach of Jones and Ireton, Waterford became their objective. To get passage over the Suir, they sent the invaluable Reynolds with a body of horse and dragoons to seize Carrick, a town on that river where there was a ferry. He took the garrison there by surprise, and it ran away. On the 21st and 23rd Cromwell himself brought the rest of the army over from New Ross, and they entered Munster at last, numbering 4,000 and 2,000 horse, and left Reynolds with a garrison to hold the crossing at Carrick behind them.[110]

On 24 November, they reached the environs of Waterford, and Oliver summoned the city to surrender. He hoped that it would give up easily after a negotiation, because the leadership there had seemed even more confused and inept than at Wexford, despite the continued security of the harbour. Ormond had made Castlehaven himself governor and sent him to the town with 1,000 soldiers to reinforce it, but the Catholic corporation had refused to accept his authority and had shut him out with his men. Cromwell was informed of this development by some of the citizens, who were now keen to negotiate with him. At this moment, however, the marquis showed his capacity for leadership and sent 200 picked men to the city, whom its leaders found acceptable. He then reinforced them with 1,300 more from the Ulster Catholic army, under one of its generals, Richard Farrell, an able man respected by the townspeople. Waterford was now temporarily safe, and Inchiquin led a strong force to retake Carrick, in order to sever Cromwell's communications with Leinster. This would have been one of the small but strategic victories over detachments of Cromwell's men which Ormond had intended to achieve. It did not work because of a deficiency of equipment, as Inchiquin's soldiers lacked long enough ladders to scale the town walls. They did have artillery enough to make a breach, but not the pickaxes needed to pull down sufficient rubble to get men through. A four-hour battle was fought in the inadequate gap, of pikemen pushing their long spears at each other, before the Irish were beaten off with the loss of 500 men. Their morale sank still further.[111]

Cromwell now set to work to tighten his grip on Waterford by sending Jones with a party to capture the fort that guarded the other side of the harbour entrance from Duncannon, at the aptly named Passage. This one was weaker both in its defences and in the resolution of its garrison, and surrendered. The fleet that accompanied the army could now enter the harbour and unload the vital siege artillery. This time, however, this apparently decisive advantage came to nothing, because of the sheer fury of a wet winter. The ground proved too waterlogged to construct batteries for the heavy guns. Constant storms prevented supply ships from sailing, so that the army was now short of food, clothing and pay, and its tents were no longer adequate cover against the deteriorating climate. The cavalry began to kill the livestock of the farmers of the district to feed themselves, and to take their wheat and barley to feed the horses, leaving neither money nor tickets promising payment in return. This, as Cromwell knew, would both ruin the local economy, which might otherwise yield taxes and supplies, and alienate the population, so he issued a proclamation against it. His soldiers were still, inevitably, falling sick in droves, so that he estimated that ten of each infantry company did so each night and that he had only 3,000 foot left fit for duty. His own second cousin, a major Oliver Cromwell, was among those who died.

The situation was accordingly hopeless. On 2 December Cromwell called off the siege and marched west towards the Munster ports that were now at his command. It was the only time in his life when he failed to take a town, city or fortress of which he had demanded the surrender. Behind him Ormond brought another large contingent of Ulster infantry into Waterford to secure it, though he claimed that the corporation had prevented him from attacking the rear of Cromwell's retreating army for fear of provoking it. The journey of that army away was itself dreadful, another violent storm lashing and drenching the moving soldiers. After a dozen miles of this, it reached a small town for the night, where it lacked food, fuel and bedding. Among those who caught cold was Oliver's lieutenant-general, Michael Jones, who was sent to Dungarvan to recover; instead, he contracted typhoid there and died. The exhausted, hungry and sickly soldiers were dispersed among the Munster towns to recuperate, while Cromwell wrote desperately to England for fresh supplies of men, ammunition, food and clothing. He claimed that these were vital to be able to continue fighting the royalist alliance, which not only still had most of the resources of the island to draw upon, but were also being supported from overseas by Catholic states.[112] In that last point, and in his evaluation of Ormond's strength, Cromwell was completely wrong. The marquis was getting no help at all from either foreign states or the exiled king whom he served. Ormond wrote to the latter saying that he would try again to retake some of the smaller towns that his enemy had garrisoned, but that the local people were now too impoverished by a decade of the ravages of war, and too distrustful of him and his soldiers, to give them any support. The only province left entirely in royalist hands was Connacht, which was now stricken with bubonic plague – another providential stroke of luck for Cromwell – and could therefore send no aid. Ormond admitted that, without supplies of money, food and ammunition from abroad, he could not take the field at all now. If no support arrived, he would be helpless when the spring campaigning season opened.[113]

WINTER QUARTERS

The story of the winter suspension of fighting in the south of Ireland is one of how Ormond continued to lack any assistance from overseas, while Cromwell received it in ample quantity from England. Between November and February, a total of 9,000 soldiers, properly armed and equipped, were sent to reinforce him, along with tons of cereals, biscuit, cheese, salted fish and beer. Almost 18,000 suits of new clothes were sent for the infantry (allowing plenty of spares), and almost 2,000 pairs of boots, stockings and breeches for the cavalry. Proportionate quantities of gunpowder, weapons, knapsacks, horse fodder and money accompanied them.[114] The Council of State was careful to send veteran soldiers as well as new recruits, issuing an order that twenty troopers be chosen for Irish service from each of the existing horse regiments in England. One of the genuinely new units was given to Cromwell's younger son, Henry, though, as part of that care which Oliver always now took to avoid accusations of zeal for personal and dynastic advancement, Henry and his men were given a place in a Munster force detached from Oliver's main one. To help those soldiers in the winter quarters who were sick enough to be hospitalized, rugs and blankets were sent over to keep them warm.[115] By the end of January of the new year 1650, Cromwell's regiments were rested, healthy, re-equipped, paid and at full strength again, ready for war.

Throughout most of December and January, Oliver restlessly moved along the Munster coast, visiting the port towns that now obeyed him and inspecting the army units quartered there. As he journeyed up and down this rocky seaboard, of small bays and peninsulas, he dealt with a variety of official tasks in his capacity as lord lieutenant.[116] He established a renewed system of judges in Munster, to provide legal opportunities for the inhabitants, with the explicit intention of encouraging Catholic tenants to seek redress against their landlords, and so win their gratitude and make them more inclined to convert to Protestantism.[117] He deployed other means of discouraging local people from Catholicism: when he visited Kinsale, the mayor of the town made him welcome and delivered him the mace of the corporation and the keys to the gates. This was a regular ceremony when Cromwell entered one of the ports that had recently defected, and the normal response was for him to return both, confirming the corporation in office. On this occasion, however, he refused to do so, on the grounds that the mayor was a Catholic and therefore could not be trusted.[118] He also disposed of the highest-level appointment possible in Munster, by getting Parliament to make Henry Ireton its lord president.[119] This office had been held by Inchiquin, the leading member of the most powerful Old Irish family in the province. It was one for which Broghill might have hoped, as the commonwealth's supporter in the most powerful New English settler family there. By giving the position to Ireton, Parliament both gratified Cromwell and reaffirmed direct English control. It also re-established Ireton formally as Cromwell's second-in-command on the expedition, after the death of Jones, to whom that place had been given from military and political expediency. If Cromwell did not yet quite trust Broghill, he was correct to do so because, while working hard for the commonwealth's cause in Munster at this time, the lord also sent secretly to Inchiquin, stating his willingness to serve him and his continued loyalty to the king.[120]

At this time, Cromwell also engaged in an important piece of public propaganda. In early December, the Irish Roman Catholic bishops had met in the middle of Ireland, at the grey medieval monastery of Clonmacnoise in its quiet lush meadow beside the River Shannon. As a group, these prelates had been among the strongest opponents of any alliance with the royalists that did not yield major concessions to their religion. As such, reviewing the poor military results of the current one, they were in a position to condemn it and so to destroy Ormond's position. They did not, however, instead issuing a declaration reaffirming the alliance and calling for unity against Cromwell and the regime that he served, as inveterate enemies to Catholicism and the Irish, and perpetrators of persecution, dispossession and massacre.[121]

Cromwell's published reply was long and careful. We do not know how much of it was his own work, and if it was, on what advice he modelled it, but he had always been a master of both publicity and persuasion, and the result lived up to his record. His scorn and loathing for the Catholic prelates was unfettered, as he termed their religion the Church of Antichrist. He accused it of having perpetrated the most barbarous massacre in history, in the form of the 1641 rebellion against peaceful and unsuspecting English settlers, and so held that God had to be against them. He declared that the Catholic religion was already illegal under the laws that British monarchs had imposed on Ireland, which he would uphold. He announced that he had come not to extirpate but to convert Irish commoners. He then made his claim that he had not massacred or transported any innocent civilians, and had come to restore English liberties in Ireland, as well as to avenge atrocities. He ended by promising protection to Catholic landowners who had not supported the rebellion, and mercy to former rebels no longer in arms who submitted voluntarily, unless they had been leaders.[122] It was a document calculated to appeal to Irish Protestants, while holding out hope of good treatment to moderate Catholics who surrendered. It studiously ignored the fact that a confiscation of most of the land remaining in the ownership of Catholics and leading royalists would be needed to repay the money advanced in England to fund the various attempts to reconquer the island since 1641. Cromwell's letters from Ireland were generally free of anti-Catholic rhetoric,[123] but there is no doubt, from his actions and declarations, that he intended the Roman Catholic religion to disappear from the land, though seemingly by disempowerment and conversion rather than by direct persecution of its lay adherents.

Even during this short and frenetic break from campaigning, Oliver found time for informal letters to England. When still trapped at New Ross, he had written to the father-in-law of his son Richard, asking that man to prompt his daughter, Richard's wife Dorothy, to send Cromwell news of how she and her husband were. His disappointment in Richard himself now showed openly, as he said that he knew that his son was too 'idle' to write. From Cork in January, he sent to one of his former close allies among the Independent peers, Lord Wharton, who, like most of that group, had parted company with Cromwell over the purging of Parliament and the regicide. He admitted that those actions had been unpleasant, but insisted that God had made them his instruments, and that there had been no alternatives. He urged Wharton to realize that truth, and also to try to persuade the king's former gaoler Robert Hammond, another one-time friend of Oliver's who had been alienated from him and had recently written him a wounding letter, to do the same.[124]

By late January, as said, Cromwell's army was fully repaired and ready for action, and he decided to launch it. Prolonged severe weather would have given Ormond a further respite, but once more luck was against the marquis and with Oliver, because the late winter turned out to be exceptionally mild. Cromwell decided to gamble that spring had indeed come early, and to take the field. It was still ridiculously soon in the year to do so, but he was in even more of a hurry than before. The situation in Britain was deteriorating, as shall be explained in the next chapter, and his recall there now seemed likely, and perhaps at any moment.[125] A less ambitious man, and one with less of a sense of personal mission and divine favour, would not have been so affected by this: he had, after all, already accomplished a great deal, and he had competent subordinates to whom to pass his army, which was now in excellent shape. Nor was there any sign of any external aid for Ormond, or anything else to salvage the marquis's vulnerable position. Oliver, however, had always, from the start of his career in the current Parliament, hungered and reached for glory and acclaim. He did so now with the same avidity and the same dramatic results.

FETHARD AND KILKENNY

The strategic problem at the opening of the new campaign was clear. Having possessed nothing in Ireland at the opening of September except Dublin and Londonderry, the English commonwealth now controlled the entire coast of the Ireland from Londonderry in the north-west, all round the east and south, as far as Baltimore in the south-west, except for Waterford. Cromwell himself had conquered it from Drogheda round to Wexford, after which the south Munster ports had defected. Venables had continued his invasion of Ulster, linking up with the Londonderry garrison, and by the end of the year they had taken the coastal towns of that province too, aided by the defection to them of most of its Protestants.[126] This meant that the commonwealth could easily continue to resupply its armies by sea, while tapping into the wealth generated by trade in the ports it now controlled. Almost nowhere, however, did it have a grip on any territory more than 20 miles inland from this coastal littoral. To sustain a continued conquest of the whole island, while diminishing the strain on English resources, it was necessary to push into the interior and annex whole districts there which could be made to contribute money, food and other materials for the republican war effort. This process Cromwell now set about initiating in Munster.

He launched an invasion of its interior in two columns. The first was sent north-east from Carrick, led by Reynolds with fifteen or sixteen horse troops and 2,000 foot, followed by Ireton with another body of men to reinforce him. They moved up into County Kilkenny to cover the eastern flank of the operation and prevent interference by Castletown's royalist units in Leinster. On 29 January Cromwell launched the second advance, leaving Youghal and pushing through the hills to its north. He reached the Blackwater valley and passed up it to the town of Mallow, in just two days. There he could cross the Blackwater and invade County Limerick. Broghill was left at Mallow with 600–700 horse and 400–500 foot to cover Cromwell's western flank. Oliver now led a small but highly mobile strike force of twelve horse troops, three companies of dragoons and 200–300 foot. He put parties into two castles and a hall on the Limerick border, accepting the surrender of an Irish garrison in one of the castles, and so enabled the county to be laid under contribution to his war effort.

His next objective was Fethard, a small town to the east, in the heart of County Tipperary, which was surrounded by stronger and more important royalist strongholds. He had clearly decided that it was vulnerable, and would give him a base in the heart of enemy territory, from which he could disrupt supplies to his foes and pick off their garrisons. It was defended itself, by an occupying force within a wall with outlying earthen bulwarks, and Cromwell made another lightning march to it, through a return of wet and windy weather, fording the River Suir with difficulty. He arrived at dusk in the shelter of its suburbs, with darkness covering the size of his force and its equipment, and summoned the surrender of the place at once. In the course of a full night of negotiation, he beat down the resolution of the governor, offering very generous terms backed up by threats. These were pure bluff, as he had too few men and no material for a siege, even lacking ladders, but it worked, and the royalists marched away. Cromwell was never a gambler – quite the reverse – and in this case had his bluff been called he could have withdrawn his force without risk or damage to it. He was, however, a very competent trickster. On hearing of the fall of Fethard, the royalist garrison of Cashel, the ancient capital of Munster, lying to the west across the Tipperary pastures, gave up and fled. Its corporation offered the surrender of the town, a more important one than Fethard, and Cromwell garrisoned it in turn. He had cut a swathe across the centre of southern Ireland in just five days, establishing a string of strongholds without needing to fire a shot.

He now moved the remnant of his strike force (having put detachments into all his new fortresses) eastward to rejoin Reynolds. The latter was now at Callan, another market town, which lay in the south-west of County Kilkenny. His men had stormed two of the three small castles in it and slaughtered the defenders, after which those of the third surrendered and were allowed to march away without their weapons. Cromwell left garrisons there while Reynolds seized another little town to the south-east, Knocktopher, to secure communications with New Ross. Oliver then took the rest of his men and Reynolds to quarter at Fethard and Cashel, where the rich countryside could support them. Levies of money and foodstuffs were imposed on County Tipperary to maintain his new garrisons there. The pause also allowed his men to refresh themselves, and four of his vital siege guns to be brought up from the coast. The usual, lowland, routes from there were still blocked by enemy strongholds, so the heavy pieces had to be taken through mountains, at this season a dark, secret land of rocks and bogs. Draught horses and oxen could not pass these, meaning that the cannon had to be dragged and pushed by hundreds of men, which was a long, hard business. After two weeks it had been achieved, and Cromwell was ready to use his renewed firepower on the remaining royalist fortresses in the area.[127]

He called a council of war, which chose first to attack Cahir Castle, a sprawling medieval fortress, planted by medieval English invaders, which guarded a crossing on the River Suir where main roads converged from Kilkenny, Dublin and the Irish midlands to run down to the Munster ports. Taking the castle would give him control of this vital route and make supplies much easier. On 24 February he summoned it to surrender; the governor did so by the end of the day, for two evident reasons. The first was that his walls would not be a defence against Cromwell's modern artillery. The second was that his own home was one of the castles seized and garrisoned earlier in the month by Oliver's strike force; the terms allowed him to go back to live there. His men were able to join the victors if they were Protestants, or go home or overseas if not. It may be that Cromwell had fired warning shots on facing the fortress, for a ball from a field piece of the period is still stuck in the wall near the front gate. He cheerfully cried up the magnitude of his achievement in taking the castle to the Council of State, boasting that he had managed to do so in a single day, while an Elizabethan viceroy of Ireland, the earl of Essex, had needed eight weeks (the true duration of that siege had actually been four days).[128]

Early March was spent enforcing the surrender of more castles in the area now controlled by Oliver and his subordinates, opening up further routes to the south coast and laying more districts under contribution to their war effort. One, at Thomastown on the River Nore, initially fired back on those who summoned it, killing a few men; the colonel sent to take it punished the garrison when it did capitulate by hanging the officers as a deterrent example. Another, at Dundrum, was taken by storm, and as at Callan the defenders were massacred, save for a few who got into a tower and surrendered on promise of their lives. To the west, Broghill enlarged his quarters at Mallow by taking a medieval fortress 6 miles off at Castletown. He had a siege gun big enough to breach the walls, whereupon the garrison surrendered; he hanged the officers for failing to do so sooner.[129]

There was therefore no overall policy adopted by Cromwell and his lieutenants of showing a greater leniency to the occupants of enemy fortresses after the massacres at Drogheda and Wexford. There was, rather, a consistent one of giving generous terms to those who surrendered immediately, but meting out a punitive and deliberate brutality to those who resisted actively, even for a short time. This was a greater severity than that which Parliament's armies had shown during the English Civil War, but was, as stated before, a continuation of the greater savagery with which the war in Ireland had been fought from the beginning. It was also applied throughout Cromwell's campaign on the island. If it did not produce slaughters in the latter part of the expedition on the scale of those which had commenced it, this was only because the garrisons on the receiving end were much smaller.

Cromwell and his officers now had a new and very important target in their sights: the city of Kilkenny, which was one of the main inland centres of Ireland and a strongpoint of medieval English rule. It also possessed a major symbolic importance in the politics of the 1640s, for it was both the traditional seat of Ormond's family and the capital of the Catholic rebel confederacy. As such, its fall would be another tremendous blow to both, and a proportionately glamorous further addition to Oliver's reputation. He accordingly prepared for an attack on it with great care. His remaining siege train was brought up from the coast, and he ordered his governor of Dublin to come west with a strong force to join him. This was a hard-bitten colonel from the English army, John Hewson, who had led one of the regiments into the breach at Drogheda and had supervised the burning out of the defenders of the steeple of St Peter's church. He had already advanced into County Kildare with 3,000 soldiers and had reduced a number of minor enemy garrisons using his own little, but effective, siege train of a culverin, demi-culverin and mortar. Now, reinforced by cavalry ordered to him by Cromwell from Wexford, he pushed forward. Castlehaven's small army of Leinster retreated before him, outnumbered, and also menaced to its rear by 1,200 men sent by Cromwell. Hewson secured the crossing over the Barrow at Leighlinbridge, where the main highway from Dublin to Kilkenny still spans the river, and so arrived to the east of the latter city. More supplies of men and material came in to Cromwell's army from England. There was not enough money to keep the soldiers regularly paid any more, but abundant food was shipped over with fodder for the horses, and so there was no need to levy much of either from the local people.[130]

Kilkenny was now isolated and vulnerable, and morale there sank further as the plague reached it. Castlehaven and Ormond were crippled financially by the refusal of the remaining towns held by Catholics to send money to them. Castlehaven claimed afterwards to have attempted to bring all his infantry, numbering 2,000, into Kilkenny to reinforce it, but that the majority of his men refused to obey for fear of the epidemic.[131]

Cromwell sent Ireton with a detachment to hem in Waterford and prevent any sallies from that city which might disrupt the main operation. He then united his army with Hewson's, 12 miles to the east of Kilkenny in the pastures, where the hedges were now showing yellow hazel catkins and grey willow buds, near the little town of Gowran. That give him a combined formidable strength of 11,000 foot and 4,000 horse.[132] Gowran's castle was occupied by Ormond's own foot regiment, reformed after the Drogheda massacre and commanded by another English royalist refugee, who had fought against Parliament in the Kent uprising of 1648. When the siege guns opened up on the castle wall, this man realized that his situation was hopeless and surrendered on the promise that the common soldiers would definitely be spared but that the fate of the officers would be left to the decision of their captors. What this meant in practice was that the officers were all shot and the priest who acted as chaplain to the Catholic soldiers was hanged.

A council of war now agreed to close in on Kilkenny, which was reached on 22 March and was summoned to surrender that evening. Cromwell informed the governor and corporation that God had punished them for their rebellion and slaughter of Protestants in 1641 by sending them first plague and then his army. There was, in fact, no evidence that the Old English population of Kilkenny had been involved in that slaughter, but as usual Oliver was making all rebel Catholics guilty by association. His exchanges of correspondence with besieged garrisons were always propaganda documents in their own right, which he preserved and forwarded for publication. He informed the recipients of this one that they would keep their lives and freedoms if they gave in immediately and if he felt generous. A relation of Ormond, Sir Walter Butler, was in command of the city and, although he had only 650 men left effective in his garrison, he sent a defiant message after two days.

The medieval city had two suburbs, both with their own walls, one adjacent and called the Irish town, the other across the River Nore. Cromwell and his officers decided to attack the main city and the Irish town simultaneously to stretch the defenders, Oliver and his main body assaulting the former while a detachment of 1,000 men went up against the latter. Two demi-cannon and a culverin opened up against the wall of the main city on the 25th and smashed a hole in it after a hundred shots, whereupon the storming party went in. It met a nasty surprise, because Butler had worked fast and hard to build two strong and complete earthworks inside the breach, hemming it in and looming over it. Their outer sides were stuck full of stakes with sharp metal points to hamper attackers, and all of the defenders in that town were ready behind them. Cromwell's men were beaten off with the loss of thirty to seventy of them, including some officers. At the same time, however, the concentration of Butler's attention and resources on the breach into the city had deflected both from the suburb, which fell to the separate attack on it as the defenders were overwhelmed. Cromwell then sent a party to storm the suburb across the river, which was taken too. A second battery was now started to smash another gap in the wall of the main town, so that both entries to it could be assaulted at once. Butler probably realized that he would be overstretched to defend both breaches, that he had now lost the suburbs and that he had absolutely no hope of help from outside. His own commander, Castlehaven, advised him to treat while he had something to trade, and Cromwell was prepared to offer generous terms to get rid of him and his men. He was further prompted to do so because the storming and sacking of the city would carry the risk of infecting the victorious soldiers with plague.

On 28 March Butler and his soldiers marched out and laid down their arms, and then moved on to safety with their goods and Catholic clergy, whom Cromwell threatened to kill if they remained. The town was promised protection from plunder, providing it paid an indemnity of £2,000. Kilkenny had proved harder to take than had been hoped – Irish royalists were starting to find effective ways of defending the breaches that the English cannon opened – but it was now secured, with all the advantages and prestige that its fall conferred on the victors.[133] At the same time, Oliver received news from England that gratified him on a purely personal level: Richard and Dorothy had presented him with a first grandchild; while he still warned Richard against an 'unactive vain spirit' and urged him to greater piety, he conceded that his son's letters 'now had a good savour'.[134]

CLONMEL AND HOME

For much of a month after this success, Cromwell himself suspended major military operations, for four reasons. The first was that his very victories, by proliferating garrisons of all sizes, consumed men and local resources at a time when the flow of recruits and supplies from England was slackening. He wrote to Parliament to complain that he was now receiving only a fifth of the money needed to keep his soldiers in regular pay, and that letters from it had become rare and increasingly out of touch with the military situation in Ireland. His second reason for marking time was uncertainty over his own position. He was now constantly hearing rumours of his imminent recall to Britain, but had as yet received no formal letter from Parliament commanding his return.[135]

Third, he had to settle an administration for all his new conquests, to gain the maximum benefit from them, and enlarge them to the north and east. A force was sent under Reynolds to occupy parts of Queen's County (modern County Laois), while another was despatched into County Carlow. Most of southern and eastern Ireland was now under republican control. Hewson was returned to Dublin (without most of his men), and on Cromwell's western flank Broghill notched up his first independent victory when Oliver ordered him to attack royalists who were advancing from County Kerry. He was given a detachment which he reinforced from the Munster ports, and surprised and routed his enemy at Macroom, west of Cork. He emulated the pattern of showing brutality where it was feasible, by having most of his prisoners clubbed to death, and hanging the most important, a Catholic bishop, when he could not persuade a local castle to surrender.[136]

The fourth distraction from campaigning which affected Cromwell at this period was a development in the royalist coalition, which offered the hope that he might make further gains without taking the field. In March 1650, trust between the two religious wings of the coalition had collapsed after so many defeats and defections, and the Catholic leaders forced Ormond to disband his remaining Protestant soldiers. Cromwell wavered between offering the demobbed men lenient and harsh terms. Eventually, on 26 April, he allowed any Protestant royalists who surrendered to his government to go abroad or to settle in territory that he controlled, with their money and goods, and start the process of retrieving their estates by paying fines and promising future good behaviour. Most subsequently accepted this offer. Ormond and Inchiquin were offered the chance to go into exile, losing their lands, but for the time being they refused to do so.[137] In the same period, the government in England acceded to Cromwell's appeals for better support. Its consignments of food for men and horses had been maintained, and between March and April it sent another 7,000 soldiers to Ireland, to join a total of 24,000 already in its pay there.[138]

Cromwell attended to all these issues while moving between places such as Carrick and Fethard, as his men rested, or besieged stray castles that held out in the areas that they now mostly controlled. At the end of April, however, he was ready to take the offensive again with his main army, against one last major target. It was an obvious one, the important town of Clonmel, upriver on the Suir from Carrick, which was the last significant centre to hold out for royalism and Catholicism in County Tipperary, and the last of all to do so between the south coast of Ireland and the territory he had now secured in the interior. It was thus at once valuable, isolated and vulnerable. Knowing this, Ormond had taken care to garrison it with many of the finest soldiers from Ulster under one of their best leaders, Hugh Dubh (Black Hugh) O'Neill, a canny veteran of both Continental and domestic Irish wars. Ormond had solemnly promised him to march to his relief within a week if he were besieged – something the marquis was completely unable to do at the time.[139] O'Neill had around 2,000 excellent infantry and just over 100 horse inside the medieval walls, and those walls were further defended by the river on one side of the town and patches of bog on the other. There was, however, a stretch on the north side that was bordered by firm ground outside and lacked the protection of a thick enough lining of soil. It thus made a perfect target for Cromwell's guns, and Clonmel's fate could well have seemed sealed when the siege train arrived four days after the army closed around its landward side in early May.

Oliver set about operations with his usual methodical efficiency, sending Reynolds with 2,500 horse to cover the approaches to the town from the north, in case of any attempt to aid it. He strongly entrenched the perimeter of his camp to protect it against sallies from the town, and had enough tents within it to shelter him and all his men. The battery was established securely, and then the bombardment began. Once more the crash of metal balls striking medieval stonework, and then the roar of falling masonry, was heard. By mid-afternoon of 9 May the expected wide gap had been created in the wall. Complaints had been voiced that it was always the foot soldiers who faced the dangers of a storm, and so on this occasion dismounted cavalry, who had the additional protection of the body armour that they wore – breastplate, backplate and helmet – were used in the assault. The attack force swept up to the breach, yelling its watchword, only to be met and repelled on a first attempt, as at Drogheda. As at Drogheda too, the defence in the gap yielded to a second and stronger wave of enemies, and fell back inside. Here, however, the resemblance ended. The more cautious of the soldiers pouring into the town may have feared the possibility of facing formidable earthworks as had happened at Kilkenny. Instead, they found something infinitely worse.

The breach had been made at the end of a street that ran straight from there into the town, and O'Neill had turned it into a death trap. He had filled the houses that lined it with his men, equipped with muskets to fire down on the attackers and heavy objects – stones, lumps of metal and spars of wood – to hurl on top of them. Those who made it past these dangers found the way blocked by a double line of freshly built ramparts, constructed of timber, stones and dung. These had firing steps behind, lined with more musketeers, pikemen and men with scythes; and two field guns were mounted at the point at which they met, to rake the street with cannonballs chained in pairs. When the attackers had filled the street, the defenders opened fire at point-blank range. The colonel leading the storming party was killed, and his men were mown down with him. For a time, those trying to fall back were pushed forward by those pressing on behind, but at last the survivors were able to turn and flee for safety. Ireton persuaded them to halt outside the wall and to hold the breach in it to allow a further attempt on the following day. The dead and dying in the street within were left to their fate as night fell. Cromwell had been waiting outside one of the town's gates, for it to be opened by his victorious men, and slowly realized that a disaster had occurred. He must have been both shocked and angry as he retired to his tent at midnight. Then the apparent miracle occurred, as a message was brought to him from the townspeople asking to negotiate. He agreed at once, and swiftly made a deal by which the citizens would be protected from plunder if they surrendered the town and all the weaponry in it by eight o'clock that morning. Nothing was said of O'Neill and the garrison, and Cromwell must have assumed that they were being left to his mercy, and revenge.

Instead, when his soldiers marched in, they found that the defending soldiers, and all their equipment and camp followers, had gone. As ever, the deficiency of the Irish royalists in resources had proved a fatal weakness, because the defence of the street had used up all O'Neill's stock of munitions, and he had nothing left with which to fight. His council of war had decided to get out of the town. Accordingly, he had told the citizens to make the best possible deal with Cromwell and had marched out two hours later in the darkness, across the bridge onto the far side of the river and away to safety. On discovering this, Oliver was naturally furious, especially when he saw the bodies of his men piled in the trap that O'Neill had prepared for them on the previous day. Nevertheless, he felt obliged to honour his promise to the citizens, and slaked his anger by sending out horsemen immediately to pursue and attack O'Neill's force. Only stragglers from it were intercepted, but the troopers butchered a couple of hundred of these. With that, the action was over.[140]

We cannot know what would have happened had the defenders possessed a better stock of munitions. One account left by the attackers stressed that cannon were being brought to the breach to smash down the defences inside it on the following day.[141] Another, in contrast, had Cromwell doubting that he could have persuaded his men to enter that hell-hole again.[142] Had they not done so, we have no idea what would have occurred: if a new gap in the wall would have been broken at a better point, or if Cromwell would have left the town to be starved out. Without any prospect of relief or resupplying, O'Neill could not have held out indefinitely.

We shall also never know how many died in the trap beyond the breach, except that we can be sure that it was a large number because neither Cromwell nor any other member of his party provided a body count: a sure sign that they had a bad one to conceal. A correspondent of Ormond writing soon after the event but who had been nowhere near Clonmel claimed that 1,500 casualties had been sustained.[143] A history of the war written later by somebody who served in Ireland in the 1640s but was not at this particular action – though he claimed to have spoken to those who were, inside and outside the town – claimed more than that number. His story of the siege, though the most vivid and detailed (and most often quoted), has implausible touches, such as profane oaths uttered by Cromwell, and cannot therefore be trusted; yet we have no figure from any more reliable source.[144] Certainly the victors realized that they had suffered a blow that needed to be downplayed. Uniquely, no despatch from Cromwell to the Council of State has survived reporting the taking of the town, either because he did not feel able to write one, or because they decided to suppress it instead of publishing it as usual. The few newspapers that informed readers of these events concentrated on the success of the capture, and usually implied that it had fallen to the storming party. As ever, Parliament's propaganda machine acted effectively to cry up successes and minimize reverses. After all, Clonmel *had* ended up as another success, even if care was needed in handling the details. In an important sense, Cromwell had just suffered the worst defeat of his military career, but providence had ensured that it was immediately followed by the achievement of the goal at which the disastrous operation had been aimed.

That, on the face of things, made a triumphant conclusion to his Irish service, as he was now directly recalled to England by Parliament for other duties. He appointed Ireton, his second-in-command, to take control of the Irish war as his lord deputy, and left him all the army in Ireland, with Reynolds, Hewson, Broghill and its other subordinate commanders. On 26 May he sailed for home from Youghal with only his own servants and a few gentlemen and officers. He was less seasick than before, and after two days he landed at Bristol, to a triple salute of cannon shot.[145] He then, at a leisurely pace, repeated in reverse the journey he had made from London almost a year before, through the limestone and chalk hills in the season of snowy hawthorn blossom, buttercups and rising green crops. On 1 June he reached Windsor, where he was saluted with more shots from the castle and was met by his wife, the Council of State and many army officers and MPs. Discussions of the state of Ireland were held with many of those people, and the exemplary courtesy with which he welcomed all comers and conferred with them was noted, as was the fact that, as usual, Cromwell attributed all his successes to God. He added with the same modesty that, should well-wishers decide to cheer him on his approach to the capital, then he would not object lest he seem ungracious. Cheer they did, as some horse troops from the regular army escorted him down the roads the next day with a swelling retinue of lords, MPs, gentry and citizens. Infantry and field artillery awaited him to salute him in Hyde Park, and he reached Westminster in the afternoon. Two days later, he took his place once more in the House of Commons, to receive the hearty thanks of the Speaker, on behalf of all members.[146]

Parliament was correct to be grateful. Cromwell had been sent to Ireland primarily to prevent its newly formed Catholic and Protestant coalition from invading England to destroy the equally new commonwealth there, and he had done so resoundingly. Ormond's set of alliances had fallen apart, leaving the Catholics to fight on alone, after a succession of rapidly sustained major defeats and extensive losses of territory. Oliver had certainly not succeeded in imposing English republican rule throughout the island, but he had taken that process to the point that his successors only had to complete the work of mopping up a weakened and disunited enemy – long, wearying and expensive though that process would be. Had he not been recalled urgently to England, he would undoubtedly have finished the conquest in person. For an episode in Irish history that is as fraught with continuing emotion as this one, there is a remarkable unanimity among recent historians of it that, as he embarked on the venture, Cromwell already held all the advantages. He had a perfect bridgehead for his arrival, and he faced an enemy who had already been defeated and left unable to face him in battle. All that Ormond and his allies could do was throw their soldiers into fortified strongpoints which Cromwell's superlative siege train could smash open within hours. That process could be sustained until there were no more refuges into which they could retire. It was aided by two other tremendous strengths in Cromwell's position: that he was consistently reinforced and resupplied from England, on a scale and with a frequency denied to any former invader of Ireland; and that he received further major accessions of strength from defecting opponents as soon as he won victories. Had either of these factors not operated, he would still have made progress, but at a much slower pace.[147]

There is equal apparent consensus, however, that Cromwell seized all these advantages and exploited them to the full, just as he had all those that had presented themselves to him in the Civil Wars in England. He had made not a single serious mistake, and his four failures can all be extenuated. The first was his inability to take Wexford peacefully and intact, which occurred because his men acted on impulse and without his orders;

and he still became master of the town. The second was the reverse before Duncannon, because it was simply too strong for his available resources. There he was not commanding in person, and he nullified the retreat by a new advance that yielded the desired result – entry to Waterford harbour – from a different direction. The third was the failure to reduce Waterford itself, which was the result of bad winter weather that rendered an effective siege impossible. Cromwell had gambled here and for once his good luck had deserted him; but he had not made any actual errors, and he left the city hemmed in by his own garrisons and unable to menace his operations. The last was the fiasco at Clonmel, and here his own culpability was limited. It made sense to breach the wall at that point, and then to attempt to storm it, and nobody in the attacking army had any experience that would have forewarned it of the lethal nature of the trap prepared inside. Once the soldiers were caught in it, it was very difficult to extricate them. Oliver himself cannot be blamed for the failure to do so, as he was not on the scene but supervising what was expected to be the next phase of the operation. Moreover, fortune then delivered him the town anyway.

In general, he acted consistently with perfect strategic and tactical skill, pushing his army at maximum speed and with maximum impact without depleting its strength fatally, and using all his superiority in numbers, support systems and firepower to greatest effect at each point. He clearly retained an excellent rapport with his officers, and so with his men, and showed an equal ability to work with and employ trusted lieutenants from England such as Ireton, Hewson and the recently added Reynolds, existing commanders in Ireland such as Jones, and able men who had just offered their services such as Broghill. His awareness of the importance of publicity and propaganda, and so the packaging of all news, was as keen as ever.

The only real controversy over Cromwell's career in Ireland, tremendous though it was and is, has been over the degree of ruthlessness with which he pursued his objectives, and his personal culpability for the mass deaths of soldiers and civilians that resulted from some of his victories.[148] The conclusion drawn here is that he must bear much of the blame, for ordering a general slaughter of the huge garrison at Drogheda and for sustaining an assault on the defences of Wexford even while negotiations were in progress for its surrender. Nor did the wholesale killing of resisting garrisons, and the selective killing of prisoners, end with those notorious cases, but was continued by Cromwell and his commanders until his departure from the land. To point out that it fitted into a long-established tradition of unusual brutality in the Irish warfare of the 1640s is to help explain it without extenuating it. Nor can any further extenuation be gained from the undoubted, and important, fact that the extent of Cromwell's own severity was subsequently grossly exaggerated in nationalist tradition.

6

SCOTLAND

THE TOP JOB

When Cromwell returned to his home in Westminster, it was not to his private house in King Street, but to the palace of Whitehall itself, because a grateful Parliament had rewarded him for his achievements in Ireland with a step up in grandeur. He and his family had been granted a luxurious suite of apartments in the detached building of the palace called the Cockpit, originally used for games and plays and subsequently converted into accommodation for favoured royal courtiers. He was also given custody of the smaller red-brick Tudor palace of St James's and its park, which ran beside the Cockpit, for business affairs and entertainments, and the final arrangements had been put in place for his custody of the full aristocratic landed estate promised to him for his services in the First Civil War.[1] Immediately his new and exalted life commenced: in the first week of June, the lord mayor and aldermen of London visited him at the Cockpit, to congratulate him on his Irish conquests. Oliver, as usual, gave all the credit to God alone in reply. The journalist who reported this termed him 'the Lord Cromwell', which was technically correct as he was regarded as Ireland's lord lieutenant, but it fitted his new status in a more general sense.[2] He had, however, little time in which to enjoy it, because he had to reckon with another military emergency. It had been developing since

January, when Parliament had first started to consider his recall from Ireland, and it now seemed critical.[3] The danger came from Scotland.[4]

Ever since the autumn of 1648, the 'Kirk Party' that Cromwell had helped to power there had controlled the country absolutely, but even its gratitude to him for this assistance, and the long association of its leaders with him and with Parliament's cause in the first Civil War, could not withstand the shock of the regicide. That was a double insult to the Scots as a nation. For one thing, it represented a fundamental alteration of the government of England, undertaken without any of the consultations between the two states that had usually accompanied attempts to settle that government after the war, as the nature of the English regime clearly had implications for both. For another, Charles I had been king of Scotland as well as England and Ireland, and the English technically had no right to kill the reigning head of another state. Moreover, their act in doing so directly breached the treaty between the Scottish government and English Parliament of 1643, the Solemn League and Covenant, which had included an agreement to preserve the monarchy; to devout people, this treaty was a covenant with God as well as between two nations. Two days after receiving the news of Charles's execution, therefore, the Scottish Parliament declared his son king of Scotland, England and Ireland. It also, however, declared that, before being admitted to Scotland, Charles II would have to accept the Solemn League and Covenant himself, which was regarded by everybody as committing him to establishing presbyterian church government in all his kingdoms.[5] And he was required to bring with him only those followers whom the current Scottish government deemed acceptable, which ruled out most Scottish and English royalists.

These terms were completely unacceptable to the new king as long as he had any other options, for they involved the outright betrayal of the principles for which his father had died and the royalists had fought. He had at that time much better prospects in Ireland, which was now dominated by his loyal servant Ormond. At the same time, instead of making concessions to the current Scottish regime, he had a good prospect of overturning it or driving it to a better deal by means of a royalist uprising in Scotland. During the mid-1640s, the leading Scottish royalist general, the marquis of Montrose, had briefly reconquered most of the country for Charles I, and Montrose now offered his services to start another rebellion in his native land. In May 1649, therefore, Charles II rejected the terms offered by the ruling regime and prepared to join Ormond. Fortunately for him, it took months for him to travel to a point from which he could embark for Ireland, and by that time Cromwell had already embarked on his victorious campaign. Charles therefore waited on events, which by the end of the year were running, seemingly unstoppably, against the Irish royalist coalition. This drove the king back towards the Scottish government, with the hope of persuading it to accept him on less offensive conditions. Montrose was ordered to proceed with his plans for invasion and rebellion in order to weaken the government position and make it more tractable. The Scots agreed to treat, but only with reluctance and division, and on the same terms as before.

The talks began in March 1650, at the Dutch town of Breda, where agreement was reached in April that the king would declare his approval of the Covenant but not actually commit himself to it, and would confirm the existing Scottish regime in power; in return, the Scottish government agreed that it would consider allowing royalists and the Engagers of 1648 back into office at a later date. Charles was now formally invited to Scotland. During May, however, his position was much weakened by two developments. The first was the defeat of Montrose's royalist rebellion. The marquis had landed in Scotland in April and gathered a small army, but within three weeks this was surprised and destroyed by an even smaller government force. Montrose was captured, brought to Edinburgh and hanged. The fact that the most brilliant and dreaded of Scottish royalist soldiers should be overcome so swiftly and easily strengthened the Kirk Party's sense of divine approval for its cause, and made it the less inclined to compromise. As a result, the Scottish Parliament rejected the treaty just signed with Charles and insisted on its original offer. This was communicated to the Scottish commissioners with the king, but concealed from him until he had set sail for Scotland, being sprung upon him halfway through the voyage. He argued furiously until he arrived off the coast of his kingdom on 23 June. Then, with the prospect of a humiliating and dangerous journey back to the Continent staring him in the face, he gave in and signed the Covenant with obvious bad grace. The new alliance was therefore founded on resentment, suspicion and distrust.

The English commonwealth, however, had no intention of waiting to see how it worked out. When news of the treaty between the king and the Scots reached Westminster, and before the king set sail, the English were already preparing for war, and Cromwell's arrival removed the last brake on action. There was nothing in the Treaty of Breda that committed the Scots to attacking the English commonwealth on Charles's behalf, but also nothing to deter them. After all, they had proclaimed him king of England as well as of their own land, and had never recognized the validity of the revolutionary English regime. If they did invade, it would not be with an inexperienced and badly led army, as in 1648, but with commanders who had defeated the forces of Charles I in three successive wars and had helped Parliament to win the biggest of those. The English government could not take the risk of leaving the frontier open. Responsibility for defence lay with the Council of State, which Cromwell had rejoined as soon as he had returned to Westminster. On 10 June it decided that Fairfax and Cromwell be directed to take the army in England to the north as soon as possible, and Parliament enacted this two days later. Thomas Harrison was chosen to command the forces left to hold down the south of England in their absence.[6] On the 20th, however, the momentous decision was taken by the council to launch a pre-emptive strike on Scotland without waiting for the Scots to start the war. Parliament agreed the next day, and ordered Fairfax and Cromwell to lead their men across the border when they reached the north.[7]

It seems likely that English and Scots had become locked into a vicious circle of suspicion, powered from England. On hearing that the king was approaching, the Scottish Parliament had ordered the nation's small standing army to muster in the centre of the country, both to keep order and to have its officers purged of any deemed to be unreliable by the ruling Kirk Party. It is possible that news of these troop movements convinced the English government that an invasion of England was being prepared, and led it to decide to strike first, to keep the ravages of war on the enemy's soil. On the other hand, knowledge that the king was making for Scotland could have made the English conclude that war was inevitable. At any rate, even before the English decided to attack, the Scots had become fearful that they would do so; on the day that the English Parliament decided to invade, the Scottish one voted to reinforce its gathering army massively. Within two more weeks it had ordered the conscription of 26,000 men. On initiating this process it informed its English counterpart that these measures were only taken in self-defence, with the English army moving towards Scotland, and denied that it had any plan for invasion itself.[8] The English Parliament replied that the Scots could not be trusted, had proclaimed Charles king of England and had now promised him assistance to conquer it (of these charges, there was no evidence for the last, while the first was only arguable). It declared that its pre-emptive attack was not intended to seize territory but to ensure English freedom and security.[9] With this, the war commenced. In truth, we shall never know what would have happened had the English republic chosen to remain on the defensive: the king would certainly have wanted to attack it, but there is no certainty that the Kirk Party would have obliged him.[10]

The immediate result of the English choice of an aggressive strategy was a crisis in the military command system. When Parliament initially ordered Fairfax and Cromwell to defend the north of England, both men had immediately accepted the mission.[11] Relations between them remained excellent, and on returning from Ireland Cromwell had been quick to visit his old commander, at his town house in the next Westminster street to his own, with great warmth.[12] On being ordered to attack Scotland, however, to everybody's initial surprise, Fairfax refused on the grounds that such an invasion was unjustified without any proof that the Scots had aggressive intentions, and would breach the Solemn League and Covenant between the nations. Those who knew him agreed that this was because of the influence of his wife and his chaplains, who strongly favoured a presbyterian system of Church government close to the Scottish model and who regarded the Kirk Party as natural allies. The Council of State immediately sent a group of its members, including Cromwell, to talk away Fairfax's reservations, but he not only held obdurately to his view but insisted on resigning his commission on the transparently fictional excuse of poor health. On 26 June Parliament accepted his resignation, at the same time as confirming the decision to invade Scotland, with immediate effect.[13]

All the accounts of the arguments that the council's deputation held with Fairfax agree that Cromwell did his utmost to persuade his old friend and leader that a Scottish invasion was inevitable, and that Fairfax needed to command the army sent to forestall it. Some of the authors also recorded their later suspicions that this was dissimulation, and that Oliver really wanted Fairfax gone in order to supplant him.[14] As ever, we cannot see into Cromwell's heart, and can only conclude that political calculation (in avoiding any show of selfish ambition), piety (in avoiding the sin of pride) and genuine affection for and gratitude to his familiar commander would all have tended to the same end: that of urging Fairfax to continue. However, when the latter proved obdurate, there was really only one obvious successor for him in the current emergency. On the same day on which Parliament let Fairfax go, it appointed Cromwell as captain-general and commander-in-chief of all its soldiers. Henry Ireton was confirmed as commanding the army in Ireland in his place.[15] Preparations for war had commenced as soon as it had been decided to mobilize the army, with regiments marching north and provisions being shipped to meet them, all through the last two-thirds of June. A new foot regiment was being raised for Cromwell himself.[16] Only a few days after his appointment, Oliver left London for the campaign.[17]

TO THE BORDER

The route he took was to Cambridge, and then across to the Great North Road, which he followed to Newcastle. Cromwell travelled in his coach, accompanied by his staff, chief officers and mounted bodyguard, and set a tremendous pace. Towards the end of the journey they averaged 24 miles per day. The landscapes crossed were familiar to him from many campaigns: a succession of ridges and valleys, with towns of stone, timber or brick, their church spires and towers rising from the bigger centres like a stand of soldiers' pikes. At this late midsummer season, the countryside between would have been filled with light green cereal crops and meadow grasses, red poppies, trees heavy with dark green foliage, and tiny green and black flies. At York the city's lord mayor and aldermen, and many local gentlemen, turned out to greet their distinguished guest and provided a dinner, after which Cromwell was careful to talk privately to some of the gentry.[18] One of the senior officers travelling with him was the dashing John Lambert, who had – as major-general in charge of Parliament's northern forces – been his second-in-command on his campaign in the North Country in 1648. Lambert was now to fulfil that role again. He later remembered how, as they passed through the towns en route, many of the inhabitants cheered them. Lambert took this as a sign that the nation had come round to support for the commonwealth. He recalled that the more politically experienced Cromwell replied that the crowds would cheer as loudly if the two of them were going to be hanged.[19]

Cromwell's care to speak privately to some of the Yorkshire gentry was part of a vigorous public relations campaign that he was waging on his way to the military front. It had started at Westminster before his departure, when he had taken the dour radical MP and soldier Edmund Ludlow aside at a meeting of the Council of State, and asked him for a one-to-one conversation. They withdrew to a nearby chamber in Whitehall Palace, where Cromwell proceeded to try to clear up any remaining tension between them, apologizing for and regretting his negotiations with the king in 1647 and claiming that he supported prospective reforms in the Church and the legal system, but had been obstructed by more conservative leaders of the new regime. For an hour he expounded the message of Psalm 110, on the day in which God would come into his true power on earth and strike down kings as part of that: this was Ludlow's sort of language. He then came to his point, which was to persuade Ludlow to go to Ireland to serve as Ireton's second-in-command, as lieutenant-general. The younger man agreed, and also consented to serve as one of a set of commissioners nominated by the Council of State to run the civilian government of that country.[20] The appointments removed one of Oliver's former critics from the central seat of power and turned him, for a time, into a grateful client. It also presaged a pattern which was to obtain for the rest of Cromwell's life, whereby he both took former opponents or critics into favour and also placed people who were not formerly comrades and allies of each other – in this case Ireton and Ludlow – in positions in which they had to work together under him. The result was to draw upon a wide range of different talent and experience. It also allowed him to put into positions under him a set of followers who had little in common with each other, so would not easily combine against him, and who owed their good fortune directly to him.

In the same period, Cromwell made other efforts to conciliate a broad range of former opponents, to build unity at the onset of the war. He intervened to help a prominent royalist leader, the earl of Northampton, make peace with the commonwealth and regain access to his estates.[21] He made his own peace with his mercurial alternate friend and foe, John Lilburne, who had eventually been put on trial for treason by the government while Cromwell was in Ireland, but had been spectacularly acquitted by the jury after a masterly defence. On his return, Oliver supported Lilburne in the Council of State over his struggle finally to get compensation from Parliament for his sufferings at the hands of Charles I's government in the 1630s. As Cromwell left London, Lilburne met him on the road out to give him thanks, and was invited to travel with him on the first day of his journey. That evening, 'Freeborn John' supped at Oliver's own table. The next morning Cromwell gave him a hug of farewell and promised to make Parliament enact the long-delayed plan for successive Parliaments elected on a reformed franchise.[22]

Oliver's diversion through Cambridge was to speak to the leaders of the university and persuade them to support the war. The royalists in the institution had been purged in 1644 and reliable parliamentarians put in, but many of the latter were monarchists and presbyterians, who had baulked at a recent requirement by the commonwealth government that the nation's office-holders, including holders of academic posts, declare loyalty to it. Cromwell met them at an inn and told them he had asked Parliament not to put pressure on those who refused to sign. The person who reported this commented dourly on Oliver's habit of making courteous and charming overtures to people when he felt vulnerable, and then crushing them when he became secure again. Like the devil, he added, Cromwell was more dangerous when behaving like a serpent than when behaving like a lion.[23]

Having reached the north, Oliver took care to reduce tensions within the army, which had largely preceded him there. John Okey, an old comrade of his who commanded the dragoon regiment, was at odds with one of his captains about the latter's religious beliefs. Contrary to general British Protestant orthodoxy, the man thought that God was present in all things, including inanimate objects, that all men were potentially godly, that divine revelation came better from people's hearts than from the Bible, and that forms of Church government were unimportant. These beliefs were representative of the kind of novel ideas that the war and revolution had let loose among radical Puritans, and they divided the regiment, the colonel being among those scandalized. The captain's critics accused him before Cromwell of misconduct, whereupon Oliver treated the man gently, promising him a court martial so that he could clear his name and be reinstated, but explaining that he had to leave his present regiment as he could not work with Okey. The captain agreed, but no court martial was forthcoming, meaning that he had been deceived into leaving the army without a fuss.[24] Nor were Cromwell's soothing words of much lasting benefit to others who received them at this time. As soon as Parliament felt more secure, the presbyterian heads of Cambridge colleges who refused formally to pledge loyalty were indeed purged.

Cromwell reached Newcastle on 9 July, met his full set of senior officers and planned the invasion in detail. The first day after his arrival was spent fasting and praying for success, five ministers preaching the righteousness of the cause, and it was decided to issue a declaration to the Scots justifying the attack. This promised mercy and liberty to all godly people in Scotland, and hailed them as brethren. It proclaimed that Charles I had been killed to prevent him from destroying English religion and freedom, and that this cause overrode the section of the Solemn League and Covenant which undertook to preserve the monarchy. It professed a readiness to adopt any form of government for the English Church that accorded with the Bible, to punish blasphemers and to allow presbyterians to practise their mode of religion freely, whatever the final structure that was decided for English religion. It then accused the Scots of provoking the war by undertaking to restore Charles II to power in England.[25] In issuing this statement, Cromwell and his subordinates were launching a propaganda campaign with the object both of reinforcing commitment to the military effort within their army and in England, and of dividing the Scots, with the hope of detaching some of them. This policy of appealing to prospective allies in the nation being invaded had worked wonderfully in the case of the Irish Protestants, and there was a chance that it would do so again. Five hundred copies of the declaration were sent into Scotland.[26]

While at Newcastle, Cromwell was also putting his army into readiness for the advance. One of his infantry colonels demanded a further two weeks to put his private affairs in order, and resigned when this was refused. Present among the experienced men gathering around Oliver was George Monck, the professional soldier who had conducted himself so obligingly over the dealings with Owen Roe O'Neill and who had clearly been promised subsequent favour. He had been invited to Newcastle, where Cromwell now offered him the vacant regiment. In doing so, he had reckoned without the independent spirit of its soldiers, who refused to accept a former royalist. They had to be allotted to Lambert instead, thus providing him with a foot unit as well as his long-standing horse regiment, but Oliver did not regard himself as defeated in the matter of employing Monck. He stubbornly created a new foot regiment by pulling companies out of the local garrisons, and so it was that Monck became one of the senior officers of the expedition.[27]

On 16 July Cromwell advanced into Northumberland to muster his invasion force.[28] Both the season and the latitude were changing. Since York the blue line of the Pennines had shut off the western horizon, and now their extension came much closer in the form of the Cheviot Hills, their slopes rising green, purple and dusky brown to the left hand. To the right, the land fell gently away to the North Sea, carrying its late summer music of sheep, crickets and skylarks. The morale of the converging regiments, and of their commanders, was raised on the march by news of a great victory in Ireland, in which the army that had once been O'Neill's had been totally destroyed by the Ulster forces of the commonwealth, and its remaining leaders beheaded.[29] At Alnwick, at the beetling black and brown castle of the medieval earls of Northumberland, Cromwell made a backward glance at his family, writing once again to the father-in-law of his eldest son, Richard. The young couple had neglected their correspondence with Cromwell, and the latter now asked Richard Mayor to take his son in hand, openly stating that the youth was lazy and could go astray.[30] It seems that his thoughts were being concentrated on the possible consequences of his own death on campaign. His army issued another declaration to the Scots, repeating its assurance that those who were godly, peaceful and co-operative had nothing to fear from it. On the 20th, its units came together at last on a moor beyond Alnwick, cheering Oliver as he rode around them.[31]

It was a first-class body of soldiers. It was large, with a total of 16,354 men, of whom 5,415 were cavalry and dragoons, in eight regiments, and

10,249 were infantry, also in eight regiments.[32] The majority were veterans, and their equipment was also of a high standard. There was a large train of mobile field artillery, but no heavy siege guns, as the object of this force was to move with maximum speed and to engage and destroy the Scottish army and so end the war: if possible, within a few weeks. It was expected that the Scots would fight soon after their assailants crossed the border.

On the evening of the 21st, Cromwell led the advance guard into Berwick, the frontier town that he had retaken for England almost two years before. On the following day, his great column of military men marched out onto Scottish territory for 4 or 5 miles, halting in the rich fields of the Merse, as he had done when entering Scotland in 1648. A proclamation had been read at the head of each regiment before the march began, forbidding any violence or pillage to be offered to Scottish civilians, in order to encourage them to collaborate and voluntarily offer supplies – just as in Ireland. As darkness fell, points of flame could be seen on the hilltops to the north: beacons lit by the Scots to warn their government and soldiers that the foe was at hand.[33]

STALEMATE

The initial consequence of the invasion was an anticlimax, whereby the English army was stuck in the Merse for three days waiting for supplies. Its sheer size made it a major logistical problem, for it cost £67,000 per month in pay, while every member of it needed a minimum each day of a pound of bread (either fresh or more usually baked hard into biscuit to preserve it), half a pound of cheese and a pint of watery beer.[34] The government had dealt well with the money, sending four months' pay north in time for the campaign, but, although it and the army's agents in London had placed huge orders for wheat, oats and beans (all for the horses), and biscuit and cheese and tents to serve the soldiers, this all had to be taken by sea to Newcastle and Berwick, and few of the ships had arrived. The north of England itself could supply only about half of the army's food, especially after its ravaging in 1648, and that only for the start of the campaign.

There was no hope of subsisting on Scottish produce, because not only was the land poorer than England, with fewer inhabitants and less productive farms, but scouts reported that most of the Scots in the districts on the line of march had disappeared, along with their livestock and food stores. In the end, the English soldiers had to move north living on bread and water, and sleeping rough in the fields for lack of tents. This made a quick victory all the more urgent.[35]

The halt, and the poor living conditions, had an immediate impact on morale. Cromwell had to issue a proclamation threatening his men with death if they continued to straggle from their units and plunder the locals. Even Oliver himself, however, was moved to merriment by the sight of a soldier with his head stuck fast in a tub of local cream. Another of Okey's turbulent dragoons got drunk and blasphemed, and was sentenced to have his tongue bored through with a hot iron. Any hope that the Scots might be persuaded to start negotiations was scotched when they sent a reply to the army's declaration. It accused the English Parliament of turning upon them after they had given it so much help, of breaking the Solemn League and Covenant, and of tolerating heretics and sectaries. It denied that it had any intention of attacking England to restore Charles II, and so condemned the English invasion as wholly unjustified.[36] With that, all-out war was finally certain, and on 25 July the army moved up the coast. The place taken by the Cheviot Hills on the western horizon was now succeeded by the Lammermuirs, even larger and steeper, and the space between them and the sea was narrower. The land remained eerily deserted, some of the soldiers not seeing more than ten adult local men during the march, and only the poorest women and children. All the rest, and the food, had been evacuated out of reach. The soldiers found a little oats and meal, and some beer hidden away, but that was all. As soon as the army had passed, armed Scots sallied out of local strongpoints to attack supply parties and cut land communications with England.

In two days the small port of Dunbar was reached, where a few more provisions were landed. Progress then continued across the neck of a broad peninsula, its centre occupied by another small town, Haddington. From there it was only a day's march to the Scottish capital of Edinburgh, and the decisive battle was expected to take place on one of the open stretches of moorland between.[37] No enemy appeared, however, and on the 27th the English army moved forward to another small port, Musselburgh, only 4 miles from Edinburgh. The next day it advanced again, and the scene that enfolded in front disclosed at last the Scottish strategy. Once again Cromwell saw the large volcanic hill, covered with coarse grass, called Arthur's Seat. To the right of that rose the drum towers and walls of the royal palace of Holyrood, and rising beyond that, its end facing the invaders, was a huge whale-backed ridge onto which the tall houses of Edinburgh were crowded, rising to another volcanic plug at the far end, on which sat the enormous medieval castle. To the right of Holyrood were scattered houses and parks, running down to the buildings of Edinburgh's port, Leith, beyond which sprawled the great inlet of sea called the Firth of Forth. The whole stretch of land between Leith and Edinburgh was now crossed by a continuous line of earthworks and ditches, representing a formidable defensive system crowded with armed men and artillery.

On 4 July the Scottish Parliament had ratified the treaty with the king and adjourned to fight the war, leaving a committee to govern the nation and make policy in its absence.[38] Official command of the armed forces lay with Alexander Leslie, earl of Leven, who had held this position in the wars with Charles I, but he was now too old and infirm to take the field. Effective leadership therefore devolved to his lieutenant-general, David Leslie, a very experienced and able soldier who had served alongside Cromwell at the battle of Marston Moor, one of the turning points of the English Civil War. As we have seen, however, he seemed to have cooled towards Oliver and appeared to have snubbed him during his visit to Edinburgh in 1648. Leslie now mustered about 12,000 foot and 7,000 horse at the Scottish capital, an army around the same size as Oliver's.[39] That said, it was much less well trained, most of its men being raw recruits, and much less well equipped. This was a powerful argument for avoiding a pitched battle, and so Leslie and the government agreed to position their soldiers behind the line of powerful defences for the capital. A defensive strategy was also made sensible by the increasingly tense relations between the king and the Scottish government. The joy of the Kirk Party on hearing of his arrival had rapidly soured when it learned of the reluctance with which he had signed the Covenant, and of the large retinue of English and Scottish royalists and Engagers – old enemies of the Kirk Party – which he had brought with him. Both the Scottish Parliament and the General Assembly of the Scottish clergy immediately ordered most of his companions to depart. Charles's response was not to comply but to argue. The Committee of Estates, which the Parliament had left to run the country, expressly forbade the king to join the army in person, whereupon the impetuous young monarch ignored that too, turning up at the lines between Leith and Edinburgh just as Cromwell appeared before them.[40]

Oliver and his officers surveyed the unexpected and formidable barrier that now loomed in front of them, and probed it throughout 28 July, attacking outworks and occupying Arthur's Seat. By evening it was clear that the defences were too strong and the defenders too numerous to make an all-out attack feasible. Moreover, rain fell all day, saturating the English army as it stood in battle order on open ground, turning that ground to mud beneath the men, and leaving them to try to sleep in the mud when night fell. It was clear that soldiers could not stay healthy long nor muskets functional in such conditions, and the rations, miserable though they were, had started to run out. The only course was to retreat to Musselburgh the next day, and as soon as this began the Scots sallied out 'like bees' on the rear of the retiring English. A hard fight was needed to drive them off, in which Lambert was wounded lightly twice and briefly captured. The Scots attacked again late in the following night, when Cromwell's army was quartered in Musselburgh. Once more they were repelled, and then the exhausted and filthy English retreated further to Dunbar, to await supplies by sea at a safer distance from the enemy. As part of a continued effort to win the Scots over, Oliver sent the wounded prisoners taken in the skirmishes back to Edinburgh, the senior officers in his own coach; but he could not afford to feed them in any case. His hungry men plundered the remaining residents of Dunbar and its district, and he tried to salvage his reputation for good behaviour towards civilians by feeding the poorer of them from his army's stores as more arrived. Five soldiers who had beaten and plundered a farmer's family were forced to sit astride wooden horses with muskets tied to their feet to pull their groins onto the bars, while the army marched past. All this did not prevent some of the locals from murdering the English soldiers when they straggled.[41]

At Dunbar Cromwell and his men were at least in relative peace, partly because of their distance from the enemy and partly because of a crisis that had erupted within the Scottish government. On reaching its army, Charles had been greeted rapturously by the soldiers, which confirmed the Committee of Estates in a well-founded belief that he was trying to take control of them. The committee ordered him firmly to retire to a royal palace across the Firth of Forth; he complied with notably bad grace. The General Assembly of the Kirk had gone into recess like the Parliament, and likewise leaving a commission to represent it; for these churchmen, the king's behaviour now seemed intolerable. On 5 August they demanded the removal of all his royalist and Engager companions, and tendered him a new declaration to test his commitment to the Kirk Party's principles. He was now expected to express his devotion to the Solemn League and Covenant, his grief at his own former sins and those of his father and mother, his readiness to grant the English the terms that Charles I had refused in 1646, and his rejection of Ormond's alliance with the Irish Catholics. With some reluctance, the Committee of Estates endorsed these demands. The king refused to sign such a humiliating document, which represented a comprehensive rejection of everything for which the royalists had fought and his father had died. The Kirk then formally withdrew its support from him until he did so.[42]

One factor that prevented the Kirk from doing so precipitately was that it found Cromwell just as offensive. On 3 August he had written to the

Commission of the Kirk, accusing the Scottish clergy of allying with wicked men and suggesting that their own beliefs and actions might be contrary to Scripture, citing texts from the latter against false priests. This of course greatly irritated them, and they returned a reply that they knew the Bible very well and were confident that breakers of oaths (including the Solemn League and Covenant) invited divine punishment.[43] Cromwell's letter to the ministers was a public piece of propaganda, and had doubtless been agreed with his senior officers, like the declaration to the Scots in July. Nonetheless it was written in a personal idiom, that of his private letters, and for the whole of his life in politics – from his first speech in a Parliament – he had manifested a visceral dislike of powerful churchmen, whether the prelates of Charles I, the Irish Catholic bishops or Scottish presbyterian clergy.

Other factors inhibited the Scots in interfering with the English at Dunbar. The defeat of their nocturnal raid on the camp at Musselburgh discouraged similar probes, and cast doubt on whether their cause had divine favour.[44] Spurred on by the ministers of the Kirk, and by allies of theirs in the army, the Committee of Estates reacted to the rejoicing shown by many soldiers at the king's visit by purging the ranks of any who were now deemed politically untrustworthy. Eighty officers were removed, and the process further disrupted military activity.[45] Just as in Ireland, the cohesion of Cromwell's army, and of the government behind it, contrasted dramatically with the divisions among their foes. On 11 August he felt able to lead his men back to Musselburgh, and the next day ships were able to land stores there at last. These included Cheshire cheeses, the first protein that his soldiers had obtained since entering Scotland, and tents to shelter them during nights in the field. Morale rose accordingly, and that evening they were marched to the south of Edinburgh, to cut off supplies to the Scottish army from the countryside there, and to see if the capital's defences were weaker on that flank.[46]

The army pitched its new tents on the Pentland Hills, that huge ridge of moorland and bog that runs south-west beyond the city and overlooks it, which at that season was a land of purple and grey heather, bleached grass, gold tormentil, green and pink mosses, bright stars of butterwort and sundew, and the grey-green of bog myrtle. Oliver admonished and entertained his men by having five of them condemned to death for plundering, as the lesser punishment had not been a deterrent, though only their commander, a serjeant, was actually hanged, on a scaffold erected on the summit of the ridge. Once more, however, the army found itself militarily stymied. Below them were the medieval defences of Edinburgh, the more effective because of the steep ridge on which the city was built. The Scottish army had simply swivelled round to man those. Any inclination on that army's part to engage the English had been further diminished by the political crisis caused by the refusal of the king to sign the declaration demanded of him by Kirk and government. On the 13th, the Kirk commission and the government committee sent a message to Cromwell reproaching him for his declarations against them but also informing him that the king would be deposed if he did not agree to the declaration currently tendered to him. This was represented as involving both Charles's condemnation of his actions and those of his parents against the godly in both nations, and his dismissal of any royalists about him. Some of the Scottish commanders parleyed with the English outposts and said they expected the deposition to take place, which would end the war. The leading officers of the Scottish army demanded a further purge of its members, and this was immediately carried out. Interestingly, when Leslie sent Cromwell news of the prospective repudiation of the king by Kirk and government, Oliver and his officers did not return encouragement, and hope of peace, but denounced the Scots for dealing with Charles at all. After two days of waiting on the hills, they were forced to march back to Musselburgh for more provisions.[47]

These duly arrived, in plenty, and included a further major instalment of pay for the soldiers and enough food and drink to furnish them for a week. More good news came from Ireland, of the surrender of Waterford, the city that had resisted Cromwell in the previous winter, and of another major Leinster stronghold, Carlow, so subduing most of that province.[48] On the other hand, the hope of an immediate end to the Scottish war faded out, as on 16 August Charles signed the declaration, having no other option if he were to remain king. This turned him in the eyes of many of the Kirk Party, and in official representation, from an unregenerate sinner to a repentant one, being purged of his sins in readiness to be born again. With this, Kirk and government closed ranks behind him again.[49]

On the following day, Cromwell marched west, to use his new supply of provisions to get back onto the Pentland Hills and to discover if the Scots could be brought to battle or talked into compliance. Once the camp was re-established, and entrenched for protection, Cromwell provided his men with another display of exemplary justice, by executing most of a party of deserters who had been rounded up and returned to him when they had reached England. The Scots, however, proved recalcitrant as before. They sent out bodies of horse to scout the English position, but would not engage. At one point, Oliver himself led out a force to tempt them to do so, and one of the enemy fired a carbine at him from too long a range to do any damage: Cromwell amused his own men by calling to the Scot that, had he been under his own command, he would have cashiered the man for such a waste of ammunition. A Scottish outpost in a mansion was stormed, but even this did not provoke Leslie's army to attack. Parties of English officers did meet to confer with parties of Scots, but again each failed to convince the other of the justice of their cause and the need to make peace on their terms. The English commanders fasted and prayed for divine guidance to resolve the deadlock. Attempts by Cromwell's men to extend the food supply by living off the country were fruitless: there was ripe corn in some of the fields between the hills and the city, but it was soon all consumed or trampled by the invaders.[50]

Once again, the English army marched to Musselburgh for fresh supplies, and once again they returned to the Pentlands. Once more, some of their leaders conferred fruitlessly with the Scots. On 27 August, David Leslie led his army west out from Edinburgh, and it seemed as if he might at last be offering battle. When Cromwell brought his men down from the hills to accept it, however, they found to their disgust that they were being invited to attack across ground that would make such an attempt suicidal. Between the armies lay a bog, seamed by a stone wall and a ditch, which would fatally disrupt the formations of either if it tried to cross. Some skirmishing and artillery fire resulted. On the next day, Cromwell's soldiers ran out of bread and heard of a possible Scottish move against their supply base at Musselburgh. They had to hasten back there through a stormy night, trees being blown down and rain stinging their faces. Much gear was abandoned on the hills. Once they had arrived, a council of war decided to retire further to what had previously been the safe distance of Dunbar, to fortify that port as a secure base for further operations, and to await re-inforcements. On 31 August the English reached Haddington in a misty evening, and beat off a Scottish attack during the night. On the next day, they offered battle in an open field near the town. When this was refused, they marched on to Dunbar. By the time they got there, tired and frus-trated, one of the foot soldiers summed them up as 'a poor, shattered, hungry, discouraged army'. Thus far, events seemed to be following the dispiriting pattern which they had repeated since July. This time, however, there proved to be a difference: the whole Scottish army was following Cromwell.[51]

DUNBAR

Disappointing and depressing as the whole campaign had been thus far, there is no sign that Cromwell and his officers intended to give it up, even though autumn was approaching. Their project of turning Dunbar into their main base testified to that. Their army was certainly diminishing, as field forces always did on active service. A bad diet and cold and wet weather would have contributed to this, but the most frequent and dreaded natural wastage of an army was always disease, and this one had not escaped. Its sheer size made some kind of epidemic likely, and especially one of dysentery, an infection carried in human faeces, which would spread rapidly because of the inadequate sanitary arrangements for so large a host. By late August it was already prevalent, and 500 sick men were shipped out of Musselburgh when supplies were taken on there.[52] On arrival at Dunbar, 2,000 more were put on vessels bound for England. These losses reduced the army to between 10,000 and 12,000 men, which meant that between a quarter and a third of the original force was gone.[53] Nevertheless, this still left a formidable army, especially in view of its quality. On hearing of Cromwell's losses, the Council of State decided to send 5,000–6,000 reinforcements, so that he had the prospect of a strike force fully restored to its original strength.[54] Moreover, some of the sick men sent off to convalesce would return.

At first sight, David Leslie's situation might look better than Oliver's. He could be plausibly claimed to have outgeneralled the latter with his stonewalling tactics, wearing down his enemy while his own army, well accommodated in Edinburgh and Leith and well supplied from the north and west of the city, had not suffered similar losses. Moreover, the same tactics might be claimed to have awarded his cause the moral high ground, with the argument that, by defending themselves without giving battle, the Scots were trying to keep the conflict to a minimum and so preserve their Solemn League and Covenant with the English.[55] Yet the achievement had been very limited. The invaders had not been defeated or deterred, and they clearly intended to remain on Scottish soil and prolong a conflict which represented a terrible strain upon a relatively poor nation, one which had a fifth of the English population and a government income equal to that of one English earl. Cromwell's army could easily make up its losses with the projected reinforcements. The seventeenth century, moreover, did not view military conflicts in entirely practical terms. It was a sensible argument that Leslie should not engage an enemy with equal numbers and superior training and equipment, but legend and Scripture were full of examples of warriors who, in a good cause and with divine approval, defeated numerically and technologically superior foes. In fact, Cromwell's losses now made his army numerically inferior. The Scots had heard that Oliver had sneered at them that nobody could have a righteous cause who hid in trenches and dared not give battle; and that rankled.[56] It was a great temptation now to strike at him when his men were tired, hungry, despondent and at a nadir of numbers, and they yielded to it.

What is not clear is how much bigger Leslie's army actually was. The figures subsequently claimed by Cromwell and his soldiers were between 23,000 and 30,000, which would have made it one of the largest armed forces ever seen in the British Isles during the wars of the 1640s and 1650s, and more than twice the size of Cromwell's.[57] The figures for casualties provided by the victors after the battle mean that it would have to have been at least 16,000 strong, but it is not clear how much larger than that it was. One of the English soldiers, watching the Scottish army from the Pentland Hills on 21 August, thought that it was only slightly larger than his.[58] A Scottish nobleman who was not with the army but was well informed on events, computed it confidently on 12 August as 12,000 foot and 6,000 horse, the losses in political purges being offset by new recruits.[59] Two other pieces of information cloud the issue. One is that in late August Leslie was expecting further newly raised reinforcements from the north, but it is not recorded if these had arrived by the time that he followed Cromwell, or how many they were, and how good.[60] The other is that an English royalist follower of the king, who had now been dismissed from his court, later put Leslie's strength at 16,000 foot and 7,000 horse, which matches the figures cited by Cromwell and his men. This information was, however, written retrospectively, and may have drawn on the estimates published in England.[61] As a result, as in 1648, we can be sure that Cromwell faced a significantly larger Scottish enemy, but not by how much he was outnumbered, nor how much quality offset a numerical advantage.

From the beginning of the campaign, Leslie's strategy had not been to avoid battle but to offer it only on ground which would make victory as difficult as possible for the enemy. His action in marching west out of Edinburgh in late August was intended specifically to lure Cromwell into attacking across a bog, but Oliver was too canny.[62] Leslie's action now was of a piece with that: on reaching the vicinity of Dunbar he put his army on the crest of a steep ridge to the south, Doon Hill, and then sent a party to seize a pass a few miles along on the road from Dunbar to Berwick. This was where the Lammermuirs rolled down to the coast at Cockburnspath, penning the road into a narrow space between hillside and sea which a few could hold against many. These moves meant that Cromwell's army was now trapped. He knew that he was in trouble and sent a message to England at once appealing for help: in it, significantly, he likened his position to that of the earl of Essex, commander of Parliament's main army for most of the English Civil War, who had likewise been pinned down on a sea-girt peninsula in 1644 and his men forced to surrender.[63] He had in theory four options, all very unattractive. One was to attack Leslie's army uphill, risking almost certain defeat. The second was to try to force a way through the pass at Cockburnspath, which would be difficult, would be equivalent to fleeing, and would risk being taken in flank and rear by the main Scots army. The third was to try to ship the foot soldiers and artillery away to England, and to use the horse to break through at Cockburnspath, which was to admit defeat in the whole campaign. The last was to dig fortifications at Dunbar, and sit tight in the hope of being supplied by sea until the Scots moved; but if the supply ships failed to arrive, the army would starve.

Leslie, however, was in a tough spot himself. Up on Doon Hill his men were completely exposed to the elements, without any tents or materials to make themselves shelters, and the weather was turning nasty again. The distance from Edinburgh was great enough to make food supplies, which would all have to come overland, difficult to fetch. Moreover, with an outnumbered enemy caught in a trap below, to await attack yet again in a secure position could look like cowardice and wasted opportunity. There was a very real chance that Cromwell's army would simply dig defences and then stay safe behind them, snug in the little town and fed from ships, until the Scottish one wasted away. All this explains why, after one uncomfortable night on the bare ridge, Leslie threw away his advantage of position and ordered his men to prepare to attack the English in Dunbar. It is also clear that the decision was not his alone, and that he was not in ultimate control of tactics. Members of the Committee of Estates were with him, and it was these people who directed him, and took the vital decision to descend the hill on 2 September.[64] It is possible, too, as one report stated, that from the ridge top the Scottish leaders could see the ships taking off Cromwell's sick soldiers, and mistook this for a general seaborne evacuation of his infantry.[65] According to this account, they thought they would be attacking a demoralized enemy attempting to escape, and one that was further diminished in numbers. Cromwell and his men believed that it had been the Scottish ministers who had hectored Leslie and his officers into abandoning their safe position: this is possible, but there is no evidence for it on the Scottish side, and the story suited the prejudices of those who repeated it.[66]

From the hilltop, before he quit it, Leslie could view the whole of the prospective battlefield. The wiry general, with his delicate regular features and pencil-line moustache, would have seen both opportunities and difficulties there. The area consisted of a small peninsula jutting out into the North Sea, just over a mile in width. The houses of Dunbar clustered round the harbour on the right side of the end of that promontory, under a ruined medieval castle. In the town's fields, across the neck of the peninsula, was stretched Cromwell's army, drawn up for battle among the corn, and treading it down: a great red and steel-grey band with its stands of erect pikes, musketeers and horsemen. In front of it a stream, the Brocksburn, ran across almost the whole of the peninsula, from left to right. For much of its course it had cut a ravine 40–50 feet wide, which represented a major obstacle for soldiers. Only to the far right, where the stream neared and entered the sea, did the land flatten out and passage across the water become easy: that was where the road to Berwick ran.

The Scottish army began to descend Doon Hill at sunrise on 2 September, but it took all day to do so, an especially long time being needed to get the artillery down the slope. By late afternoon the soldiers were stretched across a mile of ground on the southern side of the Brocksburn. Cromwell's army had spent a miserable previous night in the fields, which were too sodden to enable it to pitch tents, and remained in battle order all day, ready to receive the Scots. Crossing the ravine would be difficult, daylight would soon run out, and wind, hail and rain were setting in for the evening, so Leslie ordered his men to sleep where they were, in the fields beside the stream, and to prepare to attack when day returned. He positioned two-thirds of his cavalry and many of his infantry on his right wing, where the stream was most easily forded, in order to sweep over it onto the enemy's flank.[67] All was now in place, and the one eventuality which he did not seem to consider was that the enemy might attack first – which is exactly what occurred.

How the idea to do this was reached is not quite certain, because of different subsequent accounts. One is that sent by Cromwell to Parliament immediately after the battle, which told of how, after the Scottish army had taken up its positions on the other side of the Brocksburn, he himself went with Lambert to view those positions from where the stream neared the sea. He thought that they provided him with an opportunity, Lambert agreed, and they summoned Monck to inform him of their opinion. They then called some colonels together and got their cheerful acquiescence, after which a detailed plan of attack was worked out between them.[68] Another account is in the memoirs of one of Lambert's officers (and admirers), written decades later. It described how Cromwell called a council of war that evening, at which many colonels wanted to ship the foot soldiers to safety and send all the horse to break through the pass at Cockburnspath to England. Lambert, however, made a powerful speech that swung the meeting, including Cromwell, behind a decision to launch an attack, and to appoint Lambert himself to lead it.[69] In addition, Monck's subsequent biographer credited Monck himself with convincing the council of war of the whole scheme.[70] The three stories might be reconciled if Cromwell had instigated the whole plan, convinced Lambert and then

Monck of it, and got Lambert to present it to the council of war and Monck to support him. This is, however, speculation. The one thing that is certain is that the offensive strategy would not have been adopted had not Cromwell himself favoured it, while it remains very likely that it was his idea in the first place.

The Scottish deployment had depended on an attack across the easy terrain where the stream neared the sea, delivered by a much reinforced right wing. The English plan now consisted of a pre-emptive strike in strength against that wing, using the same terrain. The strike force would consist of both horse and foot and be launched against the horse regiments massed on the Scottish right. In the meantime, fire from the field artillery and the remaining English foot regiments would keep the centre and left wing of the Scottish units, strung out along the far side of the ravine, pinned down. The Scots had left gaps between those units, which made a co-ordinated response more difficult, and they were crammed into the narrow space between the ravine and the foot of Doon Hill. If the English attack could rout the Scottish right wing and drive it back against the rest of the Scottish force, the whole of the latter could be rolled up and put to flight. The attack was to be launched in two waves. It would be spear-headed by six horse regiments and three and a half foot regiments, with two more horse regiments and two more brigades of foot to second it and bring up field guns. All Cromwell's best officers would lead the initial assault: Lambert, Monck and two of his old and faithful cavalry commanders from the English Civil War, Charles Fleetwood and Edward Whalley, whom he had placed in first and second command of the army's horse units.[71]

Long afterwards, one of Cromwell's soldiers recalled seeing him riding around the regiments deploying for the attack in the dark, stormy night, seated on a small Scottish nag used to rough ground, encouraging the men and biting his lower lip with tension, so that blood streamed from it.[72] He was justified in being worried, because the action did not initially go according to plan. It had been intended to strike the Scots just before daybreak, when most were sleeping, but the assault troops took too long to reach position, and day had broken and the Scottish trumpets were sounding to rally their men when the attack went in, roaring the English battle cry of 'The Lord of Hosts'. They met horse units that were mostly mounted and prepared to fight, and a hard struggle was needed to get across the stream, after which the initial strike force came up against a Scottish counter-attack and was forced back. Two factors gave it eventual success. One was that the Scottish right wing consisted of horse, with foot soldiers further to their left. By contrast, the attacking brigade combined both horse and foot, and used them effectively together to deploy their respective strengths to break the enemy. The second advantage that the English plan embodied was that the attack was reinforced promptly at each weak point, from the reserve of men, every time that it stalled. At one moment, Cromwell's own foot regiment marched up and launched a pike charge to take the pressure off their comrades in the van. By contrast, most of the Scottish infantry, and their left wing of horse, were trapped between the ravine and the hillside, unable to move up to help their fellows on the right wing.

All of the leaders played their part well, Lambert leading the initial horse charge and Monck bringing up the infantry to second it, a pike in his hand. Lambert directed one of the foot regiments in the front of the operation to march round the Scottish flank and fall on it. When the regiment had broken the units in front of it, Cromwell arrived and ordered it to move left again, around the fighting soldiers. As the sun rose out of the angry sea behind, he quoted Psalm 68, 'Now let God arise and his enemies shall be scattered.' He then sent the regiment in to attack again at a weak point of the enemy. The English battle plan was therefore flawlessly directed throughout, from the top.[73] To a casual onlooker, the area to the east of the stream, near where it met the sea, would have been a chaos of thousands of struggling, slashing, stabbing, shooting, clubbing, thrusting, shouting and screaming men, among whom the English would have been distinguishable only by their red coats, and the Scots by their more variegated regimental tunics. In reality, the English units were being moved like chess pieces, guided by grand masters of the game, who seem to have had the further advantage of a greater variety of pieces to move.

This may in itself explain the result, but in addition it is possible that the concentration of English strength against the Scottish cavalry wing on the right provided numerical parity or even superiority there: virtually all the English horse were being deployed in the attack. At any rate, after an hour of hard fighting, in which most of the Scottish army had to stand idle, unable to move in its narrow pen between hill and ravine, its horsemen on the right wing broke and fled at last. With the sea to north and east and the steep Lammermuirs to the south, there was only one direction in which they could run to reach safety: west, into the ranks of their own infantry. As the frantic horsemen surged past and through them, the foot regiments caught the panic and began to break up and flee as well, leaving only a few to make individual stands and be surrounded and slaughtered. Cromwell's grip on his men did not slacken even now: he halted one foot regiment and got it to sing Psalm 117, of gratitude to their God, until more units joined it, at which point he ordered the enlarged force against the remaining Scots.

The English now found themselves either carrying out butchery on the brave enemy units that remained and resisted, or chasing the bolting mass of the others for 8 miles across the countryside towards Edinburgh. For cavalry, in particular, fleeing foot soldiers were easy game, and this explains the scale of the catastrophe that now overwhelmed Leslie's army. Between 3,000 and 5,000 men were killed, and 8,000–10,000 were taken prisoner: one of the largest national forces that Scotland had ever raised was virtually annihilated. By contrast, Cromwell's men claimed to have lost only twenty of their number. They also captured 10,000–16,000 weapons and the whole Scottish train of field artillery, munitions and baggage.[74]

Dunbar was therefore one of the greatest battles of British history. In keeping with the spirit of the age, it was a theological as well as a political and military event. To Cromwell, his men and the regime that backed them, it was the clearest possible proof that God favoured their cause and prized it above that of their enemies. The Scots and their English royalist allies apportioned responsibility for their defeat according to their own partisan sympathies. Royalists and Engagers blamed the Kirk Party, for purging its army of too many good officers and men.[75] The extremists among the Kirk Party leaders blamed Charles II, for having been insincere or insufficient in his repentance for his past sins and those of his parents, and the treaty made with him for being too lenient, a verdict officially accepted by the Commission of the Kirk.[76] Leslie himself blamed many of his officers, for abandoning their men during the stormy night to seek dry quarters.[77] A royalist observer added that the whole Scottish army had gone off guard, the infantry falling asleep in makeshift shelters made of new-reaped corn sheaves and the cavalry unsaddling their horses to graze.[78] All this may be true, but the horsemen on the right wing who had borne the brunt of the attack had fought stoutly for about an hour, and that was quite sufficient time for the rest of the army to wake up and for many of the absentee officers to return.

It seems more likely that three larger failures doomed the Scots. First, they had taken up a position on the eve of battle that would give them serious problems if they were attacked. Second, it does not seem to have occurred to them that such a pre-emptive attack would happen, let alone one expertly planned and led with a great concentration of strength at the vital place. Third, if the English leadership was superb, their own was distinctly lacklustre. While we hear plenty about what Cromwell, Lambert and Monck did during the action, there is nothing recorded of Leslie and his senior officers, save that most managed to flee fast and early enough to get safely away.[79]

Cromwell led the majority of his victorious army back to Dunbar, to pitch their tents, celebrate and scour the battlefield for booty. He released all of the prisoners who were badly wounded, about half of the total, to be carted home by friends or family, or to die en route.[80] The able-bodied were sent under guard to Newcastle and Durham, on what turned out to be a death march during which over half of them perished of malnutrition and disease.[81] In his victory despatch to Parliament, Oliver concluded by boldly, if vaguely, admonishing the MPs to thank the Almighty by implementing long-overdue reforms to improve the lot of the English people: curbing the insolent, relieving the oppressed, helping poor prisoners, reforming the abuses committed by clergy and lawyers, and doing something to palliate social inequality and economic exploitation. He termed the battle a resonant divine rejection of the Scottish clergy, for meddling arrogantly in public affairs, and exulted that some of them had fallen in it.[82]

Parliament responded to his call over the following two months, by establishing bodies to look at means to speed up legal processes and to consider electoral reform, and passing two significant measures. One ordered all legal proceedings henceforth to be in English instead of Latin or Norman French in the traditional manner, so that ordinary people could understand them. The other at last took a decisive step towards the liberty of conscience for which Cromwell had striven for so long, by repealing the laws that forced the English to attend their established Church, and allowing them to frequent other forms of Christian service, apart from the Catholic one.[83] Parliament also expressed its tremendous relief and delight at the victory of Dunbar by ordering a medal to be struck to commemorate it, which would be presented to every one of Cromwell's soldiers: something never known before in English history, and not to be known again until the battle of Waterloo. The MPs specifically insisted on having a bust of Cromwell's head and shoulders on one side, overriding Oliver's protests that this would suggest vainglory and immodesty on his part. The protests themselves, of course, enabled him to rebuff such suggestions.[84]

On the day after the battle, Cromwell was clearly still reeling from the magnitude of his victory, and of his delivery from a perilous position. He wrote not only to Parliament and the Council of State but to the governor of Newcastle, Ireton, his wife (lovingly), his in-law Richard Major, and his former ally Lord Wharton (urging him and other estranged friends such as Robert Hammond to see how his providential success showed that his cause was righteous after all). To his wife, he commented that the battle had upheld his faith that God approved of him, so crucially important to his self-belief.[85] He and his men seemed genuinely to believe that the war was now effectively over, because the Scots would not be able to recover from so shattering a blow, to both their strength and their morale. He and some of his officers who sent despatches home expected to occupy Edinburgh and Leith, and then press on to Stirling and so lay open the heart of Scotland, if the Scots did not surrender before then.[86] On the day after the battle, he sent Lambert with most of the cavalry and one foot regiment to seize the capital, and followed himself two days later.[87] The Scots had indeed abandoned both Edinburgh and Leith, as the soldiers who had manned the defences in front of them had almost all been lost. They left behind them plenty of abandoned weaponry and wealth.[88]

After just over a week of settling matters in the capital, Cromwell moved on towards Stirling, to seize the crossing of the River Forth there that gave access to the whole northern two-thirds of Scotland. He took three days to make the journey, in more gales and heavy rain which turned the roads into mud too deep for his artillery, as he pushed through the small hills of the Scottish Central Lowlands – a land of hedgerows, cattle and corn. On 17 September he came in sight of Stirling, and found himself looking at a miniature of Edinburgh: another sloping volcanic ridge with the walled town clinging to its spine and a huge medieval castle beetling on the high end. On the following day, he prepared his army to storm the place, but then called off the attack. Stirling was full of defiant Scottish soldiers – he estimated about 4,000 of them – holding strong and tall medieval defences which could not be breached without the proper siege train that he lacked. The ground in front of them was too sodden for horse to operate. The River Forth was too small there for him to bring up ships to land guns and other supplies, and too fast and deep to be forded, while the town controlled the only bridge. As usual, his men were able to carry only a week's supply of food in their knapsacks, and so could not settle down in front of the town. It was raining again. On the 19th, therefore, he abandoned any attempt to take or pass Stirling and started the march back to Edinburgh. En route he garrisoned Linlithgow, a town midway between

Edinburgh and Stirling, with an impressive royal palace, to secure his western flank. It was now depressingly clear that he was going to have to put his men into winter quarters, and that the war would continue into another year. On 21 September he dispersed his foot soldiers into billets in Edinburgh and the surrounding district. He and his officers held an all-day prayer meeting to ask God what had gone wrong.[89]

In truth, the tremendous victory at Dunbar had handed Cromwell Edinburgh and its secure and capacious port – certainly very prestigious gains, which made his position in Scotland much more comfortable and sustainable – but not much else. Neither the Scottish government nor the Kirk showed the slightest inclination to surrender, responding to their shattering defeat by regrouping north of the Forth, pouring their surviving soldiers into Stirling and strongpoints along the coast of Fife, which faced Edinburgh across the Firth of Forth, and ordering the levying of a new army.[90] Cromwell now faced a repeat of the summer's stand-off, and had won control of only the south-eastern sixth of Scotland. This was certainly the richest and most important part, but he did not even securely possess that, for the Scots still held half a dozen fortresses in it, which disrupted land communications with England. To be sure of retaining Edinburgh, Leith and Dunbar, Cromwell had to garrison them strongly, and that left his already depleted army dangerously short of field troops for any further advance.[91] In particular, it was galling that the enemy still occupied Edinburgh Castle itself, and fired down into the city, obliging him to cut the fortress off by digging trenches across streets, and to make his own headquarters at Leith, safely out of range. He tried to persuade the local ministers who had taken refuge in the castle to return to serve their parishes, promising them safety, but found himself and his army still scorned by them as sectaries and covenant-breakers.[92]

THE LONG WINTER

On settling into quarters, Cromwell regained 'great hopes' that given time he would be able to win over enough of the Kirk Party to his side to divide it irreparably and cripple the Scottish war effort.[93] Indeed, he enjoyed some success with individuals, such as a member of Parliament for Aberdeen, Alexander Jaffray, who had been captured at Dunbar and on whom Oliver himself, Fleetwood and the minister John Owen, who had joined the army in Scotland, all worked with arguments. The man came to accept both their political and their religious principles.[94] Cromwell also wrote to the Committee of Estates and to particular Kirk Party leaders, offering a renewed alliance, with the reassurance that the English republic did not intend to impose any form of religious or secular government on Scotland, but only to secure itself against Charles II and his followers.[95] In the event, the Kirk Party did split, but none of it was prepared to ally with him. As said, those of its members who had always been doubtful about the treaty with the king read the defeat at Dunbar as a divine rejection of that treaty. Their most prominent military leaders were two cavalry colonels, Gilbert Kerr and Archibald Strachan, the man who had defeated the marquis of Montrose. They found most support among the lairds and ministers of the western Central Lowlands of Scotland. It therefore made both political and strategic sense to detach both of them from what was left of Leslie's army and send them to recruit a separate regional force in that area. To conciliate them and those who shared their views, both the Committee of Estates and the Commission of the Kirk took a tough line with the king, ordering him to repent further of his sins and dismiss his remaining royalist courtiers. No greater role in government was allowed to him than before.[96]

The effect of this treatment on Charles was to make him despair of working with the Kirk Party any longer, and to bolt for the hills – literally, in that he rode for the Highlands with the intention of linking up with royalists there and defying the authority of the current Scottish government. As we have seen, the action was one entirely characteristic of his father, who repeatedly took dramatic and impulsive actions to escape tense and menacing political situations. The propulsions that lay behind such reactions were, however, different. Charles I tended to lash out, or take to his heels, when he found himself in positions in which he could not bear the strain any longer. Charles II, throughout his life, was a gambler and risk-taker, who loved to resolve problems with bold, dramatic and hazardous measures that promised to transform his situation at a stroke. The one thing that father and son had in common in this respect was that the outcome of their actions was usually disastrous. In this case, the king made his dash for the Highlands on 3 October, only to be overtaken by Kirk Party soldiers on the following day and brought back ignominiously to face the Committee of Estates.[97]

The king's escapade shattered the fragile unity of the Kirk Party. Those left in control of the Committee of Estates, and especially the nobles led by the marquis of Argyll (who had welcomed Cromwell to Scotland in 1648), were shocked into realizing that their harsh treatment of Charles had almost lost them his support and produced a rebellion in their rear. They accordingly admitted him to the committee's meetings, and so to participation in government at last, and proclaimed a pardon for the royalists who had attempted to help him. The hard-liners gathered around Kerr and Strachan, and their embryonic Western Association army in the south-west, however, decided that it was final proof that an alliance with the king was hopeless. On 17 October they issued a declaration that Charles's cause was ungodly, and stated explicitly that the Kirk Party had no right to intervene in English politics. On the other hand, the declaration also reaffirmed the need to expel Cromwell's army from Scotland. The Committee of Estates, and the Commission of the Kirk, attempted to ignore this 'Western Remonstrance' until the end of November, when the former condemned it and the latter criticized it as divisive. The Scottish Parliament reconvened at Perth, a safe distance from Cromwell, on 26 November, at which point it placed the Western Association army under the command of a cavalry general loyal to the king, Robert Montgomery. What all this meant in military terms was that, throughout October and November, Kerr and Strachan were roaming around the south-west with a force of 3,500 horse. This was too small to enable them to attack Cromwell themselves, and yet they were unwilling to co-operate further with the Scottish government, so that their resources, and those of their region, were effectively wasted.[98]

Cromwell eagerly followed these developments, and in early October he marched his army to Glasgow, one of Scotland's most important cities, the capital of the Western Lowlands and easily accessible from Edinburgh. It was a notable centre of support for the faction of Kerr and Strachan, and following the king's attempted flight Oliver hoped to make an alliance with them. Furthermore, the journey provided an opportunity to bring more territory under control, prevent the Scots from recruiting in the area, and find a way to outflank Stirling from the west. Oliver went in force, with six foot regiments and nine of horse and dragoons. He set out on the 8th, at times following the earthworks of the ancient wall that had marked the utmost limit of the Roman province of Britain. He reached Glasgow on the 11th and stayed for two days, threatening to hang any of his men who plundered the citizens, who quietly watched them march in. The 13th was a Sunday, on which he provided an object lesson in religious toleration by listening with his officers to one of his army chaplains preach in the high church of the city (the former cathedral) while a Scottish minister delivered a sermon there on the far side of a partition. All this show of friendship was in vain, as no Scots responded to his overtures, and the minister had preached against him and his cause. The most that Kerr and Strachan would say is that they wanted to treat but could not do so without the leave of their government. Cromwell was running out of food for his army, could still find no way around Stirling, and could not garrison the city without weakening his grip on Edinburgh too much. On the 14th he gave up and marched back towards Edinburgh, suffering from bad weather and muddy roads again, and finding progress harder and harder through the autumn woods, fields and low hills, until he entered the capital after three days of struggle.[99]

An episode which probably occurred on this expedition illustrates exceptionally well Cromwell's remarkable charm, when he chose to deploy it. One of the prime objects of the foray to Glasgow had been to win

Scottish hearts and minds, and he made a special attempt when he called at a mansion named Allanton House, the seat of a local gentleman, Sir Walter Stewart. The latter had fled as the English army approached, leaving his wife and children to entertain their unwanted visitors. She gave Cromwell a glass of Canary wine, whereupon he spoke a grace over it, passed it round those present and drank the family's health. He mentioned that his mother was a Stewart, hinting that they might be kin (the reality being that her family had been called Steward, and that there was virtually no possibility of a connection). One of the lady's sons handled the hilt of an English officer's sword, whereupon Oliver called him 'my little captain'. Another appeared, obviously sickly, and he showed concern and recommended taking the boy to a warmer climate. He called for wines of his own and shared them with the household, spoke a final prayer and departed, leaving Lady Stewart impressed by his courtesy and piety.[100] This reaction, however, made no wider impact on her compatriots, and it is more significant that, when news of Cromwell's Glaswegian expedition reached the rest of Scotland, it was claimed that his troopers had stabled their horses in churches and trampled the crops that had not yet been reaped.[101]

When Cromwell set out for Glasgow, snow was already lying on the hills of Fife across the sea to the north, and it was clear that winter was at hand.[102] Those hills remained effectively as remote as the Alps to him, because he had no means of shipping his men across the Firth of Forth between. With all the harbours held by Scottish soldiers, he needed large numbers of purpose-built flat-bottomed boats that could land soldiers and horses on beaches, and he had none. Instead, in the rest of October and throughout November, he tried to consolidate what territory he had. An attempt was made to bombard Edinburgh Castle, and to tunnel under the wall to plant a mine, but there were still no powerful siege guns available, while the granite of the rock on which the fortress stood was too tough for the miners, even though 2,000 men worked on the attempt each day. All that was achieved was to shoot down the Scottish national flag of the St Andrew's cross, which had waved defiantly above the castle. The long work of reducing the remaining enemy garrisons in the south-east commenced, Monck and Lambert being sent out with parties to besiege the nearest. To counteract the continuing murder and robbing of his soldiers by local people in this region, Cromwell proclaimed that retribution would be exacted from the communities of the culprits, including executions.

For their part, his men themselves behaved badly at times, accidentally burning down part of the royal palace of Holyrood and breaking up the furniture in the university and three churches for fuel. One of the captains in Cromwell's own horse regiment, Cowell, was court-martialled and thrown out of the army for allegedly denying the humanity of Christ and the existence of sin, opinions that had been proscribed in an act of Parliament passed in August. As usual in cases of religious heterodoxy, Cromwell had tried to avoid direct proceedings, warning the captain to be more discreet when complaints were first made against him, and was satisfied when the man denied the charges. When the complaints went on, he removed Cowell from his command, and finally turned against him when Cowell defied his removal, upon which Cromwell likened him to 'the Levellers' in his insubordination. At the same time, a common soldier was executed for buggery, as part of the same drive to keep the army godly.

Whalley was sent to Carlisle with a strong detachment, to open another route into England for supplies of food, equipment and recruits, and to make another attempt to treat with Kerr and Strachan. An exchange with them was secured, but did not go well, as Whalley and his officers informed the two colonels that by serving the king they were supporting Satan's cause, and were told in turn that their invasion of Scotland was ungodly. In the end, Strachan did lay down his commission and refuse to fight the English further, but Kerr broke off the talks when the Kirk ordered him to do so, and he and his small army remained a threat.[103] Its end came suddenly and unexpectedly on 1 December, and was precipitated by the decision of the Scottish Parliament to put Montgomery in charge of it, and his departure with a strong body of horsemen to take it over. This development convinced Cromwell that the reinforced western army would attack his outposts, so he left Edinburgh late on 27 November with seven regiments of horse and dragoons to make a pre-emptive strike. The expedition was a failure: Kerr retreated out of reach, and Oliver and his men found themselves floundering in the boggy pastures and hills around the Clyde valley. They were struck by gales, hail and snow, the mud pulled off the horses' shoes, the river went into flood and the troopers had to sleep on the sodden ground. After a day and night of this, Oliver led back most of his men to Edinburgh, leaving Lambert to quarter in the small town of Hamilton, beside the Clyde upstream from Glasgow, with five horse regiments, to watch the Scots.

Kerr now heard that Montgomery had reached Glasgow with most of the horse and dragoons from the main Scottish army, ready to merge Kerr's own men with his own and crush opposition to the king from the hard-liners. He decided to redeem his reputation, eroded by his miserable performance in the autumn, before he was replaced, and perhaps to prevent the takeover. This meant winning a striking victory: he chose to make a night attack on Lambert's detachment at Hamilton and annihilate it. He therefore gathered 1,200 horse and dragoons and marched on the town in the early hours of 1 December under a bright moon, which assisted the alert English scouts in seeing their enemy coming, and preparing their comrades to meet the attack. Kerr's men broke into Hamilton but found themselves outnumbered and surrounded, by troopers on larger horses. Kerr was captured, his sword hand hanging by a strip from its wrist, and Lambert chased the fugitives as far as the western sea at Ayr, with reinforcements sent to him by Cromwell, his men plundering as they rode. Montgomery retreated to rejoin Leslie's main army and Strachan surrendered himself to Lambert with other Kirk Party leaders from the region. It was the end of the Scottish western army, and of the hold of the Scottish government on the south-west of its country, which had been one of its best recruiting grounds. The Western Lowlands and Galloway became a contested territory, into which both sides in the war made forays without either exerting any real control. In the short term, the fight at Hamilton allowed Cromwell's army to claim its first victory since Dunbar.[104]

A few weeks later it could boast of another. In early December, a train of heavy siege guns was landed at Leith to reduce Edinburgh Castle. It included four mortars, which opened up on the fortress. They lobbed shell after shell over the walls, to explode inside, and soon several fires were seen to have broken out there. The garrison were already suffering a shortage of drinking water, and many had fallen sick. Under this onslaught, the governor asked permission to send to his government warning it that he would have to surrender soon if not relieved. This was refused, and the bombardments continued, interrupted at times by snow but now cracking the walls as well. After a week, the garrison agreed to surrender, and marched out on 24 December, after which Cromwell and his leading officers looked around the huge castle where they had been entertained in 1648. Some of its defenders, including the governor, elected to carry on living in the city rather than face the anger of their government.[105]

No more major military developments occurred for a long seven months. During the spring the remaining enemy garrisons in the castles and mansions of the south-east were forced to surrender by siege parties sent out with the effective new train of guns. By the opening of summer, therefore, land communications with England via Berwick were finally secure. The defenders were treated according to the usual rules observed by Parliament's armies since the Civil Wars began: those who gave up immediately were allowed to march away disarmed, while those who held out for a time were made prisoner. None waited to be stormed, and so slaughtered as the garrison of the fortified hall taken near Edinburgh in August had been. Nor were any of the prisoners from the spring sieges executed, as three of those who surrendered a strongpoint near Edinburgh to Monck had been in November, as a punishment for raiding the English quarters. All told, the treatment of Scottish garrisons was slightly better than that of their Irish equivalents had been, but there was no striking difference. The Scots were killed less frequently because they almost always surrendered on negotiated terms and included fewer individuals against whom Cromwell's men had a special animosity.[106]

Cromwell's army spent most of this period snugly quartered in the Scottish capital and its surrounding villages, and grew healthy and well rested. This process was greatly helped by the fact that, after its difficult start, the system of supply and reinforcement from England was now working efficiently. During the last three months of 1650 a total of nine foot regiments, or portions of them, were sent to reinforce those already in Scotland, together with several troops of horse and 400 more dragoons. Even if the actual numbers specified to make them up were not achieved, these would have totalled several thousand men, a mixture of veterans and new levies. Some were escorted by Whalley from Carlisle, some arrived overland from Berwick and some were landed from ships at Leith. Together they would have brought the army in Scotland up to the strength it had possessed when it invaded, and probably more.[107] A London contractor engaged to provide enough bread, baked into biscuit, each month, to feed 20,000 men per day. Parliament allocated £1,000 to build flat boats at Newcastle, suitable for shipping an attack force over to Fife.[108]

The accounts of the Council of State at Westminster reveal the immense effort made to feed, clothe and equip the soldiers around Edinburgh in the first seven months of 1651. Apart from the shipments of biscuit, it sent wheat, butter and cheese, 1,311 tons of the last alone being despatched, most from Suffolk and Cheshire. The horses received oats and hay, and the men were kept kitted out in coats, shoes, boots, hats and knapsacks. A further 2,000 tents were ordered, along with saddles and other horse harness, body armour, arms and ammunition. Fifty-six hand mills were supplied to grind grain, and thousands more men were provided to recruit both foot and horse regiments.[109] Pay was more irregular, even though £1,210,000 was spent on the army in Scotland during 1651. Even so, the foot were paid for more than three-quarters of the time and the horse more than half of it. Cromwell, notably, got his salary as general punctually and even in advance, but he may have used it to defray some of the expenses of the war.[110]

The problem was that the Scots were rebuilding their army at the same time, and from resources much closer to hand. Moreover, they were doing so on a much broader regional and political basis, representing a true national effort. In December the remainder of the Kirk Party had recognized that the loss of the whole southern third of the country had deprived it of the areas from which it had drawn most of its own support, and that it therefore no longer had the resources to carry on the fight alone. The Committee of Estates and the Commission of the Kirk therefore agreed that former enemies should be admitted to the army if they showed public repentance for their actions. Twenty-five new regiments were ordered, and entrusted to men who included Engagers and royalists; and the test of expressed remorse was not always demanded of them. The English royalists who had come to Scotland with the king were restored to his court, and he was formally crowned on New Year's Day, at Scone, where the medieval rulers of the land had been inaugurated. He subsequently took over direct control of the army, with Leslie still commanding it for him from day to day. In late May this counter-revolution was completed, as the Scottish Parliament repealed the law that reserved political office for Kirk Party members, passed after Cromwell's intervention in 1648, and royalists and Engagers were added to the Committee of Estates. By then 18,000 men had been gathered along the Forth under Leslie's command. They were not fit for an offensive, being mostly inexperienced, weak in cavalry and still divided by memories of recent enmity, and they were probably outnumbered by the army that Cromwell had around Edinburgh. They did, however, represent a formidable defence for the fortifications that had now been perfected at Stirling and along the Fife coast.[111] While Charles was as disposed as his father to sudden and impulsive actions, which were generally disastrous, he was much better at recovering from them than Charles I, because he possessed two lifelong qualities that his sire had lacked. The first was charm, and the second was simply luck.

The single military expedition that Cromwell led in early 1651 proved catastrophic for him. It started on 4 February, when he took eight foot and nine horse regiments westward again during a break in the snowstorms. He and his council of officers had decided to push Leslie's soldiers back out of the Clyde valley again, as they had intruded there, and quarter in it a while to spare the Edinburgh area. They also hoped to cross the large massif of steep hills above Kilsyth and so outflank Stirling by getting over the River Forth upstream of it. Instead their men found themselves facing an exposed and barren wilderness of bog and moor, with tangles of brown winter heather and dark peaty mud. The weather turned dreadful once more – wind, hail, snow and rain alternating with heavy frost – which made sleeping in the open too dangerous to health. It also became clear that the few passes to the Forth valley were well guarded by the enemy. After four days the attack force was back in Edinburgh.[112]

During the expedition Cromwell himself had been accommodated in houses, but this did not save him from contracting a vicious strain of dysentery, which gave him the most serious and protracted illness thus far in his life. He had been blessed with an unusually hardy constitution, which underpinned much of the success of his military and political career, but even this fractured under the impact of the new infection. In March he seemed to be mending, and joined his officers cheerfully for dinner on the 18th, but he then relapsed. After another month he rallied again and led his army into Glasgow on 19 April, to quarter it on the resources of the western lowlands, denying those to the enemy, and to attend a meeting of Scottish ministers called in that city. The hope was once more to strike a deal with those members of the Kirk Party who had now rejected the king, which would provide Scottish support for Cromwell's army at last, especially in the south-west, and perhaps furnish an alternative government to the royal one. Once more, talks led by Oliver himself and Lambert came to nothing, the very obduracy which prevented the Kirk Party extremists from compromising with Charles still equally stopping them from doing so with the English commonwealth. The horses of Cromwell's cavalry began to run out of hay and on 30 April he returned with his men to Edinburgh, where the strain of the double journey precipitated a further serious bout of his illness.[113]

This time Parliament was so worried about him that it sent permission for him to retire to England to convalesce, while the Council of State despatched two distinguished physicians to tend him. Neither gesture was necessary, however, because by late May he was clearly recovering at last. By the last day of the month he could walk in the garden of his lodgings at Leith, and on 9 June he could start a series of visits to the regiments of his army, on horseback. On the 24th he formally rejoined them to launch a new campaign.[114] His long period of disablement had not been devoid of either activity or honour. He had accepted the post of chancellor of the university of Oxford, and had encouraged Parliament to establish a third English university at Durham, to promote learning and piety in the north. He kept up loving contact with his wife and with the father-in-law of his son Richard. As so often, his tone regarding Richard was critical and disappointed, noting that his son seemed to have got into debt by spending too much on his pleasures, a situation which Oliver felt to be both dishonourable and ungodly. The fact that Richard and his wife Dorothy had now given him two grandchildren did little to palliate Cromwell's irritation.[115]

In truth, it had been a depressing half year. Cromwell had come close to death, and his long periods of disablement, without ever handing over command to another, had paralysed his army, even as the Scottish one grew ever stronger. In early June the decision was taken to pull back all the English garrisons west of Linlithgow, as the threat from Leslie's soldiers, raiding out from Stirling, was too great.[116] This opened the south-west to Scottish recruitment and supply demands again, and meant that the limits of the territory controlled by Cromwell's army were back where they had been in September. It was noted how his soldiers chafed at the inactivity to which they were condemned in their quarters around Edinburgh, and some even deserted to the king, who formed them into a unit under the English parliamentarian war hero and Presbyterian leader Edward Massey, who had accompanied him.[117] A letter from one soldier at Edinburgh on 10 June, printed in an English newspaper in mid-June, observed that 'the beauty of the summer is pouring away very fast, and yet we are not upon any action'.[118]

There was a real fear on the part of Cromwell and his officers that the Scottish army might grow large enough to be divided into two. One force would continue to pin him down along the Forth, while the other would invade England through the now open south-west of Scotland and join a royalist uprising there. To block the route of any such attempt, Cromwell ordered Harrison, left in charge of the defence of England, to bring his soldiers up to Carlisle.[119] On 16 June Oliver led his officers in a day of humiliation before God, to ask the renewed favour of their deity, at which 'deep sighs and groans' were heard. Cromwell expounded a text from the Book of Isaiah, which declared that the Almighty would never abandon his chosen people, but always uphold them against their enemies.[120] In truth, a recurrent pattern of his life was about to repeat itself: that he suffered notable afflictions, frustrations or tribulations just before he achieved his greatest successes.

BREAKTHROUGH

Throughout June, as his health returned, Cromwell readied his army for action. He formally appointed Lambert as his lieutenant, and made Monck a general, in charge of the artillery train, in recognition of his good use of it against Scottish castles. Richard Deane, an infantry colonel who had served well under Cromwell in 1648 and had since shown equal ability as a commander in the commonwealth's navy, was made general of the foot soldiers.[121] Oliver also court-martialled a number of officers, of whom the most prominent was Edward Sexby, one of the leading agitators of 1647, who had annoyed Cromwell during the Putney Debates with his intemperance and had since risen to command a foot regiment. He was dismissed for alleged financial malpractice.[122] As part of this purgative process, Cromwell imprisoned an Englishwoman who had entered the army's quarters with religious opinions of some kind of extreme radicalism.[123] In late June, thirty-three supply waggons arrived from London, the contents of which included six weeks' pay for the soldiers, and the fresh summer grass was now lush enough to feed the cavalry horses.[124] On the 25th Cromwell began to gather his army on the Pentland Hills again, and five days later it marched west, after he had treated all his senior officers and their wives to a grand dinner in his tent.[125]

This advance was occasioned by a Scottish one, by which Leslie's army had moved several miles south of Stirling, to a forest known as the Torwood, famed in national historical memory because the great medieval Scottish freedom fighter, William Wallace, had hidden from the English there. From this position, Leslie had renewed access to the recruiting grounds of the south-west, and could also threaten Cromwell's outposts. At the same time, however, it afforded Oliver a possible opportunity to bring his enemies to battle, and he came in strength with twelve horse regiments and twelve of foot, plus sixteen field guns and his dragoons. One of his officers expressed the fear that once more the Scots would 'play bo-peep', and that is exactly what happened, as Leslie again put his men into a position which Cromwell dared not attack.[126] The Scots were entrenched along a steep ridge with a small river in front which had few fords, one bridge, and boggy pastures on its banks. From this height their field guns bombarded Cromwell's camp, forcing his men to flee their tents. On 3 July he withdrew his army to Linlithgow, where he lodged, as he had often done on such sallies westward from Edinburgh, in the royal palace.[127]

It was essential for the morale of his men not to lapse into idleness, and so two days later, with fresh supplies, he began the now familiar march across the waist of Scotland to Glasgow, to prevent the Scots from recruiting there. Once again, he found himself outwitted, because on the 10th Leslie moved his army to Kilsyth to the north-east of the city, occupying another impregnable position, protected by bogs and rocky hillsides. There he could not be attacked, but could menace Cromwell's men and exploit any carelessness or vulnerability on their part. Oliver's riposte was twofold. First he put a garrison into a fortified mansion on the River Clyde, below Glasgow, to control shipping going in and out of the city. His soldiers trampled the growing corn in the fields around the city to deny it to their enemies. Then he moved his army east, at top speed, in the hope of surprising Stirling when it was lightly guarded and breaking through into northern Scotland. Leslie, however, had anticipated this, and moved even faster, so that when Cromwell approached Stirling he found the Scottish army blocking his way at the Torwood once more, in the same naturally defended position.

By 14 July Oliver was back in the palace at Linlithgow, his frustrated army quartered around him. The former parliamentarian general-turned-royalist, Massey, rapidly forced Cromwell's new garrison on the Clyde to surrender, so that his grip on the south-west was broken yet again. Meanwhile, Leslie garrisoned a nobleman's seat east of the Torwood, within striking distance of Cromwell's position. On this Oliver vented his feelings, by having it stormed and most of its garrison slaughtered. He had continued to forbid his soldiers to plunder the local civilians on the Glaswegian expedition, and executed those who did, but some of those locals still murdered his men; he had their villages looted and burned in retribution.[128] A sense of lack of progress was evident in his army. His scoutmaster commented on 'how were we tugging these ten months, and reaped nothing but disappointment'. Another of his officers commented that, if the Scots continued their stonewalling tactics until the autumn, the English invasion force would have to go home.[129] Even with the great succession of supplies reaching it from England, it still depended partly on the resources of the Edinburgh region to subsist, and these were being eaten out.[130] The brief Scottish summer was already half run.

In fact, the decisive breakthrough was imminent, and made possible by the continuing inflow of strength to Cromwell's force from England. Recruits were arriving all the time, by land and sea, to fill up his regiments.[131] As the Scots seemed to show no sign of launching a diversionary invasion of England by a second army, Cromwell called up Thomas Harrison's force from defending the English border, to swell his resources still further. It arrived in mid-July, 3,000 strong, and by then the government in England had also delivered the flat-bottomed boats, ideal for shipping soldiers over water to land on beaches, that were needed to launch an amphibious operation across the Firth of Forth.[132] This was Leslie's point of weakness: he had enough men to concentrate them on the few points where the Forth could be crossed inland, but the long and complex coast of Fife, on the north shore of its estuary, stretched his defenders too thin.

We have no precise figures for the number of men whom Cromwell had under his command by this time, but it was probably in excess of 20,000, giving him the strength to pin down Leslie at Stirling and still be able to send an outflanking thrust across the water. On the windless and warm night before 17 July he sent 1,600 soldiers stealthily over the water, to seize a small peninsula at North Ferry (now North Queensferry) where the firth was at its narrowest. They easily overpowered the defenders of a small Scottish fort there and entrenched themselves on the peninsula to make a secure bridgehead. Over the following two days, Cromwell reinforced them steadily to create a total invasion force of 5,000 horse and foot, and put Lambert in charge.[133]

On 20 July, Lambert decided to take control of the small hills just to the north of the North Ferry peninsula, between it and Inverkeithing. He led out his men and sighted an approaching Scottish detachment sent by Leslie to drive them back into the sea. Leslie's information was, however, out of date, so that he had despatched enough soldiers to overwhelm the initial landing force, but not the one that Lambert now commanded. As a result, the Scots were inferior in number, as well as probably in equipment and in the quality of their cavalry. Lambert played up expertly to his advantage of resources. He attacked his enemies at once, forcing them to turn and fight where they could face him down a slope. He himself took charge of his right wing, packing it with most of his horsemen and the best regiments of them, to strike a killing blow. The majority of that strike force engaged the Scots in front while his dragoons fired into their flank and disordered them, after which his reserve of horse swung into the crumbling Scottish flank and its rear. After fifteen minutes of this punishment, the Scots on that wing broke and fled, exposing their infantry to attack from the sides and behind in turn, when it was already wilting under the massed volleys of English shot. The rest of the Scottish force now began to disintegrate and run. The Highlanders in it, especially the Clan Maclean under its chief, fought with great courage, but this in the end merely increased the slaughter. Between 1,000 and 2,000 were killed and 700–1,400 more captured. Many of the prisoners were hacked with swords by their captors, who said they would put 'Cromwell's mark' on them: the Scots were becoming viewed more and more as mortal enemies and less as wayward former allies. Oliver's army could boast its first real victory in seven months.[134]

Moreover, the way into Fife was now secure and Cromwell could co-ordinate operations on both sides of the Firth of Forth with consummate skill and devastating effect. First, on hearing the result of the battle of Inverkeithing, with the realization that the flank of his long-established defensive position was now turned, Leslie withdrew his whole army from the Torwood and prepared to launch it against Lambert's men and crush them. Immediately, Cromwell followed him with his own main field force, compelling Leslie to halt at Stirling, to hold the line there against him. Lambert now being safe, Cromwell reinforced him further, to a strength of 7,000, and instructed him to clear the way for a full-scale invasion of Fife. This was duly done. On 24 July the small Scottish garrison on the islet of Inchgarvie, in the Firth of Forth to the east of the North Ferry crossing, was forced to surrender, and so the route across the water was completely opened, allowing troops to be moved over in daylight. By then Cromwell's main army, which had marched back rapidly from Stirling, was pouring across. By the 27th he had ten horse regiments and ten foot in Fife, with another four regiments in the process of crossing, and four left behind to hold Edinburgh and Leith. It remained to secure a proper port on the Fife shore, to ship in supplies, and the obvious choice was Burntisland, with a good harbour directly opposite Leith. On the 28th the garrison there, also a small one, accepted an offer to march away to safety before it was stormed. All was now ready for a push north into Leslie's rear with 20,000 men, provisioned for ten days.[135]

Cromwell and his council of officers had already decided on their objective: the major town of Perth on the River Tay beyond the broad Fife peninsula. This had great symbolic importance, being where the Scottish Parliament had met after the loss of Edinburgh, and where the government had often been seated. It was also a major route centre, and possession of it would block the main supply lines to Leslie's army at Stirling, making his impregnable position there rapidly untenable. Within two days the English army had crossed the rolling hills and rich cornlands of Fife, and within a day more had drained the water from the moat outside the walls of Perth that had been its main defence. The walls were now exposed to be stormed at many points, and the Scottish governor, finding himself with 1,300 men to hold them against 20,000, surrendered at once on terms that allowed him to march them away to safety with their weapons. The town was guaranteed protection from plunder; two troopers who subsequently ignored this injunction were hanged. On 2 August Cromwell's soldiers occupied Perth.

Leslie and his king had just been checkmated.[136] They had three unattractive options: to move on Perth and give battle to Cromwell's army, with inferior numbers, equipment and training; to remain at Stirling and starve or be attacked from the rear by their enemies; or to retreat north or west into the Highlands, where the land was too poor to sustain a force of the size of theirs, meaning that it would disintegrate. In fact, by the time that Cromwell took Perth, the royal army was no longer at Stirling, because Charles and Leslie had chosen a fourth option, which at first sight may have seemed the least likely: to lead all their soldiers into England. Such a diversionary strategy had long been feared by Cromwell and his men, as mentioned earlier. It had, however, been based on a scenario whereby the Scots had amassed so much strength that they could send some of their force into England while the rest still held Cromwell's army in check in Scotland. It was clear to Cromwell's officers by July that this was not so – which is why Harrison's defence force could be ordered up from the border – though the possibility of some kind of strike into England remained alive.[137]

The decision taken to respond to the loss of the royal army's whole strategic position in Scotland by launching it all into an invasion was therefore a reckless and foolhardy gamble. It depended on two presumptions. The first was that a caretaker government left behind in northern Scotland would be able to raise enough new soldiers, speedily, to pin down Cromwell there, and that the surviving towns and cities in Scottish control would endure long enough to reinforce that effect. The second was that the English royalists and Presbyterians would rise in sufficient numbers, and with sufficient rapidity, to swell the numbers of the incoming Scots to the point at which they could overpower any opposition, including units that Cromwell might send back from Scotland. Both were very shaky hopes, and if neither obtained then the chances that the royal army would be trapped and annihilated in England were considerable. The whole almost absurd venture was utterly characteristic of King Charles, who was clearly the person who decided to launch it: a bold, dazzling, imaginative and appallingly dangerous stroke of action, intended to astonish and outwit his opponents and put his fortunes to a test in which the only alternatives were triumph or disaster.

The decision to make for England was taken as the result of a series of debates in the royal council between 24 and 29 July. Charles and his English courtiers had always wanted to invade, and they now succeeded in convincing the majority of his Scottish followers that the gambit might work.[138] A minority were not convinced, so that thousands of ordinary soldiers deserted, and so did some of Charles's leading councillors, including his greatest noble, the marquis of Argyll. A selection of other leading politicians were left as the caretaker government to form a new army and hold Cromwell. The rest, together with the generals and about 12,000 remaining men, marched south on the 30th, while Cromwell was moving in the opposite direction to Perth. In one day they had reached the Clyde valley and in four more were crossing the border.[139]

There is not the slightest evidence that Cromwell set out deliberately to provoke the king into this venture.[140] Not a single letter or memoir from him or any of his officers indicates such a thing, and it would have been a much better outcome of their spectacular turning of the Scottish flank if the enemy army could have been engaged and destroyed, swiftly, on its own soil. On hearing that it was making for England, he admitted in writing that this caused concern and inconvenience, and he had to defend his strategy of leaving the way to the border open as the only means of breaking the stalemate by concentrating forces on Fife. Every indication is that the royal dash for England took him by surprise when the news reached him at Perth.[141] If so, his response was immediate and effective. He put a garrison into Perth and left Monck there with 5,000–6,000 men and the superb siege train, instructed to carry on the conquest of Scotland. Cromwell then turned the rest of his army back across Fife and shipped it over to Leith again, arriving on 4 August as the king entered England. Harrison had already been ordered back southward with a cavalry force to try to overtake the royal army and strike at its flank, while on the following day Lambert was detached with between 3,000 and 4,000 more horsemen to catch up with it and attack its rear. Cromwell followed on 6 August with 10,000 soldiers, in eight horse regiments and eight or nine of foot. Letters had been hastened to Parliament and the Council of State to inform them of developments and to warn them to mobilize the defence of England. With no royal army left in Scotland to face Monck, and with such huge strength at his disposal, Oliver had been able to set out in pursuit of Charles immediately, with forces that were already, in aggregate, larger than the king's.[142]

As early and mid-August fell away, Cromwell's coach rattled south amid his huge column of marching men, which was accompanied by the minimum of field artillery and baggage, to maximize speed. First the Pentlands, and then the Cheviots, swelled around them in their metallic early autumn hues of amethyst, jade and onyx, and then fell away behind. On the 12th Oliver crossed the Tyne at Newburn and pushed on into County Durham, staying all the way in country houses while his tired soldiers camped in the fields and were fed by nearby towns. On the 18th he was in Yorkshire, at Ripon, writing ahead to corporation leaders to get local farmers to bring in bread, butter, cheese and meat for sale to his army, which had run out of supplies. The news from Scotland was excellent: Monck had occupied Stirling and had already used his mortars to shell the terrified Highlanders in the castle there into surrender.[143]

On the other hand, it was becoming clear that Lambert and Harrison had bungled their mission to halt the royal army. They had both made excellent time, having no infantry to slow them down, and racing along the shortest route to the border, towards Northumberland, and then across the Tyne and into the Pennines. Harrison swept up the regular horse troops that policed northern England for the commonwealth, so that by the time that the two of them joined forces on 14 August, upon a moorland on the western slope of the hills, facing into Lancashire, they had 6,000 troopers. This was probably more than the king possessed, and they were now parallel to the royal army as it marched south through the same county. However, they could not attack without infantry, and for that they relied on militiamen mobilized by the English government. The Council of State had been working hard and successfully, since the news of the invasion first arrived, to concentrate regular units to shield London and to call up great numbers of country militia members, under loyal officers, to resist the Scots further north.[144] A total of 4,000 militia infantry from Cheshire and Staffordshire had concentrated to block the crossing of the River Mersey at Warrington, where the earlier Scottish invasion force had surrendered in 1648. The long bridge there represented a bottleneck at which Charles's men might feasibly be held, and Harrison and Lambert now rode south with their men, to reinforce the militia foot soldiers there and make up an army to block the passage. They reached it before the Scots did, but found that the terrain to the south of the bridge was completely unsuitable for cavalry, being divided into many small enclosures. They tried and failed to break down the bridge before their enemies arrived, and then left the militia units to try to hold it. Inexperienced and outnumbered, these made a brave attempt but gave up and retreated under a determined attack. The royal army came over the river, and Cromwell's two generals drew up their force to fight it on Knutsford Moor to the south-east. Instead, they had the galling realization that it had marched straight past them into the Midlands.[145]

The king wanted to head straight for London and take it, but most of his advisers felt that their soldiers were too exhausted after so many forced marches. It was decided to rest them in a stronghold amid the traditional royalist recruiting grounds of western England. Worcester, a populous city which had been the last to hold out for Charles I in the First Civil War, lay open to them, and was duly occupied on 22 August. Its western side was protected by two rivers, the Severn and the Teme, while the others had solid medieval walls that could be strengthened with outworks. The rich countryside around provided supplies of arms, clothing and food; a new earthwork fort was constructed with forced labour to cover the south-eastern gate; and the suburbs were burned to provide a clear field of fire. What did not arrive were recruits: after a few days only 200 had come in, instead of the expected thousands. This failure, which doomed the expedition, may be attributed to three factors. The first was that Charles had not entered England with a victorious army but a desperate one, hotly pursued by superior numbers, which could offer neither payment nor the prospect of victory. Second, the Council of State, equipped with full legal powers and large financial resources, had immediately mobilized the full strength available to it. By the last week of August, a combination of regulars and militiamen had given the council a total of 50,000 men under arms, enough to police the provinces and concentrate overwhelming force against Charles. Third, the commonwealth government had captured two key royalist agents, who had confessed the plans for the uprising to accompany an invasion from Scotland. As a result, most of the prospective leaders of that had been arrested before Charles entered England. One of the few who were not in prison, the earl of Derby, did raise a rebellion in Lancashire after the royal army passed through it, but this was crushed almost immediately by a detachment of Cromwell's army led by Robert Lilburne.[146]

By the time that Cromwell was making his way across the Midlands, therefore, Charles's invasion had ground to a halt, and his army was increasingly isolated and cornered at Worcester. On his march across Yorkshire, Oliver was joined for a time by his old commander, Fairfax, who travelled 3 miles with him in his coach, encouraging him and offering to raise a force to help. On 22 August Cromwell entered Nottinghamshire, and three days later was reunited with Harrison and Lambert at Coventry. On the following day they mustered their combined forces, with neat symbolism, at Edgehill, the first great battlefield of the English Civil Wars. Militia units had now arrived from all over the Midlands and East Anglia, and the grand total of assembled soldiers came to around 30,000, the biggest army gathered anywhere in the British Isles during the wars of the 1640s and 1650s. It poured down the Avon valley to Stratford, and on the 27th to Evesham, the horse moving ahead to face Worcester. The next day Cromwell set up his headquarters 4 miles from the city, and the closing of the net on the king's army could begin.[147] At first sight, this was going to be a very hard task. Charles may have been both trapped and outnumbered by much more than two to one, but he occupied a well-defended city. In the Great Civil War the royalist marquis of Newcastle had held York for three months in a similar situation, against enemies who outnumbered him much more seriously. The two rivers that met at Worcester, and the size of the royal army, made it impossible for Cromwell to encircle and besiege the place even with the numbers that he possessed. Instead the city would need somehow to be attacked and stormed, co-ordinating huge numbers of men, of different fighting quality and experience, across a wide terrain riven by broad watercourses, against a powerful enemy who had the advantage both of fortifications and of interior lines of communication.

Oliver and his officers now set about doing just this, at maximum speed and with the superb efficiency and unity that long experience had combined with talent to award them. The process was commenced even as Cromwell moved up to Worcester on the 28th, and consisted of the gaining of a passage across the Severn to the south of the city and the closing of that southern route as a means of escape for Charles. It was Lambert who undertook this, taking a party to the first bridge downstream on the great river – Britain's largest – from Worcester, at Upton. The Scots should have strongly secured this, as a top priority. Instead they had sent a few hundred horsemen under Massey to quarter in the village on the near side of the bridge, and had broken the centre of the latter but left a plank across the gap, to allow some traffic still to pass. This negligence seems to have been prompted by the assumption that the commonwealth's soldiers would not attack so soon, and the same complacency may account for the fact that the garrison in the village were not actually watching the bridge. As a result they only realized that there was a problem after Lambert's dragoons had got across the plank and occupied the village church, pinning down the royalists with their fire. Meanwhile, Lambert's cavalry were fording or swimming the river, and rode up to rout Massey and his men. They then repaired the bridge, allowing a large brigade of Cromwell's army under Fleetwood, the gentle-looking blonde Midlander who had served under Oliver since 1644, to cross over to hold the village, with two field guns. Worcester could now be attacked from both sides, and Cromwell himself visited Upton in the evening to inspect the position that had been established there.[148]

By 29 August, he had positioned between 10,000 and 11,000 men at Upton under Fleetwood, concentrating 18,000 under his own command to the east of Worcester, with 3,000 more coming up to join them. The royal army he intended to crush numbered 10,000–11,000 in total. He now established his headquarters in a house 2 miles south-east of the city, and, moving between there and Upton, he agreed the plan of attack with his chief officers. It depended on an innovative feat of engineering: to overcome the problem of the rivers by having two pontoon bridges, of planks fixed across boats, constructed across them. These bridges would allow soldiers to move over them and so give Cromwell simultaneous access to Worcester on its western, southern and eastern sides. Once that decision was taken, there was a pause of five days, during which he wore down the nerves of the defenders by bombarding the city with the artillery train that had just arrived for his use.[149]

The day chosen for the assault was 3 September, which was probably deliberately selected as a propitious date, being the anniversary of the amazing victory at Dunbar. To signal the connection, the same battle cry was chosen, of 'The Lord of Hosts'. The day itself dawned fine, a dreamy early autumn morning in which the hedgerows beside the two rivers – which were about to be trampled and torn – hung with dark blue elderberries and sloes, and dark red hawthorn peggles and rose hips, and the Severn and Teme glided past them brown and placid. The morning indeed remained quiet, because nothing could be done until Fleetwood's huge division (made up of four regiments of horse and eight of foot) was in position along the Teme. Something – perhaps fetching the boats to make the bridge – delayed it, so that whereas it was ready to march north at six o'clock, it was not there until early afternoon.[150] It is not clear why Cromwell gave command of it to Fleetwood instead of to Lambert, who was his appointed, and natural, second-in-command. Perhaps he wanted to keep the charismatic Yorkshireman by his side, to be deployed where there was need; or perhaps he wanted to rotate important roles among his subordinate generals; or perhaps Lambert was in some disgrace after his failure at Warrington Bridge. At any rate, by mid-afternoon all was ready at last. Twenty large boats had been propelled up the Severn to a point just above where the Teme flowed into it. As soon as they arrived, carts loaded with poles and planks raced down to the waterside, and within half an hour Cromwell's engineers had constructed the pontoon bridges, one across the Severn at that point and the second across the Teme just above its mouth. He himself supervised the process.[151]

When the bridge over the Teme was finished, Fleetwood sent over the right wing of his brigade. The left wing was deployed upstream, at the village of Powick, where the main road running south-west from Worcester crossed the Teme over a bridge. The Scots had broken that, but there was still hope of forcing a passage. Until now, the royal army had shown the same slackness of attention that had cost it the pass at Upton-on-Severn. Not knowing of the project for the pontoons, and with Powick bridge broken, it had thought itself safe behind the Teme and neither made preparations against an attack there nor kept close watch on the river. Nevertheless, the alarm was sounded when the enemy crossed on the pontoon and appeared at Powick, and bodies of horse and foot soon converged on the force emerging onto the north bank of the Teme and engaged it. Cromwell had been expecting this. He himself led substantial reinforcements (two and a half foot regiments and one of horse plus his own horse guards) over the pontoon on the Severn, from the division of his army to the east of Worcester. These bolstered Fleetwood's men and forced back the Scots. The result was that, shortly after the start of the fighting, about two-thirds of Cromwell's army was now on the west side of the Severn.[152]

The plan seemed to be to capture the whole bank of that river opposite Worcester. If the bridge across to the city could be forced, then it might be taken immediately that way. If not, then Worcester was vulnerable to assault from both sides. Its long stretches of medieval walls had no outlying defences save for the newly built fort that covered the gate to the south-east. They could therefore be stormed at several points, given the huge size of Cromwell's army, while Charles's men would be spread thin around so great a perimeter.[153] The Scots along the Teme were dreadfully outnumbered, but had the advantage of the ground, which was thickly planted with hedges and seamed with ditches that provided natural defences for musketeers and pikemen and greatly limited the movements of cavalry. They also had, for a while, the cover of the Teme, which the attackers had only crossed at the pontoon. The slow and inexorable pressure of numbers nonetheless began to tell, especially as reinforcements kept arriving from the rear and the east bank of the Severn as the front units tired. At last the republican soldiers at Powick discovered a way to ford the Teme, and came across, while comrades of theirs repaired another bridge that the Scots had broken further upstream, allowing access for three horse regiments. Together, these forces could now take the royal soldiers in the flank, who were pushed back slowly towards Worcester, still fighting stoutly from hedge to hedge.[154]

Meanwhile, the king had not been idle. For the republican soldiers outside the city, its most prominent landmark was the tall, reddish stone rectangle of the cathedral tower. This was also the main vantage point from which the defenders could observe their enemies, and in early afternoon, as Cromwell's men were getting ready to attack, Charles was on the summit of it with his chief officers, surveying the scene.[155] To the east the ground rose quite swiftly to a ridge with a large wood in the centre, along which units of Cromwell's army were drawn up, the red coats of the regular soldiers being interspersed with the various colours of the militia regiments. Oliver's headquarters was set back on its summit. To the south-west the Severn valley sprawled, a lush green patchwork of fields chequered with the yellows of the season, to where the massive serrated profile of the Malvern Hills rose dramatically to bound the view. The king and his military men decided to launch a surprise attack with their whole army later that day, on the enemy drawn up on the ridge to the east, by moving forward in two columns on either side of the wood to execute a pincer movement beyond it and smash through the centre of Cromwell's division there. There was probably also a design to close upon and capture the enemy headquarters. His other division, to the west of the Severn, would be cut off from this force by the river and unable to help. Having agreed their plan, they were distracted by the sight of the carts being hurried down to the Severn's east bank, with a large body of soldiers following, and realized that a pontoon bridge was to be constructed. Charles ordered his generals to mobilize their army immediately, and when it was ready led some down to the Teme to see what was happening there. The delay consequent on mobilization enabled the construction of both bridges to proceed undisturbed, and the royal army lost the opportunity to disrupt it, or to rake the bridge over the Teme with fire before Fleetwood's men had crossed it in strength.

In retrospect, it seems clear that what the king should have done now was to pit the full weight of his men against the attack developing across the Teme. The enemy there certainly much outnumbered them, but not by a margin that negated the advantage that they possessed thanks to the hedges and ditches. It is true that Charles may have initially suspected that the assault there was a feint, and that the main attack would develop from the east. Lookouts on the cathedral tower could, however, have kept a careful watch on that side, and interior communications would have allowed Charles to despatch defenders from one front to another. In the meantime, he could have fed reinforcements, of both horse and foot, steadily into the fight on the west bank, supporting and relieving his front-line troops constantly until this sustained resistance, and the difficulty of the ground, stalled the attack. Instead he left fewer than 2,000 foot soldiers to face the push up from the Teme, outnumbered by at least seven or eight to one, and with no cavalry support. He then led most of the rest of his army against the division of Cromwell's on the ridge to the east, according to the original plan. There was a kind of logic to this. A surprise attack in strength might break up and rout the whole of that division, and this disaster to their comrades would halt the thrust made by Fleetwood's men to the west, and so take the pressure off Charles's there. The republican soldiers to the east included some of Cromwell's best veterans, but also the newly raised militia, whose steadiness and ability was untested. Nevertheless, the king was throwing away all the advantages of his defensive position in a wild, dramatic, reckless venture that offered the prospects of stunning victory or complete disaster. It was another rash and impulsive action utterly characteristic of him, of the same sort as his landing in Scotland bound by a treaty he did not want, his attempted escape to the Highlands, and the invasion of England that had got his army into the trap at Worcester.

The sudden eruption of the royal army out of the south-eastern gate of the city, in strength, took the soldiers on the eastern ridge by surprise, and they gave ground when struck. Seeing this, Charles raced back through Worcester to the western bank of the Severn, discovered that the situation there was (inevitably) deteriorating, and detached another 2,000 infantry to bolster it. He then returned to the fight on the east side, only to find his men there already falling back. The job he had set them was just too great, as they were attacking uphill against superior numbers in enclosed fields that favoured defenders (as they did for the royal soldiers on the western side of the city). The militiamen had held firm. Moreover, on hearing of the royalist onslaught to the east, Cromwell promptly led back two of the best regiments he had brought to Fleetwood, across his bridge on the Severn, increasing the odds against the tiring royalists and taking them in the flank. He himself rode up and down, through the enemy fire, encouraging his soldiers. Struggling through the hedges, taking volleys of shot from the sides as well as the front because of the disparity of numbers, Charles's men fought with desperate courage, but eventually gave up and retreated towards the city, leaving many dead and wounded behind. The king did his best to rally them with charismatic leadership, going from regiment to regiment to encourage the soldiers, but the task was hopeless. The victorious republicans now surged forward, and the retreat of the king's men became a panic-stricken rout.[156]

The south-eastern gateway to Worcester, through which the defeated army was now pouring, was covered by the newly built artillery fort, with projecting bastions which should have made it a strong position. Instead, the routed soldiers surged around it, now hotly pursued, and in the confusion Cromwell's men swarmed over the walls of the fort and slaughtered the defenders. They could then turn its guns on the royalist soldiers still outside the city, and also fire into it, increasing the panic. Charles himself was almost caught outside, but clambered back into Worcester across an overturned ammunition cart that was blocking the gateway. With the cart in the entrance, and the enemy pursuing so hard that nobody had the time to clear it away, the gate could not be closed, allowing Cromwell's men to climb through it into the city. On the far side, Fleetwood's division had now taken the suburb on the opposite side of the bridge over the Severn, but were held there as the bridge was guarded. Charles's rash sally, however, had let the republican army in upon the eastern side, and all was now lost.

Dusk was falling on Worcester as hell broke loose inside it. Many of the royalist infantry were now trying to surrender, while the cavalry were trying to get away. There were still no republican soldiers to the north of the city, and so Leslie led around 3,000 horsemen out through the gate there, and away towards home. The king escaped by the same route, with 600 more troopers, telling the men he was leaving behind to carry on fighting. One of his English courtiers, the earl of Cleveland, a veteran cavalry commander, mustered a body of horse to cover Charles's flight and led it in a series of charges down the streets, which rekindled furious fighting. Eventually he and his surviving men were forced back to the quays along the river, where they surrendered. The other royalists who kept up resistance were gradually overwhelmed, until at midnight a final fifty troopers got away through the north gate, and the battle was over. For the victorious soldiers of the commonwealth, a dream had just come true, because they had taken a rich city by storm, and custom now accorded them the right to plunder it at will. The citizens lost virtually everything they possessed, both from their homes and from their persons, and the seats of the royalist gentry in the surrounding countryside were likewise looted bare. The militia were lavishly rewarded, in material terms, for the stoutness they had shown on the battlefield.[157]

Cromwell duly reported that he had lost around 200 men, while his army had killed about 3,000 of the royal one and taken 6,000–7,000 prisoners, with all the baggage and artillery. He inflated the magnitude of his victory, as usual, in his despatch to Parliament, which famously termed it a 'crowning mercy' on the part of God, boosting the size of Charles's force to 16,000 and claiming that the king had flung the whole of it against just half of his own army, so that Cromwell's superior numbers had not counted.[158] As day broke again, the streets were full of dead men and horses, and more human bodies littered the houses. Soldiers searched those for further loot, and for concealed royalist leaders whom they kept pulling from the 'holes' in which they had taken refuge.[159] The actual scale of the slaughter was probably the same as at Drogheda, but there was no imputation of atrocity, because the civilian population was almost wholly spared, and the dead represented a much smaller percentage of the defenders, who had made up a much bigger army. Almost all of those who had escaped away northward on horseback were rounded up exhausted in Cheshire, Lancashire and Yorkshire, including Leslie. In the end, only a few succeeded in getting away, but one was – famously – the king himself. Charles's usual amazing good luck kicked in again, as he fell immediately into the hands of loyal Roman Catholics who were adept at concealing their own priests and hid him expertly. He was then moved from one safe house to another along local royalist networks, until after six weeks he was shipped over to refuge in France.[160] As usual in his career, he had evaded the consequences of a catastrophe he had brought upon others.

Worcester has a nodal place in England's military history as the last battle ever fought between regular armies upon its soil. Just as at Dunbar, the contrast in discipline and co-ordination displayed by those armies was striking. One of the English royalists who had joined the king in the city accurately noted the difference: that Cromwell's army achieved perfect co-operation between its different units, despite its huge size and the expanse of disconnected territory across which it had to operate. Aided by the remarkable, and hugely successful, innovatory device of the pontoon bridges, reserves of soldiers were smoothly moved back and forth across the battlefield at the times when they were needed, and flung in and reinforced at critical points. By contrast, and despite its possession of interior lines of communication which allowed faster and shorter movement, the royal army failed to achieve any such efficiency of speed, precision and co-ordination.[161] Especially wasted were the thousands of Scottish horse directly under Leslie's command, which remained inactive for most of the battle, while he rode up and down before them seeking a purpose.[162] They might have been sent to bolster the flanks of the infantry trying to hold the west bank of the Severn, or galloped down the river to overwhelm the guards of the bridge of boats over it, and cut that loose, so breaking Cromwell's army in two. In the end, Leslie's only contribution to the battle, where in theory he commanded under the king, was to lead his horsemen in flight out of the city.

It is probably pointless to speculate upon what would have happened to England had Charles won the battle of Worcester because, given the odds against him, he could not possibly have done so. There is more mileage in counter-factual history when considering the battle of Dunbar because, had the Scottish leadership shown greater military ability there, there is a real chance that it would have won a crushing victory and ended Cromwell's public life. In that case, Charles II would certainly have remained as king of Scots, presiding over a limited constitutional monarchy with an intolerant presbyterian Kirk. There is also a real chance that Leslie's army would have invaded England in turn. Had its commanders shown equal skill there, they could have overthrown the commonwealth and established a monarchy and a presbyterian Church similar to those envisaged in the terms offered to Charles I in 1646, though probably with more royal powers. As Charles II would have detested such a settlement, and wished to restore the traditional monarchy and Church that his father had inherited, such a result would have been inherently unstable. As it was, the mistakes made by Leslie and his fellows, and the remarkable competence displayed by Cromwell and his, had compounded the victories achieved in Ireland to lay the whole of the British Isles, potentially, at the feet of the new English commonwealth. It remained to be seen what that regime actually signified, in the longer term.

Cromwell ordered that the walls of Worcester be demolished and the ditches outside it filled in, to render it defenceless and punish it further for its reception of King Charles.[163] More wonderful news arrived from Scotland. In the last week of August, the indefatigable Monck had laid siege to the important port of Dundee, and the caretaker government which Charles had left behind him gathered near the town to decide on a means to relieve it. They were too near, because Monck received word of their meeting and sent a strike force to surprise it. This succeeded in capturing every last member, including the aged earl of Leven, who had led the Scottish army that helped Parliament win the English Civil War. The Scottish state was thereby beheaded, and nobody was left to co-ordinate resistance to the English. On 1 September Monck took Dundee by storm, and made it an object lesson of the folly of further resistance. Of the 800 soldiers in the place, 500 were killed, together with many citizens, including eighty women. The town was systematically looted, and sixty shiploads of its wealth despatched to England: some soldiers ended up with £500 in cash each.[164] After that there was no more determined opposition to Monck's army by any notable centre of population, and the war could peter out in a series of surrenders and of sieges of a few castles. Scotland's acceptance of Charles II had cost it very dear: for the only time in its entire history, it had been properly conquered by the English, and in the process had probably lost around 10 per cent of its entire adult male population, a casualty rate exceeding that of any European state in either the First or the Second World War.[165]

Almost a week after the battle of Worcester, Cromwell left his army to disperse to quarters and the militia to march home and disband, and commenced his journey back to Westminster. On 12 September he neared it, and was met in the fields outside by the Speaker of the Parliament, the Council of State, the lord mayor and aldermen of London in their scarlet robes, and many MPs and gentry. There were also many soldiers, who lined the streets to his lodgings at the Cockpit and saluted him with volleys of shot. First in his ceremonial entry to the city came his life guard of splendidly equipped horsemen, who had taken part in the thick of the recent battle. Then marched the London militia horsemen, followed by the members of the public, and after them the Speaker's own coach, with Cromwell inside, leading a procession of 300 others. Thousands of ordinary citizens cheered and doffed their hats to him for miles along the way, and he doffed his to them: it was noted that he had deliberately refused the pomp of riding a horse like a conqueror. As ever, it was a virtuoso exercise in public relations, with piety (in showing Christian humility) and political shrewdness in perfect accord.[166] For most of the past ten years, Oliver had been away from the capital, and had ranged far more widely across the British Isles than most Englishmen of his time. Now he was back, and would never leave London again, save for brief forays into the neighbouring counties. The enormous capital conurbation was to be his home, and the setting for all his notable actions, for the rest of his life.

7

PARLIAMENT

THE PEOPLE'S CHAMPION

Cromwell's return to his metropolitan duties initially extended the hero's welcome that he had received on entering Westminster. Four days after getting home, he resumed his seat in Parliament, where he was treated to an oration from the Speaker which embodied the thanks of the House. The lord mayor of London then hosted a large dinner in his honour.[1] Parliament's gratitude took more substantial forms, as it voted him use of the enormous Tudor royal palace of Hampton Court, where Charles I had been lodged in 1647, as a country retreat. It also assigned him further landed estates, worth £4,000 a year, confiscated from the royalist duke of Buckingham, who had followed the second Charles to Worcester. Most were in the east Midlands, and to these in the following year Parliament added two more manors in Lincolnshire, three in Essex and a row of lucrative town houses in the Strand. These properties came rapidly into Cromwell's possession and the estates turned out to have been generously undervalued. His landed estate now gave him the income of one of the great aristocrats of the realm.[2] As always, he reacted to this wave of acclaim and reward with studied humility. To a fellow Puritan in Massachusetts he described himself a few weeks after his return as 'a poor weak creature, and not worthy of the name of a worm, yet accepted to serve the Lord and his people'.[3]

He immediately flung himself back into political life, and work. He resumed his place in Parliament and was constantly active there, both speaking in the House and serving on some of its committees. Only nine other members of the Council of State (out of forty) attended its meetings more than he did in late 1651. All military business was referred to him for advice, and passed to him for implementation, and he was worked hard in that capacity. He also sat on the committees for Irish and Scottish affairs, and was put straight onto a new committee for trade and foreign affairs, which included all of the leading politicians of the republic. These all met in different chambers of the former royal palace of Whitehall, which also included his home of the Cockpit: he was effectively living over the shop.[4] His own foot regiment was made the guard for Parliament and Whitehall, and lodged in St James's Palace to the north-west, of which he was the custodian. When, as an economy measure, the other regiments in the army were reduced in strength, and eight disbanded altogether, along with many garrisons, his was increased to full size.[5] In the annual election by which Parliament voted in a new Council of State, Cromwell easily topped the poll.[6] He was far and away the foremost citizen of the newly secured English commonwealth. Just as in the aftermath of the First Civil War, however, the threat lurked that a change of politics might remove him from power, and perhaps threaten the cause for which he had fought.

At least there no longer seemed any risk that such a change would be imposed by external enemies, as the army and navy of the commonwealth proceeded to complete their conquest of the former royal domain. In the remainder of 1651, the Isle of Man and the Channel Isles were taken in; during the first half of 1652, the West Indian and American colonies were secured, and virtually all the remainder of Scotland and Ireland subdued. The problem now was what to do with the powerful and extensive republic which had emerged from the revolution and wars of the previous three years. To much of the army that had created it, and the civilian radicals (still mostly concentrated in London) who supported it, a divine mandate seemed clear. This mandate was to reform political, religious and legal structures fundamentally, in order to create a new kind of polity and society, with freedom and justice better provided for as many citizens as possible. The aspiration was not merely a political but also a Christian one, as the Bible enjoined care for the poor and oppressed, and deliverance of a godly people from fiscal and ideological burdens.

This policy was articulated strongly in the newspapers of the time. The new republican regime had introduced an effective press censorship, which had put royalist and Presbyterian journalists and pamphleteers out of business. Parliament itself had its own official newsbook, to publish its actions and such news as it thought that its subjects should receive. Virtually all the other papers had been established or reshaped during the wars to report the progress of the army in Ireland and Scotland, and had become linked to the interests of the military. Most of them accordingly espoused a radical reform programme.

This programme was concerned with four areas, all of which now represented pressing problems. The first was to settle a stable and lasting form of republican government. The existing one, the Parliament purged by the army in 1648, had only ever been intended as an interim regime, to get the king executed, the royalists defeated and a new order of government established. The second problem was to overhaul the English legal system, which seemed unsatisfactory to radicals in three respects. First, the penalties for crimes were harsh, a large number of them incurring a sentence of death. Second, civil litigation was concentrated in a few overworked courts at Westminster, which enforced an extremely complex legal system that needed lengthy professional training to understand it. Legal actions therefore tended to be protracted and expensive. Third, the ability of creditors to have those who could not repay their loans imprisoned until satisfaction was provided meant that impoverished debtors could be locked up indefinitely. The third general area for reform was the unprecedented weight of taxation occasioned by the wars and the victorious Parliament's need for security. Much of that taxation was represented by the monthly 'assessment', the levy on property to pay the armed forces, but it was the excise that was especially resented: the sales tax on commodities offered in shops and markets, which extended to daily necessities such as beer (in an era when water was often unsafe to drink).

The fourth problematic area was the Church, the status of which had been left unclear in the wake of the revolution. That had disrupted the settlement of a national presbyterian system to replace the royal one run by bishops, so that there was no longer any supervisory authority to ordain new clergy and remove those who proved unfit for their duties. The whole traditional framework of parishes served by beneficed ministers was still in place, but the ministers concerned were a mixture of presbyterians and independents, representing a range of opinion concerning theology and Church government, and concerning whether they were in post to minister to all inhabitants of their parish or only to the godly among them (however they defined godliness). Moreover, the established ecclesiastical system now existed alongside a growing number of independent congregations gathered around particular preachers, themselves of very diverse views. These had possessed a legal existence since 1650, without any certainty as to how they might be regulated and how they related to the formal Church. In particular, the issue of tithes remained unresolved. Members of the new-style gathered churches now protested even more strongly that, as they did not attend public worship, they should have no obligation to pay for it. Without tithes or an effective alternative to them, however, the national system of religion would collapse, and the Protestant Reformation had added a further complication to the matter. This was that many parishes had become appropriated during the Middle Ages to religious houses, which collected the tithes for their own needs and paid the parish priest an allowance from them. When these houses were dissolved, the right to the tithes passed to the secular landowners who bought up their lands, and these gentry and aristocrats now paid ministers of the parishes concerned and pocketed the remainder of the proceeds. Tithes therefore represented a significant source of income for many members of the national social and political elite.

In the year following the decisive victory at Worcester, the newspapers bubbled with suggestions for measures to address these problems. *Mercurius Politicus* concentrated on the political and constitutional question, hammering home the message that power should not be allowed to be concentrated in the hands of a self-serving oligarchy, and that the present Parliament should therefore dissolve itself after ensuring its replacement by a succession of others, consisting entirely of elected members. It also printed a petition to the army officers from Yorkshire smallholders, calling for the abolition of tithes and the excise, a general reduction in taxation, and reform of the law to make litigation cheaper and easier.[7] *The Faithful Scout* commended tracts which condemned exploitative lawyers and clergy, and called for the abolition of salaries and fees for all legal officials, including judges, and that the law be reduced to a simple code that could be understood by anybody. It also demanded the abolition of tithes, the annual election of local officials, the establishment of county courts to hear civil actions, and the removal of all taxes save those on foreign trade. It called for county committees representing all tolerated religious groups to license preachers and eject unworthy ministers and schoolteachers. It campaigned against the excise and, in general terms, called on the army to pull down tyrants and lift up the oppressed.[8] *The French Intelligencer* fulminated against the treatment of poor debtors and also endorsed the Yorkshire smallholders' petition.[9] *A Perfect Account* inveighed against the unequal assessment of taxation and supported the call for annual elections of officials.[10] *Perfect Passages* campaigned against tithes, and for county courts, without lawyers.[11]

This journalistic context is important for an understanding of Cromwell at this time because of his long-established appreciation of the value of good publicity, and his resulting close relationship with newspapers. This had developed early in his military career, during the first year of the Civil War, when his exploits were regularly reported in the parliamentarian press, where they were extolled and magnified in a way that annoyed his colleagues in the fighting.[12] At no point is it clear how directly Oliver himself was involved in representations of himself in the press, and how much they were controlled by friends and well-wishers. What can be said is that the admiring portraits of his actions that were published would not have appeared so consistently had he not condoned or encouraged them. Had he been actively concerned in their dissemination, then he would have been sure to conceal his participation in the process, and so the extent of that participation must remain forever a matter for speculation. The upshot, however, is clear: that during the first year after his return from the wars, some of the surviving newspapers represented him not only as the greatest hero of the commonwealth but as its greatest champion of reform, of the sort that they were advocating. People with proposals or pleas for that reform were encouraged to address him directly. Even while Cromwell was referring to himself as a worm and a servant, sections of the mass media were extolling him as a colossus, and the best hope of his people for a better future.

The Faithful Scout hailed his return to Westminster with the declaration that, next to God, the nation was most indebted to Cromwell for the preservation of its freedom. In December 1651 it claimed that he was thinking of ways to free the people from heavy taxes, which, if accomplished, would make his name forever praised. Two months later it informed readers that he had declared for liberty, the easing of burdens on the people and the freedom of trade. In April 1652 it told them that he had informed a deputation asking for legal reform that he was determined to make justice impartial.[13] In December 1651 *The Moderate Intelligencer* echoed the story that Cromwell had declared the need to end heavy taxation, and credited him with making provision for the poor and with saying that he desired nothing more than the freedom of the people.[14] *The French Intelligencer* held that the smallholders' petition cited above was addressed specifically to him.[15] *The French Occurrences* added in May 1652 that he had visited several government committees to find ways of reducing the number of officials, and so the cost of them.[16]

A fellow MP noted that, between October and December 1651, Cromwell was repeatedly presented with petitions to persuade Parliament to free the nation from oppression, restore former liberties, remove tithes and the excise, reduce other taxes, simplify the law, order new parliamentary elections and grant justice to the poor.[17] A series of pamphlets were dedicated to him, which advocated between them the abolition of tithes, manorial rights, tolls on trade, hereditary titles and lawyers; complete freedom of conscience; faster and cheaper recourse to law; the recognition of lay preachers without formal qualifications; the distribution of all common and waste land among landless people; and the general overthrow of tyranny, which such writers considered still to be embedded in the legal, social and fiscal system.[18] Prominent radical preachers wrote to him personally to hail him as a patron and hero and bid him remove oppression, release imprisoned debtors and relieve the poor, taking the money from royalists, tithes, judges, officials and lawyers.[19]

The sources that mentioned this lobbying of Cromwell did not record his reactions to it, and glimpses of his opinions on the matter are few and possibly unreliable. In April 1652 he gave dinner to an Independent MP who had withdrawn from Parliament, and whom he was apparently trying to woo back. That man recorded Oliver as citing a Biblical text which spoke of God as raising up the poor and the beggar and setting them among princes.[20] A champion of the widest possible toleration of religious opinion claimed that, at a parliamentary committee in February 1652, he had heard Cromwell declare 'that he had rather that Mahometanism were permitted amongst us, than that one of God's children should be persecuted'.[21] This rings true, as the single principle to which Oliver had always been firmly attached was that of liberty of conscience for Puritans of all different shades, including those who rejected the established Church.[22] Some of those, however, claimed to have become rapidly disenchanted with him. One leader of a gathered congregation recalled eight years later that, in the autumn of 1651, Cromwell was 'accounted the head of the sectaries', and that a deputation of them attended him to encourage him in 'the glorious cause' of reform. He was friendly and bade them seek the divine will in prayer, but did nothing much to assist them in practice, and so after two more meetings they gave up on him and decided to form their own group to lobby for the removal of corrupt officials and clergy and the establishment of Christ's kingdom.[23] It was probably the same preacher who asserted in another publication of 1659 that, at one of the meetings, Oliver had said that there was no more chance of getting Parliament to answer their expectations than of making an iron bar into a lute string. He quoted Cromwell as asserting at another that there were no more than five or six good members in Parliament.[24] Cromwell's own letters show that he had a real feeling for former soldiers of his army and their widows and orphans, collectively and individually, but they do not display any broader zeal for social justice.[25]

His disassociation from some radicals was signalled in January 1652, by his role in the disaster that overcame one of the greatest of them, his old protégé, ally and opponent John Lilburne. Lilburne had, wisely, largely withdrawn into private life since his acquittal by jury in 1649, and it was ironically an aspect of that which felled him. He took up the cause of an uncle of his who had been dispossessed of a coal mine in County Durham, confiscated from a royalist and then leased to the uncle by a London merchant. The title of the merchant to it, and so the uncle, was challenged, and the property seized, by the local parliamentarian administration, led at the time by the prominent republican MP Sir Arthur Hesilrige. Lilburne joined the merchant in composing and publishing a petition against this action, which attacked Hesilrige, along with his colleagues in the local administration, in vehement terms. In January 1652, Parliament reacted furiously against the petition, as a libel against one of its members. When Lilburne was summoned to answer this charge, he compounded his usual intemperance in print with his typical intransigence in person, by refusing to remove his hat to the members. They fined him £7,000 and banished him from Britain for life, on pain of execution if he returned. Lilburne duly removed to the Dutch Netherlands.[26] Those who exiled him had seen him as a 'troubler of Israel', vexatious because of his 'turbulence of spirit', and were determined to get rid of him once and for all.[27]

Lilburne and Cromwell had remained on warm terms ever since their rapprochement in the summer of 1650, and when Oliver returned to Westminster he had allegedly renewed his expressions of friendship during a long talk with Lilburne in his gallery at the Cockpit. Yet, once in exile, Lilburne asserted that Cromwell had declared the sentence on him to be just, both in a private meeting with MPs and then in Parliament itself, putting his hand on his heart as he did so.[28] 'Freeborn John' had sympathizers in the House, and so his information is likely to have been correct: at any rate, it is certain that Oliver made no attempt to save him. He had apparently decided that Lilburne had made a nuisance of himself once too often. Certainly, the man's fate was decided in Parliament without a vote, and so Cromwell would have been facing overwhelming opposition had he spoken up for him. There was a lot of dismay at the sentence among radicals both in London and in the army, but opinion among them was divided over it and most decided to take no action.[29] Not a single newspaper came out in Lilburne's favour. There was accordingly no political risk to Oliver in letting him fall.

It is therefore certain that Cromwell was promoted in the public eye during the year after his return to Westminster as the greatest national champion of reforms designed to benefit people in general, and also that he must have been happy with this image. It would definitely have suited him politically, largely because of the sympathy for radical courses long evident in the army, on which he depended for his position: ever since 1647 its soldiers had called for the abolition of tithes, a broad toleration of religious sects, legal reform, and regular Parliaments with altered constituencies and franchise. It is less certain how much enthusiasm he actually felt for reform, and how far he favoured the specific proposals presented to him for it. Nor can we know how much he was aware of the bitter irony embedded in the situation: that the army was itself mainly responsible for the oppression of the people against which Cromwell was claimed to have set himself. The continuing enormous burden of taxation was mostly needed to pay that army, and to repay the loans that had been needed to fight the wars of the past two years, which would never have been needed had the soldiers not enforced the killing of the king. It was the army which had done most to destroy the nation's traditional liberties, by purging the majority of members from Parliament, down to an unrepresentative minority. The soldiers of course saw things differently, believing that they represented the true interests of the nation better than anybody else, and that their dramatic string of military victories over the previous six years were the only proof needed that God considered this to be correct.

The drive for reform that Cromwell had come to epitomize addressed two of the army's desires. The first was to please God by fulfilling the Christian duty to relieve the poor and downtrodden. The second was to offer the English and Welsh in general a fairer and more equitable society that would vindicate and excuse the soldiers' actions in overturning the traditional system of representative democracy and flouting the wishes of the majority of the nation.

THE PARLIAMENTARY MORASS

Cromwell's commitment to a broad reform programme was signalled by the way in which, as soon as he resumed his seat in Parliament, progress was commenced there to enact one. However, it is very likely that it would have started anyway. There were plenty of people in the House who favoured such reform, and the new power and security of the republican government, after the decisive defeat of the king and the Scots, made a turn to domestic affairs, and a lasting settlement of the new republic, the obvious course to take. It may therefore be concluded with confidence that Cromwell himself enthusiastically supported such a course, but not that he was actually in charge of it in the House, nor that he had himself a systematic programme of actions to be taken, in different areas of policy, to enact it (though both remain possible). Likewise, the extreme paucity of information about the detail of politics at this time, with few parliamentary papers and no diaries, little helpful personal correspondence or investigative journalism, and the vaguest of subsequent memoirs, makes it dangerous to draw conclusions concerning his relationships with other politicians.[30]

Nevertheless, the outline of parliamentary proceedings is plain. The day after Cromwell resumed his seat, the MPs began to debate how to call a new Parliament with both a redistribution of constituencies and a change in voting qualifications to make it more representative. A week after, on 25 September, it agreed by a majority of thirty-three to twenty-six to bring in a bill to dissolve itself and call a new-style successor. Oliver's enthusiasm for this was signalled by the fact that he acted as one of the tellers for the motion. On 8 October the House committed a bill for reform of the religious system to discussion by all its members, and revived a committee to discuss reform of the law. It then made progress on a bill of indemnity, to pardon all hostile acts committed against Parliament before the battle of Worcester, and so secure former royalists and Presbyterians under the rule of the commonwealth.[31] It was expected to exclude only the most obdurate royalists.[32]

All this was an excellent start, but by the end of February only the bill for indemnity had been passed, and it was clogged with exceptions and provisos. The latter excluded from pardon not only a list of named individuals but also anybody who had attempted to overthrow the republican government since the execution of the king, or who now refused actively to profess allegiance to it.[33] They also banned permanently from offices all those who had hitherto been removed from such offices as untrustworthy. During the rest of 1652, further limitations were added, in the shape of acts to disable all those deemed to be enemies of the purged Parliament from either holding office or participating in elections to it, and also to confiscate and sell the estates of more than 700 royalists.[34] In all the divisions on the details of these bills in which he acted as a teller, Cromwell usually features on the side of mercy, voting not to include particular categories of offender and one specific royalist among those refused pardon, and to protect another individual royalist from the loss of his estates: he won the first two divisions but lost the third.[35] It must be said, however, that these cases concerned only minor details of the measures concerned. Where he was most firm was in upholding the honour of his army, by arguing that the government should not proceed against royalists who had been promised protection for their estates in return for surrendering major fortresses at the end of the First Civil War.[36]

In the immediate aftermath of the victory at Worcester, Cromwell followed Parliament's orders in setting up military courts to try and execute, without juries, some of the prisoners taken after the battle.[37] When the most eminent of those condemned to die, the earl of Derby, appealed to him for mercy on the grounds that he had surrendered on promise of his life, Oliver did nothing to help him.[38] On the other hand, shortly afterwards Cromwell did intervene to save the lives of some Presbyterians charged with conspiring against the government while he was in Scotland.[39] Moreover, he also protected his old commander at the battle of Marston Moor, the earl of Leven, who had been captured by Monck, from close imprisonment or the confiscation of his lands.[40] And he secured the release of a sick royalist from prison, by the Council of State, on bail, after the man's doctor had assured him that the illness was serious.[41] The overall pattern is therefore of a disposition to mercy in specific cases, but not invariably, even though there is both contemporary and retrospective evidence that he was in general very enthusiastic about the Act of Indemnity.[42]

His role in promoting the push for a new Parliament is far better recorded. As said, he was a teller for the motion to launch it in September 1651. The bill struggled through October, as MPs wondered how such a Parliament could be made to deliver a body of representatives loyal to the republic.[43] On 14 November, Cromwell made a long speech to persuade the House to add a date for its own dissolution, and it duly agreed to do so, but by a majority of just two votes. Four days later it ruled that the date concerned should be at latest on 3 November 1654. That was clearly a compromise with those who had not wanted any date to be set, by agreeing on one that was three years away.[44] This prolongation of the potential duration of the present Parliament could only be justified if the members used the time to enact a full programme of reforms, or if the actual dissolution came much sooner. It soon became obvious that at least the latter development was unlikely, because the House lost interest in the bill as soon as the distant date was agreed.[45] The army had handed them a viable blueprint for a new representative system in its *Agreement of the People* in January 1649, which the MPs could have amended according to their tastes.[46] Instead of getting back to work on it, however, they ignored the matter until early May, when they at last agreed to revive the bill and discuss it weekly. Yet, after one discussion it was forgotten again, as they switched attention to the work of identifying royalists whose lands were to be confiscated.[47]

A similar story attended the attempt to enact legal reform. The revival of a parliamentary committee to discuss it, in September, met with considerable opposition from the lawyers in the House, who saw their professional standing as threatened by it.[48] Unsurprisingly, it made no apparent progress thereafter, and in January Parliament adopted a bold attempt to achieve some movement, suggested by the council of army officers led by Cromwell. This was to commission a group who were not MPs – of lawyers, officers, gentry, merchants and clergy – to consider the issue and produce proposals. Cromwell headed the committee which nominated its membership. It was chaired by a respected barrister, Matthew Hale, and over the following six months came up with many pieces of draft legislation. These included the establishment of a court for civil litigation in each county; a state system to approve last wills and testaments; a central court for appeals; the reduction of the number of offences that incurred the death penalty; and the end of imprisonment for debtors, who would be sent to labour in workhouses instead, to atone for their inability to pay. It also sent Cromwell a proposal to ban practising lawyers from Parliament and to cap their fees. This was bound to cause uproar among his fellow MPs and he apparently never delivered it to them. Nevertheless, the package of measures that the commission did send to Parliament – seven by April – represented a major overhaul of the legal system designed to deal with its most obvious current defects, which still left traditional structures of authority, and the legal profession, in place. Despite this, the entire assemblage failed to make any progress in the House, much of it disappearing in committee. The one reform actually passed was in January, before the commission met, when Parliament agreed that judges and court officials should not take any fees from plaintiffs, receiving only their salaries.[49]

Reform of the Church met the same fate. Once more, after a winter in which the committee set up by Parliament to discuss the matter had got nowhere, an external body produced a viable blueprint. This was the work of a group of churchmen and army officers who were mostly religious independents, seemingly led by John Owen, the young cleric whom Cromwell had headhunted for his Irish expedition. Oliver had remained sufficiently impressed by Owen thereafter to make him vice-chancellor of Oxford University. He himself had been honoured with appointment as its chancellor, and he made full use of it, not only by installing his own people in charge of the university, but by obtaining degrees, and the waiving of residency qualifications, for young scholars whom he favoured.[50]

Owen's group (which included such prominent members of the army as Whalley, Goffe and Okey) presented its scheme in February 1652. Their proposal centred on two bodies of mixed lay and clerical members. One consisted of local committees to license preachers, whether they were already ordained clergy or not, who were to be recommended by at least six godly people including two ministers. The other was a national commission which would tour the country to remove unfit clergy and schoolteachers. Parish ministers could choose whether to administer the sacraments to parishioners, while nobody could be compelled to take sacraments from them, and those who wished to worship outside the established Church could do so in public if they informed the local justices of the peace. Only people who denounced basic Christian principles would be silenced, and fifteen such principles were specified.[51] The document was silent on issues such as whether liberty should be extended to followers of the old Prayer Book and bishops, and whether tithes should still be enforced. Cromwell sat on the parliamentary committee to which it was referred, and where it then disappeared from view.[52] Once again, a promising programme of reform had seemingly died at that stage. On 29 April another petition against tithes was presented to Parliament, this time from Middlesex, and the House instructed the committee considering the Owen group's proposals to find an alternative form of support for parish ministers. It agreed to continue the compulsory payment of tithes in the meantime by twenty-seven votes to seventeen. The committee then initially sat twice a week to consider the matter, and received advice from groups outside Parliament, but yet again seemed to run out of steam, so that it never reported back.[53]

This pattern of inaction is so sustained that clearly a common reason must have been behind it, though it is one that must be surmised, as no MP has left an explanation on record, and the absence of almost any account of parliamentary debates removes another means for an informed answer to the problem. Certainly the purged Parliament could act rapidly and efficiently when it wished to do so: for example, in trade laws (as shall be seen) and in the case of the Act of Indemnity. It had also been formidably effective in supporting the enormous recent war effort, ensuring domestic security and imposing effective taxation and administration. The normal attendance of the House was fifty to sixty, a small and experienced group, used to working together, which, if it were only cohesive, should have made legislation easy. On the other hand, an increasing lethargy seemed to set into its proceedings in general after its achievement of military security. It passed seventy-eight acts in 1650, fifty-four in 1651 and forty-four in 1652. It had ninety-eight committees to prepare legislation in 1650, sixty-one in 1651 and fifty-one in 1652.[54] Given the sustained lobbying which it experienced from groups desiring reform of laws, and the public identification of Cromwell with the need for them, this lack of response is the more glaring. Recent historians have been agreed on the most likely reason for it: that the majority of the surviving MPs simply did not want further reforms, and this was true even of those who had actively supported the removal of the king, the monarchy and the Lords.[55]

To some extent, this was the result of vested interest. The purged Parliament included a total of forty-four lawyers, many of whom were prominent in its daily workings and had no incentive to change a system which yielded them good profits.[56] Some of its members were in receipt of income from tithes, and the overwhelming majority of them were attendees of the national Church. These considerations were not, however, sufficient in themselves to block reforming measures, of the kind advocated by the army and London radicals since 1647, and those of the Hale Commission and the Owen group. What seems more likely is that the Parliament had different priorities from the radicals, having perceived that the measures already forced upon it by the army since 1647 had alienated most of the traditional social and political elite without winning the support of the masses. It accordingly sought to play down the novelty of the commonwealth and to achieve stability, peace and security rather than further disruption and change, in the hope that such a policy might attract a lasting acquiescence in republican rule even if it could not earn enthusiasm.

Parliament's members may well have been appalled by the attacks published by radicals at this time against lawyers and established clergy, as likely to undermine the social system. Some of the problems of reform – such as how to find a viable substitute for tithes as a support for parish ministers, or how to reduce taxes while retaining an army that could guarantee the commonwealth's security, or how to ensure the election of a new Parliament that would support the republic and the army – were genuinely difficult. The number of people who wanted to worship outside the national Church was still a tiny minority, and though radicals were numerous enough in London to field thousands of people to sign petitions or attend demonstrations, this still represented a small percentage in a city of 400,000 people. Most of the population could not afford litigation in any case, and most of those who sought the punishment of debtors were not wealthy moneylenders but ordinary people whose willingness to extend credit had been abused. There could be little enthusiasm for new Parliaments when most of the population would still not be able to vote for them and most of the traditional political nation would probably be excluded from them. The 'people' at whom the reform programme was aimed were an unrepresentative fragment of the population, and when proponents of it spoke of the people they really meant those like themselves: in Cromwell's language, 'the people of God'. Those proponents themselves often lacked consensus over what exactly they wanted, and Parliament was simultaneously being lobbied by ministers and pamphleteers to safeguard the Church and the traditional social, educational and administrative system. Being unable to set its face firmly against either conservatives or reformers, and divided itself, it drifted into paralysis.[57]

From the summer of 1652, Parliament had a further reason for neglecting reform: that it had become engaged in another war. This represented the first venture of the fledgling republic into Continental European politics, and reflected its need to establish itself in international affairs. When the republic was first established, Continental states in general refused to recognize it, partly from abhorrence of the act of regicide, killing an anointed, hereditary and utterly legitimate monarch, and partly because of an expectation that it might be rapidly destroyed by a royalist invasion from Ireland or Scotland. Once it had conquered the British Isles, however, foreign powers became uneasily aware that they would now have to make a relationship with it, and their ability to do so mapped onto their own internal affairs, external relations and connections with the royal house of Stuart. Three states in particular were important in this respect. One was the Spanish monarchy, which ruled an extensive colonial empire in the Americas and also a string of territories around the eastern and northern borders of France, especially the area of the southern Netherlands which is mostly comprised in modern Belgium. That monarchy was especially abhorred by Protestant nations because it professed an especially intolerant form of Roman Catholicism which refused to allow the existence of other kinds of Christianity within its territories. It had no connections with the Stuarts, however.

The second great Western European power was France, which was also a Catholic monarchy but one better regarded by Protestants for allowing them to worship within its possessions. Since 1635 it had been locked in a struggle with Spain which it had been winning until 1648, before crumbling into a series of civil wars, produced by the strains of the foreign conflict coupled with a power struggle within the royal family, consequent on the death of the king and the succession of a young boy in his place. France was also, however, the main refuge for obdurate English royalists, because the widow of Charles I was a French princess, aunt to the current monarch, and maintained a court in exile near Paris. It was there that Charles II had taken refuge after escaping England in the autumn of 1651, and this had badly strained relations between France and the English commonwealth, which encouraged attacks on French shipping to press the French government to expel Charles and his followers. The French retaliated in kind, resulting in an undeclared maritime war.

The third mighty neighbouring state was the Dutch Netherlands, which should have had most in common with the commonwealth, as both were Protestant republics. Two factors, however, vitiated a friendship between the two. One was that the Dutch were England's main trade rivals, and had much increased their supremacy in this area while the English had been distracted by their civil commotions and wars in Scotland and Ireland. They now carried most of the goods between England and its own colonies, as well as surpassing English merchants in most foreign markets. The second problem was that Mary, daughter of Charles I and sister of Charles II, had been married to the leading noble and statesman of the Dutch republic, the prince of Orange. The two together had given much support to the English royalist cause, and the Netherlands had become the main source of military supplies for the Scottish Covenanters in their war with England. This support had been much diminished by the untimely death of the prince at the end of 1650, leaving Mary to bring up their baby son to succeed him. This development allowed a party hostile to the prince, mainly concentrated in the rich trading seaports of Holland, to take control of the state and grant recognition to the English republic. Nevertheless, the Orangists, now led by Mary, retained considerable power in the landlocked eastern provinces, and maintained a consistent hostility to the regicide

English government. They were no longer able to lead national policy, but they were still capable of blocking it.[58] There was therefore an irony in the fact that the Spanish monarchy, the foreign power most ideologically inimical to the regime of Cromwell and his colleagues, was therefore the one most friendly to it and the first prepared to recognize the new republic.

The purged Parliament was determined to rectify this situation by reaching out to the Dutch, and duly sent an embassy in the summer of 1651 to make an alliance. This failed because of Orangist opposition, and the English envoys were insulted by exiled royalists and preached against by hostile clergy. They returned with the message that the Dutch were as perfidious and ungodly as the Scots had proved, and the result was a Navigation Act rapidly passed by Parliament in the autumn to exclude Dutch shipping from the carrying trade between England and its colonies, and from bringing any goods into England. This act stung the Dutch sufficiently for them to send a peace mission in the following winter to re-establish good relations, which resulted in a draft treaty by May 1652 that restricted the ban on Dutch carriers to the English colonial trade, and ended any Dutch assistance to British and Irish royalists. Three forces, however, operated to prevent this settlement. One was the anger provoked by the English enforcement of the Navigation Act, which involved the seizure of Dutch ships that flouted it, compounded by an English insistence on searching other Dutch shipping suspected of carrying French goods, loaded onto them to avoid the English attacks on French merchantmen. This resulted in a Dutch embargo on trade with England and the preparation of a war fleet to prevent further seizures. The second was that the commonwealth decided on an aggressive enforcement of the claim long made by English monarchs to domination of the seas around England, symbolized by a demand that foreign warships salute those of England when they met in those waters. The third was the continuing hostility to the English republic on the part of the still powerful Orangist party.[59]

All these elements suddenly united on 19 May, when an Orangist admiral, commanding the battle fleet sent out to protect Dutch shipping, encountered a much smaller English squadron off the coast of Kent. He refused to salute it, whereupon an all-out fight ensued, until nightfall allowed the Dutch to draw off with the loss of two ships. Afterwards both sides denied having started the shooting.[60] Parliament immediately approved the action of its admiral, and Cromwell was despatched to Dover with another MP on the 20th to investigate the details of the affair. He travelled with an entourage of officers.[61] This may have been the first occasion on which he had left the capital since his return there from the wars, and it was a glorious season in which to travel along the chalk line of the North Downs, at the time of lark song and hawthorn blossom. Trumpeters escorted him into Canterbury for a banquet provided by the corporation.[62] Having taken depositions from officers involved in the action, he and his colleague reported to the Council of State on 24 May that the Dutch were clearly to blame, and he himself returned to Westminster two days later.[63] On receiving the report, Parliament ordered the navy to be made ready for war, and Cromwell was hard at work with preparations during the following weeks.[64] The Dutch government hurried a special envoy to Westminster to patch up peace with England, but both nations felt the other responsible for what had happened, and so each demanded terms that the other was unwilling to concede. On 30 June the Dutch withdrew all their diplomats, and immediately English warships began systematically to attack Dutch merchant shipping. On 7 July Parliament confirmed that a war was now under way.[65]

As so often, Cromwell's actions in all this are clear, but his expressed opinions hard to discern, and his private thoughts inaccessible. Stories swirl around him with respect to his dealings with foreign policy during his first year back at the heart of government, but almost none can be verified.[66] The best recorded case of a personal intervention of his does, however, suggest that he was able to take action in bold and aggressive ways. One of the main seaports of the Spanish Netherlands was Dunkirk, occupying a strategic position on the North Sea close to where it narrowed into the English Channel, near the French border. It had accordingly fallen to the French as one of their string of victories over the Spanish during the 1640s. Now that France was rent by civil war, however, the Spanish were advancing again, and laid siege to the town in March 1652. In that month, the French governor conducted negotiations with an Englishman whom he believed to be a personal and unofficial envoy from Cromwell. The Frenchman was seeking English aid to save Dunkirk, while Cromwell was interested in securing the port for England. The French government was willing to treat with England formally by May for an alliance against Spain in exchange for recognizing the commonwealth, but not to offer it more than that, including Dunkirk. This was not enough for the English republicans, and the exchange ended in July. The commonwealth then took its revenge on the French by using its battle fleet, now conducting the war with the Dutch, to destroy the naval expedition that the French sent to relieve the town. As a result, it was surrendered to the Spanish.[67] It hardly seems credible that a charlatan would have passed himself off as a representative of Cromwell to conduct such a major negotiation, or that Cromwell himself would have acted in such a manner without the support of other leading figures of the English government. This covert exchange therefore lifts a curtain for a moment on a world in which he and his colleagues were willing to contemplate ambitious foreign adventures by which to increase English power and the reputation of their regime.

How far this willingness extended to hostilities with the Dutch Netherlands is much harder to say. Samuel Rawson Gardiner declared that Cromwell's dislike for the war was 'beyond doubt', but it is doubtful that it was there from the beginning.[68] As shown, Cromwell helped compile the report that convinced Parliament that the Dutch were responsible for the clash between the fleets in May. Dutch journalists were convinced that he was one of the foremost promoters of the war, and the French ambassador subsequently reported that he had supported it at the start.[69] On the other hand, a Dutch source testified that one of Cromwell's favourite churchmen, Hugh Peters, who certainly opposed the conflict as he had worked in Holland and liked its people, brought some of the Dutch colony in London to Oliver in the first month of the war. Peters had encouraged them to petition Parliament to offer new peace terms, and it was claimed that Cromwell commended them and said he would support the initiative. Another Dutch source noted that, when some of the English leadership sent an unofficial envoy to sound out the Dutch government about treating in August, the man claimed that Cromwell was among those who desired an end to hostilities.[70] It may be that all these accounts are true, and that Oliver supported an attack on the Netherlands, but only so that its leaders could be brought swiftly to accept the English terms.

His relations with Ireland altered at this time. Since his return in 1650 he had retained his office as supreme civil and military commander there, usually described as that of lord lieutenant. For more than a year after he left, matters were in the hands of his trusted lord deputy, Henry Ireton. In November 1651, however, Ireton fell ill and died. It was a severe and unexpected blow for Oliver, and observers noted his sadness, while he told his sister that it had brought home to him the transitoriness of worldly affairs.[71] It also posed the problem of choosing a successor, but on 21 January the Council of State made the obvious recommendation to Parliament, with no sign of doubt on Cromwell's part, of John Lambert.[72] Lambert had the necessary military and political stature and ability, and had effectively been running Scotland during that winter. He duly arrived at Westminster in March, and in early May was granted £3,000 by the council, for the expenses of his retinue and journey.[73] Gossip relayed that he actually laid out far more money on that equipage than his grant, to take up his office with the greatest pomp, and that this annoyed many MPs.[74] That annoyance may have found expression a fortnight later, after Cromwell asked Parliament for leave to lay down his commission as lord lieutenant.[75] The gesture was typical of his studied modesty, and carefully nurtured image as a devoted public servant.[76] Parliament accepted his request, but it also decided by two votes on 19 May to abolish the offices of lord lieutenant and lord deputy altogether.[77]

It seems that the decision to remove the two great Irish offices was aimed at Lambert, to prevent him from wielding the power in Ireland of which Cromwell and Ireton had disposed, and was based on an alliance of the officers and administrators completing the conquest of the country, and MPs at Westminster.[78] Lambert himself certainly thought so, and reacted by refusing the reduced post with which he was now left, of commander of the army in Ireland. He stomped off in a sulk to his country seat in Surrey, at the former royal palace of Wimbledon. In his place, and on the advice of both Cromwell and the Council of State, Parliament appointed Charles Fleetwood, who, with Lambert, had been one of Oliver's two principal lieutenants in the Worcester campaign and, unlike Lambert, had been closely associated with Cromwell since the earlier part of the Great Civil War. The connection between the two was strengthened in early June when Fleetwood had married Ireton's widow, Cromwell's daughter Bridget. Oliver was confirmed as commander in chief of the Irish army, so retaining great powers of patronage in that country as well as control of all soldiers in the British Isles, and Fleetwood was commissioned as his second-in-command. Cromwell thus ensured that an utterly loyal supporter was placed in charge of this significant military force, while the civilian administration of Ireland remained vested in a commission of four MPs sent over from Westminster.[79]

It was a very favourable resolution of the affair from Oliver's point of view, but it distressed him when such a dependable follower as Fleetwood departed from his side, and in the autumn he described himself as left almost alone.[80] He also had the problem of ensuring that Lambert did not extend his resentment to Cromwell himself, and reputedly did so by encouraging the general in his sense of grievance against Parliament and paying from his own pocket to reimburse Lambert for the additional expense that the latter had laid out on an expedition that he now would not make.[81] Some of his enemies later asserted that he had secretly given leading MPs his blessing in abolishing the office of lord deputy, in order to head off the ambitious Lambert from the Irish command and secure it for the more tractable Fleetwood, and Lambert himself later came to agree with this.[82] The story reflects the suspicions that swirled around Oliver because of his genuine slipperiness as a politician and his tendency to want to remain on good terms with different groups, but in this case the truth must be forever undetermined.[83]

In all events, Cromwell emerged well from the affair, which was, in the perspective of Irish history, a minor episode in the important business of settling the land after its conquest, which was now being undertaken. In doing so, the purged Parliament had to try to reconcile two sets of undertakings. One was to pay everybody who, since 1642, had lent it money to finance the conquest of Ireland – a group including Cromwell – and to satisfy the large arrears of pay run up by the soldiers who had served there since then, and especially those who had carried out the conquest now being concluded. This required the confiscation of huge amounts of land there from royalists and confederate Catholics. The other obligation was to those last two groups, most of whom had recently surrendered to the commonwealth on terms that promised them their lives, freedom from compulsion to attend Protestant worship, and the hope of retaining at least some land, as long as they had not been involved in atrocities against Protestant settlers.

The two obligations clashed directly with each other over the supply of real estate, and in the conflict Parliament was certain to gratify its own supporters rather than former enemies. A blueprint for doing so had already been drawn up by Ireton, which divided the Irish into different categories, with differing severity of treatment. This was made the basis for the settlement that Parliament suddenly commenced on 18 May, the decision regarding Irish government being taken the following day as part of the process. The MPs now showed how fast and effectively they could work when they wished, because a complex act embodying the carve-up of Ireland was passed on 12 August. It put a possible maximum of 80,000 Irish people at risk of losing both life and property, offered another 34,000 transportation to the Continent, and deprived all the remaining Catholic Irish, and any Irish who had fought against Parliament, of one-third to two-thirds of their lands, with the remainder to be reassigned by Parliament in the poor western province of Connacht, to which they would be transplanted. Irish Catholics were not compelled to attend Protestant worship, but nor were they allowed to practise their own. There is no sign of any part played by Cromwell in the passage of this act, or any record of his views upon it: the nineteenth-century term 'Cromwellian', commonly applied to the settlement, is therefore now recognized as unjustified.[84]

Oliver's lack of apparent agency in, or direct association with, a measure of such severity may appear creditable at the present day. In the context of the time, however, it also excluded him from prominence in one of the purged Parliament's few legislative achievements. The painful truth was that, during the past eleven months, for one of the few times in his life, he had failed to deliver. He had allowed himself to be set up as the greatest champion of the reform movement, and that movement had failed to achieve almost anything of significance. To save himself from a very public loss of face, and of faith in his political capability, he now needed to accomplish one of two things. One was to persuade the MPs to pass significant reforming legislation after all, or to make way swiftly for a different body of national representatives who would do so. The other was to place the blame for the failure of that legislation to date firmly on them, and to make them pay for it. If some of the remarks credited to him were true, he had already begun to disparage the purged Parliament as a barrier to the public welfare. Time would now show which of those outcomes would occur.

ESCALATION

Cromwell would never have permitted himself to be represented as a champion of reform with such confidence had the lobby for it consisted solely of the minority of civilian radicals in the nation. He was clearly aware that now, as before, that minority was empowered because the army on which his own position depended sympathized with its agenda. The winding down of the wars left that army increasingly free to intervene in central politics once more, but for almost a year after the end of the fighting in England it did not do so. The constant promises of legislative action, and the foregrounding of its leader as the main figure likely to abet that, seem to have kept it quiet. By the summer of 1652, however, the absence of such action was becoming apparent to the soldiery, and those in Ireland in particular were acquiring an additional reason for engaging in political lobbying at Westminster. This concerned the land settlement for that nation which was eventually enacted in August. A power struggle was developing between some of the civilian commissioners sent by Parliament to govern Ireland and the army officers there, over how far the former could control the latter. It may have been sharpened by religious differences, in that the officers included an increasing number of sectaries who rejected national churches, while the commissioners and their allies tended to the retention of such churches, based on the independent model of local congregations. It was certainly worsened by the question of how the land confiscated from the defeated Irish was to be shared out, as the soldiers naturally pressed to secure the largest possible proportion of it, in settlement of the arrears of pay that they were owed for their service.[85]

Meanwhile, the army in England launched itself into action in early August. Upon the 9th the officers were drafting a petition to Parliament, and the following day Cromwell met them and agreed that it should cover a range of issues, which were finalized at a council of war held by them three days later in Whitehall Palace.[86] The Venetian ambassador noted that Oliver himself did not sign it (though the disgruntled Lambert did), and suggested that this was due to Cromwell's habitual desire to position himself above factions and act as an arbiter between them.[87] As a comment on one of Oliver's recurrent political characteristics, this has merit, but there was probably a more functional reason for his failure to subscribe the document: that it freed him to play a full role in the parliamentary discussion of it, because he was not a party to it. Certainly he must have approved of it, because it was presented by one of his longest-established and most loyal military followers, Edward Whalley, accompanied by others close to the lord general, such as Goffe, Okey and the commander of Cromwell's own foot regiment, Charles Worsley.[88] Its tone was courteous and respectful, and it did not accuse the MPs of anything, but its requests were by implication an indictment of their recent record of achievement. Those requests included the abolition of tithes, the improvement of parish ministry, the implementation of the Hale Commission's recommendations, the replacement of corrupt officials, the prevention of abuses in the collection of the excise, the repayment of poor state creditors before the wealthy, the end of payments of public money to favoured individuals, the payment of the army's arrears, a reduction in the number of state officials, the regular publication of public financial accounts, the appointment of an extra-parliamentary commission to investigate corrupt financial practices within government, and the finding of work for the poor. The petition also asked for speedy provision for a new Parliament, with qualifications set to ensure that the right sort of member was elected.[89]

In a fundamental – if to many contemporaries an uncomfortable – sense, the purged Parliament was the army's creation, and the soldiers could expect such a direct approach to its members to get respectful attention. This is indeed what seemed to happen, as the Speaker returned emphatic thanks to the officers on behalf of the House, which immediately established a large committee, including Cromwell, to frame actions in response to the petition. As a further gesture of friendship, the MPs voted to appoint one of the officers who had accompanied Whalley, John Barkstead, to command the Tower of London.[90] On 14 September they agreed to give the committee charged with responding to the petition the specific task of producing a bill to obtain a new Parliament, and by late September that committee was sitting daily to do so.[91] In early October Parliament ordered the commissioning of a body to supervise the public finances, on which no MP sat, and revived the parliamentary committee to reform the national religion (on which Oliver sat) and directed it to meet daily. They also started a bill to provide the poor with work.[92] The committee for religion invited ministers to set up conferences between different denominations of Puritan clergy to develop a new framework for the Church, and Cromwell allegedly urged that these be as broad as possible in their catchment of attendees, with sectaries attending in addition to presbyterians and independents.[93]

Once again, however, all this hopeful momentum ground to a halt, the committees concerned failed to report and the measures did not progress. Cromwell later claimed that to try to remedy this he and the army officers began to meet MPs regularly from the autumn, to share views and keep up the pressure to get results. By December they were pressing the MPs for a rapid dissolution.[94] When the annual elections for the Council of State were held in November, Cromwell once again headed the list, and his military lieutenant Harrison, who was regarded as a leading radical, was restored to a seat.[95] It was noted that a total of ten colonels had been included in the council, with the expectation that this would please the army.[96] None of this, however, did anything to quicken action from Parliament, and there were signs that Cromwell's own reputation was starting to tarnish in the House, because of the support he gave to petitions that seemed unjust to many members. He allegedly spoke to gain a London alderman damages awarded to him by the House of Lords, when the abolition of that House called the constitutional status of the award into question; for a man who wanted Parliament to overturn a verdict reached by due process in a law court; and to reprieve three men sentenced to death on good evidence for horse-stealing. Opponents in these cases got the impression that Cromwell had not bothered to learn the details of them before taking them up as part of his persona as the champion of the oppressed.[97] Towards the end of 1652 he was once more lauded in that role by the press. *The Moderate Intelligencer* reported that he was giving money to the poor and declaring that he wanted nothing more ardently than the freedom of the people and the end to heavy taxation.[98] *The Flying Eagle* praised him for allegedly calling for tax relief for people who owned no land.[99]

In the face of the now familiar paralysis of reforming legislation, moreover, some rather dangerous language was starting to bubble. An army captain in England wrote to a member of the army in Scotland, in late

August, that the Parliament seemingly intended to sit for ever, but an end would be put to it sooner than its members expected.[100] In September it was reported that at least fifty officers had met near London to decide on rules that would prevent arbitrary power and oppression on the part of the commonwealth government.[101] Royalist gossip during that month reported 'credible people' as asserting that Cromwell was preparing to dissolve Parliament forcibly, and crown Charles I's youngest son, the duke of Gloucester, who was still its prisoner, with himself as the child's protector.[102] Coincidentally or not, Parliament decided to pack off the young duke abroad, to join his relatives, two months later.[103]

At the other end of the political spectrum from royalism, leaders of gathered churches in London who had become disenchanted with the pace of reform a year before were now preaching at the former medieval friary of Blackfriars against the self-seeking ways of the commonwealth regime. The Speaker rebuked them, and Cromwell and his fellow senior army officers were displeased, even though they themselves complained of the Parliament. The sermons, however, continued.[104] Also significant was the behaviour of the army general and active MP Harrison, whose own radicalism had long reached the point at which he refused, like the more extreme sectaries, to use the traditional, pagan, names of months and weekdays. In November he wrote to a Welsh friend to hasten to London with leaders of the gathered churches of Wales, to confer over some eminent work that God was expected shortly to bring about, apparently in settling a framework for national religion.[105] By the end of the year, the French ambassador could report a story that some MPs were discussing the replacement of Cromwell as lord general, while Cromwell was calling more regiments near to London to threaten Parliament.[106]

To some extent the rising tension was produced by the strains of the needless war in which the commonwealth had become embroiled with the Dutch. In April that year, its navy commission had realized that it had less than half the money needed to send forth a battle fleet in the summer.[107] To plug the gap required further borrowing, and this made a short and rapidly victorious campaign all the more necessary. Instead, the English navy failed in its first campaign to capture any Dutch trading fleets or to win any decisive battles, and the conflict dragged on into the winter, by which time the deficit on the naval account had increased still further, to almost a million pounds.[108] Worse followed, when on 30 November the English fleet engaged a much larger Dutch one off the Dungeness peninsula of Kent, and was defeated. This humiliation drove Parliament and the Council of State into a concerted effort to ensure recovery and vengeance. The navy was overhauled and some ships and commanders replaced: one of the new admirals appointed was Cromwell's protégé George Monck, brought down from Scotland.[109] To fund this work, the monthly tax on property was raised in December by a quarter, to £120,000, and the pay of the seamen was increased to raise morale and attract recruits.[110] As before, it is hard to discern Cromwell's own views on the wisdom of the war, and indeed to have expressed them decisively would have been unwise, because his own followers were divided over it. Harrison and the preachers at Blackfriars supported a fervent prosecution of the conflict, while Peters continued to oppose it, and seems to have got into trouble with Parliament in September for urging an admiral to resign his command. It was reported that Cromwell had sheltered him from retribution.[111]

The desperate need for money sapped the regime's ability to reconcile the nation to its rule. The property tax had been greatly increased, and although, a year before, Parliament had exempted private brewing from the excise, there was now no prospect of further reduction in that hated levy.[112] The large-scale confiscation and sale of royalist estates, setting up a further barrier to the healing of wartime divisions, was similarly driven by the need to fund the navy. Moreover, the war had disappointed. As so often in this age, military defeat could be read as a sign of divine disapproval, and the battle off Dungeness delivered control of the English Channel and North Sea to the Dutch navy. English shipping had already been suffering from the depredations of Dutch privateers, and now major trade routes were jeopardized. One that was of particular importance to

Londoners was the delivery of coal from the Newcastle and Durham fields to warm the capital in winter and enable it to cook, and this was now interrupted, just as cold weather began seriously to bite. Another blow fell in January, when Denmark allied with the Dutch to exclude English trade from the Baltic. The travails of existence under the commonwealth had just become considerably worse.[113]

A discontented civilian population was still no direct threat to the regime as long as its army remained in control of the nation. The war, however, was now straining relations between the army and Parliament much further. At the opening of December, Parliament reviewed its financial figures and realized that, even after disbanding seven regiments and some dragoons, the cost of the army in Britain was still exceeding the revenue of the property tax imposed to support it by almost £400,000 a year. Cromwell's life guard of fifty gentlemen plus officers cost almost £40,000 alone. That tax now had to be increased to fund the navy as well, but a hike in its rates sufficient to pay for both services at their current size would probably not be sustainable by the national economy. The solution found was, as said, to increase the tax by a quarter, and allocate a third of it to the navy. This meant that the amount remaining to the soldiers was cut by £10,000 a month, when their pay was already sliding into arrears.[114] The inevitable solution was to reduce the army, and by the end of the month Parliament had resolved on a drastic plan to do that. Regiments and garrisons across Britain would be slimmed down immediately to fit the cost of the army into the tax now allotted to it, while the pay of the remaining soldiers was cut by a quarter. Cromwell was asked to find a further £10,000 a month in economies thereafter. All these decisions together meant that the amount that the regime was intending to spend on the army would be cut by almost a third, with a proportionate fall in its strength and influence. A further emergency economy struck directly at Cromwell himself, as Parliament voted to sell a number of the former royal palaces, including Hampton Court, which had been allocated to him as a country seat. For a short time it was removed from the list, but this was challenged and overturned two days later.[115]

The reaction of the army was immediate, as during the first days of 1653 regiments gathered around the capital and the officers held prayer meetings to ask the Holy Spirit for guidance, something that only happened when they thought that things were going wrong.[116] As in 1647 and 1649, the soldiery could be rendered uneasy by a sense that their ideological goals were not being served, but what launched them into mutinous action was a perceived attack on their material interests. Cromwell met the officers at St James's Palace on 7 and 8 January and agreed to set up a committee of them to frame a plan of action.[117] As it deliberated through the middle of the month, the prayer meetings continued, with growing agreement at them about the need to replace the existing Parliament, and to ensure a broader guarantee of safety for sects who wanted to worship outside the national Church than the one that Parliament was expected to allow. Gossip began to predict a rapid change of government.[118] The Venetian ambassador reported that Cromwell, caught once again between soldiers and MPs, 'covertly but shrewdly' encouraged the former, causing some of the latter to discuss curtailing his authority.[119] The officers successfully sought to extend some control over the navy, by persuading Parliament's Admiralty Commission to take their advice when appointing commanders.[120] On the 28th they finally approved the plan of action that had been framed, which consisted of a letter to all soldiers in the three kingdoms. It was a stinging if oblique indictment of the purged Parliament, declaring that the work of God had halted in the nation and Satan's power grown again. The people were oppressed by the obstruction of justice, and many in authority were corrupt and made good men suffer for their religious beliefs. The letter therefore declared the need to press the Parliament to end itself and produce a succession of others, and to reform the law, extend freedom of worship to all kinds of 'godly' people (but not Catholics or profane individuals), and ensure effective preaching of Christianity.[121] This was not a petition, asking the MPs to do things, but an ultimatum to them to act as directed.

Once more, Parliament made gestures to appease the military. In January it allocated lands in Ireland to satisfy the arrears of the army there, and produced a bill to clarify the freedom extended to godly Protestants while persecuting Catholics more severely. It appointed Harrison himself, one of the most prominent army officers in the House, to take the lead in finalizing the bill for a new Parliament as fast as possible. This body had already been decided to consist of 400 members, elected from the larger towns and the counties in proportion to the tax paid by those, and scrapping many small boroughs, to make representation fairer. This was in line with what the army had requested in January 1649, and it had been agreed to add members from Ireland and Scotland to create a body that spoke for all three former kingdoms. Parliament also read the report of the Hale Commission, as filtered through its own committee on legal reform, and produced a bill to set up county registries for land transactions. It revived its committee for the reform of religion. All this was the most noteworthy in that its main business remained, of necessity, the prosecution of the Dutch war.[122] The soldiers were now perceived to be growing increasingly hostile to that conflict, as it was clearly now acting against their own interests.[123]

The momentum of prospective legislation did not slacken in February. It is true that no progress was made with legal reform in the face of general opposition from lawyers and judges. However, a bill was brought in to relieve poor people and get them work, those for probate of wills and county registries were further discussed, and a prospective settlement of the Church was commenced. The basis accepted for this last was the scheme proposed by the group including Owen and Whalley a year before. Harrison seems to have made no impact on the bill for a new Parliament, perhaps because he had by now lost faith in the measure, but it was carried forward in committee, with Sir Arthur Hesilrige becoming the most prominent member.[124] The problem with all this was that it did little to please the army.[125] The first measure agreed for the future form of the Church was that it would be controlled and regulated by the government and its appointed magistrates. This begged the question of how far this regulation would extend, when the officers had already complained that some godly Protestants were already being harassed by overzealous magistrates for heterodoxy. The issue of the

Irish land settlement was also continuing to rankle. The soldiers occupying Ireland were in close contact with the army in England, and their commanders were old comrades of the officers there. Parliament had rejected a proposal to give land to families of soldiers who had died on service in Ireland, and had refused requests from the army there to allot its members estates before satisfying the state debtors, and at generous rates. Petitions to Parliament on the matter from the officers commanding the Irish army were disregarded, and the MPs decided to award that army estates at only half the value allowed to people who had lent Parliament money for the reconquest of Ireland. This ensured that the soldiers would get both less land and less profit from its resale.[126] All this suggested that the Parliament had little concern for military interests, and much for its own, as many MPs were among the state creditors owed Irish land.

At the same time, the wider context in England was of great concern to the army. Between the autumn of 1652 and the spring of 1653, Parliament received a stream of petitions and addresses calling on it to defend the national Church, and its ministry, against the attacks published and preached against it by members of sects.[127] It is clear from their behaviour that the MPs regarded the signatories as representing the nation far more genuinely than the radicals; in terms of numbers, there is no doubt that they were correct. They were also correct in an instinct that the republican regime would have a far better prospect of winning widespread public support if it appeared unequivocally as the defender of the Church and traditional ways rather than as the vehicle of innovation, and in the process proved its independence of the army: but with the soldiers breathing down their necks, the MPs were unable to do that. There was nothing inherently unreasonable and ludicrous about the measures requested by most of the radicals, military or civilian. Most of those measures, or equivalent actions to achieve the same ends, were to be enacted in the nineteenth century. At that time, however, they were produced by reform movements with a genuinely wide base of popular and elite support – movements that did not exist in the mid-seventeenth century.

It is virtually certain that, by the beginning of March 1653, the army had given up on the purged Parliament that it had created. The officers commenced a fresh series of angry meetings at St James's Palace, and Cromwell agreed with them on the 8th to set up a committee to find a way of getting a new Parliament called.[128] The febrility of the rumours now circulating reached a new pitch. In mid-March a royalist correspondent reported that only the intervention of Cromwell and Desborough had prevented the officers from deciding to expel the Parliament at once. He added that the soldiers had decided on a 'high' petition to the MPs, who would be expelled if they did not agree to it. Royalist observers were also circulating a story that some MPs were hoping to replace Cromwell as general with the more tractable Fairfax, and that the former had accordingly refused to see the latter when he came to the capital.[129] The leading MP Bulstrode Whitelocke recorded that Cromwell and his officers were now agreed that the Parliament had to be ended, and disfavoured those who argued otherwise.[130] Edmund Ludlow heard that they held several meetings with members of the House in which Oliver and his followers insisted that no more good could be expected of its present occupants.[131] Certainly radical pressure on the army to act was increasing: in mid-March a petition was published to Cromwell and his officers from the London area, calling on them as leaders of the people's army to force a Parliament poisoned by corrupt and selfish interests to reform the law, make taxation fairer and dissolve itself.[132]

Caught between Parliament and the army, Cromwell acted as he had done in 1647, when he had tried to reconcile the two but, on failing, had thrown in his lot with the soldiers who were the basis of his power. By March it was clear that he, too, was giving up on the present regime, as he virtually ceased attending the Council of State after the first week, and his appearances in the House became rarer.[133] At the same time, Parliament itself careered on, following its own course as before and ignoring the storm apparently growing around it. It was buoyed up by a resoundingly successful outcome in its efforts to wage the war with the Dutch more effectively, as between 18 and 20 February the reconstructed English fleet engaged its enemy off the south coast, between Portland Bill and Beachy Head, and won a clear victory. This actually enabled the opponents of the war to have a better chance of ending it, as the commonwealth government could now do so with honour. The French ambassador noted that Cromwell was among the people who pressed for a treaty.[134] When the government of Holland broke ranks with the other provinces in March and asked for talks, Parliament eventually agreed to respond.[135] The current churning rumour mill had it that Oliver had persuaded his army officers not to force an immediate dissolution of the House until the peace was made.[136]

This turn in foreign policy should have been amenable to Cromwell and the army. On the face of it, so too should have been the steady progress made on the bill for a new Parliament, as the current MPs worked hard to determine the redistribution of seats from which it was to be elected. They banned royalists from being elected as members for seven years, unless they had shown clear signs of repentance, and reserved the right to vote in county elections to men owning land worth at least £200. In April they ruled that future MPs had to be 'persons of known integrity, fearing God and not scandalous in their conversation'. This conveniently vague formula may have been added to other qualifications for incoming MPs, and there is much about the bill's contents that remains mysterious. It is not known how, if at all, it made provision to keep out the great majority of former Civil War parliamentarians who had not supported the purging of Parliament and the revolution that followed – who did not, in fact, want the republic or the army. The act for probate of wills was completed and passed, giving responsibility to a national commission of twenty people who were not members of Parliament, including Hugh Peters. Progress was also made on the Church, with assent to proposals that county panels of godly Christians should approve candidates for the ministry, and that men who were not ordained by clergymen could become public preachers if approved by the same process.[137]

Much in these proceedings should have been welcome to the army, but they did nothing to repair the military's relations with Parliament, for two reasons. The first was simply that the officers had now decided that the House had to go as soon as possible, whatever happened. The scapegoating instinct which was so natural to seventeenth-century politics had kicked in again. When the army was formed in 1645, it shared with most Civil War parliamentarians the belief that, once the king's royalist councillors had been removed and punished, all would be well in the nation. Then in 1647 it had presumed that this would be the case if the Presbyterian leaders were forced out, and in 1648 that it would be so if the king were killed and the House of Lords and the majority of members of the House of Commons driven from power. Now its resentment, condemnation and blame for its continued inability to achieve its political and religious aims had fastened on the remaining MPs, whom it had once regarded as the best instruments to do its will, while nurturing and preserving it. They had become viewed by the soldiers as at best worthless, and at worst corrupted and sinful evil-doers.

The second reason why the officers could not be mollified was that the government persisted in other actions which offended them, and especially their leaders. In March the Council of State ordered Cromwell to reinforce the crews of the navy with 4,000–5,000 of his soldiers, to make up the shortage of sailors. It pressed for the implementation of this in April, specifying that most of his own regiment now had to serve.[138] On 29 March Parliament received a petition from Wiltshire, which declared that Satan inspired the people who were attacking the national clergy and the payment of tithes to them. It asked for support for both, and the MPs not only thanked the bearers but replied that some of the necessary measures were already being considered and others would follow.[139] Three days later, Parliament abolished a scheme that it had established previously to compensate for the generally royalist and conservative character of the Welsh clergy by funding a team of itinerant preachers and commissioners who supported the republican regime, and who had power to eject and appoint parish clergy. These proved very active, and were especially associated with Harrison and shared his radical views. They accordingly became controversial in Wales, and in late

March a petition was delivered to Parliament against them, and for a more settled and traditional provision of ministry. To the fury of Harrison and his allies, the MPs decided to accept it, and to set up commissions in each Welsh county to approve new preachers.[140] By early April some sectarian preachers in London, and army officers who attended their meetings, were calling openly for the destruction of the Parliament.[141] Parliament also compounded the material grievances of the soldiers by pushing forward the Irish land settlement, with a division of the spoils that disadvantaged the army in Ireland and would leave a large proportion of their arrears unpaid, as the projected disbandment of the army in England in 1647, which had provoked it to mutiny, would have done. The rate of valuation given to the soldiers was raised to two-thirds of that awarded to state debtors, but that still wrote off one-third of what was owed to them, and looked mean.[142]

The question for the army was therefore not whether the Parliament would be allowed to continue but whether it could be persuaded voluntarily to put an end to itself or not. Cromwell was apparently preparing for a showdown. At the end of March, he claimed the full amount of his own arrears of pay from the Irish campaign – probably as a dissolution would make that more difficult – much as in 1647 he had claimed his arrears from his English service as the crisis between Parliament and army escalated then.[143] In early April he allegedly told Whitelocke that he wanted the House to put an end to itself as soon as possible.[144] At that period, private and heated discussions continued among the officers gathered in the compact red-brick Tudor palace of St James's, and observers expected dramatic action at any moment.[145] In the middle of the month, Cromwell appeared in Parliament himself, after weeks of absence which had caused much rumour and debate.[146] The government attempted gestures of conciliation towards him and his senior officers: the Council of State invited him to commission Lambert to command the army in Scotland, and Parliament removed his country seat of Hampton Court Palace from the projected sale of former royal residences.[147] It was too little and too late.

The long-anticipated crisis commenced on 19 April, and it was Cromwell who precipitated it. First he ordered that all the horse regiments in England should rendezvous near London, to quell any disorder resulting from the political actions to follow. Then he met the officers in council at St James's on that date; they were believed to have decided to dissolve the Parliament and constitute a body to run the country until a new representative assembly was chosen. It was hoped to obtain the consent of the MPs to both measures.[148] Oliver immediately set about attempting to do so, by inviting about twenty leading members of the House to meet him that evening at the Cockpit with senior army officers. Many did, and the argument went on late into the night. The proposal of Cromwell and the soldiers was for Parliament to dissolve itself after naming an interim government to manage the nation as the army council had decided. He gained some support from Parliament men, including allegedly his old friend, relative and ally Oliver St John, but not the majority. At the end of the evening, after some MPs had departed in distress, those who remained seemed to have agreed to hold a second meeting at the Cockpit the following afternoon, to try to settle the matter. Two or three were also said to have promised to try to persuade the House to suspend work on its existing bill for dissolution and a new Parliament, which made no such provision for an interim council of this sort, until that meeting convened.[149] It was a very shaky undertaking, and swiftly to prove insufficient.

ANOTHER MORNING JOURNEY

On 20 April 1653, Oliver Cromwell stepped out of his opulent lodgings in the Cockpit to attend the House of Commons. It was almost six years since he had left his earlier home in Drury Lane on the same errand. In those years he had risen, through some of the most dramatic political and military events in British and Irish history, to become the greatest figure in the nation. In them, also, almost all of the traditional constitutional structures of all three nations had been forcibly removed, and he was now about to remove the last. Before leaving his home that morning, he may already have had two more meetings there, after a short night of sleep. The first, the existence of which was recalled later by Whitelocke, who claimed to have attended, was of a few officers and members of the House who had returned soon after daybreak to argue further over the army's plan. It was said to have broken up when Parliament convened at nine o'clock.[150] Interestingly, Cromwell himself did not join those members heading for the House to take part, even though the vital issue of the suspension of the bill for a new Parliament was now to be discussed there. He was distancing himself from the debate, as if he already had doubts about it and was considering other courses. As the morning went on, he received at least one, and possibly three, messages from the House to warn him that his hoped-for agreement had failed, and that the MPs were hastening to complete the bill which the army now wanted to halt.[151] It seems that Sir Arthur Hesilrige, who had been away from Westminster the previous day, had dashed back there on hearing what had been proposed at the Cockpit, and had exhorted his colleagues to reject it.[152] They were only too willing to respond, and Cromwell and his officers afterwards claimed that none of those to whom they had just proposed their alternative plan were supporting it.[153]

Oliver launched himself into action. The second meeting at his home that morning was said afterwards to have been with army officers, whom he now told that the army had to persevere with the reformation of the nation, that the present Parliament would never do the job, and that a new one was too risky. God therefore needed to save England by a few, and five or six good men could accomplish more in one day than a Parliament in a hundred. The people were burdened, the law unjust and the current Parliament only sought to serve and perpetuate itself. It therefore needed to make way for a smaller body of 'unbiased men'.[154] He ordered the commander of his foot regiment, which was guarding Westminster, to summon a party of musketeers from it.[155] He then set out for the House, and did not trouble to dress as he normally would for public occasions, wearing only a domestic costume of a plain black suit with grey worsted stockings.[156] Apart from giving us the information that Cromwell was now normally a rich, though not a flamboyant, dresser, this homely costume made a strong impression that he had dashed out in a tearing hurry, taken unawares by events. This may be the simple truth, though there may also have been a deliberate visual effect contrived to convey this message, and so dispel thoughts that what he was about to do had been a contingency plan.

He made the familiar journey down King Street, through the buildings of Whitehall Palace. To his left was the pale grey stone hulk of the banqueting house, and the place in the street outside where the king's head had fallen. In front was the square Tudor gatehouse of chequered stone, with its turrets, that guarded the way into Westminster. He passed through, crossed the broad beaten-earth yard as he had now done hundreds of times, and entered the former royal palace. He climbed the steps to the House of Commons and swept into the chamber, with its high whitewashed wooden ceiling, tiers of tall, pointed windows, and rows of wooden stalls, with the attending members seated along them. In front was the Speaker, facing him from his seat on the raised dais at the end of the chamber, with the table for the clerk beneath him.[157] Cromwell took his seat on one of the benches, in his accustomed manner, while his musketeers waited in the lobby.

What happened next was probably the most dramatic scene in British parliamentary history, and one on which all accounts of it agree, though they differ slightly concerning the exact sequence of events.[158] Cromwell sat and listened to the speeches around him until the time came for the House to approve the passage of its bill for a new Parliament. Then he rose, took off his hat and addressed the MPs. He spoke at first in praise of what the House had accomplished, but then accused it of injustice and self-interest and declared that God had chosen more worthy instruments. He put on his hat, left his place and marched up and down the central aisle, kicking the floor in his rage and accusing the members of a range of vices and misdeeds, gazing at individuals as he did so as if to apportion specific shortcomings to them. He finally declared that they were no longer a Parliament, and told Harrison to bring in the soldiers waiting outside, to clear the House.

Cromwell ordered the Speaker from his chair; when he got no response to stir, he commanded Harrison to fetch him down. Harrison laid hands on the Speaker, whereupon the wretched man rose and allowed himself to be helped from his seat. A few other MPs likewise sat still at first, but they in turn gave up when Cromwell's officers began to pluck them out. As the members departed, Oliver railed against some of them individually, especially former allies of his such as Sir Henry Vane and Henry Marten. Those who tried to argue with him were shouted down, and one, Alderman Allen, who denounced Oliver's action, was arrested by the soldiers (but soon released). Cromwell did not merely insult the members individually and collectively, but abused the authority of the House, embodied in the mace that was its symbol of authority and lay upon the clerk's table. He ordered his men to remove it, terming it a 'bauble' or 'baubles', after the object carried by a jester. When the chamber was clear he had it locked up. The time was now just twenty minutes past eleven o'clock.[159]

Oliver went immediately to the council of army officers, allegedly telling them that they needed not be troubled by what had just occurred. He added that when he went into the House he had not intended to expel its occupants, but that the spirit of God had moved him to do so when he realized that they were planning to perpetuate their own power.[160] There may be a hint of truth in this, if he had still hoped that he and his traditional allies might yet turn the MPs from their course. He had, however, made no attempt to do so, and the fact that he had armed men waiting to expel the occupants of the chamber is clear proof that he had at the least prepared for that eventuality. His fury in dealing with the members probably was genuine, representing both an explosion of frustration after years of trying to get Parliament to do what he and the army wanted, and an acute sense of betrayal that all his efforts on the previous evening had been wasted. It was later said that some of the officers at the council that morning, especially his hitherto loyal dragoon commander John Okey, expressed dismay at what had happened, and that Cromwell replied that he himself could now do more good than Parliament might ever have done.[161]

It remained to sweep away the executive arm of the fallen regime, the Council of State. That defiantly met in its usual room in Whitehall that afternoon, as scheduled, and Cromwell marched in with Harrison and Lambert. He informed the council that it no longer had legal validity, whereupon John Bradshaw, currently presiding and the man who had led the tribunal which had sentenced Charles I, replied that it had. He declared that, as Cromwell had no authority to dissolve a Parliament (and there was indeed a statute of 1641 that laid down that this Parliament could indeed only dissolve itself), both it and the council were still in existence. Once it became clear that the generals were prepared to use force to clear this chamber as well, the councillors sullenly departed.[162]

The next step for Oliver and the officers was to seize and retain the initiative in representing what had happened to the public. He had always been acutely aware of the importance of journalism and other forms of propaganda, and a full-scale effort was immediately launched to ensure that it was his and his followers' version of events that was published to the nation. The first task was to destroy the bill that Parliament had been about to pass, so that no objective evidence of its nature remained against which their assertions could be checked. This was accomplished immediately, as Cromwell snatched the draft document from the hand of the clerk as he evicted the MPs, put it under his cloak and took it out with him. It was never seen again.[163]

The next task was to put his case to the nation, and this started within two days, as he and the Council of Officers published a formal defence of his actions. It declared that the army had a special favour from God, as proved by its victories, and that 'the people' had turned to it to obtain spiritual and civil liberty when Parliament made no progress towards that freedom. Cromwell and his officers had therefore urged the MPs towards vigorous reform, but had no effect, while Parliament merely grew more hostile to 'the people of God'. It then went on to accuse the MPs of having sought to perpetuate their own hold on power by filling the vacant places in Parliament with their own friends, instead of having a proper new representative body. The officers had therefore joined forces with the 'honest people' of the nation to get power devolved from the Parliament to 'men fearing God and of proved integrity', who would encourage 'God's people', reform the law and administer impartial justice until the nation forgot monarchy and was ready to elect new Parliaments that would support the republic and the reforms. Then the army could disband. Instead, the document went on, the MPs had persisted with their scheme to recruit their friends to the House. The officers were therefore compelled to dissolve Parliament to prevent the ruin of all their hopes. They would now proceed with their scheme for a reforming interim government. The declaration concluded that they could justify their action with copious evidence of the late Parliament's misgovernment, but instead would trust to God who had brought them to this action to lead them on from it. It called on all legal and administrative officials to continue in their posts, and on the 'godly' to live in harmony with everybody else.[164]

This was a classic mixture of truth and misinformation, mingled with language that obscured sensitive points. When the army spoke of 'the people' it actually meant the small radical minority in the nation which represented its main civilian allies, a fact at which alternative circumlocutions such as 'the people of God' and 'the godly' hinted. In particular, those phrases indicated people who wished to worship in gathered congregations rather than the formal parochial structure of the Church of England, who were regarded as heretics and apostates by the great majority of the English and Welsh. Cromwell's commitment to the preservation of these had been the main guiding principle of his public career. The charge against the MPs that they wanted only to fill up the existing House with their cronies was an outright falsehood, made possible by the disappearance of the bill which would have disproved it. It was a way of mitigating the fact, which the declaration admitted, that the army had realized it could not trust the country with elections.

A few days later, a second declaration appeared in a newspaper, and was published as a tract on 3 May, 'on behalf of the Lord General and his Council of Officers'. It retained the accusation that the MPs had failed to do any good for the nation despite constant pressure from the army, but dropped the one that they had intended to recruit new MPs to fill the existing House. Instead, it now admitted that they were aiming at a new Parliament, but that the latter would be dangerous. It also made two new charges against the House. One was that the MPs intended to slash the funding for the army by half again from the much-reduced level to which Cromwell had been ordered to bring it in January, so effectively crippling it as a fighting force. The document supplied no evidence for this, and none exists elsewhere: it does indeed seem hard to imagine that the MPs would have destroyed the effectiveness of a body of soldiers on whom they themselves still relied for security. The other new assertion was that the MPs had probably intended to adjourn the Parliament as soon as they had passed the bill for a new one, so depriving the army of any means to put further pressure on them.[165] Again, there is no corroborating evidence. These official declarations were backed up with unofficial letters and publications from the army's supporters, which likewise shifted their justifications in line with those made by the leadership.[166]

Cromwell's own accounts of his action also changed with time. In late May the aldermen and sheriffs of London came to him asking to have the Parliament recalled, and he replied that his expulsion of it was on good advice taken beforehand (so contradicting his earlier story that it was a divinely inspired last-minute impulse). He added simply that the MPs had to go because 'they did not perform their trust'.[167] His fullest justification came over a month later, in a speech delivered on 4 July, to people whom he regarded as allies in promoting the radical cause.[168] He represented again the picture of a godly army striving unavailingly to make the Parliament address the needs of a dissatisfied nation. He also repeated the accusation that its members had intended to deny the people the choice of a new representative body, and only to recruit the House in order to perpetuate their own power. Now, however, he asserted that, under the army's pressure, it had altered its project to a new Parliament as requested, but set about that with indecent haste and designed a body that would be offensive to both God and 'our cause'. It seemed determined 'to cross the troublesome people of the army', and to surrender hard-won liberties to the royalists. The needs of 'the people of God' were despised. Cromwell admitted that the final straw for him had been the abolition of the existing commissioners for the advancement of religion in Wales, 'to the discontent of all the good people of the nation' (and, indeed, after expelling the Parliament, he reinstated the previous commissioners on his own authority).[169]

He went on to say that by that April it was clear that the Parliament intended no good to the 'forms of Godliness in this nation' who had put it there (by which he probably meant those who had formed it by the purge of December 1648). He reported that, at the meeting at his home on the evening of the 19th, his officers had asked the MPs what security there was in the bill to ensure that the right sort of people were elected to the Parliament it proposed. Cromwell and the soldiers had insisted that a means be found to bar all Presbyterians from sitting, as well as all people who had been neutral in the Civil War or who had dropped away from active support of all that had been achieved since. These he identified as being as dangerous as royalists to the preservation of freedom of conscience to radical Puritans. The MPs had replied that the only alternative to risky elections was to keep the present Parliament going. Indeed, it is hard to see what qualifications could have been imposed which would effectively exclude all the kinds of person against whom the army objected. It is also likely, and indeed fairly apparent, that the MPs cared a lot less than the soldiers if a subsequent Parliament did indeed prove more conservative. To stop this happening, the officers demanded that the MPs devolve power to some fewer trustworthy men until the nation settled down more and accepted what the army wanted. It was Cromwell's discovery of the rejection of this plan the following morning, and the determination of the Parliament to press on with arrangements for the election of a successor, that drove him to expel the MPs. All this may actually be the truth, for it fits the known facts very well, and it may be suggested that it disposes of any need to seek a more complex reason for his behaviour on 20 April.[170]

After their ejection, almost all the MPs left the capital and scattered to their homes in the provinces.[171] There was nothing to keep them around Westminster any longer; if they remained, they would probably be suspected of sedition and arrested. Alderman Allen's brief sojourn in captivity served as a message to those who might be tempted to speak out against what had happened. A general in the Irish army who was on leave and attending the Council of Officers at Whitehall circulated some questions among it concerning the wisdom of what Cromwell had done. His colleagues were not persuaded; although he was at first spared, he was arrested some weeks later and imprisoned.[172] To publish replies to the army's justifications of its action would be to invite immediate and severe retaliation against both authors and printers, working the efficient censorship system that the commonwealth had developed. Physical resistance was not an option. The cavalry regiments around London and the foot soldiers quartered at Westminster would move in as soon as any tumults arose. In any case, the expelled MPs had no popular basis of support, either in London or in the provinces. The radicals in the nation supported the army, and the rest of the population regarded the late Parliament as the tool of the soldiers, associating it with heavy taxes, religious chaos and the destruction of the traditional political order. The nearest to an immediate reply to the army that has survived is a manuscript letter, possibly by Henry Marten, that seems to have been designed for private circulation.[173] It was a direct response to the officers' declaration of 22 April, and flatly denied that the bill that had triggered the expulsion had contained a clause to fill up the existing House. It also accused the soldiers of having taken power from the people of the nation, whom they did and could not represent, and of having got rid of the Parliament because of a suspicion that the latter was planning to disband part of the army.

As Cromwell made his way homeward at the end of the day, he and his fellow officers had just become absolute masters of the British Isles, and he the leading figure among those masters. The very last fragment of the old constitution, which might have resisted the will of the military, had been removed. As a result, they were now in charge of three formerly independent nations, the vast majority of the inhabitants of which resented their new military overlords, and all that they stood for in politics and religion, very deeply. At all levels of society, including that of the traditional ruling class in England, which retained its social and economic power, and including the huge city that still smoked and rumbled just to the east of Cromwell's home, most of the people in whose names the army had claimed to act were cowed but disaffected. The expulsion of the MPs had just earned the army a new set of enemies, who had formerly been its most effective allies and support system. It now remained to be seen if and how the God whom Oliver and his subordinates still firmly believed to be guiding their actions would enable them to rebuild something viable from the ruins of all that they had destroyed.

CONCLUSION

The Cromwell who expelled the purged Parliament was recognizably the same man as the one who had emerged from the Civil War. Yet he was not only greatly enhanced in stature and responsibilities but also altered in many of his ideas. The single great ideological foundation of his belief and conduct remained an unwavering commitment to the right of godly and sober Protestants who dissented from the prescribed doctrine, liturgy and/or governance of the national Church to worship outside it, and for those within it to enjoy some freedom of decision at parish level. He had adhered to this ever since he had been a born-again Puritan farmer, co-operating with like-minded brethren in Huntingdonshire and Cambridgeshire when they were harassed by the regime of Charles I in the 1630s. Had Charles and his advisers favoured, or even just positively tolerated, Puritans, then Cromwell would have been loyal to them. He remained prepared to support any kind of government which would allow the liberty of conscience that he was seeking. It was the drift of political developments that ensured that to obtain it he had to join first the critics of Charles I in the Long Parliament, then the wartime parliamentarian party, then the Independent party within that, and then those Independents who were prepared to accept a republic, until finally they failed him too and he was left with his army and its civilian radical allies. The fact that these were a small and utterly unrepresentative minority in the nation was reflected in the fact that his commitment to liberty of conscience for those whom he saw as the godly was itself a position shared by a small minority.

It should be stressed that what he was seeking was not toleration in the modern sense. There were a few radicals in England at this time who did call for complete freedom of belief in matters of religion, as long as the doctrines concerned conformed to contemporary notions of piety and decency. Cromwell and his allies, however, only wanted such freedom for their own kind, and for people who had been loyal to Parliament alongside them in the Civil Wars. This excluded Catholics, of course, but also all those who wanted the traditional liturgy and government by bishops, who were a great number in the nation. Moreover, there was no sign that Cromwell and those with whom he co-operated envisaged liberty of conscience as more than a temporary dispensation. They always seem to have thought in terms of a broad alliance of different forms of Puritan – of the sort that had won the Civil War and made up the army – being a temporary mechanism to achieve a future in which its different components would reunite, to achieve a national religion most acceptable to each other and to God. Cromwell assisted this process by keeping his personal preferences with respect to the ideal Church government unclear, within the broad Puritan framework of a national structure without bishops and centred on preaching Scripture. The prospect of reunion was made the more difficult by the fact that the very people who needed toleration at this time were rarely themselves tolerant. If most presbyterians believed that sects should not be allowed to exist alongside the established Church, then many sectaries believed as strongly that the established Church should be abolished, and bickered among themselves about the forms that doctrine and practice should take in its place, and how much religion should be regulated by national authorities. Likewise, the blueprints for parliamentary reform drawn up by the army and the London radicals always excluded the majority of the population from voting. The intention was that politics would be confined to people who agreed to accept their ideology.

Cromwell's own religion was one fervently and entirely fixated on the God who stood at its centre. This was to an extent unusual even among devout Puritans, and resulted in the marginalization of two figures who loomed large in the cosmos of most. One was Satan, whom most committed early modern Christians regarded as ever active in the world and a daily force of temptation with whom they had to reckon. Oliver clearly believed in him, and in hell, but almost wholly disregarded him in practice. Cromwell's relationship with the Almighty was so close, constant and direct, that he felt no risk of intrusion by the Devil: he was wholly preoccupied with the pleasure or displeasure of God. The other figure was Jesus Christ, with whom many Christians felt (and still feel) an acute and immediate interaction, as saviour, role model and mediator. Cromwell referred at times to Christ, but seemed to accord him little separate identity from his divine father, who was Cromwell's great preoccupation. Consequently, the Gospels feature relatively little in Oliver's quotations from the Bible. He was interested in portions of the New Testament that deal with the nature of faith, especially the epistles, but his God – especially in the period covered by this book – was very much the one of the Old Testament, who was directly concerned with the political and military issues that preoccupied Cromwell. In many ways, Oliver saw himself as an ancient Hebrew prophet, judge or war leader, with a direct and ongoing interaction with his deity, to enable a chosen people to achieve the divine plan for it.

As a result, he was really not concerned by, or much interested in, constitutional and governmental structures, and was prepared to work with any that promised to deliver the liberty of conscience that he sought for his kind and their allies. He would co-operate with the Presbyterians as long as they held out a hope for that; when they failed him, he turned to negotiation with the king; when he was forced from that course of action, he relied on the new Independent majority in Lords and Commons. He fully embraced the commonwealth, ruled by a single-chamber purged Parliament, when that became expedient, and scrapped it in turn when it became inconvenient. Two aspects of this sequence of events need to be emphasized. The first is that, when new constitutional thinking was needed, and blueprints needed to be drawn up, he always left this work to others, having virtually no interest in it, nor any ideas. The second is that it was not he himself who drove that sequence of events, but the army on which his power and position ultimately depended, and which was the final guarantee that freedom of conscience for 'God's people' could be achieved. When tension developed between its soldiers and the politicians currently in charge of the nation, he always began by trying to reconcile the two. When that proved impossible, however, loyalty and expediency both ensured that he would always side with the soldiers. His political targets evolved with theirs. In 1647 he was prepared to abandon the king to satisfy the soldiers, but not to accept the radical reform programme that some of them advocated with their civilian allies. By the end of 1648, as the army radicalized further, he accepted that programme, and by 1651 he was prepared to appear as the champion of it. Each time that he followed the army into a new course, he threw his abilities energetically into achieving the army's ends, and so reaffirmed its affection and loyalty.

Those abilities were formidable, and all that were already evident before 1647 were further honed and displayed in the following six years. He was a superb military leader, in every respect, and one of the finest whom England has ever produced. He was an adroit talent-spotter, never mistaken in the abilities of those whom he favoured and promoted, and able to fashion capable men from a variety of backgrounds into a united and harmonious team in which each played a part to the best effect. He was equally adroit in managing cavalry, infantry and a train of siege artillery, and deployed all in unison or in turn for maximum impact. He rarely held the initiative in choosing a setting for action, whether on the offensive or the defensive. At Preston he needed to attack his enemies, wherever they happened to be, and chose his route of approach because it was the swiftest and cut off his opponents from reinforcement. At Dunbar he was forced to fight where he was cornered. At Worcester he needed to find a way to break into a prepared enemy position. Each time he besieged a town or city, he had to locate the weakest point in its defences and crack it open: time and resources almost never allowed him the option of a protracted operation of encirclement and starvation. Yet he coped with every one of these challenges and won.

Admittedly, he was greatly aided by luck in every case. He was always given logistical support that ensured him men and equipment of the highest quality. In Ireland he faced an already weakened, outnumbered, divided and demoralized enemy who never dared face him in battle, and many of whom soon defected to him. Divisions among his British enemies also prevented them from utilizing their full available strength effectively. At his three major battles in Britain, he was opposed by inept generals who threw away all their advantages. At one he had overwhelming superiority in numbers, and at the other two the enemy tactics allowed him to negate his own numerical weakness by concentrating his strength on a section of the opposing army while most of the latter remained ineffectual. He could then break it up portion by portion. In siege warfare, his superb firepower was repeatedly deployed against walls that were not constructed to withstand it, unlike most military defences in England (and indeed Europe) by this date. When the defenders in Ireland eventually learned ways of defending those breaches, their success was immediately erased by lack of numbers in one case and lack of ammunition in another. At Pembroke, where he lacked siege artillery, he was given the time in which to reduce it by attrition. Nevertheless, he always seized the opportunities presented by his good fortune, producing plans of attack that maximized his strengths and his opponents' weaknesses, and delivering them flawlessly. Nor did he take risks: when presented with the option of battle on ground that was clearly in his disfavour, he always declined it – in Scotland repeatedly. When he faced an impossible situation in his siege of Waterford, he decamped immediately. His boldest venture was probably to invade County Tipperary with his flying column of cavalry in January 1650, and then he knew he would not face a field army there, and could make up in guile what he lacked in firepower to win towns.

Cromwell's political skills were also formidable, and well honed after so many years of practice. He remained an effective speaker, idiomatic and emotional, and was a great networker, often convening meetings of people from different groups and trying to persuade them to co-operate. He reached out to individual politicians in the same way. He always gave people a chance to state their case and to find ways in which it could be made compatible with what he and his current allies wanted. He was also willing, if it seemed expedient, to reconcile with former enemies and with former friends with whom he had fallen out: examples range from King Charles I to John Lilburne. Under the commonwealth he worked to moderate official severity towards both royalists and Presbyterians. He tried hard, and persistently, to mend relations with friends and collaborators with whom he had parted company, such as Lord Wharton and Robert Hammond, and brought some, like Sir Henry Vane, successfully back into his political fold for a time. In the army, he attempted to persuade political troublemakers to see the error of their ways, and religious troublemakers to behave more circumspectly, only turning on them if they then proved insubordinate. He repeatedly impressed people with the patience with which he could listen to various different viewpoints and the sympathy that he appeared to accord to them. His flexibility and adaptability were also notable, and he always maintained a keen sense of what was possible in given situations. He suited his tactics and behaviour to the moment, and was expert in waiting on events until he saw how the stream of them was moving, and then taking decisive action appropriate to the occasion; this could also, of course, be described as waiting until the divine will seemed to be clear and then obeying it.

As earlier in his career, these remarkable talents and virtues were combined with less appealing traits. The efforts that he made to woo and to reconcile people were coupled with a savagery towards them when they proved obdurate and inconvenient. The more crass of his insubordinate soldiers found this out, as did Lilburne, the king and the members of the purged Parliament. This ruthlessness extended to military operations. He can still be held accountable for the notorious massacres at Drogheda and Wexford, the former directly and the latter indirectly, by continuing to attack the town while surrender negotiations were in progress (even though neither slaughter was as extensive as Irish nationalist mythology has made them). Moreover, they were not aberrations. He had exulted in killing during the first Civil War in England, and subsequently directed or accepted the slaughter of defenders and execution of prisoners when minor garrisons were stormed or reduced in both Scotland and Ireland. This savage streak was linked to the explosive temper which had been a feature of his youth, and which, while carefully reined in for most of his maturity, manifested again in the heat of moments both at Drogheda and at the end of the purged Parliament.

As a politician, he retained a slipperiness and deviousness that contemporaries of many different ideological shades noted, and that were regarded by them as unusual even in the fraught, fractious, unstable and vicious political world of civil war and revolutionary England. His readiness to listen with apparent sympathy to different viewpoints was often taken as a policy of being all things to all men, until it became clear which were going to prevail and which suited his interests best. He was also regularly accused of deceiving, manipulating and manoeuvring people in order to get his own way, and of assuring them of one thing while actually doing another. Solid proof of these instances is hard to supply, but an adroit mover such as Oliver would have ensured this very absence, and the regularity of the charge, made by people who had nothing else in common, is both exceptional in the political life of the time and telling.

In blackening the reputations of adversaries, and making scapegoats of them, Cromwell was much more normal for his political culture, and for the groups within it to which he belonged. During the Civil War, he had told blatant untruths to get rid of generals from his own party with whom he had worked and whom he had come to regard as incompetent and inconvenient. Now the army of which he was a, and then the, commander carried out a series of such defamation exercises. First it accused the

Presbyterian leaders of plotting to foment a new civil war in which it could destroy the soldiers. It may well be that, when this charge was first made, the soldiers sincerely believed it, but there is no evidence for it, and good evidence against it, and once the army was in control and in a position to ascertain the facts, it quietly dropped the charge once the end had been achieved of driving out the Presbyterians concerned. Then the commanders of the army, having opened negotiations with the king and won his co-operation with them, realized that his unpopularity with much of their army rendered him a liability. They promptly turned against him, blamed him for the change with vague accusations of untrustworthiness, and drove Parliament to stop dealing with him and imprison him closely. When Cromwell expelled the remnant of that Parliament in 1653, he and his officers first accused it of a scheme to fill itself up rather than make way for full elections, after destroying the evidence that would have refuted this charge. Only subsequently did they abandon this assertion and tell what seems likely to have been the truth.

This pattern is the more telling in that, in every one of the regime changes that the army enforced – its rebellion against the Presbyterians in mid-1647, its ending of negotiations with the king in the winter of 1647–8, its purging of Parliament in late 1648 and its expulsion of the surviving MPs in 1653 – it was essentially acting in its own selfish interests, even while it spoke of the liberties of the people and the nation. The same is true of those units in it which mutinied in 1649. It is ironic that, when treating of this period, the verdict of history has tended instead to blame Charles I for the lack of settlement after the Civil War, using charges against him based on those advanced by Cromwell's army. It is undeniably true that Charles was an inept and ultimately disastrous national leader, and that his refusal to accept Parliament's terms in 1646 precipitated many of the troubles that followed. On the other hand, the Presbyterians had found a workable basis for a settlement despite him in 1647, and only the intervention of the army prevented that from taking effect, and destabilized the whole of Britain. Moreover, the problem with the king at this time was not that he was duplicitous and untrustworthy, but that his conscience compelled him consistently to hold out for a compromise settlement, between royalist and parliamentarian, to which Parliament was never quite prepared to agree. When the army leaders did draft a plan for one which came nearer to meeting the king's terms, and which Charles regarded as hopeful, they found that neither the MPs nor many of their own soldiers were prepared to support it.

Did the ideas generated by the army and its radical civilian allies nevertheless sow the seeds of later British and American liberties, as has often been suggested? Here again it is difficult to give an easy assent to a traditional assumption. It is certainly true that modern liberals and socialists have found inspiration and fellow feeling in some of the utterances of the radicals of 1647–53, and it is understandable that they should have done so. This has been achieved, however, by taking those words out of their contemporary context. The ideas and actions that directly led to modern British and American freedoms developed in the later seventeenth century and the eighteenth, out of a constitutional monarchy with Houses of Lords and Commons, and an established Church of England with prelatical bishops and cathedrals. In America they were catalysed by a colonial revolution against the motherland, enabled by the particular conditions and institutions of the settlers. In Britain they evolved organically out of the established monarchical, aristocratic and episcopal regime, enabled by its traditional democratic elements and propelled by the massive increase of urbanization, industrialization, standards of living and education that eventually transformed most of Europe.

Having said that, for the British there was a vital ingredient in this process. Not only was Cromwell's army responsible for this, but it was driven directly by the ideological commitment to which Cromwell himself steadfastly adhered: freedom of conscience for Protestants who wished to worship outside the established national Church. Without the intervention of the soldiers, it is unlikely that this commitment would have been continued after the civil war which had allowed it, and certain that it would not have been maintained with a latitude that allowed a significant body of Protestant nonconformity, in various different denominations, to establish itself securely. This meant that, when the episcopal and ceremonial pre-war system of national religion was restored with the monarchy and political aristocracy in 1660, those who rejected it had become a permanent feature of British life. They were still a minority in the nation, but one that could neither be assimilated nor persecuted out of existence, and this minority was to grow considerably in number and influence during the following two centuries. Its very existence made Britain a more pluralistic society and culture than many others, and forced it to adopt a greater than normal attitude of tolerance towards religious and ideological diversity than most states of the pre-modern era. That in turn greatly enriched the country culturally, economically and politically, and also made its subsequent achievement of precocious democracy, liberalism and pluralism much easier. This is the true gift to subsequent modernity made by the army which Oliver Cromwell led to victory and then to supreme power – and it is a great one.

NOTES

ABBREVIATIONS

BL	British Library
Bod L	Bodleian Library, Oxford
CJ	Journals of the House of Commons, London, 1803
CSPD	*Calendar of State Papers, Domestic Series* (the volumes used were edited by John Bruce, and then William Douglas Hamilton, in London, between 1860 and 1891)
CSPV	*Calendar of State Papers and Manuscripts Relating to English Affairs, Existing in the Archives and Collections of Venice* (the volumes used were edited by Allen R. Hinds, in London, between 1925 and 1926)
HMC	Historical Manuscripts Commission
L	Library
LJ	Journals of the House of Lords, London, 1803
NA	National Archives
RO	Record Office
WCL	Worcester College Library, Oxford

Note: I have credited the recent impressive new edition of Cromwell's letters, writings and speeches to John Morrill, as editor, which is what the text itself does; but it was a complex co-operative venture, with several scholars working under Professor Morrill's general direction.

1 MAY EVE 1647

1. This is, of course, based on his portraiture, from 1646 onward.
2. What follows in this paragraph is based on Charles Hoover, 'Cromwell's Status and Pay in 1646–7', *Historical Journal* 23 (1989), 703–15. For my own take on Cromwell's previous career, and the developments in it noted here, see Ronald Hutton, *The Making of Oliver Cromwell*, New Haven and London, 2021.
3. Malpas Pearse, *Stuart London*, London, 1969, 90–3; Ben Weinreb et al., *The London Encyclopaedia*, London, 2008, 250. For what follows on London, see these two works and Peter Ackroyd, *London: The Biography*, London, 2001.
4. This is my own take on the events of this period. For relatively recent narratives of them, see Austin Woolrych, *Britain in Revolution*, Oxford, 2001, 335–65; Barry Coward, *The Stuart Age*, 3rd edition, Harlow, 2003, 224–30; and Michael Braddick, *God's Fury, England's Fire*, London, 2008, 463–93. For Cromwell's own activities before 1647, and their context, see my characterization of them in *The Making of Oliver Cromwell*, some of which is summarized in the present chapter.

5. Bod L, Clarendon MS 29, f. 97.
6. John Morrill, ed., *The Letters, Writings and Speeches of Oliver Cromwell*, Oxford, 2023, vol. 1, 366–8.
7. *CJ*, vol. 5, 107–8.
8. This is the French ambassador's report in NA, PRO/31/3/84, ff. 113–14.
9. BL, Additional MS 4693A, f. 156; *CJ*, vol. 5, 133; *LJ*, vol. 9, 122. Massey spelled his own name 'Massie', but the majority of writers at his time rendered it as I have, most historians have followed them, and there is a limit to the number of historical conventions that I think it necessary to flout. For the same reason, I have followed mainstream scholarly tradition in speaking of Thomas Rainsborough instead of Rainborowe and John Desborough instead of Disborowe, though the latter forms may be more authentic.
10. On this, see especially David Underdown, *Pride's Purge*, Oxford, 1971, 18–21.
11. I accept here Austin Woolrych's definition of parties in this period, in *Soldiers and Statesmen*, Oxford, 1987, 24, as 'groups of politicians regularly associated in the pursuit of coherent policies over a wide range of issues'.
12. For the coup in the Derby House Committee, see NA, SP 21/26, ff. 34–50.
13. Context, of course, is vital to the usage here. Back in 1640–1 the radicals in English religious politics had been those who wanted to abolish bishops and the Prayer Book instead of reforming them, and to place long-term formal restraints on royal power as well as ensuring regular Parliaments to check it. By 1646 this had moved to being the mainstream parliamentarian position, and the frontier of radicalism had progressed to the position now to be described.
14. A very good recent summary of the development of the group is provided by Gary S. De Krey, *Following the Levellers*, London, 2017, 16–93.
15. The most compendious and notorious of the written attacks was Thomas Edwards's *Gangraena*, which went through successive editions in 1646.
16. On this, see especially Woolrych, *Soldiers and Statesmen*, 19–22.
17. *The Humble Petition of the Lord Mayor, Aldermen and Commons of the City of London*, London, 1646.
18. *LJ*, vol. 9, 19, 71.
19. On these, see especially Michael Patrick Mahony, 'The Presbyterian Party in the Long Parliament' (Oxford University DPhil thesis, 1973), 336–40.
20. C. H. Firth and R. S. Rait, eds, *Acts and Ordinances of the Interregnum*, London, 1911, vol. 1, 913–14.
21. Morrill, ed., *Letters, Writings and Speeches*, vol. 1, 366–8, 375–7.
22. Bod L, Clarendon MS 29, ff. 165, 203.
23. *Memoirs of Denzil, Lord Holles*, London, 1699, 82; NA, SP 21/26, passim.
24. *The Kingdomes Weekly Intelligencer* 202 (23–30 March 1647), 469, and 219 (20–27 July 1647), 605.
25. Samuel Rawson Gardiner, ed., *The Constitutional Documents of the Puritan Revolution*, 3rd edition, Oxford, 1906, 290–306.
26. Ibid., 306–8.
27. His reasoning and attitudes are displayed clearly in his secret correspondence with his wife and supporters, published in *State Papers Collected by Edward, Earl of Clarendon*, Oxford, 1767, 242–315.
28. Ibid.; *Colonel Joseph Bamfield's Apologie*, The Hague, 1685, 20; John Bruce, ed., *Charles I in 1646*, Camden Society, 1st series 63, London, 1856, 80–1.
29. J. G. Fotheringham, ed., *The Diplomatic Correspondence of Jean de Montereul and the Brothers de Bellièvre*, Scottish History Society 29 (1898), 393–431, and 30 (1899), 14–108.
30. For this, see especially Ivan Roots's entry on Gardiner in the *Oxford Dictionary of National Biography* 21 (2004), 424; J. S. A. Adamson, 'Eminent Victorians', *Historical Journal* 35 (1990), 641–57; and Timothy Lang, *The Victorians and the Stuart Heritage*, Cambridge, 1995, 139–83.

31. Robert Ashton stated that Charles never offered sincere concessions, and bungled his chances by trying all his options in turn, so ruining the possibility of a settlement by double-dealing (*Counter-Revolution*, New Haven, 1994, 16–28). Michael Young has declared that he genuinely tried to negotiate but wasted his chances by playing off different groups against each other (*Charles I*, Basingstoke, 1997, 161–5). David Scott has suggested that he had his best chance of making peace in all kingdoms in 1646 and in England in particular in 1647, but tried to sow division instead (*Politics and War in the Three Stuart Kingdoms*, Basingstoke, 2004, 130). Richard Cust has said that he had a strong hand in both years, but that his main objective was not to make peace but to restart the civil war, although he does allow that the king was willing to offer compromise (*Charles I*, Harlow, 2005, 421–7). Clive Holmes has declared that Charles aimed to bring about a new war between his old opponents rather than get the best peace terms (*Why Was Charles I Executed?*, London, 2006, 95). Mark Kishlansky (*Charles I*, London, 2014, 91–4) and John Adamson ('Eminent Victorians') have stood out in their emphasis on a need to check Gardiner's take on events at each point, and Kishlansky has been unique in his conclusion that Charles genuinely sought a settlement after the war.
32. It was, for example, stated with absolute conviction by an earlier and even more famous Victorian historian than Gardiner, Thomas Babington Macaulay.
33. *CJ*, vol. 5, 114, 126–9, 132; *LJ*, vol. 9, 112–18; *The Moderate Intelligencer* 106 (18–25 March 1647), unpaginated; Sir William Waller, *Vindication of the Character and Conduct of Sir William Waller*, London, 1793, 44–76; *The Weekly Account* 12 (17–24 March 1647), unpaginated. For differing but generally complementary accounts of the events in Parliament and army in March and April, see Samuel R. Gardiner, *History of the Great Civil War*, London, 1898, vol. 3, 223–46; Mark A. Kishlansky, *The Rise of the New Model Army*, Cambridge, 1979, 150–206; Woolrych, *Soldiers and Statesmen*, 30–47; and Ian Gentles, *The New Model Army in England, Ireland and Scotland 1645–1653*, Oxford, 1992, 148–53.
34. *CJ*, vol. 5, 152–3; Fotheringham, ed., *Diplomatic Correspondence of Jean de Montereul*, vol. 2, 128–9; *The Moderate Intelligencer* 110–11 (15–29 April 1647); Waller, *Vindication*, 77–91; *Letters from Saffron Walden*, London, 1647; *A Perfect Diurnall* 194–5 (12–26 April 1647); *The Weekly Account* 16 (14–21 April 1647), sub. 17 April.
35. *CJ*, vol. 5, 152–3; Waller, *Vindication*, 79–81.
36. Waller, *Vindication*, 79–80, is certain on this point.
37. *A Warning for All the Counties of England*, London, 1647; *A New Found Stratagem*, London, 1647; *The Kingdomes Weekly Intelligencer* 204 (6–13 April 1647), 490–1; C. H. Firth, ed., *The Clarke Papers*, vol. 1, Camden Society N.S. 49, London, 1891, 15.
38. Firth and Rait, eds, *Acts and Ordinances*, vol. 1, 924–5; Margaret Steig, ed., *The Diary of John Harington, M.P. 1646–53*, Somerset Record Society, 1977, 46; Bod L, Clarendon MS 29, f. 203; *LJ*, vol. 9, 176. For the strength of the London militia, see Lawson Nagel, 'The Militia of London 1641–1649' (London University PhD thesis, 1982). For that of the New Model in April 1647, see Firth, ed., *Clarke Papers*, vol. 1, 18–19.
39. John Lilburne, *Ionahs Cry Out of the Whales Belly*, London, 1647, 3–4.
40. Edward, Earl of Clarendon, *The History of the Rebellion and Civil Wars in England*, ed. W. Dunn Macray, Oxford, 1888, X.88.
41. *CJ*, vol. 5, 142, 148, 152–3.
42. *The Kingdomes Weekly Intelligencer* 207 (27 April–4 May 1647), 511.
43. For this, see John Morrill, 'Mutiny and Discontent in English Provincial Armies 1645–1647', *Past & Present* 56 (1972), 49–74.
44. *A Perfect Diurnall* 196 (26 April–3 May 1647), 1570.
45. *The Petition and Vindication of the Officers of the Armie under His Excellencie Sir Thomas Fairfax* (27 April 1647).
46. *The Apologie of the Common Soldiers of his Excellencie Sir Tho. Fairfaxes Army* (3 May 1647).
47. For the events in the House that day, see *CJ*, vol. 5, 157–8; *LJ*, vol. 9, 163–4; *The Moderate Intelligencer* 112 (29 April–6 May 1647), 1046–7; *A Perfect Diurnall* 196 (26 April–3 May 1647), 1572–3; Firth, ed., *Clarke Papers*, vol. 1, 430–1.
48. *CJ*, vol. 5, 162–3.

2 MUTINY

1. John Morrill, ed., *The Letters, Writings and Speeches of Oliver Cromwell*, Oxford, 2023, vol. 1, 378–9; C. H. Firth, ed., *The Clarke Papers*, vol. 1, Camden Society N.S. 49, London, 1891, 19–20.
2. *The Apologie of the Common Soldiers of His Excellencie Sir Thomas Fairfaxes Army*, 3 May 1647. I follow Austin Woolrych, in *Soldiers and Statesmen*, Oxford, 1987, 59, in accepting this as a genuine army document.
3. Firth, ed., *Clarke Papers*, vol. 1, 21–2.
4. Ibid., 22–4.
5. Ibid., 24–6; Keith Lindley and David Scott, eds, *The Journal of Thomas Juxon 1644–1647*, Camden Society, 5th series 13, Cambridge, 1999, 155–6.
6. Morrill, ed., *Letters, Writings and Speeches*, vol. 1, 379–83; *The Moderate Intelligencer* 113 (6–13 May 1647), 1058–9.
7. *The Kingdomes Weekly Intelligencer* 209 (11–18 May 1647), 530–1.
8. *A Perfect Diurnall* 198 (10–17 May 1647), 1588; *The Perfect Weekly Account* 20 (12–19 May 1647), sub 13 May.
9. Firth, ed., *Clarke Papers*, vol. 1, 33–44.
10. Ibid., 45–87; *Divers Papers from the Army*, London, 1647. Other sources, such as newspapers and Waller's *Vindication*, just summarize the information given in these.
11. WCL, Clarke MS 41, ff. 105–27. The collated document also exists, as *The Declaration of the Armie under His Excellency Sir Thomas Fairfax, as it was lately presented at Saffron-Walden*, London, 1647.
12. Among the army documents apparently from this time is one proposing annual parliaments and the sovereignty of the people: WCL, Clarke MS 41, f. 18.
13. Morrill, ed., *Letters, Writings and Speeches*, vol. 1, 389–90; *CJ*, vol. 5, 175–7.
14. *LJ*, vol. 9, 112, 160–2, 191–202; *CJ*, vol. 5, 175–80; Margaret F. Stieg, ed., *The Diary of John Harington, M.P. 1646–53*, Somerset Record Society, 1977, 50–3; *Perfect Occurrences Of Every Daie iornall in Parliament* 19 (7–14 May 1647), 150; Bod L, Clarendon MS 29, f. 279.
15. Ian Gentles is especially good on these, in *The New Model Army in England, Ireland and Scotland*, Oxford, 1992, 166.
16. This is the conclusion drawn by every historian to work intensively on the period since Gardiner proposed it, including Mark Kishlansky, Austin Woolrych and Ian Gentles.
17. Morrill, ed., *Letters, Writings and Speeches*, vol. 1, 391–7; *The Moderate Intelligencer* 115 (20–27 May 1647), 1082–3.
18. *CJ*, vol. 5, 181.
19. Robert Bell, ed., *Memorials of the Civil War*, London, 1849, 347–8; BL, Additional MS 37344, f. 84v.
20. *CJ*, vol. 5, 182–8; *LJ*, vol. 9, 207, 222–4; Bulstrode Whitelocke, *Memorials of the English Affairs*, Oxford, 1853, vol. 2, 146.
21. Firth, ed., *Clarke Papers*, vol. 1, 100–13; *LJ*, vol. 9, 226–7; *The Kingdomes Weekly Intelligencer* 211 (25 May–1 June 1647), 547–8; *A Perfect Diurnall* 201 (31 May–7 June 1647), 1607–9. NA, SP 21/26, ff. 72–3 proves that the order of the Derby House Committee, to bring the artillery train to London, was provoked by the move of the soldiers to seize it, and not vice versa.
22. Firth, ed., *Clarke Papers*, vol. 1, 425–7 (Wogan's narrative); Edward, Earl of Clarendon, *The History of the Rebellion and Civil Wars in England*, ed. W. Dunn Macray, Oxford, 1888, X.88; Clement Walker, *The History of Independency*, London, 1660, vol. 1, 31–2; *Memoirs of Denzil, Lord Holles*, London, 1699, 85; Sir William Waller, *Vindication of the Character and Conduct of Sir William Waller*, London, 1793, 139.
23. C. H. Firth, ed., *The Memoirs of Edmund Ludlow*, Oxford, 1894, vol. 1, 147–8.
24. William Walwyn, *Walwyns Just Defence*, London, 1649, 2–6.
25. H. G. Tibbutt, ed., *The Tower of London Letter-Book of Sir Lewis Dyve*, Bedfordshire Historical Record Society 38 (1958), 57.

26. *Sundry Reasons Inducing Major Robert Huntington to lay down his Commission*, London, 2 August 1648, 1–2. See also *A Back Blow to Major Huntington*, London, 1647.
27. Lindley and Scott, eds, *Journal of Thomas Juxon*, 107.
28. Bell, ed., *Memorials of the Civil War*, 347–8.
29. Bod L, Clarendon MS 29, f. 227.
30. The area has been much planted with woodland in subsequent centuries, and farmed. The presence of the bustards is recorded in the reign of Charles II, when the king's cousin Prince Rupert shot them on the heaths near Newmarket.
31. Gardiner suggested that Cromwell inserted these clauses, but Mark Kishlansky, quite rightly, pointed out that there is no evidence for this and that similar expressions are found in the regimental petitions of May: *The Rise of the New Model Army*, Cambridge, 1979, 239. Indeed, Cromwell might not even have reached the muster by then.
32. John Rushworth, *Historical Collections of Private Passages of State*, London, 1722, vol. 6, 504–10; *A Perfect Diurnall* 201 (31 May–7 June 1647), 1616; *A Solemn Engagement of the Army under the Command of his Excellency Sir Thomas Fairfax*, London, 5 June 1647.
33. Clarendon, *History of the Rebellion*, X.88–90.
34. Firth, ed., *Memoirs of Edmund Ludlow*, vol. 1, 149–50.
35. *Putney Projects*, London, 1647, 7, which has generally been credited to John Wildman.
36. These are the accounts by Holles and Waller.
37. Thomas Birch, ed., *A Collection of the State Papers of John Thurloe*, London, 1742, vol. 5, 674. The London radical William Walwyn also claimed later to have had some influence in persuading Cromwell to join the soldiers: *Walwyns Just Defence*, 35.
38. See the Presbyterian sources – Wogan, Walker, Holles and Waller – at n. 22.
39. *CJ*, vol. 5, 197–200; *LJ*, vol. 9, 232–44, 249–51; *The Moderate Intelligencer* 117 (3–10 June 1647), 1107–9; *A True Narrative Concerning The Armies preservation of the Kings Majesties Person*, London, 1647; *A Letter From his Excellency Sir Thomas Fairfax, sent To both Houses of Parliament June the 6*, London, 1647; Henry Cary, ed., *Memorials of the Great Civil War in England 1642–52*, London, 1849, vol. 1, 223–4; *The Perfect Weekly Account 24* (2–9 June 1647), sub 7 June; Sir Thomas Herbert, *Memoirs of the Last Two Years of the Reign of King Charles I*, London, 1813, 27–32. Childerley was commonly known then as Childersley.
40. BL, Additional MS 17667, f. 456. The French ambassador was also aware of this design: J. G. Fotheringham, ed., *The Diplomatic Correspondence of Jean de Montereul and the Brothers Bellièvre*, Scottish History Society 30, 1899, 161–3.
41. Firth, ed., *Clarke Papers*, vol. 1, 119–20.
42. *The Grand Designe*, London, 1647, usually credited to John Harris, sig. A3. The account in *Memoirs of Denzil Holles*, 96–7, does not seem to be independent but based on this pamphlet, which it cites. It gives a slightly different date, of 30 May, but this may itself be a mistake derived from the tract, which speaks of 'the Monday before Whitsun', which was 31 May that year, rather than giving an actual date.
43. *Sundry Reasons Inducing Major Robert Huntington*, 3. The account by Sir William Waller in his *Vindication*, 136–7, seems to be based mainly on this one, and so is not an independent witness.
44. Wilbur Cortez Abbott, ed., *The Writings and Speeches of Oliver Cromwell*, vol. 1, Cambridge, MA, 1937, 453. As Abbott points out, it is dated 4 June but must have been written on the 3rd.
45. BL, Additional MS 31116, f. 312v.
46. *A True Narrative of the Occasions and Causes of the late Lord Gen. Cromwell's Anger and Indignation against Lieut. Col. George Joyce*, n.d., but 1659.
47. Bod L, Fairfax MS 36, p. 6.
48. There is still a messy problem of times and places hanging over the whole affair. The Oxford magazine was seized by New Model soldiers by 29 May, two days before the meeting was supposed to have been held at Cromwell's house at which Joyce was authorized to take the action in Oxford: Firth, ed., *Clarke Papers*, vol. 1, 111–13. Moreover, Austin Woolrych, a

former soldier as well as a distinguished historian, noticed a logistical difficulty with Joyce's movements, in *Soldiers and Statesmen*, 106–9: if Joyce was in Drury Lane on 31 May and near Holdenby on 2 June, he did not have time to take a body of soldiers through Oxford in between. Austin proposed that Joyce made a lone dash from Oxford to London on the 31st, sending his troopers ahead towards Holdenby, and rejoined them in the Midlands direct from the capital with Cromwell's blessing a day or two later. Such an epic ride, however, strains credulity, and it may be more economical to scrap the meeting in Drury Lane as a later invention, or allow that it might have happened on an earlier date. Another economical solution would have been to conclude that Joyce might not have gone to Oxford at all, as the units from which his troopers were drawn, listed in *The Perfect Weekly Account* (see n. 39 above), were all stationed in the Midlands near Holdenby, suggesting that Joyce had raked them together there. However, the army's official account of his action, *A True Narrative Concerning The Armies preservation* (see n. 39), states in passing that some of his men had come from Oxford.

49. Herbert, *Memoirs*, 35–6; *State Papers Collected by Edward, Earl of Clarendon*, London, 1767, xxxviii; *Another letter from His Excellency Sir Thomas Fairfax to the Speaker of the House of Commons of His Majesties removall from Childersley to New-Market*, London, 1647; BL, Additional MS 18979, f. 238; *LJ*, vol. 9, 249–51.
50. Fotheringham, ed., *Diplomatic Correspondence of Jean de Montereul*, vol. 2, 159–60.
51. *CJ*, vol. 5, 193–202; *LJ*, vol. 9, 226–52; C. H. Firth and R. S. Rait, eds, *Acts and Ordinances of the Interregnum*, London, 1911, vol. 1, 953–4.
52. Fotheringham, ed., *Diplomatic Correspondence of Jean de Montereul*, vol. 2, 161–3.
53. One Londoner put the number of these ex-soldiers in and around the city as near 20,000: Lindley and Scott, eds, *Journal of Thomas Juxon*, 160.
54. In the 1640s it was clearly pronounced 'Triploe' or 'Triplow', which is how it was spelled then.
55. *A Perfect Diurnall* 202 (7–14 June 1647), sub 11 June; Firth, ed., *Clarke Papers*, vol. 1, 127–9; Waller, *Vindication*, 142–4; *The Moderate Intelligencer* 118 (10–17 June 1647), 1117; Holles, *Memoirs*, 108.
56. Morrill, ed., *Letters, Writings and Speeches*, vol. 1, 400–2.
57. The best statistics here are provided by Gentles, *The New Model Army in England, Ireland and Scotland*, 168.
58. *CJ*, vol. 5, 206–9; *LJ*, vol. 9, 255–75; Firth and Rait, eds, *Acts and Ordinances*, vol. 1, 954–6.
59. *A Representation of the Army*, London, 1647.
60. This was Whitelocke, in *Memorials of the English Affairs*, vol. 2, 162–3.
61. *A Charge Delivered in the Name of the Army*, St Albans, 17 June 1647; *Articles of Impeachment Agreed upon by the Army*, St Albans, 19 June 1647.
62. *CJ*, vol. 5, 212–17; *LJ*, vol. 9, 264–87; *The Kingdomes Weekly Intelligencer* 213 (8–15 June 1647), 162; *A Perfect Diurnall* 203 (14–21 June 1647), 1624; Firth, ed., *Clarke Papers*, vol. 1, 132–3.
63. Fotheringham, ed., *Diplomatic Correspondence of Jean de Montereul*, vol. 2, 171–87.
64. *The last Newes from the Armie*, London, 21 June 1647.
65. *LJ*, vol. 9, 288–303; *A Humble Remonstrance From His Excellency Sir Thomas Fairfax, and the Army under his Command*, London, 25 June 1647; *The Perfect Weekly Account* 26 (23–29 June 1647), sub 26 June; *Three Letters From His Excellency Sir Thomas Fairfax*, London, 28 June 1647.
66. *CJ*, vol. 5, 221–9; *LJ*, vol. 9, 288–306; Morrill, ed., *Letters, Writings and Speeches*, vol. 1, 404; *LJ*, vol. 9, 296–307; *The Kingdomes Weekly Intelligencer* 216 (22–29 June 1647), 579. The order to Whalley on 25 June (in Abbott, ed., *Writings and Speeches of Oliver Cromwell*, vol. 1) to admit the king's royalist chaplains to him despite Parliament's wishes was signed not by Fairfax but by Cromwell and an infantry colonel, John Hewson, who was another religious independent and who had risen to prominence during the army's resistance to Parliament. It is interesting to speculate that their own religious independency might have induced them to accord more liberty of conscience to Charles.

67. *CJ*, vol. 5, 223–5; *LJ*, vol. 9, 299–306; *A Manifesto From His Excellency Sir Thomas Fairfax, And The Army under his command*, London, 27 June 1647; Firth and Rait, eds, *Acts and Ordinances*, vol. 1, 958–85.
68. *New Papers From The Armie*, 13 July 1647; *A Perfect Diurnall* 206 (5–12 July 1647), 1638–9; Firth, ed., *Clarke Papers*, vol. 1, 148–50; *CJ*, vol. 5, 231–2; *LJ*, vol. 9, 319–21.
69. Firth, ed., *Clarke Papers*, vol. 1, 151–2; *CJ*, vol. 5, 234–6; *The Heads Of the great Charge, presented to the Honourable House of Commons*, London, 8 July 1647; *A Particular Charge or Impeachment In the Name of his Excellency Sir Thomas Fairfax*, London, 1647.
70. Bod L, Clarendon MS 29, f. 258; *LJ*, vol. 9, 231–7; *The Kingdomes Weekly Intelligencer* 217 (6–13 July 1647), 596; *Sundry Reasons Inducing Major Robert Huntington*, 5.
71. John Berkeley, *Memoirs of Sir John Berkeley*, London, 1699, 3–29. Berkeley's memoirs also testify to the key role played by Robert Huntington as a go-between in these negotiations, increasing the importance of the latter's testimony concerning them. Huntington himself reported that Cromwell had been foremost in talking the General Council of the army into dealing with the king: *Sundry Reasons Inducing Major Robert Huntington*, 5.
72. *CJ*, vol. 5, 240–51; *LJ*, vol. 9, 321–39; *The Moderate Intelligencer* (8–22 July 1647); *A Full Vindication and Answer of the XI. Accused Members*, London, 1647; *A Letter From His Excellency Sir Thomas Fairfax, To Mr Speaker*, London, 1647.
73. Firth, ed., *Clarke Papers*, vol. 1, 176–215; *The Proposalls Delivered To The Earl of Nottingham*, London, 1647; *A Further Proposal From His Excellency Sir Thomas Fairfax*, London, 1647; Bell, ed., *Memorials of the Civil War*, 369–71.
74. CL, vol. 5, 253–7; *LJ*, vol. 9, 339–41.
75. Bell, ed., *Memorials of the Civil War*, 379–80; *LJ*, vol. 9, 352–4; *The Moderate Intelligencer* 124 (22–29 July 1647), 1200; *LJ*, vol. 9, 245–51.
76. Historians of the period will recognize what a delicate circumlocution this phrasing is. There is absolutely no doubt that Ireton was the draughtsman of the package: Berkeley makes that clear (*Memoirs*, 23) and so does a London radical in *Putney Projects*, 13, 29–30; and a radical MP, Edmund Ludlow, reported that the generals had told him the same: Firth, ed., *Memoirs of Edmund Ludlow*, vol. 1, 157. The drafts of the proposals found by David Como in Lambeth Palace Library are in Ireton's hand: 'Making *The Heads of the Proposals*', *English Historical Review* 135 (2020), 387–432. However, he must have taken considerable advice and direction from other senior army officers, and perhaps views from other ranks. Walwyn recorded that he had been invited by the leaders of the army to Reading to provide his comments (*Walwyns Just Defence*, 6–7); and from the Putney Debates, to be considered later, and the papers found by Como, it seems that so were at least two other London radicals, John Wildman and Maximilian Petty. The parliamentary commissioners sent to treat with the army included some notable Independents, such as Lord Wharton, who were allies of the army leadership and would presumably have been consulted. As noted, Ireton also talked to Berkeley. If the proposals were intended to reunite royalists, Presbyterians and Independents, or at the least to represent an Independent plan which would be accepted by the army and the king, wide canvassing would have been essential.

    Any reasonable person would probably acknowledge this much. The matter was, however, rendered highly toxic at the opening of the 1990s, after a talented young historian named John Adamson argued that the framework of the proposals drafted by Ireton had been devised by the parliamentary Independents, and especially the lords among them: 'The English Nobility and the Proposed Settlement of 1647', *Historical Journal* 30 (1987), 567–602. This position was attacked by Mark Kishlansky, with exceptional savagery, and a bitter debate ensued between them: Mark A. Kishlansky, 'Saye What?', *Historical Journal* 33 (1990), 917–37; John Adamson, 'Politics and the Nobility in Civil War England', *Historical Journal* 34 (1991), 231–55; and Mark Kishlansky, 'Saye No More', *Journal of British Studies* 30 (1991), 399–448. For a time, it divided the community of specialists in the period. Subsequently, the following verdicts have been delivered by members of that community. David Smith pronounced the evidence for the origins of the 'Heads of the Proposals' to be very complex and ambiguous, and commented that some aspects of the matter were doomed always to be mysterious. He noted that a variety of sources supported the idea that the army officers drafted them, and that none proved beyond doubt that the Independent peers oversaw the process or masterminded the presentation of the terms to Charles: *Constitutional Royalism and the Search for Settlement, c.1640–1649*, Cambridge, 1994, 133. Sarah Barber concluded that those terms were prepared by Ireton in partnership with the Independents in general: *Regicide and Republicanism*, Edinburgh, 1998, 36. J. C. Davis stated that they were drafted by Ireton and Lambert in partnership with the Independents and were the product of Cromwell's long collaboration with the latter's leaders in Parliament: *Oliver Cromwell*, London, 2001, 153–7. David Scott declared that they were drafted by Ireton in consultation with the Independent grandees and some of the London radicals: *Politics and War in the Three Stuart Kingdoms*, Basingstoke, 2004, 149. David Farr thought that there was co-operation between the senior army officers and their allies in Parliament, but that the balance of power in the relationship lay with the army: *Henry Ireton and the English Revolution*, Woodbridge, 2006, 84. Most recently, Ian Gentles has decided that Ireton was certainly advised by Lambert and Cromwell, and possibly by the Independent politicians: 'The Politics of Fairfax's Army', in John Adamson, ed., *The English Civil War*, Basingstoke, 2009, 184. I myself agree with David Smith that the truth will probably never be known, and suggest that it is certain that the army officers had influence over the first draft of the 'Heads of the Proposals' and that it is likely that so did both the Independents in Parliament and the London radicals.

77. Berkeley, *Memoirs*, 23; Firth, ed., *Clarke Papers*, vol. 1, 212–17; *CJ*, vol. 5, 252–3; *A Perfect Summary* 1 (19–26 July 1647), 5. According to Tibbutt, ed., *Letter-Book of Sir Lewis Dyve*, 68, it was reported that agents of the army (Leonard Watson and Dr Staines) had been in London for some days, negotiating with Independent leaders such as Sir Henry Vane, Oliver St John and Lord Wharton, who were traditional allies of Cromwell in Parliament.
78. These terms are reconstructed by comparing the eventual form of the proposals with the amendments made in them before publication, as recounted below. I accord in general with the view of the process of assembly proposed by Como, 'Making *The Heads of the Proposals*'.
79. Berkeley, *Memoirs*, 30–2; Fotheringham, ed., *Diplomatic Correspondence of Jean de Montereul*, vol. 2, 195–210; Gilbert Burnet, *The Memoires of the Lives and Actions of James and William, Dukes of Hamilton*, London, 1677, 316.
80. Como, 'Making *The Heads of the Proposals*'.
81. Berkeley, *Memoirs*, 32–6; John Ashburnham, *A Narrative by John Ashburnham*, London, 1830, vol. 2, 88–90. Robert Huntington tells a slightly different story from Berkeley's, though one that can perhaps be reconciled with it: that the king had already been allowed to suggest amendments to the proposals before leaving the Reading area, and that Huntington had then carried a further draft of them to him at Woburn. Charles had said that he could not accept them as they were, but would treat on the basis of them. The set of officers then visited him as Berkeley recalled, for three hours, and promised him many amendments with which he pronounced himself satisfied. This last outcome does contrast jarringly with Berkeley's (usually accepted) portrait of a disastrous meeting: *Sundry Reasons Inducing Robert Huntington*, 7. *Putney Projects*, 13, supports some of Huntington's version.
82. A point made by Berkeley himself in his narrative cited above.
83. Burnet, *Memoires*, 317.
84. *LJ*, vol. 9, 330.
85. Ibid., 352–4.
86. Ibid., 355–65; *CJ*, vol. 5, 258–63; Firth, ed., *Memoirs of Edmund Ludlow*, vol. 1, 160–1; *The Kingdomes Weekly Intelligencer* 220 (27 July–3 August 1647), 617–19; *A Perfect Diurnall* 209 (26 July–2 August 1647), 1680–1; Bell, ed., *Memorials of the Civil War*, 379–84; Lindley and Scott, eds, *Journal of Thomas Juxon*, 162–5. There remains a strong suspicion that some of the Presbyterian leaders, and especially some of those who had been targeted by the army, were implicated in encouraging the invasion of the Houses, but final proof has always been missing: see Elliot Vernon, *London Presbyterians and the British Revolutions 1638–64*, Manchester, 2021, 153–6, for the most recent verdict on the matter.

87. *CJ*, vol. 5, 263–5; Firth, ed., *Memoirs of Edmund Ludlow*, vol. 1, 162; *LJ*, vol. 9, 358–61; *A Perfect Summary* 3 (2–9 August 1647), 18–19. The Presbyterian Clement Walker later claimed to have seen a letter from the army to the Speaker of the Commons, who withdrew after 26 July, inviting him to join the soldiers: *History of Independency*, vol. 1, 41.
88. Bod L, Clarendon MS 36, ff. 110v–112; Berkeley, *Memoirs*, 37; Ashburnham, *Narrative by John Ashburnham*, vol. 2, 90.
89. John Rushworth, *Propositions for Peace And for the King to come to the Parliament*, London, 1647; *A Declaration From His Excellency Sir Thomas Fairfax, and the Councell of Warre; concerning their proceedings in the Proposals*, Oxford, 1647.
90. *The Kings Majesties Declaration And Profession, disavowing any preparations or intentions in Him, to lay Warre*, Cambridge, 1647. The individuals who acted as messengers between king and army subsequently provided different accounts of these transactions. Berkeley, ever keen to blame Charles for the failure to reach a deal, claimed that several senior officers had been alienated by his hostility, and that he delayed sending the letter of support until the City was treating and it was no longer needed: *Memoirs*, 38–9. Ashburnham broadly agreed, but blamed the officers, and especially Cromwell and Ireton, for soliciting the letter and then, when the king sent it, snubbing it because the City had asked for terms and it was no longer needed: *Narrative by John Ashburnham*, 91–2. Huntington, however, said that the king had asked him at this point to tell Ireton that he (Charles) now depended fully on the army and placed his hopes on it, and that Ireton seemed overjoyed: *Sundry Reasons Inducing Major Robert Huntington*, 7–8. These may all be reconciled if Huntington spoke to Ireton just before the City began to treat.
91. *LJ*, vol. 9, 374–9.
92. *A Letter from the Armie Concerning the Kings Majesty*, London, 1647.
93. *A Perfect Diurnall* 210 (2–9 August 1647), 1688–91.
94. *LJ*, vol. 9, 386. Sir William Waller, one of the eleven accused MPs, later told a story of how, when the declaration was drafted, Cromwell and the Independent leader, Sir Arthur Hesilrige, hesitated overnight about concurring with it because it had a clause guaranteeing the privileges of both Houses, and the two men were reluctant to confirm those of the Lords. Waller was, of course, nowhere near them, and it is impossible to ascertain the truth of his account: *Vindication*, 191–4.
95. *Two Letters, The One, From the Right Honorable The Lord Major, Aldermen, and Commons Of The City of London*, London, 1647; Lindley and Scott, eds, *Journal of Thomas Juxon*, 165; *A Perfect Diurnall* 210 (2–9 August 1647), 1688–91; Fotheringham, ed., *Diplomatic Correspondence of Jean de Montereul*, vol. 2, 218–19.
96. Fotheringham, ed., *Diplomatic Correspondence of Jean de Montereul*, vol. 2, 219–20, 226.
97. *The Moderate Intelligencer* 125 (5–12 August 1647), 1205; *A Perfect Diurnall* 210 (2–9 August 1647), 1691–2.
98. *CJ*, vol. 5, 268–9; *LJ*, vol. 9, 374–9; Fotheringham, ed., *Diplomatic Correspondence of Jean de Montereul*, vol. 2, 226–7.
99. *A Perfect Summary* 3 (2–9 August 1647), 24; *The Kingdomes Weekly Intelligencer* 321 (3–10 August 1647), 627–8; *The Moderate Intelligencer* 125 (5–12 August 1647), 1205.
100. *Perfect Occurrences* 35 (27 August–3 September 1647), 234.
101. Ibid.; *The Kings Majesties Declaration Concerning The High and Honourable Court of Parliament*, London, 1647, 4; *A Perfect Diurnall*, 212–13 (16–30 August 1647).
102. *The Moderate Intelligencer* 131 (16–23 September 1647), 1273; *The Heads of the New Proposals*, London, 1647; *A Declaration From His Excellency Sir Thomas Fairfax, And The Generall Councell of the Army*, 18 September 1647; *The Kingdomes Weekly Intelligencer* 226 (7–14 September 1647), 665–6; *A Perfect Diurnall* 216 (13–20 September 1647), 743.
103. *CJ*, vol. 5, 270–80; *LJ*, vol. 9, 382–91.
104. *CJ*, vol. 5, 284–96; *LJ*, vol. 9, 406–25; Holles, *Memoirs*, 172–4; Walker, *The History of Independency*, vol. 1, 46–8; *The Resolutions of the Agitators of the Army, Concerning the prosecution of their late Remonstrance*, London, 1647; *The propositions of the Lords and Commons assembled in Parliament for a safe and well grounded peace*, London, 1648; *The*

Kingdomes Weekly Intelligencer 223 (17–24 August 1647), 644; Staffordshire RO, D868/4, f. 102; *Sundry Reasons Inducing Major Robert Huntington*, 8, 12.
105. *The Moderate Intelligencer* 127 (19–26 August 1647), sub 24 August; *The Kingdomes Weekly Intelligencer* 227 (14–21 September 1647), 669.
106. Berkeley, *Memoirs*, 40–2.
107. Ibid., 43; Ashburnham, *Narrative by John Ashburnham*, 98; Firth, ed., *Clarke Papers*, vol. 1, 225.
108. *LJ*, vol. 9, 434–5.
109. *Sundry Reasons Inducing Major Robert Huntington*, 9–10.
110. Berkeley, *Memoirs*, 43.
111. *CJ*, vol. 5, 309–15 (the politician who was teller with Cromwell was Sir John Evelyn); *LJ*, vol. 9, 440–2; *Papers Of The Treatie At A great Meeting of the Generall Officers of the Army*, London, 20 September 1647.
112. *A Representation From his Excellency Sir Thomas Fairfax, And the generall Counsel of the Army*, London, 1647.
113. John Lilburne, *Ionah's Cry Out of the Whales Belly*, London, 1647.
114. Richard Overton, *An Appeale From the degenerate Representative Body the Commons of England*, London, 1647.
115. HMC Portland MSS, vol. 1, 433; Tibbutt, ed., *Letter-Book of Sir Lewis Dyve*, 85–8; *The additionall Plea of Lieut. Col. John Lilburne*, n.d., 22–3.
116. *Two Letters Writ By Lieut. Col. John Lilburne*, London, 1647. The politicians named by Lilburne were Lords Saye and Wharton, and Sir Henry Vane and Oliver St John, while Cromwell's faction in the army was named as Desborough, Ireton, Whalley, Nathaniel Rich, Harrison and Scoutmaster-General Leonard Watson.
117. Tibbutt, ed., *Letter-Book of Sir Lewis Dyve*, 78.
118. *The Perfect Weekly Account* 36 (8–15 September 1647), sub 10 September; *The Heads of the New Proposals.*
119. Francis White, *The Copy of a Letter Sent to his Excellencie Sir Thomas Fairfax*, London, 1647.
120. Tibbutt, ed., *Letter-Book of Sir Lewis Dyve*, 84, 89–90; *Sundry Reasons Inducing Major Robert Huntington*, 13.
121. *CJ*, vol. 5, 312–15.
122. *Putney Projects*, 43. Cromwell's and Ireton's associates in the Commons were named here as Sir John Evelyn, William Pierrepoint, Saye's son Nathaniel Fiennes and Vane. Further material has been added from Staffordshire RO, D868/5, f. 24.
123. *The additionall Plea of John Lilburne*, passim. The ally named was Fiennes.
124. Staffordshire RO, D868/4, f. 91. The writer was one William Smith, to the royalist Sir Richard Leveson.
125. Morrill, ed., *Letters, Writings and Speeches*, vol. 1, 432–3.
126. *CJ*, vol. 5, 327–51; *LJ*, vol. 9, 467–518; Fotheringham, ed., *Diplomatic Correspondence of Jean de Montereul*, vol. 2, 301–2, 313–16; *The Moderate Intelligencer* 134–8 (7 October–11 November 1647); *The Kingdomes Weekly Intelligencer* 228–32 (21 September–2 November 1647); *The Perfect Weekly Account* 40–3 (6 October–2 November 1647).
127. For Cromwell's speeches with regard to the king in mid-October, see NA, PRO/31/9/46, ff. 130–49, a report of the papal agent in London, and the royalist newsletter in Bod L, Clarendon MS 30, f. 152, which corroborate each other.
128. For the continued popularity of the traditional service, see the classic essay by John Morrill, 'The Church in England 1642–9', in John Morrill, ed., *Reactions to the English Civil War*, London, 1982, 89–114.
129. *Sundry Reasons Inducing Major Robert Huntington*, 13.
130. E.g. Bod L, Clarendon MS 30, f. 144.
131. This point was made by a royalist in Bod L, Clarendon MS 30, f. 163.
132. *The Case of the Armie Truly Stated*, London, 1647; *The Perfect Weekly Account* 42 (20–26 October 1647), sub 22 October. For the army at this period, the best account is Gentles, *The New Model Army in England, Ireland and Scotland*, 198–9.

133. *Papers From The Armie Concerning His Excellency and the General Councell*, London, 23 October 1647; *The Kingdomes Weekly Intelligencer* 231 (19–26 October 1647), 702–7 (a garbled account); *The Moderate Intelligencer* 136 (21–28 October 1647), 1333; *The Perfect Weekly Account* 221 (18–25 October 1647), 1778–9.
134. NA, PRO/31/9/46, ff. 130–49.
135. *The Justice of the Army Against Evill-Doers Vindicated*, London, 1649, 1–3; *The Perfect Weekly Account* 43 (26 October–2 November 1647), sub 28 October.
136. Firth, ed., *Clarke Papers*, vol. 1, 226–35. A much superior transcription of Cromwell's contributions to the Putney Debates can be found in Morrill, ed., *Letters, Writings and Speeches*, vol. 1, 437–76.
137. Firth, ed., *Clarke Papers*, vol. 1, 236–79.
138. Printed in A. S. P. Woodhouse, *Puritanism and Liberty*, London, 1950, 438–9.
139. Firth, ed., *Clarke Papers*, vol. 1, 280–98.
140. Ibid., 299–362.
141. *A Cal to all the Souldiers of the Army*, 29 October 1647.
142. Firth, ed., *Clarke Papers*, vol. 1, 364–7.
143. Ibid., 367–408.
144. Bod L, Clarendon MS 30, f. 163.
145. Firth, ed., *Clarke Papers*, vol. 1, 407–9; *A Perfect Diurnall* 223 (1–8 November 1647), 1772–3.
146. *A Perfect Diurnall* 223 (1–8 November 1647), 1774–5.
147. *A Copy of a Letter Sent by the Agents of several Regiments of his Excellencies Army*, 11 November 1647; *CJ*, vol. 5, 351–2; Fotheringham, ed., *Diplomatic Correspondence of Jean de Montereul*, vol. 2, 313–16. More details could be added to the skeletal account found in these sources from the hearsay relayed by royalist agents and other foreign ambassadors. These are, however, not reliable; although Gardiner made extensive use of them, recent historians have tended to not to do so and I follow this tradition. Wild rumours with respect to political intentions and designs had been circulating in these sources and others since the spring; without any corroborating evidence these are consistently better disregarded.
148. *A Copy of a Letter*; Firth, ed., *Clarke Papers*, vol. 1, 411–15; Cary, ed., *Memorials*, vol. 1, 356–7.
149. *CJ*, vol. 5, 353–4.
150. Firth, ed., *Clarke Papers*, vol. 1, 414–30; *A Perfect Diurnall* 224 (8–15 November 1647), 1890; *A Copy of a Letter*.
151. *A Copy of a Letter*.
152. Firth, ed., *Clarke Papers*, vol. 1, 417–18.
153. *State Papers Collected by . . . Clarendon*, 380–2.
154. Bod L, Clarendon MS 30, f. 163.
155. See, for example, ibid., ff. 153, 163, 180; Fotheringham, ed., *Diplomatic Correspondence of Jean de Montereul*, vol. 2, 304–16; *Mercurius Pragmaticus* 8 (2–9 November 1647), 57–8; and *The Moderate Intelligencer* 138 (4–11 November 1647), 1360–1.
156. Ashburnham, *Narrative by John Ashburnham*, 99–101; *A Letter Written By John Ashburnham*, London, 1647; Berkeley, *Memoirs*, 45; *A Message And Declaration Sent From Colonel Whalley*, 7 December 1647; *Mercurius Elencticus* 2 (5–12 November 1647), 10–11 (used for the dates of these events, though there is no corroborating evidence in the other sources for the assertion of this royalist newspaper that Viscount Saye was the evil influence behind them); *The Kingdomes Weekly Intelligencer* 233 (2–9 November 1647), 724. It may be noted that nobody in the Putney Debates cited the king's withdrawal of his parole as a reason for hostility to him, and that this withdrawal took place after the debates had started and the tone of hostility to the king had been set.
157. *The Moderate Intelligencer* 138 (4–11 November 1647), 1358–9.
158. *An Alarum to the Headquarters*, n.d. but clearly early November 1647.
159. Abbott, ed., *Writings and Speeches of Oliver Cromwell*, vol. 1, 551–2. See *The Kingdomes Weekly Intelligencer* 234 (9–16 November 1647), 732; and *A true Relation of His Majesties private departure from Hampton-Court*, London, 1647.

160. Berkeley, *Memoirs*, 46–65; Ashburnham, *Narrative by John Ashburnham*, 101–18; *A true Relation of His Majesties private departure*; *LJ*, vol. 9, 519–22; *A More full Relation of the manner and circumstances of His Majesties departure from Hampton-Court*, London, 1647. There is no evidence here that the king had been motivated in fleeing by a wish to negotiate more freely with the Scots: Ashburnham and Berkeley, who engineered his escape, stated afterwards that the Scottish envoys were discussed as a possible destination for it, but were thought to be too untrustworthy and to require unacceptable terms. Charles left a letter to Whalley stating that he had not fled because of the warning message the colonel had shown him, which seems to contradict the one which he left to Parliament saying that he had departed in fear; but he may have been trying to protect Whalley, whom he liked, from being blamed for his escape.
161. It appears in *The Grand Designe*, published in London in early December, and was immediately repeated by a royalist agent: *State Papers Collected by . . . Clarendon*, xliii..
162. It was repeated in *A Back-Blow To Major Huntington*, London, 1648, and then by writers as different as the poet Andrew Marvell, writing in praise of Cromwell in his famous *Horatian Ode* (1650), and the republican MP and soldier Edmund Ludlow, in Firth, ed., *Memoirs of Edmund Ludlow*, vol. 1, 107–8. It may be noted that, whereas historians have generally disbelieved that Cromwell engineered the king's flight to the island, in the 1970s there was a belief articulated by writers such as Lady Antonia Fraser, Christopher Hill and Roger Howell that he might have frightened the king into fleeing because Charles's presence at Hampton Court was becoming an embarrassment. This was last expressed by Barry Coward, *Oliver Cromwell*, London, 1991, 57, and now seems to have been abandoned.
163. *CJ*, vol. 5, 357–9; *LJ*, vol. 9, 523–4; *The Kingdomes Weekly Intelligencer* 234 (9–16 November 1647), 732; *A Perfect Diurnall* 226 (22–29 November 1647), 1814–15. Clarendon, *History of the Rebellion*, X.138, states that it was Cromwell himself who broke the news to the MPs that Charles was in Wight, which seems likely.
164. *The Moderate Intelligencer* 139 (11–18 November 1647), sub 15–16 November; *State Papers Collected by . . . Clarendon*, xli.
165. *LJ*, vol. 9, 522–3, 530–1.
166. *A Full Relation Of The Proceedings at the Rendezvous of that Brigade of the Army that was held in Corkbush Field*, London, 15 November 1647; Firth, ed., *Memoirs of Edmund Ludlow*, vol. 1, 172; *LJ*, vol. 9, 526–8; *The Justice Of The Army Against Evill-Doers Vindicated*, London, 1647, 5–6; *State Papers Collected by . . . Clarendon*, xlii. The regiments invited were the horse of Fairfax, Rich, Fleetwood and Twistleton and the foot of Fairfax, Pride and Hammond. There has been disagreement among experts over whether or not Cromwell made a personal dash into disaffected regiments to cow them: see Mark Kishlansky, 'What Happened at Ware?', *Historical Journal* 25 (1982), 827–39; Gentles, *The New Model Army in England, Ireland and Scotland*, 223; and Woolrych, *Soldiers and Statesmen*, 279–80.
167. *CJ*, vol. 5, 364–8; *The Kingdomes Weekly Intelligencer* 235 (16–23 November 1647), 739; *Perfect Weekely Account* 47 (17–23 November 1647), sub 19 November; *The Moderate Intelligencer* 140 (18–25 November 1647), 1383; *A Perfect Diurnall* 225 (15–22 November 1647), 1788–90; David Underdown, 'The Parliamentary Diary of John Boys 1647–8', *Bulletin of the Institute of Historical Research* 39 (1966), 152–3.
168. Samuel Rawson Gardiner, ed., *The Constitutional Documents of the Puritan Revolution*, 3rd edition, Oxford, 1906, 328–32; Berkeley, *Memoirs*, 67. See also the king's letter to a Scottish commissioner about his optimism regarding a settlement, in Burnet, *Memoires*, 326.
169. Berkeley, *Memoirs*, 68–76; *The Kingdomes Weekly Intelligencer* 237 (30 November–7 December 1647), 749–50; *The Moderate Intelligencer* 141 (25 November–2 December 1647), 1400.
170. *Letters Between Col. Robert Hammond, Governor of the Isle of Wight, and the Committee of Lords and Commons at Derby-House*, London, 1764, 19–22.

171. In 1681 Sir William Dugdale mentioned a rumour that Cromwell and Ireton had turned against the king when he was still at Hampton Court, on intercepting a letter from the queen telling him that the Scots were raising an army for him, forwarding it to him resealed and then hearing him deny its existence: *A Short View of the Late Troubles in England*, London, 378–9. In the 1690s, Roger Coke wrote of another story, that when at Hampton Court Charles had written to his wife that when he was restored to power after a deal with the army he would be able to destroy Cromwell, who intercepted and read the message: *A Detection of the Court and State of England*, 2nd edition, London, 1697, vol. 1, 323. The most spectacular claim was published in 1742, consisting of a memoir penned by a chaplain of Roger Boyle, Lord Broghill, a politician who knew Cromwell well and will feature later in this book, and who claimed to have heard it from Boyle. It recounted how, acting on a tip-off, Cromwell and Ireton rode to London disguised as common troopers and intercepted a letter from the king to the queen in which Charles stated that he was negotiating with both army and Scots and would probably choose the latter: Thomas Morrice, *A Collection of the State Letters of the Right Honourable Roger Boyle*, London, 1742, vol. 1, 14–16. An eighteenth-century antiquary recorded a fourth-hand story that the earl of Oxford, a prominent politician of the reign of Queen Anne, had claimed to have seen a letter in which Charles told his wife he would hang Cromwell and the other officers with whom he was negotiating: Joseph Spence, *Anecdotes, Observations and Characters of Books and Men*, reprint, Cambridge, 2015, 298–9. Interestingly, in his memoirs written after the mid-1660s, Ashburnham recalled that Cromwell and Ireton treated him coldly at one point because they had seen letters from king to queen revealing that he had been talking to the Scots and Presbyterians as well as to the army in July (which he had); but this was in August, and co-operation between king and generals resumed fully thereafter: *Narrative by John Ashburnham*, 94.
172. *As The King's Cabinet Opened*, London, 1645.
173. Burnet, *Memoires*, 326. Charles's reply to them is in the National Records of Scotland, GD406/1/2177. He stated in it that many proposals 'could be fitly offered to obtain a treaty, that may be altered when one comes to treat, and there is a great difference between what I will insist on and what I will permit, for the obtaining of peace'. What he was not doing here, however, was stating that his overture to Parliament was insincere, only trying to mollify the Scots by telling them that toleration of religious heterodoxy in England had not been agreed yet, while hinting that he might in the end permit things he did not himself like (such as this) to obtain a settlement. He further said that it was his duty to try to satisfy all parties as far as he could. The context is important: that Charles was in acute danger of losing all Scottish support while not yet having secured any favour for his terms in Parliament and army, and he was trying desperately to prevent that.
174. Fotheringham, ed., *Diplomatic Correspondence of Jean de Montereul*, vol. 2, 326–33.
175. *CJ*, vol. 5, 369–70; *The Moderate Intelligencer* 141 (25 November–2 December 1647), 1390.
176. Gardiner, ed., *Constitutional Documents*, 335–6.
177. Fotheringham, ed., *Diplomatic Correspondence of Jean de Montereul*, vol. 2, 331–41; Walker, *History of Independency*, vol. 1, 67–8; *LJ*, vol. 9, 580–8, 592–600.
178. See Ireton's letter at n. 170.
179. *LJ*, vol. 536, 556–63; *A Letter From His Excellency Sir Thomas Fairfax, To The Lord Major, Aldermen and Common-Councel of the City of London*, London, 22 November 1647; *The Agreement Between The Commissioners Of Parliament, And His Excellencie Sir Thomas Fairfax*, London, 1647; Firth and Rait, eds, *Acts and Ordinances*, vol. 1, 1048–56; *The Kingdomes Weekly Intelligencer* 238–9 (7–21 December 1647); *A Perfect Diurnall* 228–9 (6–20 December 1647); *The Perfect Weekly Account* 48 (30 November–8 December 1647), sub 30 November.
180. *CJ*, vol. 5, 401–4; *LJ*, vol. 9, 614–17.
181. *The Kingdomes Weekly Intelligencer* 240 (21–28 December 1647), 780.
182. *Wonderful Predictions, Declared in a Message . . . by John Saltmarsh*, London, 1647; *A Perfect Diurnall* 230 (22–27 December 1647), 1856.

183. *State Papers Collected by . . . Clarendon*, xliv.
184. Gardiner, ed., *Constitutional Documents*, 347–53.
185. *LJ* vol. 9, 620.
186. *CJ*, vol. 5, 415–16, 426; *LJ*, vol. 9, 662; Walker, *History of Independency*, vol. 1, 67–73, which agrees with *Mercurius Pragmaticus* 8 (4–11 January 1648), n.p., and Underdown, 'The Parliamentary Diary of John Boys', 152; Berkeley, *Memoirs*, 91; Ashburnham, *Narrative by John Ashburnham*, 122. Clarendon's account of the Commons' debate in his *History of the Rebellion*, X.146, conflicts at points with Walker and Boys, and was written long after, so may be regarded as unreliable. In a letter to Hammond on the evening after the vote, Cromwell said that the Commons were aware of the king's talks with the Scots, and suspicious of them, but that they did not know their outcome: Morrill, ed., *Letters, Writings and Speeches*, vol. 1, 492.
187. For a cross-section, see the royalist newspapers *Mercurius Pragmaticus* and *Mercurius Elencticus*; *Putney Projects*; *The Grand Designe*; *A Word To Lieut. Gen. Cromwel*, London, 1647; and *The Machivilian Cromwellist*, London, 10 January 1648.

3 REBELLION

1. *CSPD (1648–1649)*, pp. 1–52. The original minute book is NA, SP 21/26, with these meetings on ff. 124–53, and the order for the establishment of the committee is in *CJ*, vol. 5, 440–2.
2. *CJ*, vol. 5, 432.
3. Ibid., 487–9; Clement Walker, *The Complete History of Independency*, London, 1661, 83; *Mercurius Elencticus* (1–8 March 1648), 1015.
4. *The Kingdomes Weekly Post* 6 (2–9 February 1648), 44.
5. *CJ*, vol. 5, 452–3.
6. *A Declaration of the Commons of England*, London, 1648.
7. Bod L, Clarendon MS 30, f. 292v. The full history of the allegation of James's murder is recounted in Alastair Bellany and Thomas Cogswell, *The Murder of King James I*, London, 2015.
8. S. R. Gardiner, ed., 'Hamilton Papers: Addenda', *Camden Miscellany* (1895), 9–10.
9. *CJ*, vol. 5, 436–7.
10. George Masterton, *The Triumph Stain'd*, London, 9 February 1648; *A Lash for a Lyar*, London, 22 February 1648; John Wildman, *Truths triumph, or Treachery anatomized*, London, 1 February 1648.
11. Bod L, Clarendon MS 30, f. 279.
12. A. C., *A Vindication of Lieut. Gen. Cromwell*, London, 7 March 1648; *A True and Impartial Relation Of the Whole matters concerning the proceedings of several Councels of War, against W. Tompson*, London, 20 March 1648.
13. *A Perfect Diurnall* 232 (3–10 January 1648), 1872.
14. Ibid., 234 (24–31 January 1648), 1883.
15. Ibid., 239 (21–28 February 1648), 1926.
16. Ian Gentles, *The New Model Army in England, Ireland and Scotland 1645–1653*, Oxford, 1991, 231–3; and *The New Model Army*, London, 2021, 105–6.
17. C. H. Firth and R. S. Rait, eds, *Acts and Ordinances of the Interregnum*, London, 1911, vol. 1, 107–14.
18. Walker, *History of Independency*, vol. 1, 78; NA, PRO/31/3/86; NA, PRO/31/9/47; Bod L, Clarendon MS 30, ff. 291–307, passim; Bod L, Clarendon MS 31, ff. 6–50, passim; Samuel Rawson Gardiner, ed., *The Hamilton Papers*, Camden Society N.S. 27, London, 1880, 148–85; Gardiner, ed., 'Hamilton Papers: Addenda', 10–24; BL, Additional MS 78198, f. 70. Occasionally a radical enemy of the government repeated the same kind of rumour: cf. *Tricks of State*, London, 18 April 1648.
19. John Morrill, ed., *The Letters, Writings and Speeches of Oliver Cromwell*, Oxford, 2023, vol. 1, 585–92.

20. *CJ*, vol. 5, 513; Wilbur Cortez Abbott, ed., *The Writings and Speeches of Oliver Cromwell*, vol. 1, Cambridge, MA, 1937, 494–9.
21. There is a fine, detailed, survey of public opinion at this period in Robert Ashton, *Counter-Revolution: The Second Civil War and Its Origins*, New Haven, 1994, 197–267.
22. Walker, *History of Independency*, 84–5; *The Moderate Intelligencer* 160 (6–13 April 1648), 1268; *The Kingdomes Weekly Intelligencer* 255 (4–11 April 1648), 902–5; C. H. Firth, ed., *The Clarke Papers*, vol. 2, Camden Society N.S. 54, London, 1894, 2–4; *A Perfect Diurnall* 246 (10–17 April 1648), 1977; *A full Narration of the late Riotous Tumult*, London, 18 April 1648.
23. *LJ*, vol. 10, 242. News of developments in Scotland had featured regularly in the main English newspapers during the previous two months. The best account of Scottish politics during this period is probably still David Stevenson, *Revolution and Counter-Revolution in Scotland 1644–1651*, London, 1977, 98–105, supplemented by John R. Young, *The Scottish Parliament 1639–1661*, Edinburgh, 1996, 189–214.
24. For an excellent account of Pembrokeshire politics during and after the war, see Lloyd Bowen, *John Poyer, the Civil War in Pembrokeshire and the British Revolutions*, Cardiff, 2020.
25. Again, the English newspapers for March and April chronicle between them the onset and progress of the uprising.
26. For the last two paragraphs, see C. H. Firth, ed., *The Memoirs of Edmund Ludlow*, Oxford, 1894, vol. 1, 183–90. There were also assertions by writers hostile to Cromwell that in March and April he sent agents into the City to woo influential and wealthy individuals there, and to interfere in its politics: Walker, *History of Independency*, 83; *Tricks of State*; Gardiner, ed., *Hamilton Papers*, 169–70.
27. *LJ*, vol. 10, 240, 247; *The Moderate Intelligencer* 163 (27 April–4 May 1648), 1293–1303; *The Kingdomes Weekly Intelligencer* 259 (2–9 May 1648), 931–4.
28. Gardiner, ed., *Hamilton Papers*, 191–2. The Independents named here as supporting the new measures were Sir Henry Vane and William Pierrepont.
29. *The Moderate Intelligencer* 163 (27 April–4 May 1648), 1294–1303; *The Armies Petition Or A New Engagement*, London, 1648; *The Kingdomes Weekly Intelligencer* 258 (25 April–2 May 1648), 295; *Perfect Occurrences Of Every Daie iornall in Parliament* 69–71 (21 April–12 May 1648); William Allen, *A Faithful Memorial Of That Remarkable Meeting Of Many Officers of the Army in England*, London, 1659 (I agree with the reasons given by Austin Woolrych, *Soldiers and Statesmen*, Oxford, 1987, 333–4, for continuing to trust this source); Henry Cary, ed., *Memorials of the Great Civil War in England from 1646 to 1652*, London, 1842, vol. 1, 392–4; Gardiner, ed., *Hamilton Papers*, 195.
30. *The Moderate Intelligencer* 164 (4–11 May 1648), 1305–6.
31. *The Kingdomes Weekly Intelligencer* 259 (2–9 May), 931; Gardiner, ed., 'Hamilton Papers: Addenda', 33. The foot regiments were Thomas Pride's, Richard Deane's and Isaac Ewer's; the horse regiments, Cromwell's own and Thornhaugh's.
32. *The Declaration of Lieutenant-Generall Cromwell Concerning His present Design and Engagement*, London, 9 May 1648.
33. *Colonell Poyers Forces In Wales Totally Routed*, London, 11 May 1648; *A true and particular Relation Of The Late Victory Obtained By Colonel Horton and Colonel Okey*, London, 1648; *A fuller Relation of a great Victory Obtained Against the Welsh Forces, by Col. Tho: Horton*, London, 1648.
34. *A Great Fight At Chepstow Castle*, London, 1648; *A full and particular Relation of the late besieging and taking of Chepstow Castle*, London, 1648; *The Moderate Intelligencer* 165 (11–18 May 1648), 1328. The regiment concerned was Ewer's.
35. The land itself is unchanged, but the eagles were exterminated in the nineteenth century: one of the last is in Swansea Museum.
36. John Rushworth, *Historical Collections*, London, 1659–1701, vol. 7, sub 26 May, in the online version; *The Moderate Intelligencer* 166 (18–25 May 1648), 1349.

37. *A full and particular Relation; Exceeding Good Newes From South-Wales Of The Surrender of Tenby Castle*, London, 1648; *The Moderate Intelligencer* 166 (18–25 May 1648), 1349, and 168 (1–8 June 1648), 1374–5.
38. *The Moderate Intelligencer* 168–72 (1 June–6 July 1648); *The Kingdomes Weekly Intelligencer* 267 (4–11 July 1648), 1002–3; *Perfect Occurrences* 76–9 (9 June–7 July 1648); *A Dangerous Fight at Pembrooke Castle*, London, 1648; *A great and bloudy Fight At Pembrook Castle*, 9 July 1648; Morrill, ed., *Letters, Writings and Speeches*, vol. 1, 516–26.
39. *CSPD (1648–1649)*, 112, 116, 140.
40. *Perfect Occurrences* 81 (14–21 July 1648), 580–1; *A Perfect Diurnall* (10–16 July 1648), 620–1; HMC Portland MSS, vol. 1, 480; *The Moderate Intelligencer* 174–5 (13–27 July 1648), 1453.
41. *The Moderate Intelligencer* 175 (20–27 July 1648), 1466–7; *Perfect Occurrences* 82 (21–28 July 1648), 408; *CSPD (1648–1649)*, 219–28.
42. *The Moderate Intelligencer* 176 (27 July–3 August 1648), 1469; *The Moderate* 3 (25 July–1 August 1648), 20.
43. *The Moderate Intelligencer* 176–7 (27 July–10 August 1648).
44. Morrill, ed., *Letters, Writings and Speeches*, vol. 1, 526.
45. *CJ*, vol. 5, 572, 649, 650.
46. Ibid., 650.
47. *The Kingdomes Weekly Intelligencer* 269 (18–25 July), 1018–23; Cary, ed., *Memorials*, vol. 1, 441–3.
48. *LJ*, vol. 10, 408–12.
49. Firth, ed., *Memoirs of Edmund Ludlow*, vol. 1, 196.
50. John Lilburne, *The Legal Fundamental Liberties Of the People of England, Revived, Asserted and Vindicated*, London, 1649, 32.
51. *The Moderate Intelligencer* 177–8 (3–17 August 1648); *A Perfect Diurnall* 263–4 (7–21 August 1648); *A full, exact, and particular Relation, Of The Chiefe Passages Of The Parliaments Army in Lancashire*, London, 1648.
52. The story of this campaign is well told in P. R. Hill and J. M. Watkinson, *Cromwell Hath The Honour, But . . .*, London, 2012.
53. For various views of the question, and of the Scots' situation, see Austin Woolrych, *Battles of the English Civil War*, London, 1966, 160–4; Simon Robbins, *God's General*, Stroud, 2003, 103–8; and Malcolm Wanklyn, *Decisive Battles of the English Civil War*, Barnsley, 2006, 191.
54. Morrill, ed., *Letters, Writings and Speeches*, vol. 1, 547–9; *The Moderate Intelligencer* 179 (17–24 August 1648), 1502; *Original Memoirs Written during the Great Civil War*, Edinburgh, 1806, 114.
55. Morrill, ed., *Letters, Writings and Speeches*, vol. 1, 552–9.
56. *The Moderate Intelligencer* 179 (17–24 August 1648), 1494; *Original Memoirs*, 114. Rushworth, *Historical Collections*, vol. 7, 1211, quotes a letter from Lambert's quarters written two weeks before Cromwell joined Lambert, putting the former's force at 5,000 and the latter's at 9,000, but this is so out of line with all the other figures that it seems likely to have been an inaccurate guess.
57. Morrill, ed., *Letters, Writings and Speeches*, vol. 1, 552–9.
58. *An Impartiall Relation of the late Fight at Preston*, London, 1648. This is Langdale's account of the campaign and battle, which exists in four or five different versions, specified and distinguished in Wanklyn, *Decisive Battles*, 187: the differences are not significant for the account given here. Malcolm Wanklyn's work, over the past two decades, has been very valuable, both in identifying the primary sources for Civil War battles and in reminding us of how little we really know about those battles.
59. Sir James Turner, *Memoirs of His Own Life and Times*, Edinburgh, 1829, 77.
60. Since 1965, Peter Young and Richard Holmes have accepted Cromwell's figure for the Scots (*The English Civil War*, London, 1974, 282), but Austin Woolrych reduced it to 14,000 (*Battles of the English Civil War*, 161). Ian Gentles (*The New Model Army in England,*

Scotland and Ireland, 259, 261, 513) reduced it further to 9,000–10,000 (excluding Langdale's men), which persuaded Woolrych (*Britain in Revolution 1625–1660*, Oxford, 2002, 416). Malcolm Wanklyn thought Hamilton probably had between 13,000 and 14,000 men at Preston itself, including Langdale's (*The Warrior Generals*, London, 2010, 282; and *Decisive Battles*, 191). Martyn Bennett allowed him just under 14,000 in all, without Langdale, and raised Cromwell's numbers to 11,200 (*Cromwell at War*, London, 2017, 153). Stephen Bull and Mike Seed also raised Cromwell's total, to around 10,000, and put the Scots at between 14,000 and 17,000 (*Bloody Preston*, Lancaster, 1998, 37, 105). Simon Robbins guessed at 14,000 Scots (*God's General*, 107). Part of the problem is that some of these estimates rely on the size of Hamilton's army in early July, before it was apparently reinforced by further arrivals from Scotland.

61. This is the common ground between the accounts in Gilbert Burnet, *The Memoires of the Lives and Actions of James and William Dukes of Hamilton*, London, 1677, 358; *An Impartiall Relation*; Turner, *Memoirs*, 62; and *A Letter from Holland*, London, 12 October 1648.
62. This is to assume that it was Cromwell, and not Lambert, who ordered them, which Oliver's authority would seem to warrant: *Original Memoirs*, 115–16.
63. The horse regiments were Cromwell's and Harrison's; the foot to the right Read's, Dean's and Pride's; and those to the left Bright's and Fairfax's: Morrill, ed., *Letters, Writings and Speeches*, vol. 1, 552–9. *The Moderate Intelligencer* (below) gives a slightly different order for these units, but Cromwell should surely be trusted better as he knew his own battle plan.
64. Morrill, ed., *Letters, Writings and Speeches*, vol. 1, 552–9; *The Moderate Intelligencer* 179 (17–24 August 1648), 1494; *Original Memoirs*, 117–18; Burnet, *Memoirs*, 358–9; *An Impartiall Relation*; *A Letter from Holland*; *A full, exact, and particular Relation*.
65. For the last two paragraphs, see Morrill, ed., *Letters, Writings and Speeches*, vol. 1, 552–9; *The Moderate Intelligencer* 179 (17–24 August 1648), 1494; *Original Memoirs*, 118–21; *Memoirs of Henry Guthry, Late Bishop of Dunkel*, London, 1702, 235; William Beaumont, ed., *A Discourse of the Civil War in Lancashire*, Chetham Society, 1864, 65–6; Burnet, *Memoires*, 359–60; *An Impartiall Relation*; Turner, *Memoirs*, 63–4; *A Letter from Holland*; *A full, exact, and particular Relation*; HMC Portland MSS, vol. 1, 175.
66. This is the unanimous and harmonious testimony of Burnet, *Memoires*, 360–1; *A Letter from Holland*; and Turner, *Memoirs*, 64–5. Burnet may depend to some extent on Turner, and there may have been a general decision among those who left accounts to pin everything on Callander, but the agreement between the sources is still impressive.
67. Sources as at n. 66, plus *Three Letters Concerning the Surrender of many Scotish Lords*, London, 28 August 1648. The parliamentarian cavalry colonel who died was Francis Thornhaugh.
68. Morrill, ed., *Letters, Writings and Speeches*, vol. 1, 552–9.
69. *LJ*, vol. 10, 408–42.
70. *CSPD (1648–1649)*, 255–6, 264–6.
71. *The Moderate Intelligencer* 181–2 (31 August–14 September 1648); *Perfect Occurrences* 89 (8–15 September 1648), 658; *Joyful Newes From The Kings Majesty And The Prince of Wales*, London, 4 September 1648.
72. *Perfect Occurrences* 90 (15–22 September 1648), 668; *CSPD (1648–1649)*, 283–4, 289; *Bloudy Newes From The North, Declaring The particulars of three several fights*, London, 1648; *The Resolution of Major-Generall Monro*, London, 1648; Morrill, ed., *Letters, Writings and Speeches*, vol. 1, 565–70.
73. *The Demands Of Lieutenant-Generall Crumwell To The Estates of the Kingdom of Scotland*, London, 1648; *The Transactions of Several Matters between Lieut: Gen: Cromwel And The Scots*, London, 2 October 1648; Morrill, ed., *Letters, Writings and Speeches*, vol. 1, 575–8.
74. Morrill, ed., *Letters, Writings and Speeches*, vol. 1, 582–90; *The Moderate Intelligencer* 184 (21–28 September 1648), 1554–5; *A Perfect Diurnall* 271 (7–14 October 1648), 2179–81; *A Letter sent from Lieutenant Generall Cromwell To The Marquis of Argyll*, London, 29 September 1648.

75. *A Perfect Diurnall* 271 (7–14 October 1648), 2179–81; *The Moderate Intelligencer* 185 (28 September–5 October 1648), 1574–5; Morrill, ed., *Letters, Writings and Speeches*, vol. 1, 592–5.
76. HMC 10th Report, Appendix 6 (The Manuscripts of the Marquess of Abergavenny Etc.), 171; *Memoirs of Henry Guthry*, 237–48; William Row, *The Life of Mr Robert Blair*, ed. Thomas M'Crie, Edinburgh, 1848, 206–8; Burnet, *Memoires*, 367–75; Thomas Birch, ed., *A Collection of the State Papers of John Thurloe*, London, 1742, vol. 1, 100–3.
77. HMC 10th Report, Appendix 6, 171–2; *His Majesties Gracious Message To the Army for Peace*, 10 October 1648; *The Moderate Intelligencer* 186 (5–12 October 1648), 1684–5. Here I accept David Stevenson's contention (in *Revolution and Counter-Revolution in Scotland*, 117–18) that Argyll and his fellows allied only reluctantly with Cromwell and used him only to bring the Engagers to terms, proved by National Records of Scotland, PA 12/2, papers of 20–25 September.
78. *CJ*, vol. 6, 37; *LJ*, vol. 10, 520.
79. *A Perfect Diurnall* 273 (16–23 October 1648), 2194–5; HMC 10th Report, Appendix 6, 172; *A True Account Of The great expressions of Love from the Noblemen, Ministers and Commons*, London, 1648; *Memoirs of Henry Guthry*, 248–9; *The Moderate Intelligencer* 187 (12–19 October 1648), 1696; Abbott, ed., *Writing and Speeches*, vol. 1, 668–9.
80. HMC 10th Report, Appendix 6, 172; *Life of Mr Robert Blair*, 209–10. The visit by the three ministers is attested in the sources at n. 79, as is the fact that the other two went back to see Cromwell but Blair did not, which would seem to support Blair's account. Nobody present seems to have left a record of what the Scottish political leaders discussed with Cromwell and his companions on the visit, which would have been even more interesting.
81. *The Moderate Intelligencer* 188 (19–26 October 1648), 1704–7.
82. Morrill, ed., *Letters, Writings and Speeches*, vol. 1, 610–13.

4 REVOLUTION

1. The full papers concerning the treaty are helpfully gathered in an appendix to Sir Edward Walker, *Historical Discourses upon Several Occasions*, London, 1705.
2. Ibid. Also *CJ*, vol. 6, 73; *LJ*, vol. 10, 564–70; and *State Papers Collected by Edward, Earl of Clarendon*, Oxford, 1773, 425–54.
3. Thomas Wagstaffe, *A Vindication of King Charles I, the Martyr*, London, 1711, 158–63.
4. Thomas Carte, ed., *A Collection of Original Letters and Papers Concerning the Affairs of England from the Year 1641 to 1660*, London, 1739, vol. 1, 185.
5. Sir Philip Warwick, *Memoirs of the Reign of Charles I*, London, 1813, 360–7.
6. *To The Right Honorable, The Commons of England In Parliament Assembled. The humble Petition of divers wel affected persons inhabiting the City of London*, London, 11 September 1648. Lilburne admitted his input in *The Legall Fundamentall Liberties Of The People of England*, London, 1649.
7. *The Moderate* 12–14 (26 September–17 October 1648).
8. *The Demands, Resolutions, and Intentions, of the Army Under the Command of Generall Fairfax*, 26 September 1648.
9. *The True Copy of a Petition Promoted in the Army by the Regiment under Commissary-General Ireton*, 18 October 1648; *The Moderate* 15 (17–24 October 1648), P2.
10. For this, see in particular *The Moderate Intelligencer* 188 (19–26 October 1648), 1703.
11. The royalist newspaper *Mercurius Pragmaticus*, in successive issues during the autumn of 1648, represented the agitation as having been stirred up by the senior officers, especially Cromwell and Ireton, and their civilian allies in the Commons, such as Henry Marten. It is simply impossible to tell how much truth, if any, there is in its assertions.
12. *The Moderate* 17–19 (31 October–21 November 1648).
13. *The Kingdomes Weekly Intelligencer* 284 (31 October–7 November 1648), 1137–8.
14. An account of the first four days of its deliberations is provided in *The Representations And Consultations of the Generall Councell of the Armie at S. Albans*, London, 1648. This includes

the information that the officers initially decided to punish royalists but to seek reconciliation with the king; but it is not clear how reliable this information is. There was certainly an impression circulating during the first week of the council that the officers would be conciliatory. On 14 November, two days before they agreed to the opposite course, a letter from St Albans stated that they had resolved not to oppose the treaty, printed in *Packets of Letters From Severall Parts of England* 35 (7–14 November 1648), 6. A foreign envoy wrote from London on the 17th that they had not yet agreed a policy: BL, Additional MS 17677, f. 283. Again, it is not clear, however, how accurate that impression was.

15. Lilburne, *Legall Fundamentall Liberties*, 29–30.
16. The unanimity was alleged in the covering letter of the remonstrance, and in C. H. Firth, ed., *Clarke Papers*, vol. 2, Camden Society N.S. 54, London, 1894, 54–5.
17. *A Remonstrance of his Excellency Thomas Lord Fairfax, General of the Parliament's Force, and of the General Council of Officers*, St Albans, 1648. The 16 November date is confirmed by Firth, ed., *Clarke Papers*, vol. 2, 54–5, as that on which the council approved it, though a committee headed by Ireton, who was probably the author, was appointed to give it a final scrutiny before presentation. A pamphlet survives, *His Majesties Declaration Novemb. 17 From the Isle of Wight*, London, 1648, which looks like an official army publication. It prints terms allegedly sent by the council of officers to the king, matching some of those proposed to Parliament in the remonstrance, and a reply from the king dated 17 November, referring a decision on them to Parliament when his settlement with the latter was concluded. Samuel Rawson Gardiner, *History of the Great Civil War*, London, 1898, vol. 3, 241–6, accepted these documents as genuine, and concluded that the king's reply had caused the officers to adopt Ireton's remonstrance and with it a different policy. However, the pamphlet is supported by no other testimony, and it would have been utterly extraordinary for the officers to have sent their own terms to the king without Parliament taking notice of them, and in the face of so much pressure from the soldiers and their civilian allies to end talks with Charles altogether and bring him to trial. Moreover, the dates do not match: the remonstrance was agreed on the 16th, the day before the king was supposed to have written his reply to the army's terms. I accordingly reject these documents as a hoax. Gardiner used them, as he did the pamphlet commented on in n. 14, as evidence for the flexible and reasonable nature of the army officers, even at this late stage, until they finally gave up on a monarch who was neither. When this doubtful evidence is laid aside, the picture looks different.
18. *CJ*, vol. 6, 76–7. On the importance of this resolution, I am in agreement with David Underdown, *Pride's Purge*, Oxford, 1971, 121–2; and Ian Gentles, *The New Model Army in England, Ireland and Scotland 1645–1653*, Oxford, 1992, 272.
19. *CJ*, vol. 6, 81–92.
20. *LJ*, vol. 10, 615–17; Firth, ed., *Clarke Papers*, vol. 2, 55–60; *Perfect Occurrences Of Every Daie iornall in Parliament* 99 (17–24 November 1648), 740.
21. Lilburne, *Legall Fundamentall Liberties*, 31–3. His detail is so circumstantial, and fits the frame of events so well, that I accept it.
22. Firth, ed., *Clarke Papers*, vol. 2, 61; *The Declaration of his Excellency the Lord General Fairfax and his General Councel of Officers, showing the Grounds of the Army's Advance towards the City of London*, Windsor, 29 November 1648.
23. C. H. Firth, ed., *The Memoirs of Edmund Ludlow*, Oxford, 1894, vol. 1, 206.
24. *The Kingdomes Weekly Intelligencer* 288 (28 November–5 December 1648), 1174.
25. Firth, ed., *Clarke Papers*, vol. 2, 65. The horse regiments were those of Fairfax, Whalley and Ireton, with troops from those of Fleetwood, Rich, Cromwell and Harrison; the foot regiments were those of Hewson, Pride, Deane and the lieutenant-colonels Cooke and Ashfold, with ten companies from others; and there were two companies of Okey's dragoons.
26. *The Kingdomes Weekly Intelligencer* 288 (28 November–5 December 1648), 1175–6.
27. *CJ*, vol. 6, 92–3.
28. The best overall account of these events remains Underdown, *Pride's Purge*, 138–48.

29. *The Humble Proposals and Desires of his Excellency the Lord Fairfax and the General Council of Officers*, London, 6 December 1648.
30. Made clear by HMC Leyborne-Popham MSS, 8.
31. *The Moderate Intelligencer* 189–90 (26 October–9 November 1648).
32. The best account of this episode is Adrian Tinniswood, *The Rainborowes*, London, 2013, 272–82.
33. *The Kingdomes Weekly Intelligencer* 284 (31 October–7 November 1648), 1142; *A Perfect Diurnall* 275 (30 October–6 November 1648), 2216.
34. *The Moderate Intelligencer* 191 (2–9 November), 1737–8; *The Moderate* (7–21 November 1648).
35. For the Civil War defences, see Nathan Drake, *A Journal of the First and Second Sieges of Pontefract Castle*, ed. W. H. Longstaffe, Surtees Society 37, Durham, 1860. For the castle itself, see Ian Roberts, *Pontefract Castle*, Wakefield, 1990.
36. *The Moderate Intelligencer* 191–3 (9–30 November 1648); *The Kingdomes Weekly Intelligencer* 286 (14–21 November 1648), 1155–6; *A Perfect Diurnall* 276–7 (6–13 November 1648); John Morrill, ed., *The Letters, Writings and Speeches of Oliver Cromwell*, Oxford, 2023, vol. 1, 65–72.
37. *The Moderate Intelligencer* 193 (23–30 November 1648), 1761–2; *Perfect Occurrences* 99–100 (17 November–1 December 1648); *The Moderate* 20 (21–28 November 1648), 173–4.
38. For this in particular, see the successive issues of the royalist newspaper *Mercurius Pragmaticus* in September, October and November.
39. Lilburne, *Legall Fundamentall Liberties*, 29.
40. HMC Leyborne-Popham MSS, 8–9.
41. *A Declaration Of The Army, Concerning The King's Majesty*, London, 1648.
42. Lilburne, *Legall Fundamentall Liberties*, 29.
43. Morrill, ed., *Letters, Writings and Speeches*, vol. 1, 523–6, 636–7.
44. Ibid., 610–13, 628–33.
45. I myself see no real ambiguity or hesitation in it, and no sense that Cromwell was carrying on an argument with himself rather than trying to persuade Hammond to fall in with the army and the civilian radicals.
46. *Mercurius Militaris* 3 (24–31 October 1648), 19.
47. *Mercurius Pragmaticus* 39 (19–26 December 1648), sig. Eee.
48. Here I line up, against majority opinion, alongside Ian Gentles (*The New Model Army in England, Ireland and Scotland*, 284–5).
49. Firth, ed., *Clarke Papers*, vol. 2, 62–3.
50. Morrill, ed., *Letters, Writings and Speeches*, vol. 1, 636–7. Lambert's task proved appallingly difficult, the castle only surrendering in late March. It was then demolished on Parliament's orders.
51. *The Moderate Intelligencer* 194 (30 November–7 December 1648), 1776; *Mercurius Elencticus* 55 (5–12 December 1648), 528; *The Kingdomes Weekly Intelligencer* 289 (5–12 December 1648), 1182.
52. Firth, ed., *Memoirs of Edmund Ludlow*, vol. 1, 211–12. Cromwell's slipperiness is a theme of these memoirs.
53. *CJ*, vol. 6, 94; *Mercurius Pragmaticus* 37 (5–12 December 1648), sig. CCC3; *Mercurius Elencticus* 55 (5–12 December 1648), 524; Clement Walker, *The History of Independency*, London, 1660, vol. 2, 34–5.
54. Underdown, *Pride's Purge*, 152–9.
55. *LJ*, vol. 10, 624–40; for the disappearance of the committee, see its minute book calendared in *CSPD (1648–1649)*.
56. *CJ*, vol. 6, 95–121; *LJ*, vol. 10, 641–2; Bulstrode Whitelocke, *Memorials of the English Affairs*, London, 1682, 357; Walker, *History of Independency*, vol. 2, 56–7.
57. Firth, ed., *Clarke Papers*, vol. 2, 71–170; Lilburne, *Legall Fundamentall Liberties*, 33–5; John Lilburne, *A Plea for Common Right and Freedom*, London, 28 December 1648; *The*

Kingdomes Weekly Intelligencer 290–3 (12 December 1648–9 January 1649); *Foundations of Freedom*, London, 15 December 1648; *The Humble Petition of his Excellency Thomas Lord Fairfax and the General Council of Officers*, London, 1649.

58. *The Moderate Intelligencer* 195 (7–14 December 1648), 1778–9; *The Kingdomes Weekly Intelligencer* 289 (5–12 December 1648), 1188–9, and 293 (2–9 January 1649), 1215; *A Perfect Diurnall* 280 (4–11 December 1648), 225–56; *The Perfect Weekly Account*, unnumbered (3–10 January 1649), 341.
59. Firth, ed., *Clarke Papers* vol. 2, 71–170, and especially 272. The best commentaries on the debates are Carolyn Polizzotto, 'Liberty of Conscience and Whitehall Debates of 1648–9', *Journal of Ecclesiastical History* 26 (1975), 69–82; Carolyn Polizzotto, 'What Really Happened at the Whitehall Debates?', *Historical Journal* 57 (2014), 33–51; Barbara Taft, 'The Council of Officers' *Agreement of the People*', *Historical Journal* 28 (1985), 169–88; and Frances Henderson, 'Drafting the Officers' *Agreement of the People*', in Philip Baker and Elliot Vernon, eds, *The 'Agreements of the People' and the Constitutional Crisis of the English Revolution*, Basingstoke, 2012, 163–94.
60. Firth, ed., *Clarke Papers*, vol. 2, 170–1, being the minutes of the meeting.
61. Ibid., 141–4.
62. *The Kingdomes Weekly Intelligencer* 290 (12–19 December 1648), 1191; Gilbert Burnet, *The Memoires of the Lives and Actions of James and William Dukes of Hamilton*, London, 1677, 379; *Mercurius Pragmaticus* 38 (15–19 December 1648), sigs Ddd2–3; *Mercurius Elencticus* 56 (12–19 December 1648), 540; *A Declaration, Collected out of The Journalls of Both Houses of Parliament* 3 (13–20 December 1648), 19.
63. *CJ*, vol. 6, 101–2, 110–11; *Perfect Occurrences* 105 (29 December 1648–5 January 1649), 784.
64. *The Kingdomes Weekly Intelligencer* 291 (19–26 December 1648), 1196.
65. Whitelocke, *Memorials of the English Affairs*, 357–9.
66. *Mercurius Pragmaticus* 41 (26 December 1648–9 January 1649), endpaper; *A Brief Narration of the Mysteries of State carried on by the Spanish faction*, The Hague, 1651, 65–6; Walker, *History of Independency*, vol. 2, 67.
67. As always when forming his pioneering narrative of events, Gardiner tended to credit most of the surviving evidence, both contemporary and retrospective, and craft it together to produce his account. This resulted in an impression of policy-making filled with sudden changes and twists, with dramatic reversals from day to day, which may be correct or may be an illusion produced by the different sources that he patched together. In practice, what has happened since is that individual historians have tended to preserve those parts of his story, and reuse those sources, which suit the particular interpretations that they have wished to argue. It is possible to construct at least half a dozen different, equally plausible and equally doubtful, accounts of what happened in English politics between November 1648 and January 1649, by favouring specific testimonies. Some of the information provided – for example, in the reports of the Venetian ambassador – is plainly preposterous, though that has not stopped it from being used occasionally in the past. For the most part, however, the worth of individual reports is simply impossible to judge. As before, there are various pamphlets from late December and early January, purporting to represent the views of the army and the responses of the king, the authority of all of which seems suspect.
68. This is true of *Mercurius Pragmaticus* and *Mercurius Elencticus*.
69. Gilbert Burnet's *History of My Own Time*, ed. Osmund Airy, Oxford, 1897, vol. 1, 79, retrospectively reported that Ireton drove the trial on, while Cromwell was 'in some suspense about it'. It is equally hard to know what to make of confident reports by royalists like those in Bod L, Clarendon MS 34, ff. 12–13, 17, that Cromwell was backing off proceedings against the king because of his growing distrust of the radicals, and that the army and parliamentary leadership were trying to negotiate a deal to spare Charles in exchange for an almost total surrender of royal powers. I stand with Dame Veronica Wedgwood, *The Trial of Charles I*, London, 1964, 232; Clive Holmes, 'The Trial and

Execution of Charles I', *Historical Journal* 53 (2010), 296–8; and Mark Kishlansky, 'Mission Impossible', *English Historical Review* 125 (2010), 844–75, in doubting the French ambassador's story of a mission by the earl of Denbigh from the army and parliamentary leaders to the king in late December to offer him a final set of terms, in NA, PRO/31/3/89, ff. 58–63. This has played a great part in narratives drawing on Gardiner, as the moment at which Charles threw away his last chance, by refusing to deal with Denbigh. Not only is it unsupported by any other source, but that the leadership should have treated with Charles after the army had so publicly set its face against doing so seems incredible. Moreover, one of the king's attendants, Sir Thomas Herbert, left a detailed account of Charles's stay at Windsor that never mentions the arrival of Denbigh: *Memoirs of the Two Last Years of the Reign of Charles I*, ed. G. Nichol, London, 1813, 142–50. I also agree with Edward A. V. Beesley, 'Aspects of the English Revolution December 1648 – May 1649' (Bristol University, PhD thesis, 2001), 34–9, that there is no solid evidence that Cromwell was trying to save the king in mid- to late December 1648, by any initiative.

70. *Mercurius Melancholicus* 1 (25 Dec 1648–1 January 1649), 7. Likewise, when the French ambassador reported on 21 December that the General Council had decided to try the king by just five votes, there is no corroboration for this: NA, PRO/31/3/89, f. 52.
71. This was reported in both Bod L, Carte MS 23, f. 425, and NA, PRO31/3/89, f. 52, but the source may have been the same.
72. Walker, *History of Independency*, vol. 2, 54; Bod L, Clarendon MS 34, f. 72.
73. The preliminary and actual proceedings of the trial are recorded in *A Perfect Narrative of the whole Proceedings of the High Court of Justice in the Tryal of the King*, London, 1649; *The Proceedings of the High Court of Justice, With Charles Stuart*, London, 1655; John Nalson, *A True Copy of the Journal of the High Court of Justice for the Tryal of King Charles I*, London, 1684; and John Nalson, *The Trial of Charles I*, London, 1740. Those in the Painted Chamber were published in J. G. Muddiman, *Trial of King Charles the First*, Edinburgh, 1928, 193–230. A series of bulletins were printed as the trial went on by Theodore Jennings, in four instalments, all headed *Collections of Notes Taken at the King's Tryall, during January 1649*. In addition, the London newspapers gave their own accounts weekly. That all these records agree almost perfectly with each other proves that we have an accurate knowledge of at least the formal process. I have added details from HMC Viscount De Lisle MSS, vol. 6, 581; and *The Perfect Weekly Account*, unnumbered (24–31 January 1649), 391.
74. There is a story made famous by Gardiner, which he found in Joseph Spence, *Anecdotes, Observations and Characters of Books and Men*, ed. Samuel Weller Singer, London, 1820, 286–7, that on the night after the king's beheading, when his body was lying in the Banqueting House watched by one of his loyal followers, the earl of Southampton, a man entered, muffled in a cloak. Southampton could not see his face, but when he gazed at the corpse, sighed, shook his head and uttered the words 'cruel necessity', the earl thought the voice and gait were those of Cromwell. The tale is on the border of credibility, because Southampton himself was not quite certain of the man's identity, and by the time it was recorded in the 1730s it was at least at fourth hand. Moreover, the setting is wrong, as the king's body did not lie in the Banqueting House that night, but was immediately embalmed, coffined in lead and removed to St James's Palace (Herbert, *Memoirs*, 194–5). Those wishing to believe the tale may argue that this is the sort of distortion which would occur in such long transmission: and it has been used to support the argument for Cromwell as a late and reluctant convert to regicide. Others would suggest that the person who invented it did not check his facts.
75. In the contemporary record, she is referred to simply as 'a malignant lady'. Only after the Restoration was her identity publicly disclosed, in two witness statements in *An Exact and most Impartial Accompt Of the Indictment, Arraignment, Trial and Judgment (according to Law) of Twenty nine Regicides*, London, 1660, 186–7, 189. This has understandably caused Jacqueline Eales, 'Anne and Thomas Fairfax, and the Vere Connection', in Andrew Hopper and Philip Major, eds, *England's Fortress*, Farnham, 2014, 163–6, to doubt the identification. On the other hand, there would have been obvious political reasons for keeping it secret at the time, and there were no denials when it was stated publicly at the Restoration.

76. For this assumption, see *An Exact and most Impartial Accompt*, 153; *The Bloody Court*, London, 1660; and *Inquisition for the blood of our late sovereign*, London, 1660.
77. *An Exact and most impartial Accompt*, 259–69; *A True and Humble Representation of John Downes*, n.d.
78. R. W. Blencoe, ed., *Sydney Papers*, London, 1825, 237–9.
79. *An Exact and most Impartial Accompt*, 187, 206–9.
80. François Guizot, *History of the English Revolution of 1640*, translated by William Hazlitt, London, 1854, vol. 2, 460–2.
81. Herbert, *Memoirs*, 194–5. Fairfax's ignorance seems partly confirmed by the Dutch envoys, who obtained from him that morning a promise to ask Parliament for a reprieve: Guizot, *History*, vol. 2, 462.
82. Samuel Rawson Gardiner, ed., *The Constitutional Documents of the Puritan Revolution*, 3rd edition, Oxford, 1906, 357–8.
83. Ibid., 377–80.
84. *The Moderate* 28 (16–23 January 1649), 261.
85. Carte, ed., *Collection of Original Letters*, vol. 1, 201–22.
86. BL, Additional MS 63743, f. 1v.
87. *CJ*, vol. 6, 130–1, 147, 150, 153.
88. *CJ*, vol. 6, 131, 145, 153.
89. We know this because we have Vane's direct testimony to it, a decade later, in *A Vindication Of That Prudent and Honourable knight, Sir Henry Vane*, London, 1659, 6–7. Cromwell may indeed have been behind the return of other MPs, perhaps many of them, and so behind their accommodation to the new regime, but such clear evidence is missing. I am nervous in general of inferring political connections between individuals during this period without evidence, which is itself rare. In lieu of it, there is a temptation to rely on two other kinds of source, namely the assertions of political enemies, mostly royalists, and social and business connections between people, which need not certainly mean political alliances. I have tended to fight shy of both.
90. Underdown, *Pride's Purge*, 208–56; Blair Worden, *The Rump Parliament*, Oxford, 1974, 25–6.
91. *CJ*, vol. 6, 158–9.
92. *CJ*, vol. 6, 132; *The Kingdomes Weekly Intelligencer* 298 (6–13 February 1649), 1250; *A Perfect Diurnall* 289 (5–12 February 1649), 2321–2. Cromwell's wish to save the Lords is testified to by both Ludlow (Firth, ed., *Memoirs of Edmund Ludlow*, vol. 1, 220–1) and a royalist (Bod L, Clarendon MS 34, f. 73v).
93. Edward, Earl of Clarendon, *History of the Rebellion*, ed. W. Dunn Macray, Oxford, 1888, XI.259.
94. *CJ*, vol. 6, 159–60.
95. NA, SP 25/62, f. 342.
96. *CJ*, vol. 6, 141–3.
97. Ibid., 147; *CSPD (1649–50)*, xlviii–lix, 6–33.
98. Carte, ed., *Collection of Original Letters*, vol. 1, 215. It is not clear how large a part Ormond's progress in Ireland played in Charles's eventual fate. One of the charges that the army made against him was that he had done nothing to stop it, and the king himself certainly gained hope from it: see HMC De Lisle MSS, vol. 6, 578. On the other hand, there is no actual evidence that it represented a crucial factor in bringing about Charles's trial and execution; moreover, it was only one item, and not a highly prioritized one, on the army's charge sheet against him.
99. *CJ*, vol. 6, 153–8.
100. *CSPD (1649–50)*, 37–40.
101. Clarendon, *History of the Rebellion*, XII.71.
102. Firth, ed., *Clarke Papers*, vol. 2, 200–9; *The Moderate* 37 (20–27 March 1649), 384; *The Kingdomes Weekly Intelligencer* 304 (20–27 March 1649), 1303.

103. *The Kingdomes Weekly Intelligencer* 305 (27 March–3 April 1649), 1308; *CJ*, vol. 6, 177, 183–4.
104. *The Moderate Intelligencer* 213 (12–18 April 1649), 1989–90.
105. Morrill, ed., *Letters, Writings and Speeches*, vol. 2, 3–41, passim.
106. John Asty, ed., *A Complete Collection of the Sermons of the Reverend and Learned John Owen*, London, 1721, ix–x.
107. Whitelocke, *Memorials of the English Affairs*, 540.
108. Ibid., 546.
109. Lucy Hutchinson, *Memoirs of the Life of Colonel Hutchinson*, Cambridge, 2013, 308–9, 322–3.
110. Instead, he published a denunciation of Cromwell: Christopher Chisman, *The Lamb Contending with the Lion*, London, 1649.
111. Firth, ed., *Clarke Papers*, vol. 2, 19–30.
112. *The Parliamentary or Constitutional History of England*, London, 1757–62, vol. 19, 49–51; *Englands New Chains Discovered*, London, 1649.
113. Lilburne subsequently recorded, in his *The Picture of the Council of State*, London, 1649, that by late March he had become angry with Cromwell and Hesilrige for attacking his group in Parliament, and this was the obvious time at which to do so.
114. *The Hunting of the Foxes*, London, 1649; *The Moderate Intelligencer* 207 (1–8 March 1649), 1926–7; *The Kingdomes Weekly Intelligencer* 301–2 (27 February–13 March 1649); *Mercurius Pragmaticus* 47 (20–27 March 1649), sig. Lll2.
115. *CJ*, vol. 6, 153–4; *The Moderate Intelligencer* 207 (1–8 March 1649), 1927; *The Kingdomes Weekly Intelligencer* 301 (27 February–6 March 1649), 1278–9.
116. *The Hunting of the Foxes.*
117. *The Second Part of Englands New Chains Discovered*, London, 1649.
118. Lilburne, *The Picture of the Council of State*; *CSPD (1648–1649)*, 57–8. The others arrested were William Walwyn and Thomas Prince.
119. *CJ*, vol. 6, 183.
120. *CJ*, vol. 6, 177, 189–90; C. H. Firth and R. S. Rait, eds, *Acts and Ordinances of the Interregnum*, London, 1911, vol. 2, 24–57, 81–104; Bulstrode Whitelocke, *Memorials of the English Affairs*, Oxford edition, 1854, vol. 3, 16; *A Perfect Diurnall* 297 (2–9 April 1649), 2410.
121. This was recalled by somebody who was himself a Presbyterian MP, and who hated Cromwell, so that he is unlikely to have invented a story to Oliver's credit, and he was ideally placed to know about the initiative: Clement Walker, *History of Independency*, vol. 2, 157.
122. *A Perfect Diurnall* 297 (2–9 April 1649), 2410.
123. *A Modest Narrative of Intelligence* 3 (14–21 April 1649), 24; *The Moderate Intelligencer* 214 (19–26 April 1649), 2011; *A Perfect Diurnall* 299 (16–23 April 1649), 2449. The foot regiments chosen were Ewers's, Cook's, Deane's and Hewson's, the horse regiments Ireton's, Scrope's, Harlow's and Lambert's.
124. *The Moderate Intelligencer* 214 (19–26 April 1649), 2001.
125. *A Modest Narrative of Intelligence* 4–5 (21–28 April 1649); *A True Narrative Of the Late Mutiny Made by Several Troopers Of Captain Savage's Troop*, London, 1 May 1649; *The Army's Martyr*, London, 1649 (whence the quotation); *The Justice Of The Army Against Evill-Doers Vindicated*, London, 1649, 10–12; *The Moderate Intelligencer* 215 (26 April–2 May 1749), 2012–14; *Perfect Occurrences* 122 (27 April–4 May 1649), 1006; *The Moderate* 42 (24 April–1 May 1649), 475.
126. *An Agreement of the Free People of England*, London, 1649.
127. *The Resolutions of the Private Soldiery of Co. Scroops Regiment of Horse*, Salisbury, 1 May 1649.
128. William Thompson, *Englands Standard Advanced*, Banbury, 6 May 1649; *England's Moderate Messenger* 3 (7–14 May 1649), 19–21; *The Impartiall Intelligencer* 11 (9–16 May), 81; *Perfect Occurrences* 122 (4–11 May 1649), 1028; *The Moderate* 44 (8–15 May),

497. Reynolds's career is summed up by Gerald Aylmer, in the *Oxford Dictionary of National Biography*, Oxford, 2004, vol. 46, 543–4.

129. This can be perceived by reading through the contemporary issues of all the newspapers cited above and below.
130. *England's Moderate Messenger* 3 (7–14 May), 19; *A Perfect Summary Of An Exact Dyarie* 16 (4–12 May 1649), 150–1; *The Kingdomes Weekly Intelligencer* 311 (8–15 May 1649), 354–6. The quotation is from *The Kingdomes Faithfull And Impartiall Scout* 16 (11–18 May 1649), 121–2. The foot regiments were those of Fairfax, Ewers and Hewson.
131. *The Moderate* 44 (8–15 May 1649), 603; *The Declaration of the Levellers Concerning Prince Charles*, London, 17 May 1649.
132. *England's Moderate Messenger* 3 (7–14 May 1649), 24; *The unanimous Declaration of Colonel Scroope's and Commissary Gen. Ireton's Regiments*, 1649; *The Kingdomes Faithfull And Impartiall Scout* 16 (11–18 May 1649), 121–2.
133. *CJ*, vol. 6, 207–9.
134. *A Declaration From his Excellencie, With the Advice of his Councel of War Concerning the present distempers*, London, 1649; *The Declaration Of Lieutenant-Generall Cromwell Concerning the Levellers*, London, 14 May 1649; *A Full Narrative Of All the proceedings betweene His Excellency the Lord Fairfax and the Mutineers*, London, 1649; *The Levellers (Falsly so called) Vindicated*, London, 1649; *A Narrative Of The Proceedings Of His Excellencie The Lord Fairfax, In the reducing of the Revolted Troops*, Oxford, 21 May 1647.
135. *A Full Narrative*; *The Levellers (Falsly so called) Vindicated*; *A Narrative Of The Proceedings*; *The Impartiall Intelligencer* 12 (16–23 May 1649), 100–1; *A Perfect Diurnall* 303 (14–21 May 1649), 2511–15; *A Perfect Summary* 17 (14–21 May 1649), 153; Bod L, Tanner MS 56, f. 40; Francis White, *A True Relation Of The Proceedings In The Businesse of Burford*, London, 1649.
136. *The humble Representation and Resolutions Of The Officers & Soldiers Of Lieut. Generall Cromwel's Regiment*, London, 1649; *A Perfect Diurnall* 305–6 (28 May–11 June 1649); *The Kingdomes Weekly Intelligencer* 315 (5–12 June 1649), 1387.
137. *The Levellers (Falsly so called) Vindicated*; *A Perfect Summary* 17 (14–21 May 1649), 153; *A Perfect Diurnall* 303 (14–21 May 1649), 2524.
138. The best accounts of this action are in *A Perfect Summary* 19 (21–28 May 1649), 156; and *A Perfect Diurnall* 304 (21–28 May 1649), 2533–4.
139. Anthony à Wood, *Annals of the History and Antiquities of the University of Oxford*, ed. John Gutch, Oxford, 1796, vol. 2, part 2, 619–21.
140. *CJ*, vol. 6, 218; *The Impartiall Intelligencer* 13 (23–30 May 1649), 103; *A Perfect Diurnall* 304 (21–28 May 1649), 2540; *The Moderate Intelligencer* 217 (10–17 May 1649), 2046–7.
141. *A Modest Narrative of Intelligence* 10 (2–9 June 1649), 80; Whitelocke, *Memorials of the English Affairs*, vol. 3, 46–7; *The Moderate* 48 (5–12 June 1649), sig. bbb.
142. *CJ*, vol. 6, 233, 240. In the course of the following winter, both Cromwell and others began at times to refer to him as lord lieutenant.
143. For a full contextualizing description, see Laura Lunger Knoppers, *Constructing Cromwell*, Cambridge, 2000, 31–5.
144. *A Perfect Diurnall* 310 (2–9 July 1649), 2633.
145. Whitelocke, *Memorials of the English Affairs*, vol. 3, 65; *CJ*, vol. 6, 254.
146. *Perfect Occurrences* 131 (6–13 July 1649), 1119; Whitelocke, *Memorials of the English Affairs*, vol. 3, 65; HMC De Lisle MSS, vol. 6, 589–90.

5 IRELAND

1. *The Moderate Intelligencer* 226 (12–19 July 1649), endpaper; *The Earl of Pembrookes Speech To Nol-Cromwell*, London, 1649 (the speech is a hostile satire).
2. *The Moderate Intelligencer* 226 (12–19 July 1649), endpaper.

3. For what follows, at present the most handy surveys are S. J. Connolly, *Contested Island: Ireland 1460–1630*, Oxford, 2007, and *Divided Kingdom: Ireland 1630–1680*, Oxford, 2008; and Pádraig Lenihan, *Consolidating Conquest: Ireland 1603–1727*, London, 2014.
4. Jane Ohlmeyer, 'The Wars of Religion 1603–1660', in Thomas Bartlett and Keith Jeffrey, eds, *A Military History of Ireland*, Cambridge, 1996, 163.
5. A good impression of events in Ireland in 1642–9 may be gained from a combination of Connolly, *Divided Kingdom*, 60–118; Pádraig Lenihan, *Confederate Catholics at War 1641–49*, Cork, 2001, and *Consolidating Conquest*, 87–126; Micheál Ó Siochrú, ed., *Kingdoms in Crisis*, Dublin, 2001; Micheál Ó Siochrú, 'Atrocity, Codes of Conduct and the Irish in the British Civil Wars 1641–1653', *Past & Present* 195 (2007), 55–86; Tadhg Ó hAnnracháin, *Catholic Reformation in Ireland*, Oxford, 2002; Geoffrey Parker, *Empire, War and Faith in Early Modern Europe*, London, 2002, 169–91; and Robert Armstrong, *Protestant War*, Manchester, 2005.
6. *CSPD (1649–1650)*, 239–57.
7. John Morrill, ed., *The Letters, Writings and Speeches of Oliver Cromwell*, Oxford, 2023, vol. 2, 64–6, 70–5; HMC Leybourne-Popham MSS, 39; *CSPV (1647–1652)*, 116.
8. *CSPD (1649–1650)*, 261; *A Perfect Diurnall* 314 (30 July–6 August 1649), 2679.
9. *Perfect Occurrences of Every Daie Iournall in Parliament* 134–5 (20 July–3 August 1649); *The Kingdomes Weekly Intelligencer* 331 (24–31 July 1649), 1442–4. For modern histories of this campaign, see the basic one in Samuel Rawson Gardiner, *History of the Commonwealth and Protectorate*, London, 1903, vol. 1, 70–99; and the recent one in James Scott Wheeler, *Cromwell in Ireland*, Dublin, 1999, 40–63.
10. *The Moderate Intelligencer* 230 (9–16 August 1649), 2190; Bulstrode Whitelocke, *Memorials of the English Affairs*, London, 1682, 402; *A Perfect Diurnall* 314–16 (30 July–20 August 1649); *A Modest Narrative of Intelligence* 19 (4–11 August 1649), 152; Morrill, ed., *Letters, Writings and Speeches*, vol. 2, 67–8.
11. *CSPD (1649–1650)*, 257; *The Moderate Intelligencer* 228 (19–26 July), passim; Henry Cary, ed., *Memorials of the Great Civil War in England*, London, 1842, vol. 2, 159–60; John T. Gilbert, ed., *A Contemporary History of Affairs in Ireland, from 1641 to 1652*, vol. 2, Dublin, 1880, 269.
12. Morrill, ed., *Letters, Writings and Speeches*, vol. 2, 70–3.
13. *The True State of the Transactions of Colonel George Monck with Owen-Roe-Mac-Art-O-Neal*, London, 15 August 1649; *CSPD (1649–1650)*, 264; Whitelocke, *Memorials of the English Affairs*, 403; *Perfect Occurrences* 135 (27 July–3 August 1649), passim; Thomas Gumble, *The Life of General Monck*, London, 1671, 28–9; Wilbur Cortez Abbott, ed., *The Writings and Speeches of Oliver Cromwell*, vol. 2, Cambridge, MA, 1939, 100.
14. In this I completely accept the account of Broghill's career in Patrick Little, *Lord Broghill and the Cromwellian Union with Ireland and Scotland*, Woodbridge, 2004. In particular I endorse his rejection (on pp. 2–5) of the famous story in *A Collection of the State Letters of the Rt. Hon. Roger Boyle, the First Earl of Orrery*, London, 1742, 9–11, that Broghill was actually on his way to join the king in 1649 when Cromwell stopped him and blackmailed him into changing sides. I do accept from this account that there was a meeting between the two men at this time, but regard the later telling of it as an attempt by Broghill to extenuate his connection with Cromwell after the restoration of the monarchy (when he had adroitly changed sides again). Broghill was also the alleged source of another unlikely later story that has already been considered, that of the 'saddle letter' in November 1647.
15. *The Moderate Intelligencer* 231 (16–23 August 1649), passim; Abbott, ed., *Writings and Speeches*, vol. 2, 104; *A Perfect Diurnall* 317–18 (20 August–3 September 1649); *Perfect Occurrences* 138 (17–24 August 1649), 1250; HMC Leybourne-Popham MSS, 35.
16. *The Moderate Intelligencer* 231 (16–23 August 1649), 2227; *A Perfect Diurnall* 317–18 (20 August–3 September 1649); Bod L, Carte MS 25, f. 210; Whitelocke, *Memorials of the English Affairs*, 406.
17. *The Moderate Intelligencer* 232–3 (23 August–6 September 1649); *A Perfect Diurnall* 318 (27 August–3 September 1649), passim; *Perfect Occurrences* 140 (31 August–7 September

1649), passim; HMC Leyborne-Popham MSS, 36. This is all ample testimony that Ireton's expedition to Munster was a serious one, and not a mere feint.

18. Morrill, ed., *Letters, Writings and Speeches*, vol. 2, 82–3; *CSPD (1649–1650)*, 294–5; *The Moderate Intelligencer* 233–4 (30 August–13 September 1649); *A Perfect Diurnall* 318 (27 August–3 September 1649), 2748; *Perfect Occurrences* 140 (31 August–7 September 1649), 1265–6.
19. *A Perfect Diurnall* 319 (3–10 September 1649), 2476; *The Moderate Intelligencer* 234 (6–13 September 1649), 2261–2; *A Modest Narrative of Intelligence* 25 (15–23 September 1649), 192.
20. Gilbert, ed., *Contemporary History*, 230, 496–9; Morrill, ed., *Letters, Writings and Speeches*, vol. 2, 97–8, 104.
21. Gilbert, ed., *Contemporary History*, 235–54; Bod L, Carte MS 25, ff. 210, 360–2, 463, 486.
22. Gilbert, ed., *Contemporary History*, 246–58; *The Moderate Intelligencer* 237 (13–20 September 1649), 2296; *Cromwelliana*, Westminster, 1810, 64; *Perfect Occurrences* 143–4 (21 September–4 October 1649); *Two Letters One from Dublin in Ireland, and the other from Liverpoole*, London, 1649; *A Perfect Diurnall* 323 (1–8 October 1649), 2688; *Two Great Fights in Ireland*, London, 1649.
23. On this see, in particular, J. W. Willis-Bund, ed., *The Diary of Henry Townshend of Elmley Lovett*, London, 1920, 134.
24. What follows is a medley of information from Robert Norton, *The Gunner*, London, 1628, and *The Gunners Dialogue*, London, 1643; William Bourne, *The Art of Shooting in Great Ordnance*, London, 1643; and Nicholas Stone, *Enchiridion of Fortification*, London, 1645, 54–64.
25. Gilbert, ed., *Contemporary History*, 260.
26. The author is painfully aware of all these points, after long years working field artillery for the Sealed Knot Society, the largest British body for re-enactment of the Civil War.
27. Gilbert, ed., *Contemporary History*, 261; Bod L, Carte MS 25, ff. 463, 486.
28. Gilbert, ed., *Contemporary History*, 261; *The Moderate Intelligencer* 237 (27 September–4 October 1649), 2296; *Cromwelliana*, 64; *Two Letters One from Dublin*; *A Perfect Diurnall* 323 (1–8 October 1649), 2694.
29. Hewson's, Ewers's and Castle's. Castle was the colonel killed.
30. The fresh regiments were Venables's and Phayre's.
31. Sources as in n. 28, plus Gilbert, ed., *Contemporary History*, 49; *Perfect Occurrences* 144 (28 September–4 October 1649), 1275; and Morrill, ed., *Letters, Writings and Speeches*, vol. 2, 125–6.
32. Denis Murphy, *Cromwell in Ireland*, Boston, 1893, 55–61.
33. Ibid.
34. Gardiner, *History of the Commonwealth and Protectorate*, vol. 1, 116–24.
35. Tom Reilly, *Cromwell: An Honourable Enemy*, Dingle, 1999; *Cromwell Was Framed*, Winchester, 2014; and 'War Criminal Allegations', in Martyn Bennett et al., eds, *Cromwell and Ireland*, Liverpool, 2021, 51–74. A subsequent and accompanying attempt to defend Cromwell's conduct at Drogheda was Philip McKeiver, *A New History of Cromwell's Irish Campaign*, Manchester, 2007, 63–106. He likewise insisted that there was no proof that unarmed civilians were killed.
36. John Morrill, 'The Drogheda Massacre in Cromwellian Context', in David Edwards, ed., *Age of Atrocity*, Dublin, 2007, 242–65; Ó Siochrú, 'Atrocity'; and Micheál Ó Siochrú, *God's Executioner*, London, 2008, 79–89.
37. Since 1990, Ian Gentles has held that the majority of the royalist officers were killed in cold blood after surrender, and called the event the moral low point of Cromwell's life (*The New Model Army in England, Ireland and Scotland 1645–1653*, Oxford, 1992, 358–60; and *Oliver Cromwell*, Basingstoke, 2011, 115). Peter Gaunt termed Cromwell's actions justified (*Oliver Cromwell*, Oxford, 1996, 116–18). Austin Woolrych agreed that he was severe but

wholly within his conventional military rights (*Britain in Revolution 1625–1660*, Oxford, 2002, 469). Martyn Bennett asserted that the killing was initially all in hot blood, and that any civilian deaths were probably collateral damage, but accepted that the slaughter continued during the following day (*Oliver Cromwell*, London, 2006, 166–7; and *Cromwell at War*, London, 2021, 172–6). James Scott Wheeler, by contrast, held that, even by the standards of the wars in Ireland, what happened was 'an appalling event' and 'the blackest episode in Cromwell's career' (*Cromwell in Ireland*, 85–8). Micheál Ó Siochrú (see n. 36) was also of this view, while Pádraig Lenihan believed Thomas Wood's story (*Consolidating Conquest*, 129). Alan Marshall thought that Cromwell had lost control of his men, and that war crimes were committed even according to contemporary notions (*Oliver Cromwell*, London, 2004, 207–18).

38. *The Moderate Intelligencer* 236 (20–27 September 1649), endpaper; *A Perfect Diurnall* 321 (17–24 September 1649), 2754, and 322 (24 September–1 October 1649), 2800; *Perfect Occurrences* 143 (21–28 September 1649), 1318–19.
39. *A Letter from Ireland Read in the House of Commons on Friday Septemb. 28 1649*, London, 1649.
40. *Perfect Occurrences* 144 (28 September–4 October 1649), 1275–86.
41. Morrill, ed., *Letters, Writings and Speeches*, vol. 2, 92–6.
42. Here I am convinced by the argument of Pádraig Lenihan, 'Siege Massacres in Ireland', in Bennett et al., eds, *Cromwell and Ireland*, 26–40.
43. Morrill, ed., *Letters, Writings and Speeches*, vol. 2, 96–9.
44. NA, SP 25/87, f. 89.
45. Morrill, ed., *Letters, Writings and Speeches*, vol. 2, 96–7.
46. *The Moderate Intelligencer* 237 (27 September–4 October 1649), 2297.
47. *A Perfect Diurnall* 323 (1–8 October 1649), 2689.
48. *A Letter of Dr Bernards to a Friend of his at Court*, London, 1660.
49. Frances Parthenope Verney, ed., *Memoirs of the Verney Family during the Civil War*, London, 1892, vol. 2, 344–5.
50. For example, *The Moderate Intelligencer* 237 (27 September–4 October 1649), 2296–7.
51. *Two Letters One from Dublin*. The arrival of the heads is confirmed by *The Moderate Intelligencer* 236 (20–27 September 1649), endpiece.
52. Lenihan, 'Siege Massacres in Ireland', 30–49.
53. *The Moderate Intelligencer* 198 (28 December 1649–4 January 1650), 1816.
54. Bod L, Carte MS 30, ff. 271–2.
55. *A True Relation of a Great Victory Obtained by the Forces under the Command of the Lord of Inchiquin*, London, 30 November 1647; *A Mighty Victory in Ireland*, London, 29 November 1647.
56. For these patterns in his earlier career, see Ronald Hutton, *The Making of Oliver Cromwell*, New Haven and London, 2021, summed up on pp. 331–3.
57. Reilly, *Cromwell*, 93–4; Reilly, *Cromwell Was Framed*, chs 2–3.
58. *The Moderate Intelligencer* 237 (27 September–4 October 1649), 2296–7.
59. *The Kingdomes Weekly Intelligencer* 331 (25 September–2 October 1649), 1513.
60. *Two Letters One from Dublin*.
61. Bod L, Carte MS 25, ff. 553–96, passim.
62. Ibid., f. 553.
63. Morrill, ed., *Letters, Writings and Speeches*, vol. 2, 199–200.
64. This is one of the themes of Hutton, *The Making of Oliver Cromwell*, summed up on pp. 330–8.
65. Here I am persuaded by Nick Poyntz, '"This day by letters severall from hands": News Networks and Oliver Cromwell's Letters from Drogheda', in Bennett et al., eds, *Cromwell and Ireland*, 253–74.
66. The argument from numbers is suggested, and its limitation acknowledged, in Morrill, 'The Drogheda Massacre in Cromwellian Context', 252–5.
67. *A Letter of Dr Bernards*.

68. Nicholas Bernard, *The Penitent Death of a Woeful Sinner*, 3rd edition, London, 1651, 311–13.
69. BL, Harleian MS 5409, ff. 34v–35v; Bod L, Tanner MS 102, ff. 17–18.
70. The publication history is described in Andrew Clark's introduction to his edition of Wood's autobiography, *The Life and Times of Anthony Wood*, Oxford, 1891.
71. In *A Letter of Dr Bernards*. The colonel concerned was John Hewson, who left his own account of the action at the church in *Perfect Occurrences* 144 (28 September–4 October 1649), 1275–6, exulting in the deaths of all the defenders of the steeple as another manifestation of God's glory.
72. This development, and its ghastly consequences, is fully explored in Mark Stoyle, 'The Road to Farndon Field', *English Historical Review* 123 (2008), 895–916.
73. See especially *Mercurius Elencticus* 24 (8–15 October 1649), 186–8; and *The Man in the Moon* 26 (17–24 October 1649), 213. The significance of these entries was first spotted by Reilly, *Cromwell Was Framed*, ch. 2. The former paper stated ambiguously that neither women nor children were spared, which could refer to a few individual atrocities but could also be read as a more general massacre.
74. E.g. *An Exact History of the several Changes of Government In England, From the horrid Murther of King Charles I*, London, 1660, 43–4; Edward, Earl of Clarendon, *The History of the Rebellion and Civil Wars in England*, ed. W. Dunn Macray, Oxford, 1888, XII.115.
75. Morrill, ed., *Letters, Writings and Speeches*, vol. 2, 97–8.
76. Ibid., 102–4; Gilbert, ed., *Contemporary History*, 267.
77. Morrill, ed., *Letters, Writings and Speeches*, vol. 2, 92–3.
78. Ibid.; *A Perfect Diurnall* 321 (17–24 September 1649), 2754; *Perfect Occurrences* 143 (21–28 September 1649), 1316.
79. *CSPD (1649–1650)*, 349–51, 368.
80. Morrill, ed., *Letters, Writings and Speeches*, vol. 2, 113–14; *A perfect and particular relation of the several marches and proceedings of the army in Ireland*, London, 27 October 1649; Gilbert, ed., *Contemporary History*, 54; *A very full and particular Relation of the great progresse and happy proceedings of the Army of the Commonwealth*, London, 1649; HMC Leyborne-Popham MSS, 55. The last wolves in the British Isles were killed in the Wicklow Mountains at the end of the eighteenth century.
81. Bod L, Carte MS 25, f. 757; *A very full and particular Relation*.
82. Bod L, Carte MS 25, ff. 608–32, passim; Gilbert, ed., *Contemporary History*, 282.
83. *A very full and particular Relation*; Morrill, ed., *Letters, Writings and Speeches*, vol. 2, 114–15; HMC Leybourne-Popham MSS, 97; *Severall Proceedings in Parliament* 3 (16–23 October 1649), 21.
84. Bod L, Carte MS 25, ff. 691–724, passim; Gilbert, ed., *Contemporary History*, 310–12; *The Memoirs of James Lord Audley Earl of Castlehaven*, London, 1680, 99; *The Taking of Wexford*, London, 1649.
85. For the account of the fall of Wexford that follows, see Bod L, Carte MS 25, f. 757 and MS 26, f. 443v; *A perfect and particular relation*; *A Letter from the Lord-Lieutenant of Ireland to the Honorable William Lenthal, Esq.*, London, 1649; *The Taking of Wexford*; *A very full and particular Relation*; HMC Leyborne-Popham MSS; and *A Briefe Relation of some affaires and transactions, Civill and Military* 5 (30 October 1649), 68. Cromwell said that the governor of the castle, James Stafford, was one of the commissioners treating with him for Synnott, which may be read as suggesting that he struck a deal to surrender the castle with him then. But all the reports from Cromwell's soldiers agree that Stafford was in the castle as it was about to be stormed, and surrendered from there. Catholic and royalist sources were unanimous in attributing the fall of the town to deliberate treachery on the part of Stafford, but there is nothing in the Cromwellian testimonies to substantiate this. Nevertheless, following Denis Murphy, it has become part of a modern Irish nationalist legend.
86. Murphy, *Cromwell in Ireland*, 93–7.
87. Gardiner, *History of the Commonwealth and Protectorate*, vol. 1, 127–34.

88. Ian Gentles limited the body count to those who put up armed resistance, those who drowned and Catholic clergy, and absolved Cromwell from ordering it. Nonetheless, he still faulted Cromwell for failing to rebuke his men and noted that an attack on a town on the brink of surrendering breached the rules of war (*The New Model Army in England, Ireland and Scotland*, 367). Peter Gaunt concluded that Cromwell had not ordered the slaughter and that the latter was not wholesale, but that he had still made no attempt to restrain it (*Oliver Cromwell*, 119). Tom Reilly emphasized that Cromwell showed a real desire for a lenient and peaceful settlement and was then taken by surprise as events fell out and had no personal part in the fall of the town. Reilly thought that the attackers had killed those who resisted, and noted that that no eye-witness spoke of civilian deaths at their hands, though he allowed that women and children may have died accidentally (*Cromwell*, 139–91). Austin Woolrych praised Cromwell for his patience with Synnott during the negotiations, and exonerated him from knowledge that the town was being attacked and his men from knowledge of the negotiations. He did, however, think it likely that Cromwell made no attempt to halt a massacre that he thought was divine judgement (*Britain in Revolution*, 470–1). John Morrill agreed that Cromwell was not in control and so cannot be blamed, and also thought that Cromwell controlled his soldiers as soon as he could. He found little evidence of killing in cold blood, and none of the murder of prisoners, but much of civilian deaths happening as collateral damage (Morrill, 'The Drogheda Massacre', 259–63). Philip McKeiver held that there was no proof that any unarmed civilians were killed, and thought Cromwell not responsible for any of the killing (*A New History of Cromwell's Irish Campaign*, 11–23). Frank Kitson declared that Cromwell neither ordered nor regretted the killing (*Old Ironsides*, London, 2004, 178). Alan Marshall thought that he had made no attempt to restrain his men once they were out of control (*Oliver Cromwell*, London, 2004, 223). Micheál Ó Siochrú corrected Denis Murphy by noting that many of the garrison were spared or escaped (*God's Executioner*, 97). In the same year (2008) Pádraig Lenihan thought that the story of the 300 women cut down in the marketplace was credible (*Consolidating Conquest*, 129). Martyn Bennett emphasized the scale of the killing, but also that the situation as the town fell was chaotic, and that Cromwell had – for once – completely lost control (*Oliver Cromwell*, 177–8). James Scott Wheeler put civilian deaths in hundreds, and noted that Cromwell made no apparent attempt to regain control over his army and showed no remorse for what it did (*Cromwell in Ireland*, 96–9).
89. Jason McHugh, '"For our owne defence": Catholic Insurrection in Wexford 1641–2', in Brian Mac Cuarta, ed., *Reshaping Ireland 1550–1700*, Dublin, 2011, 214–40.
90. A point made in *A very full and particular Relation.*
91. All points made in *A very full and particular Relation.*
92. Ibid.
93. *A perfect and particular relation.*
94. *Collections of Letters from severall parts, Concerning The Affairs of the Armies in Ireland*, London, 1649.
95. *The Taking of Wexford.*
96. HMC Leyborne-Popham MSS, 47.
97. Morrill, ed., *Letters, Writings and Speeches*, vol. 2, 114–17.
98. Bod L, Carte MS 25, f. 762.
99. *Mercurius Elencticus* 24 (29 October–5 November 1649), 215.
100. *A Briefe Relation* 17 (1–8 January 1650), 214.
101. *An Exact History of the several Changes of Government*, 46.
102. A sequence worked out by McKeiver, *A New History of Cromwell's Irish Campaign*, 123–5.
103. Morrill, ed., *Letters, Writings and Speeches*, vol. 2, 117–30, for Cromwell's letters to Taaffe; and Murphy, *Cromwell in Ireland*, 105–7, for the replies.
104. Morrill, ed., *Letters, Writings and Speeches*, vol. 2, 127–30.
105. Gilbert, ed., *Contemporary History*, 53–5, 247–317, passim; Bod L, Carte MS 26, ff. 23, 25.

106. Gilbert, ed., *Contemporary History*, 322; Cary, ed., *Memorials*, vol. 2, 155–8, 186; *Severall Proceedings in Parliament* 9 (23–30 November 1649), 87–8; *A Briefe Relation* 12 (4–11 December 1649), 129–31, and 19 (21 January–7 February 1650), 247–51; Bod L, Carte MS 26, ff. 23, 133; Morrill, ed., *Letters, Writings and Speeches*, vol. 2, 132–48.
107. Morrill, ed., *Letters, Writings and Speeches*, vol. 2, 130–45.
108. *Memoirs of Castlehaven*, 100–2; *Severall Proceedings in Parliament* 9 (23–30 November 1649), 97–8, and 10 (30 November–7 December 1649), 109–10; Bod L, Carte MS 26, f. 106. The English governor was Edward Wogan.
109. Bod L, Carte MS 26, ff. 70–301, passim.
110. Morrill, ed., *Letters, Writings and Speeches*, vol. 2, 152–6; HMC Ormonde MSS, O.S. vol. 2, 104–5; *Severall Proceedings in Parliament* 9 (23–30 November 1649), 87, 97–9, and 10 (30 November–7 December 1649), 109–10.
111. *Memoirs of Castlehaven*, 102; Bod L, Clarendon MS, ff. 40–1; Bod L, Carte MS 26, ff. 247, 256, 446. HMC MSS in Various Collections, vol. 6, 435–6; Gilbert, ed., *Contemporary History*, 58–9, 331; HMC Ormonde MSS, O.S. vol. 2, 104–5; *A Briefe Relation* 14 (11–18 December 1649), 158–9; *A Perfect Diurnall* 1 (10–17 December 1649), 9–12.
112. Morrill, ed., *Letters, Writings and Speeches*, vol. 2, 156–67; Bod L, Carte MS 26, f. 446v; Gilbert, ed., *Contemporary History*, 331; *A Briefe Relation* 14 (11–18 December 1649), 159, and 17 (1–8 January 1650), 214–18; *A Perfect Diurnall* 4 (31 December 1649–7 January 1650), 35, 39–40.
113. Bod L, Carte MS 26, ff. 381–3; Gilbert, ed., *Contemporary History*, 329–30.
114. The expert in the logistics of Cromwell's Irish campaign is James Scott Wheeler, from whom these details are taken: *Cromwell in Ireland*, 92, 118–20.
115. *CSPD (1649–50)*, 406, 454, 465; *CSPD (1650)*, 45, 50, 121.
116. *A Briefe Relation* 16–17 (25 December 1649–8 January 1650); *Severall Proceedings in Parliament* 20 (7–14 February 1650), 264–5; *A Perfect Diurnall* 7 (21–28 January 1650), 60.
117. Morrill, ed., *Letters, Writings and Speeches*, vol. 2, 169–71.
118. *A Perfect Diurnall* 8 (28 January–4 February 1650), 67–8.
119. *A Perfect Diurnall* 5 (7–14 January 1650), 42.
120. Gilbert, ed., *Contemporary History*, 331–2.
121. *Certain Acts and Declarations made by the Ecclesiastical Congregation . . . Met at Clonmacnoise*, Kilkenny, 1649.
122. Morrill, ed., *Letters, Writings and Speeches*, vol. 2, 189–202.
123. A point made ably by John Morrill in 'The Religious Context of the Cromwellian Conquest of Ireland', *Cromwelliana* (2014), 29–35.
124. Morrill, ed., *Letters, Writings and Speeches*, vol. 2, 134–5, 172–5.
125. Hugh Peters stressed that Cromwell was propelled into the field by fear of his imminent recall: *Severall Proceedings in Parliament* 21 (14–21 February 1650), 296.
126. This campaign is well narrated by Wheeler, *Cromwell in Ireland*, 104–7.
127. Morrill, ed., *Letters, Writings and Speeches*, vol. 2, 207–10; *Severall Proceedings in Parliament* 23 (28 February–7 March 1650), 322–4, and 24 (7–14 March 1650), 340–1; *A Briefe Relation* 28 (5–12 March 1650), 399–400; *A Perfect Diurnall* 14 (11–18 March 1650), 113–14.
128. Morrill, ed., *Letters, Writings and Speeches*, vol. 2, 212–15; *Severall Proceedings in Parliament* 24 (7–14 March 1650), 340–1. Cromwell's report to the council strongly suggests that there was no fighting, but an ultra-Catholic history, written later in the century and very hostile to Ormond, gave a detailed account of half an hour of fierce resistance by eighty Ulstermen in the outer court, inflicting much loss: Gilbert, ed., *Contemporary History*, 75. This history is, however, generally inaccurate, and the end of the account, in which Cromwell allowed the Ulstermen to march away to Clonmel, is incompatible with the agreed terms of surrender. The correct duration of the Elizabethan siege was noted by Abbott, ed., *Writings and Speeches*, vol. 2, 218.

129. Morrill. ed., *Letters, Writings and Speeches*, vol. 2, 215–17; *A Perfect Diurnall* 14 (11–18 March 1650), 114, and 15 (18–25 March 1650), 139.
130. *A Perfect Diurnall* 20 (22–29 April 1650), 221; *Severall Letters from Ireland*, London, 1650; *Severall Proceedings in Parliament* 25 (14–21 March 1650), 346–7; Morrill, ed., *Letters, Writings and Speeches*, vol. 2, 230; J. Casimir O'Meagher, 'Diary of Dr Jones, Scoutmaster General to the Army of the Commonwealth', *Journal of the Royal Society of the Antiquaries of Ireland*, 5th series, 3 (1893), 44.
131. Bod L, Carte MS 26, f. 602, and MS 27, ff. 1–30, passim; *Memoirs of Castlehaven*, 105–9.
132. This figure is from George Bates, *Elenchus Motuum Nuperorum in Anglia*, London, 1685, 36–7, a history of the period very hostile to Cromwell but which accords well in all other respects with the contemporary accounts of this particular campaign. It would make sense, given the scale of this combined army's operations, and no other is available from the sources.
133. *A letter from the Lord Lieutenant of Ireland to the Honourable William Lenthal Esq*, London, 1650; Bates, *Elenchus*, 38–9; *Memoirs of Castlehaven*, 108–9; O'Meagher, 'Diary of Dr Jones', 45; *Severall Proceedings in Parliament* 29 (11–18 April 1650), 408–10; *A Briefe Relation* 38 (9–16 April 1650), 469. These accounts accord in all details except the English casualties. Cromwell claimed thirty to forty, and Bates seventy. The Scoutmaster-General, Jones, said ten were killed and twenty wounded.
134. Morrill, ed., *Letters, Writings and Speeches*, vol. 2, 236–41.
135. Ibid., 234–5.
136. O'Meaghar, 'Diary of Dr Jones', 40; Broghill's despatch, printed in Murphy, *Cromwell in Ireland*, 189–90.
137. There is a good account of these negotiations in Wheeler, *Cromwell in Ireland*, 142–7. Key documents are in Abbott, ed., *Writings and Speeches*, vol. 2, 240–8.
138. Again, Wheeler is the master of the logistics here: *Cromwell in Ireland*, 149.
139. Bod L, Carte MS 27, f. 18; Gilbert, ed., *Contemporary History*, 337–8, 250–1.
140. This account of the siege of Clonmel is based on the six printed in Gilbert, ed., *Contemporary History*, 409–16; Morrill, ed., *Letters, Writings and Speeches*, vol. 2, 259; *Severall Proceedings in Parliament* 35 (23–30 May 1650), 504–5. I have pinned the date of surrender at 10 May because of a letter from a soldier bearing it that stated that he and his comrades had entered the town that morning: *Severall Proceedings in Parliament* 35 (23–30 May 1650), 504, which agrees with two of the accounts in Gilbert's edition.
141. Gilbert, ed., *Contemporary History*, 413–14.
142. Cary, ed., *Memorials*, vol. 2, 217–20.
143. Bod L, Carte MS 27, f. 131, from Sir George Hamilton.
144. This is the narrative by a soldier in Sir John Clotworthy's regiment, edited in 1873 and reprinted in Gilbert, ed., *Contemporary History*, 414–16. Among historians, Gardiner confidently asserted 2,500 casualties (*History of the Commonwealth and Protectorate*, vol. 1, 156). Ian Gentles preferred the figure of 1,500 in the source quoted in n. 143, and took it to mean killed rather than killed and wounded (*The New Model Army in England, Ireland and Scotland*, 374). Micheál Ó Siochrú cautiously accepted both totals as limits of a possible span (*God's Executioner*, 123). James Scott Wheeler thought that there had been 3,000 casualties, and 1,500 dead, representing 10 per cent of the English soldiers in Ireland (*Cromwell in Ireland*, 155–6). Alan Marshall thought that 2,000 to 2,500 fell (*Oliver Cromwell*, 232). Malcolm Wanklyn has been the vehement dissenter, insisting on a casualty figure between 500 and 1,000 (*The Warrior Generals*, London, 2010, 213, 286). At the other extreme, Martyn Bennett claimed 3,000 dead, a third of Cromwell's army (*Oliver Cromwell*, London, 2006, 187).
145. O'Meagher, 'Diary of Dr Jones', 52; *A Perfect Diurnall* 25 (27 May–3 June 1650), 278; *A Speech Or Declaration Of The Declared King of Scots*, London, 1650, 4–5.
146. *A Speech Or Declaration*, 4–5; *Severall Proceedings in Parliament* 36 (30 May–6 June 1650), 513; Whitelocke, *Memorials of the English Affairs*, 413.

147. These views were established by Gardiner and are common to all the historians since 1990 cited above, but especially those who have devoted most space to the campaign, such as Gentles, Wheeler and Ó Siochrú.
148. For lack of expertise, I make no personal intervention here in the debate among historians over Cromwell's subsequent reputation in Ireland. Toby Barnard established conclusively that his elevation to the principal bogey figure of modern Irish nationalist tradition was a nineteenth-century phenomenon, propelled largely by the new Victorian British hero-worship of him: 'Irish Images of Cromwell', in R. C. Richardson, ed., *Images of Oliver Cromwell*, Manchester, 1993, 180–206; and 'Cromwell's Irish Reputation', in Jane A. Mills, ed., *Cromwell's Legacy*, Manchester, 2012, 191–218. What remains in dispute is how much of a bogey he was before then. He was clearly one of a number of figures from the period to whom Irish tradition was hostile, but only at times and not necessarily the greatest. He is certainly the towering English villain in Irish folklore, but it is not clear whether this pre-dates his elevation to that status in mainstream nationalist culture. See Jason McElligott, *Cromwell Our Chief of Enemies*, Dundalk, 1994; and Sarah Covington, 'The Folkloric Afterlife of Oliver Cromwell in Ireland', in Bennett et al., eds, *Cromwell and Ireland*, 275–92, and *The Devil from Over the Sea*, Oxford, 2022.

6 SCOTLAND

1. *CJ*, vol. 6, 343–4, 371, 418.
2. *A Message Sent From The Lord Hopton*, London, 1650.
3. *CJ*, vol. 6, 343–4.
4. For the summary of negotiations between the Scots and Charles II given below, see David Stevenson, *Revolution and Counter-Revolution in Scotland 1644–1651*, London, 1977, 132–71, for the Scottish side of events, and Ronald Hutton, *Charles II, King of England, Scotland and Ireland*, Oxford, 1989, 37–50, for the king's viewpoint.
5. He was also required to subscribe to an earlier document, the National Covenant taken by Scottish rebels in 1638, but this only committed him to confirming the presbyterian system in Scotland, and so was less of a stumbling block.
6. *CSPD 1650*, xv–xxiii, 197–8, 207; *CJ*, vol. 6, 423–4; BL, Egerton MS 1048, ff. 113–14 (Fairfax's new commission).
7. *CSPD 1650*, 210; *CJ*, vol. 6, 427–8. Samuel Rawson Gardiner quoted despatches from the French resident in London, preserved in the archive at Paris, which show that this option had been discussed since the opening of June, along with the possibility that Cromwell might replace Fairfax or lead the invasion of Scotland while Fairfax guarded England: *History of the Commonwealth and Protectorate*, London, 1903, vol. 1, 257. As with many of the pieces of news sent by the representatives of foreign nations, it is difficult to know how much these possibilities were actually being debated by people in power, and how much they were mere speculative gossip about them.
8. Thomas Thomson and Cosmo Innes, eds, *The Acts of the Parliaments of Scotland*, London, 1872, vol. 6, part 2, 577–600.
9. *A Declaration Of The Parliament Of England, Upon the marching of the Armie into Scotland*, London, 1650.
10. When one of the commissioners who had made the treaty with Charles parted from him on his arrival in Scotland, the Scot asked the king for a declaration that he would not attack England, but await an invitation from it: Thomas Houston, ed., *A Brief Historical Relation of the Life of Mr John Livingston*, Edinburgh, 1848, 133. Even after the English government had sent its army against them, some leaders of the Kirk Party were still doubtful over whether to invade in retaliation once that army was defeated: David Hay Fleming, ed., *Diary of Sir Archibald Johnston of Wariston*, vol. 2, Edinburgh, 1919, 13. In August one of the Kirk Party grandees most favourable to the king, the earl of Loudon, promised him that, if he did everything that the party wanted, its army would invade England and restore him: *Perfect Passages Of Every Daies Intelligence From The Parliaments Army* 12 (20–27

September 1650), 91–2. This, however, was after the English republic had invaded Scotland, and even then it is not clear that most of the Scottish leadership would have endorsed his assurance.

11. *CSPD 1650*, 199.
12. *Mercurius Politicus* 1 (6–13 June 1650), 3–4.
13. *CJ*, vol. 6, 421–2; Bulstrode Whitelocke, *Memorials of the English Affairs*, London, 1682, 454–6 (original in BL, Additional MS 37345, ff. 81–4); Daniel Parsons, ed., *The Diary of Sir Henry Slingsby of Scriven*, London, 1836, 340–1 (Fairfax's letter of resignation); C. H. Firth, ed., *The Memoirs of Edmund Ludlow*, Oxford, 1894, vol. 1, 242–4; Lucy Hutchinson, *Memoirs of the Life of Colonel Hutchinson*, London, 1884, 344.
14. These are the accounts of Whitelocke and Ludlow.
15. *CJ*, vol. 6, 432, 435.
16. Ibid., 427–38; *CSPD 1650*, 210.
17. *Perfect Passages* 1 (28 June–5 July 1650), 2, has 28 June; Whitelocke, *Memorials of the English Affairs*, 447, has 29 June.
18. *Perfect Passages* 1 (28 June–5 July), 2; *A Perfect Diurnall Of Some Passages and Proceedings Of, And In Relation To, The Armies In England and Ireland* 30–1 (1–15 July 1650); *The Perfect Weekly Account* (10–17 July 1650), 531.
19. Osmund Airy, ed., *Burnet's History of My Own Time*, Oxford, 1897, vol. 1, 154.
20. Firth, ed., *Memoirs of Edmund Ludlow*, vol. 1, 244–8.
21. Cumbria RO (Kendal), WDHOTH/3/44/6/54.
22. *Liet. Colonell I. Lilburne his apologeticall narration*, Amsterdam, 1652, 12–13. Lilburne's testimony here is borne out by his letter to Cromwell in Longleat House, PO/VOL 11, ff. 89–90: I am grateful to the marquis of Bath for allowing me access to his papers. The best current account of Lilburne's career at this period, as in general, is Michael Braddick, *The Common Freedom of the People*, Oxford, 2018, 177–202.
23. Henry Cary, ed., *Memorials of the Great Civil War in England*, London, 1842, vol. 2, 223–5.
24. Francis Freeman, *Light Vanquishing Darknesse*, London, 1650.
25. John Morrill, ed., *The Letters, Writings and Speeches of Oliver Cromwell*, Oxford, 2023, vol. 2, 279–88. John Yonge Akerman, ed., *Letters of Roundhead Officers, Written from Scotland*, Edinburgh, 1856, 1, shows that the declaration was completed on the evening of 11 July, though it cannot be shown to have been distributed before the 15th. For more information on the prayer meeting, see *A Perfect Diurnall* 32 (15–22 July 1650), 369; and *Severall Proceedings in Parliament* 42 (11–18 July 1650), 214.
26. *Severall Proceedings in Parliament* 43 (18–25 July 1650), 232.
27. *Original Memoirs, Written during the Great Civil War*, Edinburgh, 1806, 127, 138; Thomas Gumble, *The Life of General Monck*, London, 1671, 34–5; *A Large Relation Of The Fight at Leith*, London, 1650; *A Perfect Diurnall* 34 (29 July–5 August 1650), 407.
28. Akerman, ed., *Letters of Roundhead Officers*, 2; BL, Additional MS 21419, f. 209; *Perfect Passages* 4 (19–26 July 1650), 28; *A Perfect Diurnall* 32 (15–22 July 1650), 376.
29. *Original Memoirs*, 128–9.
30. Morrill, ed., *Letters, Writings and Speeches*, vol. 2, 289–90.
31. *The Perfect Weekly Account* 2 (17–24 July 1650), 537; *The Impartial Scout* 58 (26 July–2 August 1650), 259; *Severall Proceedings in Parliament* 43 (18–25 July 1650), 23; Morrill, ed., *Letters, Writings and Speeches*, vol. 2, 293–4; *A Perfect Diurnall* 33 (22–29 July 1650), 382–3.
32. *The Impartial Scout* 58 (26 July–2 August 1650), 257–8. The horse regiments were those of Cromwell, Lambert, Fleetwood, Whalley, Twistleton, Robert Lilburne and Hacker, plus Okey's dragoons; the foot were those of Cromwell, Fairfax (a relative of the former general), Pride, Lambert, Maulverer, Cooke, Daniel and Monck.
33. Ibid., 260; Morrill, ed., *Letters, Writings and Speeches*, vol. 2, 297–8; *Original Memoirs*, 128–9; *Perfect Passages* 5 (26 July–2 August 1650), 33–4. The war that followed this invasion has been well treated in two overall studies a century apart: W. S. Douglas, *Cromwell's*

Scotch Campaigns 1650–51, London, 1898; and John D. Grainger, *Cromwell against the Scots*, East Linton, 1997. In addition, the various biographers of Cromwell and historians of the period have dealt with it, as noted below, and there are book-length studies of the major battles: Stuart Reid, *Dunbar 1650*, Oxford, 2004; Arran Johnston, *Essential Agony*, Solihull, 2019; and Malcolm Atkin, *Cromwell's Crowning Mercy*, Stroud, 1998.

34. James Scott Wheeler, 'The Logistics of the Cromwellian Conquest of Scotland 1650–1651', *War and Society* 10 (1992), 8; Ian Gentles, *The New Model Army in England, Ireland and Scotland 1645–1653*, Oxford, 1992, 388.
35. *CSPD 1650*, 210; John Nicholls, ed., *Original Letters and Papers of State Addressed to Oliver Cromwell*, London, 1743, 11–12; Wheeler, 'The Logistics of the Cromwellian Conquest of Scotland', 8; *A Perfect Diurnall* 34 (29 July–5 August 1650), 393–4, 401; *The Impartial Scout* 58 (26 July 1650), 260.
36. References as at n. 35, plus *Original Memoirs*, 130; and *An Answere From The Committee of Estates To a Printed Paper*, Edinburgh, 22 July 1650.
37. Morrill, ed., *Letters, Writings and Speeches*, vol. 1, 302; *A Perfect Diurnall* 35 (5–12 August 1650), 409–10; *The Perfect Weekly Account* (31 July–7 August 1650), 551–2; *A Large Relation Of The Fight at Leith*.
38. Thomson and Innes, eds, *Acts of the Parliaments of Scotland*, vol. 6, part 2, 601–2.
39. This is the estimate of the earl of Cassilis, who was an eye-witness, of the number at the end of July: George F. Warner, ed., *The Nicholas Papers*, vol. 1, Camden Society, London, 1886, 188–9.
40. Hutton, *Charles II*, 49–50, and sources given there.
41. Morrill, ed., *Letters, Writings and Speeches*, vol. 2, 303–5; *Mercurius Politicus* 10 (8–15 August 1650), 160; *A Perfect Diurnall* 35 (5–12 August 1650), 409–10, 424; *Original Memoirs*, 131–6 (the source of the 'bees' analogy); *A True Relation Of The Proceedings Of The English Army Now In Scotland*, London, 1650, 6–12; *The Impartial Scout* 59 (2–9 August 1650), 269–71; *A Large Relation of the Fight at Leith*; *Severall Proceedings in Parliament* 46 (8–15 August 1650), 681; *A Perfect Diurnall* (19–26 August 1650), 441–2.
42. Hutton, *Charles II*, 52–3.
43. Morrill, ed., *Letters, Writings and Speeches*, vol. 2, 307–10; James Christie, ed., *Records of the Commissioners of the General Assemblies of the Church of Scotland*, Scottish Record Society, 1909, 13–23; *Diary of Sir Archibald Johnston*, 10.
44. *Diary of Sir Archibald Johnston*, 6.
45. National Records of Scotland, PA 12/5, sub August 1650; James Haig, ed., *The Historical Works of Sir James Balfour*, Edinburgh, 1825, vol. 4, 89.
46. *Mercurius Politicus* 11 (15–22 August 1650), 166; *A Perfect Diurnall* 37 (19–26 August 1650), 441–2; *Severall Proceedings in Parliament* 47 (15–22 August 1650), 690–2. The same despatches from the army tended to get printed in a number of different newspapers, and also in pamphlets. I have accordingly, to save my word count, cited only the first sources in which I read them, though these tend also to be the most reliable and detailed newspapers.
47. *Mercurius Politicus* 12 (22–29 August 1650), 186; *A Perfect Diurnall* 37 (19–26 August 1650), 452–3; *Perfect Passages* 8 (23–30 August 1650), 6; *Severall Proceedings in Parliament* 48 (22–29 August 1650), 715–16; *The Diary of Sir Archibald Johnston*, 17–19; David Laing, ed., *Correspondence of Sir Robert Kerr, First Earl of Ancrum, and His Son William, Third Earl of Lothian*, Edinburgh, 1875, 283–4; Morrill, ed., *Letters, Writings and Speeches*, vol. 2, 313–16. The Pentlands offered an excellent vantage point from which to view both sides of the city and the Scottish position, and it was a strong one in the face of a sudden attack, within easy distance of the supply point at Musselburgh. The position also allowed Cromwell to cut off supplies from the south to Leslie's army. All these factors are stated in the sources. There is no sign that Cromwell feared the Scots might invade England if the way were not blocked, or that the dissension between Kirk Party and king made him halt hostilities in the hope of a settlement.
48. Sources as in n. 47.

49. *Records of the Commissioners of the General Assemblies*, 33–42.
50. *Mercurius Politicus* 13 (29 August–5 September 1650), 195; *A Perfect Diurnall* 38–9 (26 August–9 September 1650).
51. Morrill, ed., *Letters, Writings and Speeches*, vol. 2, 317–18, 324–5; *Mercurius Politicus* 14 (5–12 September 1650), 214; *Original Memoirs*, 138–44 (quotation from 143); *A Perfect Diurnall* 38 (2–9 September 1650), 454–8; HMC Earl of Eglinton MSS, 57–8.
52. *Original Memoirs*, 142; Morrill, ed., *Letters, Writings and Speeches*, vol. 2, 324.
53. Morrill, ed., *Letters, Writings and Speeches*, vol. 2, 325, has Cromwell's own computation of 3,500 horse and 7,100 foot. *Mercurius Politicus* 15 (12–19 September 1650), 227, has 11,000 in all; *A Perfect Diurnall* 38 (2–9 September 1650), 455, has 12,000; as has *A Brief Relation Of Some Affairs and Transactions, Civil and Military* 53 (20 August–10 September 1650), 812. This last figure was also reported by Cromwell's messenger to Parliament with news of the battle: Thomas Carte, ed., *A Collection of Original Letters and Papers Concerning the Affairs of England from the Year 1641 to 1660*, London, 1739, vol. 1, 380. The majority view of officers on the spot (who sent all these letters) therefore tends to the higher figure, but Cromwell's is to be respected as the work of the commander and for its precision, and it may have omitted officers or members of the army not in horse and foot units, such as artillerymen.
54. *CPSD (1650)*, 348–63.
55. This claim was actually made by one of Leslie's senior officers, Gilbert Kerr, in a parley with English officers in August: *A Perfect Diurnall* 37 (19–26 August 1650), 452–3.
56. It certainly did with a prominent member of the government: Sir Archibald Johnston: *The Diary of Sir Archibald Johnston*, 9.
57. Morrill, ed., *Letters, Writings and Speeches*, vol. 2, 326, where Cromwell said 'we heard' it was 'at least' 6,000 horse and 16,000 foot. *Mercurius Politicus* 15 (12–19 September 1650), 229–30, has between 23,000 and 30,000. *A Perfect Diurnall* 39 (2–9 September 1650), 415–16, gives 27,000, as does *A Brief Relation* 53 (20 August–10 September 1650), 812, and Cardwell's relation in Carte, ed., *Collection of Original Letters*, vol. 1, 380–3 (as hearsay). *Perfect Passages* 10 (6–13 September 1650), 75, has 24,000. Reid, *Dunbar 1650*, 39–40, thought that the totals provided by Cromwell and his men were reached by assuming that the regiments named by prisoners as making up the Scottish army were all at full strength. That would indeed provide such figures, while the strength actually achieved was much less. This is wholly plausible.
58. *A Perfect Diurnall* 38 (26 August–2 September 1650), 468–70.
59. Warner, ed., *The Nicholas Papers*, 193–4.
60. Laing, ed., *Correspondence of Ancrum and Lothian*, 289–90.
61. Edward Walker, *Historical Discourses*, London, 1705, 180.
62. This intention is proved in HMC Earl of Eglinton MSS, 57–8.
63. Morrill, ed., *Letters, Writings and Speeches*, vol. 2, 319–20, 325.
64. Leslie subsequently made this quite clear: Thomas Birch., ed., *A Collection of the State Papers of John Thurloe*, London, 1742, vol. 1, 167. His assertion was supported by Gilbert Burnet (Airy, ed., *Burnet's History of My Own Time*, vol. 1, 94–6) and the Scottish minister Robert Baillie (David Laing, ed., *The Letters and Journals of Robert Baillie*, Edinburgh, 1842, vol. 3, 111).
65. *A Brief Relation* 53 (20 August–10 September 1650), 813.
66. *Mercurius Politicus* 14 (5–12 September 1650), 233; Morrill, ed., *Letters, Writings and Speeches*, vol. 2, 338.
67. Morrill, ed., *Letters, Writings and Speeches*, vol. 2, 326; *Mercurius Politicus* 14 (5–12 September 1650), 217, and 15 (12–19 September 1650), 226–7; *Original Memoirs*, 144; *A Perfect Diurnall* 38 (2–9 September 1650), 454–5; *A Brief Relation* 53 (20 August–10 September 1650), 813.
68. Morrill, ed., *Letters, Writings and Speeches*, vol. 2, 326. Cromwell continued to retell this story for the rest of his life: Airy, ed., *Burnet's History of My Own Time*, vol. 1, 94–6. The version printed from a manuscript in Morrill, ed., *Letters, Writings and Speeches*, vol. 2, 321–2, does not fit well with other, eye-witness, accounts of the battle.

69. This was John Hodgson in 1683: *Original Memoirs*, 144–5.
70. Gumble, *Life of General Monck*, 38.
71. Morrill, ed., *Letters, Writings and Speeches*, vol. 2, 326.
72. *Memoirs of the Life of Mr Ambrose Barnes*, Surtees Society 50, Durham, 1867, 110–11.
73. Morrill, ed., *Letters, Writings and Speeches*, vol. 2, 327; Gumble, *Life of General Monck*, 38; *Mercurius Politicus* 14 (5–12 September 1650), 217; *Original Memoirs*, 147–8; *Perfect Passages* 10 (6–13 September 1650), 74–5; *A Brief Relation* 53 (20 August–10 September 1650), 814.
74. Morrill, ed., *Letters, Writings and Speeches*, vol. 2, 327–8, 342; *Mercurius Politicus* 14 (5–12 September 1650), 217, 15 (12–19 September 1650), 229–30, and 16 (19–26 September 1650), 266–7; *Original Memoirs*, 148; *Perfect Passages* 10 (6–13 September 1650), 74–5; *A Brief Relation* 53 (20 August–10 September 1650), 814. Between them, these English sources provide the range of figures given here. It should be noted that an English royalist who had come to Scotland put the number of prisoners as 5,000–6,000: Walker, *Historical Discourses*, 180. As with his figures for the army, however, this retrospective account may have been based on English claims.
75. Walker, *Historical Discourses*, 180; Airy, ed., *Burnet's History of My Own Time*, vol. 1, 94.
76. *Records of the Commissioners of the General Assemblies*, 49–52.
77. Laing, ed., *Correspondence of Ancrum and Lothian*, 297–8.
78. Walker, *Historical Discourses*, 180.
79. These conclusions would accord with those reached by historians of the battle in recent years: Ian Gentles (*The New Model Army in England, Ireland and Scotland*, 392–8); Peter Gaunt (*Oliver Cromwell*, Oxford, 1996, 128); Grainger (*Cromwell against the Scots*, 37–50); Simon Robbins (*God's General*, Stroud, 2003, 157–74); Reid (*Dunbar 1650*, 58–78); Martyn Bennett (*Cromwell at War*, London, 2017, 95–200); Malcolm Wanklyn (*Parliament's Generals*, Barnsley, 2019, 138–9); Johnston, *'Essential Agony'*, 115–60.
80. Morrill, ed., *Letters, Writings and Speeches*, vol. 2, 336; *Original Memoirs*, 148.
81. *Mercurius Politicus* 23 (7–14 November 1650), 376–7.
82. Morrill, ed., *Letters, Writings and Speeches*, vol. 2, 328–9.
83. *CJ*, vol. 6, 474–5, 485–7.
84. Henry William Henfrey, *Numismata Cromwelliana*, London, 1877, 1–2; Morrill, ed., *Letters, Writings and Speeches*, vol. 2, 419–20.
85. Morrill, ed., *Letters, Writings and Speeches*, vol. 2, 322–47.
86. For this see ibid., 339.
87. Ibid., 337; *A Perfect Diurnall* 40 (9–16 September 1650), 457–8.
88. *Mercurius Politicus* 16 (19–26 September 1650), 266–7.
89. Morrill, ed., *Letters, Writings and Speeches*, vol. 2, 364–5; *Mercurius Politicus* 17 (26 September–3 October 1650), 284–91.
90. *Mercurius Politicus* 17 (26 September–3 October 1650), 290–1; National Records of Scotland, PA 7/24, ff. 14, 21; Laing, ed., *Correspondence of Ancrum and Lothian*, 298–306.
91. As Cromwell himself made clear: Morrill, ed., *Letters, Writings and Speeches*, vol. 2, 354–5.
92. *Severall Letters and Passages between his Excellency the Lord Generall Cromwell, and William Dundas Governour of Edinburgh Castle*, York, 27 September 1650.
93. Morrill, ed., *Letters, Writings and Speeches*, vol. 2, 366.
94. John Barclay, ed., *Diary of Alexander Jaffray*, London, 1833, 38–40.
95. Morrill, ed., *Letters, Writings and Speeches*, vol. 2, 372–3, 377–9.
96. *Records of the Commissioners of the General Assemblies*, 44–69; Haig, ed., *Historical Works of Sir James Balfour*, vol. 4, 107–11; Laing, ed., *Correspondence of Ancrum and Lothian*, 300; G. R. Kinloch, ed., *The Diary of Mr John Lamont*, Edinburgh, 1830, 23.
97. Hutton, *Charles II*, 56–7.
98. Ibid., 57–9, with material added from Thomson and Innes, eds, *Acts of the Parliaments of Scotland*, vol. 6, part 2, 613.

99. *Mercurius Politicus* 20–2 (17 October–7 November 1650); *A Perfect Diurnall* 47 (28 October–4 November 1650), 585–7, 473–7; *Severall Proceedings in Parliament* 57 (24–31 October 1650), 846–7, 853.
100. James Dennistoun, ed., *The Coltness Collection*, Edinburgh, 1842, 9–10.
101. John Nicholl, *A Diary of Public Transactions*, ed. David Laing, Edinburgh, 1836, 30–1.
102. *A Perfect Diurnall* 47 (28 October–4 November 1650), 585.
103. The material of the last two paragraphs and the first half of this one may be found in Morrill, ed., *Writings, Letters and Speeches*, vol. 2, 380–2; Robert Chambers, ed., *Domestic Annals of Scotland*, Edinburgh, 1858, vol. 2, 203; *Mercurius Politicus* 18–27 (3 October–5 December 1650); *A Perfect Diurnall* 47–51 (28 October–2 December 1650); and Bod L, Clarendon MS 34, f. 36. Details of Cowell's case are given in WCL, Clarke MS 181, f. 211v. The act of Parliament is in C. H. Firth and R. S. Rait, eds, *Acts and Ordinances of the Interregnum*, London, 1911, vol. 2, 409–12. Cowell was not tried according to it but according to the articles of war: nevertheless, it established the atmosphere within which Cromwell's army operated.
104. J. Sommerville, ed., *Memorie of the Somervills*, Edinburgh, 1815, vol. 2, 437–53; Morrill, ed., *Letters, Writings and Speeches*, vol. 2, 384–6; *Mercurius Aulicus* 26–8 (28 November–19 December 1650); *A Perfect Diurnall* 53–4 (9–23 December 1650); Laing, ed., *Letters and Journals of Robert Baillie*, vol. 3, 124–5; Nicholl, *Diary*, 36–7.
105. *Mercurius Politicus* 29–31 (19 December 1650–9 January 1651); *A Perfect Diurnall*, issues 55–6 (23 December 1650–6 January 1651); Morrill, ed., *Letters, Writings and Speeches*, vol. 2, 387–403. In 1949 Kenneth Corsar published an article, 'The Surrender of Edinburgh Castle December 1650', *Scottish Historical Review* 28, 43–54, which has proved influential. In it he argued that the governor, Walter Dundas, had no need to surrender and did so from weakness of will and loss of faith in his government, reinforced by the arrival of Strachan as a captive. There is no real evidence for this, and much against it which is cited here. The most that can be said on its side is a rumour which reached a Scottish minister that one of the Scots who had surrendered with Strachan encouraged the deal: Laing, ed., *Letters and Journals of Robert Baillie*, vol. 3, 125. On occupying the castle, Cromwell's army had to repair a considerable amount of damage that its artillery had already inflicted: *A Perfect Diurnall* 57 (6–13 January 1651), 58.
106. The details of these sieges are in *Mercurius Politicus* 36–45 (6 February–17 April 1651); *A Perfect Diurnall* 60–5 (27 January–10 March 1651); *Perfect Passages* 24 (28 February–7 March 1651), 239; and Akerman, ed., *Letters of Roundhead Officers*, 15–16. The strongholds reduced in early 1651 were Hume, Tantallon, Fast and Blackness castles and Neadperth House. Those taken in late 1650 were Borthwick Castle and Roslyn and Dirleton houses. Monck's treatment of the prisoners at Dirleton House is described in *A Perfect Diurnall* 50 (18–25 November 1650), 641.
107. The regiments were two new ones from Yorkshire and Cheshire, each 1,200 strong, plus 800 of Gibbon's, 900 of Ingoldsby's, 900 of Barkstead's, the whole of Sexby's, 500 of Alured's, a whole Lancashire regiment and 400 of Wauton's: *CSPD (1650)*, 348–94, passim; *Mercurius Politicus* 25 (21–28 November 1650), 422, and 29 (19–26 December 1650), 473; *A Perfect Diurnall* 50 (18–25 November 1650), 641, and 54 (16–23 December 1650), 709.
108. *CSPD (1650)*, 464.
109. *CSPD (1651)*, 36–82. For the totals spent on the various commodities, see Wheeler, 'Logistics of the Cromwellian Conquest', 1–18, which, with Gentles (see n. 110), established the impressive extent of the commonwealth's logistical achievement in this war.
110. Gentles, *The New Model Army in England, Ireland and Scotland*, 389.
111. Hutton, *Charles II*, 59–63.
112. *Mercurius Politicus* 36–7 (6–20 February 1651); *A Perfect Diurnall* 62–3 (10–24 February 1651). As in 1650, many of the letters printed in these two newspapers are found in others, and published separately as pamphlets. To control my word count, I do not cite the other appearances, and draw mostly on these two newspapers because they

consistently have the most detailed reports. See also here Akerman, ed., *Letters of Roundhead Officers*, 6–8.

113. *Mercurius Politicus* 39–50 (27 February–22 May 1651); *A Perfect Diurnall* 63–77 (17 February–2 June 1651); Akerman, ed., *Letters of Roundhead Officers*, 10–12, 18–24; *CSPD (1651)*, 91; BL, Additional MS 21419, f. 333.
114. *Mercurius Politicus* 52–4 (29 May–19 June 1651); *A Perfect Diurnall* 79 (9–16 June 1651), 1091, 1106; *Severall Proceedings in Parliament* 89 (5–12 June 1651), 1359; *Perfect Passages* 50 (27 June–4 July 1651), 360; Morrill, ed., *Letters, Writings and Speeches*, vol. 2, 457–8; *CSPD (1651)*, 218.
115. Morrill, ed., *Letters, Writings and Speeches*, vol. 2, 420–64, passim.
116. *A Perfect Diurnall* 79 (9–16 June 1651), 1101; Akerman, ed., *Letters of Roundhead Officers*, 25–6.
117. *Mercurius Politicus* 54 (12–19 June 1651), 877; *Perfect Passages* 44 (16–23 May 1651), 308.
118. *Mercurius Politicus* 54 (12–19 June 1651), 874.
119. Morrill, ed., *Letters, Writings and Speeches*, vol. 2, 444–5; *Perfect Passages* 50 (27 June–4 July 1651), 360; *The Weekly Intelligencer of the Commonwealth* 29 (15–22 July 1651), 241.
120. *The Faithfull Scout* 29 (27 June–4 July 1651), 219; *Severall Proceedings in Parliament* 90 (19–26 June 1651), 1396.
121. *Mercurius Politicus* 52 (29 May–5 June 1651), 838; *A Perfect Diurnall* 78 (2–9 June 1651), 1088.
122. Akerman, ed., *Letters of Roundhead Officers*, 26–7. See the entry on Sexby by Sir Charles Firth in the original *Dictionary of National Biography*.
123. She was termed a 'Ranter', and it was said that Cromwell told her that she did not deserve to live: *Mercurius Politicus* 52 (29 May–5 June 1651), 831.
124. *A Perfect Diurnall* 82 (30 June–7 July 1651), 1133; Akerman, ed., *Letters of Roundhead Officers*, 30.
125. *Mercurius Politicus* 57 (3–10 July 1651), 904–11.
126. The quotation is in *Mercurius Politicus* 57 (3–10 July 1651), 904.
127. *Mercurius Politicus* 57–8 (3–17 July 1651); *A Perfect Diurnall* 83 (7–14 July 1651), 1150; *Severall Proceedings in Parliament* 93 (3–10 July 1651), 1426–7; *The Weekly Intelligencer* 28 (8–15 July 1651), 220–1; Akerman, ed., *Letters of Roundhead Officers*, 32; *Original Memoirs*, 150. The horse regiments were Cromwell's, Lambert's, Fleetwood's, Whalley's, Tomlinson's, Twistleton's, Hacker's, Okey's, Lidcot's, Berry's, Grosvenor's and one under its major, Husbands. The foot regiments were Cromwell's, Lambert's, Deane's, Fairfax's, Pride's, Goffe's, West's, Cooper's, Ashfield's, Daniel's, Monck's and Rede's. The dragoons were still Okey's regiment, though he had now also been given one of horse.
128. The past one and a half paragraphs are based on *Mercurius Politicus* 59 (17–24 July 1651), 927–8, 946–7; *A Perfect Diurnall* 84–5 (14–28 July 1651); *Severall Proceedings in Parliament* 95 (17–24 July 1651), 1466; *The Weekly Intelligencer* 29–30 (15–29 July 1651), 241–2; Akerman, ed., *Letters of Roundhead Officers*, 32–5; James Fraser, *Chronicles of the Frasers*, ed. W. Mackay, Scottish History Society, 1894, 383–4.
129. *Mercurius Politicus* 58 (10–17 July 1651), 930.
130. Ibid.
131. *Perfect Passages* 53 (18–25 July 1651), 379.
132. *A Perfect Diurnall* 85 (21–28 July 1651), 1194–5.
133. Ibid., 1192–5; *Mercurius Politicus* 60 (24–31 July 1651), 952–65; *A Great Victory God Hath Vouchsafed by the Lord Generall Cromwels Forces against the Scots*, London, 1651; *More Letters From Scotland, Of the proceedings of the Army*, London, 1651; Akerman, ed., *Letters of Roundhead Officers*, 34–5.
134. *Mercurius Politicus* 60 (24–31 July 1651), 952–65; *A Perfect Diurnall* 86 (28 July–4 August 1651), 1205–6; *A Great Victory*; Akerman, ed., *Letters of Roundhead Officers*, 35; J. Maidment, ed., *Historical Fragments Relative to Scottish Affairs*, Edinburgh, 1833, 36. It is noticeable that Lambert's despatch to England announcing his victory (in *Mercurius*

Politicus) is much more candid about his outnumbering of the Scots than Cromwell's report of it (in Morrill, ed., *Letters, Writings and Speeches*, vol. 2, 468), which counts regiments and not overall numbers to give the impression, as usual, that the enemy had been much superior in strength.

135. *Mercurius Politicus* 61 (31 July–7 August 1651), 968–75; *A Perfect Diurnall* 86 (28 July–4 August 1651), 1207; *Severall Proceedings in Parliament* 97 (31 July–7 August 1651), 1486–97; *The Armies Intelligencer* 1 (29 July–5 August 1651), 5–8; Akerman, ed., *Letters of Roundhead Officers*, 36–7; Morrill, ed., *Letters, Writings and Speeches*, vol. 2, 471–6.
136. Morrill, ed., *Letters, Writings and Speeches*, vol. 2, 476–8; *The Weekly Intelligencer* 32 (5–11 August 1651), 245; *Severall Proceedings in Parliament* 98 (7–14 August 1651), 1504–6; *Mercurius Politicus* 62 (7–14 August 1651), 988–9; Akerman, ed., *Letters of Roundhead Officers*, 37; *Original Memoirs*, 151–2.
137. *The Weekly Intelligencer* 29 (15–22 July 1651), 241.
138. Cary, ed., *Memorials*, vol. 2, 283–91.
139. HMC Portland MSS, vol. 1, 610–11; HMC Hamilton MSS, Supplementary Report, 77–8; Gilbert Burnet, *The Memoires of the Lives and Actions of James and William Dukes of Hamilton*, London, 1677, 426; *The Faithfull Scout* 30 (8–15 August 1651), 227.
140. In this I concur robustly with the view proposed more tentatively by Malcolm Wanklyn in *Parliament's Generals*, 140–1.
141. The royalist invasion of England certainly took the Council of State by surprise, according to the wife of the republican leader John Hutchinson: Lucy Hutchinson, *Memoirs of the Life of Colonel Hutchinson*, London, 1806, 323. She recounted how shocked and horrified its members were, and how furious with Cromwell, to the extent that some suspected his fidelity.
142. *Mercurius Politicus* 62 (7–14 August 1651), 988–9; *Severall Proceedings in Parliament* 98 (7–14 August 1651), 1509, 1515–16; *The Weekly Intelligencer* 32 (5–11 August 1651), 247; Morrill, ed., *Letters, Writings and Speeches*, vol. 2, 480–2; John Nicholls, ed., *Original Letters and Papers of State*, London, 1743, 71; Cary, ed., *Memorials*, vol. 2, 295–6.
143. *Mercurius Politicus* 62 (7–14 August 1651), 988–93; *A Perfect Diurnall* 89 (18–25 August 1651), 1223–4; *The Faithfull Scout* 20 (8–15 August 1651), 227; *Severall Proceedings in Parliament* 98 (7–14 August 1651), 1516.
144. *CSPD (1651)*, 307–28.
145. *Mercurius Politicus* 62–3 (7–21 August 1651); *A Perfect Diurnall* 88–9 (11–25 August 1651); *The Faithfull Scout* 31 (15–22 August 1651), 236; *Severall Proceedings in Parliament* 99 (14–21 August 1651), 1517–29; *The Weekly Intelligencer* 24 (19–26 August 1651), 257; Cary, ed., *Memorials*, vol. 2, 300–3.
146. Hutton, *Charles II*, 64–5.
147. *Mercurius Politicus* 64–5 (21 August–4 September 1651); *A Perfect Diurnall* 90 (25 August–1 September 1651), 1238–51; *The Faithfull Scout* 32 (22–29 August 1651), 243; *The Modern Intelligencer* 5 (26 August–3 September 1651), 25.
148. *A Perfect Diurnall* 91 (1–8 September 1651), 1253; *Mercurius Politicus* 65 (28 August–4 September 1651), 1039–42.
149. *Mercurius Politicus* 65 (28 August–4 September 1651), 1039–42; *A Perfect Diurnall* 91 (1–8 September 1651), 1255; *The Faithfull Scout* 33 (29 August–5 September 1651), 252–6; Morrill, ed., *Letters, Writings and Speeches*, vol. 2, 486.
150. Cary, ed., *Memorials*, vol. 2, 357–8; *Mercurius Politicus* 66 (4–11 September 1651), 1052.
151. Cary, ed., *Memorials*, vol. 2, 357–8; *Severall Proceedings in Parliament* 102 (4–11 September 1651), 1566.
152. *Severall Proceedings in Parliament* 102 (4–11 September 1651), 1566–7; *Mercurius Politicus* 66 (4–11 September 1651), 1052; Cary, ed., *Memorials*, vol. 2, 357–9. The units that Cromwell led over were Ingoldsby's and Fairfax's foot regiments and some from his own, with his life guard of horse and Hacker's horse regiment. Fleetwood already had his own horse regiment and those of Twistleton, Desborough and Kendrick, plus the foot regiments of Goffe, Deane, Blague, Gibbon, Marsh, Lord Grey, Haynes and Cobbet.

153. This is of course mere speculation, as the actual objective of the western attack was never recorded, but it is the suggestion that fits the facts of Cromwell's strategy.
154. *Mercurius Politicus* 66 (4–11 September 1651), 1053–5; *Severall Proceedings in Parliament* 102 (4–11 September 1651), 1566–7; Cary, ed., *Memorials*, vol. 2, 356–7. As usual, these accounts also appear in other sources: that in *Mercurius Politicus* was printed as a separate tract (now in Worcester Record Office), and the originals of the letters edited by Cary may be found in the Bodleian Library's Tanner manuscripts.
155. For the account of the king's actions given here and below, I rely on three sources which all agree. One is Charles's own memory, published in *Whiteladies*, London, 1660, and reprinted in A. M. Broadley, *The Royal Miracle*, London, 1912, 54–6. The second is that of the Penderell brothers, probably also gained from the king, in Thomas Blount, *Boscobel*, 3rd edition, London, 1680, 15–19. The third was provided by a royalist prisoner two weeks later, preserved in Bod L, Clarendon MS 42, ff. 151–2, and printed in *State Papers Collected by Edward, Earl of Clarendon*, London, 1773, 560–3, and J. Hughes, ed., *Boscobel Tracts*, London, 1830, 138–46.
156. The account here of the fight on the eastern side is drawn from Morrill, ed., *Letters, Writings and Speeches*, vol. 2, 488; Bod L, Clarendon MS 42, ff. 151–2; Cary, ed., *Memorials*, vol. 2, 353–7; *Mercurius Politicus* 66 (4–11 September 1651), 1053; Burnet, *Memoires*, 430–1; Broadley, *The Royal Miracle*, 55; and Blount, *Boscobel Tracts*, 15–18. The units of Cromwell's army there were his own horse regiment, alongside those of Lambert, Whalley and Tomlinson, with Harrison's whole brigade, the foot regiments of Lambert, Pride and Cooper, plus the Cheshire and Essex militia foot and the Surrey and Essex militia horse.
157. Bod L, Clarendon MS 42, ff. 151–2; House of Lords RO, Braye MS 3, f. 39, summarized in HMC 10th Report, Appendix VI: Manuscripts of the Marquess of Abergavenny etc., 175.
158. Morrill, ed., *Letters, Writings and Speeches*, vol. 2, 489–91.
159. Bod L, Clarendon MS 42, f. 152; House of Lords RO, Braye MS 3, f. 39; *A Perfect Diurnall* 91 (1–8 September 1651), 1291–2.
160. For my own take on this famous episode, see Hutton, *Charles II*, 67–9.
161. House of Lords RO, Bray MS 3, f. 39.
162. Blount, *Boscobel*, 16–17; *CSPD (1651)*, 436–7.
163. *A Perfect Diurnall* 91 (1–8 September 1651), 1291–2.
164. Cary, ed., *Memorials*, vol. 2, 345–52; Whitelocke, *Memorials of the English Affairs*, 482–4.
165. Grainger, *Cromwell against the Scots*, 146.
166. *A Perfect Diurnall*, 92 (8–15 September 1651), 1283; *The Faithfull Scout* 35 (12–19 September 1651), 265; *Another Victory In Lancashire Obtained against the Scots*, London, 1651.

7 PARLIAMENT

1. *CJ*, vol. 7, 18; Bulstrode Whitelocke, *Memorials of the English Affairs*, London, 1682, 485. It has become quite correctly the rule in recent years to deprecate the published versions of Whitelocke's various volumes of annals and return to the manuscript originals. I have, however, checked every entry I have copied from this first edition against the originals in BL, Additional MS 37345, and found them accurate word for word; this edition is readily accessible on the internet.
2. Ian Gentles, *Oliver Cromwell*, Basingstoke, 2011, 137, has provided the best study of Cromwell's overall property portfolio.
3. John Morrill, ed., *The Letters, Writings and Speeches of Oliver Cromwell*, Oxford, 2022, vol. 2, 501.
4. *CSPD (1651)*, xxv, 427–98, passim; *CSPD (1651–1652)*, 20–474, passim.
5. *CJ*, vol. 7, 25–6; *CSPD (1651–1652)*, 56, 248.
6. *CJ*, vol. 7, 37, 41–2.

7. *Mercurius Politicus* 71–9 (9 October–18 December 1651).
8. *The Faithful Scout* 45–86 (21 November 1651–10 September 1652).
9. *The French Intelligencer* 4–5 (9–23 December 1651).
10. *A Perfect Account* 59–60 (11–15 February 1652).
11. *Perfect Passages Of Every Daies Intelligence From The Parliaments Army* 63–4 (7–21 May 1652), and with a new run, 50–4 (21 May–2 July 1652).
12. This is a theme of the first volume of this biography, Ronald Hutton, *The Making of Oliver Cromwell*, New Haven and London, 2021.
13. *The Faithful Scout* 35 (12–19 September 1651), 265; 49 (19–26 December 1651), 382; 58 (20–27 February 1652), 456; and 66 (16–23 April 1652), 519.
14. *The Moderate Intelligencer* 169 (22–29 December 1651), 2630.
15. *The French Intelligencer* 4 (9–16 December 1651), 29.
16. *The French Occurrences* 2 (17–24 May 1652), 14.
17. Whitelocke, *Memorials of the English Affairs*, 488, 492. See also *A Perfect Diurnall Of Some Passages And Proceedings Of, and in relation to the Armies* 100 (27 October–3 November 1651), 1399–1401.
18. Gerrard Winstanley, *The Law of Freedom in a Platform*, London, 1652; William Sheppard, *The Peoples Priviledge And Duty Guarded*, London, 1652; *The last Newes From The King of Scots*, London, 1651; *A Declaration of the Commoners Of England To His Excellency The Lord General Cromwel*, London, 1652.
19. John Nichols, ed., *Original Letters and Papers of State, Addressed to Oliver Cromwell*, London, 1743, 85–6, 88–9.
20. Margaret F. Stieg, ed., *The Diary of John Harington M.P. 1646–53*, Somerset Record Society, 1977, 73. The text was 1 Samuel 2.8, which was often cited by defenders of the new commonwealth to justify the regicide and revolution, but Cromwell may also have meant here to signify a need to help the poor. Their companions at dinner included Sir John Danvers and Cornelius Holland, both counted among the more radical figures prominent in the republic.
21. Morrill, ed., *Letters, Writings and Speeches*, vol. 2, 530–2.
22. I defined Puritans in *The Making of Oliver Cromwell*, 32–6.
23. Christopher Feake, *A Beam of Light*, London, 1659, 38–46.
24. [Christopher Feake], *A Faithfull Searching Home Word*, London, 1659, 5–6.
25. Morrill, ed., *Letters, Writings and Speeches*, vol. 2, 523–9.
26. *CJ*, vol. 7, 71–6; *Mercurius Politicus* 85 (15–23 January 1652), 1353–7, 1364. These together represent the best accounts of the affair. G. E. Aylmer, *The State's Servants*, London, 1972, 149–50, concluded that all the evidence suggests that Hesilrige was not guilty of the misconduct with which Lilburne and his associates charged him.
27. WCL, Clarke MS 22, ff. 10, 19v.
28. *Lieft. Colonell I. Lilburne his Apologetical Narration*, Amsterdam, 1652.
29. For the spread of opinion, see *The Faithful Scout* 53 (16–23 January 1652), 411, and 54 (23–30 January 1652), 418–20; *To The Supreame Authority The Parliament of the Commonwealth of England*, London, 20 January 1652; and *A Declaration Of The Armie Concerning Lieut. Collonel John Lilburn*, London, 1652.
30. The evidence of the journal is that other MPs who supported reform included Cromwell's old friend and ally Oliver St John, his subordinate general Thomas Harrison, Sir William Masham, Sir Gilbert Pickering, Richard Salwey, Francis Allen, the army colonel Nathaniel Rich, Thomas Scot, Henry Marten, Henry Neville, Lord Grey of Groby, Sir John Danvers, Robert Bennett, Sir Thomas Westrow and John Carew. His precise relations with any of them, however, are very difficult to discern. The best overall account of parliamentary politics in this period is still that of Blair Worden, *The Rump Parliament 1648–1653*, Cambridge, 1974, which was published when the author was supervising my undergraduate studies.
31. *CJ*, vol. 7, 19–44, passim.
32. BL, Additional MS 27962N(2), f. 257v.

33. This profession of allegiance was by taking the official 'engagement' prescribed by Parliament to promise loyalty to the commonwealth. Cromwell could hardly have approved of this clause, because he had already proposed that an imprisoned royalist be released on bail without being made to take the engagement, on the grounds that the engagement was 'no medicine' for disloyalty: Morrill, ed., *Letters, Writings and Speeches*, vol. 2, 515–16.
34. C. H. Firth and R. S. Rait, eds, *Acts and Ordinances of the Interregnum*, London, 1911, vol. 2, 545–77, 591–8, 620–1, 623–52.
35. *CJ*, vol. 7, 76, 78–9, 83–8, 95, 160.
36. Mary Anne Everett Green, ed., *Calendar of the Proceedings of the Committee for the Advance of Money*, London, 1888, vol. 1, 99; Morrill, ed., *Letters, Writings and Speeches*, vol. 2, 550.
37. *CJ*, vol. 7, 15; Morrill, ed., *Letters, Writings and Speeches*, vol. 2, 497–9.
38. Whitelocke, *Memorials of the English Affairs*, 486; and see George Ormerod, ed., *Tracts Relating to Military Proceedings in Lancashire*, Chetham Society 2, 1844, 314, for Derby's letter to Cromwell. I prefer the unequivocal testimony of Whitelocke, who was in the House, to that of the Florentine ambassador Amerigo Salvetti, who reported a rumour that Cromwell had tried hard to save Derby's life on condition that he obtained the surrender of the royalist-held Isle of Man: BL, Additional MS 27962N(1), f. 254.
39. Stieg, ed., *The Diary of John Harington*, 69; *CJ*, vol. 7, 15; *Mercurius Politicus* 71 (9–16 October 1651), 1140.
40. *CSPD (1651)*, 465; Longleat House, Whitelocke Letters XII, ff. 42, 61.
41. Morrill, ed., *Letters, Writings and Speeches*, vol. 2, 515–16.
42. The contemporary evidence is from Salvetti, in BL, Additional MS 27962N(2), f. 257v; the retrospective from C. H. Firth, *The Memoirs of Edmund Ludlow*, Oxford, 1894, vol. 1, 345. Neither is a wholly reliable authority, but the agreement between them seems significant.
43. WCL, Clarke MS 20, f. 21; *CSPV (1647–1652)*, 201.
44. WCL, Clarke MS 20, f. 52v; *CJ*, vol. 7, 36–7.
45. Salvetti was of the opinion that the slim majority to set any date was only secured because of the pressure of Cromwell and, behind him, the army: BL, Additional MS 27962N(2), f. 273.
46. Much emphasis has formerly been placed by historians upon two passages in the retrospective memorials of Bulstrode Whitelocke, one of the leading MPs in the purged Parliament and the one placed second after Cromwell in the 1651 election of the Council of State. In the first, apparently dated in early December 1651, Cromwell called a meeting of MPs and army officers, including Whitelocke, to discuss a future form of government. In the entry, the lawyers argued for an element of monarchy, and Whitelocke for the restoration of Charles II, while the officers opposed this, and Cromwell allowed instead for 'somewhat with monarchical power in it'. In the second, dated in November 1652, Cromwell and Whitelocke met in St James's Park and the former proposed that to force the Parliament to improve its performance some higher power was needed, and asked whether 'a man might make himself king'. Whitelocke again urged the restoration, on conditions, of the Stuarts. The original entries are in BL, Additional MS 37345, ff. 170–1, 240v. Modern historians have generally accepted these accounts as valuable insights into the thinking of the republican leaders, and of Cromwell, at these times. In 1990 I suggested that they were unreliable, having been written long after the time, and under a genuinely restored Stuart monarchy, when Whitelocke had 'the strongest possible motive for portraying himself as a covert royalist': Ronald Hutton, *The British Republic 1649–1660*, Basingstoke, 1990, 2–3. In 1996, Peter Gaunt commented that, although the accounts did echo Cromwell's idiom of speech, as found in his letters and orations, there was no corroborative evidence for them (*Oliver Cromwell*, Oxford, 1996, 137–8), but in general experts continued to cite them unproblematically. John Morrill's entry on Cromwell in the *Oxford Dictionary of National Biography*, vol. 14, 338, called the evidence that Cromwell was thinking of a restoration of monarchy fragmentary, treacherous and retrospective, but concluded that it could not altogether be discounted. In 2022, however, Jonathan Fitzgibbons launched a sustained attack on the credibility of Whitelocke's passages, echoing my suspicions about his motives in

writing them, and showing how little they fitted the context of the time to which they were attributed: '"To settle a government without somthing of monarchy in it": Bulstrode Whitelocke's *Memoirs* and the Reinvention of the Interregnum', *English Historical Review* 137 (2022), 655–91. I accept his conclusion that both episodes seem to have been 'fabricated, if not wholly invented' in the 1660s.

47. *CJ*, vol. 7, 131, 136. Salvetti reported a long debate among the MPs about the form of a future Parliament, in which they were completely divided over a range of different proposals: BL, Additional MS 27962N(2), f. 357v.
48. WCL, Clarke MS 20, f. 10.
49. The best accounts of the commission are in Worden, *The Rump Parliament*, 271–3, 279; and Mary Cotterell, 'Interregnum Law Reform', *English Historical Review* 83 (1968), 689–704. The minutes of the commission are BL, Additional MS 35863, and there is further information in *CJ*, vol. 7, 58, 73–4, 76, 107, 110; *The Faithful Scout* 59 (27 February–5 March 1652); and WCL, Clarke MS 20, ff. 73v, 79v, and MS 22, f. 19.
50. Morrill, ed., *Letters, Writings and Speeches*, vol. 2, 526–36.
51. *Proposals For The furtherance and propagation of the Gospell*, London, 2 February 1652.
52. Morrill, ed., *Letters, Writings and Speeches*, vol. 2, 530–2.
53. *CJ*, vol. 7, 128; *Perfect Passages* 63 (7–14 May 1652), 265.
54. These useful statistics were compiled by David L. Smith, 'The Struggle for New Constitutional and Institutional Forms', in John Morrill, ed., *Revolution and Restoration*, London, 1992, 16–18.
55. For the historians concerned, see n. 57 below.
56. This statistic was worked out by Austin Woolrych, *Commonwealth to Protectorate*, Oxford, 1982, 7.
57. This conclusion is shared by the two works most comprehensively devoted to the study of this Parliament and its regime: Worden, *The Rump Parliament*, and Sean Kelsey, *Inventing a Republic*, Manchester, 1997. It was endorsed by Austin Woolrych, in *Britain in Revolution 1625–1660*, Oxford, 2002, 515–16; and Clive Holmes, *Why Was Charles I Executed?*, London, 2006, 121–46.
58. Recent historians have shied away from a comprehensive study of the commonwealth's foreign policy, largely because of the barriers of language and travel involved. The basic narrative therefore remains that in Samuel Rawson Gardiner's *History of the Commonwealth and Protectorate*, London, 1903, vols 1 and 2, the product of Gardiner's admirable patience and dedication in acquiring proficiency in Dutch, French, Italian and Spanish, and travelling to state archives abroad.
59. This account generally follows and endorses that of Steven C. A. Pincus, *Protestantism and Patriotism*, Cambridge, 2009, 1–100, and the sources cited there, with a little more emphasis on the part played by trade rivalries.
60. Gardiner's remains the best account of this action, in *History of the Commonwealth and Protectorate*, vol. 2, 177–9, to which I have added some political input from Pincus, *Protestantism and Patriotism*, 69–100.
61. *CJ*, vol. 7, 135–6; *A Perfect Diurnall* 128 (17–25 May 1652), 1902. The other MP was Dennis Bond. The order to them to proceed is obvious from what followed, but seems to be missing: that in *CSPD (1651–1652)*, 249–50, does not seem to be to them.
62. HMC 9th Report, Appendix, 164.
63. Steve Pincus has laid out the sources for the report, and made clear its conclusion, in *Protestantism and Patriotism*, 72. I have provided the dates from *CJ*, vol. 7, 135–6; *CSPD (1651–1652)*, 256; and *Mercurius Politicus* 103 (20–27 May 1652), 1624.
64. *CJ*, vol. 7, 136; *CSPD (1651–1652)*, 256–89, passim; Morrill, ed., *Letters, Writings and Speeches*, vol. 2, 542.
65. *CJ*, vol. 7, 147–50.
66. Gardiner assiduously collected them, with his usual impressive diligence, from both contemporary and retrospective sources, in his *History of the Commonwealth and Protectorate*, vol. 2, 154–68. Less happily, having done so he adopted his usual approach to

source material, which was to credit virtually everything, thus giving Cromwell's activities both a frenetic energy and a lack of coherence that they probably did not have in reality. The Venetian ambassador, but nobody else, reported a rumour that a rebel French prince, Condé, had sent an agent to Cromwell in October 1651 to ask for military aid, whereupon Oliver replied that he would come himself with a huge army if the prince would turn France into a Protestant republic. A Spanish diplomat relayed another rumour that rebels in the French port of La Rochelle had offered to Cromwell to hand it over to the English, whereupon he had looked it up on a map but taken no action. A French churchman among the rebel leaders later claimed in his memoirs that Cromwell had sent a leading political ally, Sir Henry Vane, on a mission to him to discuss an alliance, but there is no other evidence for this, and the dating provided in the account is impossible. There may be some truth in one or more of these tales, yet as things stand they cannot be accorded the status of fact. The former army officer Edward Sexby claimed later that the Council of State had sent him on a mission to the rebel French city of Bordeaux to treat with it, which seems very likely, but Gardiner assumed that Cromwell was personally responsible for this, which is again just speculation. Likewise, he thought it certain that Oliver was the unnamed English leader whom an agent of the French government reported in February 1652 to be negotiating with both the rebel prince and the French Protestants for an advantageous alliance – but it is not.

67. The papers for this negotiation were printed by Gardiner in 'Cromwell and Mazarin in 1652', *English Historical Review* 11 (1896), 479–509. The despatches from the English agent to Dunkirk are in BL, Additional MS 32093, ff. 285–91.
68. Gardiner, *History of the Commonwealth and Protectorate*, vol. 2, 181.
69. Wilbur Cortez Abbott, ed., *The Writings and Speeches of Oliver Cromwell*, vol. 2, Cambridge, MA, 1939, 551–2.
70. These are recorded in Gardiner, *History of the Commonwealth and Protectorate*, vol. 2, 187–8. The other leaders named by the envoy were Sir Henry Vane, Bulstrode Whitelocke and Dennis Bond. Historians in general have found it difficult to decide exactly who were the enthusiastic advocates of war in Parliament: see ibid., 180; Worden, *Rump Parliament*, 301–3; and Pincus, *Protestantism and Patriotism*, 90–116.
71. Whitelocke, *Memorials of the English Affairs*, 491; Morrill, ed., *Letters, Writings and Speeches*, vol. 2, 522.
72. *CJ*, vol. 7, 79; *CSPD (1651–1652)*, 113.
73. *CSPD (1651–1652)*, 233; *CSPV (1647–1652)*, 217.
74. Lucy Hutchinson, *Memoirs of the Life of Colonel Hutchinson*, London, 1806, 327.
75. WCL, Clarke MS 22, f. 94, states this clearly, and no source contradicts it.
76. Edmund Ludlow, left in command of the army in Ireland, heard that Cromwell had been compelled to the step by hearing that MPs were murmuring against the office of lord lieutenant, as more suitable to a monarchy: Firth, ed., *Memoirs of Edmund Ludlow*, vol. 1, 318.
77. *CJ*, vol. 7, 134. It is hard to tell what was going on here. The tellers for the motion were Sir Arthur Hesilrige and Henry Marten, and those against it Bulstrode Whitelocke and Thomas Harrison. All were men with whom Cromwell had collaborated previously, and it is difficult confidently to see any party lines between them at this stage. It is probable that Oliver himself was still in the House when the vote was taken, and there is no evidence of whether he participated in it. There is more sign of his position being at stake in another division two days later, when, again by two votes, it was decided to postpone further discussion of Irish affairs for a week (*CJ*, vol. 7, 135). By then Cromwell had departed for Dover, and it seems likely, though not proven, that the decision was taken to suspend matters until he had returned and could participate. The tellers for the motion were traditional allies of his, his military lieutenant Charles Fleetwood and Sir Henry Vane, although the tellers against were once more Hesilrige and Marten. Again, it is hard to say how much political weight hung on these decisions.
78. Here I am persuaded by John Cunningham, 'Divided Conquerors', *English Historical Review* 129 (2014), 842.

79. *CJ*, vol. 7, 142, 152; Whitelocke, *Memorials of the English Affairs*, 511; HMC 6th Report, Appendix, 436; Morrill, ed., *Letters, Writings and Speeches*, vol. 2, 552–4; WCL, Clarke MS 22, newsletter of 12 June.
80. Morrill, ed., *Letters, Writings and Speeches*, vol. 2, 562–3.
81. Hutchinson, *Memoirs*, 328.
82. Ibid., 327; Thomas Birch, ed., *A Collection of the State Papers of John Thurloe*, London, 1742, vol. 6, 660. In this latter source it was confirmed by Lambert that Cromwell had encouraged him in his anger against Parliament.
83. It may be noted that Edmund Ludlow, subsequently an enemy of Cromwell himself, recorded that Oliver was annoyed by the move to exclude Lambert from the lord deputyship: Firth, ed., *Memoirs of Edmund Ludlow*, vol. 1, 318.
84. This story is laid out, and the conclusion reached, in two separate, and impressive, studies: John Cunningham, 'Oliver Cromwell and the "Cromwellian" Settlement of Ireland', *Historical Journal* 53 (2010), 919–37; and John Morrill, 'Cromwell, Parliament, Ireland and a Commonwealth in Crisis 1652', *Parliamentary History* 30 (2011), 192–214.
85. Here I accept the argument of Cunningham, 'Divided Conquerors', building on that of Sarah Barber, 'Irish Undercurrent to the Politics of April 1653', *Historical Research* 65 (1992), 315–26.
86. *A Perfect Account Of The daily Intelligence from the Armies* 8 (4–11 August 1652), 670; *A Perfect Diurnall* 140 (9–16 August 1652), 2085; WCL, Clarke MS 24, f. 5. A pamphlet bought in London on the 10th claimed that most of the officers had started the process by signing a declaration to Cromwell to address what they called the oppressions of the people. This allegedly asked for a new Parliament; the abolition of taxes and the provision of full accounts for public money; the removal of some law courts and the publication of the posts held by legal officials, and their salaries; and relief for impoverished people held in prison: *A Declaration Of The Armie To His Excellency The Lord General Cromwel*, London, 1652. It seems impossible to tell how authentic this claim was, or whether it represented another unofficial radical initiative to provoke action. Edmund Ludlow much later recorded in his memoirs that the officers had debated a petition to Parliament to dissolve, whereupon Cromwell sent Desborough to warn them not to put that sort of pressure on the MPs. He then arrived to reinforce this message himself to the soldiers, only for them to tell him that they had taken up the idea for the request to dissolve because they had thought he wanted it: Firth, ed., *Memoirs of Edmund Ludlow*, vol. 1, 348. Ludlow, however, was often hazy about dates, and it is impossible to tell where to locate this episode, if it indeed occurred.
87. *CSPV (1647–1652)*, 270.
88. *To the Supreme Authoritie the Parliament of the Commonwealth of England. The humble Petition of the Officers of the Army*, London, 1652.
89. Ibid.
90. *CJ*, vol. 7, 164–5; *A Perfect Diurnall* 140 (9–16 August 1652), 2085. Whitelocke, *Memorials of the English Affairs*, 516, recorded that many MPs nevertheless thought the soldiers arrogant, and that Whitelocke himself urged Cromwell to curb them. This may well be true, but once again it is possible that Whitelocke was subsequently trying to whitewash his actions at this time.
91. *CJ*, vol. 7, 178; WCL, Clarke MS 24, f. 30.
92. *CJ*, vol. 7, 188–92.
93. N. H. Keeble and Geoffrey F. Nuttall, ed., *Calendar of the Correspondence of Richard Baxter*, Oxford, 1991, vol. 1, no. 99. When I tried to check the original, in Dr Williams's Library, London, I found that it had just closed down, permanently, and its collections were unavailable until further notice.
94. Morrill, ed., *Letters, Writings and Speeches*, vol. 2, 669–70; Whitelocke, *Memorials of the English Affairs*, 526.
95. *CJ*, vol. 7, 219–21.
96. *CSPV (1647–1652)*, 317–18.

97. These cases were noted in the paper in Henry Marten's archive, cited in n. 173, below.
98. *The Moderate Intelligencer* 169 (22–29 December 1652), 2630.
99. *The Flying Eagle* 5 (25 December 1652–1 January 1653), 40.
100. HMC Leyborne-Popham MSS, 104.
101. *The Weekly Intelligencer of the Commonwealth* 91 (21–28 September 1652), 603.
102. George F. Warner, ed., *The Nicholas Papers*, vol. 1, Camden Society N.S. 40, London, 1886, 310.
103. *CJ*, vol. 7, 226.
104. Feake, *A Beam of Light*, 43–6; *A Faithfull Searching Word*, 5–6.
105. Joseph Meyer, ed., 'Inedited Letters of Cromwell, Colonel Jones, Bradshaw, and Other Regicides', *Transactions of the Historic Society of Lancashire and Cheshire* N.S. 1 (1860–1), 214–18.
106. NA, PRO/31/3/90, f. 521.
107. *CJ*, vol. 7, 220.
108. Ibid.
109. Ibid., 222.
110. Ibid., 228, 245.
111. Meyer, ed., 'Inedited Letters', 217; Feake, *A Beam of Light*, 44; *CSPV (1647–1652)*, 283.
112. The exemption is recorded in *CJ*, vol. 7, 50.
113. The best military history in English of this phase of the war, and account of its impact, is probably still Gardiner, *History of the Commonwealth and Protectorate*, vol. 2, 176–213.
114. *CJ*, vol. 7, 224–5.
115. Ibid., 237–42; *CSPV (1653–1654)*, 9; *CSPD (1652–1653)*, 95.
116. NA, PRO/31/3/90, f. 559v; WCL, Clarke MS 24, ff. 92, 98v.
117. *Mercurius Politicus* 136 (6–13 January 1653), 136; *A Perfect Diurnall* 161 (3–10 January 1653), 2424; WCL, Clarke MS 24, f. 100.
118. NA, PRO/31/3/90, ff. 562, 575; *CSPV (1653–1654)*, 12.
119. *CSPV (1653–1654)*, 12.
120. WCL, Clarke MS 24, f. 104v.
121. *Mercurius Politicus* 139 (3–10 February 1653), 2113–16; *The Moderate Publisher* 83 (28 January–4 February 1653), 713; WCL, Clarke MS 24, ff. 107, 112.
122. *CJ*, vol. 7, 242–53, passim; Firth, ed., *Memoirs of Edmund Ludlow*, vol. 1, 334; Whitelocke, *Memorials of the English Affairs*, 526.
123. *CSPV (1653–1654)*, 21, 30.
124. *CJ*, vol. 7, 253–62, passim. The Venetian ambassador commented on the general opposition of the legal profession to the proposed law reforms: *CSPV (1653–1654)*, 30.
125. Whitelocke later identified February as the month in which the officers began openly to speak against the MPs as worthless: *Memorials of the English Affairs*, 526.
126. Barber, 'Irish Undercurrents to the Politics of April 1653', 327–30; Cunningham, 'Divided Conquerors', 854–6.
127. Blair Worden portrayed this context well in *Rump Parliament*, 321–6.
128. WCL, Clarke MS 24, f. 123v.
129. Bod L, Clarendon MS 45, ff. 204–6.
130. Whitelocke, *Memorials of the English Affairs*, 527.
131. Firth, ed., *Memoirs of Edmund Ludlow*, vol. 1, 350.
132. *To His Excellency The Lord General Cromwel . . . The Humble Remonstrance of many Thousands in and about the City of London*, London, 14 March 1653.
133. His attendances were tabulated by Wilbur Cortez Abbott, ed., *Writings and Speeches of Oliver Cromwell*, vol. 2, Cambridge, MA, 1939, 622. Between 8 March and 7 April he only attended the council once, and there is no trace of him in Parliament between mid-March and mid-April.
134. NA, PRO/31/3/90, ff. 613, 620.
135. This course of events is given in detail in Pincus, *Protestantism and Patriotism*, 101–26.
136. Bod L, Clarendon MS 45, ff. 204–5.

137. *CJ*, vol. 7, 263–77, passim; WCL, Clarke MS 25, f. 8v; Bod L, Clarendon MS 45, f. 222v; *Mercurius Politicus* 48 (7–14 April 1653), 2368.
138. *CSPD (1652–1653)*, 261, 266–7.
139. *Severall Proceedings in Parliament* 183 (24–31 March 1653), 2890–2.
140. *CJ*, vol. 7, 274; WCL, Clarke MS 25, f. 1v; Bod L, Clarendon MS 45, ff. 206, 269.
141. Bod L, Clarendon MS 45, f. 223, the writer of which was a witness of these events, and not reporting a story.
142. Cunningham, 'Divided Conquerors', 857.
143. It was Ian Gentles, in *Oliver Cromwell*, Basingstoke, 2011, 137, who noticed this.
144. Whitelocke, *Memorials of the English Affairs*, 528. The lack of any additions to this entry displaying Whitelocke's apparent enthusiasm for a Stuart restoration suggests that the record is a genuine one. The French ambassador subsequently held (in NA, PRO/31/3/90, f. 655) that the army officers had presented another petition to Parliament in early April, but there is no mention of this in the Commons' journal.
145. WCL, Clarke MS 25, f. 7v.
146. Ibid., ff. 7v, 8v; Bod L, Clarendon MS 45, f. 293. My policy with rumour, especially when reported by individuals outside the government and army such as foreign ambassadors and royalist correspondents, is to set aside, as unsubstantiated, reports – especially of dramatic kind – that do not occur in more than a single source. So, at this period, I have parked in that category the stories that Cromwell had offered his resignation to the officers if a challenger appeared for his office (which none did); that four of the regiments most violently hostile to the Parliament had been sent away to Scotland; and that Cromwell had got into an altercation in the House with another MP, about its dissolution, which had to be stopped by the other members after Cromwell's antagonist had remarked that it was time for a new general. These are found in Bod L, Clarendon MS 45, f. 222; and in *CSPV (1653–1654)*, 60, 64. Likewise, I have not repeated the different accounts of factions within the army officers and MPs, given in Clarendon MS 45, ff. 140–1, as they do not seem to match the course of events. I have shelved the assertion in James Heath's *Flagellum*, London, 1663, 134, that, at the Cockpit in early 1653, Cromwell said it was better to trust a few good men to do the necessary work than Parliament or the people. It matches Oliver's actions, but is in a late and utterly unreliable source. The same is true of the story attributed to the MP Henry Neville in Isaac Kimber, *The Life of Oliver Cromwell*, London, 1724, 233–4, that Cromwell told a group of leading London ministers that the supreme law was the safety of the nation, and that having nine out of ten men against him did not matter if the tenth was the only one with weapons. There is no contemporary evidence of such a meeting.
147. *CSPD (1652–1653)*, 279; *Mercurius Politicus* 149 (14–21 April 1653), 2385.
148. WCL, Clarke MS 25, f. 10.
149. Accounts of the meeting survive from both sides: Whitelocke, *Memorials of the English Affairs*, 529; and Morrill, ed., *Letters, Writings and Speeches of Oliver Cromwell*, vol. 2, 674–6. They agree on the facts stated, while Whitelocke said that the proposal was for a council of forty which mixed MPs and army officers, and Cromwell only that the MPs were asked to devolve government to some trusted men. A newsletter sympathetic to the army likewise stated just that the proposal at the meeting was to put the nation into honest and able hands: C. H. Firth, ed., *The Clarke Papers*, vol. 3, London, 1899, 1.
150. Whitelocke, *Memorials of the English Affairs*, 529.
151. Whitelocke (ibid.) states that one of Cromwell's officers, Richard Ingoldsby, brought him the news. Bod L, Clarendon MS 45, f. 334, reported that Harrison sent a message. Cromwell stated afterwards that he had received no fewer than three before acting: Morrill, ed., *Letters, Writings and Speeches*, vol. 2, 676.
152. Or so he claimed six years later: John Towill Rutt, ed., *The Diary of Thomas Burton*, London, 1828, vol. 3, 98.
153. Morrill, ed., *Letters, Writings and Speeches*, vol. 2, 616.

154. This is the testimony of John Streater, quartermaster-general of the foot soldiers in Ireland, who was visiting England and among the officers at Westminster on that day: *Secret Reasons of State*, London, 1659, 2–3.
155. This may be inferred from the fact that, when Cromwell entered the House, the soldiers were already with him, left outside awaiting a call: Morrill, ed., *Letters, Writings and Speeches*, vol. 2, 607–8.
156. Ibid.
157. The physical layout of the chamber was described in Hutton, *The Making of Oliver Cromwell*, 55–6.
158. Sir Charles Firth collated them all in 'The Expulsion of the Long Parliament', *History* N.S. 2 (1917), 129–43, in an attempt to hammer out a definitive narrative. I lack his confidence in a historian's ability to privilege one account over another with absolute certainty. The best records of what happened are that by Whitelocke, *Memorials of the English Affairs*, 529, of which I am less dismissive than Firth; that probably by Algernon Sidney reprinted in Morrill, ed., *Letters, Writings and Speeches*, vol. 2, 667–9; and that probably by Harrison, repeated by Ludlow in Firth, ed., *Memoirs of Edmund Ludlow*, vol. 1, 351–4. These are supported in outline by the republican and royalist newsletters printed in C. H. Firth, 'Cromwell and the Expulsion of the Long Parliament in 1653', *English Historical Review* 8 (1892), 530–4; and *CSPV (1653–1654)*, 64. Details are added by the subsequent recollection of one MP in 1659, in Rutt, ed., *Diary of Thomas Burton*, vol. 3, 209; and the alleged words by Harrison in 1660, in *The Speeches and Prayers of some of the Late King's Judges*, London, 1660, 2. Morrill, ed., *Writings, Letters and Speeches*, vol. 2, 613–15, prints (without endorsement) an alleged speech made by Cromwell in the course of his action, preserved in BL, Additional MS 37682, ff. 34–36v. I accept Firth's verdict that its language suggests it is an eighteenth-century fake: 'The Expulsion of the Long Parliament', 205–6.
159. Recorded by Elias Ashmole, for the purposes of astrology: C. H. Josten, ed., *Elias Ashmole*, Oxford, 1967, vol. 2, 642.
160. Streater, *Secret Reasons of State*, 2–3.
161. Firth, ed., *Memoirs of Edmund Ludlow*, vol. 2, 356. Ludlow's informant was probably Okey himself, just as Harrison probably was for the expulsion, as the three men drew together politically later in the 1650s.
162. Firth, ed., *Memoirs of Edmund Ludlow*, vol. 2, 356.
163. Ibid., 355.
164. Morrill, ed., *Letters, Writings and Speeches*, vol. 2, 615–20.
165. Ibid., 624–6.
166. E.g. Firth, ed., *The Clarke Papers*, vol. 3, 1; John Spittlehouse, *The Army Vindicated*, London, 1653; *The Army No Usurpers*, London, 1653; *A Letter Written To a Gentleman in the Country*, London, 3 May 1653. Sometimes these went beyond what the army dared to say: Spittlehouse, a former soldier, declared that the gathered churches and the army were the only true citizens of the commonwealth, and that all others should be banned from elections.
167. Bod L, Tanner MS 52, f. 13.
168. Morrill, ed., *Letters, Writings and Speeches*, vol. 2, 664–710.
169. Ibid., 623.
170. I am not much given to the use of Occam's razor, for life in reality seems so complex and messy that the simplest available explanation for something may not necessarily be the correct one, but in this case there may not be any such problem. There has, however, been a historiographical one, which has occasioned an extensive debate among experts over the past fifty years. It was started by Blair Worden in the glittering launch of his career with the work which culminated in his first book, *The Rump Parliament*. He proved conclusively that the bill that was almost passed on 20 April had not been intended to fill up gaps in the existing House, as the officers had at first asserted and as historians, as usual following Gardiner, had accepted. He was less confident in finding alternative explana-

tions for Cromwell's hostility to it, and for the army's initial insistence that it was for recruitment, not proper elections. He did not believe that the army had deliberately misrepresented the bill, as he thought Cromwell was not cold-blooded enough for such a deception, and wondered if Cromwell had been misinformed that a recruitment clause had been added to the bill on the fateful morning and discovered his mistake too late. He also perceived, however, that the new Parliament summoned by the purged one would probably be still more conservative, and that Cromwell, tending as usual to his army's views, had chosen godly reformation over constitutional propriety when they became irreconcilable. In addition, Worden showed that the purged Parliament was not especially corrupt or self-seeking for a body of its time. His work was extended by another excellent scholar, Austin Woolrych, in *Commonwealth to Protectorate*, Oxford, 1982, 68–99. He suggested four possible reasons for Cromwell's behaviour on 20 April: that he had believed that the Parliament was about to replace him as lord general; that he needed to seize back the position of leader of the radicals, which would slip if he spared the MPs; that he had temporarily turned against elected Parliaments; and that he had found a defect in the bill. Woolrych rightly thought the evidence for the first three too slight, and so the fourth most likely. Like Worden he could not believe that the army officers would lie about the bill, and proposed that Cromwell had made a mistake on the fatal morning, but in Austin's formula this consisted of not realizing that a recruitment clause had been dropped from the bill, rather than thinking one had been added. However, he also went on to suggest that the army may simply have become afraid of the kind of Parliament which the projected elections would produce. Finally, the leading historian of the army at this period, Ian Gentles, found the idea of a mistake made on 20 April plausible, and also endorsed the importance of the question of qualifications of future MPs. He concluded that the action on that morning was a desperate act of self-preservation by Cromwell and the army, linked to the army's frustration with Parliament's behaviour and Cromwell's desire to retain or augment his role in national decision-making: *The New Model Army in England, Ireland and Scotland 1645–1653*, Oxford, 1992, 435–6. I do not think that as canny and well informed a politician as Cromwell would have made any mistake as to the contents of the bill, and I do believe that Cromwell and his allies would tell deliberate lies: it is a theme of both the first volume of my biography of him and this one that he and they did exactly that, at times, to get rid of political opponents. I also, however, endorse the other suggestions of my distinguished predecessors.

171. See the newsletters printed in Firth, 'Cromwell and the Expulsion of the Long Parliament', 530–4.
172. Streater, *Secret Reasons of State*, 3.
173. It is among Marten's papers at the Brotherton Library, Leeds. I have used the transcript in C. M. Williams, 'The Political Career of Henry Marten' (Oxford University DPhil thesis, 1954), 528–58.

INDEX

Subheadings under significant entries, whose locators appear frequently through the text and extend over more than one calendar year, are indexed chronologically for ease of narrative continuity.

INDEX